HARRY DEXTER WHITE

A Study in Paradox

DAVID REES

MACMILLAN

6 0037878 4x

SBN 333 01917 2

First published in Great Britain in 1974 by
MACMILLAN LONDON LIMITED
London and Basingstoke
Associated Companies in New York
Dublin Melbourne Johannesburg and Madras

PRINTED IN THE UNITED STATES OF AMERICA

For permission to reprint copyrighted material, the author wishes to thank the fol-
lowing: Chatto & Windus, Ltd., for an excerpt from *The Magnetic Mountain* by
C. Day Lewis, Chatto & Windus, Ltd., 1933, reprinted by permission of the pub-
lisher; Devin-Adair Company, Inc., for excerpts from *Out of Bondage* by Elizabeth
Bentley, Devin-Adair Company, Inc., 1951, reprinted by permission of the publisher;
R. F. Harrod and St. Martin's Press, Inc., for excerpts from *The Life of John Maynard
Keynes* by R. F. Harrod, Macmillan Press, Ltd., and St. Martin's Press, Inc., 1951, re-
printed by permission of Macmillan Press, Ltd., and St. Martin's Press, Inc.; Harvard
University Press for excerpts from *China and the Helping Hand* and *China's Wartime
Finance and Inflation, 1937–1945* by Arthur Young, copyright © 1963 and 1965, re-
spectively by Arthur Young, used by permission of Harvard University Press, publishers;
John Morton Blum and Houghton Mifflin Company, Inc. for excerpts from each of three
volumes of *From the Morgenthau Diaries* by John Morton Blum: *From the Morgenthau Diaries: Years of Crisis, 1928–1938*, *From the Morgenthau Diaries: Years of
Urgency, 1938–1941*, *From the Morgenthau Diaries: Years of War 1941–1945*, by
John Morton Blum, Houghton Mifflin Company, Inc., 1959, 1965, 1967, respectively,
reprinted by permission of the author and the publisher; William Heinemann Ltd.
and Houghton Mifflin Company, Inc., for excerpts from *The Coming of the New
Deal* by Arthur M. Schlesinger, 1958, reprinted by permission of William Heinemann Ltd., and Houghton Mifflin Company, Inc., publishers; McGraw Hill Book
Company, Inc. for excerpts from *Sterling-Dollar Diplomacy*, by Richard N. Gardner,
McGraw Hill Book Company, Inc., 1969, reprinted by permission of the publisher;
Methuen & Company, Ltd. for an excerpt from *Die Mutter* by Berthold Brecht,
published in *Brecht: A Choice of Evils* by Martin Esslin, Methuen & Company, Ltd.,
1965, reprinted by permission of the publisher; Princeton University Press for excerpts from *Economic Planning for the Peace* by E. F. Penrose, Princeton University
Press, 1953, reprinted by permission of Princeton University Press; Whittaker Chambers and Random House, Inc., for excerpts from *Witness* by Whittaker Chambers,
published by Random House, Inc., 1952, copyright © 1952 by Whittaker Chambers,
reprinted by permission of Random House, Inc., and by permission of Whittaker
Chambers; Stanford University Press for excerpts from *Ex-Communist Witnesses* by
Herbert Packer, Stanford University Press, 1962, reprinted by permission of Stanford University Press.

HARRY DEXTER WHITE

. . . He is noble, wise, judicious, and best knows
The fits o' the season. . . .
But cruel are the times, when we are traitors
And do not know ourselves, when we hold rumour
From what we fear, yet know not what we fear,
But float upon a wild and violent sea,
Each way. . . . —MACBETH

By DAVID REES

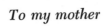

To my mother

CONTENTS

PART IV. THE PROBLEM OF GERMANY

PART V. LAST ACT, 1945–48

PROLOGUE

CARDS OF IDENTITY

Who was Harry Dexter White? He was born in Boston, Massachusetts, in October, 1892, and died in Fitzwilliam, New Hampshire, in August, 1948. He was brought up in Boston and served in France as an officer in the United States Army in the First World War. He then went to Stanford University, California, and Harvard, where he was awarded a doctorate and taught economics. After a brief period as a professor at Lawrence College in Wisconsin, he joined the United States Department of the Treasury in 1934, the beginning of his official career.

Promotion was rapid, and White soon won the confidence of the Secretary of the Treasury, Henry Morgenthau, Jr. As Director of Monetary Research in the years immediately preceding the American entry into the Second World War, White gained much practical and administrative experience in the internal and external affairs of the Treasury Department. During 1941 he was appointed as assistant to Henry Morgenthau.

On December 8, 1941, the day following the Japanese attack on Pearl Harbor, Harry Dexter White was given the authority of Assistant Secretary of the Treasury by Henry Morgenthau. White held this authority, but not the formal title, along with his two other positions in the Treasury. His new responsibilities included supervision of the foreign operations of the Treasury, and in 1943 he was put in charge of his department's relations with the American Army and Navy.

White's influence, therefore, during the war years was probably greater than that implied by any of his official titles. He was the author of a last-minute proposal for a general settlement between the United States and Japan in the weeks preceding the Pearl Harbor attack. Some of White's suggestions were incorporated in the final "ultimatum," as it was regarded in Tokyo, which was given by Secretary of State Cordell Hull to the Japanese envoys on November 26, 1941.

A few months later, in early 1942, White took the leading part in the formulation of American policy for the postwar international financial order. The White Plan became the historic basis of the structure of to-

9

day's International Monetary Fund. With Lord Keynes, White was the dominating figure at the Bretton Woods Conference of July, 1944, when the Fund and its twin institution, the International Bank for Reconstruction and Development, were born.

Another influential, but perhaps less well-known, part played by White was his role in the long, complex and tortuous negotiations between the United States government and Nationalist China during the Second World War.

In White's own words, he "participated in a major way" in the drafting of a United States Treasury paper for President Roosevelt on the treatment of postwar Germany. Known to posterity as the Morgenthau Plan, the paper inspired the "Quebec Memorandum," which was initialed by Roosevelt and Churchill during their second wartime conference in that city in September, 1944. The memorandum approved by the two leaders on that occasion looked forward to the transformation of the postwar Reich into "a country primarily agricultural and pastoral in character."

Following his attendance at the Octagon Conference, White continued to be closely involved in American policy-planning for postwar Germany. But in this sphere his influence inevitably began to contract following President Truman's accession in April, 1945, and Morgenthau's departure from the Treasury three months later.

However, he had been formally appointed Assistant Secretary of the Treasury in January, 1945. The importance placed at this time by the American government on the Bretton Woods institutions presaged a new phase of his career. White attended the important inaugural meeting of the Fund and the Bank at Savannah, Georgia, in March, 1946. His nomination as the first American Executive Director of the International Monetary Fund had been approved by the Senate the previous month. When the Fund began work in May, 1946, White presided over the first meeting of the Board of Executive Directors.

Slightly less than a year later, White resigned from the Fund in a letter to President Truman written at the end of March, 1947. He left Washington and took up work in New York as a financial and economic consultant, also spending some time at his newly acquired summer home at Fitzwilliam, New Hampshire.

In September, 1947, White suffered a severe heart attack, and it was from a second coronary attack that he died at his summer home, Blueberry Hill, Fitzwilliam, in August, 1948.

Both at the time of these great events, and later, there seems to have been little doubt as to White's importance.

Following his resignation from the Fund in the spring of 1947, the Executive Board passed a formal resolution which stated that White had been "preeminent in the establishment of the International Monetary Fund and the International Bank for Reconstruction and Development.[1] In his biography of Lord Keynes, Sir Roy Harrod has written that "but for White's assiduity and galvanic personality, a large scheme of the kind for which Keynes was working in Britain would never have come to birth at Bretton Woods.[2]

An American historian, Professor Earl Latham, writing in the 1960's, considered that Harry Dexter White was "one of the most influential men in international affairs in the 1940's, entrusted by the Secretary of the Treasury, Henry Morgenthau, with vast responsibility and discretion . . . his part in public affairs was of tremendous significance for the national policy. . . .[3]

Regrettably, however, there has been some difficulty in assessing White's historical role. In a Chicago speech in November, 1953, over five years after White's death, the then Attorney General Herbert Brownell stated that "Harry Dexter White was a Russian spy. He smuggled secret documents to Russian agents for transmission to Moscow."

Soon after, former President Harry Truman revealed that serious accusations involving espionage had been made against White late in 1945 and early 1946, but it had been practically impossible to prove these charges with the evidence then at hand. Pending an intensive secret investigation, White's appointment to the Fund had been allowed to take its course. But when the necessity for secrecy came to an end, Mr. Truman said, White had been "separated from the Government service promptly."

In further congressional testimony at this time, Attorney General Brownell considered that "conclusive" evidence had appeared after White's death.[4]

Clearly, therefore, history has been kinder to the Bretton Woods institutions than to one of their principal authors. The charge that White may have been involved in what was essentially ideological espionage brings the question of divided loyalty to some of the events in which he took part. Here we shall attempt to describe and to analyze such events, rather than to accuse or defend White. When the charges against White are noted, denials or rebuttals will be also noted when necessary.

However, the first charges against White had been broached in his lifetime. There followed the single occasion in which he was asked about these matters. With perhaps excusable hyperbole, it has been described as "one of the most unusual, most dramatic and perhaps inexplicable scenes of all U.S. history."[5]

The scene was set in the summer of 1948 by the appearance in Washington before the House of Representatives Committee on Un-American

Activities of two self-confessed members of the Communist underground in the United States.

The committee, as has been related in Walter Goodman's recent comprehensive study, *The Committee,* had first been conceived in the 1930's as a bulwark against Nazis and Bundists. It had been set up as a special, temporary committee of the House in 1938. Long before its permanent establishment as a standing committee in 1945, it had dedicated itself, under the guise of ferreting out Communists, to a scatter-gun inquisition of liberals, progressives, welfare state enthusiasts and radical dissenters of every kind.

Perhaps the committee was indifferent to the real issues posed by authoritarian organizations. What Martin Dies, the first committee chairman, represented "was an aching nostalgia for pre-World War I America. He stood for the small town populated by a few hundred neighborly descendants of early settlers and against the cities with their polyglot masses. He stood for a style of life that was being shaken by industrial unions, by the Negro awakening, by revolutionary currents of every sort."[6]

Now, in 1948, the committee was surrounded by events even more challenging and perplexing than the prewar period that had given it birth. As Walter Goodman has written, "It was the year of the end of democracy in Czechoslovakia, and Soviet blockade in Berlin, of domestic spy scares, security checks, deportations and harassment of Communists; of the dismal fling of the Progressive Party. It was an election year, filled with decisions. . . ."[7]

On July 31, 1948, Elizabeth Terrill Bentley appeared before the committee. She said that during the war, from 1941 to 1944, she had worked as a courier for Soviet Intelligence, the NKVD, in the United States. She was in contact with at least two separate networks. Altogether Miss Bentley named some thirty former government employees, the majority of whom had worked in quite responsible positions, as participants in these espionage activities. The most senior of the officials named was Harry Dexter White.

Miss Bentley said that White gave information to one Nathan Gregory Silvermaster, a leader of one of the underground espionage groups, which was relayed to her. White had known where the information was going. He would help to place people with Communist sympathies in government employment, but she did not know whether he was a "card-carrying" Communist or not. Miss Bentley did not know White personally; she was repeating what she had been told by Silvermaster and others.[8]

Interviewed by the United Press, White said that he was shocked by

Miss Bentley's statements and that he would seek permission to refute them. (The committee had already decided to subpoena all those named by Miss Bentley.) White also said that he had been questioned by a Federal Grand Jury inquiring into Communist activities in the United States, and which had heard Miss Bentley.[9]

Three days later, on August 3, another self-confessed underground agent appeared before the committee—David Whittaker Chambers. He stated that he had worked for the Communist Party underground in Washington in the 1930's, which he claimed was then headed by one J. Peters. According to Chambers, the primary underground organization named after its leader, Harold Ware. But during 1936 an "elite group," composed of promising officials who were expected to rise in the government service, was detached from this parent group. Its paramount objectives at that time were "power and influence" rather than active espionage. Certain people not in the Ware group had been added to the "elite group," and one of these was Harry Dexter White.

Chambers went on to say that he was the link between this elite group and J. Peters. He could not state whether White was a Party member but "he certainly was a fellow traveller so far within the fold that his not being a Communist would be a mistake on both sides." When Chambers had broken with the Communist Party in 1937 he had asked White to break away from "the Communist movement." Chambers had left White "apparently in a very agitated frame of mind, and I thought I had succeeded. Apparently I did not."[10]

Although Chambers had not mentioned White's name specifically in connection with espionage, he had, unlike Miss Bentley, asserted that White was known to him personally during the course of these alleged clandestine activities.

On Friday, August 13, 1948, Harry Dexter White appeared before the House Committee in Washington. He was no stranger to Capitol Hill and in the spring and summer of 1945 had played an important part in piloting the Bretton Woods legislation through Congress.

Formally dressed, his manner frank, White took the oath and outlined his distinguished career. He told the Congressmen that he was now a "sort of financial and economic consultant" living in New York.[11]

White emphatically denied the charges of Miss Bentley and Whittaker Chambers. Judging from pictures, he had never met them, and he repudiated the charges of espionage and of Communist affiliations: "The principles in which I believe, and by which I live, make it impossible for me to ever do a disloyal act or anything against the interest of our country, and I have jotted down what my belief is for the committee's information."

My creed is the American creed. I believe in freedom of religion, freedom of speech, freedom of thought, freedom of the press, freedom of criticism and freedom of movement. I believe in the goal of equality of opportunity, and the right of each individual to follow the calling of his or her own choice, and the right of every individual to an opportunity to develop his or her capacity to the fullest.

I believe in the right and duty of every citizen to work for, to expect and to obtain an increasing measure of political, economic and emotional security for all. I am opposed to discrimination in any form, whether on grounds of race, color, religion, political belief or economic status.

I believe in the freedom of choice of one's representatives in Government, untrammelled by machine guns, secret police or a police state. . . .

White ended his credo to applause from the public gallery, applause which was repeated at intervals throughout the hearing.

In reply to questions, White stated frankly that he knew Silvermaster, "a very fine chap," and considered him innocent. Although it was "disconcerting" that a number of the people named by Miss Bentley or Chambers had worked for him in the Treasury, it was not strange, as the department was a large one, expanding at that time, and White considered himself "a pretty good judge" of competence in his field as he hired new staff.

In answer to other questions, he reminded the committee of the beliefs of the Founding Fathers with regard to Star Chamber proceedings, of the provisions of the Bill of Rights and of "all the paraphernalia that stands for Anglo-American justice."

White skirmished brilliantly with the committee, dominating its proceedings, and forcing the chairman at one stage to ask him to "please be responsive to the questions." When asked if he were the author of the Morgenthau Plan, White quickly shot back, "Did you also hear that I was the author of the famous White Plan?" After saying that he had "participated in a major way" in a memorandum (on Germany) which was sent to President Roosevelt, White asked if he could comment. The inquiring Congressman now preferred that he didn't. It was "immaterial."

The committee's procedure was self-defeating, and with one exception there was little sustained questioning. However, Chambers had said that he knew White. Evidently, one Congressman considered that here was an elementary issue of fact that might be explored before other weightier issues such as alleged espionage or possible Communist affiliations could be examined. Perhaps it might be possible, by questioning both men in turn, to develop some corroborative evidence as to the truth or falsity of Chambers' simple statement. The question of identity could be crucial to the whole proceedings.

Were there any possible circumstances, Representative Richard Nixon wanted to know, in which Chambers, known by his underground pseudonym of "Carl," could have met White? Pictures of Chambers taken in August, 1948, were produced:

WHITE: I say I have no recollection of ever having met him. It was twelve or fifteen years ago. I must have met anywhere from 5 to 10,000 people in the last fifteen years, but I have no recollection. It may be that he did meet me, and it may be that I did chat with him.

NIXON: In the event that you had met that individual, Mr. White, on say, as many as three of four occasions, would you recollect whether you had or had not met him?

WHITE: The oftener I was supposed to have met him, the more nearly would it be that I would have remembered. It partly depends on where, what the conversation was. I should think so, three or four times, I do not know.

NIXON: Well, assuming that a meeting did occur on as many as four occasions, would your testimony be that you do not recollect having met this person?

WHITE: My testimony would have been the same. I do not recollect ever having met him. It is possible that I may have met a chap like that in any one of a dozen conferences or cocktail parties or meetings.

NIXON: Suppose you had met this individual on four occasions by himself, and were engaged in conversations with him, would you recollect whether you did or did not?

WHITE: I should think I would—I should think I would, but I am not sure.

NIXON: And you do not want to say then that if you had met him on three or four occasions, whether you do or not remember having met him?

WHITE: I do not recollect ever having met him. . . .

NIXON: Your testimony is that you did not during the year 1935 or 1937—

WHITE: I do not recollect having met that individual.

NIXON: I am sorry, but I did not hear you. You what?

WHITE: I said I do not recollect having met that individual. I am
merely repeating what I said before. . . .

Representative Nixon returned again to this issue, to clear it up "for the
record," but White was emphatic. Only some months later, when Chambers elaborated on his original story involving White, did this exchange
assume a possible added significance. But by then it was too late for
White to help Richard Nixon or anyone else seeking clarification of
Chambers' story.

During the journey back from Washington to his summer place in New
Hampshire, White's heart gave way again, and he died in Fitzwilliam on
Monday, August 16, 1948. The reports of his death, among them a front
page story in the New York *Times*, mentioned his vigorous rebuttal of the
charges against him, along with the details of his career.

Inquiries continued into what would be referred to as the case of
Harry Dexter White.

PART I

FROM BOSTON TO THE TREASURY

1892–1934

1

BOSTON BOYHOOD

Boston seemed to offer no market for educated labour. A peculiar and perplexing amalgam Boston always was, and although it had changed . . . it was not less perplexing. One no longer dined at two o'clock; one could no longer skate on Back Bay; one heard talk of Bostonians worth five millions or more as something not incredible. Yet the place still seemed simple. . . .

—Henry Adams, *The Education of Henry Adams*

Comparatively little is known about Harry Dexter White's early years, but the main outlines are reasonably clear.

Conventional wisdom has usually decreed, probably rightly, that the curiosity we feel about the forebears and upbringing of famous men and women may be justified by their subsequent influence on character. Indeed, the greater the belief that this early interaction of environment and heredity is a decisive matrix of character, the greater the conviction that an understanding of the whole man and his actions may be found in these early years. Possibly so. Within this framework, however, the rival claims of nature and nurture are necessarily inconclusive. Their essence is that of the unique complexity of the human personality itself confronted with other people and diverse surroundings.

It will continue to remain uncertain, therefore, why a man so remarkable as Harry Dexter White should be so different from others who shared the same family and early life. What is certain, according to the Boston City Hall records, is that Harry White—the middle name was to be added later—was born on October 9, 1892, at 57 Lowell Street, Boston, Massachusetts. This record of birth gives his father's name as Isaac White, a peddler, his mother's name as Sarah White, and both are listed as natives of Russia. The Massachusetts state record lists an unnamed boy born on the same day to the same family at 59 Lowell Street, Boston. Here, too, the father's name is given as Isaac.[1]

Lowell Street lay at the foot of Beacon Hill—at the time of Harry White's birth a declining middle-class area of tenements, shops and dwelling houses, sometimes known as the millinery district of Boston. White's birthplace, below the elevated railroad of the Massachusetts Transit Authority, was replaced in 1906 by another structure. Today, in another cycle of rebuilding common to many cities all over the world, the district where White was born is being redeveloped with high-rise apartment blocks and other buildings—Boston's West End Development.

Some confusion exists over the background of White's family. In his carefully researched series of articles on White published in the Boston *Globe* in November, 1953, Boston newspaperman Charles L. Whipple stated that according to a boyhood friend, Nathan Krock, White had a sister, Bessie, and three brothers, Benjamin, Nathan and Abraham, the latter living in New York. Nathan White, who died in 1955, and whose book on Harry White was published privately by Bessie the following year, states, however, that Harry White was "the youngest of seven children."[2]

According to Nathan White, the family had emigrated to the United States from Lithuania, then, of course, a part of the Czarist Empire. The immigration record shows that the family's date of arrival in Boston was April, 1885. Harry Dexter White's death certificate of August, 1948, issued by the State of New Hampshire, together with the Massachusetts file copy, as White was cremated in Boston, also lists the parents' birthplace as Lithuania. The possibility exists, then, that the White family may have consisted of more than five children, some of whom may have died or left the family circle when young, either before, or more probably after, the family's arrival in the United States in 1885.[3]

Some further confusion exists over the family name. According to a listing of the Boston Board of Assessors in 1892, the appropriate notation for 57 Lowell Street shows a Jacob, not an Isaac White, as tenant, although of course White's father may have used his different first names at different times. In his listing the word "White" is scratched out, the word "Rith" written above, in its turn topped by "Weit."

The Federal Immigration records, which also note details of naturalization, show that Jacob Weit, peddler, of 57 Lowell Street, Boston, was granted American citizenship on June 18, 1892. Weit's date of birth was given as August 1, 1860, former allegiance Russia, and date and port of arrival in the United States as April 2, 1885, Boston. These facts complete the record.

But a second immigration record, filed in the same archives of the Federal Building in Boston, indicates another naturalization petition granted to Jacob White on May 6, 1897. Except for the surname, date, and the address given as 109 Salem Street, Boston, the data are the same as in the first immigration record. Presumably this second petition was filed in order to regularize the change of surname. In those days, of course, wives automatically acquired American citizenship when it was granted to the husband.[4]

These matters are further clarified by Harry Dexter White's New Hampshire death certificate, which with the Massachusetts file copy, gives his father's name as Jacob White, his mother's maiden name as Sarah Magilewski and their birthplace Lithuania. Except that their birthplace is given as Russia, the same information on the parents' names is given in White's marriage certificate of February, 1918, noted in Chapter 2 below. In June, 1946, White himself told an inquiring newspaperman that "my family immigrated to this country in the early eighties from Europe, and it is my understanding that the name in the old country was Weiss, but was altered at the suggestion of the immigration authorities."[5]

It seems probable, therefore, that the first Federal Immigration record of 1892, together with Nathan White's account and Harry White's own death certificate, sums up most of the known details of the White family background. Jacob and Sarah Magilewski Weit arrived in Boston from Lithuania in April, 1885, were naturalized four months before Harry's birth in October, 1892, and the family change of name to White was regularized at the latest by May, 1897.

White's first twenty-five years were dominated, one way or another, by the family hardware business which, according to Nathan White, had been set up in 1892, the year of his birth.

As the business slowly expanded, the White family was listed by city directories in 1894 as living at Prince Street, Boston, but the following year Jacob White was back in 57 Lowell Street, occupation "dry goods." As we know from the 1897 immigration record, by that year Jacob White's address was in Salem Street, away from the shadow of the El. In 1900 Jacob White was again listed as a peddler living at 100 Salem Street, where in 1953 neighbors remembered his crockery shop.

In September, 1901, Harry White entered the Old Eliot School in Boston, reputed to be one of the oldest public grammar schools in the United States, and which had been attended by John F. (Honey Fitz) Fitzgerald, grandfather of President Kennedy. The school records show that Harry White listed his address on entering the school as 7 Salem Street, and that he remained in the Eliot School until at least the sixth grade. The records, however, do not show the date of White's discharge from the Eliot School, which was torn down after the Second World War.

According to Charles Whipple, White apparently graduated from the Eliot School at the age of fourteen in 1906, the year the family moved to Dyer Avenue in Everett, a northern suburb of Boston. (Nathan White says this move to Everett was made in 1904.)

In any case, White certainly entered Everett High School in 1906, and completed a four-year course in three years, graduating in 1909. During this time in high school, he commuted to Boston in the evenings, taking his books with him, so that he could help in the family business. He was already a sports enthusiast, particularly interested in tennis and baseball. White's high school classmates later remembered him as "the youngest, smartest and one of the smallest—a retiring boy, but witty."

Perhaps because he had graduated in three years, White's grades were good but not brilliant. The Boston *Globe* recorded, with a picture, on June 25, 1909, that Harry Dexter White—the first recorded use of the middle name—was the youngest three-year graduate from Everett High, and that he would not be seventeen until December 24 that year. As far as is known, no one has ever explained White's use of the acquired middle name.

White was not able to pursue his formal education after graduating from Everett High. According to Nathan White, his mother had died in 1901, and two months following his graduation from high school in June, 1909, his father, Jacob White, also died. White spent the next two years clerking for the family hardware and crockery business, now known as J. White's Sons. By now the firm was a going concern, and sometimes during this period White would take over as a store manager, invariably bringing his books and pencils with him. Soon, J. White's Sons had grown to four hardware stores.[6]

After two years working for the family business, White enrolled in September, 1911, at the Massachusetts Agricultural College (now the University of Massachusetts) at Amherst. He gave his birthday as October 29, 1892, the date he was to use for the rest of his life, his religion as Hebrew, and his future profession as farming. It was necessary to take an entrance examination in three subjects, and while he passed in English he failed in American history and civics. He soon passed in both subjects in a second examination, but left college after one semester in February, 1912. As a freshman, his average mark was 80.8, but his best, 99, was in military science. His academic career was over for ten years.

Family affairs had now required White's return to the business, and for the next five years, until April, 1917, White was "a hard working hardware man." "The hours were long in those days," Nathan White tells us:

It was all work save for an occasional dance or theatre. But [Harry] had a host of friends and whenever they got together, his ready wit made him the spark plug of the group and there was never a dull moment. Sunday was a day for rest and recreation, but for several years, right up to the entry of the United States into World War I, he spent his Sunday mornings teaching the senior class of boys at the Home for Jewish children at Dorchester. The boys worshipped him.

He also directed them as a Boy Scout troop and was a dominant factor in their moral and ethical development.[7]

During this period between 1912 and 1917, White, in his early twenties, moved several times in Boston and its environs. He is recorded as living in Myrtle Street and at Pinckney Street, Beacon Hill; in Wanopah Street, Roxbury, and then successively at Harlem and Esmond Streets in Dorchester. Apart from his work at J. White's Sons, he also spent time at the North End Union, Boston, a settlement house, where he was recorded on the honor roll after the First World War.[8]

Understandably, White was restless at this time. As the youngest son of an industrious family, his attempt to persist in his schooling had been necessarily sacrificed to the demands of the family business. Yet White's abortive attempt to continue his education while working, and his activities in social work illustrate an understandable ambition to better himself, a wish for success in his own right.

Underlying this familiar conflict between family duty and personal ambition lay the challenge of the proud city in which White spent his first twenty-five years.

The challenge was symbolized in the name of the street where he was born, with its mocking, aristocratic echoes to a young man of White's background. True, the Lowells and the Cabots and many of the other famous patrician families of Boston, had once been adventurers and revolutionaries. The American Revolution itself would perhaps have been neither possible nor successful without Boston's contribution.

This outpouring of Boston's talent had led to the city's remarkable intellectual and financial primacy in the nation's life from Washington's time to that of Lincoln. Then, in the later nineteenth century, Boston had been overtaken by New York. But there was an inner certainty about Boston in the early twentieth century that would hardly notice the aspirations of many more secure than the young Harry White.

Invoking Quincy's view of the city, that reluctant Bostonian, Henry Adams, commented that "the tone of Boston society was colonial. The Bostonian always knelt in self-abasement before the majesty of English standards; far from concealing it as a weakness, he was proud of it as his strength. The eighteenth century ruled Boston long after 1850. . . ."[9] By 1906, when White was entering Everett High School, an English visitor, H. G. Wells, found a distinctive sterile beauty in the city: "There broods over the real Boston an immense effect of finality. . . . The capacity of Boston, it would seem, was just sufficient, but no more than sufficient to comprehend the whole achievement of the human intellect, up to, let us say, the year 1875. Then an equilibrium was established. . . ."[10]

In this Antonine community, Richard Whalen has remarked for the scion of another nineteenth-century Boston immigrant family, "For an aspiring Yankee who arrived after the Civil War, the upper reaches of society were closed. For an Irishman on the scene a generation or two later, the situation was hopeless. Money might be made, but money in itself meant little. Everyone's place had been decided long ago."[11] For someone of White's birth and resources, no matter how diligent or intelligent, that place was not necessarily one of advantage.

The way out for White, as for many of his generation caught in the same chain of events all over the world, came at last in April, 1917. On April 2, in a peroration received with thunderous applause, President Woodrow Wilson told Congress that "the day has come when America is privileged to spend her blood and her might for the principles that gave her birth and happiness and the peace that she has treasured." The war resolution was quickly passed by Congress, and on April 6, 1917, the United States and Imperial Germany were at war.

Six days later, without waiting to be drafted, Harry Dexter White enlisted in the United States Army.[12]

2

SOLDIER AND STUDENT

. . . at no time since Lincoln's has there been a man more fitted to lead
than you. [We] await instructions. . . .
                    —HARRY DEXTER WHITE to ROBERT M. LA FOLLETTE,
                                                    February, 1924

ON HIS enlistment in April, 1917, White applied for admission to the
officers' training camp at Plattsburg, New York. Nathan White suggests
that, although he was handicapped by the fact that he had spent only one
term in college, Harry White's mark of 99 percent in military science may
have helped toward his acceptance for this officer training course.

When he enlisted, White was in his twenty-fifth year. The "smallest,
smartest" student of his class at Everett High School was now 5 feet 6
inches tall. But White's lack of height may have been compensated for by
his determination to pass the great test of his generation. As far as his
appearance was concerned, White was to say in later years that the
distinctive moustache which he first grew during his service in the First
World War was necessary to make himself look older. He was, of course,
younger and smaller than many of the men he commanded.

At the end of the summer's training at Plattsburg, White was commissioned as First Lieutenant in the infantry. According to Nathan White,
his brother was one of a group of five men in his company selected for
advanced training with several hundred other officers in an "Iron Battal-
ion." Once this second course was over, White was assigned to Camp
Devens in Massachusetts which had been established to help train the
thousands of recruits pouring into the Army in the winter of 1917–18.[1]

Like many another soldier at this time, White decided to get married before he was sent overseas. His bride was Anne Terry, a twenty-two-year-old student. She filed their marriage intention at Boston City Hall on February 18, 1918, listing herself as born in Russia, the daughter of Aaron Terry and Sarah Atkins, also Russian-born. White's address was given as Camp Devens, his father's name as Jacob White, his mother's maiden name as Sarah Magilewski, also Russian-born. Anne Terry White, the mother of White's two daughters, later became a well-known author of children's books on the general subject of archaeology and prehistory.

The marriage license was issued two days after the intention was filed, and on February 22, Washington's birthday, the couple were married at Boston's Temple Israel.[2]

In the Boston City Hall marriage intentions, White's occupation was originally listed as "military service," but these two words were crossed out and replaced by "Soldier U.S.A." In fact, soon after his marriage White was sent to France with the 302nd Infantry Regiment, an organic part of the United States 76th Infantry Division. Later, he transferred to the 163rd Infantry Regiment of the 41st Infantry Division. Neither regiment, as given by Nathan White, saw combat in France, or, according to the Office of the Chief of Military History, participated in a named campaign. By the end of the war the 41st Division was designated the 1st Depot Division, American Expeditionary Force.[3]

It seems probable, therefore, that White spent his time overseas in a relatively uneventful way in the American Army's large training and service-of-supply camps in France. Following the armistice of November, 1918, White's regiment returned to the United States. It was demobilized at Camp Dix, New Jersey, in February, 1919. White was mustered out a First Lieutenant of the Infantry, and he went back to Boston and J. White's Sons.[4]

As with many other "Soldiers U.S.A." after 1918, life would never be quite the same again for White. For a short time he worked once more in the family hardware business, but as Nathan White writes, "life in the army had changed his outlook." He left the family business for good in 1919 to take up the post of head of an orphan asylum for dependents of American Expeditionary Force servicemen killed in the war. Then, in 1920, he became the director of Corner House, a settlement house on New York's West Side. Two years later, in 1922, he became financially interested in a boy's summer camp, of which he was for a short time a director.[5]

But by 1922 White had decided at last what he wanted to do. His army service had been the way out of Boston. Now he was to make really sure of the break with the past. Possibly this new course had been in his mind for ten years, ever since circumstances had forced him to leave college in 1912. In February, 1922, the married veteran, nearly thirty years old, enrolled at Columbia University in New York. He had decided on an academic career.[6]

White's experience in the 1st Depot Division in France had probably been less eventful than Ernest Hemingway's war in the auto-ambulance or e. e. cummings' encounters in the enormous room, let alone the scenes of carnage witnessed by Robert Graves or Siegfried Sassoon. But White had worn an overseas cap and was sure of himself. Ignoring the lost generation of the Jazz Age, he would concentrate at the age of thirty on the immensely practical task of building a new career from the beginning.

When he first enrolled at Columbia in February, 1922, White had decided to study government. But after three terms he left to move across the continent to Stanford University at Palo Alto, California, which he entered as a junior in the summer quarter of 1923. By now he was studying economics. He later told a friend that he had "realized that most governmental problems are economic, so I stayed with economics."[7]

While he studied at Stanford, White and his wife lived at Los Gatos on the San Francisco peninsula, about thirty miles from the Pacific coast. At thirty-one he was, of course, ten years older than the average student and apparently took little part in student activities. But White had not come to Stanford to look for distraction. In October, 1924, he was awarded an AB in economics "with great distinction," and symbolizing this academic success he was elected a member of Phi Beta Kappa. A year later, in June, 1925, he was given an AM in economics.[8]

A Stanford University professor who knew White at this time later described him as "aggressive and brilliant."

He was the type of student who would disagree with this professor in class and present a well-conceived argument to bolster his point, but he respected the opinions of others. White knew exactly what he was going to do. When he was an undergraduate here [in Stanford], he had already decided he was going to take his PhD at Harvard, and said that he was then going to take up an academic creer. I don't recall that he had any individualistic characteristics of manner or dress, and at that time he did not display any so-called left-wing tendencies.[9]

Nevertheless, a copy of one of White's letters which has survived from this period shows that his interests were not completely intramural during these years on the Pacific coast when he laid the foundations of his subsequent career:

Senator Robert M. La Follette   Los Altos, Calif.
Washington, D.C.   February 29, 1924
Dear Sir,

The writer represents a group of men consisting for the most part of mature graduate students of Stanford University, who are in thorough accord with your ideas and your policies. They are particularly desirous of having your consent to become a candidate for the office of the President of the United States in 1924, for they feel that in no other way can the principles which you represent be brought more forcibly to the people. They fully appreciate the additional burden which such action would place on your shoulders, but they unanimously believe that you have at least ten more years of good fight left in you and know that you will be able to carry on the fight for a truly democratic government most effectively as President of the United States. They have no illusions about the difficulty of election, but this merely serves to make them more determined to support you.

They are able and enthusiastic workers and most of them are good speakers; all of them yearn to serve your cause. Most earnestly they urge upon you the fact that at no time has our country been more in need of a leader, and that at no time since Lincoln's has there been a man more fitted to lead than you. They await instructions as to how they can best further your cause.

Very truly yours,

HARRY D. WHITE[10]

Robert Marion La Follette (1855–1925) had long excited the enthusiasm of many idealists besides White and his "mature graduate students" at Stanford. A lawyer and a Wisconsin Republican, he had practiced in Madison before becoming successively a member of the House of Representatives, Governor of the State and Senator from 1905 until his death. Years after these events, in 1957, he was voted, along with Henry Clay, Daniel Webster, John C. Calhoun and Robert A. Taft as one of the five greatest men ever to grace the upper chamber.

A staunch defender of agrarian interests against the railroads and Eastern finance, "Fighting Bob" had inevitably become spokesman for American progressivism during his long career, and he had opposed, on broadly pacifist grounds, the entry of the United States into the First World War.[11]

When White drafted his letter, it seemed as if the 1924 presidential election would be a remarkable contest. The Republican administration of Calvin Coolidge was still discredited by the Teapot Dome scandals of the Harding era, while the Democrats, who eventually nominated John

W. Davis, after 103 ballots, were regarded by many on the left as a relatively conservative party.

La Follette, traditionally the standard-bearer of progressivism, was unlikely to be adopted by the Republicans. But the Conference for Progressive Political Action, the most important progressive grouping within the labor movement, began turning toward him, as La Follette alone had the stature to lead a third party. Irving Howe has written of this time that "any American, who, for whatever reasons wanted a new political movement on the national scene now had cause for optimism and hope."[12]

It was to this movement, apparently, that White and his friends now gave their support. In the event, of course, the Republicans voted down La Follette and nominated Calvin Coolidge in their Cleveland Convention in June, 1924. On July 4, also in Cleveland, the C.P.P.A. nominated La Follette as an independent presidential candidate, with Burton K. Wheeler as his vice-presidential running mate. Refusing to have anything to do with the Communists, La Follette's platform called for the public ownership of water and railroads, strict public control of natural resources, recognition of agriculture as a national industry and other progressive policies.

Although La Follette won only thirteen electoral college votes in the 1924 presidential election, in which Coolidge was returned, he and his progressive movement polled five million votes in the country. This was a considerable achievement, "but disappointing to those who expected more immediate victories—the whole third party movement began to wither away."[13] La Follette died the following year.

In this early political commitment White had therefore supported with some passion a movement with little significant political effect at the time, and one probably not central to the preoccupations of most Americans as the boom roared on to the crash of October, 1929. But, in any case, despite the hopes of some of La Follette's supporters, the third party adventure in 1924 was as much an idealist protest against the prevailing political system as it was a search for political power in its own right.

In view of this it seems possible that White's background may have been one of the reasons that led to his support of La Follette at this time of his life. An inevitable "cultural shock" was bound to affect any family immigrating to the United States, one that could have been especially sharp in Boston, as we have seen. As Theodore Draper has pointed out, America was a land of immigrants, and the disproportionately large number of immigrants on the radical left was as much a result of their rejection by the predominant political institutions and parties as the reverse. Poverty was another of several factors. It was here on the Fundamentalist Left that the dream of American equality came true for some, with the result, as Draper puts it, that "a large proportion of Socialists were immigrants, but a small proportion of immigrants were Socialists."[14]

Of course, White, as an ambitious veteran trying to make up lost time, would have different problems. Besides, the La Follette movement with its populist and progressivist roots looked back to an indigenous, precapitalist political Arcadia, rather than to the imported, postcapitalist Utopias of the socialists, whatever their precise persuasion. But for someone brought up in patrician Boston with its "Last Hurrah" machine politics, the third party of 1924 may well have seemed an attractive political choice when compared with the traditional political coalitions.

What, perhaps, is also significant, quite apart from the politics of the time, is that White took the lead as a spokesman of this largely graduate group when still an undergraduate, although, to be sure, a "mature" student who already knew what he wanted in the next stage of an ascending career.

Now, in 1925, he was to leave the Pacific coast and return to the East, to Harvard.

had grown a lot then, but at Harvard he was not an outstanding personality.

A Boston lawyer, who during this period was tutored by White at Harvard, has confirmed this impression of a man who was both a good teacher and personally withdrawn: "He seemed very easy to get along with, an excellent mind, could make very penetrating economic criticism, and all in all, an excellent teacher. . . . White taught some sections of Economics A [a freshman, elementary course] but money and banking was his field. He had no close relationship with anyone. . . ."[4]

In the summer of 1932, after six years of teaching at Harvard, White apparently realized that his chances of promotion to the Faculty of Arts and Sciences there were slender. He then took the post of Assistant Professor of Economics at Lawrence College, Appleton, Wisconsin. Perhaps his conquest of Boston had not been so certain after all.

In the autumn of 1932, at the age of forty, Harry Dexter White left Cambridge for Lawrence College. The following year, White was promoted to Professor of Economics at Lawrence, but he felt marooned and unhappy at Appleton and said so, apparently thinking that the work was beneath his capabilities. His colleagues once again considered him a fine teacher, but he was not particularly liked. A fellow professor at Lawrence later remembered White as "very intelligent, well informed, but opinionated and assertive." Politically he was considered by another professor as an "ardent New Dealer, as much anti-Communist as anyone."[5]

The then president of Lawrence College, Henry M. Wriston, later president of Brown University, has summed up by saying that during these two years White was regarded as,

a very conservative man, as conservative as Adam Smith. I might say a probably better characterization would be that he was a classical economist. He was a very fine teacher recommended by an expert on anti-Marxianism. I can only tell you what I knew about him at Lawrence. At that time there was not the slightest trace of Marxianism in his teaching. He was a good teacher and I never heard any adverse comment concerning his views. He left Lawrence of his own accord because he wanted to better himself. I never saw him again.[6]

White's reputation as a conservative economist had been cemented by the publication in the summer of 1933 of *The French International Accounts 1880–1913*. The book was listed no. 40 in the Harvard Economic Series which included such volumes as Jacob Viner's study of the Cana-

dian balance of payments, S. E. Harris on Federal Reserve Policy, and
J. C. Hemmeon on the British Post Office. White's book was dedicated to
F. W. Taussig, and in the preface he thanked, among others, Dr. L. B.
Currie, a fellow instructor in Harvard, who had read the manuscript, and
Dr. A. G. Silverman of the National Bureau of Economic Research, with
whom the author had discussed the theory of international trade.[7]

In his preface White remarked that the book was one of a series the
purpose of which was to test and verify the doctrines of the orthodox
theory of international trade based on the gold standard. The French
situation described in his book was interesting because gold played an
important part in the monetary and banking system, capital exports
played an important part in the French foreign accounts, and because the
size of these capital exports in prewar years had been a source of domestic controversy. Statistical material for the project was poorer than expected, and his conclusions, wrote White, were to be received with
greater caution than would be the case in a comparable study of England, Canada or the United States. The period covered by the study was
chosen, of course, to avoid the effects of the upheavals of 1870 and
1914.

White's book was divided into two parts. The first part was devoted to
the construction of a balance sheet of the French international accounts
of the period, and an analysis of the important items with a view to
tracing the mechanism of adjustment of these accounts, the way equilibrium was restored between debtor and creditor. The second part
explored the French monetary and banking system in relation to this
mechanism of adjustment—the heart of the study—and also discussed
the interrelated movements of commodities and capital. The terms of
trade over the period were analyzed and finally an attempt was made to
evaluate the effect of these capital exports as a whole on France.

The book was written with great clarity, and besides the technical
analysis of the French balance of payments, there was also a succinct
outline in White's introduction of the neoclassical theory of how capital
payments were adjusted between countries on the International Gold
Standard. In its simplest form, the traditional doctrine held that a transfer of capital modified the exchange rate, so inducing a flow of gold. This
latter movement of specie then altered interest rates, credit and price
levels of the countries involved, so facilitating exports from the lending to
the borrowing country, while of course reducing imports from the latter
to the former as equilibrium was once again restored.

This remarkable, elaborate (and idealistic) formulation of the classical
economists and their successors explained the intricate self-adjusting
mechanism which lay behind the huge expansion of world trade in the
nineteenth century based on the International Gold Standard. The for-

mula was only ceasing to be received wisdom in the United States and Great Britain at the very time when White's book was published. The legacy of war, reparations, high tariffs, shifts in international trade and other unpredictable political factors showed at last that the world of the balanced budget and the International Gold Standard had ceased to exist in its classical sense by 1914. But this was the broad economic tradition in which White conceived and wrote his book on the French balance of payments.

His conclusions pointed out that, while it had been generally supposed that the huge foreign investments of France yielded a net revenue large enough to make a continuous excess of imports possible, the net revenue in fact for the period under study "was no greater than the total exports of capital for the same period." French industry had been deprived of funds, and countries which had borrowed from France, unlike those which had drawn their capital from the United States or Great Britain, had not spent the money in the creditor country. Moreover, yield in foreign investments was only equal to that on domestic loans, and the real yield was less, "since equal returns imply equal risk." It was questionable whether France as a whole had benefited. As for the assumptions of neoclassical theory, White suggested that the traditional formulation was "not the complete explanation" of the forces at work. He suggested that the classical explanation postulated an "undisturbed world" and that it exaggerated such factors as gold flows and the influence of sectional price changes. He went on to mention the movement of exchange rates between countries on and off the Gold Standard and fluctuating capital exports as factors that had not in the past been given sufficient emphasis. He concluded:

> The French experience in the matter of capital exports leads to the conclusion that the orthodox attitude toward unrestricted capital exports is open to criticism; the assumption that the capital exports benefit both the country and the world at large is not unassailable. . . . The study of French foreign investments supports, in my opinion, the growing belief that capital exports are not always beneficial to the exporting country and that some measure of intelligent control of the volume and direction of foreign investments is desirable. . . . The ramifications of exporting a large portion of a country's savings are too complex, and the consequences too important to permit the continuance of capital exports without making some attempt at evaluating their effects on the well being of the country at large.[8]

These conclusions, made from within the traditional assumptions, were equally valid, White implied, for the United States, Great Britain and other industrial countries.

The book on the whole was well received. The *American Economic Review* remarked that the study was handicapped by the dearth of official data on the subject, and that "the conclusions are suggestive rather than definitive, as the author repeatedly warns us." Despite this, and because of the deductive as much as the inductive analysis, White's book constituted "a valuable addition to the literature on international trade and finance."[9]

In the *Journal of Political Economy*, Roland Wilson commented that the statements of the French accounts were more of a tribute to the author's industry and ingenuity than to the reliability and extent of the recorded statistics. The reviewer went on to say that there were a large number of statistical weaknesses in the first part of the book, "both in the raw materials with which Mr. White has to contend, and in the methods by which he attempts to bring order out of the chaos. He is meticulous in explaining the former, and at times overconfident in his use of the latter. A fair criticism of the estimates [of capital exports] in detail would extend to a volume in itself."

The second part of White's book, was "ably executed. Despite the skill which Mr. White brought to bear on this side of the study, it is disappointing that the results are not more conclusive."[10]

In Britain, the *Economic History Review* discussed White's book against the general background of work being done on the theory of international trade at that time. White tended to confirm the view, wrote Leland H. Jenks, that "economic processes must be viewed as proceeding from the variable combination of a considerable number of factors." The reviewer found himself "highly sympathetic with the author's conclusion and respectful of his diligence." Despite faulty data White had weighted "interpretation heavily with logic and common sense." He also noted White's comments that English conditions may have been "very different" from those in France during this period under study.[11]

The Boston *Transcript* commented respectfully that the compilation of French trade figures was "a distinct contribution in the statistical field,"[12] but perhaps one of the shrewdest comments came from R. L. Buell in *Books* magazine: "The one outstanding weakness of his book is that it does not adequately stress the fact that French foreign investments before the war were controlled by the Quai d'Orsay for political and military reasons. Consequently, no general conclusions as to the effect of wisely made foreign loans can be made from French experience."[13]

Perhaps not all governmental problems were economic.

Yet quite apart from the cut and thrust of the reviewers, there was an irony about the timing of the publication of White's book that transcended any of the volume's carefully threaded arguments. Composed, as we have seen, as a doctoral thesis in the late 1920's, and placed quite explicitly in the classical economic framework, the book appeared four years after the beginning of what J. K. Galbraith, another Harvard economist, has called "the most momentous economic occurrence in the history of the United States, the ordeal of the Great Depression."[14] The world economic system that White had outlined in his narrative of the French accounts was already a thing of the past.

In 1933, the year White was made a professor at Lawrence College, the American Gross National Product (total production of the American economy) was nearly a third less than in 1929. Not until 1937 did the physical volume of production recover the 1929 level, and then it slid back again. Until 1941, when the Depression had been succeeded by global war, the dollar value of American national production still remained below the 1929 level.

The human consequences of the Great Depression were incalculable. During 1933 nearly 13,000,000 people, about one in four of the labor force, were out of work. The Federal Reserve Board index of industrial production (1923–25 = 100) had declined from 126 in June, 1929, to 57 in 1932. Total value of finished commodities at current prices had fallen from $38 billion to $17.5 billion in the same period, and farm prices had fallen by over 50 percent. Prosperity was still far around the corner.[15]

This catastrophe in the United States, where the cities were stricken, and where the rural areas simmered in a state of angry discontent, was only a part of the disintegration of the world economy. Here trade fell even faster than production. By 1932, world trade in manufactures was but 59.5 percent of the 1929 figure. Everywhere economic barriers went up in a desperate attempt to preserve minimal trading positions. New, destructive political forces were unleashed in Europe, symbolized above all by the rise of Hitler.

Such events posed unanswered questions, perhaps especially compelling to one who had both been involved in the La Follette movement of 1924 and who was at the same time an analyst of the classical economic system.

In White's papers in Princeton University Library there is a "Memorandum Prepared by L. B. Currie, E. T. Ellsworth, and H. D. White," dated January, 1932, when White was still at Harvard, which outlines remedial measures. The paper suggests that the administration should combat the Depression, "which had cost more than the Great War," by canceling all debts and reparations, by creating an administration of public works, by reducing tariffs, and by the purchase by the Reserve banks of $1 billion of securities to increase liquidity.[16]

An undated memorandum by White in the same file attacks Samuel Crowther's book, *America Self-Contained,* which was published in 1933. Crowther, a former collaborator of Henry Ford, had suggested in a symptomatic defense of economic nationalism that the capitalist system could save itself without planning if it imposed a "prohibitive" tariff backed by an "absolute embargo." Such measures were criticized by White.[17]

The influence of such general anti-deflationary measures, as outlined in this January, 1932, memorandum by White and his colleagues, on the events of the early New Deal is well known. But throughout most of the worst years of the Depression both parties were equally devoted to the orthodox principles of tight money and a balanced budget. President Hoover had announced a tax cut in November, 1929, a month after the Wall Street crash, and he had later asked businessmen to keep up wages and maintain investment. But although both these measures were on the right side of increasing income, they were without effect.

By the 1932 presidential election campaign, therefore, it appeared that most responsible economic advisers were against expansionist measures to check deflation. Even economists not particularly committed to budget balancing, as Herbert Stein has suggested in his recent study, *The Fiscal Revolution in America,* thought that budget deficits might be harmful rather than helpful. The Age of Keynes was still to come, and in any case national economic independence from the Gold Standard was necessary before the "new economics" could be technically possible. During this early period of the Depression, therefore, budget balancing was virtually a doctrinal matter for the Republicans, while the Democratic Party platform in 1932 also insisted on a "federal budget annually balanced on the basis of accurate executive estimates within revenue."

Roosevelt himself stated at the close of the 1932 campaign that his platform advocated "a sound currency to be preserved at all hazards." The fear of inflation, rather than of deflation, also ruled out the possibility of low interest rates and cheap money. At the time, as Galbraith has written, such attitudes were "above party."[18]

The inspired pragmatism of Roosevelt's first months in the White House after March, 1933, moved away, of course, from the orthodox formulas. But there was still no certainty that the Platonic dogmas would not reassert themselves, or that the Depression could be cured. As we have seen, White was opposed to the orthodox nostrums of deflation and he was also hostile to draconian tariffs. It appears from a letter probably drafted late in 1933 that by this time he was beginning to suspect that the answer to the Depression might not be found in the methods improvised hitherto by the New Deal.

Sometime, probably late in 1933, Professor Taussig apparently wrote to

White at Lawrence College asking him if he would review some books for the *Quarterly Journal of Economics*. An undated draft of White's reply from Appleton, which survived in White's papers at his home near Fitzwilliam, New Hampshire, shows that he intended to tell Taussig that he would be glad to review "Viner's and Habirle's books."[19]

> Lawrence College,
> Department of Economics
> Appleton, Wisconsin.

Dear Professor Taussig,

Thank you very much for keeping me in mind. I shall be glad to review Viner's and Habirle's books and hope the results meet with QJE standards.

I have just finished reading The Theory of Protection and Int. Trade by M. Manoilesco, and am writing a review of it. The seeming authoritativeness of the book and its claims of a new defense for protection is apt to influence readers not well versed in the theory of int. trade. The review of the book in the March[20] number of the Econ-Jour. is not in my opinion sufficiently critical. I do not believe the book important enough for the QJE so shall offer the review to the Journal of Political Economy. I hope it's accepted, but in any case I had to answer the argument to my own satisfaction.

My interest has been aroused by the growing claims that our domestic economy must be insulated against critical disturbances, and that a greater (degree) restriction of imports could supply the insulation. This plea for virtual economic self-sufficiency needs, I believe, more critical treatment than has been forthcoming. I am wondering whether it may not be possible to develop feasible means of rendering our domestic affairs less sensitive to forcing disturbances without sacrificing either stabilizing influences of int. econ. relations or the gains from for. trade. The path, I suspect, may lie in the direction of centralized control over foreign exchanges and trade. I have been spending the spring and summer reading and thinking about the problem but my opinion is as yet unsettled. I am also learning Russian in the hope that I may get a fellowship which would enable me to spend a year chiefly in Russia. There I should like to study intensively the technique of planning at the Institute of Economic Investigation of Gosplan. I expect to apply for a Social Science Research fellowship tho my hopes of an award are not high. Kindest greetings from Mrs. White and myself. We think and speak of you very often.

> Sincerely Yours,
> HARRY D. WHITE[21]

However, within what must have been at the most a year from the writing of this letter, a *deus ex machina* in the shape of Professor Jacob Viner of Chicago University decreed that White would not go to Moscow to study the "technique of planning" at Gosplan, but to the Treasury in Washington.

> Treasury Department,
> Washington, June 7, 1934

Dear Mr. White,

The Treasury Department is undertaking a comprehensive survey of our monetary and banking legislation and institutions, and with a view to planning a long term legislative program for the Administration. The preliminary studies are to be made from about June 20th to Sept. 20th, under my general direction. I am very anxious to have your assistance in the conduct of this study, and I hope that you will be able, and willing, to come to Washington for this purpose for the period indicated. The Treasury of course is prepared to arrange a mutually satisfactory basis of remuneration for your services. If you are interested will you please wire me "collect government rates" as soon as possible, and I will send you further particulars.

> JACOB VINER[22]

Professor H. D. White,
Lawrence College, Appleton, Wis.

On June 9 White accepted the invitation and wired Viner at the Treasury from the telegraph office at Appleton, Wisconsin, "Will be very glad to come to work with you."[23] Viner then wrote the same day from Washington, hoping that White could report to him on June 20, and suggesting that White would be paid one-third of his academic salary, with a $200 pension allowance.[24]

White did not return to teach in Appleton. His summer assignment in Washington would last for thirteen years.

PART II
MATTERS OF STATE
1934–41

4

THE NATURAL POINT OF CONTROL

In governments, as in households, he who holds the purse holds the power. The Treasury is the natural point of control to be occupied by any statesman who aims at organization or reform.

HENRY ADAMS, *The Life of Albert Gallatin*

WHITE's first few months in Washington could have been typical of those many from outside the traditional ranks of government who flocked to the capital during the administrative and intellectual turmoil of the early New Deal.

His special summer assignment was dated, as we have seen, from June 20, 1934, and his report for Professor Viner, "Selection of a Monetary Standard for the United States," was dated September 22.[1] White therefore resigned from this temporary assignment as Economic Analyst in the Office of the Secretary of the Treasury on October 4. The following day he was gazetted "Special Expert, Chief Economic Analyst," working for the United States Tariff Commission, at a salary of $5,600. But he held this post for less than a month, resigning "without prejudice" on October 31.

The next day White became Principal Economic Analyst in the Treasury's Division of Research and Statistics at the same salary. The appointment, which was for "emergency work," was to continue until the following June, but it marked the formal beginning of White's career in the Treasury.

All three of these appointments were "excepted" ones, like so many at this time. This meant that White had been appointed, under the appropriate statutes or executive order, without recourse to the usual civil service examinations—although not, of course, without making the necessary civil service applications. Not until January, 1942, when White was already one of the most powerful men in the Treasury, was he classified as an established civil servant under the sweeping provisions of the Ramspeck Act of 1940.[2]

White had entered the Treasury when some of the most significant reforms of the early New Deal had already become law. Barely eighteen months before, on March 4, 1933, with the banks closed, and with about a quarter of the labor force out of work, President Roosevelt, facing the gravest domestic crisis since Lincoln in 1861, had stated in his rousing inaugural that he might have to assume wartime powers. In addition to the domestic financial crisis, much of the flight of "hot" money that had entered the United States after its exodus from London in 1931 was now being withdrawn, so adding foreign pressure on the dollar to the internal breakdown.

Roosevelt's overall objective was to save the system not to change it. Thus, restoration of confidence and a modicum of financial stability was even more urgent than the implementation of the reforms passed by Congress during the Hundred Days, when the famous alphabetical agencies had been created by such measures as the Agricultural Adjustment Act, the Tennessee Valley Authority Act and the National Industrial Recovery Act.

During March and April, 1933, therefore, the President had taken drastic measures to stop the domestic hoarding of gold and its shipment to Europe, both developments which had helped to precipitate the near panic of the banking crisis. The export of gold was forbidden, except under license, its private hoarding was proscribed and all domestic gold was to be delivered to the Federal Reserve Banks. However, continued pressure on the dollar abroad, combined with demands for inflationary measures in Congress, led to the Treasury announcement on April 19, 1933, that no gold export licenses would be issued. The abandonment of the strict gold standard was followed the next day by an executive order imposing a gold embargo which left the dollar free to find its own level.

Over the next four weeks the dollar declined 17 percent in value from its former gold parity, but the tenacious problem of deflation and low prices remained. Roosevelt was quite explicit in announcing his policy of a managed currency combined with controlled inflation. On May 7 he stated that "the Administration has the definite objective of raising commodity prices to such an extent that those who have borrowed money, will on the average, be able to repay that money in the same kind of dollar which they borrowed."[3]

The Thomas Amendment to the Agricultural Adjustment Act passed on May 12 gave the President broad powers to reduce the gold value of the dollar by up to fifty percent. This legislative phase of the break with the golden past was completed when in June Congress abrogated the gold payment clause in public and private contracts, an act upheld by a narrow 5–4 Supreme Court decision in February, 1935. However, Roosevelt still had to square the political circle between inflation and deflation.

But by now the general economic philosophy of the New Deal was quite clear. Before 1933 the Hoover Administration, as we have noted, had sought to preserve the economy by tariffs, while staying on the International Gold Standard. Roosevelt was, on the contrary, trying to maneuver the economy free from such international arrangements, while seeing little point in specifically raising tariffs: "The conservative version of economic nationalism was thus nationalist in trade, internationalist in finance; the liberal version, internationalist in trade, nationalist in finance."[4]

Roosevelt's belief that no foreign commitments should undermine his program of domestic recovery was dramatically expressed by his "Bombshell" message to the London Economic Conference in July, 1933. In that conference Continental countries still on the Gold Standard wished to stabilize the gold value of international currencies. Great Britain, two years after its own abandonment of gold in September, 1931, now looked with sympathy on such proposals; beset with their own economic difficulties, the British wished to keep the pound low in relation to the dollar.

Of course, such a stabilization of the dollar, barely a few weeks after the beginning of Roosevelt's attempted currency manipulation would have made it hard for prices and credit to rise in the United States. Such proposals would have aroused the inflation lobby on Capitol Hill; and besides Roosevelt was temperamentally opposed to having his hands tied. Even a vague conference declaration on the merits of stabilization and the Gold Standard was unacceptable, and the almost contemptuous tone of the "Bombshell" of July 3 wrecked the conference. The President's commination against the "old fetishes of so-called international bankers" was generally disapproved in Europe, but applauded by Keynes and a group of Oxford economists headed by Roy Harrod and J. M. Meade.[5]

In the United States the "Bombshell" at least showed who was in control, and for the next few months prices moved upward, a result perhaps of both monetary depreciation and the work of the alphabetical agencies. In the autumn, as demands for inflationary measures were again heard, the administration embarked on a gold-buying program under the influence of Professor George Warren. This, it was hoped, would push up the internal price level. As Henry Morgenthau later described this process, it seems hardly a particularly irrational one in the history of our time:

The actual price [of gold] on any given day made little difference. Our object was simply to keep the trend gradually upward, hoping that commodity prices would follow. One day, when I must have come in more than usually worried about the state of the world, we were planning an increase from nineteen to twenty-two cents. Roosevelt took one look at me and suggested a rise of twenty-one cents. "It's a lucky number," the President said with a laugh, "because it's three times seven." I noted in my diary at the time: "If anybody knew how we really set the gold price through a combination of lucky numbers etc. I think they would really be frightened." But he rather enjoyed the shock his policy gave to the international bankers. Montagu Norman of the Bank of England, whom F.D.R. called "old pink whiskers," wailed across the ocean: "This is the most terrible thing that has happened. The whole world will be put into bankruptcy!" . . . The President and I looked at each other, picturing foreign bankers with every one of their hairs standing on end with horror. I began to laugh. F.D.R. roared. . . .[6]

Opposed to Roosevelt's monetary manipulation, the Undersecretary of the Treasury, Dean Acheson, left the administration following what he has described as "a spectacular row" in November, 1933. As the Secretary, William H. Woodin, was already seriously ill, Roosevelt appointed his friend Morgenthau Acting Secretary of the Treasury, which further increased the President's control over these matters.

When Morgenthau succeeded in his own right to the position of Secretary of the Treasury on January 1, 1934, the time was ripe for an abandonment of the gold-buying program and a consolidation of Roosevelt's monetary policies of the past year. The President's "special monetary message" to Congress on January 15, 1934, proposed a stabilization of the dollar at between 50 and 60 percent of its formal gold value, the profits from devaluation to go to form a $2 billion Exchange Stabilization Fund managed by the Treasury. This fund would be partly analogous to the Exchange Equalisation Account set up by the British after their own abandonment of gold in September, 1931. The proposed Bill also vested in the Government the title to all gold held by the Federal Reserve.

The Gold Reserve Act, passed by Congress on January 30, gave the President powers to devalue between the above limits; Roosevelt already possessed, of course, under the Thomas Amendment, powers to devalue by 50 percent. The act also partially neutralized those political groups demanding inflation, for lobbying in future on the value of the dollar would have to be directed to Congress rather than to the White House, and moreover, the price of gold would not be under constant scrutiny. The subsequent Silver Purchase Act of June, 1934, authorizing the administration to buy the metal up to a quarter of the value of the government gold reserve was a victory for the influential silver bloc and the inflation lobby, but the political price paid for the Gold Reserve Act could have been greater in the circumstances.[7]

On January 31, 1934, the day following the passage of the Gold Reserve Act, a Presidential proclamation put the law into effect. The new value of the dollar was established at 59.06 percent of its previous official value against gold of $20.67 per ounce, and the revised official price of gold was therefore set at $35 per ounce. The Treasury would buy gold at this price, and sell the metal at the same rate to foreign central banks of countries on the gold standard.

Coming after Roosevelt's earlier measures, the act meant that now an unprecedented degree of government control existed over the exchange and gold value of the dollar as the Administration sought to protect the American price and credit structure from international pressure. The new banking legislation, which would recast the Federal Reserve, together with the Securities Act, was all part of the same general process. Soon the currency was stabilized at its new value, and in May, 1935, Morgenthau was able to report to the nation that the dollar was sound.

Therefore, by the time Harry Dexter White joined the Treasury, whatever Roosevelt's difficulties as the economy remained depressed, the specter of financial collapse had vanished. In this process, as the power of government replaced the power of business, much of the leverage of the old monetary system had passed from lower Manhattan to Washington, where it reposed in the Treasury, subject as always, of course, to the discretion of the President.

The use to which these crucial measures of the early New Deal were put depended less on the law and the statutes than on Roosevelt's personality. In an age that has come to remember him as the shrouded figure of Yalta, the rousing of the country from the slough of the Great Depression can sometimes seem like an episode from before the nuclear flood. But to those who lived through it the slump was the great cataclysm, the invisible scar of today's older generation.

This Roosevelt well understood in his efforts to restore the country's confidence. He was the first truly modern president as he made the White House the focus of national life. The enormous problems he faced were only matched by his courage and his determination to rescue the American *via media* from the scourges of tyranny and chaos that seemed only too evident in other parts of the world.

Intensely conscious of this mission, Roosevelt once defined his philosophy as that "of a Christian and a Democrat—that's all." But this idealism was always balanced, fortunately, by an equally intense grasp of the practical realities of political power and the regrettable but certain limits of human character.

The Hudson Valley squire, who looked on the White House as a virtual family property, had also been Assistant Secretary of the Navy, a governor of New York, and over twenty years in Democratic party politics. He was a relative of one of the most activist presidents of all before his own incumbency in the White House. "No president this century," Robert Neustadt has reported,

> has had a sharper sense of personal power, a sense of what it is and where it comes from, no one had more hunger for it, few have had more use for it, and only one or two could match his faith in his own competence to use it. . . . No modern president has been more nearly master in the White House. Roosevelt had a love affair with power in that place. . . . And happily for him, his own sense of direction coincided in the main, with the course of contemporary history.[8]

Roosevelt's application of this almost mystically apprehended power was as bewildering to memoir-writing contemporaries as it has been to historians. In Arthur Schlesinger, Jr.'s classic description of the decision-making process:

> The first task of an executive, as he evidently saw it, was to guarantee himself an effective flow of information and ideas. . . . An executive relying on a single information system became inevitably the prisoner of that system. Roosevelt's persistent effort therefore was to check and balance information acquired through official channels by information acquired through a myriad of private, informal and unorthodox channels and espionage networks. At times he seemed to pit his personal sources against his public sources. From the viewpoint of subordinates, this method was distracting when not positively demoralizing. . . .

The link between this flow of information into the White House and the actual decision would be the time of postponement, a period not only to ruminate over the forces involved, but, as important, to keep his own freedom of action among the passionate and ambitious men who surrounded him:

> His favorite technique was to keep grants of authority incomplete, jurisdictions uncertain, charters overlapping. The result of this competitive theory of administration was often confusion and exasperation on the operating level; but no other method could so reliably insure that in a large bureaucracy filled with ambitious men eager for power the decisions, and the power to make them, would remain with

the President. . . . Coexistence with disorder was almost the pattern of his life.

Finally, when all the relevant forces had been assessed, the actual decision was at hand. For Roosevelt these preliminaries were vital in deciding whether his policy would really result in action, the end of policy:

> He evidently felt [Schlesinger goes on] that clear-cut administrative decisions would work only if they expressed equally clearcut realities of administrative competence and vigor. If they did not, the balance of administrative powers would not sustain the decision, then decision would only compound confusion and discredit government. And the actualities of administrative power were to be discovered, not by writing—or by reading Executive orders, but by apprehending through intuition a vast constellation of political forces. . . . Situations had to develop, to crystallize, to clarify; the competing forces had to vindicate themselves in the actual pull and tug of conflict; public opinion had to face the question, consider it, pronounce on it—only then, at the long, frazzled end, would the President's intuitions consolidate and precipitate a result.[9]

These labyrinthine processes of intelligence gathering, calculation and finally decisions were thus some of the means by which Franklin Roosevelt sought to outmaneuver, and to dominate, the forces against him. There could never be any simple, rational explanation of this process. As Rexford Tugwell once put it, "Franklin allowed no one to discover the governing principle." But throughout the twelve years of Roosevelt's presidency, no one was nearer to understanding that principle than Henry Morgenthau.

Henry Morgenthau, Jr., who was forty-two when he became Secretary of the Treasury in January, 1934, had been born in 1891 in New York City. The family background was originally German, and Morgenthau senior had made a notable career in business, real estate and politics, becoming Woodrow Wilson's ambassador to Turkey during the First World War.

Although he had studied at Cornell University, Henry Morgenthau, perhaps overshadowed by his father, had not found a true sense of direction until a convalescent period in Texas convinced him that the land was the key to the good life of the individual, the community and the family. Farming became Morgenthau's passion, and in 1913, when Harry Dexter White was immersed in the Boston hardware business, the young Jeffersonian bought a thousand acres at East Fishkill, Dutchess County, New

York, where the outliers of the Berkshires fall to the rolling country of the Hudson Valley. Here at Fishkill Farms, as the estate was known, Henry Morgenthau made his home.

During 1915 Morgenthau first met his Dutchess County neighbor, Franklin D. Roosevelt, Assistant Secretary of the Navy, who was also active, of course, in Democratic politics in New York and Washington. At this Hyde Park meeting, Roosevelt tried without success to make his neighbor run for county sheriff. But the two men liked each other, and Morgenthau and his wife, Elinor, soon became firm friends with Franklin and Eleanor Roosevelt. As Roosevelt's career flourished, Morgenthau remained anchored to the land, while retaining a marginal interest in politics. When polio seemed to have wrecked Roosevelt's high political hopes, Morgenthau played games and talked with him for hour after hour at Hyde Park. Sometimes the Morgenthaus joined the Roosevelts for a winter cruise through the Florida Keys.

Although he tried his hand at potatoes, corn, rye and a dairy farm, his extensive apple orchards became Morgenthau's special enthusiasm. Later in life, the Secretary of the Treasury used to attribute his enduring financial conservatism to his difficulties (and perseverance) in cultivating the McIntosh, the Courtland and Golden at Fishkill. With such preoccupations, Morgenthau and his wife became increasingly immersed in the life of Dutchess County.

In 1922 Morgenthau bought the *American Agriculturist*, a local paper, and continued its policy of advocating such causes as rural credit and conservation. As the two men's political interests began to converge, it seemed a rational choice for Roosevelt, when he became Governor of New York in 1928, to summon Morgenthau to Albany, the state capital, to become chairman of his Agricultural Advisory Commission and later New York's Conservation Commissioner. Following Roosevelt's election to the White House, the tall, reserved, sometimes inarticulate gentleman-farmer who invariably wore pince-nez, was called to Washington by the new President. He was asked to preside over the liquidation of the Federal Farm Board, then to head its successor, the Farm Credit Administration.

In these tough assignments Morgenthau showed that he had administrative drive and competence, combining a financial conservatism with strong humanitarian instincts for the victims of the Depression. More important perhaps at this time was the fact that, while of different temperament, Roosevelt and Morgenthau shared similar backgrounds. Neither were radicals, neither were intellectuals, and both possessed a patrician feeling for the land and for public service.

Perhaps most important of all was the fact that as a friend of almost twenty years Morgenthau could be trusted as few others by the man in the White House. Once Roosevelt gave Mrs. Morgenthau a picture of Morgenthau and himself in an open automobile and wrote across it, "For Elinor, from one of two of a kind."[10]

Inevitably this friendship developed into a more significant political relationship when Morgenthau took over the Treasury. Located at Pennsylvania Avenue and 15th Street, only a few yards away from the White House, and balancing the State Department on the other side of the executive mansion, the Treasury is guarded by the statues of two of its former Secretaries. On the south side of this imposing Greek Revival structure of granite stands Alexander Hamilton, the first director of the nation's finances. On the north side, facing Pennsylvania Avenue, is Albert Gallatin, the clever Swiss who had been the right-hand man of Jefferson and Madison, and in whose biography Henry Adams had written: "In governments, as in households, he who holds the purse holds the power. The Treasury is the natural point of control to be occupied by any statesman who aims at organization or reform."[11]

With Roosevelt in the White House, even Adams's insight was for once overtaken by events, but there could be little doubt that at this time the Treasury remained the most remarkable department of the American government. Besides implementing the new monetary legislation of the New Deal, the Treasury continued to buy gold and silver and to keep the country's accounts Its budget was exceeded only by the armed forces, and its work included functions that in Great Britain would be undertaken by the Home Office, the Board of Trade, the Ministry of Works, Customs and Excise and Scotland Yard.

Thus the United States Coast Guard, which patrolled the American sea frontiers, was responsible to Morgenthau, as was the Bureau of Narcotics, the Secret Service which guarded the President and fought counterfeiters, the Public Health Service, the Procurement Division, a purchasing agency which built public buildings, the Bureau of Internal Revenue, the Bureau of Customs and the Alcohol Tax Unit. This last organization not only pursued minor bootleggers and smugglers, but also unchastized gangsters of the Prohibition era such as Dutch Schultz, a quest in which Morgenthau, with his puritanical instincts, took a keen personal interest.

In all these and other activities Morgenthau regarded himself not only as the custodian of the public purse but, as his official biographer, John Morton Blum, puts it, "a keeper of the public conscience."[12] It was this conception of his office that was partly responsible for Morgenthau's decision to preserve the voluminous diaries of his eleven and a half years in the Treasury, saved in his own words, "in order to make possible a book showing what government is like."[13] Appropriately enough, the nine hundred volumes of the Morgenthau Diaries are kept in the Franklin D.

Roosevelt Library in Hyde Park. But, as Professor Blum has written, while the Diaries sometimes include reflective observations, they are really "a collection of the papers that crossed the Secretary's desk, letters and memoranda, incoming and outgoing; or verbatim minutes of meetings held in his office; of stenographic transcripts or condensed summaries of other meetings he or his subordinates attended; and of verbatim conversations he held on the telephone. At their fullest, the Diaries provide a minute by minute account of his days in office."[14]

However, neither Morgenthau's formal political support of Roosevelt, as shown in the Diaries, nor the early Dutchess County friendship, fully explain the powerful alliance between the two men after 1933. Although, of course, Roosevelt took his counsel from no one man—far otherwise— among his senior advisers Morgenthau remained consistently closer to him than anyone else. From the early days of the New Deal, when Morgenthau, cruising with FDR off the New England coast on the warship *Indianapolis*, read the newly drafted "Bombshell" message to the London Economic Conference, to the last night of Roosevelt's life when he dined with the President at Warm Springs discussing postwar German policy, the friendship endured.

Thus Morgenthau's influence with Roosevelt transcended the political and institutional leverage of the Treasury, and conversely the President had more than a friendly Cabinet member. In one of its simplest manifestations the relationship meant that, in Morgenthau's words, "Mr. Roosevelt often asked me to do things for the Government which had nothing to do with regular Treasury work. He would usually ask these things of me after some Cabinet member had failed with the result that I made many enemies."[15]

Rather more significant than Morgenthau's role as the administration's whipping boy was the fact that, whatever reforms Roosevelt sought to impose on the economy, the Democratic Party or the country, Morgenthau stood outside any precise political allegiance, pressure group or ideology in his single-minded devotion to Roosevelt. In John Morton Blum's words, "Morgenthau's first joy in life was to serve Roosevelt, whom he loved and trusted and admired."[16]

When, during 1937–38, there was a possible question of Joseph Kennedy succeeding to the Treasury, Roosevelt was emphatic. He told James Farley, "I think Henry Morgenthau has tried to carry out my plans in every respect. I wouldn't put Joe Kennedy in his place, for example, because Joe would want to run the Treasury in his own way, contrary to my views and plans."[17]

In the early days of the New Deal, according to Arthur Schlesinger, Morgenthau shared his close comradeship with Roosevelt only with Louis Howe and Harry Hopkins. Of Roosevelt, Schlesinger writes, "His three friends were a middle-class newspaperman, a Jew and the son of a harness maker."[18]

Later, in the 1930's, with the dictators on the march, and when the President had of necessity to listen to the caution of the State Department on many issues, it was apparently with Morgenthau's denunciations of the Axis that he instinctively agreed. As Professor Blum has written, "If Cordell Hull was Roosevelt's book of rules, Morgenthau, as Mrs. Roosevelt often said, was her husband's conscience."[19]

As executant, friend and "conscience," Morgenthau had a peculiarly close relationship with Roosevelt. After 1941, of course, he had nothing to do with the planning of grand strategy, which remained the prerogative of Roosevelt as Commander in Chief, acting in consultation with Churchill and the Combined Chiefs of Staff. But here again, outside this military hierarchy, as the political and economic problems of the postwar world began to surface, Morgenthau's influence reasserted itself, as it was essentially not based on the forces that motivated most of Roosevelt's advisers, whether civilian or military.

Finally, no matter what the specific issue at hand or the immediate balance of forces inside the administration, Morgenthau was able to benefit from his special understanding of the near chaos of Roosevelt's administrative methods.

The demiofficial historians of American foreign policy from 1937 to 1941, William Langer and Everett Gleason, have outlined in some detail how Roosevelt's intense awareness of his prerogatives meant that he used his powers without paying too much attention to effective staff work, to say the least, another complicating factor in the application of the governing principle.[20]

Hence, whatever his objectives in dealing with the rivalries in his administration, Roosevelt's methods sometimes meant that, in Herman Kahn's words, conflicts were resolved by permitting "each opposing side to believe that he agreed with it."[21]

In this melee, Morgenthau, close to the apex of power, in and out of FDR's office, an administrator himself and his interests not confined by any petty jurisdictional constraints, was at a great advantage, for, in Langer and Gleason's trenchant words, he was "more accustomed to the President's bizarre administrative methods."[22]

Inevitably, therefore, as White's career progressed in the Treasury, and as he became Morgenthau's principal adviser, he was the beneficiary of some of the authority that fell by the osmosis of power from Roosevelt to Morgenthau. As the problems of the Depression gave way to those of the war and the postwar world, that authority remained as intangible as the governing principle, but also as certain as the friendship between the two Hudson Valley squires.

In addition to the results of his own energy and talents, therefore, some of Harry Dexter White's later influence stemmed less from any formal title or delegation of responsibility than from his degree of access to Morgenthau. This access became increasingly easier as his work took him closer to the central interests of both the Treasury and the country. But first White had to serve an apprenticeship at "the natural point of control."

5

APPRENTICESHIP

The ideas of economists and political philosophers, both when they are right and when they are wrong, are more powerful than is commonly understood. Indeed, the world is ruled by little else. . . .

—John Maynard Keynes

White's report of September, 1934, to Professor Viner on the American monetary standard, which effectively opened his formal Treasury career, was a comprehensive paper.

In his foreword White sensibly pointed out that the "ultimate goal of monetary and banking legislation and policy is the promotion and main-tenance of prosperity." In White's opinion, therefore, a return by the United States to the pre-1933 gold parity would be "a crushing blow" to American exports. To establish too low a parity on the other hand would mean an inflow of gold and other funds, which could just as easily be withdrawn again in a crisis.[1]

If a fixed gold parity was required, White summed up, the safest choice was the existing gold content of the dollar, which had, of course, been established earlier in the year when the new price of gold had been set at $35 per ounce. If the British did not return to the traditional Gold Standard, White thought, it would be most unwise for the Americans to do so.[2] Such conclusions but endorsed what Roosevelt and Morgenthau had already decided.

Nevertheless, despite the restoration of a large degree of financial con-fidence following the Gold Reserve Act of January, 1934, and Roosevelt's smashing victory in the off-year Congressional elections in November, when the Democrats were returned with an increased majority to the House and the Senate, the economy was still far from healthy. The Amer-ican national income for 1934 was $48 billion, nearly $40 billion below the 1929 figure; and, while unemployment had declined from the peak of 1932–33, ten million people were still out of work.

In an "Outline Analysis of the Current Situation," written during February and March, 1935, White elaborated on these problems. Mentioning the unemployment figure of 10,000,000, White went on to record that inflationary groups in Congress were still demanding large spending programs, that the taxation demanded by the government's social security measures was likely to prove unpopular, and that Huey Long and the radio priest, Father Coughlin, were "rapidly gaining mass support for extremely radical programs." On the other hand, the believers in orthodox finance still advocated a balanced budget.

There were two principal avenues to the tackling of the unemployment problem, White went on. The first lay in a comprehensive public works program. This should be combined with improvements in the banking system to stimulate the expansion of credit, to enable the government to finance its program smoothly and to create a bulwark against inflation. Many measures on these lines had already been set in hand by the administration; the question suggested by White was whether they were adequate.

The second avenue to recovery outlined by White was a "reestablishment of international monetary equilibrium, without jeopardizing our long run program of stabilizing domestic business at a high level of real income," combined with a promotion of imports and exports. These measures were complementary and "each approach is dependent upon and influences the other. The program must be viewed as a whole rather than two separate problems."[3]

In a further memorandum at this time for George Haas, head of his Division of Research and Statistics, White returned to these themes. He pointed out that, although progress had been made by the government since 1933, they were not out of the wood, that there were no "adequate grounds for the certainty that conditions will improve in 1935" and that the activities of the demagogues meant that the situation was "loaded with dynamite." No separation exists, White went on, "between domestic and international monetary problems, or between domestic business activity and foreign trade."[4]

White was not alone in his thinking on these lines for the necessity of tentatively attempting to restore international monetary equilibrium. As the New Deal's early emphasis on a partly managed economy yielded during 1935 to one stressing the virtues of a thriving mixed economy, propelled partly by deficit spending, Morgenthau himself was becoming aware of the benefits of some sort of international monetary stabilization. Such a preoccupation was one that transcended domestic differences in emphasis between the First and Second New Deal. Moreover, after investigating European business conditions, Professor Viner had reported to the Secretary in March, 1935, that he believed private investment in the United States was impeded by the risks consequent upon the fluctuations of the dollar abroad.

Another incentive to stabilization was that the free or managed floating rates which existed at this time between most of the world's leading trading countries also helped to bring about erratic shifts of labor and other resources as production lurched between demands for home, then for overseas markets. Lack of international agreement also encouraged mercurial flights of "hot" money and gold from country to country, but ultimately these and other symptoms were but a reflection of a deeper inability to cooperate of the countries stricken by the Depression and its aftermath. As well as Viner, Herman Oliphant, the Treasury's general counsel until his death in 1939, and a former advocate of domestic inflation, had now come to believe that the time was ripe for some sort of stabilization.

Roosevelt himself was lukewarm on the subject. The President apparently believed that other countries would not agree until their internal price structure had risen to their own satisfaction (as it had in the United States), but he hoped Morgenthau could work to avoid another round of competitive international devaluation.

There were also problems with the State Department, for during April, 1935, Cordell Hull, the Secretary of State, had circulated a memorandum to American embassies in Europe stating that the United States should cooperate with the British on the basis of conservative monetary policies, including the restoration of the pre-1933 dollar-sterling exchange rates. An enraged Morgenthau protested to Roosevelt, who was also apparently angry, and the offending memorandum was withdrawn, with a recognition by the State Department of the Treasury's jurisdiction over stabilization negotiations. So concluded an early exchange in the personal and administrative duel between Hull and Morgenthau that would last for nearly a decade.

However, the chief unknown factor at this time in Morgenthau's tentative plans for Anglo-French-American stabilization lay in England, where there was a certain coolness on this subject as a result of the breakdown of the 1933 London Conference. In early April, Morgenthau had told the French ambassador in Washington that he believed in stabilization between the three countries, going on to speculate whether France and the United States could together force the British hand. In keeping with this general policy, during his radio address in May, 1935, announcing that the dollar was sound, Morgenthau also said, "We are not unwilling to stabilize."[5]

But Morgenthau realized that these cautious moves were not enough,

and that the British must be sounded out properly. In April, 1935, therefore, Harry Dexter White, now considered in the Treasury as "an able
young economist . . . a man of extraordinary energy and quick intelligence,"[6] had been sent to Europe. White was to report on exchange and
monetary conditions in Belgium and Holland, but also to explore the
prospects of rapprochement with London.

It was his first mission abroad for the Treasury.

White was preceded on his mission by a letter from Cordell Hull, dated
April 4, to American diplomats and consular officials in Europe, which
introduced him as a "special agent" of the Treasury and asked the foreign
service to provide such "courtesies and assistance as you may be able to
render, consistently with your official duties."[7]

In one of the earliest references to White in the Morgenthau Diaries,
the Secretary of the Treasury, in a telephone conversation on April 23,
approved a State Department telegram to the Hague emphasizing that
White was in Europe to study exchange conditions and the operations of
the market, and was "not in any way authorized to negotiate on military
matters or enter into discussion of policy."[8]

The State Department placated, White arrived in London at the end of
April, staying for over two weeks before embarking at Southampton in
the middle of May. According to his report presented to Haas in June,
most of the businessmen he talked to in England "thought there would be
no advantage in having sterling fixed to gold. They feared a repetition of
events following 1925. They have come to believe that the lack of prosperity from 1925 to 1931 in England was caused chiefly by a return to the
Gold Standard at $4.86 and are in accord with the policy announced by
Chamberlain that the conditions are not yet ripe for stabilization."

White elaborated by saying that almost all the exporters he met had
said they sold their goods in the sterling areas—a manifestation of the
general contraction of world trade since the Depression—and were thus
not much concerned with the fluctuation of sterling in terms of gold.
White was surprised to find so little concern, "—almost a complete lack
of interest—in exchange problems, Gold Standard and the like among the
businessmen. In fact, many of them claimed and apparently believed that
when the price of sterling changed in terms of other currencies, it was the
other currencies that moved and not sterling."

What was significant, White reported, was that the British public was
not demanding any further depreciation of sterling and did not favor a
return to the Gold Standard. The government could continue its policy of
inaction on monetary matters without losing popular support.

Some of the economists White talked to saw matters from a different
perspective. In the London School of Economics, Professor T. E. Gregory

and Professor Lionel Robbins believed, according to White, that Britain should return to the Gold Standard "as soon as possible" at a sterling rate of about $4.80.* Unless this was done, the L.S.E. professors believed, there was a grave danger of recession in trade, the breakup of the sterling bloc, "and a destructive competitive race in successive currency depreciations."

These two men did not believe, White went on, that the dollar was significantly overvalued in relation to sterling or that the British Government would consider a return to gold. As the next best alternative to the Gold Standard they favored a *de facto* stabilization. If the American Government were to make such proposals, London would have to accept if the terms were reasonable or "be placed in the very embarrassing position of appearing to oppose settlement of international monetary difficulties."

John Maynard Keynes, perhaps the most distingusihed British economist, also told White that a *de facto* stabilization was desirable, but, White reported, he doubted if the British Government would be willing until the sterling rate was lower than at present. Keynes went on to say that one of the obstacles in the path of stabilization lay in the difficulty in obtaining informal agreement with the United States. The British felt that ultimate authority in Washington lay with "certain groups in Congress," and that any tentative arrangement made by the American Administration could therefore be overruled. The way out, Keynes thought, was cooperation between the British, French and American treasuries which did not involve any congressional or parliamentary action.

Senior officials in the British Treasury took the position that stabilization was their goal, but that it would have to come after the removal of underlying economic obstacles. It was felt that the dollar was undervalued in relation to the pound and that, therefore, sterling should go to a lower rate before any attempt to peg rates could be made. A return to gold was considered most unwise, and on the whole the Treasury in London preferred to wait before taking any action on any stabilization proposals.

At Lazard Brothers, the merchant bankers, R. H. Brand (later Lord Brand) felt that *de facto* stabilization could and should be arranged, and he believed the initiative would have to come from the United States. The coming general election in Britain and the lack of public enthusiasm for such proposals made this necessary.

* After Britain had gone off gold in September, 1931, sterling had at first oscillated considerably, but the government had then set up the Exchange Equalisation Account which gave the Bank of England power to intervene in foreign exchange markets to keep such fluctuations down. Britain was thus kept on a managed floating rate, and Scandinavian and Commonwealth countries linked their currencies to the pound. Sterling at the end of March, 1935, was quoted at about $4.81.

White had also talked to some British political figures on these problems. Hugh Dalton and George Lansbury of the Labour Party emphasized to him that Labour was against a return to the Gold Standard. They held, as Roosevelt did, that the purchasing power of the domestic currency was more important than fixed exchange rates. Stabilization was secondary to this factor. Both men believed no large deficit spending would be done by the British Government in the coming year.

Harold Macmillan, the Conservative backbencher, "one of a group who favor long-range planning and increased expenditure," also told White that the amount of deficit spending by the British government in the coming year would be small. It would be only enough, Macmillan thought, to furnish some "window dressing" to steal some of Lloyd George's thunder and reduce the strength of his political appeal. The reference to David Lloyd George's program of increased public expenditure to beat the Depression in Britain was a reminder that there were still nearly two million unemployed in the country at this time. The stabilization possibilities in which White was interested were of more than academic interest to those concerned in Great Britain as well as in the United States.[9]

Although White's report indicated the lukewarm attitude of the British toward stabilization in the spring of 1935, the idea mentioned in London of some sort of agreement between the national treasuries concerned pointed the way to the eventual solution of the Tripartite Pact of September, 1936. But, besides clarifying Morgenthau's ideas on stabilization, White's mission was successful for other reasons. His general experience during these stabilization discussions was useful practical training for his later work as Director of Monetary Research when he had the responsibility of looking after the operations of the American Exchange Stabilization Fund. Moreover, White had met in London such men as Keynes, Robbins and Brand with whom he would negotiate later in wartime Washington.

But for the present stabilization prospects hung fire, even after the uncertainty in the political atmosphere in London was removed when the National Government was returned in the British general election of October, 1935. Then, in early 1936, as the franc weakened, the precarious international monetary equilibrium seemed seriously threatened as the French considered devaluation or exchange control as a way out of their difficulties. Such a devaluation would face London, as well as Washington, with the prospect of another round of competitive devaluation.

By the summer of 1936, therefore, the British were reconciled to the American position of avoiding formal international stabilization negotiations while attempting to reach practical arrangements to keep existing exchange rates. A parallel problem was whether the British could buy gold from the United States, as it was United States Treasury policy, following the Gold Reserve Act of 1934, to deal in the metal only with the countries on the Gold Standard.

These matters now came to a head at the end of August, 1936, when, two months after the formation of Léon Blum's Popular Front Government in Paris, the outflow of gold from France precipitated a devaluation crisis in that country. Negotiations proceeded between London, Paris and Washington on the basis of accepting a French devaluation of about 30 percent, the creation of a French stabilization fund, and an understanding between the three countries to maintain within tacitly agreed limits the new exchange rates. The dollar-sterling cross-rate would of course remain broadly the same, a central feature of the proposed agreement.

Roosevelt himself favored a $5 pound—sterling was being quoted at $5.07 just before the announcement of the Tripartite Pact—and was certainly not willing to let the dollar-sterling cross-rate drop to its traditional figure of $4.86 in the weeks before the 1936 presidential election. White for his part thought at this time that a $5 pound might be too high. But the British took the figure of $5 for granted, with a ten-cent variation either way, a rate which the Americans thought could be maintained. In general, it was British policy to let the pound find its own level.

Eventually, after tense negotiations the "Tripartite Pact" between the three treasuries concerned was announced on September 25, 1936, a declaration which was greeted hopefully as opening new prospects of international monetary cooperation.[10] Later, in October and November, two further developments buttressed the Pact. First, Morgenthau stated that the stabilization fund of each country could trade in gold as it bought and sold foreign exchange, so altering in effect the previous Treasury policy on gold sales. Secondly, Belgium, Holland and Switzerland adhered to the principles of the Tripartite Pact, which meant that these three countries as well were able to exchange gold with the United States on the same terms as France and Britain.

In all these operations the appropriate national stabilization fund was a useful instrument of monetary cooperation in helping to control exchange fluctuations and in separating internal credit structure from gold flows. But, as White himself wrote in an undated memorandum of this time on "Stabilization Funds and International Trade," which survives in his Princeton papers, such funds "can perform no miracles. . . . Like all machinery, it can be ill-used, or not used at all; but, when improperly used, it is not the fault of the instrument, but rather of the policies."[11] White's remarks on this occasion underlined the fact that in these negotiations Morgenthau had pursued a consistent policy aimed not only at domestic American recovery, but also at attempting to rationalize monetary arrangements between other democratic countries hit by the Depression.

Nevertheless, after another eighteen months of spiraling international crisis, the French were forced to devalue again in the spring of 1938, when the franc was pegged to the pound. French internal economic policies had not been consistent with those in Britain and America. The pound, meanwhile, remained on a managed floating rate until the beginning of the Second World War, when it was fixed to the dollar at $4.03. Events, and the continuing economic nationalism consequent upon the Depression, rather than Morgenthau's policies themselves, were to blame for the relative ineffectiveness of the Tripartite Pact.

It was during this period of 1935–36, when the stabilization negotiations remained an enduring preoccupation of the Treasury, that White became one of the men who regularly advised Morgenthau, along with Viner, Oliphant, Haas, Archie Lochhead, an international exchange specialist, and Wayne C. Taylor, a former banker, now Assistant Secretary of the Treasury.[12]

White was also gradually promoted at this time. His initial appointment as Special Economic Analyst was renewed for a year in July, 1935, and, effective October 1, 1936, he was given a raise of $900 to $6,500 and made an Assistant Director of the Division of Research and Statistics. Until this promotion his pay had come from the Treasury appropriation for "Expenses, Emergency Banking, Gold Reserve and Silver Purchase Acts." But from July, 1937, when he was given another thousand dollar increase, his salary was paid by the Treasury from the internal appropriation of the Exchange Stabilization Fund. This seemed a rational arrangement for one who was not an established civil servant.

For most of his succeeding Treasury career, until January, 1945, when he took up a presidential appointment as Assistant Secretary, White continued to be paid from this source. The $2 billion Fund had, as we have soon, been set up under the 1934 Gold Reserve Act from the profits of devaluation, and its powers, like those of the executive over the gold content of the dollar, were regularly renewed thereafter by Congress. But the Fund was quite separate from the usual civil service appropriations voted by Congress, and its handling was an internal Treasury matter.[13]

Some additional authority was given to White during this period when in February, 1936, he was appointed as Treasury representative on the interdepartmental Committee on Foreign Trade Agreements. Later, in December, 1937, White was authorized by Morgenthau to sit in on behalf of the department on some meetings of the National Munitions Control Board.[14]

As White rose in the Treasury, therefore, his life began to reach some sort of equilibrium which had been lacking during his later academic career. Hardly frustrated, he was now able effectively to translate his grasp of his subject into the immensely practical day-to-day work of helping to administer a department never far from the brink of crisis. Moreover, White and his family had soon discovered a congenial area to live in on the northern outskirts of Washington. During his early years in the capital, White had lived on Kalmia Road, in a northwestern suburban area of the District of Columbia, not far from Rock Creek Park, near Silver Spring, Maryland. By late 1936 he had moved to an address on Connecticut Avenue, but by the end of 1938 the family had settled down in an eight-room house at Fairfax Avenue, Bethesda, Maryland, where they remained until after the war. Again, the pattern was typical of many who had moved to Washington to work in government during this time.[15]

To White's colleagues in the Treasury, his appearance would change little over a decade. In his middle forties when he first began to make a mark in the department, he was a man of slightly less than medium height, stocky in build, with a round face displaying a characteristic moustache and blue eyes covered by rimless spectacles. He dressed quietly, with an occasional taste for loud ties and for sports shoes in summer, but was generally unobtrusive in appearance.

An underlying tension appeared in his jerky walk, and in argument where he could be unnecessarily blunt and sardonic as he displayed a usually unfaltering command of his subject. He had few interests outside the Treasury apart from chess and music, and early in his official career he became known in the department for his capacity for hard work, and for his ability to explain technical matters in terms of political possibilities. As responsibility and the power that went with it became his, the playful, wisecracking assurance of his early years in the Treasury could merge into the impatience of an abrasive public manner. But in general White's first years in Washington were characterized personally by a balance between the apparent frustration of the later years in Harvard and at Lawrence College, and the abrupt behavior, noted by some, that appeared during the later wartime years when his authority was at its peak.

Quite apart from the diligence of this obviously gifted man, however, together with his flair for converting economic theory into administrative practice, qualities which would have been welcomed by any finance minister, White's influence in the Treasury at this time was probably enhanced by the conflict of views in the administration over the recession of 1937–38.

Partly, perhaps, the roots of the recession lay in the conflicting ideas

within the New Deal. While Roosevelt had boldly experimented with a
wide range of emergency measures in the early years of his first administration, his style of government precluded any thoroughgoing attempt to
launch a systematic program of deficit spending per se.

Given the balance of forces within the Democratic Party, perhaps such
a program would not have been politically possible, and in any case
Roosevelt himself looked forward to a time when the budget could be
balanced again.

However, at the end of 1934, Roosevelt had appointed to the Federal
Reserve Board the Utah banker, Marriner S. Eccles. Eccles, independently of any doctrine, advocated large-scale compensatory government
deficit spending to alleviate the Depression. He had taken with him to
the Federal Reserve Lauchlin Currie, White's former Harvard colleague,
who had worked briefly in the Treasury, and was now of general Keynesian persuasion on the subject of deficit budgeting. As the ideas of the
First New Deal, with its emphasis on the integration and management of
the economy, yielded to those of the Second New Deal, stressing the
necessity of revitalizing industry, so deficit spending as a program became more acceptable to the administration.

Worried by the prospect of inflation as economic recovery slowly continued during 1936, however, the Federal Reserve System in July of that
year had limited reserve requirements to the banks. Later, following
Roosevelt's great victory at the polls in the November presidential election, and after due consultation, Morgenthau decided to limit the inflationary potential of gold flowing into the United States from a politically
unstable Europe by placing the metal, together with newly mined domestic gold, in a "sterilized" inactive account. This would prevent it from
being added to the credit base.

By the summer of 1937, auguries of a possible coming recession only
indicated to Morgenthau the necessity for a balanced budget. The Treasury's Research Division, where White was now an Assistant Director,
saw things differently. Low interest rates, new residential construction,
and a calculated increase of purchasing power could maintain recovery as
long as federal spending did not decrease. Within the Treasury, Herman
Oliphant, White and others had begun to think in Keynesian terms.
Morgenthau disagreed, thinking that recovery was contingent on business
confidence and that "in his view only a balanced budget could sustain
that confidence."[16]

On October 19, 1937, the stock market collapsed with 17,000,000 shares
changing hands, precipitating an intense policy debate in Washington
that would continue for six months before firm remedial action was taken
by Roosevelt.

One of the results of the 1937–38 recession, however, was to bring out

Keynes's influence in administration circles. As we have seen, the earlier relief measures of the New Deal were essentially emergency programs. Seen in another perspective, personal relations between Roosevelt and Keynes were inconclusive. Frances Perkins' account of their meeting in the White House in May, 1934, related that, while to F.D.R. Keynes left "a rigmarole of figures," the great Cambridge economist for his part had supposed that the President was "more literate, economically speaking." In Sir Roy Harrod's words, "the preponderant opinion amongst those in a good position to know is that the influence of Keynes [on Roosevelt] was not great."[17]

Perhaps the gap between the two men at this time could not be bridged. But, with the publication of Keynes's landmark work, *The General Theory of Employment, Interest and Money*, in 1936, Keynesian ideas began to be of increasing importance in Washington. Keynes had, of course, long advocated expansionist economic measures in his intellectual campaign against financial orthodoxy. One of the cornerstones of the *General Theory* was the concept of the "multiplier" which explained how an increase in government spending on public works could mean a rise in spending throughout the economy which would be a multiple of the original increase. Perhaps even more important was the fact that, as Harrod has described it, the *General Theory* was "an analysis in terms of fundamental economic principle, of the causes of unemployment."

Thus, while before 1936 the case for expansionist measures could be dismissed by the orthodox, this was not really possible after the publication of the *General Theory*. The corpus of Keynes's work was becoming respectable, and he would become increasingly influential.

However, while Keynesian influence was increasingly part of the intellectual background in Washington, such ideas probably did not play any direct role in the eventual decision of the administration to deal with the recession. During the winter of 1937–38, the fight inside the government was joined between supporters of deficit spending such as Harry Hopkins and Marriner Eccles, whose ideas were essentially pre-Keynesian, and those who supported orthodox budget-balancing economics, "of which the Secretary [of the Treasury] was the most influential spokesman" (Blum).

White's general position was reasonably clear early in the debate. Within the Treasury, he, Oliphant and others had begun to think in Keynesian terms. During October he told Morgenthau and Viner in one of their meetings that, while he believed the government should move in the direction of a balanced budget as soon as business conditions permitted, "it would be wrong to balance the budget by deflationary measures such as increasing taxes or reducing government expenditure."

Marriner Eccles, Chairman of the Federal Reserve during this period, has commented to the writer on White's wider views on these matters at this time: "He was a believer in compensatory spending. He was also a strong believer in reforming our tax system so as to bring about a better distribution of income between the rich and the poor. In some ways, he was opposed to the independence of the Federal Reserve System and felt that it should be completely controlled by the Treasury. I always felt he was rather unfriendly toward me as Chairman of the Federal Reserve Board."[18]

However, while prepared to avoid raising new taxes, Morgenthau himself continued to oppose increased government expenditure, and his more specific approach during the next few months was to advocate monetary means to combat the recession. The measures "sterilizing" gold were eased in February, 1938, and on March 22 White submitted a memorandum in line with Morgenthau's views on "Monetary Possibilities." This memo listed a whole range of "monetary steps which are inflationary in character which the administration has the power to adopt without additional legislation." These measures included reduction in the reserve requirements, increases in the portfolio of the Federal Reserve banks and ranged all the way to further devaluation of the dollar.[19]

In keeping with this approach, Morgenthau continued to argue strongly for a monetary solution to the recession, querying the necessity for further public works programs. But another lurch downward on the stock market at the end of March had convinced Roosevelt that he must attempt to spend his way out of the recession, a decision which was supported by Harry Hopkins and others. The Treasury calculated the federal deficit for fiscal 1939 might be $4–5 billion. The result was that "for all his loyalty to the New Deal, for all his love of Franklin Roosevelt, [Morgenthau] could see no choice but to resign. It was the blackest hour of his career."[20]

Realizing later that he could hardly abandon Roosevelt at this time, Morgenthau changed his mind, although years after he still thought that a balanced budget should have been given a chance. On April 14, 1938, Roosevelt introduced a $4 billion emergency spending program which, besides substantially extending the American credit base, and calling for new appropriations, included large sums for increases and innovations in the New Deal's public works programs. The economy began to turn up, and as far as the foreign exchange situation was concerned, White told Morgenthau in September, as the Munich crisis approached, that if the pound continued to drop toward the $4.80 mark the British should be approached under the terms of the Tripartite Pact.[21]

The struggle over the emergency program had shown that in general White's advice was that of a moderate Keynesian who believed in the benefits of government intervention in the economy. It was a position supported by many in Washington on completely empirical grounds. No doubt Morgenthau realized that, in view of his own orthodox approach, it would strengthen his position to have such an adviser close at hand. Inside the Treasury, moreover, the internal balance of power justified a promotion for White. The Under Secretary, Roswell Magill, was generally conservative, and John W. Hanes, who succeeded to Magill's office later in 1938, had strong sympathies with the business community and Wall Street.

Accordingly, on March 25, 1938, White was appointed Director of Monetary Research, his salary of $8,000 to be paid from appropriation on the Exchange Stabilization Fund. The position, which is said to have been made especially for him, involved a certain amount of bureaucratic surgery within the Treasury. Under Morgenthau's Treasury Department Order no. 18 of the same date, the new Division of Tax Research and the Division of Monetary Research were carved out of the Division of Research and Statistics, the remaining shell of which continued to be responsible for the library, the graphic section, the stenographic section and the statistical section. These service units would be used by the new divisions, "and to the extent that consolidation is found practicable" the administrative personnel records of all three divisions would continue to be kept by Research and Statistics. Funds previously allotted to the latter department would now be proportionately available to the new divisions on a personnel basis.

With regard to the Division of Monetary Research the order became effective immediately, and the functions of the division were defined, not too precisely, as follows:

> The functions of the Division of Monetary Research will include the preparation of analyses and recommendations to aid the Secretary of the Treasury in the formulation and execution of the monetary policies of the Treasury Department in connection with the [Exchange] Stabilization Fund, and other operations under the Gold Reserve and Silver Purchase Acts, and economic analyses relating to customs activities of the Treasury Department and the Secretary's duties under the Tariff Act. The Division will function under the immediate supervision of the Director of Monetary Research, who will report to the Secretary through the Technical Assistant to the Secretary.[22]

A month later, on April 25, this formal appointment was in effect ratified when White joined the "9:30 Group" of Morgenthau's senior officials. On that day the meeting included Haas, Archie Lochhead, Oliphant, Herbert Gaston, a veteran assistant of Morgenthau's, Acting Director of the Budget Daniel Bell, and Assistant Secretary Wayne Taylor. Invariably present at these meetings was Mrs. Henrietta Klotz, who had been the Secretary's personal secretary since the 1920's and who sometimes alarmed Morgenthau's visitors with her stenotyping machine:

> H. M. JR. I thought you people would be interested to know that I've invited Harry White to become a regular member of the 9:30 staff.
> KLOTZ. Glad to meet you.
> H. M. JR. Want to make a speech, Harry?
> WHITE. I think I've made so many, probably the best thing I can do now is to keep quiet.
> H. M. JR. Don't get many chances—better make it now. Archie, read this will you . . . ?[23]

One stage of White's apprenticeship was over.

White's appointment as Director of Monetary Research and his arrival in the 9:30 Group gave him a considerable voice in the Treasury's affairs. The Division of Monetary Research remained his primary base in the department, and when he became Assistant Secretary during 1945–46, he continued to retain overall responsibility for the division. It was from this administrative base, of course, that his role in the wartime monetary negotiations stemmed.

Moreover, the terms of reference of the division were not too narrowly drawn, and there were few governmental problems at home or abroad that did not involve money or exchange problems—as in the case of the Tripartite Pact or the Treasury's dealings with such countries as Brazil and China. In any case, with the rise of the Axis Morgenthau tended to take the whole world for his province, especially after Roosevelt's "Quarantine-the-Aggressor" speech in Chicago on October 5, 1937. The implementation of a new active American foreign policy, which the speech implied, was hesitant and ineffective owing to a combination of the neutrality laws, isolationism and a "violently negative" public opinion.[24] But the war clouds on the horizon were quite visible, and it was inevitable that White should now play a growing role in matters affecting the Treasury's foreign relations, as well as the domestic economy.

On July 7, 1937, three months before Roosevelt's "Quarantine" speech, Chinese and Japanese troops had clashed at the Marco Polo bridge near Peking, and with the opening of "the China Incident" there would be no peace between the two countries until August, 1945. As early as the spring of 1936 White had been involved in the Treasury negotiations with the Chinese Nationalist Government of Chiang Kai-shek, and from this time until Morgenthau's departure from the Treasury nearly ten years later he would continue, in different ways, to be involved in the Treasury's negotiations with the Chinese. In the department's external dealings, it was only with the British that White had a longer connection.

The Treasury's wide-ranging operations had meant that White had become involved in China's affairs before the outbreak of fighting in July, 1937. During 1931–32 the Japanese Kwantung Army had seized Manchuria, consolidated their conquests into the puppet state of "Manchukuo," and later on moved to take over Jehol. Soon the influence of the Japanese extended into Chahar, Hopeh and other parts of North China. Thus, long before the opening of wider hostilities in 1937, Nationalist China had been deprived of valuable industrial and agricultural resources.

Another serious problem for the Nationalists was the American silver-buying program, made under the Silver Purchase Act of 1934.[25] During 1934–35 silver was drained out of China, raising the value of the historic Chinese silver dollar to new high values, which consequently helped to bring about deflation, credit restriction and slump. In November, 1935, the Chinese nationalized silver, and went over to a managed currency, with new legal tender notes known as *fapi*. The unit of the yuan or the Chinese dollar (C$) was to be maintained at about 30 cents or 14½ pence by the Central Bank of China, not formally linked to either sterling or the dollar.

Following this currency reform Morgenthau, at the request of the Chinese, initiated a silver-purchasing program, which could be implemented without too much reference to the State Department, which was generally chary of provoking the Japanese. Then, in April, 1936, the Chinese banker K. P. Chen arrived in Washington to discuss further silver sales to the United States, which both sides saw as a means of buttressing the Nanking regime against the Japanese.

After his first meeting with Chen, Morgenthau received a memorandum from Haas and White of the Research Division recommending the purchase of Chinese silver, which would help to stabilize the new currency. They also suggested that as a reciprocal concession the yuan be pegged to the dollar; as the larger proportion of Chinese trade was in sterling, it was the dollar-yuan ratio which was adjusted when the cross-rates between the two Western currencies fluctuated.

Morgenthau now decided to offer to buy Chinese silver at the rate of five million ounces per month for the rest of 1936. He told Roosevelt that unless the Japanese were diverted by a conflict with Russia, Chinese chances of pulling through were poor, and this weakness might be alleviated by the United States' purchasing their silver. The Silver Purchase Act, as will be recalled, authorized the Treasury to buy silver until it equaled one-quarter of the monetary reserve, so there was plenty of leeway for such action within the law.

On April 17, Harry Dexter White evaluated at Morgenthau's request this silver-purchase program. It would not, White thought, increase the Chinese reserves much, but it would strengthen the expectation of silver holders that the government could maintain the silver rate. This effect could be increased, White suggested, if the Treasury bought more silver and bought it faster than Morgenthau had proposed, and if the Chinese were loaned $50,000,000 against silver deposited in the United States.[26]

Eventually, in May, 1936, a silver-purchase agreement was signed between the Treasury and the Chinese Finance Ministry on the basis of $20,000,000 advance against silver placed in the United States. Morgenthau intended to buy 75,000,000 ounces beginning with the purchase of 12,000,000 ounces by June 15, continuing with 9,000,000 each month until January, 1937. The Chinese could have payment in gold if they so desired, and the Treasury release on the agreement looked forward to further stabilization measures.

White's interest in the Chinese situation at this time was not restricted to advising the Secretary on the silver-purchase agreement. In a forty-four-page screed for Morgenthau, written in early 1936, typed with single spacing, on the "Economic Situation in China," White dwelt at some length and detail on the history, geography, politics, family customs and other aspects of the country as well as the economic prospects.[27]

He commented that Chiang Kai-shek was "a virtual dictator although his actual power is more limited than either Hitler or Mussolini." This "modern feudalism" cramped the revenue of Nationalist China and made difficult a unified foreign policy. Transportation, production and the finance of the country were in a bad way. On the question of who would gain most if the yuan were pegged to either sterling or the dollar, White remarked that a link to sterling would mean more to the British than a comparable link to the dollar would mean to the United States. This was partly because of Britain's extensive foreign trade, and traditional role in international finance, and partly "because the U.S. is a coming nation and England is a going one."

White concluded that the American silver-purchase program would improve the China trade and help prevent depreciation of the yuan, and that the United States in its turn could obtain assurances that nothing prejudicial to its interests would be arranged between China on one hand, and England and Japan on the other. The United States might suggest a de facto pegging of the yuan halfway between the movements of the dollar-sterling cross-rate, so avoiding the impression that the Chinese currency was tied to sterling.

In fact, the arrangement by which the dollar moved, rather than sterling, in the Central Bank of China's quotations of the yuan, an arrangement which had bothered Morgenthau during the April, 1936, discussions with K. P. Chen, was revised soon after the American agreement to buy Chinese silver. The solution, in September, 1936, was to widen the spread between the buying and the selling rates of the two currencies to prevent, if possible, further changes in the official Chinese quotation. This prevented the appearance of a pegged Chinese currency and was also a minor point gained, perhaps, by the coming nation over the going one.[28]

The Treasury's continued interest in the silver-purchase program, which undoubtedly strengthened the Nationalist regime on the eve of the Japanese invasion, was shown by a further agreement between Morgenthau and H. H. Kung, the Chinese Finance Minister, on July 8, 1937; the accord was reached before the news of the fighting near Peking reached Washington. Now the United States agreed to take 62,000,000 ounces of Chinese silver at the rate of 45 cents an ounce. Including this deal, the aggregate of American silver purchases between 1935 and the outbreak of war in China during July, 1937, came to $94,000,000, while the grand total, 1935–41, was $252,000,000.[29]

However, the outbreak of war in July, 1937, meant that the Treasury in the future would be unable to project the silver-purchase program as a purely financial operation between the two countries. Yet as Arthur Young, the former American adviser to the Chinese Nationalist Government has written, the American silver-purchase policy had a number of unforeseen results. It helped to force China off the historic silver standard initially, yet had China been on this silver standard when Japan attacked in 1937, "it would have been impossible to finance extended resistance in the first place." But, as events turned out, as the climate of opinion in the Treasury changed, and as the printing presses in Chungking worked ever faster, the managed currency appeared as a two-edged sword. It afforded means to finance a long and bitter resistance, "but it also led to the inflation which was a major cause of the downfall of the government on the mainland."[30]

Later, during the changed circumstances of the Pacific war, White would again be involved in measures for supporting the Chinese currency. But during late 1937 and 1938 the emphasis inside the Treasury changed from the silver-purchase program to finding more direct means of financing and supporting the Generalissimo in his resistance to the Japanese. Here, too, White was involved.

In September, 1937, as the Japanese armies began to move into central China, the Treasury's Research Division reported to Morgenthau that the peace of the world was "tied up with China's ability to win or prolong its resistance to Japanese aggression. It is our opinion that a Japanese victory will greatly increase the chances of a general world war." Roosevelt, on the recommendation of the State Department, had not recognized a state of war in China, which meant that the Neutrality Acts did not apply to the participants.[31]

Following the President's "Quarantine" speech in October, 1937, it soon transpired, however, that there were no immediate prospects of material aid for China, or any possibility of any sanctions against Japan. American trade with Japan continued. Against the indirect opposition of the State Department which, for its part, preferred to avoid entanglements without the national will or the power to sustain them, Morgenthau continued to buy Chinese silver. A new arrangement was made in December, 1937, with Roosevelt's approval. But, in general, the President, after an angry reaction following the sinking by the Japanese on the Yangtze of the American gunboat *Panay* in December, 1937, remained cautiously aware of the isolationist sentiment in the country and Congress.

By this time, the embattled Chinese had found new friends, willing for their own reasons to prolong Nationalist resistance to the Japanese. The former alliance of 1924–27 between Moscow and Chiang Kai-shek was now revived. Since the mid-1930's, as a result of the growing threat from Germany and Japan, Soviet policy toward Nationalist China had gradually changed, and in August, 1937, a "non-aggression" pact was concluded between Moscow and Nanking.

In the next two years Soviet purchase credits of $250,000,000 for military items were extended to China, transactions that were handled with special secrecy, sometimes by Chiang Kai-shek directly. Russian arms reequipped ten Chinese Nationalist divisions, a Soviet military advisory mission of about five hundred men, including several officers, was dispatched to China, and five flights of Soviet aircraft guarded Hankow, Nanking, Chungking and Lanchow in the northwest, the terminal point of a 1,700-mile Central Asian transport link with the Russian border.[32]

The understanding between Moscow and Nanking was reached only a few weeks before the September, 1937, "united front" agreement between the Kuomintang and the Chinese Communist Party. This move had been under discussion since the beginning of the year, but it stemmed from the call of the Seventh Comintern Congress of 1935 for the creation in the colonies and semi-colonies of an "anti-imperialist united front," albeit centered around the Soviets. At this time, of course, the Chinese Communists under Mao Tse-tung were approaching their Shensi destination of Yenan after their epic Long March from Kiangsi.

A year later, the Anti-Comintern Pact of November, 1936, between Germany, Italy and Japan, which looked forward possibly to some sort of coordinated attack against the Soviet Union, together with the kidnapping and release of Chiang during the Sian Incident the following month, had brought out Stalin's preoccupation with the Generalissimo as the "only possible" Chinese national leader.[33] This was the setting for the second *de facto* Soviet alliance with the Chinese Nationalists.

As John Erickson has written, the Japanese, concerned that the Russians might move through Outer Mongolia to link up with new northern Chinese Communist base areas, credited Stalin with greater revolutionary boldness than appears to have been the case: "Since *raison d'état* now ruled, it was with Nanking rather than Shensi that Stalin had entered into formal relations."[34] According to Arthur Young, who discusses the subject in some detail, during the first one-and-a-half years of the Sino-Japanese conflict, "Russian aid utilized [by China] was nearly three times as great as Western aid. But thereafter Russian aid tapered off, while American and British aid grew."[35]

Nevertheless, as the Japanese continued to win military successes in China, existing foreign aid to the Nationalists seemed quite inadequate. In May, 1938, the Treasury was told that, in spite of the American silver-purchase program, the Chinese government was desperately short of dollars, as most of its resources were now pledged in one way or another. Morgenthau now thought an American loan to China would provide the best help, but the State Department was divided, and Hull, who maintained his view that it was inopportune to force a showdown with Tokyo, thought that a loan would involve the United States in the Sino-Japanese conflict.

In China, after the fall of Nanking in December, 1937, the situation deteriorated steadily to the extent that both Canton and Hankow were lost to the advancing Japanese in October, 1938. By now the Nationalist Government had retreated through the Yangtze gorges to Chungking in Szechuan, out of the reach of Japanese tanks, but not of the invader's aircraft, as the Generalissimo's new capital came under massed air attack.

The debate on support measures for China continued in Washington throughout the summer, and the Munich crisis of September, 1938, added new urgency to Morgenthau's pleas. At this time White had unsuccessfully proposed countervailing tariff duties against Germany, with the ultimate sanction of a trade embargo, but Roosevelt was not inclined to adopt such drastic Treasury measures for economic pressure against the Axis.

But underlying any argument over specific measures at this time was Morgenthau's crucial belief, recorded by John Morton Blum, that the State Department was timorous, conventional and dominated by the foreign-office mentality—"the notion that you got things done by being a generous host at diplomatic banquets."

In Morgenthau's view, Hull was obsessed by his trade agreements program as a key to peace and misled by the Anglophilism and hesitancies of the career diplomats. The State Department as a whole had failed to recognize the danger of Japanese militarism and European fascism, which had released forces that could not be controlled politely. Morgenthau thought of the silver-purchase program, as of the Tripartite Pact, as a means of stiffening resistance to these forces. Thus, during 1937 and after, Blum goes on, Morgenthau "acted in his own sphere more often and more vigorously than before, and also he urged upon the President a more forceful general policy than any other member of the Administration, save Harold Ickes, was yet prepared to advocate."[36]

This conflict with the State Department, with its elements of personal, political and institutional antagonism, sometimes exacerbated willy nilly by Roosevelt's methods, was seen in a different perspective by Hull who later wrote in his memoirs:

> The Secretary of the Treasury, Henry Morgenthau, Jr., who ranked next to me in the Cabinet, often acted as if he were clothed with authority to project himself into the field of foreign affairs and inaugurate efforts to shape the course of foreign policy in given instances. He had an excellent organization in the Treasury Department, ably headed by Harry White, but he did not stop with his work at the Treasury. Despite the fact that he was not at all fully or accurately informed on a number of questions of foreign policy with which he undertook to interfere, we found from his earliest days in the Government that he seldom lost an opportunity to take long steps across the line of the State Department jurisdiction. Emotionally upset by Hitler's rise and his persecution of the Jews, he often sought to induce the President to anticipate the State Department or act contrary to our better judgment. We sometime found him conducting negotiations with foreign governments which were the functions of the State Department. . . .[37]

This internecine rivalry now came to a head under the pressure of Munich and the deteriorating situation in China. During the European crisis, Roosevelt had stated that the United States had "no political involvements" on the Continent, but following the Munich settlement, which gave the Sudeten territories to Nazi Germany, Morgenthau returned to the attack with a proposal for a credit to China. He told White to prepare a case which he would present to Roosevelt.

White then drafted a long letter stating that it was

> yet possible for our financial and moral aid to be of decisive help to China. . . . Must we wait until Japan has completed her conquest before we see what we should have done? . . . Mr. President, I am

taking the liberty of pleading China's cause so earnestly because I
know you see the matter as I do. . . . All my efforts have proved of no
avail against Secretary Hull's adamant policy of doing nothing
which could possibly be objected to by an aggressor nation. . . . A
substantial aid to China will have infinitely more effect in striking a
blow for democracy than trade agreements with half a dozen more
countries. . . . What could be so effective a check to aggression, Mr.
President, as a successful defense by China? . . .[38]

Morgenthau thought White's draft "swell," but thought it needed pol-
ishing and the inclusion of another foreign policy cause of his, that of
loans for Latin America, a "financial Monroe Doctrine." These ideas he
outlined to White, at the same time asking Herman Oliphant to help
White with the redrafting. White was to keep working until the letter
was right. Eventually "the strongest statement on foreign policy [Mor-
genthau] had yet ventured" (Blum) for the President was ready for
signing on October 17. It was a hard, forceful plea for American resistance to the Axis, excluding some of White's strictures on Hull, and
ending with specific suggestions for aid to China and Latin America. It
was with "special urgency" that he pleaded the case for China, Morgenthau wrote.[39]

Eventually, after further deliberations, and after Chiang Kai-shek had
shown that he meant to keep on fighting after the heavy losses of the
autumn, an American credit of $25,000,000 for China was announced in
December, 1938. Hull was out of the country on a conference when the
statement was made. American credits from that date to the opening of
the Pacific war totaled $120,000,000; the Treasury continued to maintain
and expand an influential role in the developing American relations with
Chungking.[40]

Important as Morgenthau's letter of October 17, 1938, was in influencing the policy of increased aid for China, more important was the Secretary's conviction that after this time, "no matter what domestic issues
arose, his constant preoccupation was with American defense and foreign
policy. In a sense he had gone to war. When war actually came, it simply
increased the tempo of his work. His letter of October 17 marked for him
and his department a major turning point."[41]

With the drafting of Morgenthau's personal declaration of war White's
apprenticeship in the Treasury had come to an end.

6

THE SECRET AGENT

In the sphere of political and revolutionary action, relying partly on violence, the professional spy has every facility to fabricate the very facts themselves, and will spread the double evil of emulation in one direction, and of panic, hasty legislation, unreflecting hate, in the other. However, this is an imperfect world. . . .

—JOSEPH CONRAD, *The Secret Agent*

. . . the revolution is never stronger than the failure of civilization.

—WHITTAKER CHAMBERS, *Witness*

IT WAS during this period of White's relatively rapid rise in the Treasury that, according to Whittaker Chambers, he became involved in the work of another expanding organization in Washington—the Communist underground.

White's devotion to the work of the Treasury during this period of 1934–38 seems not only evidence of his own bulldog pertinacity, but of the wider achievements of Roosevelt's gradualist measures. Yet, in spite of the successes of the New Deal in restoring confidence, there were those in the United States who believed, as they did in other Western countries, that reformist measures were not enough.

The shock of the slump had been followed by the revolutionary successes of Hitler, who became Chancellor in January, 1933, just a few weeks before Roosevelt entered the White House. The cycle of depression, unemployment, fascism and eventual war seemed to many inevitable. Yet this cycle in itself, so again it seemed to some, was but the prelude to a new rebirth of society. The outlines of that society could be seen in the Soviet Union, a state that soon appeared to be the one sure bastion against fascism.

"Get the notion of liberty out of your head," wrote Lincoln Steffens, the veteran American journalist, to a friend at this time. "The truth from now on is always dated; never absolute, never eternal. . . ." "Russia just now is a sort of heaven," Steffens believed during 1935, "where humans have got rid of the great primitive problems of food, clothing and a roof. . . . That leaves the Russians with minds for philosophy, art and science. Now civilization may begin."[1]

In *Die Mutter*, written during 1930–32, as the Weimar republic disintegrated, Bertolt Brecht saw certainty emerging out of the contemporary absurdity. Communism

> . . . is not madness, but
> The end of madness
> It is not chaos
> But order.
> It is the simple thing
> That is hard to accomplish. . . .[2]

A British poet, C. Day Lewis, wrote in a poem published in *The Magnetic Mountain* in 1933:

> . . . Drugs nor isolation will cure this cancer:
> It is now or never, the hour of the knife,
> The break with the past, the major operation. . . .

Between the poet's vision of the break with the past and the clandestine operations described by Chambers, "a tight little world beyond the law, turning upon an axis of faith and fear,"[3] there seems a great distance. Yet, as we have seen, events in the 1930's moved with sometimes bewildering speed.

In the early years of the decade, following the Sixth Comintern Congress held in Moscow in 1928, the party line held that a Third Period of revolutionary attainment was at hand, one that would result in triumph as the contradictions of the capitalist system deepened. In practice, during the Third Period, liberals, socialists and other reformers were attacked by the Communist Party. It was a time of comparative isolation for the revolutionaries in the West.

Hitler's accession in January, 1933, and the implied threat of an attack upon the Soviet Union meant, of course, that the tactics of the Third Period seemed obsolete in the age of the Third Reich. With this realization in Moscow came the evolution of the new line that called for collective security and a united front in which the emphasis was less on the class struggle than on the defense of the Soviet Union. This was the policy that was promulgated by Dimitroff in the famous Seventh Comintern Congress of 1935.[4]

The coming of the United Front, which followed the Stalinization of the Western Communist parties after the victory of the General Secretary in the Soviet Union's internal politics, was more than just a change in the party line; it was the advent of an entire political and cultural style. Although the Popular Front in the European sense of Communist participation in the government was hardly possible in the United States, Jefferson, Jackson and Lincoln were seen to be hailed by the Party, which, as Irving Howe has written, was "now to become like any other organization."[5] In a wider context the defense of the Soviet Union was linked in the Popular Front ethos with the survival of civilized values, and thus loyalty to one's own country could conceivably be reconciled, in the minds of some, with allegiance to Moscow.

In other ways, moreover, the strategy of the Popular Front was but a reflection of "politics" in a total sense catching up with life as the full significance of the Depression became obvious to members of the middle classes. Chambers, the personification of the Third Period revolutionary, has noted that as early as 1932 "an entirely new type of Communist made his appearance, not singly but in clusters, whose members knew each other, influenced one another and shared the same Communist or leftist views. A surprising number came of excellent American families. Nearly all were college trained."[6] In Britain, it has been suggested that 1933 "is generally recognized as the year in which the university left finally metamorphosed from a small network of private commitments to an obviously noticeable political movement."[7]

Of some of these "entirely new" recruits, perhaps Machiavellians rather than revolutionaries, Nathaniel Weyl, a self-confessed member at one time of the underground in Washington has written that:

Under Stalinist leadership the lineaments of the archetypal Communist had entirely changed. The resolute and romantic organizer of street war had been put away into a museum. Into his place had stepped the iron bureaucrat—the well-dressed, soft-spoken, capable executive who sat in the board room or on the Government committee. This man with a briefcase led a secret life of his own. If Communist rule should be proclaimed in his country he would move to the head of the table.[8]

The new model Bolshevik, Leslie Fiedler commented years afterward, "was the more valuable as he seemed less radical."[9]

As we have seen, during White's second year in Lawrence College, Wisconsin, he had written during 1933–34 to Professor Taussig in Harvard "suspecting" that the path for protecting the economy lay not in a program of self-sufficiency but "in the direction of centralized control over foreign exchange and trade."

White's mind was not made up. He was learning Russian in the hope that he might be able to obtain a fellowship "to study intensively" Soviet planning techniques in the Institute of Economic Investigation of Gosplan. At a time when the progress of "the Soviet experiment" was regarded with both hope and curiosity by many in the West, such an interest in developments in Russia was hardly uncommon.

As a student of the classical economy White may have felt that the old system was broken beyond repair. And as a former enthusiastic supporter of La Follette, White may also have felt that Stalin was dealing in a radical, idealistic manner with a contemporary challenge, in perhaps the same spirit that "Fighting Bob," a true democrat if ever there was one, had attempted to deal with the very different problems of an earlier America.

Similarly, the collection of "Workers Song Books," dating from 1934, found among White's papers in his Fitzwilliam home after his death is hardly evidence of anything but a possibly sentimental regard for Soviet Russia. Perhaps the song books were not White's in the first place. It remains possible that, even if they were, quite apart from politics, White may have been drawn toward Russia from a sort of family feeling at a time of upheaval.[10]

In any case it seems reasonable to assume from his letter to Professor Taussig that during 1933–34, about the time he went from Lawrence College to Washington, White was interested in developments in Russia, as were many of his generation.

Whether, of course, White's interest in Russian affairs at a time of crisis in the national as well as the international scene led him to further involvement with the Soviet cause at this time, as stated by Whittaker Chambers, is another question.

Chambers himself was born in Philadelphia in 1901, and died on his Maryland farm sixty years later. His account of his unhappy early years, his attachment to the American Communist Party in the 1920's, and to the conspiratorial underground during the 1930's, culminating in the later Hiss trials, is one of the best known personal and political stories of our time. In his various testimony, and in his famous autobiography, *Witness*, White was necessarily one of the subordinate characters in the development of the main story.[11]

As far as White is concerned, Chambers' story, briefly, is as follows. While working as the editor of *New Masses* in the summer of 1932,

Chambers, following the instructions of Max Bedacht, a Party function-ary, was sent into "underground work." Chambers was to sever all con-tacts with the "open" Communist Party, of which he had been a member, was to live like "a respectable bourgeois" and was to be known as "Bob." Chambers later discovered that he had been enrolled by "the Fourth Section of the Soviet Military Intelligence, though no one in the appara-tus ever told me that fact, and it would be years before I was sure of it."[12]

For his entire six years spent in the underground, Chambers claims that he was "the official secret contact man between a succession of Soviet apparatuses and the Communist Party, U.S.A."[13] The head of the American Party underground, who worked with Chambers for much of this time, was the man known as J. Peters, a man of many names, one of the two or three most powerful men in the Party, who had once been an official of Bela Kun's Hungarian Soviet government. Peters, who was variously known as Alexander Stevens, Mr. Silver, Isidore Boorstein, Steve Lapin and Steve Miller, had originally studied law in the Univer-sity of Debrecen, Hungary, and his real name was Alexander Goldberger. He was also the author of a manual party organization.[14]

During 1934–35, Chambers was in contact, in Washington, with Har-old Ware, son of a veteran American Communist, Mother Bloor, "as American as ham and eggs," and leader of a Communist group whose members worked in various American government agencies. This was not an espionage group, writes Chambers, although eight members of the Ware group did eventually take part in Soviet espionage, and historically this group was one of the roots of the Soviet networks later described by Elizabeth Bentley. The Ware group, of which White was not a member, was also more than a Marxist study group as it recruited new members into the underground, attempted to staff government agencies and influ-ence policy. Chambers goes on to write that a directorate of seven men eventually managed a group of perhaps seventy-five, and that the group was under Peters' supervision as part of the American underground.[15]

Although the Ware group was a background and a base for Chambers, his activity had another significance. During 1934, J. Peters had thought that "the most likely ones" in the Ware group could be used more effec-tively. As security was compromised in any case by having so many promising Communists in one group "where everybody knew everybody else," it was decided to pull out these promising members and place them "in another distinct underground—a parallel apparatus—much more rig-orously segregated and subdivided. . . ."

Duplication of networks was standard practice, Chambers remarks, and another objective was penetration of old-line departments, such as the State Department, rather than the New Deal agencies which the

Party could infiltrate at will. The second, special or parallel apparatus, as Chambers calls it at different times, would be a reserve, Fourth Section, "sleeper apparatus" to be activated later. Soon Chambers, known as Carl, was introduced to Ware, and a little later "Bill," a Soviet contact, arrived to supervise him. Sporadic attempts at spying were now mounted, and the second apparatus waited to be triggered into active espionage.[16]

According to Chambers, one of these preliminary attempts at sporadic espionage began White's involvement in the underground. This was during 1935, as far as one can tell from Chambers' chronology. Ware was instrumental in this initiation, for, Chambers goes on, White was "a great friend" of one of Ware's contacts, "Wilton Rugg." J. Peters at this time had concocted a plan to help finance the American Communist Party by selling American government documents to the Russians, who no longer supported the Party financially as a result of the rigors of the Five Year Plan.

Rugg told Ware that White was ready to turn over certain official Treasury documents to him, which then would be collected and photographed by Chambers, armed with a Leica. The documents from White arrived on schedule, were duly photographed, but Rugg was an hour late when Chambers went to meet him to return the papers. As a result of this violation of the conspiratorial rule of strict punctuality, Chambers refused to have anything more to do with Rugg, "since I held that any Communist who would endanger a man like Harry White by coming an hour late to an appointment was unfit for underground work." Chambers, of course, had not met White personally at this time.[17]

From time to time, Chambers goes on, J. Peters suggested White as a candidate for the second apparatus, but Chambers still refused to have anything to do with Wilton Rugg. When the network was activated in September, 1936—its life was to last until April, 1938, when Chambers finally broke with the Communists—the problem of providing a contact with White was solved through the agency of Abraham George Silverman of the Railroad Retirement Board. Silverman's chief duty "was to keep Harry Dexter White in a buoyant and cooperative frame of mind," and he, Silverman, had been engaged in underground activity before he met Chambers, who traces him back to the Ware group. The second apparatus was now supervised by Colonel Boris Bykov of the Fourth Section, whom Chambers knew as "Peter." But the Chambers apparatus was only part of a larger Soviet Military Intelligence network run by Bykov from New York.[18]

Silverman cooperated readily with Chambers, taking when necessary a briefcase of Treasury documents from White, passing these papers on for them to be copied in a photographic workshop in Baltimore. But sometimes White would meet Chambers directly, for soon after Silverman had come into the picture he had introduced White to Chambers, delaying, as the latter puts it, "only until he was satisfied that I could handle that odd character."

White had been in touch with the Communist Party for a long time, Chambers says, not only through his close friend, Silverman, but through other party members now in the Treasury. In addition to supplying original documents, White also wrote and passed on "a weekly or fortnightly longhand memo covering documents that he had seen, or information that came to him in the course of a week's work in the Treasury Department."[19]

The relationship between Chambers and White developed:

He was perfectly willing to meet me secretly; I sometimes had the impression that he enjoyed secrecy for its own sake. But his sense of inconvenience was greater than his sense of precaution, and he usually insisted on meeting me near his Connecticut Avenue apartment.

Since White was not a party member, but a fellow traveller, I could only suggest or urge, not give orders. This distinction White understood very well, and he thoroughly enjoyed the sense of being in touch with the party, but not in it, courted by it, but yielding only as much as he chose. He talked endlessly about the "Secretary" [Henry Morgenthau, Jr.] whose moods were a fair barometer of White's. If White's spirits were up, I knew that the Secretary was smiling. If he was depressed, I knew that the Secretary had had a bad day. For some time, White seemed casual in his manner toward me. I sometimes found myself wondering why I troubled to see him. But when once, quite by chance, I kept away from him for two or three weeks, I discovered that he was plaintive and felt neglected by the party, was very friendly and cooperative. I never really worried about White. . . .[20]

Chambers goes on to add that Silverman and White were almost fraternally close, that Silverman's sympathy was essential to White's resolution, and that "each in fact was a tower of weakness—a leaning tower. But as they leaned together, they held each other upright." Silverman was a party member, and of the nine men in the second apparatus, two were fellow travellers, one of whom was White. In Chambers' opinion these two were so deeply engaged in Communist espionage that "the organizational differences between them and their Communist co-workers were largely metaphysical."

In sworn Congressional testimony in Washington during August, 1951, Chambers summed up by saying that he knew White "rather well," and that White had been a source of his Soviet apparatus. He had given "both original Government documents and a weekly or fortnightly written memo summarizing information which had come to him in the course of his activities." White, Chambers went on, "was not a member of the Communist Party as near as I know, and I have reason to believe that is true because he was reluctant to accept any form of discipline. I had the impression that he was a man of such character that he very much enjoyed being of the Communist Party but not in the party and not subject to its discipline. In that relationship he was willing to go to great lengths to assist them."[21]

According to Chambers, as Christmas 1936 approached, Colonel Bykov, a coward who jumped at the sight of window shoppers at the R.C.A. building in New York as if they were members of the *Geheimpolizei*, wanted to give his sources a big sum of money. Chambers protested, saying they were Communists on principle. At Bykov's reply, "Who pays is boss, and who takes money must also give something," Chambers records that "something in me more lucid than mind knew that I had reached the end of an experience, which was not only my experience." Instead, Bykov handed over $1,000 to buy four expensive Oriental rugs as a gift from a grateful Soviet people to White, Hiss, Silverman and Julian Wadleigh. Silverman and White were "clearly impressed," Chambers remarked, and "on the four rugs we marched straight into active espionage."

Next, Colonel Bykov wanted personally to inspect his chief sources, but only in White's case, after a meeting in Washington, Chambers asserts, did he stimulate enthusiasm lacking before. This was because White, more than any of the others, enjoyed the feeling that he was in touch with "big important people." The volume of documents produced by the Washington sources was high, but White was the least productive. Bykov suspected that White was holding back, and fumed to Chambers, "*Du musst ihn kontrollieren*" ["You must control him"]. Chambers then went to J. Peters, whom he was seeing regularly in 1937, explained the problem and asked for a Treasury Department Communist to "control" White. Peters suggested Harold Glasser as "an ideal man" for the purpose, since White himself had guided Glasser into the Treasury. Glasser was then posted from the American to the Soviet underground, and soon assured Chambers that White "was turning over everything of importance that came into his hands."[22]

During 1937, Chambers writes, he began to break with Communism in what was to be "a profound upheaval of the spirit." The crisis was precipitated by the developing Stalin purges ("'Where is Bukharin?' Bykov asked me slyly . . ."). Chambers took practical steps to ensure his survival and his identity for when he deserted from the underground "about the middle of April, 1938." He needed a hiding place, an automobile, a weapon, an official identity such as a record of having worked in Washington and "a life preserver, in the form of official documents stolen by the apparatus, which, should the party move against my life, I might have an outside chance of using as a dissuader."

Consequently, Chambers writes, he secreted the documents which appeared in the Hiss trials and one of White's memos summarizing developments in the Treasury. These were hidden in his wife's sister's home in Brooklyn, in a disused dumbwaiter shaft, in an arrangement with Chambers' nephew, Nathan Levine.[23]

Soon after he deserted from the Communists, Chambers goes on, he decided to attempt to frighten some of the members of his former apparatus out of the underground. Some time "in the fall of 1938" he drove to Washington from Baltimore, with the intention of seeing Wadleigh, Silverman and White. (He later visited Hiss, he writes in *Witness*, just before Christmas.) He called White from a drug store near the Treasury, and when they met White was delighted, wondering if Chambers was coming back to Washington "to work." Chambers replied that he had left the Party, and was present to break White away from the apparatus, otherwise he would denounce him.

Chambers had never liked White, as he makes clear here, because of a certain "pushing quality." But Chambers believed he had frightened White out of the underground. Both men were embarrassed, and when they left the drug store a street photographer tried to snap them, but Chambers spun White around. "White was abjectly grateful and I never saw him again."[24]

About a year later, on September 2, 1939, the day following the German invasion of Poland, barely a week after the Nazi-Soviet Pact, Chambers describes how he met Adolph Berle, the Assistant Secretary of State, in Washington, to warn him about the underground. Chambers said that the ugly word espionage was never mentioned, and that while J. Peters and other underground members were mentioned—*vide* Berle's well-known memo of the conversation taken at the time which is reproduced in *Witness*—the names of White and Silverman were not mentioned by him, as he still thought he had broken them away from the Communists. Two years later, Chambers writes, he first mentioned White's name to the FBI.[25]

As far as the wider implications of the underground were concerned, Chambers records that he believed political espionage was "a magnificent waste of time," as there was little that an intelligent man with a sense of history could not work out for himself. But Chambers also considered that his second apparatus constituted a formidable danger, as "no government can function with enemies dedicated to its destruction posted high and low in its foreign or any other service." Much more dangerous than espionage, Chambers considered, was the power to influence policy, which was always the Party's ultimate ambition.

As for the ethics of espionage, Chambers considered that for the Party members the problem of conscience had been settled long before when they accepted the program and discipline of the Party. For the fellow travellers, such as White, it had been settled at the moment when they decided to cooperate with the Communist Party: "Of fellow travellers who cooperate to the point of espionage it must be observed that in effect they have become Communists, whatever fictive differences they maintain." To those involved, espionage would appear as a moral act, "the more deserving the more it involved . . . personal risk," committed in the name of a faith on which hinged the hope and future of mankind, against a system which was bankrupt.[26]

Later, during 1951–52, when he came to write *Witness* on his Maryland farm, Chambers recalled White sauntering down Connecticut Avenue at night, a slight furtive figure, nervous and watchful at the contact, carrying a book of Bible stories retold for children by his wife. "In a shady side street beyond Connecticut Avenue, White slips the book under my arm. I still have it. . . ."[27]

We must now examine, first, White's own rebuttal of part of Chambers' story and, second, the wider defense of White put forward by his brother, Nathan White, in the book, *Harry D. White—Loyal American*. Then we shall discuss the so-called White Memorandum which Chambers produced after White's death, and which, he alleged, was in White's handwriting and which contained notes on White's official work for the underground.

First, as we have seen in our Prologue, there is White's own appearance in the original HUAC Hearings in August, 1948. In his statement, "My Creed is the American Creed," he strongly repudiated any allegations of any sympathy whatsoever with any authoritarian ideology as he denied the story of Chambers (and Miss Bentley). In this testimony before the House Committee, Chambers, it will be recalled, had stated that White was a member of a policy-influencing rather than an espionage group, but that he, Chambers, had tried to break White from the Communist movement with his own defection. Chambers did not allege that White was a Party member.

White, after inspecting some current photographs of Chambers taken in 1948, stated that he had met between five and ten thousand people in the previous fifteen years, perhaps he met such a man, but that he had no recollection of ever meeting Chambers. He repeated this firm statement several times to Richard Nixon; and, as for Chambers' allegation that he had tried to break him away from the Communist movement, White commented: "That I would have remembered. And that I can affirm without any qualification or hesitation or shortness of memory or breath could not possibly have been so." He then repeated again to Nixon: "I do not recollect ever having met that individual."

Although most of the people White was asked about on this occasion were those named by Miss Bentley, White stated that he knew Silverman "very well." Glasser, who, White confirmed, was employed in his division in the Treasury, had been the subject of an inquiry by the FBI "close to 1940," attempting "to ascertain . . . whether he was a Communist." White stated that Glasser was an extremely competent and able economist, one that he had been proud to have in his service.[28]

Lord Jowitt has written of White's appearance before the Committee that, while it is impossible to form a conclusive judgment merely from a transcript of evidence, "I have seldom read the evidence of a witness who struck me so forcibly as being a witness of truth."[29]

We now turn to the wider defense of Harry White by his brother, Nathan White. In his study defending his brother, Nathan White remarks that in the references to Harry Dexter White in *Witness*, "there are numerous lapses and contradictory statements."[30] Nathan White goes on to show, for example, that Chambers, on three different occasions, gave three dates for the interview with the FBI, when Chambers says that he first gave White's name to the authorities. In the HUAC Hearings of August, 1948, it was 1943; in the second Hiss trial of 1949, May 14, 1942; in *Witness*, as we have seen, it was 1941.[31]

Then there are the possible discrepancies in Chambers' story of his attempt to break White away from the underground. In *Witness*, Chambers states that he did not tell Adolph Berle in September, 1939, of White's role in the underground. But, while Berle later agreed with Chambers that White's name was not mentioned, the writer Isaac Don Levine, who was with both men during this meeting, wrote in the magazine *Plain Talk* for October, 1948, that White's name was mentioned. Nathan White goes on to suggest, perhaps not altogether convincingly, that if indeed Chambers did not tell the FBI about White until 1941–43, when he came to the conclusion that he had not broken White away from the underground, "How could he have known that, if he were having no contact of any kind with erstwhile Communist associates?"

Another episode related by Chambers closely involving White is the alleged trip to Peterboro, New Hampshire, with the Hisses, in August, 1937. Chambers writes in *Witness* that White was staying at "a country place" near Peterboro, New Hampshire, a property belonging to Lauchlin Currie according to Chambers' testimony in the second Hiss trial. (This property was quite separate from the house in nearby Fitzwilliam,

N.H., which White bought in 1947, and where he died the following year.) Chambers goes on to write that White was pressing a scheme for monetary reform on the Soviet government, a project which Chambers sensed "was extremely important to White." Colonel Bykov was at first lukewarm, but then suddenly instructed Chambers to obtain White's scheme. As White was on vacation, obtaining the plan was "the underground problem of the week," and Chambers did not tell Hiss the reason he had to see White.

Chambers claimed in the Hiss trials that on the way to see White the party of three saw a stock company performance of *She Stoops to Conquer* near Peterboro, which a local group did perform at the time. But other details such as where the party stayed at Peterboro and near Thomaston, Connecticut, could not be confirmed. White was dead, Hiss denied the story, Currie did not testify, and according to Cooke's account of the episode in the Hiss trials, Chambers' story was "practically discredited, only to have one plausible doubt keep it alive."[32]

There is also the confusion about the dates between which Chambers worked for the underground. Nathan White mentions three occasions on which Chambers said that he began his active career in that secret world in 1934, but on another occasion the year given was 1935. To Adolph Berle, and to the State Department officer, Ray Murphy, who interviewed him during March, 1945, and August, 1946, Chambers said that he left the Party during 1937, a date he initially mentioned before the House Committee in early August, 1948. By the end of August, 1948, Chambers was giving the date of "about 1937 or 1938, early 1938," later fixing on the second week of April, 1938, or mid-April, 1938, as the date on which he finally fled from the underground.

Why, then, asks Nathan White, did Chambers advance the date of his break? The reason, Nathan White goes on to suggest, was because the documents which Chambers claimed had been secreted in the Brooklyn home of his wife's nephew, Nathan Levine, as a "life-preserver" from 1938 until their retrieval by him in November, 1948 had in fact been "discovered" before this latter date. Chambers had then adjusted his story accordingly: "There never has been any corroboration of Chambers' statement that all the documents and film he submitted [in November, 1948, to the authorities] were actually in the envelope he alleged he had secreted ten years before."[33]

Nathan White goes on to give other examples of discrepancies in Chambers' story. For example, Chambers claimed that, as a means of establishing his identity to save him from the vengeance of the underground, he worked, thanks to Silverman's intervention, in the National Research Project (of the WPA) from October, 1937, to January, 1938, after which date he disappeared. But the documents Chambers recovered in November, 1948, showed that he was still working for the Bykov apparatus as late as April, 1938. This, Nathan White suggests, is further evidence that Chambers simply adjusted his account to tally with the documents that he obtained by means other than that given in his final story of his connection with the Communist underground.[34]

These arguments advanced by Nathan White in defense of his brother lead to an important objection to Whittaker Chambers' story of the complicity of Harry White in the underground.

In the original HUAC Hearings of August, 1948, Chambers had stated, as we have seen, that he knew White as part of a policy-influencing group in which "power and influence were the paramount objectives" and not espionage. Three months after White's death, on November 14, 1948, as the libel suit with Hiss proceeded, Chambers retrieved, he tells us, from the dumbwaiter in Nathan Levine's former Brooklyn home, the so-called White Memorandum, together with the other documents, notes and microfilm that were to feature in the Hiss trial.

With the exception of the microfilm, submitted to House Committee officials on December 2, 1948, after briefly reposing for a day in the famous pumpkin, the notes and documents were turned over to Hiss's lawyers and to the Justice Department on November 17 in the Baltimore pretrial libel examination. At the same time, the White Memorandum was turned over by Chambers on that day to the Justice Department. During the second Hiss trial, in the IPR Hearings of 1951, and in *Witness*, Chambers maintained that the White Memorandum was part of the material that White had regularly transmitted to him during his espionage activities.[35]

The point is that, if Chambers were telling the truth after he produced the White Memorandum in November, 1948, then he had either lied or omitted to tell the truth about White's espionage activities for almost ten years, keeping the story until three months after White's death. The evasions had continued from the Berle interview of 1939, through the two interviews with Ray Murphy, the State Department security officer, in 1945 and 1946, when White was mentioned as part of a Communist group but not as a spy, to the sworn HUAC testimony given by Chambers in August, 1948. Chambers had also lied under oath to the Federal Grand Jury in New York inquiring into Communist activities, before which he had appeared in October, 1948, denying he knew anything about espionage. According to Alistair Cooke, Chambers in the first Hiss trial conceded "seven specific acts of perjury before the grand jury."[36]

Lord Jowitt considers that it was not until he found himself confronted with the libel suit that Chambers revealed the existence of the hidden cache of documents, thereby making it quite plain either that he suppressed the fact of their existence or that his later story "was a complete fabrication . . ."[37]

Chambers himself, aware of the implications of his perjury, stated in the second Hiss trial and in *Witness* that as he believed in a God of Mercy, he had initially lied about his espionage activities because he wished to do as little harm as possible to the individuals involved, and that time was important in any case for people who wished to break with the Communists. Eventually, the pressures of the developing libel suit in the fall of 1948 and a feeling for the country's security had forced him to reveal the documents in the Brooklyn dumbwaiter.[38]

The question really is: Was Chambers trying to tell the truth for the first time when he narrated his later, expanded story of the underground and the Bykov network of which White's alleged espionage activities were an integral part?

Of central importance in assessing the truth of Chambers' story about White is the significance of the "long memo on yellow foolscap in the handwriting of Harry Dexter White,"[39] retrieved in a sealed envelope, along with the Hiss notes, typed documents and microfilm, from the dumbwaiter shaft in his wife's sister's home in Brooklyn, on Sunday, November 14, 1948.

The so-called White Memorandum was shown to Chambers' lawyers in Baltimore the next day, November 15, and entrusted to them along with the alleged Hiss material, excluding the microfilm. As is well known, the Hiss notes and documents were then presented in the course of the pretrial examination of the Chambers-Hiss libel suit at Baltimore on November 17, 1948. On the same day the alleged White Memorandum was "turned over to the Justice Department," Richard Nixon told the House of Representatives in January, 1950.[40]

These notes, which Chambers asserts were given him by White for transmission to the Soviet, consisted of four double-sided sheets on yellow foolscap, containing twenty-one paragraphs of varying length, all handwritten in pencil.[41]

Following Chambers' production of the alleged White Memorandum, photostats were examined by a government handwriting expert, Harold Gesell, of the Veterans' Administration, and compared with photostats of some examples of White's handwriting. Gesell reported that, subject to examination of the original documents which he had not seen, the notes submitted were in White's hand. (See Appendix A for the text of the White Memorandum and the report of the government handwriting expert.)

However, the expert was in error as far as the back of the fourth sheet of the memorandum was concerned. This simply bore the notation, in an obviously different hand from the other pages, "65 big sheets, 4 little slips," and clearly refers to the Hiss documents and notes respectively which were submitted at the Baltimore pretrail examination on November 17, 1948. There is also a reference in the Gesell report to the effect that the White Memorandum concerns State Department activities. This should, of course, indicate Treasury Department activities, although much of the information in the memorandum does indeed concern foreign affairs.

Several questions are raised by the White Memorandum. In the first place, as we have seen, Chambers states that the memorandum from White which he passed on to the Soviet was an example of a weekly or fortnightly summary containing information which Bykov was eager to obtain.

But as Nathan White points out, the memorandum from the three dated paragraphs covers a period of at least thirty-seven days from January 10, 1938, to February 15, and as most of the paragraphs are undated the period may well be longer. Nathan White therefore concludes that the claim by Chambers that White's written reports covered a period of one or two weeks "is therefore obviously entirely without foundation."[42]

Parenthetically, perhaps it should be remarked that as this period of early 1938, according to Chambers' own story, was that of withdrawal from the underground, his contacts with White may have been of a less regular nature than previously. But undoubtedly here is another discrepancy in Chambers' story, as Nathan White brings out. As one paragraph begins "About one month ago the Pres. asked Sec M," it certainly seems at this time in early 1938 that White's alleged reports were not on the weekly-fortnightly basis described by Chambers years later.

A corollary of Chambers' statement that White submitted a regular report to Soviet Intelligence is that this information was of interest to the Russians. Quite aside from whether the information was confidential or not, this assumption is contended by Nathan White.

Of the figures in the White Memorandum listing American silver purchases from China, not released at the time, Nathan White asks, "What possible harm to China or the United States could there be in this paragraph?" On another matter in the White Memorandum, the notes on the mission to London of Captain Royal E. Ingersoll, USN, to discuss, *inter alia*, naval liaison with the British in the event of war with Japan, Nathan White points out that the Ingersoll mission was mentioned in general terms in the New York press in early February, 1938. Admiral William Leahy, moreover, had answered questions on the mission before Congress at this time, stressing its secret nature.

Although the White Memorandum covered this period, there were no references in it to these press comments, Nathan White writes. He goes on to suggest that the logical explanation is that the Memorandum was thus not an intelligence report, as it omitted these press stories, but something composed "for the writer's later use," an *aide-mémoire*, in fact.

In much the same way, Nathan White considers that the reference in the alleged White Memorandum to the Van Zeeland Report could hardly be considered important or confidential enough to interest the Russians. This report, on the development of international trade, was drafted by the outgoing Belgian prime minister for the British and French governments and published on January 26, 1938. It was available to other countries, including Russia. But if White had commented that it was "not taken seriously," his opinion, as a Treasury employee, would be as authoritative as that of most American officials at this time.

As for the paragraph in the White Memorandum which records a possible attempt by the Treasury Assistant Secretary, Wayne Taylor, to press Morgenthau into a Hungarian debt settlement, Nathan White considers this, because of its apparent triviality and the rhetorical phrasing of the memo, "the clearest possible proof that the memorandum was not intended for perusal by the Russians."[43]

In this refutation of Chambers' allegations, therefore, Nathan White, while accepting that some of the information in the White Memorandum was confidential, strongly rebuts the suggestion that it would be of interest to the Russians. As for the matters which were not confidential, why should a spy pass them along? What remains probable is that some of the information was, at the time, considered confidential, as the writer of the memorandum indicates twice in Q2, for example.

It has already been noted "that there has never been any corroborating evidence that the White Memorandum was included with whatever material Chambers claims he secreted in Levine's possession."[44] Nathan Levine did testify that Chambers gave him an envelope for safekeeping in 1938, that it was sealed then, and that it was sealed when he took it out of the dumbwaiter to give it back to Chambers in November, 1948. When Levine stepped back into the kitchen after clearing up the dust from the dumbwaiter, Chambers was holding some papers. Chambers did not at this time mention the contents of the envelope to Levine. As far as this aspect of the White Memorandum is concerned, what is sure is only that Chambers had the memorandum in his physical possession when he showed it to his lawyers and produced it at Baltimore in mid-November, 1948.

Now we come to what Nathan White calls "the one sentence that really proves that the entire memorandum was never intended to be the report of a spy."[45] This sentence on Q2 obverse of the photostat of the White Memorandum reads:

Purchases of Japanese goods by _____

————are decreasing rapidly while our exports to these countries are increasing.

(The rule represents blank space on the photostat, space which is conveyed by three asterisks in the *Congressional Record* text of the memorandum.)

Nathan White argues that if the memorandum was prepared for the Russians, there are only two possible explanations for the omission of the names of the countries in the sentence quoted above. Under the first hypothesis,

the writer would have had no reason to write the sentence if he were not going to include the names, unless the entire memorandum was a rough first draft of material to be typed, the names to be given to the typist later. But if this were the procedure, there was no need of leaving a blank space at the beginning of the second line in addition to the one at the end of the first line, which would have been sufficient. Furthermore, he would not have given the courier for the Russians the roughly prepared pencilled first draft but would have given him the finished typed copy.

Therefore, Nathan White concludes, the hypothesis that the writer deliberately omitted the names of countries to which American exports were increasing "can be dismissed as unsound."

The second hypothesis put forward by Nathan White is that "the names were originally written in the sentence but were subsequently erased by someone other than the writer." He goes on to note that Japan's exports declined by more than fifty percent in the three months from October, 1937, to January, 1938, and that "this serious decline in its overall exports undoubtedly included those countries which were at the same time increasing their purchases in the United States." He then explains that the latest figures for American exports available during January and February, 1938, were the figures for the last quarter of 1937. These figures showed that, of the twenty-one countries (except Japan) whose imports from the United States went up, as a monthly average, in the last three months of 1937, the United Kingdom, British India and the Soviet Union showed the greatest percentage increase.

Nathan White then assumes that these three countries fitted the requirements of the ellipsis in the White Memorandum as states which simultaneously decreased their purchases of Japanese goods while increasing their imports from the United States. He goes on to say that, since there is enough room in the blank spaces for the names or initials of these three countries, it is "evident" that the Soviet Union was included in the names written in the sentence originally. The implication is: Why should a Soviet agent, as Chambers alleged, be sending the Russians figures about their own trade?

> In the enlarged photostat copy made by the writer [Nathan White concludes] there is a faint evidence of the capital letter "S" near the end of the blank space in the first line. None of the other countries in the entire list of twenty-one (in the trade figures of the last quarter of 1937) have the capital letter "S" in the spelling which would place it where the evidence shows it originally was written.
>
> Furthermore the fact that all the names were erased is additional evidence that the USSR was one of the countries originally written in this sentence. There is no other possible reason for the erasure of all the names to have been made. For it is obvious that the inclusion of the USSR among the countries named would have provided the best proof that the entire memorandum was not intended as information to the Soviets. A Soviet agent would not report to his Soviet contacts that the USSR was increasing its purchases in the United States. . . . However since the erasure of the USSR alone would have left a tell-tale blank space, it becomes necessary to erase all the names. It does not matter who made the erasure. The fact that the names were erased is clear proof that the erasure was made to prevent the discovery of indisputable evidence that the [White] memorandum was not written as a report to Russia. . . .[46]

Clearly, Nathan White assumes here that the handwriting in the memorandum was that of Harry Dexter White. Presumably, as his brother, he would be familiar with Harry White's hand. Yet, as Nathan White goes on, there still remains the question of whether the White Memorandum was a forgery, as the United States government handwriting expert stated that his conclusion was subject to verification of the original, which he had not seen. Even on the assumption that the memorandum is not a forgery, Nathan White writes, why would Harry Dexter White give information as a spy to a man of Chambers' background and reliability?[47] "That such action actually took place is beyond belief."

Essentially, therefore, Nathan White's case against Chambers' story of the White Memorandum is that, if not a forgery, the memorandum was an *aide-mémoire* perhaps stolen after White's death and tampered with to make it seem an incriminating piece of evidence. In any case, much of the information in the White Memorandum could hardly be of any interest to the Russians. "The answer is obvious. Chambers never had any other of White's papers. The one memorandum he did produce may have been a forgery, or if genuine, could have been pilfered after Mr. White's death."[48]

Lord Jowitt, who accepts that the memorandum was in White's handwriting and contained some confidential information, believes that the notes in the memorandum "would appear to be either some sort of diary, or the raw material from which a diary could be constructed; or else they may be letters which White intended for some friend in the Treasury who was presumably absent from Washington at the time they were written."[49]

Less convinced perhaps of White's role as a diarist, Professor Earl Latham has commented that, if the White Memorandum was an *aide-mémoire*, there is no suggestion how something written in 1938 could have been stolen from White's effects after his death ten years later: "But even if it were an *aide-mémoire*, if Chambers had received it from White in 1938, a prima-facie case is established for the assertion Chambers made that he was receiving confidential information from White."[50]

Subject to the qualification of the handwriting expert at not having seen the originals, it seems clear therefore that, prima facie, the so-called White Memorandum was in White's hand, was in Chambers' physical possession in November, 1948, and did contain confidential information. Discussing the memorandum, Richard Nixon told the House of Representatives on January 26, 1950:

> These facts have definitely been established: First. A Government handwriting expert, Mr. Harold Gesell of the Veterans' Administration, has established that the documents were in Mr. White's handwriting. Second. Mr. Chambers, a confessed espionage agent, had the documents in his possession. Third. A substantial portion of the information contained in these documents was of a confidential nature.

How these sheets came into Chambers' possession, and their significance, Professor Herbert Packer has commented, are matters "on which we have only the word of Whittaker Chambers. But it cannot be denied that their existence in his possession requires some explanation."[51]

The forces in the background of the story that Chambers told about White were not the forces of a decade later when the Witness came at last publicly to tell his tale. Apart from the problems raised by Chambers' evasions, his dramatic literary style and his affinity for absolutes, it is worth bearing in mind, perhaps, that Colonel Bykov, as a Soviet Military Intelligence officer, was "obsessed" with all information that could relate to the 1936 Anti-Comintern Pact between Germany, Italy and Japan.

Chambers goes on to remark that Bykov, "in the Russian fashion, pre-ferred the dragnet or volumetric production of documents."[52] Hede Massing, who in her account of *This Deception* tells us that she worked in an NKVD network in Washington in the 1930's, also comments on this Soviet intelligence process of collecting as much information as possible for evaluation: ". . . how can anyone understand or follow this strange routine of reporting and reporting about everything and everybody, this sifting and sifting of people, without explanation, without an obvious reason?"[53] Clearly, the amount of information to be collected was stressed by Soviet Intelligence.

From the Russian perspective, there were good reasons for this inten-sive intelligence operation during 1936–38, the period when Chambers was active with his alleged "sources." Behind the United Front, as we have seen with Soviet policy toward China at this time, lay the urgent problems of defending the Soviet Union. With the military industrializa-tion of the Soviet Union not yet completed, with the Red Army high command about to be torn apart in the Stalin purges, faced with a potentially hostile coalition of capitalist and fascist states, there were urgent, specific problems of national security that faced Moscow as it sought to make the most of its political, as well as its strategic, resources. This was not a phantom situation.

"During the years from 1933 to 1938," George Kennan has written in his *Memoirs,*

it was well understood in Moscow that the Soviet Union did not have the strength to sustain alone, without aid from outside, a German attack. . . . There was a sudden enthusiasm for Collective Security. The Soviet press developed marked solicitude for the precarious posi-tion of the Western Democracies in the face of the Nazi menace. Litvinov went to Geneva, spoke eloquently of the dangers of aggres-sion, of the indivisibility of peace and of the hopelessness of supposing that war, once begun, would not become universal. The Western powers, he argued, should agree to fight at the first sign of German aggression. . . . Litvinov's efforts tided over a difficult period, during which both German and Russian armaments were built up. But they did not succeed in drawing the Western powers into obligations which would compel them to fight Hitler if the latter embarked on a policy of expansion; and the chances of accomplishing this looked progressively dimmer as Nazi power increased and Western appease-ment continued. . . .[54]

Kennan goes on to remark that, with Munich, the Kremlin's road lay open to explore an understanding with Germany because that agreement "dispelled all serious hopes in the prospects of inducing the western world to fight Hitler except in direct self-defense." To what extent, then, could White, if Chambers' allegations were true, have helped the Soviet during the time he is supposed to have worked with the Bykov apparatus?

As a rising official in the Treasury, who was promoted to Director of Monetary Research in March, 1938, White, as we have seen, was involved in matters other than purely technical Treasury affairs. At the same time, the Treasury was increasingly involved with aspects of government that would not have been possible before 1933. But besides being in a position to pass official papers to Chambers, White was also able to report on Morgenthau's growing interest in the anti-Axis cause and his diplomatic initiatives such as those on the tripartite stabilization talks and the development, through such means as the silver-purchase program, of a positive American policy toward Nationalist China—then, of course, supported by the Russians. White, then, would have been able to help the Russians to assess the possibility (or otherwise) of the United States being drawn into an understanding with the other democracies.

Of course, as we have seen, the reaction to Roosevelt's "Quarantine-the-Aggressors" speech of October, 1937, made the development of an interventionist American foreign policy hardly possible at this time; but, from the viewpoint of someone in Moscow trying to assess the drift of American policy, an agent able to report on Morgenthau's access to and influence with the President could conceivably have been of some use. In the event, of course, the obstacles in Morgenthau's path as he sought to commit the United States to an interventionist position may have been one of the factors that propelled Moscow toward the pact of August, 1939; but that would not be for White to decide.

In any case, if he did work for Chambers, White would hardly have been the fictional spy who breaks open safes and rifles filing cabinets. The documents would have been written by him or presented to him in the course of his work, and his reports, trivial or not, would have been those of high-level political intelligence, which Moscow, in the sensitive climate of those years, may well have found more useful than the conventional secret documents which are supposed to be stolen by spies.

In this context, therefore, it is perhaps conceivable that the notes in the alleged White Memorandum of early 1938 could be of use to someone attempting to assess some of the influences on the evolution of American policy at this time.

The Ingersoll mission, raising the question of how far Britain and America were prepared to cooperate in the Far East, the continuing progress of the American silver-purchase program from China, the reported State Department belief that "British moves toward Germany and

Italy" would "reduce substantially" the fear of European war, a military report of Japan's oil-storage facilities, and Herriot's statement that, if Premier, he would "quickly strengthen" French ties with the Soviet Union were all strands in the great debate at the time of whether the Western powers would stand up to the Axis. The outcome of this debate was of interest to Moscow.

To a controller demanding a "volumetric" production of information, no matter how apparently insignificant, it might still be possible to consider, therefore, passing on the fact that the American official figures showed that Russia was increasing its exports from America. In the atmosphere of fear and urgency that Chambers described, it is at least conceivable that scribbled, incomplete notes might be written by someone participating in such an intelligence operation. Such a process might be "unsound," but not impossible. We cannot say for certain.

What does seem reasonably certain is that if White had decided to help the Soviet government as "a moral act" in the way outlined by Chambers, that former Boston hardware man who had gone through Harvard to the Treasury would not have been deterred ultimately by the risks and the all-encompassing fear which Chambers describes as surrounding the operations of "the second apparatus."

7

WAR AND THE TREASURY

. . . I want to make it clear that it is the purpose of the nation to build now with all possible speed every machine, every arsenal, every factory that we need to manufacture our defense material. . . .
—FRANKLIN D. ROOSEVELT, December, 1940

As WHITE's apprenticeship in the Treasury—and perhaps his time as a member of the underground described by Chambers—came to an end during 1938, the course of events between Munich and Pearl Harbor meant that new and varied responsibilities inside the Treasury would soon be his.

When Morgenthau, toward the end of 1938, was given the task of supervising foreign procurement orders for aircraft and other supplies by Roosevelt, this was the beginning of a process that would give the Treasury a central role in the slowly developing American preparedness program.

Although, as we have seen, the negotiation of a $25,000,000 credit for China had been a major preoccupation in Washington during the closing months of 1938, the Munich crisis had shown Roosevelt and Morgenthau without any doubt that the chief threat lay in Europe.

In England, Winston Churchill, in the Munich debate in the House of Commons in early October, had described the agreement as "a total and unmitigated defeat" for Britain, and had called for rearmament to meet the inevitable: "Do not suppose that this is the end. This is only the beginning of the reckoning. This is only the first sip, the first foretaste of a bitter cup. . . ." A few weeks later Roosevelt considered that the United States now faced the eventual possibility of an attack across the Atlantic as a result of the reestablishment of German power in Europe.[1]

The Nazi occupation of Prague in March, 1939, meant that on the domestic front the Treasury soon discovered that it possessed extensive powers over foreign exchange and assets, and that the department could, in a national emergency, regulate arms trafficking and shipping, along with other controls.

Draft executive orders embodying these powers were prepared for Roosevelt, but on another precautionary measure of economic warfare—a program of preemptive buying of strategic materials—Morgenthau was hardly successful. Following the Secretary's instructions, in April, 1939, Harry Dexter White prepared a paper stating that the Axis powers would need strategic commodities such as tungsten, nickel, rubber and manganese to the tune of about $100,000,000 monthly. Not without realism, White doubted whether the United States, together with Britain and France, could absorb these supplies in the absence of cooperation by other countries including Russia, and a favorable domestic political climate.[2]

On April 11, however, Morgenthau suggested to the President a billion-dollar program for the preemptive buying of strategic materials, so helping to check Axis aggression. Roosevelt "seemed intensely interested," Morgenthau noted, but nothing came of the scheme. The presidential assessment of what was politically possible at this time in the field of economic defense was underlined when Roosevelt appointed a committee to investigate stockpiling, asking Congress for a $10,000,000 appropriation. This was a sum rather less than that suggested by Morgenthau.[3]

A further demonstration of the limits of the possible in the spring of 1939 was shown by the expiry of the "cash-and-carry" provisions of the Neutrality legislation on May 1. This meant that in the event of war Britain and France "would be unable to buy and transport American arms and munitions even in their own ships."[4]

However, during this difficult period of 1939–40, when Roosevelt was intensely aware of isolationist opinion in Congress, he was still able to create an embryonic supply organization for aiding Britain and France. Shortly after Munich the President issued an executive order giving the Treasury's Division of Procurement authority to determine purchasing policy for aircraft as well as other military items. On December 17, 1938, Roosevelt assigned Morgenthau the task of dealing with all foreign orders for munitions, "thereby laying the foundation for coordinated treatment of what was to become the major problem of foreign aid for the European democracies."[5]

This was, of course, only the beginning. Following the outbreak of the European war in September, 1939, Morgenthau became Roosevelt's agent for dealing with the Anglo-French Purchasing Mission. Later, following the fall of France and during the Battle of Britain, Morgenthau was extremely active, along with Stimson and Knox, Roosevelt's new service secretaries, in expediting aid for Britain, whether munitions or aircraft, or in the deliberations that led to the famous Anglo-American "destroyers for bases" deal in September, 1940.

In view of Morgenthau's involvement with British supply, it was natural that the Treasury should be given the vital task of the drafting of the Lend-Lease legislation in December, 1940, when Roosevelt decided to do away with "the silly, foolish, old dollar sign." When the Lend-Lease Bill became law in March, 1941, responsibility for administering the program was given to Hopkins, but Morgenthau continued to support the interventionist cause as one of the leading "all-outers" in Roosevelt's cabinet.

Later differences with the British over such issues as postwar German policy were a reflection of Morgenthau's passionate commitment to his causes. Lord Beaverbrook, Churchill's Minister of Aircraft Production in 1940, stated to one of his representatives in Washington at this time that the British could never repay their debt to Morgenthau.[6]

Some insight into White's thinking during this period, when much of Morgenthau's energies were becoming gradually absorbed with the problem of British supply, can be seen from a long paper which he gave to the Secretary on March 31, 1939.[7]

It was a fateful month. Speaking to the Eighteenth Party Congress on the tenth, Stalin had denounced the democracies who were accustomed "to have others pull their chestnuts out of the fire." On the fifteenth the Germans had occupied Prague, and two weeks later on the thirty-first, the day of White's memorandum, Neville Chamberlain had given a unilateral guarantee to Poland in the British House of Commons.

In his exordium of March 31, White remarked that recent events had shown that the Axis hoped to get its future gains out of the British and French empires, rather than from Russia. Modestly, he went on to write that Morgenthau's letter to Roosevelt of October 17, 1938 (which he had helped to draft) had been "100 percent accurate in its prophecies and analyses." The need for an aggressive policy against the Axis was greater than ever, and "there is nobody on the horizon who can or will push that program unless you and the President do." American foreign policy, White went on, should move along three fronts at this time.

The first front was Latin America, where progress in bringing that area "into the United States orbit" had yielded negligible results in the last six months. On the other hand, Franco's victory in Spain had meant that the strength of the aggressor nations in Latin America had greatly increased. The State Department, White wrote, was pursuing its traditional policy, and was not interested in pushing assistance programs to the area. Unless this policy changed Latin America would rapidly succumb to Axis penetration. If the Latin American program was left to the State Department, nothing substantial would come of it. If results were to be achieved, economic assistance for the area should be "unqualifiedly" under Morgenthau's leadership.

Second, White's paper advocated "further substantial aid to China," going on to recommend a new $100,000,000 credit. There was a very good chance that as the fighting there was on such a large scale China could "seriously weaken, if not neutralize, one important nation in the aggressor bloc." A loan would stiffen Chinese resistance and offset the effects of the neutrality legislation.

The third point in White's memorandum discussed American relations with Russia:

The time is now opportune for an arrangement with Russia which would accomplish four things:
(a) Be an important factor in helping recovery in the United States.
(b) Make substantial contributions to our surplus-cotton problem.
(c) Settle the outstanding debts between Russia and the United States and clear the decks for future economic collaboration between the two most powerful countries in the world, which, irrespective of their political differences, constitute, for the present, at least the core of resistance against the aggressor nations.
(d) Bring pressure to bear against the Chamberlain government to seek closer military collaboration with Russia in stopping German aggression.

White then went on to argue that "the proposal in its bare outlines" consisted of two parts. The first was a settlement of governmental and private debts between the two countries, which would cost the Russians between $15–20,000,000 per annum for an unspecified period. The second, the heart of this memorandum, was a suggestion for a $250,000,000 Russian loan at 8 percent, repayable over ten years. This credit would be used to finance the purchase of $150,000,000 worth of surplus American cotton products, the rest on machinery, manufactures and leather goods. The difference between the cost to the American government of borrowing and the 8 percent interest could be applied to the settlement of the Soviet debt to the United States.

The effect of such a loan, White remarked, would be "startling" on both the current American business situation and the international political situation. The American cotton textile industry would thus have its "biggest boom" for years, and the benefits to the machine goods and leather industries would "give some added legislative support" from the cattle and industrial states. Germany and Japan would be warned that the

United States meant to support "the enemies of aggression." In Britain, Chamberlain would find it difficult to avoid taking similar steps.

Of course, the demand for some sort of agreement with the Russians against the Axis was widespread in the democracies at this time, a linchpin of the Popular Front. But perhaps Munich, compounded by Chamberlain's hesitancy with regard to an understanding with Russia, was reason enough from Stalin's viewpoint to explain the caution and suspicion in his speech to the Eighteenth Party Congress.

Moreover, to say the least, the story of the parallel Russian negotiations in the summer of 1939, almost farcical with the British, labyrinthine with the Germans, and the terms of the subsequent Nazi-Soviet Pact, show that Stalin was unlikely to be influenced by a $250,000,000 American credit, even if it had been possible to deliver the surplus cotton. For the time being, the Germans could offer Moscow neutrality in a war between Hitler and the democracies. In any case, as Langer and Gleason have written, "it appears almost certain that if Stalin meant to conclude an agreement with the democracies at all, it was only on the basis that Soviet Russia be given what amounted to a free hand in the Baltic States and Finland."[8] Here were tangible assets of national power.

Yet White's paper has a deeper interest in providing a framework for some of his later initiatives. His belief, for example, that significant arrangements could be made between countries on an economic basis "irrespective of their political differences" remained one of his preoccupations. In his paper of May, 1941, to Morgenthau, as we shall see in the following chapter, he again suggested that large credits be advanced to Russia, and to Japan, as a means for coming to wider political agreement. By 1944–45 the proposed Russian loan had grown first to $5 billion and then to $10 billion as a part of a postwar settlement. The corollary was that economic power was as important in this sort of bargaining as political or military power, a solvent to "political differences."

Closely associated with this thread in White's March, 1939, paper is his parallel concern with American national interest, as he saw it. There is the reference above to bringing Latin America "into the U.S. orbit." Again, the 8 percent terms of the proposed $250,000,000 Russian loan were an indication of White's concern with another aspect of national interest in dealing with "the other most powerful country in the world." But given the view, expressed in this paper, of an underlying identity of interest between America and Russia, some of White's later quasi-diplomatic initiatives fall into a framework which can be seen in embryonic form in this paper of March, 1939.

In his paper of March, 1939, to Morgenthau, White had suggested that "our international policy move along three fronts at the same time." In line with his own suggestion, to what extent was White involved in the Treasury's dealings with Latin America, China and the wider field of American relations with Russia which merged into the general crisis of the war?

The fear of the Roosevelt Administration over Axis penetration in Latin America had led to the Lima Conference of December, 1938, where the American republics had stated their determination to defend democratic principles. At this conference the United States sponsored a resolution calling for regular meetings of the treasuries of the republics. But, beneath vague principles of hemisphere defense, there were differences once again between the Treasury and a State Department committed to the gradualist Good Neighbor approach.

Brazil was a case in point. The State Department tended to favor the interests of private American investors in any negotiations for assistance, while the Treasury emphasized the necessity for economic development. Yet confidence was necessary in the first place if any private investment from North America was to take place. After some intense bargaining, an American credit of $19,000,000 was granted to Brazil in April, 1939, but the Treasury had wished for the approval of the larger amount of $50,-000,000. Morgenthau now became interested in the idea of a Bank of North and South America which could perhaps bypass the State Department's influence on these matters.[9]

White's interest in these problems can be seen in several papers written by him for Morgenthau during 1939–40. In June, 1939, he told Morgenthau that Latin America presented "a remarkable opportunity for economic development." The program of economic assistance for the region "should be placed under the supervision of a Cabinet member who would approach the problem from a broad gauged point of view, who would not be bound by the traditions of his organization." As we have seen from his earlier paper of March, 1939, such an administrative arrangement would not have precluded Morgenthau. Such development measures, White said, was not exploitation as control would remain with the borrowing country.

Another memorandum for the Secretary in September, 1939, put forward specific proposals for stabilization and railroad construction credits for Brazil. Later, in March, 1940, White returned to this general subject stating that lending "on a comprehensive scale" was only feasible in the hemisphere, and that $2 billion could be absorbed by the Americas in five years. The result might be "the establishment of the Americas as a tight economic unit." Such measures, if possible, would no doubt have brought the region even closer "into the U.S. orbit."[10]

The differences between these hopes and the actual programs implemented by the Treasury remained considerable. White's growing interest in these matters had been reflected by his appointment as Treasury representative, in April, 1939, to the interdepartmental Executive Committee on Commercial Policy, which had as its purpose "the systematization of the handling of American commercial relations with foreign countries."[11] But his chief work in this field during 1939–40 was on the proposed scheme for an Inter-American Bank.

Eventually, the charter of the proposed new institution, chiefly White's work, was approved by the Inter-American Financial and Economic Committee in February, 1940. But some of the larger republics such as the Argentine and Chile did not subscribe, ratifications were not deposited, and in the face of differences between the republics the scheme fell through. However, Adolph Berle of the State Department told Morgenthau that White had "worked unceasingly, and . . . handled the final stage of the negotiations in the American committee with entire success."[12]

But the Treasury's hopes for a more positive role in inter-American affairs had hardly borne fruit, and the State Department remained master of the field with its modest but relatively successful political negotiations for hemisphere solidarity. As far as White was concerned, the chief value of the abortive bank negotiations was the experience it gave him in the work of planning international institutions, experience useful in later events leading to Bretton Woods.

However, at the Havana Conference of June, 1940, Cordell Hull, as part of a broader program of hemisphere defense, had suggested that friendly Latin American governments should approach the Treasury for economic assistance. White, who had attended the conference, was one of those delegated authority by Morgenthau to deal in the Treasury with Latin American matters, and later in September he became the Treasury representative on Nelson Rockefeller's Committee on Inter-American Affairs.[13] But once again divergences between Washington and the Latin American republics (and between and inside the republics) made negotiations generally inconclusive.

Eventually an undramatic financial agreement between the Treasury and Mexico was ratified in October, 1941.[14] But it was with the Cuban Republic of General Fulgencio Batista, president from 1940 to 1944 and again after 1952, that White became most closely connected during this period of the Treasury's involvement with Latin American matters. Batista's Cuba was, of course, an ally of the United States during this period, declaring war on the Axis in December, 1941.

In September, 1941, White was appointed head of a technical mission to Cuba that included experts from the Federal Reserve and the Farm Credit Administration. The mission, to be responsible to the American ambassador in Havana, was sent in reply to a request for help on monetary and banking matters by Havana, and its recommendations were to be transmitted through the State Department.[15]

Three successive reports were submitted from the mission by June, 1942, dealing with the reorganization of Cuban finances.[16] Eventually, after protracted delays, a Cuban central bank law, based largely on the White mission's recommendations, was passed in 1948. Although Spruille Braden, a former American ambassador to Havana, stated in December, 1953, that the mission's plan would have led Cuba into "economic chaos and bankruptcy," the World Bank reported after a study of the Cuban economy in 1950 that the Cuban peso was "one of the world's strongest currencies."[17]

As far as White's larger plans for Latin American were concerned, the rising wartime demand for the region's raw materials and commodities obscured the long-term political and economic problems of the area.

But in China there seemed no solution to the fighting as, following the rapid Japanese advances of 1938–39, the war became a stalemated test of endurance. In these years immediately preceding the wider Pacific war the Chinese aimed to wear down the Imperial Japanese forces in the huge spaces of their country.

For their part the invaders hoped for a crumbling of the Nationalist regime by setting up puppet regimes in occupied territories, attacking the yuan, and by attempting to cut off Chiang Kai-shek's precarious supply lines to the West which ran through French Indochina and the Burma Road from Kunming to Lashio.

Following White's suggestion of a $100,000,000 loan to the Nationalists in his paper of March, 1939, he continued to press for financial assistance to China. On September 26, 1939, the Chinese ambassador, Hu Shih, told Morgenthau that the first American credit to China was almost exhausted, and he was wondering if his government could have "another life saving injection in the form of a loan."[18]

Morgenthau replied that the ambassador was "to sit down" with White and the Treasury Director on the Import-Export Bank, and go into the matter more fully. The Chinese soon asked for $75,000,000, and on November 22 White suggested to Morgenthau a figure of $35,000,000, secured against Chinese tin. Such a loan, White said, would "materially lengthen" China's staying power and "decrease her dependence upon Russian assistance."[19]

In another long memorandum for Morgenthau on November 20, White suggested a much more ambitious scheme to help China. He proposed in some detail legislation setting up a "Gold Investment Committee." As the American gold reserves were now approaching $20 billion, White suggested, there was a large surplus over the figure of about $8 billion needed for domestic monetary needs.

Part of this surplus could be used "to provide ample funds to carry out our Latin America programs, to make a loan to China and to participate in reconstruction loans elsewhere after hostilities cease—all without additional appropriation of funds by Congress." The Chairman of the Gold Investment Committee would be Morgenthau, and White suggested that the proposed Bill could "strengthen the monetary systems of the rest of the world without weakening our own."[20]

Eventually a $20,000,000 credit was granted to China in April, 1940, and another $25,000,000 in September. Like the first American credit, these sums were for non-military purchases, but the problem remained first, to get supplies to Nationalist China, and second, to maintain the currency there and the confidence that went with it.

White was involved in both these problems during 1940–1. As far as the transportation problem was concerned, an ingenious scheme emerged during the visit to Washington in the summer of 1940 of T.V. Soong, a former finance minister and now chairman of the Bank of China. During discussions with Roosevelt and Morgenthau, the idea of a triangular deal between Russia, China and America was discussed. Russia would sell strategic materials to the United States, while delivering their value in armaments to the Chinese over the Central Asian route.

In a special study for Morgenthau, White commended such a triangular deal, invoking a sum of perhaps $200,000,000 worth of strategic materials such as chromite, mercury and asbestos. Because of strained Soviet-American relations in July, 1940—the United States had frozen the assets of the invaded Baltic states—the scheme hardly got off the ground, and later in September it was still found impracticable owing to State Department opposition and Russian indifference.[21] With its reopening in October, 1940, after three months' closure, the Burma Road continued to be the chief supply route into Nationalist China, although some supplies still came from Russia via Sinkiang. A precarious air link flown by the China National Aviation Corporation (CNAC) from Hong Kong to Chungking lasted until December, 1941.

As far as the second problem of currency support was concerned, Roosevelt, on November 30, 1940, announced a $50,000,000 credit to China "for monetary protection and management." Another $50,000,000 purchase-credit was announced at the same time with the aim of upholding Nationalist China's morale, and a British credit of £5,000,000 was also promised. (Chungking was also eligible for Lend-Lease after March, 1941.) Following a maze of debate in all three countries over the rival claims of stabilization in a free market compared with the virtues of working through a form of exchange control, a three-power stabilization agreement was signed in April, 1941. The tripartite Stabilization Board, which had its head office at Hong Kong, and which worked through the banks in the Shanghai international settlement, as well as in free China, was set up by August, 1941. In July Morgenthau had turned over to White full responsibility for the Treasury's stabilization policy in China.[22]

A new element in these stabilization operations was the freezing of Chinese assets by the United States and Britain in July, 1941. Such a move had been recommended as a way of obtaining greater government control over Chinese foreign resources by Lauchlin Currie, an Administrative Assistant to Roosevelt, after he returned from an economic mission to Chungking early in 1941.

It was a move also demanded by Chiang Kai-shek. Yet the parallel freezing of Japanese assets by the United States, the British Commonwealth, and the Dutch East Indies following Roosevelt's executive order on July 26, in effect initiating a policy of economic sanctions against Japan, only emphasized how intertwined with stabilization operations was the crucial strategic duel between Tokyo and Washington. Against this deteriorating situation in the background, in its work from August to December 7, 1941, the tripartite Stabilization Board spent $23,000,000, half as much in three and a half months as previous stabilization operations in China had cost in over three years.[23]

Even so, this was a relatively minor figure compared with the sums involved in some of White's other projects, although according to Arthur Young the Board's operations in fixed, overvalued exchange rates of *fapi* encouraged hoarding and set the scene for the expensive American backing of the Chinese currency after December, 1941.

Essentially, stabilization operations in China at this time were of secondary importance, as White perhaps realized. For, as we shall see, he had already drafted sweeping quasi-diplomatic proposals at the end of May, 1941, for the reconciling of Japanese, Russian and American interests in the Far East.

However, on July 2, 1941, the Imperial Conference in Tokyo decided that in carrying out its plans "with reference to the southern regions," the Japanese government would "not be deterred by the possibility of being involved in war with England and America." In the event, the freezing order of July 26 was a partial Western response to the Japanese occupation of southern Indochina already in train. In Tokyo, Joseph Grew, the American ambassador, wrote in his diary in early August following these events: "The obvious conclusion is eventual war."[24]

The third point of White's memorandum of March, 1939, had hoped for the bettering of relations between "the two most powerful nations." But events between that date and June, 1941, which willy nilly brought about a *de facto* alliance between the United States and Russia, were directed from Berlin and Tokyo rather than from Washington and Moscow.

Five months after White's paper was drafted, the Nazi-Soviet pact of August, 1939, and the later "Winter War" between Russia and Finland had led to deterioration in Soviet-American diplomatic relations. But despite the Nazi-Soviet Pact, the objectives of Germany and Russia could be divergent, and Stalin's seizure of the Baltic States, Bessarabia and northern Bukovina in the summer of 1940 showed that Moscow had interests of its own. The State Department now came gradually to explore the possibility of exploiting supposed differences between Moscow and Berlin. This was also a means of putting pressure on the Japanese, as the crisis in the Atlantic was indivisible from that in the Pacific. Meanwhile, the British, in a hardly enviable strategic situation following the fall of France, had already decided to approach the Russians.

On June 26 Churchill had sent a personal message to Stalin, his first official one, stating that the two powers were well placed to resist German domination of the Continent, and that the time had come for Russia and Britain to reestablish contact.[25] There was no answer, but in a meeting with Stalin in early July the new British ambassador, Sir Stafford Cripps, had tried to convince him that Russia's interest lay with Britain as a completely victorious Hitler would turn east.

Stalin felt that Germany was the only real threat to the Soviet Union, that he was not aiding Hitler more than necessary, and that for the present the Soviet must try to avoid conflict with Germany. To the German ambassador, Von Schulenberg, Molotov reported the conversation as one in which Stalin had stated that he "did not see any danger of the hegemony of any one country in Europe and still less any danger that Europe might be engulfed by Germany. . . . Stalin was not of the opinion that German military successes menaced the Soviet Union and her friendly relations with Germany. These relations were not based on transient circumstances, but on the basic national interests of both countries."[26]

Two draft papers by White, written at this time, tended to recognize this impasse. The first, dated June 15, 1940, stated that the United States was apparently faced with a combination of Germany, Japan and the Soviet Union. But, White wrote, Russia was different from the other two powers as she was "not interested in the near future in territorial expansion," and that foreign trade was not important to the Soviet. Germany remained the chief enemy and "the fact that Russian aggression takes the form of ideological propaganda rather than military aggression should not be obscured by the differences between the ways of life of the U.S. and Russia."

In another memorandum two months later White stated that "our budgetary and monetary problems of a few years ago seem insignificant" because defense was now "the all-important matter." Foreign policy was no longer a departmental matter, White went on, for if we are pursuing the wrong policy nothing will save us. The State Department was filled with "budding Chamberlains, Daladiers, and Hoares: I am convinced that the time has come when a strong, clear cut foreign policy must be formulated and endorsed for the State Department to execute."

White believed that the United States was doing everything possible to help England, but that if Germany won there were only two possible policies. One was futile appeasement of the conquerors, the other was bound up with the question: "What practicable steps may we take to promote a parallel line of action with Russia such as will give us promise of much greater strength in world negotiations and greater security?" He went on to list such measures as more aid for China, a stronger policy against Japan, including a trade embargo of crude oil and scrap, and a three-way arrangement for sending arms to China.[27]

The fate of the proposed triangular arrangement to assist China has been noted above, but during September, at the end of the month after the Japanese occupation of Northern Indochina, an embargo on American iron and steel scrap to Japan was decided upon, as well as a new loan to China. However, despite continuing Soviet-American contact, the elusive decision to promote "a parallel line of action with Russia" remained at least partly a prerogative of Stalin.

Hence, during Molotov's famous visit to Berlin in November, 1940, when the Führer dangled the apportionment of the British Empire as "a gigantic world-wide estate in bankruptcy" before the impassive Russian, it appeared that the Soviet foreign commissar "was in agreement with everything he had understood." It would be easier for the Russians to give specific replies to the Führer if Soviet interests in the Balkans and the Black Sea were "clarified."[28]

Nevertheless, despite the grandiose language of the Berlin conversations, Hitler had probably already decided to eliminate the Soviet Union, a decision that by June, 1941, would certainly bring about "a parallel line of action" between Moscow and the Anglo-Americans.

On July 31, 1940, two weeks after the directive had been issued on the sixteenth for Operation Sealion, the invasion of England, Hitler told Colonel-General Halder, Chief of the Army General Staff (OKH), in a conference at the Berghof, near Obersalzberg, that,

Britain's hope lies in Russia and America. If the hope in Russia collapses, hope in America likewise disappears since the elimination of Russia will mean considerable strengthening of Japanese power in the Far East. Conclusion: Russia must be liquidated as soon as possible.[29]

Planning now went ahead to attack in the spring of 1941, and when the Tripartite Pact between Germany, Italy and Japan was signed in Berlin on September 27, Sealion had already been postponed by Hitler.

The Tripartite Pact was, of course, implicitly directed against America in its "defensive" provisions, yet an inherent weakness of the "world triangle" was the ambiguity felt in Tokyo regarding the Japanese obligation to intervene militarily with the Pact's European members.[30] The dilemma of Japanese policy—whether to try for a long-term accommodation with America, or to strike for a new order in Asia, while liquidating the China Incident—remained. It was this crux, emerging explicitly from the American-Japanese negotiations of 1941, that led White to put forward diplomatic initiatives of his own on this subject, which will be discussed below.

As far as White's wider hopes for a Soviet-American understanding was concerned, the inconclusive tone of the Berlin discussions in November and Molotov's continuing demands of the Germans subsequent to the conference meant that Hitler's mind was made up. He was not going to be blackmailed by Stalin, and on December 18, 1940, Directive no. 21 for Operation Barbarossa was issued: "The German Wehrmacht must be prepared to crush Soviet Russia in a quick campaign. . . ." As James V. Compton has written, Barbarossa would be "the final solution of the Russian question which would bring him in turn the solution to everything else, including the need to deal with the incomprehensible British and the impudent Americans. It was to be a race between the inevitable conquest of Russia and the staying power of the Anglo-Saxon bloc."[31]

Moreover, in the spring of 1941, if the Japanese-Soviet neutrality pact of April blocked the Russian back door, Stalin's apparent refusal to listen to Anglo-American warnings of the coming German offensive meant that Barbarossa was given an even sharper cutting-edge. According to John Erickson, "the idea of strategic surprise had been consigned to a sort of Stalinist perdition; war was not considered an immediate possibility." Hence the Russian cry on the morning of June 22, 1941: "We are being fired on; what shall we do?"[32]

Now at last "the two most powerful nations" of White's paper of March, 1939, were following "a parallel line of action," one formally initiated by the Hopkins mission to Russia in July, 1941.

Yet it was to be a close-run thing. On September 11, 1941, Roosevelt's "shoot first" order committed the United States Navy to the undeclared war against the enemy below in the North Atlantic. But on the next day, September 12, which Alan Clark has called "the low point of the fortunes of the Red Army for the whole war,"[33] the Germans broke out of their bridgeheads across the Don. On the sixteenth the fast-moving panzer spearheads of Guderian and Von Kleist, striking from north and south in a giant encircling movement, met on the Ukraine steppe at Lokhvitsa. Berlin claimed over 600,000 Russian prisoners. The panzers started to regroup for the final drive on Moscow.

This supreme crisis during 1940–1, when the American "national effort was still but a half-hearted one,"[34] meant that "Henry Morgenthau had been exercising some of the most vital functions of the War Department and even of the State Department not by a process of usurpation but by default."[35] White's position in the Treasury, therefore, at this time, was inevitably one of growing importance. If his first four years in the department had been a time of apprenticeship, the years leading to Pearl Harbor were a time of preparation for his later responsibilities.

Yet White's progress through the ranks of the civil service was as measured as his actual rise in the Treasury, in terms of power and responsibility, was meteoric. Following his appointment as Director of Monetary Research in March, 1938, he was given another $500 per annum in January, 1939, and a similar increase to $9,000 in March, 1940, was his last until he left the Treasury for the International Monetary Fund six years and several worlds later.[36]

For one whose work dealt so closely with plans for moving the nations, this was hardly magnificent remuneration, but then White himself, in many ways apparently a model of the totally dedicated public servant, would hardly have expected any different. Perhaps a greater recognition of his work was his appointment on August 5, 1941, as an Assistant to the Secretary of the Treasury. He was to continue as Director of Monetary Research and in addition would perform "such other duties as may be assigned from time to time."[37]

By this time the Division of Monetary Research was closely involved in the Treasury's preparations for economic warfare as well as maintaining its designated role in the department's work. At the heart of this effort lay the important (but unspectacular) work of the Foreign Funds Control Office headed by John Pehle. Even before the freezing of the Japanese assets in July, 1941, the Treasury had established control over the deposits of European countries taken over by the Axis. The chief function of Foreign Funds at this time was, therefore, regulating the $7 billion assets of thirty-three foreign countries and their nationals. This work not only stopped Axis countries and their associates from using their funds in the United States, but also regulated American firms with Axis connections. There was further control over American exports and imports, which could if necessary prevent any trade with a designated country.

Foreign Funds worked closely with other nascent defense agencies as well as with the Maritime Commission, the Securities and Exchange Commission, the State Department, the FBI, Army Intelligence, the Office of Naval Intelligence and the British. One of White's assignments was to represent the Treasury on the interdepartmental committee assigned with foreign funds control. White always had "a couple of people" in on the work of Foreign Funds, Edward H. Foley, Oliphant's successor as the Treasury's General Counsel, told Morgenthau in December, 1941, and White agreed with Foley's remark that "nothing has been done on Foreign Funds . . . that Harry's people did not know about and did not approve." White's Division of Monetary Research contained a group of economists who studied related problems, and there was also an investigative unit.[38]

To assist in this work and other associated activities of the Treasury, the Division of Monetary Research prepared background studies. During April, 1941, White forwarded to Morgenthau a list of more than 150 papers issued by the division in the first three months of the year. Their subjects included such matters as the "Current Argentine Situation," "German Military Expenditures," "Chart of Reorganization of British Government Machinery for War Effort," "The Economic Situation in Japan," "Madagascar Graphite" and "Bulletins Put Out by Military Intelligence for the Secretary."

These specialist studies dealt with political, military, economic and strategic developments throughout the world, providing a first-rate internal intelligence service for Morgenthau. The Division of Monetary Research, White noted, also drafted weekly reports on gold and capital movements in the United States, expenditures of the Bank of England and of the Bank of France from their special accounts in the New York Federal Reserve Bank, besides, as White put it, "participation in preparation of some of the statements and speeches by the Secretary."[39]

In addition to this ever-growing work of his division, with the extension of the war White began to take an increasing role in the Treasury's relations with other countries. His role in negotiations with the Latin American republics has been noted. Now, following the so-called Hyde Park agreement between Roosevelt and Canadian Prime Minister Mackenzie King in April, 1941, planned as the economic equivalent of the Ogdensburg defense agreement of August, 1940, between the two countries, White was appointed in June, 1941, to the United States Canadian Joint Economic Committee.

Two months later, in August, White joined the interdepartmental committee on the use of Lend-Lease funds between the two countries in carrying out the Hyde Park agreement. He thus became a participant in

the development of American foreign relations north of the 49th Parallel
as well as south of the Rio Grande.[40]

During the same month, August, 1941, following the setting up of the
Economic Defense Board (called the Board of Economic Warfare after
Pearl Harbor), White was appointed as Morgenthau's alternate on the
Board. A consolidated memorandum from White to Morgenthau in October listed in detail the Treasury's responsibilities in administering economic defense controls on shipping, foreign funds and property and the
purchase of strategic materials.[41]

Finally in this period immediately before Pearl Harbor, White was also
active in Lend-Lease negotiations with Whitehall. In a meeting in his
office in the Treasury in October, 1941, he told the British representatives
that his group would be, on specific, rather than general matters, "a sort
of court of second appeal" from decisions of the Lend-Lease administration.[42] So far from White's later, wartime responsibilities being some
occult manifestation, there was hardly anyone in the higher reaches of
the Treasury apparently better qualified by the time of Pearl Harbor to
deal with the foreign relations of the department.

But, as the Germans neared Moscow, and as time ran out in the Far
East during these last days before Pearl Harbor, White, like many in
Washington, was involved in the final negotiations with Japan. He had
already proposed "a deal of tremendous proportions"[43] to wean Japan
away from the Axis and so prevent the Pacific war.

ALL-OUT DIPLOMACY

An "all-out" effort involves in diplomacy as in military strategy the fullest use of every economic and political advantage.
—HARRY DEXTER WHITE, May, 1941

As HE became ever more involved in the slowly growing American defense program during 1941, White twice advanced sweeping proposals to reconcile American and Japanese interests in the Far East.

In the background to White's proposals lay the serious American attempt to negotiate differences with Japan during 1941, an attempt based on a relatively realistic assessment of the balance of forces involved. As a result of the "ABC-1 Staff Agreement" of March, 1941, the British and American military had reached provisional agreement on a joint war strategy. The main effort in the Atlantic against Germany was to be balanced by a defensive role in the Pacific. The corollary of this was to see if some sort of understanding between Japan and America could be reached in the Pacific, so weaning Tokyo away from the Tripartite Pact.

Talks had thus begun in Washington in March, 1941, between Cordell Hull and the Japanese ambassador to the United States, Admiral Kishisaburo Nomura, in the former's Carlton Hotel apartment, later in the Wardman Park. Essentially the Japanese dilemma was that the Konoye government in Tokyo could hardly both come to an agreement with the United States and resolve the China Incident to the satisfaction of the Japanese military. In the background were Japan's larger ambitions for a "Greater East Asia Co-Prosperity Sphere."

As far as Japan's links with the Axis were concerned, the reservations in Tokyo's attachment to the Tripartite Pact were a reflection of this confusion in Japanese objectives. As James Compton has written, "revisionist powers may unite in their grudge against the established order, but the vision of a corrected order to say nothing of details of timing, priority and area of operations may all reveal painful differences. This is what plagued German-Japanese relations from the start."

Compton has remarked that although the framework of German-Japanese relations during 1941 remained the Tripartite Pact of September, 1940, which was sometimes presented by the American government as a tightly coordinated conspiracy, in fact the disintegration of trust between Berlin and Tokyo continued to run its course. The Germans might invoke Triangle solidarity in urging the Japanese to attack Singapore or Vladivostok and to take a firm line with Washington. But the Japanese were trying to avoid commitment until they were ready, and as a firm military alliance the Pact was "moribund."[1] The Soviet-Japanese neutrality agreement of April, 1941, moreover, clearly enhanced Tokyo's freedom of action.

The eventual outcome of these divergences between the chief Axis partners, the Japanese declaration of war against Britain and America at the very time of the stiffening of Russian resistance outside Moscow, represented "a near lunatic ignorance of strategic possibilities on the part of the Axis leaders," it has been suggested by Professor Masao Maruyama.[2] F. L. Woodward, the historian of British foreign policy during the Second World War, has written that it is possible to argue that a different Japanese strategy, an attack northward to the Soviet Union and westward to the Indian Ocean, "might have had a decisive influence upon the course of the war in Europe."[3]

But whatever these divergences between the leaders of Germany and Japan during 1941, they were hardly greater, after all, than those between Washington and Tokyo. In April, Hull had laid down to Nomura the four principles which would give the American position in the talks with Japan. Hull's stand, a characteristic distillation of his almost Wilsonian moralistic approach to international affairs, meant the two countries were to respect the integrity of all nations, support the principle of noninterference in internal affairs, that of equality, including commercial equality, and finally not to change the status quo in the Pacific except by peaceful means.

Clearly, American national interest was also closely related to the integrity of China, and thus Hull's four principles were essentially an attempt to link the demands of national security with those of national idealism. For its part Tokyo, as Herbert Feis has written, "did not want to argue principles; abstract principles which took no account of place, time or degree. It wanted an end to American aid to China, a lifting of the embargoes, economic independence, a commanding place in the Far East."[4] Later, in November, 1941, Hull summed up the differences between the two positions by saying of these talks that they always "seemed to come to a certain point and then start going around the same circle."[5]

However, in mid-May, 1941, despite the obscurities over the Japanese proposals for China, and the generally pro-German attitude of Foreign Minister Matsuoka, Langer and Gleason have written that "there was in fact a better chance for the solution of the American-Japanese issue than at any point during the pre-Pearl Harbor period. The opposition to Matsuoka was evidently widespread and influential, and if led by a stronger personality than Prince Konoye, might well have imposed its will on the Foreign Minister."[6]

Besides, it was also important for the American position to play for time in view of the imminent German attack on Russia, which was known to Washington and London not only from routine intelligence sources but from the American cryptanalytic operation giving mastery of the Japanese diplomatic codes—Magic. Relatively, therefore, in these weeks before Hitler's drive eastward, the American bargaining position was hardly one of overwhelming strength, and this condition was compounded by the vocal domestic isolationist coalition whose strength Roosevelt could not for a minute ignore.

Nevertheless, Matsuoka stood his ground, and the impasse between the two countries remained, with Tokyo awaiting the outcome of the war in Europe before deciding whether to move north to Siberia or south to the Pacific.

It was at this critical time that White drafted his first proposal of new directions in American policy toward both Japan and Russia. The untitled memorandum in White's Princeton papers is headed May, 1941, "not final," and it was submitted to Morgenthau for inclusion in the Diaries on June 6.[7]

Once again, as in his earlier draft of Morgenthau's "declaration of war" in October, 1938, or his foreign policy paper of March 31, 1939, the burden of White's introduction to his proposals was a critique of the State Department's approach and with it what White took to be the practices of conventional diplomacy. But now, in May, 1941, just as the international situation was even more threatening than in those earlier years, so White's criticisms of the "half measures, miscalculation, timidity, machinations or incompetence of the State Departments of the United States, England and France" is more prolonged, almost violent in its exasperation.

Drawing an analogy between diplomacy and the use of military power, White stated that, to be effective, diplomacy must use modern weapons: "An 'all-out' effort involves in diplomacy as in military strategy the fullest use of every economic and political advantage." These political advan-

tages of a rich and democratic country, White stated, "must be utilized to
the fullest in modern diplomatic activity if it is to have any chance of
success, just as our military forces in preparation for defense or in actual
warfare must make intelligent use of our geographical position, our rich
resources, our vast labor power, technical equipment and democratic
traditions."

White contrasted the use of such total diplomacy with the "pathetic"
efforts of American diplomacy, which, he wrote, "consisted of a nineteenth century pattern of petty bargaining with its dependence on subtle
half promises, irritating pinpricks, excursions into double dealing and
copious pronouncements of good will alternating with vague threats—
and all of it veiled in an atmosphere of high secrecy designed or serving
chiefly to hide the essential barrenness of achievement. Our diplomatic
maneuvering is proving as futile in strengthening our international position or in keeping us out of a difficult war as was the equipment and
strategy of the Polish army in the task of defending Poland. . . ."

Modern diplomacy, White continued, calls for "swift and bold action,"
not cautious negotiations. The United States should talk in terms of billions of dollars, not millions; "we should be dealing with all-embracing
economic, political and social problems," not minor trade objectives or
small national advantages. Instead of facing realities, "we persist in en-
joying costly prejudices; where we should speak openly and clearly, we
engage in protocol, in secret schemes and subtleties."

His proposed program, White concluded, would be called visionary. It
would be laughed at by the professional diplomats, but their "traditional
method" would not lead to any better results than had the efforts of their
colleagues in France and England. "I am convinced that the proposal is
workable and could be spectacularly successful." But, White warned,
unless pushed by high officials outside the State Department, his plan
would not be adopted.

White's "proposed program of diplomatic effort" consisted of two parts.
The first dealt with American relations with Japan, the second relations
with Russia; but each was complementary in its objective of detaching
these countries from the German connection.

So that the United States could concentrate forces in the Atlantic
against Germany, White proposed a comprehensive accommodation with
Tokyo. The United States Navy would be withdrawn from the Pacific;
Manchuria would be recognized as part of the Japanese Empire; a
twenty-year nonaggression pact would be signed between the two countries; a $3 billion loan would be granted to Japan; the American Immigra-
tion Act of 1917 limiting Japanese entry would be repealed; America
would abandon its extraterritorial rights in China, and induce Great

Britain to do likewise and to retrocede Hong Kong; and a joint $500,000,-000 stabilization fund would be set up by the two countries.

For their part, the Japanese would withdraw their forces from the remaining areas of China and Indochina, while abandoning their extra-territorial rights in the former country; lease to the American government for three years such naval vessels and aircraft as the United States would select, up to half of the existing Japanese naval strength; grant the United States and China most-favored-nation treatment in the Japanese Empire; and sign a ten-year nonaggression pact to include Britain, China, the Dutch East Indies and the United States.

White then went on to propose an arrangement with the Russians to detach them from their pact with Germany. The United States would let Russia purchase up to $300,000,000 worth of goods or materials a year; admit 5,000 Russian technicians and 50 military attachés; grant Moscow a $500,000,000 credit; conclude a five-year Mutual Economic Assistance pact; and extend to Russia most-favored-nation treatment.

The Russian side of the arrangement would mean that Moscow would embargo trade with Germany; stop its external propaganda; settle its debts with the United States; admit 5,000 American technicians and 50 military attachés; and sell $200,000,000 worth of commodities annually to the United States. White concluded, "The advantages of the terms indicated are so great, and the disadvantages so small, that it is difficult to believe either the Japanese or the Russians would hesitate to accept the offer."

White's proposals were, or course, abortive at this time. The Treasury was not directly involved in the American-Japanese negotiations, and more to the point perhaps, Morgenthau was busy with the wider issues of the preparedness program. The problem of detaching Stalin from Hitler, moreover, ceased to become an issue on June 22, 1941, a day whose events, despite all previous indications, stunned Tokyo.

But White's suggestion in his memorandum that Manchuria could be offered to Japan as part of an overall settlement was a reminder by him that China's independence still lay at the heart of the impasse between Tokyo and Washington. Besides the precarious military and economic situation of Nationalist China, with which White was involved on a day-to-day basis as a result of his responsibilities for stabilization activities, there was also the simmering internecine conflict between the Kuomin-tang and the Chinese Communists. Here White, during the spring of 1941, obtained the services of an agent extraordinary to report to the Treasury.

Earlier in the year White had asked Ernest Hemingway, then off to

China on another journey to war, "to look into the Kuomintang-Communist difficulties and try to find any information which could possibly be of interest to you," as the novelist later wrote to Morgenthau at the end of July, 1941. Hemingway's itinerary had included Singapore, where his wife, Martha Gellhorn, had presciently considered the defenses "inadequate," and Hong Kong, where the writer thought "morale high, morals low." In China, Hemingway had visited the war zone, and met the Generalissimo and Madame Chiang Kai-shek. Back in the United States, Hemingway had then reported to the Office of Naval Intelligence in Washington.[8]

The novelist had also reported to Morgenthau in Washington, and following his return to his Havana home he wrote a long letter to the Secretary on July 30, which was then forwarded to Morgenthau by White on August 14 with a digest of Hemingway's shrewd and vivid observations.

Hemingway stated in this letter that in his opinion civil war was "inevitable" between the Nationalists and the Communists unless there was an agreement between Moscow and Chungking to make part of the country "Soviet-China with a defensible frontier." A Kuomintang official had told Hemingway that the Japanese were a "skin disease"; the Communists were a "heart disease." At the same time, the novelist considered that the United States could delay civil war by making clear that it would not finance such a development in any way.

Hemingway considered that the Nationalist government had become a form of dictatorship under the stress of war, but that the Communist evaluation of their own war effort should not be accepted completely as the part played by the central government had been "a hundred times greater." Noting the inflation in China, Hemingway thought that its effects on army officers' pay was "a greater threat to Chinese continuance of the war—not this year, but for next year—than . . . any other destructive possibility."[9]

At this time, the full import of the "difficulties" between the Chinese Nationalists and the Communists lay in the future. When White forwarded Hemingway's report to Morgenthau in mid-August, the Imperial Conference decision on July 2 to opt for a southern advance, and the American freezing order of July 26 meant that time was running out between the United States and Japan. In Washington, the American Pacific Fleet based at Pearl Harbor was regarded as a deterrent; while Admiral Yamamoto, the Commander in Chief of the Japanese Combined Fleet, saw it as a target.

Since January, secret planning had proceeded on the Admiral's "Operation Z" for a surprise carrier strike against the battleships at Hawaii. Yet another skein in this situation was the uncertainty in Washington where the blow would fall in the event of war. This confusion between political expectation and strategic surprise, between "signals" and "noise," was actually exacerbated by the necessity for secrecy within the Magic circle, as Roberta Wohlstetter has shown in her remarkable study of Pearl Harbor.[10]

By the Imperial Conference of September 6, "the machinery of war was to be placed in high gear; it was to be stopped only if Konoye managed to win American assent to terms which had up till then been rejected."[11] When in fact the terms were turned down by Hull on October 2, the era of talk had already ended. Feis has commented that the two governments "still remained separated by unyielding differences in purpose. The terms offered by the Japanese government would have permitted the country to emerge rewarded from its ten year venture in arms and stratagem . . . the terms offered by the American government meant that Japan accepted defeat. . . . They would have meant, also, a triumphant China."[12]

There was no real prospect of success in the talks between America and Japan after July, 1941, as Langer and Gleason have written: "The truth of the matter was that the policies of the two powers were no longer reconcilable. Whether the discussion rose to high levels of moral principle or dropped to mundane considerations of concrete issue, the conflict persisted."[13] During the first week of October, 1941, the Tokyo spy ring led by Richard Sorge and Osaki Hotsumi, reported to Moscow center that "a Russo-Japanese war was unlikely and that Japan would initiate hostilities against the United States within the following weeks."[14]

In Washington, however, it was still considered that there was "a good deal of evidence to support the hypothesis that Japan would attack the Soviet Union from the east while the Russian army was heavily engaged in the West."[15] White's amended proposal for a Japanese-American rapprochement now emerged again in the last weeks preceding the Pacific war, as the Japanese carriers actually began staging to carry out the Z Plan.

Following the resignation of Konoye, a weak moderate, in mid-October in favor of General Tojo, the personification of the militarists, another Imperial Conference met in Tokyo on November 5. It decided that if no accord was reached with the Americans by November 25 on either of its proposals A and B, a restatement of Japan's general position and a plan for truce or *modus vivendi* respectively, then the decision for war would be put before the Emperor. Among the general military orders that were

issued from Tokyo on this day was Yamamoto's "Secret Operations Order
No. 1":

> The Japanese Empire is expecting war to break out with the United
> States, Great Britain, and the Netherlands. War will be declared on
> X-day. This order will become effective Y-day. . . .

On November 7 Yamamoto provisionally set the date for the Pearl
Harbor attack for December 8 (Tokyo time), while on the tenth the
strike force was ordered by its commander, Admiral Nagumo, to "complete battle preparations" by November 20 and rendezvous at Hitokappu
Bay, Etorufu Island, in the Kuriles.[16]

By the tenth, Plan A had in effect been turned down by Cordell Hull.
A Japanese envoy of ambassadorial rank, Saburo Kurusu, was now flying
to Washington, where he met Roosevelt on November 17. All eyes were
on the last stages of the battle for Moscow, and on the same day Roosevelt wrote out for Hull a proposal for a temporary easing of the tension
which was based on sending some rice and oil to Japan in exchange for
an undertaking that no further troops would be sent to Indochina or
Manchuria. Some State Department officials were also working on their
own draft *modus vivendi*.

At this stage, on November 17, White submitted to Morgenthau a long
memorandum on Japanese-American relations which was immediately
caught up in the complex last-minute negotiations between the two countries which have been fully recorded in Chapter 27 of Langer and Gleason's *The Undeclared War 1940–1941*.

White's "forward" to his paper of November 17, which was entitled
"An Approach to the Problem of Eliminating Tension with Japan and
Insuring Defeat of Germany," was essentially a recasting of the introduction to his memorandum on a Pacific settlement of May, 1941, which we
have noted above. He returned to his earlier theme that "an 'all-out'
effort involves in diplomacy as in military strategy the fullest use of every
economic and political advantage. . . . If there was ever a time when
diplomacy could secure its most brilliant victories, now is that time!"

> If the President were to propose something like the appended agree-
> ment and the Japanese accept, the whole world would be electrified
> by the successful transformation of a threatening and belligerent
> powerful enemy into a peaceful and prosperous neighbor. The prestige
> and the leadership of the President both at home and abroad would
> skyrocket by so brilliant and momentous a diplomatic victory—a
> victory that requires no vanquished, a victory that immediately
> would bring peace, happiness and prosperity to hundreds of millions

of Eastern peoples, and assure the subsequent defeat of Germany! The proposal is workable and could be spectacularly successful, if Japan could be induced to accept the arrangement.[17]

In this "all-out diplomatic approach" White proposed that the American government withdraw most of its naval forces from the Pacific; sign a twenty-year nonaggression pact with Japan; promote "a final settlement" of the Manchurian problem; place Indochina under a five-power commission of the United States, the United Kingdom, France, China and Japan, giving most-favored-nation treatment to these countries until the end of the war in Europe; give up its extraterritorial rights in China and induce the British to give up theirs, together with Hong Kong; ask Congress to repeal the 1917 Immigration Act; negotiate a trade treaty with Japan granting most-favored-nation treatment and other concessions including an agreement to keep raw silk on the free list for twenty years; grant a twenty-year $2 billion credit to Japan; set up a joint stabilization fund of $500,000,000; remove restrictions on Japanese funds in the United States; and use American influence to eliminate sources of friction between Japan and its neighbors.

In exchange for these acts, Japan was to withdraw all its forces from beyond the 1931 frontiers of China and from Indochina; withdraw support from any Chinese government other than that at Chungking; replace the yen with military scrip in China; give up its extraterritorial rights in China; extend a billion-yen reconstruction loan to China; withdraw all troops from Manchuria provided that the Soviet did likewise from the "Far Eastern front"; sell to the United States up to three-quarters of current Japanese output of war materiel including naval, air, ordnance and commercial ships on a cost-plus-20 percent basis; grant the United States and China most-favored-nation treatment in the Japanese Empire; and negotiate a ten-year nonaggression pact with the United States, the United Kingdom, China, Dutch East Indies and the Philippines.

These terms would be offered to Japan for a short time. If rejected, such action would at least rally American opinion and create serious division inside Japan. Minimum concessions, to be obtained from Japan, concluded White, should be the withdrawal of troops from the Asian mainland and the sale to the United States "of the bulk of her current production of armaments," otherwise Japan could prepare for later aggression. The minimum objectives must be to free the American, British and Russian forces from the Pacific.

Tactfully deleting some of White's introductory criticisms of what he thought was the inadequacy of American foreign policy, Morgenthau forwarded the paper to Hull and Roosevelt on November 18.[18] Morgenthau thought that White, "while shooting in the dark," had written a "very amazing memorandum of suggestions." Morgenthau, not a member of the Magic circle, unaware of the full extent of the differences between America and Japan in their talks, was impressed by White's positive tone, believing that his suggestions pointed the way to an end of aggression in the Far East and the preservation of China's integrity.[19]

The State Department was also receptive to the proposals of White's diplomacy. Maxwell Hamilton, Chief of the Division of Far Eastern Affairs, wrote to Hull on the nineteenth that, while White's paper needed some revision, all officers of his division agreed with him that this was "the most constructive" proposal they had seen.[20] On the twenty-first, when Hull conferred with high Navy and Army officers, and showed them a toned-down version of the Treasury paper as a preliminary version of an American *modus vivendi*, the response was that "the document was satisfactory from a military standpoint." Even a temporary peace in the Pacific would help to complete defensive preparations in the Philippines and to continue material assistance to the British.[21]

Despite this promising beginning, the crowded events following the Japanese presentation of their Plan B on November 20 now meant that White's memorandum surfaced, after significant mutations, as a part-inspiration of the final, uncompromising Ten Point program which was eventually given to the Japanese ambassadors by Hull on November 26.

This last stage of the negotiations had begun with the presentation on the twentieth to Hull of Tokyo's Plan B, which it will be recalled was a Japanese version of a *modus vivendi*. This final proposition by Tokyo had suggested, in brief, a Japanese withdrawal from Indochina in exchange for a resumption of commercial relations between the two countries, and a cessation of American aid to China. As a stopgap arrangement it was not so far from the State Department's own conception of a *modus vivendi*, but perhaps events had by now gone too far to make any such arrangement acceptable to the coalition of which Hull was the spokesman. In any case, as Feis has remarked, Plan B "would have marked only the start of new disputes, not the end of old ones."[22]

However, Hull's characterization of Plan B as "clearly unacceptable" did not mean that the search for a settlement was over. But now, as a result of frequent redrafting, the White proposals of the Treasury memorandum became merged in a lengthy State Department reply to Plan B. This was a composite paper which consisted of an American draft of a three-month stopgap *modus vivendi*, combined with a proposal for a long-term general settlement between the two countries known as the Ten Points. By the twenty-fifth, the third, final draft of the truce or *modus vivendi* was ready, together with the last draft of the Ten Point proposal and a statement explaining the relation between the two; as Langer and

Gleason have written, "the text of the Ten Point long-range agreement having been based on a much attenuated version of the White-Morgenthau memorandum of November 17."[23]

So much for the outline progress of White's paper through the bureaucracy. But by the twenty-fifth events had already overtaken its author's hopes for a settlement. In the first place, Japanese military preparations were proceeding as planned, although on November 22 Tokyo had extended the deadline from November 25 to 29. After that date, according to the famous Telegram 812 from Foreign Minister Togo to Nomura, which was intercepted by Magic, "things are automatically going to happen."[24] On the same day, moreover, Yamamoto sent out in an impregnable naval code an operations order to the carrier strike force:

> The Task Force will move out from Hitokappu Wan [Bay] on 26 November and proceed without being detected to rendezvous set for 3 December.
> X-Day will be 8 December.[25]

The upshot of this accelerating Japanese military activity was that on the twenty-fifth news reached Washington of a large Japanese convoy moving south off Formosa (the Malayan expeditionary force). This news, together with the tone of Telegram 812, created a fresh sense of crisis.

A second factor which led to the abandonment of any further serious negotiations was the political opposition to the *modus vivendi* which had been canvassed with the Allied ambassadors. Chiang Kai-shek bombarded Washington with demands that no further concessions be made to Tokyo. Churchill telegraphed Roosevelt on the night of November 25–6 that Chiang was having "a very thin diet" and that a Chinese collapse would "enormously increase" joint difficulties.[26] The Dutch had doubts. Together with domestic opposition in some quarters to any "appeasement" of Japan in the *modus vivendi*, these factors were bound to make Hull sensitive to any charges of sacrificing principle to expediency as the price of even a temporary settlement. But in any case the evidence from Magic could not be exorcised.

In this groundswell of opinion against any last-minute truce with Tokyo, Morgenthau and White were now active, the former also having received a cable from Chiang Kai-shek asking that no concessions be made to Japan. Yet, paradoxically, White's proposals of November 17 went, of course, beyond any scope of the *modus vivendi*. Even if accepted by any Japanese government these proposals would by no means have guaranteed the salvation of China, given the relative strength of the two countries at this time.

White now drafted a Morgenthau letter for Roosevelt protesting against "a Far Eastern Munich," stating that to sell China "to her enemies for thirty blood stained pieces of gold will not only weaken our national policy in Europe as well as in the Far East, but will dim the luster of American world leadership in the great democratic fight against fascism. . . . I know that should these stories be true . . . you will succeed in circumventing these plotters of a new Munich."[27]

A longer draft of a letter by Morgenthau on the same lines was not sent to Roosevelt when Morgenthau realized that he had been misled by Chinese anxieties over these last-hour exchanges between Tokyo and Washington.[28]

As part of these developments, when the fate of the *modus vivendi* was in the balance, White sent an "urgent telegram" to Edward C. Carter, the former Secretary-General of the Institute of the Pacific Relations in New York. White asked Carter to come to Washington to lobby against making any concessions to the Japanese.

The following morning, when Carter met White, whom he later said he knew only as "a name of a financier who was influential in the office of the Secretary of the Treasury," he was told that his help had been sought to prevent the "sell-out" of China to Japan. This had now been averted, there was going to be no sell-out, and, White told Carter, "the situation was such that every friend of China could be satisfied."[29]

In this process, which led to the presentation of the Ten Point Note, White's own diplomatic initiative on Japanese-American relations was now dead. As the extent of the military crisis between Japan and the Allies became clear, White may have argued that if the threat from Tokyo to the Soviet Far Eastern flank could not be neutralized by ambitious economic proposals, as he had suggested, there was no alternative to supporting firmer measures which might well precipitate war.

On the morning of the twenty-sixth, Hull, beset by the maze of military and political complications surrounding the development of the American *modus vivendi*, had decided, as he told Stimson, "to kick the whole thing over." He recommended to Roosevelt that in view of the opposition of the Allies, and other factors, he withhold delivery of the *modus vivendi* to the Japanese and instead present "the comprehensive basic proposal," the Ten Point general statement of American long-term objectives in the Pacific. This was presented to Nomura and Kurusu at about five o'clock on the evening of November 26, 1941.

The terms of the Ten Point proposal are well known.[30] In short, Japan and the United States were to abide by the four principles which Hull had adumbrated; the two countries would sponsor a "multilateral non-aggression pact" among all countries concerned in the Far East, including the British Empire, China and Russia; "the Government of Japan will withdraw all military, naval, air and police forces from China and Indo-china. . . ."

Here was the most uncompromising statement of the American position that had emerged during these negotiations. The influence of White's thinking in his proposals of November 17 was evident in the list of Japanese concessions demanded; but there were no corresponding concessions by the United States. White's Cobdenite plan for a sweeping Far Eastern settlement had emerged as a stern outline of America's maximum political (and strategic) demands, clad in Hull's characteristic language of high principle. So far from being the opening shot in the new diplomacy, the Ten Point Note was the hard, succinct product of classical diplomacy facing the abyss of total divergence of national objectives between two great powers.

In Tokyo, the Japanese characterized the Ten Point Note as an ultimatum. Herbert Feis, while considering that the Note was not an ultimatum, writes that in this document there was "a denial of all that Japan had set out to do by stratagem or force." In the view of Langer and Gleason, "in substance if not in form, the Ten Point Note did constitute America's final terms for the indefinite future, and this was recognized by those who formulated it. In this sense it was an ultimatum. . . ." The next day, November 27, Hull told Stimson that "I have washed my hands of it, and it is now in the hands of you and Knox—the Army and Navy."[31]

It was already known from Magic that the Japanese regarded their Plan B as the very minimum terms they were prepared to accept. They would not have accepted Hull's *modus vivendi*, let alone the Ten Points. Moreover, unknown to the Americans, the Z-force carriers had already left Hitokappu Bay en route for Honolulu at around 0600 local time on November 26, about twenty-four hours before Hull's delivery of the Ten Point Note to the Japanese ambassadors in Washington.

Washington now waited for the blow to fall in Malaya, the Philippines, Siam, the Dutch East Indies. Meanwhile, on December 1 the Imperial Conference, presided over by General Tojo, took the formal decision for war, with no word spoken by the Emperor. The next day, December 2, Admiral Yamamoto put out a two-part message in the invulnerable Admirals code to the Pearl Harbor task force, now lost in the North Pacific: NIITAKA-YAMA NOBORE ("Ascend Mount Niitaka")—"Launch the attack on the enemy as previously arranged." The second part read "1208"— "The date for commencement of hostilities has been set for December 8." A diplomatic message for Hull breaking off the talks was timed for delivery twenty minutes before the first Japanese aircraft appeared at Pearl Harbor.[32]

The story of the "Day of Infamy," December 7, 1941, east of the date line, has been often told. Morgenthau was in New York, about to fly to Tucson, Arizona, for a vacation. As the news from Hawaii reached the city after lunch, a special aircraft took him instead to Washington, where White had spent the weekend at home.

Later on X-Day, the United States Navy's monitoring station at Bainbridge Island, Puget Sound, near Seattle, picked up a Magic intercept on the Tokyo-Washington circuit. The message was in clear, it was in English, and it was teletyped to the desk of a watch officer in the Communications Security Section of the Navy Department in Washington. The teleprinter rapped out the letters: C . . . I . . . R . . . C . . .

It was Circular 2507 from the Tokyo Foreign Ministry to all diplomatic missions abroad: "The Imperial Naval Air Force has damaged three United States battleships and sunk three in the Battle of Hawaii. Those sunk were the *Arizona* . . . the *Oklahoma* . . . and the *West Virginia*."[33]

White's initiative for peace in the Pacific was over. History's prize for all-out diplomacy had gone to the Japanese.

PART III

THE TIME OF POWER

1941–44

9

ASSISTANT SECRETARY

. . . Harry D. White . . . will assume full responsibility for all matters with which the Treasury has to deal having a bearing on foreign relations. . . .

—TREASURY DEPARTMENT ORDER no. 43, December, 1941

AT eleven o'clock on the morning of December 8, 1941, the day following the "Battle of Hawaii," and a few hours before Congress declared war against Imperial Japan, Morgenthau met in the Treasury with his senior staff. Among those present were Daniel Bell, the Under Secretary, Edward Foley, General Counsel, and Harry Dexter White.[1]

"In order to have the least friction, as far as I am concerned," Morgenthau told his colleagues, "and to make life easier for me . . . I want to give Harry White the status of Assistant Secretary. I can't make him an Assistant Secretary. I want to give him the status just as though he were, and he will be in charge of foreign affairs for me."

Morgenthau had previously discussed the arrangement with his staff. Everybody except Merle Cochran, he reported, was "entirely agreeable." Cochran, a special adviser on monetary affairs to Morgenthau, had been lent to the Treasury from the State Department, and had now requested to be transferred back there. That meant, Morgenthau said, "that the things I have to pass on, that I have to know about, that have to do with foreign affairs, Harry has to know about." As far as Foley's area of jurisdiction was concerned, if a foreign matter came up for Morgenthau's attention, Foley would first discuss it with White and then both men would see the Secretary.

"I want it all in one brain," Morgenthau went on, "and I want it in Harry White's brain. He will tell Bell as much as he wants to know . . . when it is some question of foreign matters, Harry will come in and see me, and I will give him a decision, and when the decision is made, he will tell you about it. If it in any way crosses anything you have got, he will come first and see you and ask your views. . . . But there has to be one brain cell. . . ."

White was to "handle China," and he would discuss the future operation of the Exchange Stabilization section with Daniel Bell. Foley suggested that White sit in on Foreign Funds Control whenever possible, instead of only occasionally, as previously. The minutes of Foreign Funds could be sent to White. But in the past, Foley said, as we have already noted, nothing had been done by Foreign Funds that White's Division of Monetary Research did not know about and approve.

Cordell Hull now spoke to Morgenthau on the telephone, to be told that from now on White would represent the foreign affairs of the Treasury and deal with the State Department. The Secretary of State considered White "a mighty suitable man . . . a very high class fellow . . . capable." When Morgenthau remarked that Cochran was not pleased by the appointment, Hull asked whether he had wished the post for himself. Morgenthau replied yes, and the conversation between the two Secretaries ended with Hull promising to take up the matter of Cochran's return to the State Department with "my folks."

A week later, on December 15, Treasury Department Order no. 43, signed by Morgenthau, confirmed White's new role, as well as putting him in full charge of the Stabilization Fund:

> On and after this date, Mr. Harry D. White, Assistant to the Secretary, will assume full responsibility for all matters with which the Treasury has to deal having a bearing on foreign relations. Mr. White will act as liaison between the Treasury Department and the State Department, will serve in the capacity of advisor to the Secretary on all Treasury foreign affairs matters, and will assume responsibility for the management and operation of the Stabilization Fund without change in existing procedures. Mr. White will report directly to the Secretary.[2]

Given the status and the power within the department of Assistant Secretary, if not the formal title, White had thus been delegated responsibility for the Treasury's foreign relations with the American entry into the war. He still, of course, retained his formal position of Director of Monetary Research and remained an assistant to the Secretary. Advice for Morgenthau on the more traditional functions of the Treasury, such as taxation and debt management, remained the responsibility of Daniel Bell, Under Secretary from 1940 to 1945, who like Morgenthau was of generally conservative disposition on fiscal policy. There were two other Assistant

Secretaries to help in the direction of the department: John L. Sullivan, a political appointee, and Herbert Gaston, who had been with Morgenthau in different posts since the end of the 1920's.

The immediate concern of the Treasury in December, 1941, was how to raise, without precipitating inflation, the huge sums of money needed for not only financing the American war effort but many of the activities of the Allies in the global struggle against the Axis. Some idea of the extent of these fund-raising activities, which have been outlined in detail by John Morton Blum in his biography of Morgenthau, may be grasped by the fact that during the Second World War the American national debt increased by some $200 billion, most of it borrowed in the war-loan campaigns of 1943–45.

A corollary of this overall operation was that the war absorbed about half the American gross national product, compared with a quarter during the First World War. Although it was policy to keep interest rates as low as possible, the annual servicing charge on the increased national debt during the war "nevertheless roughly equalled the relief appropriations of 1935 which had seemed astronomical to most New Dealers, as well as to their conservative opponents."[3]

In this unparalleled funding operation, which covered more than half the cost of the war, Morgenthau was concerned that the Treasury's borrowing should be conducted, as far as possible, with the objectives of keeping interest rates down and inflation within reasonable bounds.

It was important, therefore, to keep the price of federal securities at par, for if the price of a bond fell below par the yield would, of course, rise with a consequent added charge to the taxpayer, both present and future. On the American entry into the war the Treasury thus obtained the cooperation of the Federal Reserve System, which stood ready thereafter to advance funds to the banks on American government securities at par, so helping to keep their price up.

By this and other measures, the war was financed at a low interest level. During the First World War, the average rate of interest on the American national debt rose from 2.36 to 4.22 percent, while in contrast, between July, 1939, and the end of the Second World War the average interest rate fell from 2.53 to 1.94 percent. John Morton Blum considers this policy one of Morgenthau's "greatest accomplishments" during his years in the Treasury.[4]

Moreover, both Morgenthau and Roosevelt believed, against opposition, that a voluntary effort could raise the money needed to meet the cost of the war not covered by taxes, an effort also helping to head off the inevitable inflationary pressure on the wartime price of goods and services. Most of the increase in the national debt during the war was covered by the extensively promoted war-loan campaigns, which emphasized the war itself rather than thrift as a selling point, and which were supported by a host of groups and individuals, from chambers of commerce to labor organizations, and from copywriters to clergymen.

Inevitably as the war progressed, as speculation in securities rose, and as banks and other institutions increased their holdings of war bonds, the effectiveness of the war-loan campaigns tended to diminish. Yet if holdings by the banks in the increased national debt were larger than Morgenthau wished, just as the proportion of revenue from taxation was smaller than the Treasury desired, inflation was held in reasonable check in the United States during the war. No doubt the doubling of the American national product during the war was also partly responsible for this achievement.

Behind the growing preoccupation of White and Morgenthau with foreign affairs and the shape of the postwar world as the fighting moved ever nearer to Berlin and Tokyo lay, therefore, the successful day-to-day work of the Treasury, frequently unspectacular, of funding victory in the first place.

The Treasury was less successful in the struggle with Congress over its wartime tax proposals, which went on for some two years after Pearl Harbor. Along with his belief in voluntary fund-raising in the war-loan program, Morgenthau also held that wartime revenue legislation should be in the tradition of the social objectives of the New Deal by distributing "the burden of taxation on the principle of ability to pay" (Blum).

During early 1942, as the full impact of total war production began to hit the American economy, it was initially even more important to attempt to control inflation than to raise revenue. This meant that the Treasury had to sponsor ever stiffer tax proposals on individual and corporate wealth, so widening the gap between the department and the House of Representatives Ways and Means Committee, which held the Congressional purse strings firmly in its grasp.

In July, 1942, with the contested revenue bill for that year moving slowly through Congress, and with inflation still a major hazard, White suggested the need for compulsory savings. A little later he supported the proposal of the Treasury's new General Counsel, Randolph Paul, for the collection of taxes at source. During 1943, White went on, industrial workers, like other Americans, should pay taxes on their 1942 income, as well as taxes for the current year, through payroll deductions. As the workers would object to such proposals, there was no point in asking their opinion of such measures. Morgenthau was shocked: "The little fellow on the bench doesn't get his chance to be heard." Morgenthau was also hesitant because payroll deductions already included such items as social security, savings bonds and union dues.[5]

The problem remained, and by the end of July, 1942, the Treasury had evolved a new scheme of "expenditure rationing," by which each family or individual in the country would be able to spend only the amount of money for which the government had issued coupons, so controlling total demand. During the following month this proposal developed into a projected spendings tax, a graduated impost supplementary to income tax, levied on the whole sum spent by a family.

On September 22, White returned to the subject of expenditure rationing, which, he recommended to Morgenthau in a strongly worded memorandum, would be the "most effective" way to control inflation. He went on to urge that the Treasury should "attempt to get further increases in individual income surtaxes and other progressive taxes, as increases became politically possible from time to time."[6]

When the 1942 revenue bill was passed by Congress in October of that year, it provided for some taxation at source, but the spendings tax had been rejected by the legislature and the Act also omitted the Treasury's proposals for tax reform and social security revenue. Like the essentially bureaucratic concept of expenditure rationing, the spendings tax was hardly "politically possible" at a time when Congress was ready to assert itself over the executive in domestic matters.

The controversy over the 1942 tax bill was only the beginning of a great triangular revenue debate between executive agencies such as James Byrnes' Office of Economic Stabilization, the Treasury and Congress. Moreover, there was a shift away from the administration in the Congressional off-year elections of November, 1942. Although an interim tax measure was passed on the Hill in the summer of 1943, the saga of the fight over the chief revenue bill for that year continued with Morgenthau maintaining his stand on corporate taxes and social security provisions against the opposition of the House Ways and Means Committee and the Senate Finance Committee. In general, Congress believed that the revenue bill was dangerous to the economy and to business solvency, as well as being oppressive to the taxpayer.

Eventually, the revised bill emerging from the conference committee of the two houses of Congress was so unsatisfactory to the Treasury that some of Morgenthau's staff urged him to recommend a presidential veto. In a Treasury conference on January 31, 1944, White thought that "the bill should be vetoed. I think that the President could gain stature by vetoing. . . . This is a lousy Congress and deserves to be slapped." Morgenthau, who soon came to think that Roosevelt should let the bill through without his signature, told his colleagues that it was no longer a question "of how I feel about it, but a question of how the President feels about it." The conference ended with Morgenthau organizing a twenty-five-cent sweepstake for his colleagues, not participating himself, on "whether he will veto, or whether he won't." The pool was to be held by Mrs. Klotz; White put his money on "not veto."[7]

Two weeks later Roosevelt decided to veto the bill and White lost his twenty-five cents. But it was the Treasury, and not Congress, which was slapped down. Alben Barkley, the Senate Democratic Majority Leader, resigned, and both houses dramatically overrode the presidential veto. Although Roosevelt patched matters up with a "Dear Alben" letter, "the damage was done. Congress had passed a revenue act over a veto for the first time in American history, and Congress had so routed the Administration that debate over taxation ceased for the duration of the War."[8]

Not all the Treasury's proposals during the war were so open to Congressional scrutiny. But there seems little doubt that the experience over the wartime revenue bills was a contributory factor in the care and circumspection with which White and Morgenthau consulted Congress during the concurrent development of their plans for the postwar international monetary system, and the legislation that followed the Bretton Woods Conference.

It was frequently said during these times that Roosevelt had replaced "Dr. New Deal" with "Dr. Win-the-war." Morgenthau had gone further. Within a few days of Pearl Harbor he had already asked White, in accordance with his new responsibilities for the Treasury's foreign relations, to prepare outline plans for the international monetary arrangements of the postwar world.

10

THE WHITE PLAN

. . . One thing is certain. No matter how long the war lasts nor how it is won, we shall be faced with three inescapable problems; to prevent the disruption of foreign exchanges and the collapse of monetary and credit systems; to assure the restoration of foreign trade; and to supply the huge volume of capital that will be needed virtually throughout the world for reconstruction, for relief and for economic recovery. . . .

AN EARLY DRAFT of the WHITE PLAN, 1942

A WEEK after Pearl Harbor, on December 14, 1941, Harry Dexter White was directed by Morgenthau to prepare a memorandum on the establishment of an inter-Allied stabilization fund. That fund, Morgenthau said, "should provide the basis for postwar international monetary arrangements."[1]

This directive, which put White in charge of Treasury planning for postwar international financial policy, in addition to his other responsibilities, led directly to the framing of the White Plan. In London, John Maynard Keynes and the British Treasury, as we shall see, were also working on proposed postwar financial arrangements. Eventually the planning that was begun in London and Washington during 1941–42 led to the twin institutions of the Bretton Woods Conference of July, 1944, the International Monetary Fund and the International Bank for Reconstruction and Development. Behind the upheavals of global war from Pearl Harbor to the Normandy landings lay, therefore, the frequently unspectacular work on these financial institutions which their authors assumed would have a considerable effect on the state of the postwar world.

As we have seen, White's career had in many ways been a preparation for this central part of his work in the Treasury. Fully aware of the wider implications of the Depression, his initial report to Professor Jacob Viner in 1934 had emphasized the "ultimate goal" of the maintenance and promotion of prosperity. Later, White's part in the events which led to the "Tripartite Declaration" of 1936 had involved him in the broader international aspects of recovery with this Anglo-French-American stabilization agreement.

White's subsequent work in connection with the operations of the American Exchange Stabilization Fund, the abortive Inter-American Bank, and the Cuban Financial Mission all pointed toward his being given responsibility for the "inter-Allied stabilization fund." His own remarkable talent, as some saw it, for acquiring and retaining responsibility inside the Treasury would not have been a bar to the added duties of preparing the draft of a new international stabilization fund.

Yet the underlying inspiration of the White Plan, as it soon came to be known, was one of more than merely rationalizing international financial arrangements for the postwar world. White and Morgenthau hoped to eliminate the gyrations of the international economy which, they held, had helped to lead to the Depression and its train, the war. Governments, not bankers, should therefore direct monetary policy.

In his biography of Morgenthau, John Morton Blum remarks that the Secretary of the Treasury was proud of his role in the framing of the 1936 Tripartite Declaration. He visualized a broader and wider international financial accord which would preclude competitive devaluations and exchange controls. Moreover, Morgenthau looked forward to the continuing cooperation of the wartime allies and assumed that the United States, as the richest of the three wartime allies, would benevolently exercise the largest influence in the proposed new institutions. From the first, Professor Blum writes, Morgenthau "envisaged a kind of New Deal for a new world." Such a view, as we see, was implicit in the White Plan.

In a letter to President Truman in March, 1946, Morgenthau remarked that his primary objective during his years as Secretary of the Treasury was to "move the financial center of the world from London and Wall Street to the United States Treasury and to create a new concept between the nations of international finance." The Bretton Woods agreements, Morgenthau wrote to Truman, were to have been the "crystallization of that program," with the Fund and the Bank "instrumentalities of sovereign governments and not of private financial interests."[2]

During the early months of 1942 White produced three drafts of a proposed Fund and a Bank which survive in his papers at Princeton. What seems to be the first draft is an undated typescript, written presumably at the beginning of 1942, entitled, "Suggested Plan for an United Nations

Stabilization Fund and a Bank for Reconstruction of the United and Associated Nations." Another typescript is dated March, 1942, and a third mimeographed draft was produced in April of that year.[3]

White's proposals, as presented in the first undated draft, were both striking and idealistic, forming an unmistakable departure from prewar financial practices. The White Plan hoped to prevent "the disruption of foreign exchanges and the collapse of the monetary and credit systems; to assure the restoration of foreign trade; and to supply the huge volume of capital that will be needed virtually throughout the world for reconstruction, for relief, and for economic recovery."

Solving these economic and financial problems would help to solve basic international issues. "If we are to avoid drifting from the peace table into a period of chaotic competition, monetary disorder, depressions, political disruption, and finally into new wars within as well as among nations, we must be equipped to grapple with these three problems and to make substantial progress toward their solution . . ."

The Fund and the Bank were thus to be the chief means of conducting postwar international financial relations. The Stabilization Fund would have resources of $5 billion, subscribed in gold, local currency and securities from member countries, with voting in proportion to national quota. National domestic financial politics would be subordinate to the operation of the proposed international institutions, as the Fund's resources would become available for countries facing temporary balance-of-payments difficulties.

In return for this added international liquidity, members of the Fund would have to surrender some sovereignty in dealing with the problems of adjusting their balance of payments. Exchange controls and the right to vary exchange rates would be circumscribed. There would be Fund supervision over domestic financial policies. No country could draw more than its quota from the Fund.

The associated plan for the Bank—there was no provision for "development" as separate from "reconstruction" in this first draft—was to provide the "huge volume" of capital to repair the ravages of war and so smooth the transition from wartime to peacetime conditions. For this work of relief, reconstruction and recovery, the Bank would have a capital of $10 billion for long-term loans at low interest rates. It would also engage in activities to stabilize world commodity prices and to help alleviate impending economic depression by contra-cyclical lending.

While either agency could work without the other, they were clearly complementary, as the short-term work of the Fund would facilitate the restoration of long-term equilibrium by the Bank. Liberal commercial policies, involving a lowering of tariff barriers, were clearly a corollary of the new postwar world of the White Plan.

By May, 1942, White had completed a final first draft of his proposals for a Fund and a Bank. In forwarding these proposals to President Roosevelt on May 15, 1942, Morgenthau wrote enthusiastically that he was convinced that "the launching of such a plan at this time has tremendous strategic as well as economic bearing. It seems to me that the time is ripe to dramatize our internal economic objectives in terms of action which people everywhere will recognize as practical, powerful and inspiring."

Later on the afternoon of the fifteenth, Morgenthau told White on the telephone that Roosevelt had liked his plan, but that he had told the President that it could only happen "if you get behind it." Then, Morgenthau would take the program to Cordell Hull. White considered this a "very good move."[4]

With Morgenthau's access to Roosevelt and the "New Deal" reputation of the Treasury, the State Department soon recognized the Treasury's primacy in postwar financial planning. But the State Department retained responsibility for commercial policy, and negotiations begun informally with the British in 1943 eventually led to the later General Agreement on Tariffs and Trade (GATT) and the proposed International Trade Organization.

On May 25, 1942, a Cabinet-level committee met in Morgenthau's room in the Treasury to consider the proposed financial plans. Besides White, representatives from the Treasury, the State Department, the Federal Reserve System and other agencies were present. There was general enthusiasm, and it was agreed to set up an interdepartmental subcommittee, the "American Technical Committee," to develop the financial proposals.

The Technical Committee first met on May 28, 1942, with White as its chairman, so centralizing both administrative and expert responsibility for the development of the proposed financial institutions in his person. Two other Treasury officials who sat on this committee, and who gave White much assistance in the development of the financial institutions were Edward M. Bernstein and Ansel F. Luxford.[5] Bernstein was an economist of international repute. Luxford, who had worked in the Treasury since 1935, with one break, usually in the General Counsel's office, was to become the chief legal adviser to the American delegation at Bretton Woods, as well as an Assistant to the Secretary of the Treasury.

At first White was inclined to press for a formal international conference as soon as possible. But in July, 1942, the Treasury accepted State Department advice to postpone such a gathering pending preliminary conversations with the British and a few other allies. That same month a draft of the White Plan was sent to London for Keynes to see. In August, a copy of the British plan for postwar financial operations, Keynes's "International Clearing Union," arrived in Washington for White. From this time on the two countries worked together on postwar financial planning.

Keynes had rejoined the British Treasury in the summer of 1940 as a policy adviser to the then Chancellor of the Exchequer, Sir Kingsley Wood. Although he had a room in the Treasury he was not a civil servant and drew no salary. After returning to London from a visit to the United States in the late summer of 1941, Keynes, who was to be made a baron during 1942, had begun to think about British participation in a possible postwar multilateral trading system. His plan for a Clearing Union, as eventually published in 1943, was designed in his own words to "obtain the advantages, without the disadvantages, of an international gold currency." The Clearing Union, if successful, would moreover substitute for the gold standard "an expansionist, in place of a contractionist, pressure on world trade."

During 1941–42 the International Clearing Union achieved the status of a British Cabinet paper, and Roy Harrod has recorded, "at first . . . was indeed regarded as impractical, a sketch of something one might achieve in a world not realised. . . . But in the course of discussion, comment and re-drafting, gradually, over a period of many months, by an imperceptible process, it came to be recognized as the main Treasury plan."[6]

The Keynes Plan, while sharing the wider objectives of the White Plan, differed from it structurally in several important aspects. To preserve both exchange stability and financial liquidity, so avoiding the paralyzing deflation which had spread from country to country between the wars, the Clearing Union would make available large overdraft facilities to members. These facilities would be related to members' share of prewar world trade, and would be expressed in "bancor," an international unit of accountancy and exchange issued by the Clearing Union.

The formula suggested in the Keynes Plan meant total overdraft facilities of some $26 billion. This figure was large enough to enable members to do away with exchange restrictions, and at the same time to expand their economies without fearing the inflationary effect on their current balance of payments. With its large facilities, relief and rehabilitation functions could also be undertaken by the Clearing Union.

Unlike the Fund proposed by the White Plan, the Clearing Union would have no fixed quotas. Instead surpluses and deficits would be reflected in credits and debits on the account of the Union, expressed in "bancor." The Keynes Plan was thus explicitly expansionist and provided a completely closed clearing mechanism. Its primary objective was to counter domestic deflation, rather than inflation.

Politically, of course, the Keynes Plan was more adventurous than the White Plan, and during 1942–43 preliminary talks continued between the experts of Britain and America, the two countries which would have to

take the chief responsibility for any new international financial arrangements. As a background to these financial talks were the larger aspirations of the postwar planners.

The White Plan, like the Keynes Plan, looked forward to a new trading
order in which the international community and its component nations
would benefit. Planning would have to proceed at first, as we have noted,
on a bilateral basis between the two chief trading countries. Many differences remained to be reconciled between (and within) Britain and
America before the issue could ever be taken to an international conference. Yet in both countries there was also considerable resolve to avoid
the mistakes that had led to two world wars in one generation. White was
not alone in his apparent determination to work toward a new world.

The proposed break with the past was especially marked in the United
States, considering the isolationist legacy and the strong influence of
orthodox finance. Moreover, as the world's richest nation, no matter what
cooperation would be coming from other countries, the primary financial
responsibility for any new institutions would have to be underwritten by
the United States. In the United Kingdom on the other hand, the supporters of Imperial Preference were reluctant to abandon the Ottawa
Agreements of 1932 on grounds of both prudence and sentiment. Many
other Britons were loath to abandon national economic defenses against
any new depression. In any case, the wartime liquidation of Britain's
overseas assets indicated caution in designing the postwar world.

But even before the emergence of the White Plan, the two countries
had attempted to compose their differences of approach to economic
matters in the Atlantic Charter of August, 1941, and the Mutual Aid
Agreement of February, 1942. The later White-Keynes negotiations, the
Bretton Woods agreements and the subsequent debates in Congress and
Parliament on the new financial institutions were thus all part of a continuing drama in which White quite frequently played a central role.
Moreover, White's own departure from the International Monetary Fund
in the spring of 1947 came at a time which marked the end in some ways
of the wartime hopes and assumptions for a new world.

On the American side, as Richard N. Gardner has commented in his
classic study, *Sterling-Dollar Diplomacy*, the postwar planners, with the
"lessons" of Woodrow Wilson's unhappy experience in peacemaking in
mind, and whatever their own internecine rivalries, were determined
that some detailed planning on the postwar world should take place
during the fighting. They were also sure that the United States should
play an active part in the postwar United Nations Organization. Thirdly,
they recognized that the breakdown of the earlier peace settlement owed
much to economic factors.

Consequently, many of the postwar planners, throughout the administration, in line with the influential beliefs of Cordell Hull, tended to assume the efficacy of adumbrating general principles of international political conduct. Hull's own enthusiasm for his "four principles" during the American-Japanese negotiations of 1941 has been noted, for example. The planners also tended to reject the need for any balance of power or of international alliances, and were influenced by what Hull termed the "universal" approach to world order. Again, economic institutions by themselves, operating in some sort of political vacuum, were seen as an important means of restoring harmony to a shattered world. These ideas, laudable in themselves, based on high principles, but sometimes, perhaps, pressed too far, Richard Gardner has described as Legalism, Universalism and Economism.

As part of their basic economic objectives of constructing a postwar multilateral trading system, with fewer and diminishing obstacles, many of the influential postwar planners on the American side aimed not only at reducing tariffs and similar trade barriers as a commercial policy. In line with Hull's special enthusiasm, they hoped to eliminate trading "discrimination," by which they usually meant the British Imperial Preferences. As Dean Acheson has summed up:

> Mr. Hull's establishment had drawn its blueprints from Wilsonian liberalism and an utopian dream. They were founded on a refurbished and strengthened League of Nations, which assumed continued cooperation of the wartime alliance in banishing war and the use of force. Economic arrangements—even the new ideas of Maynard Keynes—were to be brought into conformity with the classical economic goals of removing obstructions from the free movement of goods, people and funds as means of expanding trade and development. And economic development was to take on an evangelistic character in support of social justice and democratic institutions.[7]

In some important ways, White's own initiatives reflected these assumptions, although of course the Treasury was sometimes in conflict with the State Department and other agencies over jurisdiction. As we have seen, White's proposed quasi-diplomatic overtures to Russia and Japan in 1939 and 1941 placed some political significance on loans and economic arrangements. Later in the war, during March, 1944, a proposed $5 billion loan to Russia was partly justified by White on the grounds that it would, per se, "provide a sound basis for continued collaboration between the two countries in the postwar world."[8] By January, 1945, the amount of the suggested loan to the Russians had doubled. In the same way, perhaps, White's introduction to his initial draft on the Fund and the Bank, noted above, assumed the comprehensive wider value of the proposed financial institutions. Quite consistently, as we shall see, White later defended the Bretton Woods agreements before the appropriate Congressional bodies in "universal" terms.

At the same time, of course, there was a strong nationalist thread in White's thinking on the proposed financial institutions in that the dollar, pegged to gold, was seen as the anchor for the stability of the world's exchanges. John Morton Blum has commented that White "sought openly, with the Secretary's approval, to make the dollar the dominant currency in the postwar world. An ardent nationalist in his monetary thinking, White also championed postwar international monetary cooperation, the objective of his tireless efforts to establish the International Monetary Fund. In that cooperation White expected the United States and the United Kingdom to provide the lead, with the United States as the senior partner."[9]

As far as the wider objectives of the postwar planners were concerned, White himself wrote after the war, in May, 1948, that it was expected

> that the early postwar years would witness a degree of unity and good will in international political relations among the victorious allies never before reached in peace time. It was expected that the world would move rapidly—to use the phrase Wendell Willkie made famous—toward "One World." Economic maladjustments were, of course, contemplated and it was fully expected that the transition from a wartime to a peacetime world would be costly and difficult. But it was also fully expected that once hostilities ceased, each month would see substantial progress toward the successful completion of the transition. A few years at most were to see the major part of the transition completed. No influential person, as far as I remember, expressed the expectation that international relations would worsen. . . .[10]

As perhaps befitted the embattled position of the British, their response to this view of the postwar "One World" was hesitant but not necessarily unsympathetic. As far as the cause of multilateral trade was concerned, Churchill himself was an old free trader and though, as E. F. Penrose has commented, "he acquiesced in a certain degree of protection as a *fait accompli*, he still thought there was a general presumption on the side of free trade and felt no enthusiasm for the system of Empire Preferences adopted at Ottawa."[11]

Penrose, who was the economic adviser to the wartime American ambassador to Britain, John G. Winant, goes on to comment that Churchill's objections and hesitations over this subject arose less from his personal views than "from a desire to preserve Cabinet unity and to bring undivided energies to bear on the conduct of the war."

Within the War Cabinet, Anthony Eden, the Foreign Minister, and Sir John Anderson, Chancellor of the Exchequer after September, 1943, were aware of the necessity for American support, not only for winning the war, but for restoring Britain's position in the postwar world. There was clearly a connection between American goodwill and British support for the wider American postwar objectives.

A particularly influential supporter of financial and commercial collaboration between the two countries was Lord Cherwell, Churchill's adviser and friend, and Paymaster-General after 1942. Cherwell was inclined to the idea of freedom of trade, and "ridiculed" supporters of economic bilateralism who stated that after the war Britain would be in a strong bargaining position.

Cherwell drew the analogy of a man going into the Ritz, and pleading that he was in a strong bargaining position because he was so hungry—regardless of his means for paying for what he wanted. "The Prof" pointed out "again and again" in Whitehall that the proposed International Monetary Fund was far more flexible than the gold standard. In general, Cherwell held that if there were no rules in the postwar world there would be anarchy which would be disastrous for a nation such as Britain which depended so much on foreign trade.[12]

Other support in Britain, on idealistic grounds, for the necessity of "universal" postwar institutions came from the leaders of the Labour and Liberal parties, which were represented, of course, in the coalition government. The League of Nations had always been popular with members of these parties, the cause of Empire was suspect, and as in the United States, there was growing hope for postwar collaboration between the great powers.

Moreover, in the specific case of a multilateral trading system, influential academic economists in the wartime civil service were fully aware of the classical liberal tradition which had sustained British policy throughout much of the nineteenth century. Free trade in the classical sense was hardly possible, but with safeguards for the transitional postwar period Britain might well benefit from liberal trading policies. Influential in the wartime commercial and financial negotiations with the United States were two distinguished academic economists, supporters of a liberal trading system, Professors Lionel Robbins, head of the Economic Section of the War Cabinet Offices 1941–45, and James Meade, his successor.

As for Keynes himself, who would have to negotiate with White on the proposed postwar financial institutions, during the 1930's he had supported, out of necessity, autarchical measures of national self-preservation in economic matters. But preceding the drafting of the International

Clearing Union, his views were reverting to his earlier liberal attitudes on international trade:

The autumn of 1941 was for Keynes a time of deep reflection and heart searching. Then, as afterwards, he was acutely conscious of how great Britain's balance of trade difficulties would be once the war was over. . . . How should we then proceed? He was advised on every side that it would be needful to maintain something like the wartime system, suitably modified, of tight controls, of blocked accounts, and bilateral bargains. . . . Yet he revolted against all this. He, like the Americans, disliked reverting to the law of the jungle. His instincts were for international cooperation. If these instincts had been dormant in the years before the war, that was because such cooperation seemed impracticable; the internationalists tended to be those who had not accepted Keynesian economics, and to hand arrangements over to them would, in his judgement, be fatal. . . . But was the world changing now? . . . Perhaps the time was ripe to apply Keynesian thought on a world scale; that would be much better than doing so on a national scale only.[13]

Yet, influential as were the supporters of a multilateral trading system, the opposition in Britain was also powerful. On the right were the supporters of Imperial Preference, their political arguments buttressed by the appeal of an empire at war. Veteran politicians such as Leo Amery, Secretary of State for India, and Lord Beaverbrook, a minister and a friend of Churchill's, were in the van here. Beaverbrook, in particular, was concerned at a possible return to the rigidity of a new gold standard with a liberal multilateral regime.

On the British left, socialists and other radicals saw, almost doctrinally, in postwar multilateralism a prescription for further depression as an inevitable consequence of the capitalist system. Other moderates on the left, arguing from recent history, suggested that British living standards, the balance of payments, and levels of employment would be hazarded in a multilateral regime. There was a fear that employment would be "exported" from the United States in the event of a further depression.

In the financial (and commercial) wartime negotiations, therefore, there was a strong British desire to retain some safeguards for the British economy, together with the wish to keep some Commonwealth preferences. As we shall see, both White and Keynes were very aware of these political factors, and on the American side there was an equally strong awareness of what Congress would tolerate as the defender of national sovereignty and the dollar. From the beginning there was bound to be a difference in national emphasis on postwar planning. Could these differences be surmounted as was being done in the area of military strategy from the Roosevelt-Churchill "Arcadia" conference of December, 1941, onward?

A beginning was made to synthesize the differing viewpoints in the Atlantic Charter of August, 1941. Despite strenuous representations by the State Department to obtain a join commitment to the removal of "discrimination," Article Four merely stated the desire of the two countries "with due respect for their existing obligations, to further the enjoyment by all States, great or small, victor or vanquished, of access, on equal terms, to the trade and to the raw materials of the world which are needed for their economic prosperity." From his Placentia Bay meeting with Roosevelt the Prime Minister cabled the War Cabinet that the phrase, "with due respect for existing obligations," safeguarded the British relationship with the Dominions. A fifth article of the Charter recognized without any precision the desire of the two countries to bring about "the fullest collaboration between all nations in the economic field with the object of assuring, for all, improved labor standards, economic development and social security."

However, the vagueness of the Atlantic Charter's economic provisions ensured that a second attempt was soon made to define common objectives.

This came with Article VII of the Mutual Aid Agreement, signed on February 23, 1942, with the object of regularizing the provision of American Lend-Lease supplies to Britain. After eight months of tenacious negotiation,[14] the United States and the United Kingdom here agreed, in accord with the statutory demand of the Congressional Lend-Lease legislation that the President had to find some "benefit" in exchange for Lend-Lease assistance, "to promote mutually advantageous economic relations" in the final settlement. This promise by Britain was thus the famous "consideration" which the American executive could hold eventually to Congress as the "benefit" for Lend-Lease.

But the undertaking by the British to promote postwar multilateral trade was carefully qualified. Article VII stated that the final Lend-Lease settlement between the two countries was to provide for "agreed action" directed to the expansion of "production, employment and the exchange and consumption of goods." Only then did this clause refer to the eventual provision for "the elimination of all forms of discriminatory treatment in international commerce, and to the reduction of tariffs and other trade barriers."

Thus there was no provision for the direct abrogation of "discrimination," and in any case its "elimination" was predicated both on the expansion of production and employment, and the reduction of tariffs.

Emphasizing these reciprocal, rather than unilateral obligations, the last sentence of Article VII stated, with another qualification on overall conditions, that at an early date "conversations shall be begun between the two Governments with a view to determining, in the light of governing economic conditions, the best means of attaining the above-stated objectives." The ambiguity between intention to negotiate and the actual execution of agreement remained to be resolved between the two countries, but what was certain was that the clause provided for mutual obligations over tariffs, preferences, employment and economic policies generally.

Thus Article VII "became the basic legal framework for postwar planning in the economic field" (Gardner). As we have seen, with the drafting of the White Plan and the Keynes Plan at the very time of the signing of Article VII, progress was already being made in the financial field. To what extent did these plans contribute toward the ambitious objectives of the postwar planners?

An early meeting in London between the authors of the White Plan and the Keynes Plan showed that, in spite of their broadly similar objectives, there were considerable differences in detail.

During October, 1942, White and Morgenthau were in England on a general tour of inspection, completing arrangements, among other matters, for the Anglo-American occupation-currency in the impending North African landings.[15] An unofficial "off-the-record" meeting between White and Keynes was now arranged by the American ambassador, and the two men came together in Winant's room in the Embassy. Their relationship had changed since their earlier meeting in London in 1935. Present were experts from both countries, including E. F. Penrose, who records that "the exchange of views was left almost wholly to Keynes and White. It was lively and at times acrimonious but exceedingly fruitful. There was a substantial area of agreement but there were also sharp differences."[16]

Keynes considered that the Fund proposed by the White Plan was not large enough, while White thought that it would be impossible to get more money out of Congress for the American share. White also thought that Keynes's suggestion to use the Clearing Union as a means of financing postwar relief and rehabilitation was not politically possible. Keynes attacked the concept of a Fund with subscribed capital, but White insisted that this alone would be acceptable to Congress.

As far as exchange rates were concerned, Keynes stated in this meeting that the White Plan's proposal to allow exchange variations by only a four-fifths majority of Fund member votes would not be acceptable to the British. In view of their expected postwar financial difficulties, the British must obtain freedom of action over exchange rates. There were also differences over the voting system to be created with the new institutions, for in the White Plan, where the United States would have the largest quota, the Americans would be predominant. In the Keynes Plan, where, in Penrose's words, "the nations were arrayed according to their prewar commercial position," the British took a leading position.

According to Penrose's account, Keynes "heatedly argued" that the subject matter being complicated, it was essential that America and Britain should work out a plan themselves, invite the Russians in order "to allay suspicion," and perhaps the Dominions, "and then set it up and invite the rest of the world to join." Here White maintained that such an arrangement would create suspicion of "an Anglo-Saxon gang-up."

In concluding his account of this meeting, which raised issues of continuing relevance to international financial problems, Penrose remarks that the very act of bringing these differences into the open had "the greatest effect on subsequent preparations, in Whitehall and Washington." Both White and Keynes agreed that as a result of this exchange of views they would return to their colleagues with proposals for modifications on a number of points.

Confidential exchanges now continued between the two sides during the winter of 1942–43, and drafts of the two plans were then published in April, 1943. Work on White's Bank project lagged and this draft was not published until November, 1943.[17]

As Richard Gardner has remarked in *Sterling-Dollar Diplomacy*, both plans aimed to promote a multilateral payments system in which external financial equilibrium could be maintained with levels of full domestic employment.

Success depended technically upon three factors. Could the restoration of financial equilibrium be established in the transitional postwar period? Could the Stabilization Fund and the Clearing Union provide enough liquidity to give member nations confidence to abandon financial restrictions? Thirdly, would it be possible to devise an acceptable method of adjustment to deal with the inevitable fluctuations in member nations' balance of payments? Some of these fundamental problems had been discussed in the Keynes-White meeting in London during October, 1942, but now agreement acceptable to the British and American governments would have to be reached.

As far as the transitional problem was concerned, the White Plan, as the Keynes Plan, was designed to operate in a state of global political and economic equilibrium. Both plans therefore primarily provided a means of clearing exchange, rather than dealing with long-term problems such as relief, reconstruction and development, which would have to be dealt with by other agencies. In the White Plan such capital assistance was to be provided by the Fund's twin, the Bank, and while the Clearing Union made some provision for relief and reconstruction, it was not specifically designed to remedy long-term problems.

As we have seen, in its original form the Bank, which lacked the word "development" in its early 1942 draft, had the huge capital of $10 billion, a sum worth perhaps over double that figure at today's prices. In later drafts, development was given equal prominence with reconstruction in the Bank's functions, but draft publication was delayed, and soon the Bank's more ambitious functions such as contra-cyclical lending were dropped. There was an increasingly conservative mood in Congress during 1942–43, as we have noted, and White was bound to take such political developments into account. The Clearing Union, with its resemblances to an international central bank, could make long-term credits possible, as envisaged in Section IX, but its chief emphasis was on stabilization of current accounts.

In an enthusiastic article in the *American Economic Review* in March, 1943, White outlined his belief in the benefits that currency stabilization could bring to the international order. He remarked that success depended primarily on "the participation and leadership of the United States," and went on to bracket together the Fund and the Bank when he wrote that they could together "also provide a large part of the capital needed for reconstruction."[18] Essentially, however, the transition from war to peace would have to be resolved politically before the Fund could operate as White intended.

To deal with the problem of global liquidity, there was some contrast between the projected resources of the Stabilization Fund and the Clearing Union. The White Plan suggested a Fund of some $5 billion, with members' quotas representing their maximum liabilities as well as their maximum drawing rights. Voting, of course, was geared to subscription, which would have given the United States a virtual veto in the Fund. Under these provisions the American liability would be limited to its national contribution, about $2 billion.

In the Clearing Union, on the other hand, based as it was on the overdraft principle, national facilities indicated the drawing rights of members, but not their total liability, which could be increased if necessary in terms of bancor, the Keynes accounting unit. As the Clearing Union was a closed system, American credit liability was theoretically limited only by the total demand of all other members. This liability could amount, therefore, to $23 billion, the sum of all quotas minus the

American contribution. The Fund's liquidity was thus restricted to the aggregate of its quotas, while that of the Union could be expanded according to circumstances.

The two proposed financial organizations also differed in their outline of the circumstances in which this liquidity could be made available. White's Stabilization Fund, with its more limited resources, could restrict the sale of currency to members in certain circumstances, implying discretion in its operations. The Clearing Union, on the other hand, was "passive" rather than "active" in its operations as it made resources automatically available, a point on which the British were insistent in negotiation.

Finally, and crucial if any lasting Anglo-American agreement was to be reached by both the technicians and the politicians, were the provisions for adjustment in the White Plan. The money advanced or sold by the Stabilization Fund was for purely short-term purposes, pending the elimination of balance-of-payments difficulties. Exchange controls and variations in national exchange rates were not seen as usual means of adjustment by both White and Keynes. One of the chief objectives of both the Fund and the Clearing Union was to restrict such measures, exemplified above all by competitive devaluation, which had of course bedeviled international financial relations in the 1930's.

The third way of adjusting toward equilibrium was for a member country to make appropriate changes in its price-income structure, deflating in the case of debtor countries, inflating in the case of creditor countries. In the past, as we have seen, such changes would come about automatically under the Gold Standard. The first draft of the White Plan, in early 1942, stated that Fund members would be obliged not to adopt any measure promoting either serious inflation or deflation without the consent of a majority vote by Fund members. This would avoid giving the Fund any formal deflationary basis, envisaging mutual adjustments by both creditor and debtor.

When the White Plan was published in April, 1943, the Stabilization Fund no longer had the authority to demand internal adjustments on the lines above, a compromise with the claims of national sovereignty. But Fund members were still to "give consideration" to the Fund on internal economic policies which would bring about "a serious disequilibrium" in the balance of payments of other countries. Moreover, White proposed that drawing rights were specifically limited, as a debtor country could, after two years, only withdraw more than its quota if approved by a four-fifths majority of Fund member votes. In addition, such overdrawing was contingent on carrying out Fund-approved measures to correct the balance-of-payments equilibrium. The underlying problem, which White was attempting to solve in a truly creative manner, was how to reconcile national sovereignty with the efficient operation of the Fund, as one country's credit was another's debt.

In general, such measures provided for putting pressure on debtor countries, while the Clearing Union, possessing greater facilities, was rather more tolerant, with its specifically expansionist bias, of the debtors. But what of the vital position of creditor countries? Could they be made partly responsible for adjustment? In the Keynes Plan, "the real sanction against the creditor country lay precisely in the large credit that it would pile up in due course. The idea was, that when it saw this credit grow, it would feel forced to take remedial measures" (Harrod).

Now, in the autumn of 1942, White saw that, with the more limited liability of the Stabilization Fund, some other form of sanction would have to be devised against a creditor nation if the Fund was to be a credible instrument. Thus emerged the famous "scarce-currency" clause which does not appear in the early drafts of the White Plan. The new draft indicated that, if the Fund holdings of a creditor nation's currency dropped below a certain level, such currencies could be declared "scarce" and rationed by the Fund. A Fund report could be issued to the creditor outlining measures to restore equilibrium. Further sanctions against the creditor could include authorization of the debtor country to apply discrimination against the creditor's exports, so helping to restore the balance of payments. Part of the onus for adjustment was thus put on the creditor in this clause which appeared in Section III of the published Stabilization Fund.

This draft provision first appeared in a version of the White Plan dated December 16, 1942, which reached London in February, 1943. Sir Roy Harrod has vividly described, in *The Life of John Maynard Keynes*, his own discovery of the "scarce-currency" provision of the White Plan during a crowded wartime journey from London to Oxford:

This was a very remarkable concession. If the United States was really to maintain over a term of years the oppressive role of creditor, which all predicted for her, it would mean that she was by this clause authorising other nations to discriminate against the purchase of American goods, to take in each other's washing, and to maintain their own full employment in the presence of an American depression. . . . This then was the big thing. For years we had complained of the United States' attitude as a creditor. For months we had struggled in vain to find some formula which would pin them down to a share of responsibility. Now they had come forward and offered a solution of their own, gratuitously. This was certainly a great event. For it was the first time they had said in a document, unofficial it was true, and noncommittal, but still in a considered Treasury document, that they would come in and accept their full share of responsibility when there was a fundamental disequilibrium of trade. As I sat huddled in my corner, I felt an exhilaration that comes once or twice in a lifetime. . . .[19]

With the draft publication of the Stabilization Fund and the Clearing Union in April, 1943, it became clear that any technical compromise between the two countries would have to be politically acceptable to British and American opinion. In Britain, the White Plan was regarded by critics as both financially orthodox and deflationary. In the United States, financial circles considered the Keynes Plan inflationary and experimental. Isolationists were also suspicious of its internationalist assumptions. In both countries critics believed national sovereignty would be compromised.

There was also the influential view put in a New York *Times* editorial on March 30, 1943, that "the gold standard was, without any international agreements, the most satisfactory international standard that has ever been devised." Correspondingly, in Britain, Robert (later Lord) Boothby, who was to emerge as one of the most forceful parliamentary critics of Bretton Woods, stated in the House of Commons in May, 1943, that the White Plan was "the end of all our hopes of an expansionist policy and social advance."

Boothby told the writer that his opposition to the Fund stemmed from his belief that "in a world of chaos" it was best to keep exchange rates as flexible as possible. Moreover, Fund liquidity was inadequate, Boothby considered, bearing in mind the American official price of gold, $35 per ounce.

As a first move toward international agreement, therefore, White, Keynes and their colleagues would now have to draft an acceptable compromise between the politics of the dollar and that of the pound. Well aware of these considerations, White once said during the Anglo-American financial negotiations in the autumn of 1943 that "he regarded himself as a middleman between two sovereign powers, the American Congress on one hand, and the British Cabinet on the other."[20]

11

GOLD FOR CHINA?

. . . This yellow slave
Will knit and break religions; bless the accurs'd; Make the hoar leprosy
adored. . . .

—*Timon of Athens*

. . . Gold constitutes one of the most effective war chests; gold constitutes
the most effective and safest store of international purchasing power
known. . . .

—Harry Dexter White

White's part in the financial negotiations which led to the Bretton Woods
Conference of 1944 was perhaps the most widely known of his extensive
wartime responsibilities. But, from the first weeks following Pearl Harbor
to the very end of the Pacific war, the Treasury was increasingly concerned with the problem of American relations with another wartime
ally, Nationalist China. Here White, who had earlier supported the Nationalist cause, came to play an increasingly important role.

With the opening of the Pacific war it appeared that Sino-American
relations had never been closer. The Japanese offensive across the Far
East and the Pacific put a new and urgent emphasis on preserving the
Nationalist regime which had fought alone for over four years against
Japan.

In Chungking hopes were raised as the United States and the British
Empire formally became China's allies. Generalissimo Chiang Kai-shek
assumed the post of Allied Supreme Commander of the China Theatre.
From the United States Lieutenant General Joseph Stilwell went to
Chungking in early 1942 to take up the post of chief of staff of Chiang's
proposed joint Allied staff, as well as commander of American forces in

the China-Burma-India theater and of "such Chinese forces as may be assigned him." During the Roosevelt-Churchill Washington ("Arcadia") Conference of December, 1941–January, 1942, the Prime Minister was conscious of the existence on the American side "of a standard of values which accorded China almost an equal fighting power with the British Empire, and rated the Chinese armies as a factor to be mentioned in the same breath as the armies of Russia."[1]

Yet already, in these few weeks of the Pacific war, there lay the seeds of Stilwell's Laocoön-like struggle against the command, strategic, economic and political problems that were to bring his mission to its unhappy end in 1944. In the Arcadia Conference the two leaders had agreed on the primary task of defeating Germany. Second in priority was the war across the Pacific toward Japan. According to Henry Stimson, the American Secretary of War, in "Anglo-American grand strategy" the China-Burma-India theater "was a poor third. Yet in its strategic and political significance this part of the world was of enormous importance. . . . Strategically, the object of American policy in this area was to keep China in the war, and to strengthen her so that she might exact a constantly growing price from the Japanese invader."[2]

The overriding necessity of keeping China in the war seemed obvious enough. During the war period as a whole, according to John K. Fairbank and his colleagues, "National Government forces tied down most of Japan's troops in China, roughly half her armies overseas and suffered the great part of China's three million or more battle casualties."[3] At the same time, Arthur Young has commented, China drained away "perhaps thirty-five percent of the cost of Japan's war effort."[4] Important, too, was the fact that in a war fought by Imperial Japan under the slogan "Asia for Asiatics," the Anglo-Americans obtained considerable political benefit from Chiang's refusal to come to terms with Tokyo. In late January, 1942, Stimson told Morgenthau that China must "at any price" be kept in the war.[5]

But quite apart from the higher strategy there was the practical problem of how to help China. The Japanese conquest of Burma in the spring of 1942 cut the Burma Road and with it land communications from China to the West, a grave blow to the Nationalist regime which dictated the future course of the war in the C.B.I. theatre. Apart from the tenuous Central Asian link with Russia, Nationalist China was virtually besieged with the Japanese successes in Burma. The only remaining link with the West was the 600-mile Hump air route between Assam and Kunming over the unsurveyed 20,000-foot peaks of the Himalayas. The Hump route, usually flown during 1942–43 by two-motored C-47 transports without navigational aids, was destined, in the words of the official American Air Force historians, to be "the proving ground, if not the birthplace of mass strategic airlift."[6] Despite the Air Transport Command's later successes in 1944–45, this was not apparent early in 1942.

From the opening of the Pacific war, therefore, one of the most effective ways in which the United States could help its beleaguered Chinese ally, and attempt to further its own policies in China, was by money. On December 30, 1941, the Generalissimo asked Washington, through the American ambassador, Clarence Gauss, for a $500,000,000 loan. The British Government was asked at the same time for a loan of £100,000,000.

In this crisis atmosphere, with its prospect of the disintegration of the Nationalist regime following Japan's spectacular Pacific victories, time was of the essence in showing American confidence in the Generalissimo. On January 9, 1942, Roosevelt wrote to Morgenthau that he was "anxious to help Chiang Kai-shek with his currency. I hope you can invent some way of doing this." The following day Cordell Hull told the Secretary that as "an act of wartime policy," a loan of $300,000,000 should be organized for China with "the greatest possible expedition."[7]

The Chinese leaders were anxious to impress Morgenthau with the political significance of the loan. In a message on January 9, H. H. Kung, the Chinese Finance Minister, declared that "a political war loan" of $500,000,000 was needed. The loan's chief justification was "political above all . . . to demonstrate that China's confidence in the allied powers was matched by equal confidence in China of the allied powers, in the most crucial months of the emergency before us."[8]

As custodian of the public purse, Morgenthau was hesitant about the sweeping nature of the proposed loan. He was interested in a scheme for paying the Chinese troops with dollar currency. But, after a meeting with T. V. Soong, Morgenthau reported to his staff on January 13 that the Chinese Foreign Minister had told him, "How can [Chiang] say where he is going to use five hundred thousand troops? He has got to have them in reserve and then use them." But, Morgenthau went on, Soong knew that he would keep any promises: "I mean, I wouldn't promise two or three hundred million dollars and then have it come out . . . twenty million."[9]

The Generalissimo was firm, and in a personal message to Morgenthau on January 21 said that he regarded the loan as an "advance to an ally fighting against a common enemy, thus requiring no security or prearranged terms."[10]

Later in the month, after a meeting with Stimson and General Marshall, Morgenthau's reservations about the loan were allayed. Marshall considered the situation in the Far East critical, and Stimson, as noted, thought Chiang should be kept going at any price. But Maxim Litvinov, the Russian ambassador, thought that the Chinese request was "blackmail," Morgenthau told Harry Dexter White. The Russian had asked Morgenthau during their meeting if negotiations could be "dragged out."[11]

White was now present at a meeting on January 30 in Hull's office with Morgenthau, the Secretary of State and his advisers. All agreed that a loan of $500,000,000 should be recommended to Congress. Later in the day there was general support in a Cabinet meeting for the proposal. Roosevelt would send a message to Capitol Hill, and the State, Treasury and War departments would join in promoting the necessary legislation which would leave the administration free to work out precise terms. Within the next few days both Houses of Congress passed a joint resolution which was signed by the President on February 7. It provided:

> That the Secretary of the Treasury, with the approval of the President, is hereby authorized on behalf of the United States to loan or extend credit or give other financial aid to China in an amount not to exceed in aggregate $500,000,000 at such time or times and upon such terms as the Secretary of the Treasury, with the approval of the President shall deem in the interest of the United States.[12]

At the same time the British government announced a £50,000,000 loan to China "for war purposes."

The Bill appropriating the funds was signed on February 13, and three days later Morgenthau told Chiang that the unanimity and promptness with which the American government had responded to his request was evidence that "your confidence in the support of the United States is well founded." The Generalissimo, Morgenthau said, was "the personification of the heroism and courage of the Chinese people."[13] Moreover—and more important—it was eventually decided that the formal agreement on the loan between the two governments would have no provisions for joint consultation, as the Chinese were strongly opposed to any limitation on their freedom of action or their sovereignty. In retrospect, we can see that later American reservations over the implementation of the credit stemmed in part from the absence of such provisions.

Instead, Soong was to write a letter, following the formal agreement, that the United States would be kept "fully informed" on the use of the loan. Signed on March 21, 1942, the agreement deferred repayment terms until after the war, and the two countries were in accord that the $500,000,000 should be transferred "in such amounts and at such times as the Government of the Republic of China shall request." The joint statement by Morgenthau and Soong at this time saw the loan as a manifestation of the desire of the United States to aid China without stint in "our common battle for freedom."[14]

As we have seen, even in the Bretton Woods negotiations there were serious differences between the closest of allies. Within months the ideal-istic language of the "common battle for freedom" had begun to turn into Chinese-American recrimination as differences of national objectives refused to be papered over by the war, and as the proceeds of the loan turned into sand with the mounting Chinese inflation.

But in early 1942, it came to be forgotten, necessity was all, and the loan appeared as a bargain. On February 9 Morgenthau appeared before the House Appropriations Committee and stated that the United States might not get a dollar back from the half billion. Whereupon, according to the transcript, a Congressmen said, off the record, that "he supposed that even so we might consider ourselves amply repaid by Chinese partic-ipation in the war." The Secretary replied that he agreed.[15]

With the signing of the Sino-American agreement in March, 1942, White would soon come to play an important part in the implementation of the loan by the United States Treasury. The preamble to the agreement stated that the promised money would be used, *inter alia*, to strengthen the Chinese war effort by supporting the economy, increasing production, improving communications, prevention of hoarding, and to "retard the rise in prices, promote stability of economic relationships, and otherwise check inflation." Eventually the credit was used in the following way (figures in millions of dollars):

To back American dollar securities in China	$200m.
Purchase of gold for sale in China	220m.
Purchase of bank notes	55m.
Textiles shipped to China in 1945–46	25m.
	$500m.[16]

As will be seen from these figures, despite the ambitious terms of the preamble, the major part of the loan was used in an attempt, by the sale of dollar-backed securities and gold, to drain off surplus money and so restrict inflation in China. For underlying all wartime Chinese-American relations was the effect of the rise of prices in China which came to influence most political relationships in China's internal and external af-fairs.

By the end of 1941 average prices in China had risen about twenty-fold from the January–June, 1937 base. But, despite the favorable political effect of the American and British credits in early 1942, prices now began to rise faster than ever. The occupation of China's most productive cities, the closing of the Japanese blockade in early 1942, the shortage of goods, the inability or unwillingness of the authorities to impose efficient controls, taxes and credit restrictions, all were factors in the great Chinese inflation. There was also the recourse to the printing press in the face of these difficulties, which many observers believe to be the primary cause of the inflation. Arthur Young, the financial adviser to the Chinese government from 1929 to 1947, has written that:

> China's wartime inflation was caused chiefly by monetary excesses, and to a much less extent by nonmonetary factors. In the first year of fighting the government made a good showing by limiting to 37 percent the cash deficit covered by bank credit. But thereafter the figure ranged between 69 and 83 percent. After the first eighteen months, during which China lost control of the main areas where modern style banking existed, approximately 80 to 90 percent of this credit gave rise to expanded note issue. Thus the chief source of wartime receipts was the printing press. Expansion of credit to the government dwarfed expansion in the private sector. . . . During an inflation such as China's, the rate of turnover mirrors confidence or the lack of it, which affects propensity to spend. As the buying power of money falls, people are less willing to hold it, and they convert it into goods more and more quickly. The rise of general prices, first caused primarily by the increase of note issue, becomes itself a cause of further price rises by hurting confidence as the inflation progresses. This is the vicious circle of inflation.[17]

The twenty-fold increase in the average retail market prices in the cities of Nationalist China between 1937 and 1941 was only the beginning. By the end of 1942 prices had increased by about 66 times from the 1937 base; by the end of 1943, 228 times; by the end of 1944, 755 times; and August, 1945, when the war ended, the price index stood at 2,647. (See Appendix B.) During the next three years prices rose by more than another 2,500 times.

The inflation had a destructive effect on the government of Nationalist China, as Ernest Hemingway had prophesied as early as the summer of 1941. The government found it increasingly difficult to provide for its employees, military and civil; and, as corruption grew, morale and efficiency dropped. Hoarding and speculation flourished, bringing about a virtual redistribution of property, savings and income. The intellectuals, in the universities and elsewhere, began to repudiate the regime, which lost reputation both at home and abroad—a development which influenced inevitably American negotiators with Chungking during the war. Altogether the Chinese inflation seems a notable illustration of Keynes's remark that "Lenin was certainly right. There is no subtler, no surer means of overturning the existing basis of society than to debauch the currency."[18]

John K. Fairbank and his colleagues have commented that "Nationalist China's deterioration during eight years of wartime attrition reflected both the impact of overwhelming circumstances and an inadequacy of leadership, in proportions still being debated."[19] Inseparable from this process was the inflationary spiral that ripped apart the Chinese social order, providing a major cause, along with political and military factors, of the eventual collapse of the Nationalist Government.

Given the intensity and the implications of the inflation, the initial use by the Nationalist Government of the resources of the American credit was hardly auspicious.

In March, 1942, Chungking decided to sell two kinds of dollar-backed securities to the public to absorb Chinese legal tender of *fapi*. Accordingly $200,000,000 was transferred to the Chinese account in the Federal Reserve Bank of New York. It was necessary to offer the securities at the best possible price to make the issue a success, and for $100,000,000 of "U.S. Dollar Savings Certificates" the exchange was set at the rate of twenty yuan or Chinese dollars (C$) to the American dollar, a rate of 20–1, or five cents. For the second $100,000,000 issue of "Allied Victory U.S. Dollar Loan," an even more preferential rate of six cents to the yuan was set.

Central to the whole fiasco of the dollar securities was the accelerating depreciation of *fapi*. In 1937 the yuan-dollar cross-rate was C$3.36–$1, and in July, 1942, the official parity was set as C$20–$1, a rate which remained for the rest of the war. The Chinese government was adamant that a lower rate would adversely affect the inflationary situation, and prestige and considerations of national sovereignty were obviously involved in its insistence on the 20–1 rate. But although the 20–1 rate was about a sixth of the prewar figure, average prices in China by the end of 1942 were already about 66 times those of 1937. American dollar-notes could be sold for an average figure of C$32–$50 during the second half of 1942, and by the first seven months of 1943 the rate was already C$44–95.[20]

But the American dollar-backed securities remained open for subscription at the same price for some eighteen months after issue at their fixed price, a boon for speculators, as the free-market rates for dollar notes soared. An American dollar note could be converted by early 1943, therefore, through buying *fapi* on the free market, to between two and five times its value in yuan at the official 20–1 rate. Thus the dollar securities were being sold at a slow and completely unrealistic rate, often to speculators who would defer buying as prices rose. When at last the issues were closed in August and October, 1943, the government banks stepped in at the last moment to buy.

The potential drawing power of the securities had thus been lost by keeping the fixed-rate subscription open as the printing presses rolled, and there were also rumors that insiders had benefited. Eventually the Division of Monetary Research compiled a list of Chinese banks and companies connected with H. H. Kung and T. V. Soong, which, it was alleged, had bought dollar securities. It was rumored that some members of the Soong family, which included Madame Chiang and Madame Kung, had benefited, although as Herbert Feis puts it, "the evidence of that was evanescent."[21] But as well as the direct effect of the financial mismanagement, possibly even more damaging to the regime were lingering reports of inside speculation. In a survey of the Chinese financial scene at the end of 1943, Morgenthau reported to Roosevelt that sale of the securities had "made no significant contribution to the control of inflation" in China.[22]

With the relative failure of the issue of the dollar-backed securities, White now began to play an important, and eventually a central part, in the Treasury's arrangements for sending gold to China from the 1942 credit. The metal was needed by Chungking for a gold-sales program to the public designed to attack inflation by absorbing surplus purchasing power.

The use of gold as an anti-inflationary device had been suggested by the Chinese as early as October, 1942, and the message was passed to the Treasury by their man in Chungking, Solomon Adler. Adler had been sent to the Far East by the Division of Monetary Research in July, 1941. During 1942, now based in Chungking, he had been made acting American member of the tripartite Currency Stabilization Board in China. When the Board's operations were wound up in 1944, Adler remained as the Treasury's representative in China, reporting to White. In his message of October, 1942, to the United States Treasury, Adler reported that, for the purpose of "mopping up *fapi*," H. H. Kung wanted to establish a free gold market and was thinking of using $20,000,000 from the 1942 credit for this purpose.[23]

A few weeks later, in December, 1942, Morgenthau told Chungking that he was doubtful about the proposal "unless China would benefit in some way by the purchase of additional gold." But, in February, 1943, $20,000,000 of gold was transferred to the Chinese account in New York. Later in the month White considered that neither taxes nor controls had dealt with inflation in China, which was caused by lack of foreign goods and increasing government expenditure.[24]

In July, 1943, Kung asked Morgenthau for an additional $200,000,000 of gold from the credit, stating that Roosevelt had approved such a transfer in principle to Madame Chiang. Kung elaborated that "the chief purpose for the proposed purchase and sale of gold is to withdraw large quantities of notes now in circulation. The fact that each ounce of gold is worth about 8,000 yuan shows the psychology of Chinese people toward gold." On July 15 Morgenthau told Roosevelt that the Treasury had agreed in principle to Kung's request. Morgenthau went on to remark that the Chinese had been told they were using assets that could be used after the war, and that "it had been made clear that the Treasury was acquiescing to the Chinese proposal because the Government of China deems that the sale of gold to the public will aid its war effort to fight inflation and hoarding and that therefore the decision to purchase the gold is primarily the responsibility of the Chinese Government."[25]

It was a responsibility that the Chinese were willing to assume. After a formal request from Chungking, Morgenthau agreed, on July 27, 1943, in a message to Kung, to provide $200,000,000 of gold "on receipt of request" from the Chinese Government:

> Washington July 27, 1943
>
> The Treasury agrees to the request of the Government of China . . . that $200 million be made available from the credit on the books of the Treasury in the name of the Government of the Republic of China for the purchase of gold. In order to avoid unnecessary raising of funds by the United States Treasury, it is suggested that transfers from the credit of the Chinese Government for the purchase of gold be made at such time and in such amounts as are allowed by existing facilities for the transportation to China of the equivalent amount of gold. . . . On receipt of requests from the Government of China that a specific amount should be transferred from the credit of the Government of China . . . and be used for the purchase of gold, the necessary action will be taken to consummate these requests. . . .[26]

At this stage the Treasury evidently recognized the principle of using gold to raise funds for war purposes as a noninflationary process. On September 22, White informed Morgenthau that the Treasury hoped to sell $20,000,000 of gold in India and the Middle East during the next three months to cover costs. White went on to say that the Chinese had asked for $50,000,000 of gold, "in accordance with your promise to make the gold available. I have taken the position that the gold is available as rapidly as they can ship it."

However, a week later, on September 29, in a memorandum of a conversation with Morgenthau, White recorded that he had told the

Secretary that "I thought we ought to be tough with the Chinese on the question of earmarking $200,000,000 of gold for gold sales which they could not make before the gold was shipped to them. The Secretary agreed. He said he thinks we should be tough with them in this matter and he told me to go ahead and let them have the gold only as rapidly as it could be shipped to China."

Negotiations on an official level now went on with the Chinese in Washington. There was no immediate urgency over gold shipments at this time, as there was still $20,000,000 of gold from the credit earmarked in the Chinese account as well as Morgenthau's promise to deliver $200,-000,000.

On November 10 the Chinese representatives cabled Chungking that White had assured them that there was no difference whether the gold was on earmark in the Federal Reserve Bank or on the book of the Treasury. White had also stated, said the Chinese, that "whenever we need Treasury can make transfer at any time." White had then proposed a revolving fund of $10,000,000 of gold, but this suggestion lapsed as Kung hoped for larger transfers. From the Chinese viewpoint, it was unfortunate this offer was not taken up.[27]

Gold sales now began in China from the small stocks held by the Central Bank in Chungking, and the first delivery was made from the original $20,000,000 on earmark in New York. The first million dollars' worth, weighing slightly less than a short ton at $35 an ounce, left New York for Miami on September 28. It was then flown around the world via South America, the Middle East and the Hump, arriving in Chungking on November 19. Over $10,000,000 of gold had been sent to China by the end of 1943.[28]

The sale of this gold at first helped the Chinese currency, and on December 14 Kung cabled Morgenthau: "You will be pleased to know that the recent gold shipment is one of the outstanding factors contributing to the strengthening of *fapi*, because people think that the arrival of gold has increased the much needed reserve of the currency, thereby influencing the stability of prices."[29]

But soon events were to show that Kung's optimism over the results of the gold-sales program was premature.

White's suggestion to Morgenthau in September, 1943, that the Treasury "ought to be tough" over the question of earmarking $200,000,000 of gold for Chungking came at a crucial time in Sino-American relations. From the Chinese viewpoint, major aid from the United States had not come in the two years since Pearl Harbor, despite the high hopes raised by the 1942 credit. Whatever the reasons, for the three years 1942–44 the percentage of all American Lend-Lease aid delivered to China was 1.5, 0.4,

0.4.[30] Altogether, for the 1941–46 period, total American Lend-Lease aid to China was $1.5 billion, 3 percent of the aggregate of $50 billion, and about half was delivered after VJ-Day. In Chungking there was thus resentment that China, having fought Japan alone for over four years, was now being neglected in the priorities of global war.

Despite the American enthusiasm for treating China as a great power, as exemplified in the October, 1943, Moscow Declaration by the four powers, and the Cairo Conference between Roosevelt, Churchill and Chiang the following month, the economic and political situation inside China continued to deteriorate. As early as July, 1942, Stilwell noted in his diary that the Chinese Communist forces had "spread pretty well all over North China."[31] With the Russian position more secure after Stalingrad, it was reported from Moscow in August, 1943, that "for the first time since the Sino-Japanese war the Soviet press was emphasizing the role of the Communists in the struggle against Japan."[32]

Perhaps more important for Chiang at this time was the deterioration in Sino-American relations which formed the background to White's actions over the gold promise to Chungking.

In the melancholy and complicated story of Sino-American relations during the war as told by Herbert Feis, Tang Tsou and the official American Army historians, Charles Romanus and Riley Sunderland, there emerges the belief held by many observers and officials, civil and military, on the American side that, in Arthur Young's words, "China was seeking to exploit the United States."[33] It came to be believed that Chiang was less interested in common goals and the future objective of "one world" than in survival. Feis has described this feeling as follows:

> The worldwide war against the Axis had to be won. But while it was being won the Chiang Kai-shek regime wanted to be sure that it would survive in power. It was convinced that the maintenance of its position was essential for an orderly and unified China after the war. Hence it was afraid to take military chances; the loss of the capital, Chungking, might mean the end of the government, no matter what victories might be won elsewhere. It was afraid of making demands which might cause local military commanders and politicians to desert; and afraid of offending elements within the Kuomintang by radical measures of reform. Never out of mind was the knowledge that up north the Communists were waiting their chance to extend themselves and gain power; the government was determined they should not get it.[34]

These contradictory objectives were exacerbated by what would have been inevitable differences over priorities between America and China, and between the United States and Great Britain, opposed to a north Burma campaign, skeptical of the attempt to make China a great power, distrusted in turn by Chiang. There was the difference of emphasis on land and air operations in the China theater as personified by Stilwell and Claire Chennault, the 14th Air Force Commander in China. Most notorious of these tangled relationships was the famous vendetta between Chiang and Stilwell, who thought of the Generalissimo as "the Peanut . . . the little bastard . . . an ignorant and arbitrary stubborn man."[35] Underneath this feud was the very real issue of Stilwell's proposed reform program for the Chinese Army, which could, of course, have threatened Chiang's own power structure. Equally, Stilwell's fulminations were an expression of the General's awareness of the huge stakes at hand, the way the war was going to be won in the CBI theatre, the way of China's development after victory. Regrettably, this personal acrimony between the General and the Generalissimo obscured most of these issues.

Moreover, although the Cairo Declaration of December, 1943, stated that "all the territories that Japan has stolen from China such as Manchuria, Formosa and the Pescadores shall be returned," the outcome of the Cairo Conference has been described by Romanus and Sunderland as a "watershed." Until the summer of 1943 it had been assumed that China would be a main base in the offensive against Japan. After Cairo, with the successful amphibious "island-hopping" campaign in the Pacific, and the development of the B-29 long-range bomber, the strategic importance of the China theatre decreased as a direct attack against Japan across the Pacific was envisaged by the Washington planners.[36]

Relations between Washington and Chungking were therefore not easy during 1944 when the question of the gold shipments came to a head. Chiang's request for a billion-dollar loan after Cairo had lapsed. But throughout most of that year the Treasury and United States Army were engaged in hard, almost acrimonious, bargaining with the Chinese over the cost of American war expenditures in China.

Although the United States was prepared to pay for B-29 bases and other outlays, and in fact did pay altogether $392,000,000 for wartime *fapi* expenditures, the negotiations were bedeviled by the Chinese insistence on maintaining the C$20–$1 official exchange rate. The average free market rate in early 1944 was already about 200–1. Eventually the main issue was solved in November, 1944, when Morgenthau and Kung agreed on a lump sum, giving a rate of 74–1, but building the B-29 Chengtu bases further speeded the Chinese inflation, dislocating the economy of Szechwan.

These negotiations remind us of a remark in Tang Tsou's magisterial survey of Sino-American relations in the 1940's, in which he comments that, despite the bitterness of Stilwell's feud with Chiang, there was a grain of truth in the American's "realism," for "when there is a conflict of interests an essential objective of foreign policy must at some point be pursued by the use of power."[37]

Stilwell himself was of course the foremost proponent of the bargaining or *quid pro quo* policy. But while Roosevelt considered during 1943 that this was "exactly the wrong approach," because ineffectual, to deal with Chiang, pressure was put on the Chinese during 1944 over both the negotiations on war costs and Burma operations, including at one stage a threat to limit Lend-Lease. In a conference on American war expenditures in China with Morgenthau and White in January, 1944, General Somervell, head of the Army Service Forces, stated that the Army was prepared to stop building airports in China, and that Chiang could be broken by withdrawing American support from him and "buying" one of his competitors with $100,000,000.[38]

Others, outside the Treasury, for widely different reasons, therefore felt that there was room for toughness in dealing with the Generalissimo's own highly developed bargaining skills. On the other hand, the State Department, taking a rather different view of events in the Far East, felt a longer-term approach was indicated. In August, 1942, for example, Stanley Hornbeck, the State Department's political adviser on Far Eastern affairs, wrote that Chiang knew "that in the military councils in Washington and London the majority of the conferees are preoccupied primarily with considerations of occidental security and there still prevails the centuries-old concept of occidental superiority in practically all things relating to capacity and importance."

But as the Treasury and the War Department, perhaps inevitably, took the lead in dealing with Chungking, the State Department, Feis writes, "was crowded out, and it vaguely knew it."[39] Increasingly, as the end of the war approached, events in China, and American policies to deal with them, were approaching impasse. One of the few certainties in the situation was the continuing spiral of the great Chinese inflation. Between December, 1943, and December, 1944, the price index rose from 228 to 755. More and more in Washington, as in China, American officials began to doubt, with the accelerating Chinese inflation, with the new Allied Pacific strategy, and the eventual recall of Stilwell, whether the earlier American objective of making China a great power could be sustained.

In this climate of uncertainty, the 200 tons of bullion promised by Morgenthau to Chungking soon came to assume a new, almost symbolic, significance. As the operating Treasury official, White was custodian of this war chest.

Chinese anxieties were now increased, rather than assuaged, by the results of the Cairo Conference. Following their return to Cairo from their meeting with Stalin at Teheran, Roosevelt and Churchill canceled the proposed Allied amphibious operation in the Bay of Bengal ("Buccaneer"). The decision in effect downgraded the CBI theatre. It was followed by Sino-American friction over Chiang's request for a billion-dollar loan from the United States. The gold promised under the 1942 credit now became central to relations between the two countries.

On December 18, 1943, Morgenthau reviewed for Roosevelt the financial state of China. He considered a billion-dollar loan unnecessary and undesirable. Present Chinese assets in the United States could be better used for reconstruction by China. As far as an anti-inflation program in China was concerned, Morgenthau thought that the sale of dollar-backed securities had made no significant difference to inflation, as noted, and that the gold-sales program had not been sufficiently tried in China to warrant definite conclusions.

Morgenthau quoted Kung's letter of December 14 on the positive effects so far of the gold shipments, remarking to the President that he was in complete sympathy with "your position that no stone be left unturned to retard the rise in prices." As one measure, the Secretary recommended that all American expenditures in China be met by buying yuan on the open market by gold and dollars.

Secondly, Morgenthau recommended, "Accelerate the shipments of gold purchased by China to twice the amount we have previously planned to send. It should be possible to raise gold shipments from $6,000,000 a month to about $12,000,000. At the present price for gold in the open market this would be equal to the present 3.5 billion of yuan that is being issued."[40] This suggestion clearly indicated Morgenthau's wish, despite other issues, to help China with the problem of inflation, and send as much gold as could be used to absorb *fapi*.

On January 19, 1944, emphasizing the President's concern with the gold-sales program, Roosevelt spoke to Morgenthau on the telephone during a conference in the Secretary's office on American war costs in China. According to the minutes of the meeting taken by White, "The President said he remembered we were sending them about $12,000,000 of gold a month. White said it was less than that. The President said we should tell the Generalissimo in the cable that we would send them about $25 million of gold a month. . . ." (Shipments for the last two months of 1943 were about $10,000,000.)

The Treasury drafted a message for Chiang Kai-shek dated January 19 which included the statement that "the Air Transport Command has agreed to make facilities available to the Treasury for shipment of gold to China so that we may hope to be able to ship about $25,000,000 a month." The statement was omitted from the message as sent to Chungking, but at least it showed that White did not consider transportation difficulties a serious reason for not sending gold, as he was to tell Morgenthau in May, 1945.[41]

Within China the demand for gold continued to rise as the military situation deteriorated. During May, June and July, 1944, gold sales came to over $6,000,000, most of it sold in July. The program pulled in about 2.3 billion yuan in this month, as opposed to note issue of 6.3 billion. In the first half of 1944, only about $2,000,000 of gold had been sent from the United States to China, and only about half that had arrived before June 30. As there was still $6,000,000 of gold at hand in Chungking at the middle of the year, White could have argued that he was carrying out Morgenthau's earlier instructions of September, 1943, to send the metal "only as rapidly as it could be shipped and sold." But the total amount of gold delivered was rather less than the $25,000,000 monthly which Roosevelt had contemplated in January, 1944.

On July 12, as the shortage began to be felt, Chungking asked for immediate air shipments. According to Arthur Young, this was the moment when the operating officials of the Treasury began to go back on Morgenthau's promises and to depart from the letter of his instruction. No gold was sent until August 3 when $3,000,000 was sent by sea, not reaching Chungking until September 23. Three more consignments, altogether over $4,000,000, were sent by air in August and September, as Chinese reserves dwindled. The last of the air shipments over the Hump arrived on October 3: "Then China was out of gold."[42]

Although the news from the other war fronts in 1944 was good, this was a bad period for the Nationalist regime. Adler's biting reports to White from Chungking during this period, an intriguing mixture of gossip and political analysis, and those of Irving Friedman, of the Division of Monetary Research, who replaced Adler for a time in 1944, emphasized without too much diplomatic tautology the apparently bottomless venality, inefficiency and confusion of the Kuomintang as it lurched from crisis to crisis. Other selected reports by American diplomatic and military observers forwarded to White by Adler contrasted this epic disintegration with the amiable, forward-looking atmosphere in Yenan.[43]

However the most immediate threat to the Generalissimo's power at this time came from the last major offensive launched by Imperial Japan in China, Operation "Ichigo." This aimed at clearing a through rail link from Peking to Canton, eliminating Chennault's air bases in East China, and generally weakening the Nationalist regime. Following a major attack south across the Yangtse in May, the Japanese relentlessly reinforced success and in November Kweilin, in Kwangsi province, with its important American air bases, fell to the attackers.

The crisis meant that Stilwell, the leading advocate of the *quid pro quo* policy of pressure on Chiang, was recalled in October after a final showdown with the Generalissimo. But, according to the China White Paper of 1949 "there was little reason to believe that the Japanese if they so elected would not have the capability of attacking Chungking and the vitally important American base at Kunming." In Tang Tsou's words, the Japanese "appeared to threaten the very existence of the Nationalist Government. This was the gravest crisis of the seven years of the Sino-Japanese war."[44]

Fear of mass evacuation of Chinese cities before the advancing Japanese now forced up the price of gold in China. Demand soared. On October 2 White and Adler met with three Chinese representatives in White's office in the Treasury in Washington to discuss renewed Chinese requests for gold.[45]

The Chinese produced a telegram from Chungking which stated that as the initial $20,000,000 of gold from the credit was exhausted, "and as sales still extremely heavy and recent arrivals far from being adequate to meet outstanding contracts, please request U.S. Treasury immediately transfer $20,000,000 or more if possible out of $200,000,000 and ship by plane."

White now raised the merits of sending $200,000,000 of gold in the existing situation. He pointed out that the gold would be of enormous use to China for postwar reconstruction as well as for reorganization of the currency. Gold sold in China would have little anti-inflationary effect as the economic situation was due to "the acute scarcity of goods." White also considered that much of the gold would disappear into hoards.

The Chinese then said that the gold sales had achieved some beneficial effect and that to stop selling gold "would send prices skyrocketing."

White then took up the question of the discrepancy between the official and the free-market price of gold. With a spread amounting sometimes to C$5–6,000, someone was making a profit, and it was not the government; and the Secretary "had shown some interest in this question."

T. L. Soong, the Foreign Minister's brother, for the Chinese, expressed surprise that the spread had been so high and went on to argue that the main reason for the difference between the price sold by the Central Bank and the free-market rate was "the non-availability of supplies in Chungking." If the gold were available, the Chinese claimed, the discrepancy could be obliterated, as spot gold controlled the market.

White, according to the minutes of the meeting, "pointed out that it was cheaper for the Central Government to print *fapi* than to absorb *fapi* in exchange for gold at a time when the dent that was being made by the sale of gold was not significantly large." In July, the Chinese said, two billion yuan had been absorbed by gold sales, Adler adding that the note issue was nine billion.

The Chinese considered that United States Army expenditures had been the "major factor" in the deterioration and alluded to the good relations between the Chinese and the United States Treasury. White said that there was no question of that; but for these good relations, the Treasury would not be interested in how China used the gold. White was anxious, he said, to see that China got the maximum advantage from the gold.

At the end of the meeting, Hsi Te-mou of the Central Bank stated that Kung was anxious to get more gold from the credit. The Chinese Finance Minister was, in fact, asking for $150,000,000 of gold. The Chinese stressed that cessation of gold sales "would have very serious effects at this time." In reply to a question by Adler, the Chinese admitted that it appeared to have been a mistake to have lowered the official price of gold in July. White then concluded the meeting by saying that he would "take up the matter with the Secretary and get in touch with the Chinese again."

White's arguments on this occasion hardly betray much enthusiasm for accelerating gold shipments, but the Chinese evidently believed that gold should be sold at a time of wartime crisis rather than kept for after the fighting. Gold had been fetching good prices in China, and the dollar equivalent of the official price of gold during the first nine months of 1944 was $89–100 per ounce. Even though the dollar price declined after this time because gold was sold mostly for future delivery, the Chinese apparently relying on the United States Treasury, the average rates for the next nine months to mid-1945 ranged between $37–51 per ounce on the official market and $66–87 on the free market. From the Chinese view, gold sales would also divert *fapi* from commodity speculation. These measures were of course, however, palliatives.

Given this high price of gold, and bearing in mind, again with hindsight, that China's inflation was due to note issue rather than to "the acute scarcity of goods," it still seems curious for White to have argued that it was cheaper to print *fapi* than to absorb it, at this time, by selling gold. The Chinese stated in this conference that gold had absorbed C$2 billion in July, when note issue, according to Young, was C$6.3 billion rather than the $9 billion mentioned by Solomon Adler.

For the four quarters July, 1944–June, 1945, gold sales as a percentage of note issue were 27, 29, 52 and 28 respectively. As the note issue itself was about 80 percent of the cash deficit in Nationalist China in 1944–45, the overall proportion covered by gold sales was less than these figures. But the Chinese thought a beginning had been made—quite apart, of course, from the general question of whether anything could have been done to arrest the Chinese inflation at this late stage. Moreover, whereas a short ton of gold, worth about a million American dollars, could raise, at the rate of C$20,000 an ounce, about $560,000,000 for the Chinese Treasury in Chungking, a ton of C$20 notes flown over the Hump was worth only C$20,000,000 in China.[46]

One of White's chief points in the October conference with the Chinese was the implications of the gap between the official and free-market price of gold. Here the Chinese were insistent that the very shortage of gold increased the spread between the two prices. They maintained, as did Arthur Young, in his later memoirs of the period, that it was difficult for them to raise the official price, with its consequent negative effect on confidence, in such an inflationary situation without having more spot gold at hand to control the market. Sales in gold futures, also necessary, according to the Chinese, to help to retain confidence at a time of crisis and acute gold shortage, also added to the demand for the metal from the United States.

With this background the results of the October conference between White and the Chinese financial representatives were hardly propitious from Chungking's viewpoint.

At this stage, according to Morgenthau's biographer, the Secretary "had little interest in the transaction. He had delegated responsibility for assessing the Chinese request to White because the matter seemed relatively trivial." On October 5 White told Morgenthau that he had "stalled" on gold shipments to China during the summer because of the discrepancy between the official price of gold and the price at which the banks actually sold gold. White suspected that someone was making a profit, probably T. L. Soong, T. V. Soong's brother, whose bank dealt with American gold.[47]

White, however, recommended to Morgenthau that he should tell Kung, who had asked for $20,000,000 of gold during the closing stages of the negotiations on American war costs in China, that he was going to get his amount. Accordingly, this token sum of $20,000,000, the first installment of the $200,000,000 promised in July, 1943, was transferred to the Chinese account on October 13.[48] But gold under earmark in New York did not mean gold in Chungking. In early November, $3,000,000 was sent by sea to China, and a similar amount followed in a month's time, delivered the same way. No more gold was then sent until April, 1945, when $1,200,000 went by sea.

In China, prices and with them the cost of gold continued to rise during the winter of 1944–45. Between the third and the fourth quarter of 1944, the average value of the yuan broke from 209 to 441 per American dollar, and the spread between the official and the free price of gold widened from over 1,500 to 6,000 yuan. When the official price of gold, set in November, 1944, was raised, probably too sharply, from C$24,000 per ounce to C$35,000 in March, 1945, the free-market rate immediately jumped to $60,000 and prices were out of line again. (See Appendix B.)

Clearly, the fiasco of the dollar-issue securities in China, the rumors of inside speculation, and the bargaining over the American war costs in China influenced the Treasury's attitude toward the Chungking regime in the later war years. There was, too, the general disenchantment with the Nationalists, shared with other departments, after earlier overenthusiasm for China's great-power claims. Yet Stimson was surely right in his appreciation that "this part of the world was of enormous importance."

With so many problems in dispute between Chungking and Washington, and with the Chinese zealous of defending their sovereignty, the controversial issue of the gold transfers from the 1942 loan, although it was made without any "strings," seems to have been seen by White and his associates as a way of bargaining with the Chinese. The primary responsibility for delaying the gold shipments was White's, as became clear in the rather surprising denouement of the entire episode in May, 1945. Then Morgenthau suddenly resolved the confusion that had arisen with the Chinese over the Treasury's commitments and its actions over the gold.

12

AN OFFENSIVE WEAPON OF WAR

The wide geographic scope of military operations in this war and the great development of techniques of economic warfare have made money an important offensive and defensive weapon of war.

—ANNUAL REPORT OF THE SECRETARY OF THE TREASURY, 1944–45

YET FOR all White's involvement in the planning for the postwar multilateral trading regime, and his growing role in the attempts to solve the Chinese puzzle, military victory over the Axis in Europe was, after all, the chief priority of the Anglo-American war effort.

Only with the destruction of the Nazi regime could the conditions for the lasting peace envisaged by the postwar planners be created in the first place. As we have seen, the power of decision in Anglo-American grand strategy rested primarily with Roosevelt, Churchill and their Combined Chiefs of Staff. Formally, therefore, the Treasury role in the occupied and liberated areas of North Africa and Western Europe was inevitably subordinated to military factors. In addition, the State Department technically possessed authority over political and economic policy in the liberated (not occupied) areas.

However, in practice, the Treasury had to be represented in the discussions which led to the arrangements for the creation of military currency in the war zones. The department was responsible for fixing exchange rates, and for assistance on general fiscal matters. As these responsibilities were an aspect of the department's foreign relations, White was active from an early stage of the Allied counteroffensive against the Axis, in consultation with the State and War departments, together with the British. He took part in the financial planning for the Allied invasion of French North Africa in the autumn of 1942, and was also closely involved in the setting of the military exchange rate for occupied Italy and Germany.

Moreover, in the case of the delivery by the American government to the Russians of the duplicate printing places of the Allied Military marks for occupied Germany, White played an important and perhaps central role.

That these matters had more than a purely military significance was recognized at the time. During the war, occupation currency, circulating with indigenous currency, was used by the major powers more than ever before. As Vladimir Petrov has noted in his recent study of Allied military currency in the Second World War, in addition to the traditional functions of paying troops and compensating owners of requisitioned property, occupation currency served as "a major means of manipulating the economies of occupied territories."[1]

Frequently, of course, war-torn economies refused to act as predicted, and there was an inevitable degree of shortsightedness on the part of the occupiers. There was also perhaps a more fundamental contradiction between the partially punitive monetary objectives of a military occupation and the conditions of an enduring settlement which the war was supposed to bring. But, as in the case of the American JCS 1067, the directive for the American zone of Germany, which indicated that no steps were to be taken to maintain the existing economic structure, the financial regime imposed by the victors was less a military expedient than an arm of wider policy.

As one of Morgenthau's wartime reports stated,

> The wide geographic scope of military operations in this war and the great development of techniques of economic warfare have made money an important offensive and defensive weapon of war. Providing this weapon in its most efficient form has required careful and detailed planning far in advance of military operations. Just as we need many varieties of military weapons, of ships and planes, so we have found that the effective conduct of war on the financial side required a variety of currency measures designed to meet varied and changeable situations. . . .[2]

In July, 1942, Roosevelt and Churchill reached agreement on their plans for an Allied landing later that year in French North Africa. The "Torch" operation would be under the command of Major General Dwight D. Eisenhower, then the newly appointed American commander in the European theatre.

During the initial planning phase of "Torch" in July, 1942, White suggested that the dollar be used by American troops as a military currency because of its power in commanding goods and services. At the same time, for security and administrative reasons, White thought these dollars should be denoted with a special overmark to distinguish them from domestic American currency. White went on to propose that these dollar bills to be used during "Torch" as an initial "spearhead" currency should bear a distinct yellow seal. The British, meanwhile, proposed to use as a spearhead currency British Military Authority (BMA) pound notes.

The War and State departments agreed with White's proposal for yellow-seal dollars as a North American "spearhead" currency. But some of White's suggestions at this time looked forward to later (and wider) military operations. For the forthcoming occupation of friendly countries, White suggested that a military currency similar to indigenous tender should be used as soon as territory was won. For the Axis countries, White considered that the dollar be used pending a permanent settlement with the Allies.[3]

As the planning for "Torch" progressed, with its new deadline of November 8, 1942, the next problem which concerned White was the setting of a cross-rate between the occupation dollar and the pound on the one hand, and the North African franc on the other. As Churchill, unlike Roosevelt, tended to support General de Gaulle, the British suggested that the North African exchange rate should be related to that found in Gaullist French Colonial Africa south of the Sahara, and proposed a figure of 43 francs to the dollar, 172 to the pound. This figure probably overvalued the franc, but the British considered it would have a good effect, political and otherwise, in North Africa.

However, in Washington, the Treasury thought that such a rate would quickly depreciate and suggested what was considered a more realistic figure of 75 francs to the dollar, 300 to the pound. Hull and Stimson supported Morgenthau, who, at this juncture, a few weeks before the "Torch" landings, left Washington for talks in London. But White was to accompany the Secretary and would discuss the financial arrangements for "Torch" with the British.

White, with Morgenthau, arrived at Prestwick, Scotland, from the United States on October 15, and were received with some ceremony on their progress through Britain at war.

From Prestwick the two men were flown to London in the personal DC-3 of Major General Carl Spaatz, the United States Eighth Air Force commander. They were met at Northolt by Ambassador Winant and Brigadier General Bedell Smith, Eisenhower's Chief of Staff. In Claridges, where Morgenthau and his party were based, Sir Kingsley Wood, the British Chancellor, called on the Secretary before a Savoy dinner with British Cabinet members.

During the next ten days, this tempo was maintained. White, as we have noted, met with Keynes, Winant and F. F. Penrose to discuss, "off the record," the Stabilization Fund. Another day saw White in an extended session with the "Torch" planners at Norfolk House in St. James's Square. Morgenthau lunched with Winston Churchill at 10 Downing Street, and dined with the King and Queen at the Palace. Later White and Morgenthau visited operational airfields of the Eighth Air Force and RAF Bomber Command, and inspected British war factories in the industrial Midlands. On the evening of October 23, which saw the launching of Montgomery's offensive westward at Alamein, the two men spent the night with the Royal Navy Commander in Chief, Portsmouth.

The mission ended on October 27, after White and Morgenthau had lunched at the Bank of England with the Governor, Montagu Norman. Later that day, the two men left Paddington for home via the Atlantic Clipper: "Despite certain mishaps the Secretary, Dr. White and General Dalquist left in a special coach on the Bristol train at approximately 2350 hours."[4]

Eventually, after White's discussions on the matter with the British in London, and further, separate, discussion on the Roosevelt-Churchill level, the North African exchange rate in the wake of "Torch," which went ahead as planned, was agreed at 75 francs to the dollar, 300 to the pound. But the French authorities in North Africa continued to protest that this rate was unfavorable. Eventually, after the Casablanca Conference between the President and the Prime Minister in January, 1943, the cross-rate was changed to 50 francs to the dollar, 200 to the pound; technical factors were less important than considerations of politics and prestige.

However, in the labyrinth of French North African politics, with Washington and London sometimes following different policies toward the rivalry between Generals de Gaulle and Giraud, friction continued. Following the creation of the new French Committee of National Liberation (CLN) in June, 1943, further attempts were made to rationalize financial matters in North Africa.

Under reciprocal-aid agreements, in return for Lend-Lease aid to the French Army, the CLN was to open a special local currency account for Allied military expenditure, thus assuming part of the cost of the occupation. But the cost of "troop pay" was to be reimbursed by the Allies. Later, after disagreement and compromise between London and Washington, which had hoped in vain to issue a new "Allied Military" currency in North Africa, American-printed notes were circulated under CLN supervision, and the old North African tender withdrawn. But only after tedious and time-consuming negotiations were the North African French authorities—in the eyes of the Anglo-Americans—able to help the war effort.[5] For the next major military operation in the great crusade, the invasion of Italy, different arrangements were indicated.

At the Casablanca Conference of January, 1943, code-named "Symbol," Roosevelt, Churchill and their Combined Chiefs of Staff decided to invade Sicily following the capture of Tunis. The Allied air offensive against Germany and Italy was to be stepped up. There was the ultimate objective of forcing Italy out of the war. As these military decisions were accompanied by the Anglo-American demand of "unconditional surrender" from the Axis, the outlook for Italy was not reassuring.

The frustrations of the Allies in French North Africa had shown that an alternative was needed to temporary invasion currency as a means of attempting to rationalize the costs of occupation. Yellow-seal dollars, in particular, made it difficult for the local authorities to assume part-cost of the occupation, and in any case weakened the local currency. As the planning for the invasion of Italy was initiated, White now pressed for the issue of a single Allied Military (AM) currency in Italy, which could be used as a legal supplemental tender alongside the lira. The British, too, were in favor of a common occupation currency for Italy.

White's position in these and future negotiations on AM currency was strengthened at this time in early 1943 when Morgenthau granted him formal jurisdiction over Treasury matters in foreign areas occupied by the American armed forces. In his letter to White on February 25, 1943, Morgenthau wrote:

Effective this date I would like you to take supervision over and assume full responsibility for Treasury's participation in all economic and financial matters (except matters pertaining to depositary facilities, transfers of funds and war expenditures) in connection with the operations of the Army and Navy and the civilian affairs in the foreign areas in which our armed forces are operating or are likely to operate. This will of course include general liaison with the State Department, Army and Navy and other departments or agencies and representatives of foreign governments on these matters.

Previously, these duties had been the responsibility of the Treasury Under Secretary, Daniel Bell, but, as he told Morgenthau and White on February 22, there was "a limit" to the work he could undertake.[6]

With this new authority in addition to his earlier jurisdiction over the Treasury's foreign relations, White now took part as Treasury representative in the preparatory work for the invasion of Italy and Sicily being conducted by the *ad hoc* Committee on Monetary and Fiscal Planning. This was an Anglo-American planning group which met in Washington.

As Italy was an enemy power, the Allies could make arrangements without worrying about indigenous factions or whether they were to treat the country as occupied or liberated territory. In the deliberations of the *ad hoc* committee White took a hard line toward Italy for, as Paul Y. Hammond has remarked, "the Treasury approached the fiscal and monetary problems of the Italian 'liberation' with a far greater emphasis on punitive objectives than did the State or War Department officials."[7]

However, as a result of events in French North Africa, White's arguments for the issue of AM lire as a common supplemental currency won support despite the objection that a deluge of military currency would only further damage the Italian economy, thus increasing Allied liabilities. Unlike the widely circulating yellow-seal dollars and BMA pounds, which were to be used now only as a spearhead currency in the invasion of Sicily, the proposed AM lire could be restricted to Italy.

Moreover, as all the Allied forces in Italy, besides the British and Americans, could use AM lire, the notes could be debited immediately to Italian account, so making the vanquished responsible for any necessary war costs in one bookkeeping operation. Hence, AM lire would be issued at par with the existing Italian lire, and by the authority of Allied Military Government.[8] The Combined Chiefs of Staff directive largely accepted these Treasury arguments that the AM lire was an Italian currency for Italian account.

Just as important as the innovation of the AM lire was the dollar-pound-lira exchange rate. In the *ad hoc* committee, White opposed the 50–1 cross-rate between the lira and the dollar proposed by the State Department, and supported by some British members. This rate for the lira was too high, White considered, too favorable to the Italian fascists, and would cost the Army twice as much as the 100–1 figure which White suggested. It was better to begin the occupation with a 100–1 rate and then to increase it, if necessary, rather than the converse. The *ad hoc* committee eventually agreed on an AM-lira cross-rate of 100 to the dollar, 400 to the pound, and the State Department was also persuaded. The rate almost certainly overvalued the dollar (and the pound), however understandable the passions of the time and the wish also of the military to give Allied soldiers an advantage.

Fascism, war and invasion all meant that inflation was inevitable in Italy once the Allies landed in Sicily in July, 1943, and on the mainland two months later. Then came the proliferating black market, belated application of controls, and heavy troop-spending at the overvalued rate of exchange, together producing a chaotic situation. The Italian price index rose from 600 at the time of the Sicilian invasion (100=1938) to 3,500 in April, 1944; a United States Foreign Economic Administration report by Adlai Stevenson at the end of 1943 considered that "to the country at large, the rate of 100 lire to the dollar came as a surprise and a shock . . . and reduced the lira to about a quarter of its assumed value."[9]

Years later, a British official historian of the Italian occupation wrote that "there can be no doubt that on the basis of purchasing power the lira at the moment of occupation was worth a good deal more than one cent . . . the historian finds it hard to resist the conclusion, official arguments notwithstanding, that the degree of inflation that actually occurred might have been reduced by an initial exchange rate giving greater value to the lira." Perhaps this episode shows, as Paul Y. Hammond has suggested, that in the field of applying economic techniques White's talents were less obvious than the imagination which he had used in the initiation of economic objectives: "Apparently a result of White's approach to economics was a tendency to apply the meat cleaver rather than the scalpel; this is to say, to place little faith in economic controls, but rely instead on a favorable arrangement of economic power. In financial planning for Italy he had fought for what many people considered an unduly hard economic policy as exemplified in a low rate for the lira, a policy many considered unwise."[10]

Personal inclination, too, may have been also a factor in this approach, and this would soon become apparent in the Treasury's planning for the occupation policy for conquered Germany.

Eventually, of course, the victors themselves had to bear much of the cost of the political and economic dislocation in Italy following the armistice in September, 1943. Later, in 1944, partly for American domestic political reasons, the stern Allied attitude toward the Italian "co-belligerent" regime, functioning under the Allied Control Commission, began to change, and slowly aid began to reach the country. But economic conditions remained bad. Whatever gains had been hoped for by the introduction of the AM lire were probably more than canceled out by the inflation of the occupation, exacerbated by the high troop-spending.

In northwest Europe another set of circumstances obtained. Such Allied countries as Belgium, Holland and Norway, jealous of their sovereignty, did not want Allied military currency with their liberation. During early 1944, therefore, the United States and Britain reached agreement that, following the liberation, specially printed national currency would become available in these countries.

In France, on the other hand, Roosevelt was insistent that AM francs, similar to the AM lire, would be used as a supplemental currency when Eisenhower's troops landed in Normandy in June, 1944. But, from the Free French viewpoint, it was important that Morgenthau, sympathetic to the Gaullists, had agreed to the CLN suggestion for a 50–1 franc-dollar rate during conversations with Pierre Mendès-France in Washington. This, of course, was a rate similar to that set in French North Africa.[11] Technically, at least, this figure tended to overvalue the franc rather than the dollar, but in any case the overriding problems were rather those of French prestige and the political relationships among Roosevelt, Churchill and de Gaulle. For the General it was surely all-important that his "Anglo-Saxon" adversaries had recognized his provisional government by the autumn of 1944.

Clearly some progress had been made in the planning for military currency between the Italian armistice and the Anglo-American invasion of Normandy in June, 1944. But the outstanding problem at the beginning of 1944 was that of Germany, where there would be no indigenous regime or even a "co-belligerent" administration on the Italian model following defeat. Here direct military government was envisaged and Anglo-American arrangements for the production of German currency would have to be coordinated with the Russians. In the spring of 1944 White took an important part in the negotiations which led to the eventual production in both the United States and Russia of the AM marks for the conquered Reich.

Acting with the knowledge and approval of the British Embassy in Washington, White had first discussed the matter of a common German occupation-currency with Soviet representatives late in 1943. The matter was referred to Moscow. Then, in early 1944, Eisenhower's Supreme Headquarters Allied Expeditionary Forces (SHAEF) in London, considering the introduction of AM lire a success, asked for a supply of AM marks for Germany. It was agreed between the two Western allies that the notes should be printed in the United States. The Treasury's Bureau of Engraving and Printing produced designs and plates, and in view of the urgency, arranged for the AM marks to be printed, using an offset process, by the Forbes Company in Boston, an old, established company of banknote printers.

On January 29, 1944, the American ambassador in Moscow, W. Averell Harriman, told Hull that the British Government "feels it most desirable that all occupation forces use the same currency as far as possible. . . . Great importance is attached by the British Government to the Russian Government's participation in this arrangement." The Soviet attitude was not clear, and on February 8 Cordell Hull cabled to Harriman that the printing of the AM marks would have to start by February 14: "We are very desirous of ascertaining whether the Soviet expects us to use this kind of currency and if not, what type of currency they contemplated using?"[12]

Pending the Russian clarification, however, on February 9 Harry Dexter White sent photostat copies of the designs of the AM marks to Andrei Gromyko, then the Soviet ambassador in Washington. (The British were also shown the designs and approved them.) White asked Gromyko if he could send the details to Moscow so that the Soviet Government could be "informed as to our plans here." White added that present plans called for production of notes to the value of 10 billion marks. As joint issue of the AM marks was hoped for, rather than joint printing, this seemed a sensible procedure on White's part.[13]

On February 15 developments took a new turn. Harriman reported to Hull that Molotov, the Soviet Foreign Minister, had written to him that the Soviet Government was ready to cooperate with the Americans and the British in issuing occupation currency for Germany. The Russians approved the designs with the words "Allied Military Authorities." But Molotov had also written that some of the currency should be printed in the Soviet Union "in order that a constant supply would be guaranteed to the Red Army." For this purpose, Moscow would have to be provided with models of paper and colors, a list of serial numbers, and plates of all the denominations.[14]

The Soviet request was apparently unexpected by the Treasury. The Director of Engraving and Printing, Alvin W. Hall, considered that duplicate printing would create serious complications. As it was against the traditional security rules which safeguarded the printing of banknotes, the contractor would not agree to such duplication, and it was doubtful if he could be forced to do so. Removal of such precautions might result in national or international scandal, and moreover the production of the notes, to guard against forgery, had to proceed in controlled conditions, hard to reproduce: "To remove from the country . . . complete designs in the form of plates . . . would be extremely unwise."[15]

Hall's objections were submitted in writing to Under Secretary Daniel Bell, who agreed with him. The corollary of these objections was, of course, that either the three powers agreed to use the projected AM marks or that the Russians print their own military currency of their own designs on their own plates.

In a meeting in Bell's office on March 7, White, within whose jurisdiction the matter came, was troubled by Hall's approach, thinking a refusal could be construed by the Russians as an expression of lack of confidence. Bell defended Hall, however, saying that the Treasury had never made plates available to anyone. Delivery of duplicate plates to the Russians might mean that the American contractor would refuse, on security grounds, to print AM marks. Bell also thought that enough marks could be delivered to the Russians, without the need to send plates.

According to the report of the meeting, by W. H. Taylor of the Division of Monetary Research, White was loath to turn down the Soviet request without review. It was Allied currency that was being printed, and Russia must be trusted "to the same degree and the same extent as the other allies." White wondered if it might be possible to discuss the matter with Gromyko, while reviewing it with Secretary Morgenthau. If it was decided not to send the plates to Russia, the matter should be cleared with the State and War departments to prevent the Treasury later being charged with not considering political implications, and rejecting the Russian request to send the plates "on a narrow accountancy basis."[16]

But resistance within the Treasury to the Russian request for the duplicate plates was firm. On March 8, Morgenthau, Bell and White met to discuss the issue. A cable to the Russians turning down their request, drafted by Bell, was not sent, as Morgenthau decided instead to discuss the matter personally with Ambassador Gromyko. Doubtless it was hoped that the Secretary could persuade the Russians in this way to withdraw the request for the plates.

White's suggestion on March 7 that any decision not to send the AM duplicate plates to Russia should be reviewed came at a time when Western hopes of Big Three understanding, both during the war and after, had never been higher.

A few months before, in October, 1943, the Moscow Declaration by the four powers, including China, looked forward to a new international organization to maintain international peace and security. On his return home from the Foreign Ministers' Conference in Moscow, Hull told a joint session of Congress, where there was now an overwhelming majority in favor of American participation in a new world organization, that as the provisions of the Moscow Declaration were carried out, "there will no longer be any need for spheres of influence, for alliances, for balance of power, or any other of the special arrangements through which in the unhappy past, the nations strove to maintain their security or promote their interests."[17]

Following the Teheran Conference of November, 1943, between Roosevelt, Churchill and Stalin, the President, according to Robert Sherwood, believed that when Russia could be convinced that "her legitimate claims and requirements—such as the right of access to warm water ports—were to be given full recognition she would be tractable and cooperative in maintaining the peace of the postwar world."[18] Churchill remarks that at the end of that conference, "I felt that there was a greater sense of solidarity and good comradeship than we had ever reached before in the grand alliance."[19]

These hopes were widely shared in the United States and Great Britain, not only on the left, but on the right where the discipline, courage and tenacious nationalism of wartime Russia, equated with the system, found their admirers. As perspicacious and detached a commentator as Walter Lippmann considered that Wendell Wilkie's *One World* and Joseph E. Davies's *Mission to Moscow* were the two finest analyses of the Soviet Union in print.[20]

Whatever the Western hopes for Soviet intervention in the Pacific war, which was promised by Stalin at Teheran, there was a reinforced conviction in Washington and London after that conference that Soviet cooperation was necessary for a lasting peace and that American, Russian and British interests could be reconciled. This, then, would be the political underpinning of the trading structure soon to be formally agreed at Bretton Woods.

As far as the central problem of the peace was concerned, the three leaders at Teheran had talked sternly in terms of dismembering or partitioning Germany. Even Churchill, with his reservations about Soviet policy, and perhaps less detached in considering the future of Western Europe than the President, tells us that he stated that the Allies would assure a fifty-year peace by preventing German rearmament, by the supervision of factories, "and by territorial changes of a far-reaching kind."[21] During the early months of 1944, moreover, the tripartite European Advisory Commission, meeting in London, was slowly formulating plans for ruling occupied Germany through separate zones, rather than joint administration. In view of these Allied aspirations at the time, there was no urgency on specific economic grounds for a common occupation-currency. Rather, a common military currency in the prostrate Reich was seen as a symbol of the desired harmony.

However, bearing in mind the general Western desire to harmonize relations with Russia, and to act together in administering postwar Germany, the suggestion that duplicate plates be delivered still pointed to an important departure from the Italian experience of military government. In this case, control of the printing of the AM lire remained with the United States, and the notes were issued on demand to the British and the other Allies with troops in Italy. There was a uniform exchange rate, and, whatever the political differences on Italy between London and Washington, the occupation operated under the Allied Control Council which was responsible to the Supreme Allied Commander, Mediterranean. Agreed directives on financial and other matters thus meant there was joint administration of occupied Italy.

But, whatever the high hopes for the Rooseveltian "Grand Design" on inter-allied unity after Teheran, there was no agreed Allied policy over Germany, even between the United States and Great Britain. There was a feeling on some levels in Washington, in any case, that the exclusive allied relationship between Britain and America would become less necessary as Soviet-American objectives might be less in conflict than Anglo-

Soviet ones. And both Roosevelt and, to a lesser degree, Churchill wished to avoid firm commitments on major issues at this stage of the war, so preserving both freedom of action and the wartime alliance itself.

Thus White's invocation of the spirit of Allied unity over the delivery of the plates had to be balanced with the consideration that with delivery the United States would lose control of the printing as well as the issue of the AM marks without any concrete joint arrangements having been made for the occupation of Germany. Both the United States and Great Britain, moreover, would be responsible for any joint occupation arrangements which would later be agreed by the political leaders. The duplicate plates were, therefore, in effect a blank check drawn on the Bank of Inter-Allied Unity.

For their part, it has been suggested, the Russians were aware of the economic advantages of a common occupation-currency for Germany, "provided of course that the Soviet Government could produce it without any control from the West."[22] Doubtless the Russians would have considered that the means to print their own AM marks, virtually a form of reparations, was only their due after their wartime losses and sacrifices.

On the evening of March 18 Morgenthau and White met with Gromyko at the Secretary's home. According to White's record of the meeting, Gromyko said that he had explained to his government the difficulties involved in delivering duplicate plates, but that Moscow still wanted them. Morgenthau said he was sorry that the Soviet government still wanted the plates after his explanation, and he had not expected that they would. The Forbes Company was insistent that they could not go on with the contract if duplicate plates were given out. Morgenthau stressed that the United States was prepared to give the Soviet government any amount of the AM currency it wanted. But if they were given plates, the printing would be delayed beyond the time schedule given by the Army.

The Secretary went on to suggest that Gromyko send representatives to the Forbes plant to see the magnitude of the task involved, but Gromyko repeated that he doubted very much if such a visit would make any difference at all to the request of his government. The meeting ended with Morgenthau's promise to find out the time needed by the Treasury to print currency on its own, and also to see how long it would take the Russians to begin production if duplicate plates were sent them. Gromyko would be told the results of this review within two days.[23]

The issue by now was even clearer, and in the Treasury Bell and Hall stuck to their guns, with Morgenthau still undecided.

On March 21, Alvin Hall drafted a memorandum for Morgenthau

setting out again his objections to giving the Russians the duplicate plates. Hall stated that the Forbes Company held that the Russians could not produce exact duplicates of the notes even if they had the plates. Forgery would be easy. If the Russians obtained the plates, moreover, there would be a delay of about six weeks before production could begin. This period was in addition to two weeks for the manufacture and shipment of the duplicate plates.

At the same time, if the Forbes Company canceled its contract, there would be a six-to-eight-month delay before the Treasury could fulfill the SHAEF order. However, the production schedule of the Forbes Company meant that the Russians could obtain unlimited amounts of these AM marks much sooner than if the notes were to be produced in the Soviet Union. If, Hall suggested, the Russians wanted to print their own notes, they could do so from their own designs. The Treasury would be glad to help the Soviet government and could engrave plates from which the printing could be done in Russia. Hall considered that the production of a separate AM currency by the Russians need not raise "any economic or financial difficulties." Concluding, paradoxically, with the essence of White's argument, he added, "However, it may be politically undesirable at this time to give the appearance of lack of financial uniformity among the three powers."[24]

After reading Hall's arguments the next day, Morgenthau desisted from making any decision. But the Secretary sent a letter to Admiral William Leahy, the President's Chief of Staff, which in effect asked the Combined Chiefs of Staff to make the decision. Morgenthau outlined the Russian request, pointing out the delay in printing the AM marks that would occur if duplicate plates were given to the Russians, and that Eisenhower would not be able to obtain the delivery of half the total order of 10 billion AM marks that he had requested by mid-April. "It would therefore be appreciated," Morgenthau wrote, "if you would place this matter before the Combined Chiefs of Staff and advise me promptly whether in their opinion the military situation would afford such delay as would be involved in the event that duplicate plates were made available to the government of the U.S.S.R."[25]

Hall's memorandum was sent with this letter to Leahy, and at the same time copies of both were sent to Cordell Hull, who then cabled Harriman in Moscow stating that "it is not expected that the Combined Chiefs of Staff will favor delivery of plates to the Russians."[26]

Before writing to Leahy on March 22, Morgenthau had evidently decided to make one further attempt to convince Gromyko. On March 21 White was instructed to see the Russian ambassador and to read to him Hall's memorandum with its objections to sending the duplicated plates.

That evening, White called at the Soviet Embassy, and told the ambassador that Morgenthau was sending a letter to the Combined Chiefs of Staff, together with the Hall memorandum. Gromyko was not taken with the arguments therein and according to White's memorandum of the meeting for the Treasury files, the ambassador

> asked a number of questions with respect to the details and I tried to expand on the reason why it would require six to eight months to produce marks in the Bureau of Engraving and why it might be unwise to have the Army take over the Forbes plant under the War Powers Act and attempt to operate it. He kept coming back with a question which he asked a number of times, namely, why the Forbes Company should object to giving a duplicate set of plates to his Government. He said that after all the Soviet Government was not a private corporation or an irresponsible government. . . . He remained unimpressed.
>
> . . . He wanted to know whether our Government was ready to suggest to his Government that it could print its own designed mark currency. I told him such was not necessarily the view of our Government; but was merely an expression of the possibility of the memorandum and that it would have to be cleared through other departments and doubtless with the British before it could be regarded as an official specific proposal. He seemed interested in the possibility of printing their own currency but he was clearly disappointed and skeptical as to the reasoning contained in the memorandum.[27]

For over two weeks following Gromyko's hint that the Russians might "go it alone" in printing their own occupation currency in Germany, there was no word from Moscow. Then, on April 8, Harriman reported to the State Department that Molotov was adamant in his request for the duplicate plates. In a note received the same day, the Soviet Foreign Minister had rejected the Treasury arguments against transferring the plates: "The Soviet Government cannot consider as sound the objections set forth. . . . The Soviet Government in this connection has taken into reconsideration the point of view of Soviet specialists who believe that it would be a disadvantage for the common Allied cause if such military marks were not printed in the Soviet Union. . . . In the event the reply is in the negative, I must point out that the Soviet Government will be forced to proceed with independent preparation of military marks for Germany of its own pattern. . . ."[28]

The final decision would now have to be made, and meanwhile, in the

Treasury, White's arguments were apparently having some effect on his colleagues. White held that, as the United States had stated that the Russians could have any amount of American-printed AM marks, it would make little difference if the Russians were to print their own. In addition, White argued, if the Russians were to print their own currency in Germany, it would have to be recognized by the United States, and "in any case, the United States had not been doing enough for the Soviet Union all along and that if the Soviets profited as a result of this transaction we should be happy to give them this token of our appreciation of their efforts."[29]

It also seems possible that in White's thinking at this time delivery of the plates to the Russians may have been linked with wider proposals of his for aid to the Soviets. In response to a request from Morgenthau for proposals of postwar aid to Russia, White had forwarded on March 7, as we have noted earlier, a memorandum to the Secretary suggesting a $5 billion credit to the Soviet Government. The memorandum was submitted on the same day that White, in conference with Under Secretary Bell, questioned the recommendation not to send the plates to the Russians. White had suggested in this paper that Soviet purchases, over thirty years, of American industrial and agricultural products would be paid for by Russian strategic materials. Such arrangements could mean important markets for both countries and would provide "a sound basis for continued collaboration between the two governments in the postwar period."[30] Later, in January, 1945, the suggested credit amount was doubled, and, against the general background of the Treasury proposals for occupied Germany, it became part of wider plans for postwar aid to Russia.

In any event, as seems possible from White's remark to Bell on March 7, that the issue of the duplicate plates should not be settled "on a narrow accountancy basis," White was temperamentally unlikely to have too much sympathy with the case against giving the Russians the plates. As in the case of the pettifogging approach of the State Department toward the American-Japanese negotiations of 1941, which, as we have seen, White had dismissed in his critique of traditionalist diplomacy, the issue of the duplicate plates may well have demanded what White considered to be the practice of "all-out diplomacy."

While the Russians had been considering their final position on the duplicate plates, now revealed in Molotov's note, the matter had been moving through the military bureaucracy in Washington.

The Combined Civil Affairs Committee, part of the Anglo-American Combined Chiefs of Staff establishment, had discussed the matter at the Pentagon on April 1. Major General G. N. Macready said that the British

Government was against producing two sets of AM notes of similar design on the grounds that the entire issue might be discredited. From the State Department, James C. Dunn, Director of the Office of European Affairs, reported that the Soviets were still asking for the plates. Decision at this stage was postponed for more discussion.[31]

By April 12, when a meeting on the American side of the Combined Civil Affairs Committee was held in the office of John J. McCloy, Assistant Secretary of War, some of those present knew of the Soviet intention to go ahead on their own, if necessary. Major General John H. Hilldring, head of the United States Army's Civil Affairs Division, reported that the problem of the duplicate plates was "too hot" for the Combined Chiefs of Staff; the combined Civil Affairs Committee had recommended that the matter should not be settled on military grounds. The decision was a political one.

Dunn considered that the matter should be settled by the Combined Chiefs on technical grounds; it seems possible that the State Department also wished to avoid responsibility for decision. The Treasury representatives from White's Division of Monetary Research, W. H. Taylor and L. C. Aarons, supported Dunn, and pointed out that Morgenthau had asked Leahy on March 22 for a judgment from the Combined Chiefs after outlining the technical aspects of the Russian request. Dunn then told the meeting of Molotov's note and the possibility that the Russians might print separate currency.

Evidently this news had some effect on the meeting. Hilldring hoped on military grounds that the three allies in Germany would all use the same military currency. Dunn considered that "it would have a very nice effect upon the German people if we all used the same type of currency." Taylor thought that, if the United States failed to provide duplicate plates, the Russians would not only embark on a currency of their own but they might establish "monetary and financial programs of their own."[32]

The Combined Chiefs of Staff still declined to accept responsibility. The next day, April 13, General Macready told the Combined Civil Affairs Committee that in his view, in their reply to Morgenthau through General Marshall the same day, the Combined Chiefs had taken the matter of the currency plates out of military hands. It had been returned to the State Department, the Foreign Office and the two Treasuries. In spite of a feeling that it would be desirable to have one Allied occupation-currency in Germany, the official position that this did not extend to delivering duplicate plates apparently remained unchanged by the evening of the thirteenth. In the 1947 hearings on these matters, for example, General Hilldring considered that the Russians had made what he considered "a very plausible and reasonable case" for delivering duplicate plates; in 1960 Hilldring and his aide, Colonel Hilliard, were also very positive that "to the last everybody in the Combined Civil Affairs Committee was against giving the plates to the Russians."[33]

General Marshall's letter of April 13 was delivered to White on the morning of the fourteenth. Marshall stated that the schedule of furnishing SHAEF with AM marks should be met by May 1. After that, "if the United States Treasury and the State Department, in conjunction with the Foreign Office and the British Treasury, decide to furnish duplicate plates to the Soviet Government, it appears that this action could be taken any time after May 1, 1944, without interference with General Eisenhower's requirements for Allied military mark currency." If the Soviet Government needed the money urgently, Marshall said, about 2 billion marks could be made available to them immediately. The letter, as indicated, returned the matter to the civilians, as the Combined Chiefs were not taking any decision.[34]

White now acted quickly. About 9:30 A.M. he asked Alvin Hall, Director of the Bureau of Engraving and Printing, to come to his office. Present also were W. H. Taylor and Ansel Luxford, of the Treasury General Counsel's Office. According to Hall's account of the meeting, White told him that "the Combined Chiefs of Staff had directed that the glass positives [of the AM plates] be turned over to the Russian Government." Luxford thought the Forbes Company might stop printing the AM currency, and for this contingency a draft presidential order had been prepared authorizing the Army to take over the printing plant or have it taken over by the Treasury. Hall asked that this should not be done, as he thought he could convince the company that they should follow a Combined Chiefs of Staff decision. He was not shown Marshall's letter.

Those present then went to see Morgenthau. After further discussion Morgenthau stated that the plates could be given to the Russians. Apparently Morgenthau implied that he had not been fully informed on the matter. He considered that had he known "all the facts, a decision would have been made at a much earlier date." Before the meeting ended, Hall told Morgenthau that it would be fair to tell the Forbes Company what was going to happen. In reply Morgenthau "emphatically stated that under no circumstances should the Forbes Company be informed that duplicate plates would be dispatched to Moscow . . . the military and political status of affairs were such as to require complete cooperation with the Russian Government, and that the transaction should be considered a military secret."[35]

At the end of this meeting Morgenthau spoke on the telephone to Dunn of the State Department and then to Gromyko. The Secretary told

Dunn that Gromyko was being told that the plates would be delivered to the Soviet Government and asked whether the State Department would approve, so sharing the responsibility. A little ambiguously, Dunn said that from the political viewpoint, apart from military or technical considerations, "if possible it was highly advisable to have the duplicate plates furnished to the Soviet Government," so that the three Allies would have the same occupation-currency in Germany. In our opinion, Dunn went on, faced with the Soviet intention to produce their own currency, "it would be a pity to lose the great advantage of having one currency used by the three armies which itself would indicate a degree of solidarity which was much to be desired."

Marshall's letter was not mentioned, Morgenthau was very glad to have this expression of the State Department's view, and Dunn's memorandum of the conversation noted that "in order to convince the Soviet Government of our sincerity in the desire to have the closest collaboration it becomes essential that we make every effort within our possibility to furnish the plates to that Government."[36]

Morgenthau then asked Gromyko to see him in his office that afternoon. When Gromyko arrived, Morgenthau told him that the American Government, anxious to cooperate with the Soviet Government, had decided to make available a set of the AM mark duplicate plates. In reply to a question from Gromyko, Hall then said that the plates, the formulas, and specimens of the ink and paper would be ready the following week. If necessary, Morgenthau said, he would be glad to send representatives of the Bureau of Engraving and Printing to Moscow to facilitate Soviet production, but Gromyko said no further help would be needed. The ambassador was given a memorandum recording the decision.[37]

After this decision had been made on the fourteenth, the Foreign Office, in a message received by the Treasury the next day, also agreed to the transfer. While concerned about the possibilities of forgery the British stated that they realized "how desirable it is politically . . . to comply with Russia's present request which seems to indicate a welcome readiness to cooperate." Provided the American authorities were satisfied, the British agreed that the plates should be sent to Russia.[38]

Accordingly, on April 21, 1944, the duplicate plates of the AM marks, together with the necessary specimens, were sent in a War Department automobile to the Soviet Embassy in Washington. The plates were then flown to Moscow via Alaska and Siberia. According to Petrov's study of occupation currency, the three Western allies later put into circulation in their zones of post-Potsdam Germany, excluding the Berlin enclave, a total of about 10.5 billion AM marks, which had, of course, been printed in the United States. Soviet issue, on "a very conservative estimate" Petrov calculates, was 78 billion.[39]

White's important role in the transfer of the duplicate plates seems to have been obscured or confused, unwittingly or not, in two ways. The first concerns the background to the formal decision to transfer the plates, the second touches on the allegations of White's complicity in the underground.

On April 27, 1944, the transfer of the plates was regularized by a memorandum from Under Secretary Bell to Alvin Hall of the Bureau of Printing and Engraving.[40] Bell wrote that in accordance with the decision taken by the Secretary at a meeting in his office on April 14, and attended by Hall, White, Taylor and Luxford, Hall was authorized to make plates and specimens available to the Russians. The Bell memorandum went on to say that the decision was only taken after careful deliberations within the Treasury Department "and after an exchange of letters between the Secretary and the Combined Chiefs of Staff. In a letter of April 13, 1944, to the Secretary, General Marshall, on behalf of the Combined Chiefs of Staff, suggested that the material requested by the Soviet Government be made available to it. . . ."

Bell's memorandum noted that conversation in which Dunn tentatively cleared the decision, and also the Foreign Office message which, of course, came the day after the decision was made. But apart from recognizing that the formal decision was Morgenthau's, the chief interest of this memorandum is that it describes Marshall's letter as one which "suggested" transfer. Moreover, in the 1947 hearings on Occupation Currency transactions, many of the high-level witnesses also thought the sanction for Morgenthau's decision came from this letter of Marshall's. But Marshall certainly did not "direct" the transfer of the plates as White told Hall, and it remains an open question whether the letter from the Combined Chiefs, in returning the matter to the civilians, can be construed as a "suggestion" to deliver the duplicate plates to the Russians. The letter equally left open the possibility that the Soviets might be given 2 billion of the American-printed AM marks.

Neither, as far as is known, is there any evidence that there was any Presidential-level review of the decision. In the 1947 hearings, for example, the distinguished former Assistant Secretary of State for War, John J. McCloy, stated that he "had an impression" that the matter of the plates was "of such importance" that either Cordell Hull or Morgenthau had seen Roosevelt.[41] But the formal decision was Morgenthau's alone, as he acknowledged to his biographer: "My decision was correct both politically and militarily. The Russians had been holding up the Germans while the United States and England prepared for the invasion. There was every reason to trust them."[42] But it also seems plain that the initiative throughout the episode for the decision on the duplicate plates came from Harry Dexter White.

A second source of the confusion over the decision on the duplicate plates arises from some of the testimony of Elizabeth Bentley on White's role in the transaction.

Miss Bentley's wider allegations regarding White will be discussed below. But perhaps it should be noted at this juncture that in *Out of Bondage* she wrote that an alleged member of the underground, W. L. Ullmann, an Air Force officer employed in the Pentagon, and a former colleague of White's, "brought me samples of the marks the United States was preparing for use in Germany. The Russians were delighted, as they were planning to counterfeit them. However, due to a complicated ink process, this proved impossible—until I was able, through Harry Dexter White, to arrange that the United States Treasury Department turn the actual printing plates over to the Russians."

In her testimony to the Mundt Subcommittee in 1953, Miss Bentley amplified by stating that she had been instructed by her Soviet Intelligence contact either in late 1943 or early 1944 that the Russians were very interested in the German occupation-currency and she was therefore to get in touch with N. G. Silvermaster and Ullmann of the underground Silvermaster group. White was to be asked to procure samples of the occupation currency. In their next meeting, two weeks later, or the next meeting after that, two or three samples of AM currency were produced by Ullmann, wrapped in a newspaper. However, either two weeks or a month later, these samples were returned by the Russians because they had been unable to photograph them "so that they would be useful." White was then asked by the Silvermasters to turn the plates over.[43]

In view of the development of the story of the duplicate plates on the official level, Miss Bentley's story seems of limited significance because, as early as February 4, 1944, as we have seen, White had openly sent design photostats of the AM marks to Gromyko. In addition, Alvin Hall testified in the 1947 hearings that sample specimens of the printed marks were also sent to the Russians before regular production started, although no date of dispatch was given. Why, therefore, should the Russians press for delivery through underground channels?

Miss Bentley also testified in 1953 that the Russians merely asked for an unspecified number of samples; yet eight denominations, of different design, were involved and would have been necessary for counterfeiting. As for Miss Bentley's statement that the Russians were unable to photograph the two samples that were produced, there seems no doubt at all that from the beginning of 1944 the Russians were promised AM marks in quantity. What was at issue was not whether they would be able to obtain AM marks, but whether they would obtain the plates. Counterfeiting would thus have been a possibility from the very beginning of the negotiations. But possession of the duplicate plates legitimized Soviet issue of AM marks without restriction.

There seems little doubt that Miss Bentley's story, with its emphasis on the conspiratorial delivery of samples to the Russians, and its elaboration in the interim committee report, confused the issue. What was germane to the decision on the plates was that Morgenthau and other individuals and departments, who had nothing to do with the Communists, were all agreed, in different degrees, on the necessity of inter-allied harmony at a critical time of the war. In this climate of opinion there was, perhaps, a tendency to subordinate technical factors and longer-term national interests to the spirit of Allied unity. Whatever his motives, it was left to White, with his determination, his sense of timing and his awareness of the attitudes and forces involved on the official level in Washington, to play a critical and perhaps decisive role in the eventual decision to deliver the duplicate plates to the Soviets.

Following the decision to send the duplicate plates to Russia on April 14, 1944, the question of the Allied exchange rate for the AM mark now had to be decided. This was the troop pay exchange rate. At this stage of the planning for the occupation of Germany, no general cross-rate for foreign trade was contemplated. The Reich would be cut off from other countries at the end of hostilities, and any external trade would be completely subject to the direction of the Allies.

On April 18, White met with Russian official representatives in Washington to discuss the AM mark exchange rate. The United States hoped to place AM marks into common circulation at par alongside Reichsmarks as soon as the occupation began. An agreed cross-rate between Allied domestic currency and AM marks would thus enable the Allies to calculate, so they hoped, future German liability for the military marks put into circulation.

There was not much Soviet interest in the matter at this stage, as the Russians awaited instructions, but they were agreeable to the common circulation of AM marks and Reichsmarks. As far as the AM cross-rate was concerned, the Western Allies still had to agree among themselves.

The British wanted a rate of around 20 cents for the mark or a mark-dollar cross-rate of 5–1; the State Department favored a slightly lower rate for the mark, but was clearly aware of the fact that a high purchasing power for the occupation mark would tend to disrupt any price and wage structure in the occupied country. (In these discussions, the nominal, existing rate for the Reichsmark was taken as 40 cents, 2½ to the dollar.) The American War Department, which hoped eventually to maximize its spending power in occupied Germany, suggested 12½ cents.

For its part the Treasury was arguing for a 10–1 rate or a 10-cent mark. As in the discussions on the occupation lire, the underlying question was the extent to which the victors' currency should be overvalued. Here, as in the case of Italy, White was a strong (and effective) exponent of maximizing the value of the dollar (and the pound) in the AM rate.

In a Treasury discussion on May 25 over the mark-dollar cross-rate, White suggested to Morgenthau that "you ought to have the highest rate you can have some chance of holding because if there is a depreciation of the mark after the occupation forces get in and we have the responsibility, it will be very bad for many reasons. . . . Therefore there is no sense in having a higher rate than can be maintained and the controls are going to break down, prices are going to shoot up. We don't believe you can even hold a ten cent rate . . . it's a question of fighting for as low a rate as we can get. . . ."

Morgenthau remarked that the Treasury was going to fight for a ten-cent rate, which was much higher than it should be but lower "than the other fellows say. Germany of all places, I would like a rate which we could hold. . . . I want you to give me a rate at which it will get better and not worse." In bargaining with other agencies, White added, he had suggested a five-cent mark—a mark-dollar cross-rate of 20–1—and Morgenthau told him to "stick to it."[44]

Later that day during luncheon at the White House, Morgenthau and White told Roosevelt that the Treasury favored a five-cent mark. But Roosevelt suggested that the occupation begin without a fixed exchange rate. Perhaps the Army could purchase goods and services in dollars. A few days later, on June 1, White, in a Treasury conference, argued on the lines Roosevelt had suggested. He thought it would be best to postpone decision, and pay the troops according to the nominal rate of forty cents to the mark, with adjustment later when conditions had settled. White remarked that a high rate would inevitably depreciate, and with a low rate the inevitable inflation would be blamed on that rate. Morgenthau, however, did not accept the suggestion of the nominal rate: "Haven't you people thought this thing up because you don't think you can win on a five cent rate?"[45]

Morgenthau, who wanted White's original figure of an AM mark worth between 5 and 10 cents, now left the matter to White. The State Department was advocating a figure of between 12 and 18 cents, while the British stuck to 20 cents. Once again, the advocates of a higher, rather than a lower, value for the AM mark wanted a troop pay cross-rate that would at least help to ensure economic and financial stability under the forthcoming occupation of Germany. But at the same time an overvalued rate for the dollar (and the pound) would naturally be welcomed by the troops.

From Moscow, Ambassador Harriman reported that the Russians would simply give their troops whatever marks seemed necessary, without bothering about a formal exchange rate at this stage. As the Russians held their own plates for the AM marks, there was no need for such inter-allied agreement on their part. Eventually, the State Department and the Treasury agreed on a ten-cent rate for the AM mark, the figure originally suggested by White. This was an overvaluation of the dollar, based on the nominal rate of 40 cents, of 300 percent.[46]

In July, 1944, the Anglo-American *ad hoc* Committee on Financial Planning, meeting in Washington, considered the AM mark cross-rate. This was a separate group from the *ad hoc* Committee on Monetary and Fiscal Planning noted earlier, but had much the same membership, and was part of the Combined Chiefs of Staff establishment. The British were still in favor of a twenty-cent rate for the AM mark, a rate of 5–1. Harold Glasser, for the United States Treasury, repeated White's view of a ten-cent military mark, or a rate of ten to the dollar. (White was at Bretton Woods when this meeting was held.) Eventually, after negotiations, the British Treasury acceded to the White figure of 10–1 in September. This meant an equivalent rate of 40 AM marks to the pound. The decision was then communicated to SHAEF in September.[47]

By this time the matter of the AM marks had ceased to be a problem for the planners. On September 11, 1944, the first troops under Eisenhower's command, from the American 1st Army, crossed the German border in the Eifel region. White's active interest in the occupation policy to be pursued for the conquered Reich had by now moved beyond the problems of the AM mark.

MISS BENTLEY'S NEW WORLD

We will build a new world, I thought to myself, a world in which there will be no suffering, no poverty, no pain. . . .

—ELIZABETH BENTLEY,
Out of Bondage

IN VIEW of White's increasing responsibilities in many critical spheres as the war progressed, it is necessary to examine Elizabeth Bentley's story of his alleged involvement in the work of the underground at this time.

It will be remembered that after Chambers had deserted his former comrades in April, 1938, he came to assume, he tells us, that he had frightened White away from the underground. A few months later, in the spring of 1939, Chambers himself surfaced in the bourgeois world with his employment on *Time* magazine in New York. He began to make a new life for himself.

However, according to Elizabeth Bentley's sworn testimony in 1948 and 1951, and her autobiography *Out of Bondage*, published in the early 1950's, White resumed his connection with the Soviet underground in Washington during the war, at the time of his ever-increasing involvement in great events, passing secret information and attempting to assist the Soviet in other ways.[1]

The highlights of Miss Bentley's story of her years in "bondage" are probably as well known as that of Chambers', yet a brief outline is necessary here to bring out White's place in the conspiratorial activities she describes, and in which, she alleged, he was active from 1941 to 1944, and possibly afterward.

Born in New Milford, Connecticut, in 1908, Miss Bentley, who died in 1963, was brought up in genteel poverty, graduating from Vassar College in 1930, at the beginning of the Depression. She went on to do postgraduate work at Columbia University, before studying in Italy. Returning to the United States in 1934, revolted by fascism, she went back to Columbia for secretarial training, and joined the Communist Party in 1935:

> . . . my first acquaintance with the Party came during the famous "united front" period, when the Communists had, to all intents and purposes, abandoned their former revolutionary arms and presented themselves as being the leaders of a coalition of all progressive forces to beat back the tide of war and fascism. . . . We will build a new world, I thought to myself, a world in which there will be no suffering, no poverty, no pain. . . .[2]

The next three years were relatively uneventful for her as a run-of-the-mill Party member. During early 1938 she joined the staff of the Italian Information Library in New York, and her consequent knowledge of fascist propaganda activities in the United States was useful to the Party. Later in 1938, on instructions, she was detached from the open Party, told not to meet in any way other Party members, and to be responsible to just one contact, "Timmy." Her cozy description of these developments is in complete contrast to the awareness and drama of Whittaker Chambers. As Rebecca West has written, in entering the Communist Party, it was as if she had joined the Women's Institute, and in entering the underground, "it was as if her Women's Institute had put her as candidate for the County Federation and she had been elected."[3]

It was some time before Miss Bentley discovered that Timmy was Jacob Golos, a Russian-born American citizen, a member of the three-man Control Commission of the American Communist Party and an agent of the Soviet state security organization, the NKVD. Golos was also head of World Tourists, Inc., a travel agency set up by the Party, which sometimes acted as a cover for various other illegal activities. During 1940, after Golos had been prosecuted for failing to register as an agent of the Soviet Government, as the agency had a contract with Intourist, he set up a new front, U.S. Service and Shipping Corporation, with Miss Bentley as vice-president and later secretary. By this time, she was Golos' assistant as well as his mistress.

Following the German invasion of Russia in June, 1941, Golos, says Miss Bentley, received orders from the NKVD that Moscow must be "completely informed" about developments in the American government, and that as many trusted comrades as possible must be placed in strategic positions in Washington so that intelligence could be relayed to the Soviet Union. In July, Golos told Miss Bentley that he had made contact with the leader of a band of Party members and sympathizers "who had been gathering around him a group of people . . . employed in sensitive jobs in the Government where they will be able to collect valuable information for us." The leader of the group was Nathan Gregory Silvermaster, an economist employed in the Farm Security Administration, born in Odessa, who had come to the United States in 1915 via Harbin, Manchuria and Shanghai, and who had worked for the federal government since 1935. Miss Bentley, known as "Helen," was to be the courier between Silvermaster and Golas.[4]

Besides Harry Dexter White, according to Miss Bentley, the Silvermaster group included Virginius Frank Coe, Soloman Adler and William Ludwig Ullmann, employees at one time or another of the Division of Monetary Research, Mrs. Sonia Gold, a Treasury private secretary, Irving Kaplan from the War Production Board, George Silverman, a civilian economic adviser to the Assistant Chief of the Air Staff during the war, and Lauchlin Currie, presidential administrative assistant. Ullmann was drafted in October, 1942, to be posted during the following year as an officer in the Army Air Corps headquarters in the Pentagon building. Adler, as we have seen, represented the Treasury in Chungking from early 1942 to 1945, with occasional breaks in the United States.

Miss Bentley went on to say that following Golos' death, in November, 1943, she took over another network, the Perlo group, named after Victor Perlo, in March, 1944. Perlo worked in the War Production Board during the war and after December, 1945, in the Division of Monetary Research. This group also included Harold Glasser, White's one-time assistant and Charles Kramer, employee of various Senate committees; but its core was in the WPB rather than the Treasury. Although Silvermaster and Perlo were her chief contacts, employees of other organizations such as the Office of Strategic Services were in contact with her on an individual basis, but she considered that "by far the most valuable" of her sources were in the Silvermaster group.[5]

What the Russians wanted to know "was practically limitless." Besides military intelligence and information on other possible Soviet agents within the American government, they were particularly interested in political intelligence such as negotiations between the United States and Great Britain, and loans to foreign and allied countries. In her duties as courier, Miss Bentley visited Washington twice monthly to see Silvermaster, but sometimes the Silvermasters brought additional material to New York for her. Perlo invariably came to New York, and Miss Bentley collected Party dues from members in both groups.

At first, production of the Silvermaster group was meager and consisted largely of so-called political data, such as Lend-Lease transactions, from the Treasury. But by spring, 1943, production of military and political intelligence had increased to "fabulous" amounts, and once Miss

Bentley told Golos that she had brought him "the entire Pentagon." By this time she was collecting forty rolls of 35mm. film every two weeks, with about thirty-five frames on each spool. The actual microphotography was done in the Silvermaster basement, leaving the Russians themselves to do the developing. Ullmann was the principal photographer, usually using a Contax, assisted by Miss Bentley and Mrs. Silvermaster. Miss Bentley also made stenographic notes on information which Ullmann had taken out of his office on small scraps of paper. An itemized list of documents was made for the Soviet, and the microfilm was then placed in Miss Bentley's capacious knitting bag for the journey from Washington to New York, Golos and the Russians.[6]

Miss Bentley identified White as a member of the Silvermaster group in the House Hearings of 1948, though she stated in her sworn testimony that she did not know whether he was a "card-carrying" member of the Communist Party. But she said, White "gave information to Silvermaster which was relayed to me."[7] White had realized that such information would find its way to the Communist Party, she had learned from Silvermaster. It should be observed that Miss Bentley did not say that she knew or had met White, and that unlike Chambers, she did not produce any documentary evidence to substantiate her allegations.

According to *Out of Bondage*, the figures of the Silvermaster group Elizabeth Bentley dealt with personally were the Silvermasters themselves and Ullmann, apart from a fleeting contact with George Silverman in the house on Thirtieth Street. But,

> one of the most important members of the group was Harry Dexter White. . . . According to Greg [Silvermaster] he had been tied up with the revolutionary movement for many years, although no one seemed to know whether he had been a member of the Communist Party. He had been giving information to the Russians during the thirties but ceased abruptly when his contact, who was later identified as Whittaker Chambers, turned "sour" in 1938. Some two years before I came into the picture Harry became very friendly with Greg, told him all about his past activities, and offered to give him what help he could. . . .[8]

White, whose first serious contact with Silvermaster is thus placed here during 1939, was in a position to influence policy in pro-Soviet directions, Miss Bentley remarks, and he also received data from other "strategic departments." He used his influence to help Silvermaster when the latter, briefly transferred to the Board of Economic Warfare, was under fire from the intelligence authorities in 1942 because of alleged Communist affiliations. He also helped "our people" to get into sensitive positions in government, and to place "new contacts" in the Treasury:

> For all this he was essentially a timid man and, as Greg put it, "he doesn't want his right hand to know what his left is doing." To keep him peaceful, Greg had to tell him that his material was going to one man in the American Communist Party's Central Committee, and nowhere else. Although he indubitably knew that it was in reality going to Moscow, he didn't care to think about such things. After the unhappy outcome of his dealings with Whittaker Chambers, White had promised his wife, who was not a Communist and disliked his revolutionary activities, that he would stay out of espionage in the future, and he lived in terror that she would find out that he had broken his word.[9]

In the general development of her story following these remarks on White, Miss Bentley remarks that members of the Silvermaster group had ever-increasing access to confidential material. They "brought secret material to the Silvermaster home at night, where it was photographed on microfilm, and then returned to the files the first thing in the morning before its absence could be discovered." Because of the department's policy of exchanging information, there was also "a steady stream of political reports from the Treasury which included material from the Office of Strategic Services, the Navy, the Army, and even a limited amount of information from the Department of Justice."[10]

In sworn testimony in August, 1951, before the Senate Internal Security Subcommittee, Elizabeth Bentley elaborated on White's role in the Silvermaster group, as she understood it.[11] Before answering questions on the espionage side of the Silvermaster operation, she was asked about the program of moving other agents into strategic government positions.

She stated that White and Currie were the "most important" members of the group: "They had an immense amount of influence . . . and their word would be accepted when they recommended someone." In general, Miss Bentley said, "whoever we had as an agent in the Government would automatically serve for putting someone else in. . . . Once we got one person in he got others, and the whole process continued like that." But the group would use White (and Currie) if possible, assuming that the actual process of penetration would be White's affair. On the associated subject of influencing policy, Miss Bentley remarked that "on our instructions" White "pushed hard" the Morgenthau Plan for postwar Germany.

As far as White's alleged espionage activities were concerned, Miss Bentley stated that she was unable to say whether he was a Party member, "but to all intents and purposes he was because he followed its discipline." She repeated that White had been frightened away by Chambers' defection, and that the Silvermasters had brought him back into their group: "His attitude was that I am going to help you, but my right hand doesn't want to know what the left is doing. Therefore he didn't want to meet anyone he knew to be a Soviet agent, he wanted to pass it through Silvermaster to me." Adler's reports to White from China, for example, were "relayed on to us."

She further testified that many confidential government records came to her from White, all labeled from "Harry" because Soviet agents "like to know who is providing what." Sometimes White would send carbon copies of confidential documents, Miss Bentley said: "Many, many times those documents were photographed in the Silvermasters' cellar because they couldn't be spared." In the early days, Miss Bentley continued, Ullmann would bring out the material: "Sometimes Harry was leery about bringing it out himself. Sometimes it would be given to Bill Taylor." (W. H. Taylor, who, Miss Bentley testified later, she had never met personally, denied her charges, as will be seen below.) Miss Bentley went on to say that Ullmann, when giving her a report from White, would type on it, "from Harry." The documents would then be photographed in the Silvermaster basement for delivery to the Russians in New York.[12]

There were two other aspects of White's alleged clandestine activities on which Miss Bentley elaborated in these hearings. She stated that "we were so successful in getting information during the war largely because of Harry White's idea to persuade Morgenthau to exchange information . . . there were seven or eight agencies trading information with Secretary Morgenthau." When Senator Ferguson referred Miss Bentley to a previous remark in executive (secret) session that White was planning to "integrate" all intelligence material coming into the Silvermaster group, Miss Bentley replied that White not only had a plan, "but we put it into effect." This plan was initiated in the first place, she said, because White knew the information "would come across his desk." (A letter from Morgenthau's administrative assistant to an inquiring Congresswoman in July, 1944, listed eighteen interdepartmental committees on which White had represented the Treasury. The information passing through these committees would be, of course, of varying importance, and White would sometimes send one of his assistants to represent him, but he would presumably be in a position to assess fully the work of these various bodies.)[13]

Second, Miss Bentley went on to say that when she finally "turned over" the Silvermaster group to the Russians in September, 1944, after some months of argument, "my Soviet contact told me that they did not believe in having such large groups for security reasons because if someone turns sour they know too much." Miss Bentley added that "Bill," one of the Russians who had succeeded Golos as her link with the Soviet, "intended to put White directly in contact with a Soviet superior . . . and possibly with the smaller fry he could put two or three in one group. But he definitely mentioned putting White and Currie in direct contact."

She added that Bill was her Soviet superior and that she was "quite sure" the plan to put White in direct contact with a Soviet agent went through:

> SENATOR FERGUSON. Why do you say you think it went through?
> MISS BENTLEY. Because after this Soviet contact had taken over the Silvermaster group he requested me to stay on with them for three months. In talking with Silvermaster he told me that they had already put the plan into effect, and that they were about to make contact with Soviet agents, so I am convinced it went through.[14]

The death of Golos and continuing Soviet insistence that Miss Bentley should "turn over" her groups and agents to them on security grounds meant that she began to view her underground activities with a different perspective. During 1944 she increasingly came to feel that the idealism, as she saw it, of the American Communists and sympathizers was being exploited by the Soviet for their own ends. By early January, 1945, all her contacts had been turned over.

Lonely, exhausted, disillusioned, and now caught between conflicting loyalties, she decided to leave the Party. As in Chambers' case the withdrawal symptoms were agonizing, and "it took me a year to more or less get it out of my system and get to the point where I could get into the frame of mind of going to the authorities about it."[15] For Elizabeth Bentley, the liberating hopes of the mid-1930's had turned, a decade later, into a nightmare.

In August, 1945, at New Haven, Connecticut, in her native New England, Miss Bentley reported to the FBI. Later, she was put in touch with the Bureau's New York office. For a time she retained some of her underground contacts at the request of the FBI, but during 1947 she appeared with her story before a Federal Grand Jury in New York. There were no indictments. It was Miss Bentley's story rather than Chambers' that led to the House Hearings of 1948 in which she first publicly mentioned White's name in connection with the underground.

Clearly, there is much in Miss Bentley's story, both in its general outline and in its references to Harry Dexter White, that is open to challenge. Her allegations about White are, as noted, hearsay as, apart from a fleeting contact with Silvermaster, she tells us that of the Silvermaster group she personally met only the Silvermasters and Ullmann.

Unlike Chambers, Miss Bentley brought with her no documentary evidence to sustain her story. On her own account she must have carried, at least, many hundreds of rolls of microfilm between Washington and New York for the Russians from Silvermaster, yet not a spool of this film survives to corroborate her story. The absence of such evidence hardly adds to the credibility of her testimony.

Then again, as Professor Earl Latham, a dispassionate analyst of the Bentley story in his Fund for the Republic study of *The Communist Controversy in Washington*, puts it, credence of Miss Bentley's account requires "some toleration of contradiction, invention, and ambiguity. Her book contains inaccuracies, verbatim reports of conversations she could not have reproduced without steno-type or tape recorder, touches of romantic explanation, and quick girlish excursions into speculation, desolate either of knowledge or perception."[16]

One of the errors in her story lay in the case of William Henry Taylor, a former member of the Division of Monetary Research, who was alleged by her in the 1948 House Hearings and the 1951 IPR Hearings to have been a member of the Silvermaster group. Taylor repeatedly denied that he had been a Communist or had participated in espionage activities, and when a Washington newspaper called him part of an espionage ring he sued for libel and the newspaper settled out of court. An adverse judgment against Taylor's loyalty by the United States International Organizations Employees Loyalty Board—Taylor had worked in the International Monetary Fund following the Treasury—was reversed by the Board in a rehearing and Taylor was vindicated.[17]

Taylor was represented before the Board by the former New Deal congressman from California, Byron Scott, who presented to the Loyalty Board a long statement listing what I. F. Stone has called "a whole series of contradictions and discrepancies" in Miss Bentley's story.[18]

Of these thirty-seven discrepancies, one, noted above, referred to Miss Bentley's statement in July, 1948, during the HUAC Hearings that Earl Browder gave the name of Silvermaster to Golos in July, 1941. Browder was actually in Atlanta jail from March, 1941, to May, 1942, and reference to him in this alleged link-up was omitted in *Out of Bondage*. Another discrepancy of Miss Bentley's 1948 testimony noted by Byron Scott was that Ullmann, through a connection with the office of an Army Air Corps general, was able to procure for Silvermaster the date of the Normandy landings in 1944. Scott pointed out that the general in question was in the Army's Civil Affairs Division, and that according to Eisenhower's own account D-Day was postponed for twenty-four hours at the last moment because of weather.[19]

It was also pointed out that at one stage in the 1948 House Hearings, Miss Bentley stated that she did not contact Perlo till 1944. Yet, on another occasion in the same hearings, she had stated that she had turned over some Party dues from the Perlo group to Golos, in his lifetime. Golos died in 1943. However impressive this list of discrepancies noted by I. G. Stone, the latter error certainly may have been a passing confusion of dates as, apart from this one reference to the dues Miss Bentley was consistent in the 1948 House Hearings, the 1951 IPR Hearings and *Out of Bondage* in stating that Golos died in 1943 and that she took over the Perlo group in 1944.[20]

I. F. Stone has written that the "clincher"[21] in the vindication of Taylor was a purported letter from Ullmann to Taylor which the Board had to consider. This letter suggested that Taylor was appointed to the Treasury as a result of a plot. Taylor, comments Professor Herbert Packer in his study of the testimony of Chambers, Bentley and others, *Ex-Communist Witnesses*,

> adduced persuasive evidence that he had never received such a letter and that the letter was in fact a fabrication. His clearance followed. It must be attributed in major part to the Board's conviction that it was dealing with a case of manufactured evidence. . . .
>
> If we take the Board's determination of a general position, Taylor's position was vindicated. But the circumstances were such that we cannot say with any degree of certainty that his vindication constitutes a repudiation of Miss Bentley's position. Much more will have to be known before we can either affirm or deny that Miss Bentley was a truthful witness.[22]

As with the case of Chambers, with the difference that Miss Bentley brought no alleged corroborative evidence with her from the underground, the problem is to attempt to assess whether the discrepancies and inaccuracies in Miss Bentley's testimony are central or marginal.

In what is perhaps the best available critical examination of the Bentley story, Professor Herbert Packer has examined the extent to which Miss Bentley has been corroborated by others, the extent to which she has been contradicted, and the significance of the gaps in her story.[23]

As far as the White case is concerned, Professor Packer first mentions Chambers' testimony that White, while not perhaps a Party member, was a willing collaborator with the underground. As we have seen, Professor Packer considers that the means by which the foolscap sheets in White's alleged handwriting came into Chambers' possession is a matter "on which we have only the words of Whittaker Chambers. But it cannot be denied that their existence in his possession requires some explanation."

According to Professor Packer, White's alleged involvement is further corroborated by the fact that Chambers mentioned him to the FBI in 1942 and to Ray Murphy, of the State Department, in March, 1945, before Miss Bentley first went to the FBI in August, 1945. "That sequence of events," Packer goes on,

> appears to rule out the possibility that Chambers fabricated his account after learning of Miss Bentley's. It does not rule out the possibility that Miss Bentley fabricated her account after learning of Chambers'. But in order to seriously entertain that possibility we would have to assume that she was led by the FBI to name White, on the strength of their existing suspicions about him. That could not be believable unless the FBI is to be accused of incredibly sloppy investigative techniques or worse. It seems most reasonable to assume that what probably happened was what appears to have happened, namely, that Miss Bentley and Chambers, independently and without knowledge of each other's stories accused Harry Dexter White of complicity in espionage activity at two different times. And that is corroboration of a kind that cannot lightly be dismissed.[24]

Professor Packer also considers Chambers "an important corroborative source" for Miss Bentley's identification of certain members of the so-called Perlo group. He points out that Miss Bentley names Perlo and Charles Kramer as meeting in John Abt's Central Park West apartment in 1944, while Chambers names these three as members of the Ware group a decade previously. That testimony of Chambers on the Ware group, Packer reminds us, was "further corroborated" by Nathaniel Weyl, who testified he was a member of this group for some time.

Moreover, Earl Latham, after an examination of this and other sections of Miss Bentley's testimony concludes that it is "possible that the [Perlo] group had its roots originally in the Ware cell . . . so that a third of the Ware group is accounted for in the Perlo group."[25] Taken as a whole, this particular segment of Miss Bentley's testimony does indicate an element of possible coherence and also continuity with parts of the Chambers story.

Chambers' testimony, it should be remarked, also partly corroborates Miss Bentley's identification of certain members of the so-called Silvermaster group. According to the memorandum written by Adolph Berle on September 2, 1939, Chambers that day in his description of the underground mentioned Adler ("Schlomer *Adler*? [Sol Adler?]"), Coe ("Frank Coe—now teacher at McGill"), and Currie ("Laughlin Currie: Was a "fellow traveller"—helped various Communists—never went the whole way"). In March, 1945, before Miss Bentley went to the FBI, Chambers talked about the underground to Ray Murphy, the State Department officer, who recorded him as saying that "Harry White of the Treasury was described as a member at large but rather timid. He put on as assistants in the Treasury, Glasser, a member of the underground group, and an Adler or Odler, another party member. The two Coe brothers, also party members, were put on by White." Glasser, of course, as we have seen, was later described as a member of the Perlo rather than the Silvermaster group, by Miss Bentley. Espionage was not specifically mentioned in either interview.[26]

Further corroboration of Miss Bentley's story, Professor Packer goes on, comes from Louis Budenz, the former managing editor of the New York *Daily Worker*, who "corroborated Miss Bentley's account of the position of Jacob Golos in the Communist hierarchy and her assertion that Golos was engaged in directing espionage activities. He also had some peripheral contact with Miss Bentley herself, although he was not in a position to corroborate her account of the activities in which she engaged."[27]

There is also the question of what weight is to be put on the testimony of the alleged independent Bentley contacts, outside the Silvermaster and Perlo groups, those of Bernard Redmond, Robert Miller and Duncan Lee, who, in Professor Packer's words, said "that they knew Miss Bentley, although all claimed that the relationship was an innocent one."[28] Similarly, in the parallel case of William Remington, who was found guilty in 1953 by a court on one charge of perjury in a matter which had nothing to do with Miss Bentley, and on another charge of perjury in denying ever having given Miss Bentley information to which she was not entitled, "Remington himself admitted having given Miss Bentley a wide range of miscellaneous information."[29]

The specific issue here was the classification of the information, and not Miss Bentley's general story: "At the very least," Packer considers,

the testimony of Redmond, Remington, Miller and Lee serves to establish that Miss Bentley was indeed busily engaged in making and sustaining contacts with government officials in wartime Washington. It also establishes that she used different aliases with different people and that she had a propensity for clandestine meetings. All this is perfectly consistent with, and goes a long way toward confirming Miss Bentley's own account of what she was doing. She plainly thought that she was in the espionage business. But the crucial issue is what they thought. And this is placed squarely in issue by the testimony of those who admitted knowing Miss Bentley.[30]

What other testimony is there to support the general credibility of the Bentley story, given that the evidence of these "independent" contacts was far from conclusive? Professor Packer goes on to discuss the relevance of the concept of "guilt by association," the significance of the invocation by some of those named by Miss Bentley of the Fifth Amendment, and a 1953 statement by the Director of the FBI on the extent to which Miss Bentley's allegations had been checked by the FBI and the courts.

On the sensitive matter of guilt by association, Packer points out

> the problem is one of assessing probabilities. If X is a member of the Communist Party, he is more likely to commit espionage for the benefit of the Soviet Union than he would be if he were not a member of the Party. Thus stated the proposition is truism, but is a truism that cannot be ignored. Absent other evidence, a charge of espionage activity carries more weight if coupled with evidence of Communist affiliation than it would be if there was no such evidence . . . the question is not whether it is proper to take into account evidence of Communist activity in evaluating a charge like Miss Bentley's. Rather the question is how much weight to ascribe to such evidence.[31]

As Professor Packer writes, there seems to be little doubt that at least some of the persons named by Miss Bentley were engaged in some form of Communist activity. Silvermaster, for example, the alleged leading figure in the chief Washington network, was reported by the United States Civil Service Commission in 1942 to have engaged in a variety of Communist activities. The report came to the conclusion that "Nathan Gregory Silvermaster is now and has for years been a member and leader of the Communist Party and very probably a secret agent of the O.G.P.U."[32]

However, the detailed evidence in such reports is only rarely published, remaining uncorroborated, and thus bringing us back to some of the problems raised in the first place by the Bentley testimony.

The refusal of many of those named by her to answer pertinent questions before Congressional committees is sometimes quoted as corroboration of Miss Bentley's story. Those who invoked the Fifth Amendment's privilege against self-incrimination included Silvermaster, Glasser, Perlo, Silverman, Kaplan, together with Coe and Ullmann on some occasions. In a critical examination of the proposition that invocation equals guilt,

Professor Packer remarks, for example, that Attorney General Herbert Brownell, in his statements on the White case in November, 1953, appeared to believe in this "logical chain" between invocation and guilt.

Packer goes on to point out that the complex question of waiver means that the protection of the Fifth Amendment may be waived if the witness answers certain questions that may have a relation to others. To avoid being compelled to answer questions on Party membership, which rightly or wrongly a witness considers might involve him in possible criminal liability, the same witness might refuse to answer any question on, say, Miss Bentley. Packer considers that such use constitutes a proper protective invocation as a means of avoiding waiver.

Second, a refusal to answer a question might mean, apart from guilt, that the witness wished to be left alone. Or the witness might "desire to avoid a perjury prosecution based on a conflict between what the Witness believes to be truthful answers and contradictory statements made by someone like Miss Bentley." In short Packer considers "a witness who invokes the Fifth Amendment may be guilty of contempt of Congress (because of improper invocation) rather than of whatever substantive offense he is being questioned about."[33] Packer goes on to remark that "little or no corroboration" is afforded Miss Bentley's story by the fact that some of those accused by her of complicity in espionage activities have invoked the Fifth Amendment. He points out that Frank Coe, for example, after refusing at one stage to answer questions on espionage, later denied, in 1956, such involvement. William Ludwig Ullmann, too, denied the espionage charge to a grand jury in 1956, under the provisions of the Immunity Act.[34]

Professor Packer thus emphasizes that we ought "to be wary of relying" on Fifth Amendment invocation as "proof of the truth" of Miss Bentley's testimony.

Finally Professor Packer discusses the extent to which Miss Bentley's evidence has been corroborated by its general endorsement by the Director of the FBI. In November, 1953, in circumstances which will be discussed later, J. Edgar Hoover stated that "all information furnished by Miss Bentley, which was susceptible to check, has proven to be correct. She has been subjected to the most searching of cross-examinations; her testimony has been evaluated by juries and reviewed by the courts and found to be accurate." At the same time, Hoover said that as far as White was concerned, the information on him in a report sent to the White House in February, 1946, "came from a total of thirty sources, the reliability of which had previously been established." One of these sources was Miss Bentley.[35]

There are two statements here. The first is that the FBI was satisfied, "on the basis of its own investigations, that Miss Bentley's story is true"

(Packer). The second is that the courts (and juries) have found her testimony accurate.

As for the first statement, Professor Packer writes that Hoover's statement suggests that there are "adequate answers" to the ambiguities covering the circumstances in which Miss Bentley went to the FBI in 1945.[36] As we shall see later, during her initial public appearances in 1948 Miss Bentley stated that she had been in contact with the FBI, over the general essence of her story, since a visit to their New Haven field office on August 21 or 22, 1945. However, when Attorney General Brownell and Mr. Hoover testified on the White case to a Senate subcommittee in November, 1953, they seemed to suggest, on the basis of declassified FBI reports, that it was only in early November, 1945, that the Bureau learned of Miss Bentley's allegations of White's complicity in the Silvermaster ring.

The matter was not conclusive, there could have been an explanation, and here was an episode, Packer comments, to wit, the extent that Miss Bentley's final contacts with the Russians overlapped with her first FBI interviews, which was clearly "susceptible to check," as Mr. Hoover put it. But commenting on Miss Bentley's story in a more general way Packer writes: "How much of her testimony has been checked? What is the corroborative evidence? It is helpful to know that Mr. Hoover is satisfied. It is even helpful to know that Mr. Hoover's satisfaction has satisfied others. But all that is no substitute for having the evidence made public, so that it can be scrutinized and assigned its due weight by anyone sufficiently interested to want to appraise it."[37] Clearly this is an area in which the demands of security and high policy preclude full revelation of the FBI's sources and knowledge.

As far as Hoover's remark on the Bentley charges having been found accurate by the courts is concerned, Packer considers this "an overstatement. The main outlines of her story have never been put in issue in a court trial." The professor mentions the four trials in which Miss Bentley was a witness, concluding his discussion of this factor by saying that "her court appearances constitute no more than a makeweight in the assessment of the extent to which her story has been corroborated and accepted."[38]

To what extent has Miss Bentley's story been contradicted? Professor Packer points out that direct external contradiction comes only from interested witnesses. They are those "whom she had accused who have been willing to risk the possibility of perjury indictments by denying the truth of her testimony under oath."

In addition to White's emphatic denial of any complicity which has been noted, Currie, Sonia Gold and, on occasion, Coe and Ullmann of the Silvermaster group denied Miss Bentley's charges, besides W. H. Taylor whose denial and vindication by a loyalty board have been noted. Others of Miss Bentley's alleged independent contacts who denied her charges included Remington, Lee, Miller and Redmond. Unlike members of the Silvermaster group these men stated that they did know Miss Bentley.

With the exception of Remington none of these cases have been subjected to judicial scrutiny, Professor Packer observes. The Remington case was inconclusive as far as the wider Bentley story was concerned and "it is equally true of course that Miss Bentley's story cannot be regarded as having been shaken by any of these other denials, untested as they are."

Nor can it be concluded, as some have suggested, that the American government's failure to bring perjury charges against those who have denied Miss Bentley's accusations is evidence of the weakness of her charges. Packer points out that this contention "evaporates entirely" when the peculiar requirements for a federal perjury prosecution are examined.

American federal courts demand in such a case either two witnesses, such as Mrs. Remington and Miss Bentley in the Remington case; or one witness plus corroborating circumstances such as Chambers' evidence and the documents typed on the Hiss typewriter in the Hiss case. The obvious reason why no prosecutions were initiated against those who denied Miss Bentley's charges was that there was no corroboration, and Packer comments, lack of corroboration "is far from being the same thing as contradiction."

Chief among the internal inconsistencies in Miss Bentley's story, Professor Packer goes on, is the question of her activities during August–November, 1945, including the problem of whether she was under FBI surveillance when she met a Russian contact. Here, as we have noted, there may have been "adequate answers" which satisfied the authorities.

But other inconsistencies, Packer comments, "appear to result mainly from her tendency to add details in order to add an air of verisimilitude to her story. These instances do not bulk large in the total context of her story. They do not suggest that she is lying. All they do, along with everything else that we have discussed, is to point toward a need for more information than we now possess."[39]

The chief, and irremediable gap in information is, of course, the total absence, as Packer describes it, of any of the fruits of Miss Bentley's years in the espionage business. Then too, several people mentioned by Miss Bentley, such as Mrs. Silvermaster, never publicly testified after the main allegations became public knowledge in 1948.

On the other hand, there is clearly further information in the voluminous FBI files, not only deriving from Miss Bentley's questioning by the

FBI, but from the circumstances surrounding the FBI surveillance of Golos and his enterprises which Miss Bentley frequently records in *Out of Bondage*. With her death in 1963, and that of Silvermaster the following year, it seems unlikely, but not inconceivable, that further material will appear—or be released—to fill these gaps in what Packer calls "the important, tantalizing, but still unresolved account rendered by Elizabeth Bentley."[40]

The difficulties of evaluating the Bentley story are thus not inconsiderable. In his final assessment, Professor Packer refers to her vagueness, evasiveness, the lack of corroboration of her story, yet states, "hers is clearly no story invented out of the whole cloth." Indeed Miss Bentley's relations with Golos and Remington are amply corroborated and "most of her contacts had ideological affiliations that might well have predisposed them to cooperate with her." Finally, taking her story as a whole, the refusal of many of those named by her to come forward with denials or explanations "must weigh heavily in any judgment formed on the basis of a record as indeterminate as the present one."

"In lawyers' terms," Professor Packer concludes, "I would say that Miss Bentley has made out a prima facie case, that the burden of going forward is on those who would disprove her account, but that she is not entitled to a directed verdict in her favor."[41]

Fred J. Cook has concluded in another examination of the Bentley story that "no definitive verdict can ever be given on the overall validity of the Bentley testimony, but it is infinitely suspect,"[42] while Professor Latham, in his wide and deep examination of Communist activity in the United States, considers Miss Bentley's main disclosures "are believable, are not to be brusquely dismissed as malicious mania, and are still largely unrefuted."[43]

Clearly, then, if one accepts the main outlines of the story, if the facts on the whole were as Miss Bentley says they were, then some members of the Silvermaster group knew the kind of activity in which they were involved. But did the conspirators necessarily include Harry Dexter White? As White, by common agreement, did not meet Miss Bentley, there is a wide spectrum of possibility from innocence to indiscretion through sympathy and complicity to absolute commitment. There is the role of possible intermediaries. There is the classification of the material allegedly passed. Nathan White, for example, in his defense of his brother, suggests that the material Miss Bentley carried from Washington to New York was not classified information at all but press releases and United States Government Printing Office material.[44]

On the other hand, we have Miss Bentley's sworn testimony in 1951, relatively detailed by her standards, that as the operations of the Silvermaster group expanded, White became the mainspring, because of his high responsibilities, of an integrated intelligence operation, and was about to be turned over to the direct supervision of a Soviet contact during late 1944. This would imply some degree of motivation and awareness on White's part. If Miss Bentley was telling the truth here, presumably there could be no doubt that White's right hand would at last know what his left was doing.

Closely related to the charges of espionage against White made by Miss Bentley and Whittaker Chambers are the intertwined accusations of supervising infiltration into "strategic" government positions and of influencing policy. "He was in a position not only to give valuable information but also to influence US policy into a pro-Soviet direction," Miss Bentley writes of White. "He gave recommendations to any of our people who needed to get into more sensitive positions . . . and he placed new contacts in the Treasury Department."[45]

Like Miss Bentley, Chambers instances the Morgenthau Plan "for the destruction of Germany" as an example of White's influence on policy-making, going on to comment, as we have seen, that "the power to influence policy has always been the ultimate purpose of the Communist Party's infiltration. It was much more dangerous, and, as events have proved, much more difficult to detect, than espionage, which beside it was trivial, though the two go hand in hand."[46]

As far as White's influence on national policy-making is concerned, the record is clouded and certainly "difficult to detect." Inside the Treasury, as we have seen, White was given real responsibility after Pearl Harbor, but once again, before and during the war, policy was the outcome of many forces. In a general sense, as Earl Latham has noted, the policies of the American government "tend to emerge only with great difficulty from the crosspull of a thousand pressures. This is true even when the management of policy is in the hands of the President at a time when he is supported by majorities in Congress and a mandate at the polls, neither of which the Communists had."[47]

In the major preoccupation of his official career, the negotiations leading to Bretton Woods and after, White "regarded himself as a middleman between two sovereign powers, the American Congress on one hand, and the British Cabinet on the other." Here the role of the author of the White Plan was that of a tenacious and enlightened negotiator for American interests, generally recognized as such by the British side. Similarly, in his proposals to Morgenthau during 1939–40 for the guidelines of the Treasury's Latin American policy, his approach was if anything that of an American nationalist. His involvement in Latin American affairs culminated in the White mission to Cuba, whose object, later partly implemented, was to bolster the finances of General Batista's Cuban regime.

Regarding White's proposals in May, 1941, for a triangular Pacific *détente* between the United States, Japan and Russia, there is no evidence that they were considered on a policy-making level. His later November, 1941, proposals, involving the United States and Japan in a general understanding, based on principles of economic self-interest, were put forward when the time for such an approach had passed. In their passage through the bureaucracy they emerged instead as a near-ultimatum—the Ten Point Note. When the decision to present this final note was in balance, White asked Edward Carter of the IPR to come to Washington to lobby against a temporary truce or *modus vivendi* with Japan, but when Carter arrived Roosevelt and Hull had decided to present the Ten Point Note to Japan, as we have seen.[48]

There may be a presumption that an attempt could have been made to influence policy here, but no evidence exists that such an attempt actually took place. So far from being able to work on a high level to propel the United States into war with Japan, so diminishing the possibility of a Japanese attack on the Soviet Union, White was certainly not part of the policy-making process at this time, as has been noted.

But as he became involved in the campaign against the *modus vivendi* in November, 1941, White may well have realized, in view of the deepening military crisis, that his earlier proposals for American-Japanese understanding were not relevant. He may thus have argued that if the potential Japanese threat to the Soviet Far Eastern flank could not be turned by economic proposals, events would have to take their course, and that war between Japan and America might best help the Russians. In any case, Churchill, Chiang Kai-shek and the other Allies were also pressing the American government to take a firm stand against the Japanese. What remains interesting about the episode, as far as White is concerned, is not that he influenced policy but that he assumed as late as November, 1941, that the sweeping proposals he advanced in his memorandum could affect the impasse between the United States and Japan.

White's role in three other episodes, the delayed delivery of gold shipments to China, the case of the duplicate plates of the AM marks, and the development and aftermath of the Morgenthau Plan are all rather different cases.

As we shall see below, in May, 1945, White told Morgenthau, who had overlooked his commitment to send $200,000,000 of gold to China, that the Treasury had no legal grounds for withholding the gold and that "what we were doing was skating on thin ice and offering excuses." Whether, in the face of political and economic developments in Nationalist China during the latter years of the war, the gold could have made any significant contribution to alleviating China's inflation is perhaps an open question. However, White's foot-dragging on the gold shipments probably helped to prevent the emergence of a more positive Treasury policy on Chinese aid, as Morgenthau was by no means unsympathetic to the Chinese cause and eventually expedited the gold shipments, as will be seen. At the same time, other American agencies were critical of the Chinese Nationalists, and American policy generally was diffuse and at the mercy of events (and geography). White therefore hardly influenced policy as such, rather its execution in one sector—a critical one, to be sure.

There is another pattern again in the decision to deliver the duplicate plates to the Russians, for this episode took place against a background, in which inter-allied harmony was considered all-important. The conspiratorial circumstances described by Miss Bentley were irrelevant, for White, in promoting the decision on the plates, was working in a policy framework where cooperation with the Russians was considered necessary. What distinguished White's initiative was his readiness to assume responsibility in an ill-defined zone between civilian and military agencies. Then Morgenthau made a formal decision.

With the struggle over the Morgenthau Plan (which was abandoned) and the emergence of the JCS 1067 zonal directive, which incorporated some elements of the plan, it seems clear that without Morgenthau's dynamic lobbying, and the leverage of the Treasury Department, these drastic proposals for the treatment of the Reich might never have been seriously considered. Yet the proposals to turn Germany into "a fifth-rate power," and which did, to a certain extent, influence the JCS directive, do seem to have originated with White, and the extent and nature of his role in these developments will be noted. The Morgenthau Plan was favored by those who were neither Communists nor their sympathizers, and the climate of the time demanded a stern peace with Germany. On the other hand, such features of the plan as territorial partition combined with the removal on a large scale of capital equipment was not incompatible with Soviet practice or objectives. *Cui Bono?*

But it seems reasonably clear that with the exception of White's stern, perhaps extreme, proposals for Germany, so far from influencing policy, White's forte was taking the initiative in selected areas where policy was vague, confused, disputed or nonexistent. Then, perhaps, White's brand of bureaucratic "all-out diplomacy" could prove effective when supported by the Treasury Department and its powerful Secretary.

There remains the allegation that White and his colleagues helped each other to infiltrate American government departments. As we have seen, according to Miss Bentley, White was one of the leading organizers in this alleged patronage operation mounted by the underground.

When he appeared before the House Committee in August, 1948, emphatically denying the Bentley-Chambers charges,[49] White confirmed that Frank Coe, Glasser, Ullmann, Adler and Sonia Gold had worked for him in the Division of Monetary Research. After White had left the Division in January, 1945, formally to become Assistant Secretary of the Treasury, succeeded as head of Monetary Research by Coe, Perlo had worked for the Division. White believed that Kaplan had worked for another section of the Treasury. (Kaplan had joined the Division in July, 1945, before being sent to occupied Germany under Foreign Funds Control.)

White stated that he knew Currie, Silverman and Silvermaster well, and had known them for years. He knew Perlo "not very well," and Charles Kramer "not too well." White had played volleyball and baseball with Kaplan—not a very good player—and tennis with Ullmann, who was excellent. White had also played table tennis in the Silvermaster basement, but the place was cluttered up, the players had to chase the ping-pong balls, and he had not noticed a photographic darkroom there,[50] he said as the questioning digressed at this point.

White went on to say that as Director of Monetary Research he would have employed or approved the employment of the people mentioned above, and in any case would have interviewed them before they entered the Division. The FBI had interviewed him about Glasser's alleged Communist affiliations in 1940, and he was proud to have him in his Division, but he had not interceded on Glasser's behalf.

When Silvermaster had told White in 1942 that he was being asked to resign from the Board of Economic Warfare by the security authorities, including the Office of Naval Intelligence, because of alleged Communist connections, White had interceded on Silvermaster's behalf with Assistant Secretary of the Treasury Herbert Gaston, who was on the appropriate loyalty review board. (Silvermaster was later transferred back to the Farm Security Administration.) White had known Silvermaster for a number of years, had discussed world affairs with him often, and when he had asked him if he were a Communist Silvermaster had denied it, and shown White his statement denying the allegations of the security authorities. This White had accepted. White was sure Silvermaster was innocent of Miss Bentley's charges.

When White was asked if he considered it strange that many of the people named by Miss Bentley had worked for him, or knew him well, he remarked that it was "disconcerting" but not strange. The Treasury was the largest cabinet level department, at the time of his colleagues' employment it was a rapidly expanding department, "because we had been given responsibilities far in excess of anything we had," and the Treasury needed all the good men it could get. Professional competence was the criterion, and in his field White considered himself "a pretty good judge."

Frank Coe told the committee in the same hearings, when asked about the composition of the alleged Silvermaster group:

> So far as I can see these were never a group in any shape or form. They never acted as a group. . . . The nearest they ever came to being a group, to my knowledge, was in the playing of volleyball. They used to meet, or a number of these people used to go out Sundays and play volleyball. I personally didn't do it because I didn't get up that early.[51]

As Professor Packer has observed, it would take a separate book to document the "astonishing interrelations"[52] between the forty-three persons named by Miss Bentley in her various appearances as members of the underground, some of whom, as we have seen, appear also in the Chambers canon.

Some of these "interrelations," based on the publication of federal employment records, may be briefly noted here. White, for example, asked Coe in 1939 to come to the Division of Monetary Research for a temporary assignment from Toronto University, following Coe's connection with the Treasury which went back, like White's, to 1934. When Glasser, the Assistant Director of White's division, was sent abroad in 1940, White recommended that Coe succeed him, and later in the war, after Coe had worked in the Foreign Economic Administration and other agencies, Coe replaced White as Director of Monetary Research when White formally became Assistant Secretary of the Treasury. Glasser, already back in the Division, then replaced Coe as Director when Coe went to the International Monetary Fund as head of the Office of the Secretary in June, 1946. Earlier, Coe had hired Perlo to the Division in December, 1945, and soon Perlo was rated "excellent" by Glasser.[53]

Ullmann, too, who had joined the Division of Monetary Research under White in 1939, was recommended for promotion by Coe, as Assistant Director, in June, 1941, and after his wartime Pentagon service, was rehired by Coe as Director in November, 1945. He was soon rated "excellent" by Glasser.[54]

Another case was that of Irving Kaplan, who, Miss Bentley said, had paid his dues to the Perlo group but had given information to the Silvermaster group ("Somehow the two groups got a little scrambled at that point"). According to Chambers, his employment in the National Research Project (of the WPA) in 1937–8, necessary during the flight from Colonel Bykov, was arranged by Kaplan, an employee of that organization, after Chambers had been personally referred to Kaplan by Silverman. During most of the war, Kaplan worked as statistician for the War Production Board, where he gave among his references Silverman and Currie, the latter intervening with Robert Patterson, the War Under Secretary, when Silvermaster was under fire in 1942 from the security authorities in the circumstances noted above.[55]

Later, effective July 12, 1945, Coe hired Kaplan as an economic adviser in the Division of Monetary Research, but the same day Kaplan was temporarily assigned to Treasury Foreign Funds Control and sent to Germany on the decartelization staff of the U.S. Group, Control Council. Back in the Division of Monetary Research by the end of the year Kaplan was soon rated "excellent" by Coe, and giving White as one of his Civil Service references at this time, was transferred to the Office of War Mobilization and Reconversion in May, 1946. Kaplan left government in 1947 to join the United Nations Organization and later declined to answer many questions about his career in Washington, including whether he had known White, on Fifth Amendment grounds.[56] What did seem certain was that Kaplan, an economist with the Pacific Gas and Electric Company in San Francisco before coming to Washington, had made a more interesting career in government after leaving the West.

Not all these "interrelations" involved departmental transfers. When questioned, White told the House Committee in August, 1948, that he had asked Silvermaster to come to the 1944 Bretton Woods Conference because "I thought it would be an excellent thing to have an economist and a man who knew Russian there to help in the interpretation and in the discussions." Silvermaster had fallen ill, White said, and he was of no use. Silvermaster later confirmed that White had arranged for him to attend the conference as a consultant—he was described as one of the technical secretaries of the American delegation—but "a severe attack of asthma" had forced him to leave Bretton Woods after a day or two.

Coe, however, the Assistant Administrator of the Foreign Economic Administration, had remained behind in the White Mountains as Technical Secretary-General of the conference. Ullmann, too, was in New Hampshire in July, 1944, as Assistant Secretary, Conference Management. An Army captain at the time, he had been borrowed for the conference from the Pentagon by the Treasury, the arrangement, Ullmann later thought, having been made by White. The following year, in April, 1945, Ullmann had also accompanied White as his assistant to the United Nations San Francisco Conference, where White was Treasury technical adviser.[57]

This particular line of inquiry initiated by Miss Bentley's general testimony on White must, however, be viewed against the fact that there were difficulties at Bretton Woods over the size of the Soviet quota of the

International Monetary Fund. Clearly a Russian-speaker such as Silver-master could have been useful as White maintained. Ullmann, too, the alleged photographer-in-chief of the Silvermaster group, was a former employee of White's and it might seem understandable why he should be seconded from the Pentagon to Bretton Woods.

Coe was another highly capable, former Division of Monetary Research man, and one who had attended some of the earlier interdepartmental conferences in Washington on the Fund. Adler, who was also at Bretton Woods to report to White after returning from Chungking at the beginning of July, was needed for conferences with White, Morgenthau, H. H. Kung and others on American war costs in China. These meetings took place at the same time as the Monetary Conference.

Yet if Miss Bentley's story was true in its essentials, it remains conceivable that the Russians may have been interested in obtaining confidential information from outside official channels on the deliberations of the Bretton Woods delegates. As we have seen, the Russians' interest in collecting information was not confined to conventional military or strategic items.

Following the conference, Lord Keynes went to Ottawa for financial discussions with the Canadian Government. Keynes returned to Ottawa later in 1944 for further talks. The Canadian Royal Commission of 1946, inquiring into Soviet espionage in the country, found that a Bank of Canada employee, Eric Adams, who gave material to a Soviet Military Intelligence network, collected secret information dealing with Keynes's financial discussions in Ottawa with the Canadian Government on both his 1944 visits.[58]

In its 1953 report on the testimony, and surrounding evidence, of thirty-six alleged members of the underground, the Senate Internal Security Subcommittee concluded that "they used each other's names for reference on application for federal employment. They hired each other. They promoted each other. They raised each other's salaries. They transferred each other from department to department, from congressional committee to congressional committee. They assigned each other to international missions. They vouched for each other's loyalty and protected each other when exposure threatened."[59]

Nevertheless, to conclude that some sort of hermetic organization created by White and some of his colleagues inside the Treasury was solely responsible for the advancement and mobility these men achieved inside the federal bureaucracy would hardly be correct. Thousands flocked to new government posts during the New Deal and the war, and professional accomplishments, buttressed by the familiar middle-class grapevine, meant that for many promotion and mobility were a commonplace in the 1930's and 1940's. White and his colleagues were surely a part of this process.

To assume, therefore, that those named by Miss Bentley were advanced simply for nonprofessional reasons, would be to ignore their manifestly high competence. But other factors may have entered the picture. As Earl Latham has suggested, far from being a master conspiracy planned from the beginning, as it was represented in some quarters years afterward, Party members or sympathizers may have arrived in Washington for all sorts of reasons, their casual, semi-clandestine political connections only systematically being used for infiltration and espionage as the mainspring of the Popular Front continued to unwind into the war years.[60]

Moreover, the differing goals of agitation and infiltration or espionage were mutually exclusive. Inevitably, however, any patronage operation closely associated with clandestine information-gathering would eventually mean that adherents of the underground would have other propellants in their careers than the usual professional, class and social ones.

White may have been telling the truth, therefore, when he told the committee in August, 1948, that competence was his guide in hiring colleagues. If such was the case, it should of course be emphasized that White (and the other officials noted above) were doing no more than their duty in the complex process of promotion and preferment we have referred to. But, equally so, if the testimony of Miss Bentley (and Chambers) was, on the whole, true, then White may not have been telling the whole truth about the matter.

One final question therefore remains. How can we reconcile the story of the witnesses with the considerable risks that White must have taken if what they said was true?

"Is Joe getting the stuff?" was the question, Miss Bentley tells us, that Victor Perlo once anxiously asked her in a Central Park West apartment: "A deep hush settled over the room; no one seemed to breathe."[61] The essence of what Professor Earl Latham has called "the companionate subversion" was not only its enthusiasm, but its gregariousness.

As we have seen, early as 1934, J. Peters, according to Chambers, considered it poor organization "where everybody knew everybody else," for the Ware group was essentially a promotional "cell" and not a compartmented espionage organization. In spite of Peters' concern to remedy this state of affairs, Chambers himself knew, in varying degrees of acquaintanceship, so he says, the members of his "special apparatus" which allegedly included Harry Dexter White. Almost a decade after the launching of the Ware group, the alleged Silvermaster group was still conducted as a collective espionage enterprise, its members linked pro-

fessionally and socially. Such conduct seems the antithesis of the supposedly arcane laws of espionage, of which both Miss Bentley and Chambers
write in a sometimes suggestive fashion.

Yet if we are to believe Miss Bentley and Chambers, in the critical time
of the 1930's and again after June, 1941, collection of intelligence material took precedence with the Russians over strict application of the well-
worn rules of espionage to protect their sources. As David Dallin, who
accepts the Bentley-Chambers testimony, has written, "collective espionage" as practiced by the Washington groups was, from Moscow's viewpoint, a "highly dangerous" form of intelligence activity: "In the course
of decades and at great cost, Soviet intelligence had learned and enforced
the principle that its agents and subagents must not be let into the secrets
of other Soviet agents, that the number of people in the know must be
kept to a minimum. . . . Espionage carried out by a 'cell' is contrary to the
rules of conspiracy."[62]

It will be recalled that according to her story, "Bill," Miss Bentley's
Soviet contact, pointedly told her in 1944 that the Russians did not believe in using such large groups as the Silvermaster organization "for
security reasons, because if someone turns sour, they know too much."[63]
The previous operations described by Miss Bentley had thus been carried
out at great risk to all concerned, a risk necessarily accepted by their
Soviet organizers, but perhaps not fully appreciated by all those allegedly
involved in the companionate subversion.

However, it was this process of "turning over" Miss Bentley's contacts
to the Soviet *apparat* that helped to bring about her own defection. But
as David Dallin has again commented, it was the revelation of the methods used by the Washington groups, as much as the fact of espionage
itself, which helped to bring about the subsequent uproar, "for only a
fraction of what was revealed would have become known had Soviet
espionage rules been followed in the U.S. during the war."[64]

Miss Bentley had not only "turned sour," she had also known far too
much. It was the broken dream of her new world that, as we shall see,
helped to end White's official career during 1946–47, besides going on to
precipitate, almost a quarter of a century ago, "a controversy of historical
bitterness."[65]

14

TOWARD BRETTON WOODS

The purposes of the International Monetary Fund are (i) To promote international monetary cooperation through a permanent institution . . . (ii) To facilitate the expansion and balanced growth of international trade. . . .

—ARTICLE I, INTERNATIONAL MONETARY FUND,
BRETTON WOODS, July, 1944

WHATEVER White's involvement in the Treasury's relations with China, and his interest in the planning for occupation currency, his chief preoccupation during the middle years of the war remained the development of the proposed postwar financial institutions. Here the author of the White Plan continued, with Keynes, to take a leading part in the negotiations which culminated in the Bretton Woods Conference of July, 1944.

Following the publication of the draft plans for the Stabilization Fund and the Clearing Union in April, 1943, discussions continued between the two countries, together with the British Dominions. A draft of the White Plan was circulated to the finance ministers of the countries allied against the Axis.

Then, in September, 1943, a British mission led by the Minister of State, Richard Law (later Lord Coleraine), arrived in Washington to discuss economic matters between the two countries. The mission included Keynes, Lionel Robbins and other British experts, both from London and the British Embassy in Washington.

The proposed postwar multilateral trading regime could not be implemented by financial institutions alone. Tariffs and other trade barriers would have to be adjusted, for without changes in commercial policy, it was believed, the Fund and the Bank could hardly cope with the anticipated payments problems of the postwar world. At the same time, White wrote, it was hoped that, "With the Fund, countries can undertake reciprocal tariff reduction knowing that such agreements will not be defeated by offsetting action on the exchanges."[1]

Hence the preliminary Anglo-American talks in Washington on commercial policy in the autumn of 1943, described by Richard Gardner as "taking place in the spirit of a university seminar rather than that of a formal international conference," were complementary to the negotiations on the financial institutions between White and Keynes.[2] The State Department's Division of Commercial Policy, led by Harry Hawkins, looked forward to "a multilateral convention on commercial policy" negotiated "among as many nations as possible."

In the Economic Section of the British War Cabinet Offices, James Meade had produced, as Penrose describes it, "a plan for an international commercial union of countries to reduce trade barriers to low levels." Commercial Union covered many of the points that were eventually incorporated into the proposed, but never ratified, International Trade Charter of 1947–48. But on commercial policy, in spite of differences, the British and the Americans were thinking along parallel lines. In these Washington talks on the commercial policy aspects of Article VII, which eventually led to the General Agreement on Tariffs and Trade (GATT) of 1947 as well as the abortive Trade Charter, there was a wide measure of agreement by the experts.

It was agreed, for example, that commercial policy and employment policy were interdependent. High levels of income and employment must be primary postwar objectives. The necessity for abolishing quantitative import restrictions was recognized. So was the need for discovering a suitable formula to reconcile the "reduction" of tariffs with the "elimination" of discrimination as suggested in the sibylline ambiguities of Article VII.

However, these were exploratory talks on principles, and in any case Commercial Union was not at this stage British policy. Opposition inside the British government meant that work on a commercial compromise was not resumed until 1945. It was over the more advanced details of the financial institutions that White and Keynes would now have to reach practical agreement if an international conference was to be called.

In July, 1943, prior to the Washington financial talks of September and October, White had written to Keynes with some agreed minimum conditions for American participation in an international stabilization fund. White stated that the proposed fund should be based on the contributory rather than the overdraft principle, and that the American commitment should be limited to $2–3 billion. The United States must also have a veto over the gold value of the dollar, then pegged at $35 per ounce. In August, 1943, Keynes replied accepting these proposals in principle, saying, however, that for British acceptance of such a fund greater provision must be made for exchange flexibility.[3]

This was the starting point of the Washington financial talks. The British, Harrod remarks, had agreed among themselves that they would have to accept the American wish for a fund of "limited liability," and "we may be sure that it was with heavy heart that Keynes abandoned his structure."

On the other hand, in view of their abandonment of the overdraft principle of the Internationl Clearing Union, the British now hoped to negotiate for greater flexibility in the structure of the proposed fund. They also wished to propose a maximum American subscription of $3 billion in a fund of about $10–12 billion. They hoped for a recognition of the automatic "passivity" of the fund in its operations, so eliminating any interference with national sovereignty as members sought fund resources.

Clearly, too, in view of the more restricted resources of the White Plan as opposed to the Clearing Union, the "scarce-currency" clause would now take on added significance in the negotiations. The existence of the clause was vital not only for the British negotiators in Washington, but for the British Cabinet in London.

As both sides in Washington began to realize that an acceptable compromise could be reached on the fund, Harrod comments that "the procedure actually adopted that White's Stabilization Fund was taken as the basis for an agreed draft, and Keynes was asked to erase all that he objected to and add what he wished. The resulting document was then discussed paragraph by paragraph in great detail."[4] Eventually, as we shall see, after further consultations by the experts during the winter of 1943–44, the agreed draft of what was basically a modified White Plan was published in April, 1944, as *Joint Statement by Experts on the Establishment of an International Monetary Fund.*[5]

With few alterations, the key provisions of the *Joint Statement* were then incorporated into the Fund Articles of Agreement signed at Bretton Woods in July, 1944. Because of the time spent on the complicated structure of the Fund, and a realization that the lending powers of the International Bank would have to be curtailed, work on this latter project lagged until the meeting of experts at Atlantic City, New Jersey, in June, 1944. However, the Articles of Agreement of the International Bank for Reconstruction and Development were also duly signed at Bretton Woods. But without the accord reached in the Washington talks between White and Keynes in the autumn of 1943, the Bretton Woods Conference would hardly have been a success.

How then did the Washington talks of 1943 between White, Keynes and their colleagues resolve the problems of the liquidity issue, of the balance-of-payments adjustment mechanism and, thirdly, of the expected transitional period from war to peace?

As far as the problem of liquidity was concerned, with the abandonment of the Clearing Union, the United States eventually agreed by the time of Bretton Woods to raise the total size of the Fund to $8.8 billion. Of this the American quota was $2.75 billion, that of the British $1.3 billion in sterling and gold, and voting was related to each country's quota, making the American vote the preponderant one. The essential structure of the White Plan remained unchanged, but the enlargement of the size of the Fund was of great importance.

One of the most influential Treasury technicians to work with White on the development of the Fund, Edward M. Bernstein, who coined the term "limited liability" to define the alternative American approach to the Keynes plan, has pointed out to the writer that "the American technicians, and particularly Harry D. White, were aware that a larger Fund would be preferable. The initial U.S. proposal for a $5 billion Fund of which the United States would contribute $2 billion was clearly too small."

Bernstein went on to comment on some of the chief considerations on the liquidity issue that White and his colleagues had in mind during the 1943 Washington negotiations, and afterward, with their British counterparts:

One result of the bilateral discussions of the U.K. technicians and the U.S. technicians was that the United States yielded to the United Kingdom (and it was a major point) on the size of the Fund. Another result was the specific inclusion of a provision for the quinquennial review of quotas designed to provide a means for the general increase in quotas. By the time of the Bretton Woods conference, U.S. support for the Fund was well-established, particularly in the Congress, and the opposition of the American Bankers Association could be almost (but not entirely) ignored, so that the U.S. technicians were less concerned about a larger Fund. The aggregate quotas at Bretton Woods were $8.8 billion. This was somewhat more than the maximum the U.S. technicians had in mind (they would have been satisfied with about $8 billion) and probably a little less than the minimum the U.K. technicians had in mind (about $10 billion). About half the excess above $8 billion (say, $400 million) was due to the need to satisfy the Russian demand for near-parity with the United Kingdom on quotas. The rest of the excess was the result of the tremendous pressure from European countries and from India for an increase in their quotas above the amounts proposed by the United States.

There were many ancillary questions that concerned the United States and precluded a larger Fund. For example, the United States wanted a quota for itself that would be at least equal to the aggregate quotas of the Commonwealth. This was more a political question than an economic question—although it was not unreasonable on straight economic grounds. I doubt that anybody really feared that the Commonwealth would attempt to outvote the United States in the Fund, but this was a ready answer to those in Congress who might have such fears. As the maximum the United States could subscribe to the Fund without a budget appropriation (as it was done as a public debt transaction) was $3 billion—the resources of the U.S. Exchange Stabilization Fund—this placed another limit on the size of the Fund as it would be necessary to have a larger U.S. subscription to make the Fund liquid. . . . It was essential, in our view, for the United States to know the maximum amount it would have to finance through the Fund.[6]

But a corollary of the relatively smaller amount of resources in the Fund, as compared with the Clearing Union, was that Keynes took the position at Washington that a Fund member should have automatic access until it had withdrawn resources equal to its quota. The United States, on the other hand, in the words of John Parke Young, "argued that the Fund should exercise control over all drawings on the Fund's resources and that no members should have an automatic right to utilize these resources."[6a]

Full agreement on this difference was not achieved at Washington. However, talks continued and the eventual compromise at Bretton. Woods, in Article V of the Articles of Agreement, stated that a Fund member would be "entitled" to buy currency from the Fund provided that it was "presently needed" for making payments consistent with the Articles of Agreement.

But, while "passivity" seemed to be conceded here, another section of Article V stated that the Fund could limit its assets when it considered that these resources were being used in a manner contrary to the purpose of the fund.[7] Here the Fund was necessarily "active," as White had wished. The ambiguity remained to be decided in practice. White and Keynes continued to debate this point at the inaugural meeting of the Fund at Savannah, Georgia, in March, 1946, when, inevitably perhaps, the American view prevailed.

A second way in which the British sought to preserve their freedom of action in negotiating over the Fund in Washington was through the development of a suitable mechanism of adjustment in case of balance-of-payments difficulties.

The large resources of Keynes' Clearing Union would have cushioned members, it was believed, from balance-of-payments difficulties. In a retreat from the consequent relative stability of exchange rates proposed by the Clearing Union, Keynes now sought ways of protecting internal domestic economies by obtaining a recognition from the Fund of each member's right to vary its exchange rate. The published draft of White's Stabilization Fund in April, 1943, had stated that variations in exchange rates would only be possible when there was a "fundamental disequilibrium" in a member's balance of payments. Moreover, in the 1943 White Plan, a four-fifths majority of the Fund would be needed to sanction such a change. As the United States had one-quarter of the votes in the proposed Stabilization Fund, it could thus veto proposed parity changes.

Under the eventual compromise incorporated into the Bretton Woods Articles of Agreement, the Fund had no power to prevent a currency depreciation of up to 10 percent. Above this figure, subject to a "fundamental disequilibrium" in a member's economy, the Fund was required to concur in the change proposed. Moreover, under the same Article IV, Section 5(f) of the Bretton Woods Agreements, the Fund could not oppose a currency depreciation on the grounds of the "domestic, social, or political policies of the member proposing the change." Keynes believed that these provisions would thus protect domestic expansion from international deflationary forces. The problem of possible inflationary disequilibrium remained.

With this move away from the relative exchange stability once envisaged by both White and Keynes, there was also a decreasing emphasis on the rights of the Fund to demand changes in internal domestic policies as a means of reaching payments adjustment. As we have seen, the published draft of White's Stabilization Fund in April, 1943, had stated that Fund members should "give consideration" to Fund views on domestic policies which could bring about balance-of-payments difficulties.

The British were opposed to a phrasing which could justify Fund interference in domestic matters, and the above provision relating to the internal responsibilities of possible debtor members was dropped by the Americans. But in the eventual Articles of Agreement it was stated in Article XII, Section 8, that the Fund could pass its views to members "on any matter arising under this agreement." The Fund could also by a two-thirds majority issue a public report to a member country on monetary or economic conditions which tended to produce a "serious disequilibrium" in the international balance of payments of members.

Between these provisions and those which explicity precluded Fund interference in domestic matters there was a fine balance which once again could only be resolved with the actual working of the Fund. But both sides in the Washington negotiations had seen that a compromise was necessary on this thorny subject of Fund responsibility toward domestic policies. White himself was quite aware of this aspect of negotiations. Harrod relates in his biography of Keynes that when, during the negotiations, the British proposed that the right of immediate withdrawal from the Fund be recognized White objected. But E. M. Bernstein reminded him that, without such a provision, "this may mean a lot of trouble for us in Congress," and White eventually agreed with the British on this point.

Critical to the whole problem of the adjustment issue under the Fund was, it will be recalled, the extent to which White's "scarce-currency" clause put the onus for adjustment on the creditor. In some ways the clause was further strengthened as a result of the Washington talks. Under Article VII Section 3(b) of the Fund Articles of Agreement, the Fund was authorized both to ration scarce creditor currency and to allow members temporarily "to impose limitations" on the freedom of exchange operations in that currency. Each Fund member was to have "complete jurisdiction" in "determining the nature of such limitations."

But, as Richard Gardner has pointed out, in some ways this drafting of the scarce-currency clause did not provide a totally effective mechanism of adjustment. If a scarcity of the said currency developed *outside* the Fund, members might still be affected and be forced to devalue.

There remained, too, the extent to which the *creditor country* could be compelled to make adjustments. Absent from the Fund Articles signed at Bretton Woods was the specific provision of the White Plan that the Fund could issue a report to the creditor country with recommendations for restoring equilibrium, so placing a special responsibility on that country for action. Here, perhaps, the Americans had seen a possible threat to their own sovereignty. The absence of such specific responsibility was certainly invoked by White during the Congressional debates on Bretton Woods.

But perhaps one of the single most important results of the White-Keynes negotiations in Washington was the British conviction that the scarce-currency clause would be of crucial importance in dealing with the expected postwar economic imbalance between the United States and the rest of the world. On his return to London in October, 1943, Keynes wrote to the Chancellor of the Exchequer, Sir John Anderson, that the scarce-currency clause "puts the creditor country on the spot so acutely that in the view of all of us, the creditor country simply cannot afford to let such a situation arise." Keynes went on to write that "if the Americans really live up to their present proposals, it will be the U.S.A. and not the rest of us which will get into real trouble, if the U.S.A. develops a favourable balance of payments which is not adequately disposed of by foreign lending in some way."

In a statement for British Ministers drafted after the return of the Law Mission, Keynes wrote that the scarce-currency clause was "a revolutionary change for the better compared with the position in the inter-war period."[8] Thus the Washington talks had reached a wide measure of creative agreement on the proposed amount of liquidity, the structure, and the mechanism of adjustment of the proposed Fund.

The difficulty of finding a way to bridge the transitional postwar period proved more intractable. As we have noted, the original draft of the White Plan in 1942 had mentioned the "huge volume of capital" necessary for reconstruction. During 1942–43, with a weather eye on Congress, White had revised many of the ambitious proposals for the International Bank. The project was only very briefly discussed during the Washington financial negotiations.

Then, following the publication of a revised draft of the International Bank in November, 1943, there were further exchanges between London and Washington. The British did not expect to draw on the Bank's resources. In any case they anticipated that their own postwar difficulties would be large enough to preclude them from lending to other countries on an extensive scale. The Americans concurred that on the whole the Bank should primarily guarantee private loans, thus limiting the Bank's role as a lending institution in its own right. It was tentatively agreed that only a small part of the Bank's capital should be called up, the rest remaining as a reserve. Behind these talks on the Bank lay the fact that, while withdrawals from the Fund were related to quotas, borrowings from the Bank would be unrelated to capital subscription. Hence the reluctance on the part of many countries to volunteer large subscriptions for the International Bank.

Following the June, 1944, meeting of experts at Atlantic City, the Bank emerged at Bretton Woods, as we shall see, as a relatively conservative institution. The spirit of White's ambitious first draft survived in Article I, which stated that among the Bank's functions would be that of "the restoration of economies destroyed or disrupted by war." But, with the restricted development of the Bank during 1943–44, there was little possibility that its ambitious earlier functions could be fulfilled.

Originally, moreover, White had intended that the Stabilization Fund should attempt to liquidate, as part of the transitional process, the accumulated sterling balance. But this solution tended to confuse the long-term problem of the British wartime debts to overseas countries with the short-term operations of the Fund. In any case, the British preferred for political reasons to deal with these commitments on a bilateral basis, hoping to restore some of the importance of the prewar sterling area.

By the time of Bretton Woods, therefore, both countries were agreed that the problem of the sterling balances should be left out of the Fund's operations. The transitional problem, described by White in a later draft of the Bank proposals as how to "facilitate a rapid and smooth transition from a wartime to peacetime economy in the United Nations,"[9] remained.

With this problem in mind, Keynes wrote to White in December, 1943, suggesting that a new section on "transitional arrangements" be inserted into the Fund agreements. Such a provision would allow the British and other countries, as a consequence of the war, to maintain for a short time sterling-area arrangements and agreements. This temporary departure from the envisaged multilateral trading regime provided for an interim postwar period of three years in Article X of the *Joint Statement* of April, 1944. But, in Article XIV of the Fund Agreements at Bretton Woods, the period was extended to five years. After this period, members were to consult with the Fund as to whether to retain restrictions. Logically, therefore, Article XIV also stipulated that the Fund was not responsible for relief and reconstruction in the postwar period.

Taken as a whole the original supranational tendencies of the White Plan had been qualified, in the final Fund agreement, by the demands of national sovereignty and the expected exigencies of the postwar transitional period. Moreover, the Anglo-American compromise, which was basically adopted at Bretton Woods, left the matter of access to the Fund's resources to be decided in practice. Here there was ambiguity as to whether the Fund's dispensations were automatic or not.

At the same time, there was significant provision for varying exchange rates, and thus more national freedom from Fund supervision in this matter. With the scarce-currency clause there was a somewhat indeterminate, but politically important, provision for creditor responsibility in adjusting a Fund member's balance of payments. With the scaling down of the Bank's functions, the transitional problem had been attacked by allowing for a postwar period when wartime exchange restrictions and other measures would be perpetuated.

In the event, for all their concern, the dislocation of the war had been underestimated by the Anglo-American negotiators, as was the associated magnitude of the reconstruction problem and the postwar "dollar shortage." But it was understandable at the time why Keynes, with the provisional technical agreement on the Fund, looking forward to "a revolutionary change for the better."

However, the objectivity and the achievement of the Anglo-American talks in Washington on the Fund would hardly have been possible without the devoted work of the participating experts. Harrod comments that a group of honest technicians trying to solve problems on their merits had been turned into "a group of friends working together for a common cause." Yet withal, it was the collision of will and intelligence between White and Keynes that was the decisive catalyst in the Washington talks.

Keynes was not a full British delegate in Washington as he was on later visits to the United States, as the talks were exploratory. But he was sorely tried, we have it on Harrod's authority, by White's "rasping truculence." Behind the scenes, the authors of the White Plan and the Keynes Plan eventually became cronies and went off to the baseball game together. The friendship grew.

Yet the contrast between the scion of Eton, King's College and Bloomsbury and the offspring of Lowell Street, Harvard and the United States Treasury was an intriguing one. Keynes, a world figure ever since Versailles and *The Economic Consequences of the Peace*, possessed an incomparable aura of achievement and was preeminent in his field. It was only with the publication of the White Plan in April, 1943, and the Bretton Woods Conference over a year later that White became widely known outside the United States Treasury. Both men's self-assurance, sustained by different roots, different achievements, could verge on arrogance. While Keynes, perhaps, represented the greater intellectual force, White personified the power and the will without which no agreement was possible. Was it not a draft of the White Plan that lay between the two men?

Dean Acheson, Assistant Secretary of State from 1941 to 1945, was a close friend of Keynes during the Washington negotiations, and a fellow American negotiator with White on British Lend-Lease matters. He was a member of the American delegation to Bretton Woods. Discussing White with the writer, Acheson remarked that he had a "great respect" for White whom he yet considered "utterly ruthless" in his character. Yet paradoxically, Acheson went on, White was more conservative and less radical than Keynes in his conception of the Fund. Moreover, White was "profoundly jealous" of Keynes.[10]

With this maze of subterranean differences between White and Keynes, it seems hardly surprising that their negotiating relationship was a stormy one. The two men would sit side by side at the top of a long table, the British and American experts on either side. "Well, Harry," Keynes would remark, "what shall it be today, passivity, exchange stability, or the role of gold?"

Informality would lead to discussion and disagreement and then to anger. Papers would be thrown on the floor, differences would be made up. White would be taken out of his depth by the older man—who could not be taken out of his depth by Keynes?—and retaliate by reminding

Keynes of his stronger negotiating position. Once, Harrod writes, White ironically referred to Keynes as "Your Royal Highness." But one element in this situation was that White probably felt that he had to show his Treasury colleagues that he was not "soft" on the British negotiators.

Yet, "what a satisfaction it must have given White to negotiate on equal terms with the great man himself!" Well might one veteran of these negotiations remark: 'The happiest moment in the life of Harry White came when he could call Keynes by his first name.' "[11]

On April 21, 1944, Morgenthau announced in Washington that the technical experts of the United Nations had agreed on the principle of an International Monetary Fund. The release of the *Joint Statement* did not commit any government, of course, but was instead a practical recommendation to the countries concerned on postwar monetary arrangements.

The experts having agreed, the next stage was the preparation of the long-desired international conference. These preliminaries coincided with the mounting crescendo of the war in the West as the Allies prepared for the Normandy landings. On May 25, therefore, Roosevelt endorsed plans for arrangements which had been made by Morgenthau, White and Dean Acheson. It was agreed that the "United Nations Monetary and Financial Conference" should meet in July. The site would be the salubrious resort of Bretton Woods in the White Mountains of New Hampshire, where there were excellent hotels and a cool summer climate.[12]

In London there were rumblings of the controversy that would continue from the publication of the *Joint Statement* until the Bretton Woods Agreements (and the Anglo-American Loan) were finally approved by Parliament in December, 1945. Already in March, 1944, Keynes had written to White from the Treasury in Whitehall noting that the *Joint Statement* was likely to be attacked in Britain as "no better than the gold standard."[13]

In the debate on the *Joint Statement* in the House of Commons on May 10, Keynes's prescience was justified. Speakers from right and left combined to attack the Fund as a threat to the pound and to the sterling area as well as to British living standards. The new system was seen as one which inflexibly precluded bilateral trading policies.[14]

The American Embassy in London reported to the State Department on May 13 that in an informal conversation Keynes had stated that "incredible stupidity" had been shown in the debate. However, Keynes thought that the Monetary Plan "can be passed." The Embassy went on to report Keynes as saying that he "constantly kept political factors in mind during the drafting of the Monetary Plan and frequently put in phrases which spiked the guns of hostile critics or allayed the fears of

honest doubters without making any difference whatsoever to the substance of the plan."[15]

A few days later, on May 23, Keynes robustly defended the assumptions of the *Joint Statement* in the House of Lords. He outlined, as he
had for British ministers, the value of the scarce-currency clause as a
means of financial adjustment. He placed great emphasis on the national
freedom to vary exchange rates. Repudiating any return to the gold
standard, Keynes described as "near frenzy" the assumption that Britain
could survive economically by a system of bilateral agreements and
barter trading with the Dominions. Keynes appeared to suggest that
Fund resources, equivalent to the British quota, would be unconditionally available.

Replying to concern expressed in the Commons over the postwar transitional period, Keynes also emphasized that the reconstruction problem
would perhaps be dealt with by new Anglo-American measures, "another
chapter of international cooperation, upon which we shall embark shortly
if you do not discourage us unduly about this one." In any case, pending
the solution of the transitional problem, Britain would be free to retain
wartime sterling-area restrictions.[16]

In June, as preparations for the Bretton Woods Conference went
ahead, some sixty representatives from fifteen countries met with American experts at Atlantic City, New Jersey, to study the proposals that
would be formally considered by the conference. White was in the chair,
and Keynes arrived later in the month from England. Some questions,
such as the extent of the transitional period, and the final amount of some
of the national quotas, where considerations of political prestige were
concerned, remained to be settled at Bretton Woods. But there were no
serious disagreements over the Fund at Atlantic City.

Moreover, preliminary discussions on the International Bank at Atlantic City went well. These plans looked forward to a total capital of about
$10 billion, with the American subscription about one-third of the total.
But only about 20 percent of national subscriptions would be on call.
While the Bank could make direct loans from its own capital, its primary
role, as White saw it, would be to guarantee private loans for reconstruction and development. This guarantee would be backed by more than
forty nations. There was thus a wide consensus of international agreement on the purposes of the Fund and the Bank at Atlantic City.[17]

After three years of work by the American and British experts, assisted by
the technicians of the other Allies, the United Nations Monetary and
Financial Conference opened at Bretton Woods on July 1, 1944. The
American delegation included Morgenthau as chairman, Fred Vinson,
Director of Economic Stabilization, Dean Acheson, E. E. Brown the

banker, and Marriner Eccles of the Federal Reserve. Besides Harry Dexter White there were four members of Congress, two Democrats and two Republicans. The chairman of the British delegation was Lord Keynes. Other members, including experts who had previously negotiated with the Americans, were Professor Lionel Robbins, Professor D. H. Robertson of the British Treasury, Redvers Opie of the British Embassy in Washington, and R. H. (later Lord) Brand, the British Treasury representative in the United States.

The formal task of piloting the proposals hammered out by White, Keynes and the other experts through an international conference attended by the representatives of forty-four countries was a formidable one. White was insistent that all amendments should be considered, and three commissions were set up. The first, under White's chairmanship, looked after the Fund, while the second, under Keynes, was responsible for the development of the Bank. A third commission, chaired by Eduardo Suarez of Mexico, dealt with residual matters.

The chief work of the commissions was carried out in subcommittee, and White and Keynes sat apart in their offices to deal with matters as they arose. "For three and a half weeks," White later wrote, "these experts labored 14 to 16 hours a day in committees and subcommittees, going over every provision, studying every suggestion, discussing in greatest detail every point of differences. Each line of each provision was subjected to the closest scrutiny. . . ."[18]

Eventually, agreement was reached on the Bank. With its authorized capital of $10 billion, it was confirmed that only 20 percent of its capital would be immediately subject to call, and only 2 percent of each country's total subscription would have to be paid in American dollars or gold. The nominal American subscription would be $3.175 billion, that of the United Kingdom $1.3 billion. But stressing the relatively conservative nature of the Bank, its maximum amount of loans and guarantees was limited to 100 percent of its capital, not a multiple as White had once envisaged. As the cooperation of the international banking community would necessarily be needed for its successful operation, the Bank emerged at Bretton Woods as essentially an underwriting institution which would complement rather than replace private investment.

Other questions that were dispatched at Bretton Woods included an agreement to extend the transitional provisions of the Fund from three to five years. It was also agreed that the headquarters of the new agencies should be located in "the territory of the member having the largest quota." This phrasing was adopted following Keynes's protest, for the British were reserving their position at this stage on a formal proposal explicitly to locate the new institutions in the United States.

Finally, after prolonged negotiation that had lasted throughout most of the conference, the Russians agreed at the final plenary meeting on July 22 to provide a full subscription of $1.2 billion to the International Bank, equivalent to their Fund quota. The decision was greeted with much applause, and thus made Russia third to the United States and the United Kingdom in its formal financial support of the new agencies.

On July 22, 1944, the Articles of Agreement of the International Monetary Fund and the International Bank for Reconstruction and Development were signed by the delegates at Bretton Woods.[19]

The primary means through which the Fund's purposes were to be achieved included the provision that members would undertake to keep their exchange rates as stable as possible, confining fluctuations to narrow limits, and to make no changes unless essential to correct a "fundamental disequilibrium" in their payments situation. Beyond certain variations, as we have seen, exchange rates could only be adjusted after consultation or with the concurrence of the Fund.

In addition, par values of members' currencies were to be stated in terms of gold (or American dollars at "the weight and fineness" of July 1, 1944), and gold was to be accepted by members in settlement of account. Fund members agreed not to engage in discriminatory currency practices, except with Fund approval, or to impose restrictions on current account international payments. Existing restrictions were to be abandoned, as noted, following the postwar transitional period. The Fund was to be governed by a board of executive directors, functioning in the Fund's headquarters, and, as a necessary ballast to the idealistic purposes of the Fund, voting was weighted according to the size of a member's quota. Essentially, therefore, the system set up at Bretton Woods in July, 1944, was based on the two props of relatively fixed exchange rates and the general convertibility of the dollar against gold at the rate of $35 per ounce of gold. The ultimate guarantee of the Bretton Woods system lay in the preponderant strength of the American economy.

With agreement reached, Morgenthau, in his closing address to the conference, in language reminiscent of Roosevelt's first inaugural, remarked that the agreements would drive the "usurious money lenders from temple of high finance." The new agencies would be "foundation stones for the structure of lasting peace and security." Morgenthau went on to say that the "only genuine safeguard for our national interests lies in international cooperation."

In a letter to Roosevelt the same day which reflected the general enthusiasm at the closing of the conference, Morgenthau considered that the Soviet decision to raise Moscow's Bank subscription illustrated the Russian "desire to collaborate fully with the United States."[20]

The conferences had thus ended on a euphoric note of "a New Deal for a new world," and the signing of the Bretton Woods Articles of Agreement marked the apex of White's career. Keynes himself had recognized this when in his closing address he remarked that "no similar conference within memory has achieved such a bulk of solid lucid construction. We owe this not least to the indomitable will and energy, always governed by good temper and humour, of Harry White."

From this peak the two men's lives once again diverged. Keynes went on to Ottawa for financial talks with the Canadian government. On July 24, two days after the final session at Bretton Woods, the War Department in Washington issued orders that White was "appointed an official courier on a special mission for the President of the United States, traveling to the United Kingdom."[21]

Within little more than a week White was en route to London, energies released after his triumph at Bretton Woods for participation in perhaps the most far-reaching of all the grand designs in which he was involved during his career. He would soon be deeply immersed in the drafting of what came to be known as the Morgenthau Plan for postwar Germany.

PART IV

THE PROBLEM OF GERMANY

1944–45

15

THE CARTHAGINIAN PEACE

The problem is not the destruction. The problem is population.
—HARRY DEXTER WHITE, September, 1944

IN EARLY August, 1944, in his fifty-second year, his prestige and influence in the Treasury at its height following the successful conclusion of the Bretton Woods Conference, White left Washington for London with Morgenthau.

The Secretary was making the trip to discuss Lend-Lease and the problem of the British dollar balances in London, and also to inspect Treasury financial arrangements for liberated France, where, as White and Morgenthau arrived in Britain, the Anglo-American armies under General Eisenhower were beginning their spectacular breakout from the Normandy beachhead. Clearly, the end of the war in Europe was in sight, but Morgenthau was not at this time expecting to become specifically involved in questions of Germany's future. Immersed in the developments leading to Bretton Woods, he had given little thought to such questions, passionately committed as he was, of course, to the Allied cause.

As the aircraft swung out over the Atlantic on August 6, Morgenthau later recalled, one of his assistants, White, "pulled out of his briefcase" a copy of "a State Department memorandum" on German reparations: "I settled down to read it, first with interest, then with misgivings, finally with disagreement." While favoring controls over German war potential, the paper envisaged the eventual reintegration of Germany into the world economy.

The provision in the paper that German reparations should be taken out of current production over a period of some years, White explained, would mean that Germany would again become the heart of industrial

Europe. The German industrial plant would be reconstructed, and when reparations were completed Europe would be dependent on Germany, while that country, capable of maintaining its own economy and producing reparations, would not be dependent on Europe.

In Morgenthau's view, the paper that White had shown him failed to deal with "the basic question," the establishment of conditions that would prevent Germany from attempting to dominate Europe for a third time. The Secretary decided to find out more about Allied policy for Germany.

Landing at Prestwick, Scotland, at midnight on August 6, the official party was soon ensconced on a special train taking them to the south of England. At noon the next day, White and Morgenthau arrived at Eisenhower's headquarters near Portsmouth, for lunch with the Supreme Commander.[1]

At the center of the wartime policy discussions in the Allied capitals over the future of Germany, and which had long preceded White's flight to England in August, 1944, lay indeed "the basic question" of international security. How could a future resurgence of German power be prevented by the Allies? How could the Allies root out National Socialism? How could the victors preserve their own interests after victory was won?

The remarkable story of Nazi aggression and atrocity meant, of course, that there was strong sentiment in the Allied countries in favor of the strict punishment and reform of Germany. In the United States and Great Britain there was central agreement that there should be strict denazification, demilitarization, some form of reparations and the trial of those responsible for Nazi crimes. The associated view of Nazism as a criminal conspiracy placed stress on individual responsibility and was, of course, formally enshrined in the Nuremberg International Military Tribunal set up by the Allies.

In addition to these measures, opinion on the left, discerning an apparent connection between capitalism and Nazism, tended to stress that structural reform, or nationalization, was essential to control German heavy industry. But this approach certainly implied a differentiation between Nazis and non-Nazis, unlike the views of Lord Vansittart, who emphasized in his wartime speeches and writing the "incurably bellicose" nature of all Germans, a view usually described as a conservative one. In addition to strict controls over German war potential, and possible decentralization of the Reich, Vansittart advocated a prolonged reeducating occupation by all the Allies. There was, of course, no precise demarcation between these mooted solutions to the problem of European security in the public discussion.

The difficulties of attempting to form some sort of agreed Allied policy toward Germany while the war was still being fought were, as we have seen above, insuperable. To be sure, at the Teheran Conference, the three wartime leaders had taken a stern line. Roosevelt, who expected American troops to be withdrawn from the Continent after the war, had suggested splitting Germany into five autonomous states and three international zones, including the Ruhr and the Saar. Churchill had advocated the isolation of Prussia and the creation of a Danubian confederation, while Stalin, in the Prime Minister's words, thought "it was far better to break up and scatter the German tribes."

In any case, Roosevelt himself may have believed, as a corollary of his views expressed at Teheran, that the problem of security from Germany, given the desired continuation of the wartime alliance, would be partly solved, willy nilly, by the inevitable extension of Russian power. In a conversation with Cardinal Spellman on September 3, 1943, the President was in a candid, "realistic" mood. After the war, he told Spellman, "it might be assumed that Russia will predominate in Europe." Roosevelt hoped, although it might be wishful thinking, "that the Russian intervention in Europe would not be too harsh. . . . European countries will have to undergo tremendous changes in order to adapt to Russia, but he hoped that in ten or twenty years the European influences would bring the Russians to become less barbarian. Be that as it may . . . the European people will simply have to endure the Russian domination in the hope that in ten or twenty years they will be able to live well with the Russians. . . ."[2]

However, Churchill's remark that the discussion at Teheran was only "a preliminary survey of a vast historical problem" shows that the wartime leaders were in no hurry to take precipitate decisions. Anxious to avoid commitments while the alliance was still necessary to win the war, aware of the power and prerogatives of Congress, Roosevelt and, to a lesser degree, Churchill adopted what John L. Snell has called a "policy of postponement" on wider issues. The policy was, of course, tacitly admitted by the wartime emphasis in the United States and Great Britain on the generalities of the Atlantic Charter and the military imperatives of the Casablanca formula of unconditional surrender.

Officials on a less exalted level in London and Washington found the postponement of decision frustrating, but a great deal of preparatory work was done in the middle war years. In Whitehall, as early as 1942–43, a British interdepartmental committee under Sir William Malkin, the legal adviser to the Foreign Office, considered the problems of "economic security" and reparations in connection with postwar Germany. The emphasis was on limited reparations in kind, and the studies begun under Malkin were later carried out under another Whitehall interdepartmental group, the Economic and Industrial Planning Staff. Later, during 1944, these economic studies were complemented by the political deliberations of the Armistice and Postwar Committee, a ministerial committee under the chairmanship of C. R. Attlee, the Deputy Prime Minister.

In the deliberations of this committee the Foreign Office had argued in favor of the thesis that the United Kingdom was unlikely to obtain its political or economic objectives in Germany if the country were reduced to chaos. Eden also was not sure that it would be wise to enforce the partition of Germany. True to the policy of postponement, immersed in other, even more urgent problems, no formal decision on German partition had been taken by the British War Cabinet by the time of the Yalta Conference in early 1945.[3]

However, progress had been made in other directions. A few weeks before the Teheran Conference, the Moscow Conference of foreign ministers discussed Germany. Hull had presented an American view of postwar Germany, and there was tacit agreement with Eden and Molotov on the minimum provisions of a joint zonal occupation, enforced by an Inter-Allied Control Commission. There was no enthusiasm among the foreign ministers at this time for German dismemberment as such, and the Moscow Conference set up the tripartite European Advisory Commission (EAC) to study and make recommendations to the three governments on "European questions connected with the termination of hostilities which the three governments may consider appropriate to refer to it." The first formal meeting of the EAC then took place in London in January, 1944.

During the spring and summer of 1944, the EAC, meeting in Lancaster House, slowly reached provisional agreement on the German instrument of surrender, control machinery, and zonal areas, subject to the reservation that both the United States and the United Kingdom wanted the northwestern zone of Germany. However, the United States War Department tended to regard all matters concerned with the German surrender and the subsequent occupation as military ones. This meant that the State Department was unable, in effect, to obtain military clearance in Washington for its wider directives on postwar Germany to be submitted for tripartite negotiation by Ambassador Winant, the American member of the EAC.[4]

The differences between the State and the War departments did not mean that the United States Army was averse to seeing conquered Germany treated as a going concern. The concept of "military necessity" provided doctrinally, in Paul Y. Hammond's words, "for rapid reconstruction in order to alleviate the burdens upon Allied supplies, both for relief and military purposes."[5] And although the Army's Civil Affairs Division believed in protectively confining its operations to technical tasks, eschewing the wider policy areas as it followed a course of "limited liability" in such matters, the Combined Chiefs of Staff had informally approved a significant directive for Eisenhower which had been dispatched on April 28, 1944.

The directive, CCS-551, which provided for the Anglo-American military government, under SHAEF, of Germany prior to surrender or defeat, decreed in its political guide that, while Nazism was to be eliminated, law and order was to be preserved, and normal conditions were to be restored "as soon as possible, insofar as such conditions will not interfere with military operations."[6]

Finally, in the most ambitious attempt to define American policy toward Germany, there were the State Department's plans for "a stern peace with reconciliation," which had been further refined since the Moscow Conference of October, 1943. In the spring of 1944 the department reached internal agreement on a program which envisaged the eventual return of Germany into the world economy, opposed partition, and emphasized the necessity of avoiding German economic collapse. Control, not destruction of German heavy industry was foreseen, and of course such objectives were in harmony with Cordell Hull's wider postwar objectives, and the tentative work of such British groups as the Malkin Committee.

In June, 1944, the State Department presented its general position on economic objectives and reparations to the Executive Committee on Economic Foreign Policy, an interdepartmental group set up in April under the chairmanship of Dean Acheson, Assistant Secretary of State. The ECEFP consisted of representatives of the State, Treasury, Commerce and Agriculture departments, together with other agencies. Harry Dexter White was the Treasury representative, and State hoped that committee agreement would help the department to obtain full clearance for Winant's directives from the military. These directives could then be negotiated on a tripartite level by the EAC in London.

Eventually, two important papers on postwar German policy were approved by the ECEFP on August 4, 1944. The first, on general objectives, emphasized the necessity of preventing a collapse of the German economy. The chief portion of the second paper, "Report on Reparations, Restitution and Property Rights," was a recommendation on a reparations agreement, and this of course was the "State Department memorandum" shown by White to Morgenthau en route to London. The paper recommended that reparations in kind from inventories, capital equipment and current production should begin as soon as possible after hostilities ceased, and continue for five to ten years. The whole tone of the paper with its preliminary suggestion of "the eventual reintegration of Germany into the world economy," and the American objective of an "early return to a multilateral system of international trade and finance" placed it in the mainstream of much of the work of the postwar planners we have noted above in connection with the background to Bretton Woods.[7]

White himself, busy at Bretton Woods, had not been able to attend the meetings of the ECEFP, and had thus sent substitutes, Harold Classer and Norman Ness. As White later told Morgenthau, he had become acquainted with the results of the work of the ECEFP in the week after Bretton Woods Conference, which had ended on July 22. White was not in agreement with the policy papers, felt that they were "not in line" with the Secretary's views, and had accordingly told the Treasury representatives to reserve the department's position when the papers were approved on August 4. "En route to England," White commented, "I called the Secretary's attention to the [Reparations] report...."[8]

In any case, even without the reports of the ECEFP, White could have little doubt of the course of Allied preparations for the conquered German economy. On July 15, two Treasury representatives from the Division of Monetary Research attached to the American Embassy in London, W. H. Taylor and E. C. Aarons, reported to White that it was "really amazing" that among the various American and British agencies there, including SHAEF, the Combined Civil Affairs Committee, and the EAC, there were "two basic assumptions."

The first was that the Allied military should cause minimum disturbance to the German economy, and the second assumed that reconstruction of German industry "was vital" in order that Germany might become the industrial supplier of devastated Europe. Such a view, reported Taylor and Aarons, "leaves us cold."[9] White's energies in the months to come were now to be fully employed in attempting to change these "two basic assumptions."

On August 7, 1944, White and Morgenthau lunched with Eisenhower in the general's mess tent at his headquarters at Southwick House, near Portsmouth. Present also was Fred Smith, another of Morgenthau's assistants, and a former New York advertising executive, who had accompanied the Secretary on the trip to England.

According to Smith's account of the meeting, White, speaking on Germany, questioned the Army's standing instructions that Civil Affairs was to move up and quickly bolster the economy to prevent Allied troops from bogging down "in a morass of economic wreckage." Unlike liberated countries, the situation in Germany was entirely different. Germany, White said, "was the end of the road." Once conquered, the country did not need to support a fighting force. Yet, said White, the Army directive had not been altered to suit the changed situation. As it now stood, Civil

Affairs would move up, the mark would be established, utilities would be repaired, and life "would be reestablished on as high a plane as feasible as quickly as possible." White went on to say: "What I think is that we should give the entire German economy an opportunity to settle down before we do anything with it."

Eisenhower, according to Smith, stated that he was not interested in the German economy and personally he would like to "see things made good and hard" for the Germans for a while. The general said that talk of letting Germany off easily came from those who feared Russia. This was a problem, Eisenhower considered, because "the strength of Russia is fantastic." The general went on to say that the whole German population is "a synthetic paranoid," and he could see no point in bolstering their economy or taking any steps to help them. According to Morgenthau's account of the meeting, Eisenhower considered that the best cure would be "to let the Germans stew in their own juice."

In his own account of this meeting, in *Crusade in Europe*, which has no reference to White, Eisenhower writes that during the conversation Morgenthau stated that the rate of monetary exchange in occupied Germany should avoid giving that country any advantage. In the ensuing general conversation, Eisenhower insisted that the Germans must not be allowed to escape a sense of guilt. Germany should be responsible for reparations to war-ravaged countries, the war-making power should be eliminated, possibly by "strict controls," or preventing the manufacture of aircraft, and the Germans should be permitted and required to make their own living, not assisted by the United States. "Choking off natural resources would be folly," Eisenhower said, and he considered one suggestion he had heard that the Ruhr mines should be flooded as "silly and criminal." (White later opposed wrecking the Ruhr mines.)

Clearly there need not have been any contradiction between bringing home a sense of guilt to the conquered, and a longer-term program of reparations and controls which were no part of the future Morgenthau Plan. According to Morgenthau's own account, however, it was this conversation with Eisenhower and White that set his ideas "percolating." The veteran farmer of Jeffersonian persuasion knew "that people who lived close to the land tended to be tranquil and peace-loving by nature, to be sturdily independent and hostile to outside tyranny. Why not make Germany predominantly a nation of small farmers?"

While Smith's account of the meeting implies that Eisenhower helped to fire the Morgenthau Plan, in 1953, when White's alleged Communist affiliations were under public discussion, Smith was quoted as saying that Eisenhower had said nothing about making Germany an agrarian nation. Smith considered that the plan was hatched in the mind of White, who sold it to Morgenthau, and that Eisenhower "walked into it." What does seem certain is that when Morgenthau returned to Washington from England he believed that Eisenhower agreed with his outline ideas for postwar Germany, and was a potential ally in the coming battle with the State Department.[10]

Following the meeting with Eisenhower, Morgenthau left for a tour of the Normandy battlefront, but as Smith puts it, "he was anxious to get back to the thing that was consuming him," and soon returned to England. Here the Morgenthau party was based at Redrice, an elegant, classical-style country house built in the early Victorian age. The house was near Andover in Hampshire, near the edge of Salisbury Plain, where part of the ancient estate had been leased by the United States Army for the duration.

During Cabinet-level talks in London over the British dollar-balances and associated Lend-Lease problems, Morgenthau sounded out Sir John Anderson, the British Chancellor, on postwar German policy. Sir John was studiously noncommittal on Morgenthau's proposal to turn the Germans "into small agricultural land holders," since he believed that Germany should be allowed to make nonmilitary items. In another meeting with Winston Churchill, the Prime Minister told Morgenthau that Britain was "bankrupt," but the Secretary came away with the feeling that Churchill, "while having minor reservations," was "a supporter" of his plan for Germany.[11]

White had not been idle, as became evident when Morgenthau called a conference at Redrice on August 12. It was in this appropriately pastoral setting that the essence of what soon became known as the Morgenthau Plan was first unveiled before a group of high American officials. Present besides White were Ambassador Winant, his political adviser on EAC matters, Philip Mosely, his economic adviser, E. F. Penrose and Walter Radius, a State Department expert on communications and transportation. From the Treasury there was Josiah E. DuBois, a senior department lawyer who had accompanied White and Morgenthau to England, and W. H. Taylor and L. C. Aarons, the Treasury officials in London. Present, too, was Colonel Bernard Bernstein, also a former Treasury official, and now the head of the Finance Section, Civil Affairs Division, SHAEF.

Winant and his party had driven down from London, and over lunch Morgenthau asked Penrose for an account of the British planning on postwar Germany. Winant's economic adviser then outlined developments in Whitehall, and in reply to a query from Morgenthau suggested that the British "were not a vengeful people." After questions and a subsequent summing up by White, the party broke up and reassembled in the afternoon sunshine on the wide lawn surrounding the house, today the playing fields of the boys' boarding school that occupies Redrice. During the adjournment, Mosely had expounded the State Department's views on postwar Germany to Penrose and White. There was "nothing to indicate," Penrose records, that White had studied the subject or formulated even the barest outlines of any "plan" on it.

Morgenthau now outlined in simple terms his program for Germany. He feared both America and Britain favored a "soft peace," and this attitude would lead to a third world war if it were accepted. The only way to prevent such a war was to destroy Germany's economic as well as her military capacity to wage modern war, to cripple Germany economically and deprive her for as long as possible of the power to take aggressive action again. German industries must be destroyed, and Germany converted into a pastoral country. As there was little likelihood that the United States would be willing to keep troops in Germany to enforce sanctions against the country, destruction of German industry would cripple Germany's power to rearm. Chaos in Germany was inevitable, Morgenthau said: There would be no fraternization, and the destruction of German industry would enable the British to take over Germany's markets.[12]

Colonel Bernstein now said that SHAEF administrators currently being trained would "take over and control" Germany, and that such an attitude would lead to an assumption of responsibility for economic and financial affairs. The planners would attempt to control inflation and reinvigorate the German economy. The Army's attitude, Bernstein summed up, would result "inevitably in a desire to do a good job."

Morgenthau asked Winant about the work of the EAC. Anxious in any case to avoid commitment in view of his position as American representative on the commission, the ambassador replied that the EAC did not initiate policy as such, but followed the instructions of the governments concerned. It was in Washington that these policy questions were decided for the United States.

White now spoke, by bringing what Penrose calls "sequence and interconnection" into Morgenthau's remarks. He said that he had gone over both American and British position papers on Germany. The only difference between the two countries was that, while the State Department thought a strong Germany could be rebuilt in ten years, the British thought it could be done in five. "What we want from Germany is peace," White said, "not reparations." White went on:

To return Germany as a respectable member of the family of nations would be to put Germany in a position where she could again endeavor to become ruler of the world. Twice in our generation she had tried and the third time she might well be successful. Our objective was to see that Germany was never again in a position to wage war. Everything else was incidental to that objective. If, to obtain that objective, it was necessary to reduce Germany to the status of a fifth-rate power, that should be done.[13]

The reduction of Germany's power to this level was the leitmotif of the subsequent debates on the Morgenthau Plan, and unlike Morgenthau, White never seems to have placed much emphasis per se on the value of turning the Reich into an agrarian community. "Whatever might be thought of the opinions of Mr. Morgenthau," Penrose comments, "it was impossible to deny the resourcefulness of Dr. White in mastering the main points of the interdepartmental committee's report just before the meeting and in transferring the Secretary's sketchy and spasmodic exposition of his views into a clear, amplified and well organized restatement composed in fifteen minutes after Mr. Morgenthau had finished speaking, and coming as nearly as possible to clothing a bad thesis with an appearance of intellectual respectability."

Another proposal of Morgenthau and his advisers in the ensuing discussion was that, as the Germans were responsible for inflation in their own occupied territories, so the Allies should give them a taste of their own medicine, with the occupying powers having no responsibility for financial reconstruction. When, at the close of the Redrice conference, Penrose asserted that it was impossible, aside from other aspects of the question, to turn Germany into an agricultural country because of the ratio of population to cultivable land, Morgenthau replied that the surplus population should be dumped in North Africa.[14]

However, White's arguments did not go uncontested at Redrice. Philip Mosely strenuously challenged White's views on Germany, insisting that this approach "was basically destructive of the American goals for postwar Germany." (Before becoming Winant's political adviser, Mosely had worked on the drafting of the State Department's position papers on postwar Germany and had attended the Moscow Conference with Hull, as a member of the American delegation.)

Such treatment of Germany, Mosely went on, would replace a German hegemony on the Continent with a Russian one. It would prevent any attempted Western reconciliation with Germany and the eventual reintegration of that country into the Western community. Such a policy outlined by White would drive the Germans into dependence on the Soviet Union. These were hardly American objectives. At the very least, Mosely held, the Russians could exploit such a situation with selective deliveries of food and industrial equipment, and in any case it was impossible to consider seriously White's proposals in a vacuum apart from the wider postwar scene. To these arguments, White did not reply directly.

Moreover, Mosely told the writer as he discussed the Redrice conference, he privately objected to what he thought was White's attempt to use the power of the United States to pursue personal feelings of hostility toward Germany, and he came to wonder whether these drastic proposals could be explained on White's part by some wider political motivation. Mosely told the writer that he considered White to be the originator of the Treasury proposals for postwar Germany.[15]

The Redrice conference was only the beginning of the turmoil over the Treasury plan for Germany. On August 13, the day following the conference, White, Morgenthau and Winant lunched with Eden at his London home. After lunch, according to White's minute, the Foreign Secretary remarked that at Teheran "Uncle Joe" Stalin "was determined to smash Germany so that it would never again be able to make war." At Teheran, Eden said, the Big Three had decided that the EAC was to consider the problem of German dismemberment and prepare a program. Eden promised to show the Teheran minutes to Morgenthau, while White told Eden that some British Treasury technicians were thinking of a restoration of the German economy because of the prewar trading patterns between the two countries. Eden "appeared shocked," White recorded.[16]

White and Morgenthau continued to pursue the theme of German partition. On August 15, in a meeting at Eden's room in the Foreign Office at which Winant was present, the Foreign Secretary began by reading out the Teheran minutes which indicated that the EAC was to report to the three governments on the problem of German partition. Sir William Strang, the British member of the EAC, remarked that a divided Germany could not produce reparations, to which White replied that peace, not reparations, was the main objective.

In reply to White's question, Winant, who had attended the conference, stated that he knew of the Teheran decision to refer partition for study by the EAC, but that he had not received instructions from his department to work on the proposal. The State Department had not been formally told of the Teheran decision, did not support German partition anyway, and the matter had been buried in a subcommittee of the EAC.[17]

Although Eden had remained silent on one of these occasions when Morgenthau had outlined his version of Germany's future, the Secretary was convinced, erroneously, that he was supported in general by the Foreign Secretary.[18] On the other hand, Morgenthau believed that the State Department, the British Treasury, the SHAEF planners and the EAC thought in terms of a unified, reconstituted Germany. With the formative stage of what would soon be known as the Morgenthau

Plan behind him, White now left Redrice for Washington. Within the next few weeks, many of the hitherto unchallenged assumptions of the postwar planners with regard to Germany would be overthrown.

With the return of White and Morgenthau to Washington on August 17, two weeks of intense activity began as Morgenthau lobbied on the Cabinet level and with the President, while White, assisted by other Treasury staff, prepared detailed departmental proposals on postwar Germany.

Morgenthau's first visit, on the eighteenth, was to Hull, who was apparently ignorant of the Teheran decision to have German partition studied by the EAC, and who poured out his general frustration over the delay in clearing the State Department's directives to Winant in London. The next day Morgenthau saw Roosevelt, but the President was not too concerned when Morgenthau told him that no American officials were examining the problem of German partition, thinking that the matter could be resolved by personal contact between himself and Churchill.

But Roosevelt, according to Morgenthau, believed that "we have got to be tough with the German people, not just the Nazis," and it seems clear enough that Roosevelt had little general sympathy with the advocates of a lenient peace. Shortly after seeing the President, Morgenthau appointed a special Treasury committee of White and two senior departmental lawyers, Ansel F. Luxford and John Pehle, Director of the War Refugee Board, to draft the Treasury's proposals for postwar Germany. The committee would enlist the help of other Treasury staff.[19]

The combination of Morgenthau's political influence and White's imagination and drive was a formidable one. Morgenthau, moreover, had an aversion to Germany and German militarism dating from his father's ambassadorship to Turkey in the First World War, and as we have seen he had long been in the van of the anti-Nazi cause. Added to all this were the reports, reaching Washington from 1942 onward, of the Nazi mass murder of European Jewry.

It would have been remarkable if White, an equally committed anti-Nazi, had not been affected by these developments. In any case, White's longstanding belief in "all-out diplomacy" with its swift, dramatic readjustments of political and economic power was evidence of his temperamental attraction toward comprehensive solutions of international problems, perhaps the complement of the idealism which had fired the White Plan for the Monetary Fund. Now, in drafting the Treasury's proposals for Germany, White was centrally involved in issues that transcended in importance even the evolution of the postwar international monetary system.

The drastic nature of White's ideas for settling the German problem had been evident at Redrice. Moreover, drawn toward the Soviet Union by an emotional sympathy at the very least, as we have seen, White may have felt in the late summer of 1944 that the irreversible crushing of the Reich would help to lead to postwar Soviet-American understanding. If the Russians achieved a dominant position in Europe as a result, this might be a price worth paying for solving the problem of security from Germany. Here White may have been looking ahead more than Morgenthau, for whom the elimination of German power in the cause of "peace" seems almost to have become an end in itself.

In addition to the deployment of White's formidable bureaucratic talents in the coming campaign, the collective voice of the Treasury was also a powerful asset. Colonel Bernstein, for example, was regarded in SHAEF as virtually a Treasury representative, and as Paul Y. Hammond has remarked, Treasury discipline meant that there was "a solidarity of viewpoint outside the Department," no matter what disagreements inside the Treasury. Luxford and Pehle, for example, disagreed with aspects of the Morgenthau Plan, Luxford favoring some form of German reparations, Pehle concerned with the element of retribution, but both men would defend Treasury policy with other agencies. In any case, as Hammond puts it, with Morgenthau and many of his associates "there may have been more of a disposition to try and fix the problems of foreign affairs once and for all than was characteristic of State and War department officials."[20] Clearly White thought in these terms in formulating his proposals for postwar Germany.

Finally, in these weeks that saw the debate on the Morgenthau Plan, events themselves contributed to the speed with which the Treasury proposals were formulated and considered. Following the fall of Paris on August 25, the SHAEF intelligence summary reported the next day that the end of the war in Europe was "almost within reach." "As General Eisenhower's forces advanced to the German border," Stimson and Bundy remark, "it became clear that the armies had outrun the policy makers."[21] This was the gap that White now sought to fill as he worked on the Treasury proposals for Germany in the last days of August, 1944.

Morgenthau had apparently failed to arouse Roosevelt's interest over the EAC's omission to discuss German partition, but in England Colonel Bernstein had given the Secretary a copy of SHAEF's *Handbook of Military Government for Germany*. The *Handbook*, drafted by SHAEF's "German Country Unit," emphasized in some detail the military's reconstructionist principles for the guidance of British and American civil affairs officers in Germany. It had not been finally approved.

In a meeting with Morgenthau in the Treasury on the morning of August 25, White emphasized that the contents of the *Handbook* meant that the military were "practically going to attempt to run the country."

The *Handbook* was in harmony with the presurrender Combined Chiefs of Staff directive (CCS-551), and said White, unless they get other orders in London, "that is what it will be." Morgenthau now went to see Roosevelt, and he took with him a "Memorandum for the President," drafted by White and his staff, which underlined what the memorandum called "the type of thinking and planning upon which the program of military government for Germany is being formulated." One of these passages quoted from the *Handbook* indicated that "the first concern of military government will be to see that the machine works."

Events themselves seemed to be working against this assumption. With the rapid German military collapse in France, Eisenhower had cabled the Combined Chiefs in Washington on August 23, suggesting that as a central German government might not now survive the end of the war, SHAEF should be relieved of the responsibility for controlling the German economic system. The message underlined the need for a new post-surrender directive to supplement the presurrender instructions of CCS-551.[22]

At the same time, the question of the AM mark exchange rate for troop pay erupted again, with the British proposing a rate of five marks to the dollar, the State Department eight. According to a Treasury "Memorandum for the President," dated August 25, and prepared by Harold Glasser of White's staff, the continued British-State Department view was that a high troop purchase power and a low exchange rate for the mark would disrupt the German price and wage structure, thus retarding "rapid rehabilitation and recovery." Morgenthau was not put out by this suggestion. "Somebody's got to be tough with the Germans," he told Assistant Secretary of War McCloy on the telephone during his conversation with White over the *Handbook* on the morning of the twenty-fifth. "I'm going to propose that we have a military rate for our soldiers of twenty German marks to the dollar."

This 20–1 rate, equivalent to a five-cent mark, it will be recalled, had been suggested by White as a bargaining position in these negotiations three months before. But it may have been that Morgenthau now fully realized the implications of the overvalued AM mark that White had fought for, as a ready-made means of partly implementing the Treasury program for Germany. Eventually, as we have seen, a rate of 10–1 was agreed with the British.

Thus, as the first indications of the nascent debate in Washington on a German policy reached London in late August, Eden learned on September 1 from Halifax, the British ambassador, that Morgenthau "was urging upon the United States Government that the occupying powers in Germany should not go out of their way to maintain or reestablish the German economy. Morgenthau apparently thought that a severe inflation, as happened after the first war, would burn into German minds that war spelt economic ruins."[23] This aspect of the Treasury program had, of course, already been outlined at Redrice.

Following Morgenthau's delivery of the *Handbook* and the accompanying memorandum to Roosevelt on the morning of the twenty-fifth, the President had lunch with Stimson. There was a discussion in general terms of Morgenthau's views over Germany, for the two Secretaries had met for an inclusive talk on August 23, when Morgenthau had suggested that a committee of Hull, Stimson and himself should confer on Germany to "draw up a memorandum for the President so that he will have it before he meets Churchill again." Stimson was opposed to Morgenthau's views, but now he in turn suggested to Roosevelt the formulation of a Cabinet Committee of the three Secretaries to consider postwar German policy. This suggestion was approved by Roosevelt in a Cabinet meeting on the afternoon of August 25. Later Harry Hopkins was asked to coordinate the work of the committee for the President.[24]

During the Cabinet meeting on August 25, Roosevelt had remarked that the Germans should have simply "a subsistence level of food," and now, after having read the *Handbook* overnight, he issued a reprimand in a memorandum to Stimson which began "This so-called handbook is pretty bad." The President emphasized that Germany was a defeated nation, that Army soup kitchens would be sufficient to feed the Germans three times a day, and that "there was no reason for starting a WPA, PWA or CCC for Germany when we go in with our army of occupation."

Distribution of the offending *Handbook* was at once suspended. Then, on September 15, after it had been found impossible to erase the offending sections, the *Handbook* was issued with a flyleaf insertion emphasizing, at the suggestion of the Combined Civil Affairs Committee, that: (1) No steps should be taken beyond those necessary for military purposes for the economic rehabilitation of Germany; (2) Relief supplies except those necessary to prevent disease and disorder that might interfere with military operations should not be imported or distributed; (3) No Nazi sympathizer or Nazi organization should be continued in office for the purpose of expediency or convenience. In a Treasury conference on September 6, White considered these revisions "a definite improvement."[25]

More important, perhaps, than either the setting up of the Cabinet Committee or the temporary suspension of the *Handbook* was the President's new awareness of the Treasury approach to the German problem.

Morgenthau now left Washington for a break at his Dutchess County estate at Fishkill, and was not back in the Treasury until Labor Day, Monday, September 4. He remained in occasional contact with White, who continued with his work of drafting the Treasury proposals for

Germany, assisted by Treasury staff and other consultants. On the twenty-eighth Morgenthau was expecting Harry Dexter White "to carry the ball," and reminded him that they only had until the week ending September 10 to get the Treasury proposals to the President. Roosevelt would then meet Churchill at Quebec. By the thirty-first the Secretary hoped that White's men would attack the problem by taking the Ruhr "and completely putting it out of business." White replied that the problem had been discussed "at some length." There was, however, a political problem of the 18,000,000 Germans who would be put out of work. Morgenthau considered an "International TVA" manned by "a couple of million Germans" could work on projects all over the world.[26]

Amply supplied with a plethora of details on the history, geography and past administration of Germany, together with charts of central Europe from *Goode's School Atlas*, White carried on with his work of literally drawing the map of the new Germany.

On September 1, 1944, White and his colleagues completed the Treasury proposals for the Cabinet Committee, "Suggested Post-Surrender Program for Germany," sending the original, marked top secret, to Morgenthau at Fishkill.[27]

The first formal draft of what would now become known as the Morgenthau Plan—although of course White had been instrumental in its conception and formulation—was "a detailed and comprehensive scheme for permanently reducing German power."[28] This would be done by territorial cession to other countries, partition, deindustrialization and by stipulating that no steps would be taken to revive the German residual economy after the war.

At the Teheran Conference, the leaders had informally and tentatively agreed that the postwar borders of Poland should be moved westward to the vicinity of the Curzon line and the Oder, and that the Soviet Union should claim Königsberg, besides discussing the wider proposals of German partition we have noted above. Herbert Feis has thus remarked that while the Treasury proposals on the German economy and German partition were much more drastic than measures which the American State and War departments had in mind, "Yet it could be argued, I think, that they were just a runaway ride along the course which Roosevelt and Stalin had marked at Teheran."[29] Even so, these "startling proposals" (Feis) introduced a new dimension into the discussions over American postwar policy for Germany.

The Treasury program suggested that "the position of the United States should be determined on the following principles." First, German disarmament should be enforced by "the total destruction of the whole German armament industry as well as those parts of supporting industries having no other justification." Poland should be given that part of East Prussia not given to the Soviet Union, together with "southern" Silesia, while France should be ceded the Saar and adjacent territory "bounded by the Rhine and Moselle rivers."

The remainder of Germany was to be divided in three parts. An international zone governed by "an international security organization to be established by the United Nations" was to include the Ruhr, the Rhineland, and northwest Germany including Bremen and the Kiel Canal. Rump Germany was then to split into two separate North and South German states, the first consisting of parts of Prussia, Saxony and Thuringia, the second consisting of Bavaria together with parts of Württemberg, Baden "and several smaller states." Importation of capital into the zone "should be discouraged."

Reparations, White's draft proposed, would not be demanded "in the form of current payments and deliveries." Instead, reparations would come out of existing German resources (left after the destruction of the armaments and supporting industries). The primary source of reparations would thus be the capital removal of "industrial plants and equipment" from the Ruhr-Rhineland. "International Zone," and both North and South German rump states. White's reparations program also included "forced labor outside Germany" and the total confiscation of all German assets abroad. There were no limits on the extent of the proposed capital removal of German industry. White's paper also emphasized that the internationalization of the Ruhr-Rhineland area would in no way interfere with the destruction of the armaments industry, supporting industry, and the capital removal of other industry as reparations. Ownership of any remaining properties in the Zone would be transferred to the International organization.

All Nazi Party members, Nazi sympathizers, "Junkers," and military and naval officers were to be disenfranchised and banned from public office. Membership in the SS and the Gestapo would constitute the basis for inclusion in compulsory labor battalions to serve outside Germany.

The only Allied responsibility for the German economy would be to facilitate military operations and occupation, and Allied Military Government would not assume responsibility for price controls, rationing or any measures designed "to maintain or strengthen the German economy."

The primary responsibility for policing Germany would be left to Germany's Continental neighbors: "Specifically, these should include Russian, French, Polish, Czech, Greek, Yugoslav, Norwegian, Dutch and Belgian soldiers." There was no mention of British and American troops, and under this program United States troops could be withdrawn within a relatively short time."

On September 2 the deputies of the three members of the Cabinet Committee met to confer in Harry Hopkins' office in the White House, prior to the meeting of the three Secretaries. White represented the Treasury, McCloy the War Department, and from the State Department were J. W. Riddleberger, Chief of the Office of Central European Affairs, and H. Freeman Matthews, Deputy Director of the Office of European Affairs. The deputies agreed that a postsurrender Draft Interim Directive should be prepared, with Treasury participation, for Eisenhower, so beginning the protracted negotiations over what was soon to be known as the JCS 1067 directive for the American occupation-zone of Germany. But the primary business of the meeting was the presentation of the Treasury and State department drafts on German policy.

White now presented the Treasury program on Germany and, according to a minute by Riddleberger, "gave a lengthy interpretation of this plan which in its general tenor was more extreme than the memorandum itself. . . . In explaining this plan, Dr. White insisted that no trade would be permitted between the proposed international zone and the rest of the Reich, and he emphasized that the productivity of this zone should not in any way contribute to the German economy. No recurrent reparations deliveries would be demanded and reparations would be dealt with by transfer of territory, equipment and labor service."[30]

Later the same day, Riddleberger and Matthews expounded a State Department paper on the treatment of Germany, which while emphasizing the principle of strict denazification, opposed forcible partition and advocated a federal system of government for the Reich. The State Department stood by the general economic principles approved by the ECEFP on August 4, 1944, and considered that a "wrecking program" to deindustrialize Germany would lead to "the liquidation or emigration" of millions of Germans. Riddleberger was now asked to draft a memorandum for the Cabinet Committee which should attempt to reconcile the Treasury and State department positions.[31]

The next day, September 3, State returned to the fray, pointing out to Hopkins that the tripartite zonal measures for Germany discussed with the British and the Russians in the EAC were incompatible with the Treasury proposals. According to Hull's memoirs, Hopkins appeared to see the validity of these objections, maintaining that the President and Hull should keep in step on "all plans" for Germany.[32]

However, the previous day, September 2, as White met with the other deputies in the White House, Morgenthau had already presented the Treasury proposals to Roosevelt, who had driven over from Hyde Park for tea with Morgenthau at Fishkill. As at Redrice the surroundings were appropriately pastoral as Morgenthau elucidated, in the shadow of his great orchards, the Treasury proposals drafted by White. According to

Morgenthau, Roosevelt listened "very closely" to what he had to say, and seemed to be "in complete sympathy," but avoided any basic policy discussion, so of course preserving his freedom of action. However, the President did tell Morgenthau that he considered it "psychologically and symbolically" very important that aircraft, including gliders, marching and uniforms, should be denied to the Germans.[33] But clearly the initiative over policy for Germany was still very much with the Treasury as Morgenthau returned to Washington for the meetings of the Cabinet Committee.

Back in the Treasury on Monday, September 4, Labor Day, for a group meeting on Germany with White, Under Secretary Daniel Bell, Assistant Secretary Herbert Gaston, John Pehle and others, Morgenthau passed on for inclusion in the department's program for Germany the President's wishes for the prohibition of aircraft, uniforms and marching. On the battlefront Patton's tanks were across the Meuse heading for the Reich border, the British had liberated Brussels, and everywhere the Wehrmacht was falling back to the West Wall. But the chief subject of the two meetings in the Treasury attended by White that day was the disposition of the Ruhr in the Treasury program. Before the war the area, as usually defined, had contained about 6,000,000 people, producing about 70 percent of German coal, iron and steel, besides holding other major industries which altogether accounted for about one-third to one-half of German exports. Other areas of Germany and western and central Europe were, of course, partly dependent on the Ruhr in one way or another.

Morgenthau had returned from Fishkill convinced that the White committee's plan of September 1 left the Ruhr "intact."[34] He told his staff that the memorandum which White had sent him at Fishkill "didn't go far enough" toward "the complete closing down of the Ruhr." Yet this was hardly so, as White's proposals had called not only for the total destruction of the whole German armaments industry but "those parts of supporting industry having no other justification." In addition, there was no limit to the extent of the proposed removal of remaining heavy industry from the Ruhr (and the rump German states) as reparations. This proposed destruction and large-scale capital removal of industry would in any case have taken place after the effects of Allied wartime bombing of the Ruhr and elsewhere and general military operations preceding Germany's defeat.

White remarked that Morgenthau's proposal that the Ruhr "be locked up or wiped out" was "a troublesome point" as there was the problem of what to do with 15,000,000 people. This figure and the alternative of 18,000,000 also used by White related to the whole of the Reich. Yet clearly implementation of the original White proposals of September 1 would have resulted in a considerable displacement of population, as the destruction and capital removal of industry would take place, as we have noted, from the whole of Germany, including not only the International Zone but the two rump German states. White now suggested that an alternative to the complete destruction of the industrial Ruhr, including the coal mines, as advocated by Morgenthau, was to put the remaining resources of the area "under international control to produce reparations for twenty years." This arrangement, of course, would have dealt with the *residual* resources of the Ruhr after the destruction and removal of industry already advocated by White, but such a proposal might conceivably have made the overall program more acceptable politically.

Morgenthau, however, was insistent, and White considered that if all Ruhr industry were closed down, "of course you wouldn't have to do a great deal of destruction if that were the policy. If you told the various allies that you were going to do that and they can come in and strip it, they will take a good deal of it away. But they would have to do some destruction. The problem is not the destruction. The problem is the population."

Some of the Treasury staff entered objections, but White did not agree with "these half-way marks." Speaking again of the Ruhr he considered that

> there is no doubt—let's assume for a moment you could get rid of population satisfactory [*sic*]—or 90 or 75 percent of them—just have an agrarian populace—an international organization could very easily be perpetuated to see that nothing is done there because they are confronted with minor problems; then it is a policing job under international law which you can carry on indefinitely. But I don't think it is possible to pursue that if you have them produce some things and not others or if you have them cut down their production because it is merely a case of expansion. But if you can solve or you are ready to accept the consequence of that degree of shift of population, that is the price; if you are willing to pay that price now then I think the Secretary is wholly right. That is all.

This was the price White was apparently willing to pay as he rationalized—and perhaps justified—the means implicit in his program for postwar Germany from its inception:

> . . . if there is no way for them to make a living, they will move out. If you are willing to accept the consequences of an act of that kind, which will show itself in the following fashion, there will be

great unemployment in the Ruhr. Tremendous unemployment. There will be breadlines. Now, there are two ways of meeting it. Either you can prevent starvation by providing a minimum amount of foods so they can stay in breadlines as long as they can stand it and when they can't, they will go somewhere else where the lines are shorter. You don't have to drive them out. I don't think you want to say that anyone found in this area after such a time will be moved bodily. You provide some sort of transport to move them out; you provide a certain amount of bread rationing to keep them alive, and you close down the means of livelihood. That is all you have to do. I say that is all. I mean that is a ruthless decision, but it is not physically impossible or economically impossible and if it is decided to do so it is not politically impossible.

White then remarked to Morgenthau that his proposal to allow residual reparations from the Ruhr was made because, after foreign governments had stripped the area of "any machinery they want," they would still leave "something" there. Tonnage could be built up, "a half-way measure that never pleased or satisfied us." If his suggestion was out, White said, referring to the Ruhr, "I am wholly in agreement with you that the only thing to do is to root it out provided you can get away with it politically."

Morgenthau wanted Army engineers to go "into every steel mill, every coal mine, every chemical plant, every synthetic gas business, or whatever there is and put dynamite in and open the water valves and flood and dynamite that and then the great humanitarians could sit back and decide about the population afterward." The Ruhr, Morgenthau said, would become a "ghost area" like the silver mines in Nevada.

In a further conference on Germany on the afternoon of September 4, White told Morgenthau, without any response, that "some of the boys" thought the Ruhr mines should be left to produce coal. But, on the general program of destroying Ruhr industry, White went on to say that Harold Glasser "was talking of the splendid job which the German engineers did in the destruction of all industrial plants in Naples. The American Army engineers said it was the best job of a highly skilled technical destruction that they had ever seen. So it does require engineers of a high order to do it, and they could do it then. But the part that gave us pause was we thought that the machinery that was in the factories ought to be removed."

The meeting ended with Morgenthau emphasizing that he wanted to make Germany so impotent "that she cannot forge the tools of war." White was to revise the Treasury plan for Germany, in the context of the day's discussion, for a meeting of the Cabinet Committee.[35]

Later that day, September 4, on the eve of the first meeting of the Cabinet Committee, White, McCloy and Stimson dined with Morgenthau. There was an awareness of the difference between the two Secretaries, but no overt disagreement. According to White's memorandum of the table talk, Stimson and McCloy were not convinced of the need for partitioning Germany, and Stimson "doubted the wisdom of destroying the Ruhr." The Secretary of War thought that such a course would force into starvation 30,000,000 Germans, the difference in population between mid-nineteenth-century Germany, before industrialization, and the present. (White considered the figure to be 18,000,000, Morgenthau informed his staff the next morning.) The Secretary of War, recorded White, did not believe that the way "to prevent future war was to destroy Germany."

In his diary, Stimson recorded that at the dinner there was divergence between those in favor of a firm peace, and those supporting "a Carthaginian solution."[36]

With the ends and means of the Morgenthau Plan apparently clarified within the Treasury, as far as they ever would be, and with Roosevelt due to leave Washington for his Quebec meeting with Churchill within a week, the Cabinet Committee on Germany now met on the morning of September 5 in Hull's office. White was busy with the redrafting of the Treasury proposals on Germany which would be completed later that day, and others of his staff were framing the Treasury version of the Draft Interim Directive for Eisenhower. But the chief thrust of the Treasury argument on Germany was now carried by Morgenthau at the Cabinet Committee.

Hull presented to the committee Riddleberger's compromise memorandum on Germany, which, it will be remembered, had been written in an attempt to reconcile the differences of the deputies in the White House meeting of September 2. The paper outlined common ground on demilitarization and denazification, but suggested that a decision on German partition and reparations should be postponed, pending Allied agreement. A final section, however, capable of possibly differing interpretations, proposed that German living standards be held down "to a subsistence level," and that the German economic position of power in Europe "must be eliminated."[37]

In the ensuing discussion, Stimson, who could not accept this final section, found himself isolated. Hopkins wanted to prohibit German steel production, Morgenthau verbally advocated his full policy of an agrarian Germany, and Hull, who was not well, apparently sided with Morgenthau, leaving Stimson as the only member who opposed German deindustrialization. Eventually it was agreed that Hull would submit his department's paper to Roosevelt, and that Morgenthau and Stimson would each submit written statements of their views on it to the President.

Stimson, who recorded in his diary that in "all the four years that I have been here I have not had such a difficult and unpleasant meeting," remarked in his memorandum for the President that in the Cabinet Committee "the position frankly taken by some of my colleagues was that the great industrial regions of Germany known as the Ruhr and the Saar should be totally transformed into a nonindustrialized area of agricultural land." (The Saar, in the Treasury plan, was supposed to be ceded to France.) Stimson went on to deploy arguments that would be used with increasing frequency by the opponents of the Morgenthau Plan:

I cannot conceive of such a proposition being either possible or effective and I can see enormous general evils coming from an attempt to so treat it. During the past eighty years of European history this portion of Germany was one of the most important sources of raw materials upon which the industrial and economic livelihood of Europe was based. . . . I can conceive of endeavoring to meet the misuse which Germany has recently made of this production by wise systems of control or trusteeship or even transfer of ownership to other nations. But I cannot conceive of turning such a gift of nature into a dust heap. . . .

War is destruction. This war more than any previous war has caused gigantic destruction. The need for the recuperative benefits of productivity is more evident now than ever before throughout the world. . . . Moreover, speed of reconstruction is of great importance, if we hope to avoid dangerous convulsions in Europe. . . .

Nor can I agree that it should be one of our purposes to hold the German people "to a subsistence level" if this means the edge of poverty. This means condemning the German people to a condition of servitude in which, no matter how hard or effectively a man worked, he could not increase his economic condition in the world. . . .

My basic objection to the proposed methods of treating Germany which were discussed this morning was that in addition to a system of preventive and educative punishment they would add the dangerous weapon of complete economic oppression. Such methods, in my opinion, do not prevent war; they tend to breed war.[38]

The entire matter was still in flux on the afternoon of the sixth when the Cabinet Committee met with Roosevelt. Hull again presented the State Department compromise paper of September 4, while Morgenthau argued from the now amended White proposal of September 1, in effect a second formal version of the Morgenthau Plan, dated September 5. The revised Treasury program, drafted by White and his staff, and forwarded to the members of the Cabinet Committee and the President on the sixth, proposed not only the "total destruction" of the German armaments industry but "the removal and destruction of other key industries which are basic to military strength."

Within the internationalized zone of the Ruhr, the Rhineland and northwest Germany (see map on page 444), "this area should not only be stripped of all presently existing industries but so weakened and controlled that it cannot in the foreseeable future become an industrial area. . . . Within a short period, if possible not longer than six months after the cessation of hostilities, all industrial plants and equipment not destroyed by military action shall either be completely dismantled and removed from the area or completely destroyed. All equipment shall be removed from the mines and the mines shall be thoroughly wrecked."

The second draft of the Treasury plan further stated that all people in the International Zone should be made to understand that this area will not again be allowed to become an industrial area: "Accordingly all people and their families within the area having special skills or technical training should be encouraged to migrate permanently from the area and should be as widely dispersed as possible. . . ."

Besides incorporating Roosevelt's prohibitions on aircraft, uniforms and parades, and a provision in the appendix that the Nazi "arch criminals" should be executed on arrest, the Treasury draft of September 5 followed the other provisions of the earlier version of September 1.[39]

In this meeting of the Cabinet Committee with the President on the sixth, Roosevelt, who had read Stimson's memorandum of the previous day, considered that Germany could live "happily and peacefully" on soup kitchens. Stimson also recorded in his diary that Roosevelt seemed not to agree with Morgenthau's view on dismantling the Ruhr, thinking instead that the products of the area could furnish raw materials for British industry. Stimson felt that he had gained ground, and evidently so did Morgenthau, for he requested another meeting with the President on Germany.

Later in the day, Morgenthau reported to his staff that there had been "a very unsatisfactory meeting over there with the President." But, Morgenthau reported, Roosevelt had gone into something quite new. The President said that he had been thinking of Dutchess County in 1810, and that "there was no reason why Germany couldn't go back to 1810 where they would be perfectly comfortable but wouldn't have any luxuries." White intervened to say "that would dispose of many millions of people."[40]

Within the Treasury, negotiations continued between the department and Army over the SHAEF *Handbook* revisions, which as we have seen, White considered "a great improvement." More important, perhaps, as that battle was now won, were the preparations by White and his staff, including Glasser, W. H. Taylor and J. E. DuBois, of a final, third, draft of the Morgenthau Plan, together with a group of associated briefing papers for Roosevelt, which Morgenthau referred to as the "Black Book." "The only possibility you might consider, for tactical reasons," White told Morgenthau on the afternoon of September 8, "if you think it wise, is not to speak of completely obliterating the Ruhr, but leave the coal mines."[41]

On the same day, Hull told Morgenthau that he had been asked to go to Quebec, but that he was too tired to attend the conference. The Secretary of State hoped, however, that Roosevelt would confine discussions to military matters, and not discuss the partition and economic future of Germany.

These preliminaries preceding the second meeting of the Cabinet Committee came to a head on September 9. Roosevelt was due to leave Washington later that day for his meeting with Churchill in Quebec.

Before the Cabinet Committee assembled, White presented Morgenthau with a third, final version of the Treasury proposals for Germany, now entitled "Program to Prevent Germany from Starting a World War III."[42] There were only minor alterations from the second draft of September 5, as the paper called for the "total destruction" of the German armaments industry and other key industries, basic to military strength, together with the stripping of the Ruhr and the partition of Germany. As in the earlier drafts, a truncated Reich was to be occupied by Germany's Continental neighbors, and American troops were to be withdrawn within a short time. A new detail in this Gothic canvas was Article 10, "Agrarian Program," which stipulated that "all large estates should be broken up and divided among the peasants and the system of primogeniture and entail should be abolished." Tactfully, the Morgenthau Plan now suggested that, instead of wrecking the Ruhr coal mines, "all equipment shall be removed from the mines and mines closed." The sole purpose of the military in control of the German economy would be to facilitate military operations and occupation.

White then read out the titles of the briefing papers, drafted under his supervision, which would accompany the Plan to Quebec: "Reparations Mean a Powerful Germany," "Economic Restitution by Germany to United Nations," "German Militarism Cannot Be Destroyed by Destroying Nazism Alone," "It Is a Fallacy that Europe Needs a Strong Industrial Germany," "Why the Resources of the Ruhr Should Be Locked Up and the Equipment Removed." Another paper drafted by White, "Is

European Prosperity Dependent Upon German Industry?" concluded that "the statement that a healthy European economy is dependent upon German industry was never true, nor will it be true in the future."

Morgenthau thought that White and his staff had done "a perfectly amazing good job," and that the material would be "very useful" to the President at Quebec. Morgenthau was hoping that "out of this thing" would come a directive from the President "as to his policy."[43]

It was hardly surprising that there was no meeting of minds in the Cabinet Committee. Stimson had written another powerful memorandum for Roosevelt, dated September 9, stating that he was "unalterably opposed" to the Treasury program which he considered "wholly wrong." The Secretary of War considered that the committee should make interim recommendations on the basis of the State Department paper of September 4, while removing the references therein to keeping German living standards down to "subsistence levels." Stimson also thought that the German "arch criminals" should be tried by at least a "rudimentary" Bill of Rights. He had an open mind on German partition and the internationalization of the Ruhr.

According to Morgenthau, Roosevelt, at the Cabinet Committee, approvingly read out the title of the Treasury paper, "It Is a Fallacy that Europe Needs a Strong Germany." The President thought that this was the first time he had seen this stated, but he agreed with it. Hull said little, but apparently agreed with Morgenthau's views. In reply to a question from the President whether he wished to come to the conference, he stated he was too tired. Toward the end of the meeting, Roosevelt said that both monetary and military problems would be discussed with Churchill at Quebec. If the financial situation was brought up, he would want Morgenthau at the conference.[44]

On the whole, it seems clear that Roosevelt characteristically reserved his position on the differing view of Morgenthau and Stimson. But by his attitude to the *Handbook*, by his belief that the Germans should be nourished by soup kitchens, if necessary, and by an apparent concern for the postwar British economy and German economic predominance, the President was also closer to Morgenthau on Germany than to his other advisers when the Cabinet Committee ended.

That evening the President left for Quebec bearing the "Black Book" of the Morgenthau Plan and was accompanied as far as Hyde Park by Morgenthau. Here Roosevelt broke the journey overnight, while Morgenthau went to his neighboring home at Fishkill, a convenient stopover should Roosevelt summon him to Quebec.

White's pursuit of the reduction of Germany, which had led him from Redrice to the meetings in Hopkins' White House office, would now take him to the Anglo-American conference. On September 13, following Roosevelt's summons the previous day, Morgenthau arrived at Quebec; he was soon followed by White. The "Octagon" Conference had held its first plenary session earlier that day attended by Roosevelt, Churchill and their combined Chiefs of Staff at the Citadel in Quebec.

"OCTAGON" AND AFTER

This program for eliminating the war-making industries in the Ruhr and the Saar is looking forward to converting Germany into a country primarily agricultural and pastoral in its character.

—The Quebec Memorandum, September 15, 1944

On September 13, 1944, the opening day of the "Octagon" Conference, Harry Dexter White arrived at Quebec. Arrangements for the Second Quebec Conference had been under high-level Anglo-American discussion for some time, and Churchill had sailed from the Clyde on the *Queen Mary* on September 5. The Prime Minister was met by the President at Quebec on September 11, and the two leaders now made their home at the Citadel. Following a triumphant general survey of the war in the first plenary meeting on the thirteenth, attended by the Combined Chiefs of Staff, Churchill cabled home to the War Cabinet that the conference had opened "in a blaze of friendship."[1]

Inevitably, much of the agenda of the conference was dictated by military necessity as Roosevelt, Churchill and their Combined Chiefs planned the ending of the war in Europe and the final campaigns against Japan. Churchill tells us that on the voyage out he was by no means convinced that Germany would be defeated in 1944. But Sherwood remarks that at the conference there was "general belief" among "the higher authorities" that Germany would surrender "within a matter of weeks or even days."[2] The Allies were unprepared for total victory in Europe, and it was from this contingency that the two vital nonmilitary matters with which White was concerned at Quebec now sprang. These were Anglo-American policy toward defeated Germany, and the extent of continued American Lend-Lease aid to Britain in the interval between the defeat of Germany and that of Japan, or "Stage II," as it was known in London, "Phase II" in Washington.

In the opening session at Quebec the offer had been made by Churchill, and accepted by the President, of the participation of the British fleet in Pacific operations under American command. It was hoped elements of RAF Bomber Command would follow. But, Churchill writes, "the planning date for the end of the war against Japan was set for the time being at eighteen months after the defeat of Germany."[3] With this time schedule, Stage II Lend-Lease clearly had great relevance to the entire problem of Britain's progress from a wartime to a peacetime economy, the transitional problem not fully solved by the Bretton Woods negotiators. As Penrose describes it, the War Cabinet had agreed that the Prime Minister should take up the question of American aid with the President at Quebec so that with the ending of the war Britain would be able "to increase its exports, and perhaps reduce its imports, to the extent needed to reach a new equilibrium in its international transactions."[4]

Closely associated with these hopes in Whitehall was the question of the British gold and dollar reserves, which had stood at the figure of about $4 billion a year before the war. The reserves had almost been exhausted when the Lend-Lease Bill was passed in the spring of 1941. What Churchill called "the most unsordid act in history" would mean that in the course of the war the British Commonwealth countries received about $30 billion of aid, some $26-27 billion of this amount going to the United Kingdom. But there were inevitably some anomalies in the implementation of Lend-Lease despite Roosevelt's 1942 promise of "equality of sacrifice" in the financial costs of the war. Congress was understandably jealous of its prerogatives with the purse strings, there was no clear-cut promise by the United States that some repayment would not be asked, and American businessmen were concerned that Lend-Lease goods and supplies to Britain would be used in commercial competition with the United States. The British government, therefore, in the "Export White Paper" of September, 1941, undertook not to use Lend-Lease goods and materials in the British export trade.[5]

Another major source of difficulty was the level of the British dollar reserves, as Washington exerted pressure in the middle years of the war to keep the figure of these reserves at a total of not much more than $1 billion.

Here a motivating factor was that of "bargaining power," and as in the exercise of the *quid pro quo* policy over the Chinese bullion, White played an important role. Partly the attempt to limit the British reserves was due to the administration's sensitivity to Congressional opinion. But in the Treasury, and in the State Department, as Richard Gardner puts it, leading figures "were reluctant to surrender the 'bargaining power'" which forgiveness of Lend-Lease might give them in persuading the United Kingdom to embrace a policy of multilateral trade." More specifically, Gardner comments, "the lower the level at which British wartime reserves were kept, the greater would be the British dependence on American postwar assistance. And the greater the dependence, it was argued, the greater would be the chance of gaining acceptance for American views on multilateral trade."

On the other hand, Professor Gardner notes, the British were worried that their reserves "would prove too small to provide an adequate margin of safety against the uncertainties inherent in a multilateral regime."[6]

During 1943, accordingly, White and Morgenthau had urged against the expansion of the British gold and dollar reserves, as the total figure began to climb again, assisted by the wartime dollar expenditures in the sterling area. According to Professor Blum, White had resisted the expansion of these reserves "more vigorously" then Morgenthau. Thus, in November, 1943, after reviewing recent negotiations, White recommended, in a memorandum intended for Roosevelt, discontinuing certain nonmilitary items of Lend-Lease to bring the British balances down to about $1 billion.[7]

In a lunch on November 17, 1943, attended by White, Morgenthau, Halifax and Sir David Waley, a British Treasury representative, Morgenthau stated that if the British could help him over the level of their reserves, "he could say that so long as he was Secretary of the Treasury that he would try to help the British Treasury meet its difficult postwar problems." Waley, concerned over the need to maintain sufficient British reserves for the postwar period, considered that, according to White's minutes, "his Government could not very well leave themselves in a vulnerable financial situation on the promise that the American Government would make available to them through one means or another substantial sums after the war."

The meeting ended inconclusively, and after the British had left Morgenthau and White briefly "explored the possibilities" of obtaining bases or access to raw materials from "countries like India and Malaya etc." in return for help in building up the British balances.[8]

During March, 1944, Churchill entered the controversy with a telegram to Roosevelt protesting the suggestion of reducing the British reserves to a billion dollars as one "which would not be consistent either with equal treatment of Allies or with any conception of equal sacrifice or pooling of resources. . . . We have already spent practically all our convertible foreign investments."[9]

There the matter rested until Quebec, when the end of the European war was in sight. But according to Morgenthau's report on the non-military matters discussed at Quebec to the members of the Cabinet Committee on Germany, as recorded by White, "Churchill seemed to be interested solely in the Lend-Lease arrangements, whereas the President was thinking of policy toward Germany and was not very interested in Lend-Lease arrangements."[10]

Following the arrival of Morgenthau and White at Quebec on September 13, both these matters in which White had been so closely involved became the subject of separate, not formally connected agreements, between the President and the Prime Minister. British hopes for Stage II Lend-Lease would apparently be fulfilled. And on the question of postwar Germany, as Herbert Feis puts it, Churchill was now "persuaded to assent to a course close to that marked out by the Treasury."[11]

Some of White's part in the conference and also some of the process by which Roosevelt and Churchill came to agree on both German policy and British Lend-Lease may be seen through the contents of five memoranda made by White at Quebec between September 13 and 15. These papers were then placed in Morgenthau's "Presidential Diary," a separate compilation from the Morgenthau Diary, in which Roosevelt's Secretary of the Treasury recorded conversations with the President, often within hours.[12]

The scene for later agreement at Quebec was set on the afternoon of Wednesday, September 13, when Roosevelt asked Morgenthau to tea. The Secretary was told that he had been asked to Quebec so that he "could talk with the Prof" (Lord Cherwell). It was also suggested that Morgenthau come to dinner that evening. Roosevelt then told Morgenthau that he could discuss "anything" with Cherwell, with the exception of the projected military occupation zones of Germany, and the question of German partition. But, Roosevelt said, "You can talk about the fact that we are thinking of internationalizing the Ruhr and the Saar, including the Kiel canal."

Roosevelt had sent for Eden: "Churchill, Eden, yourself and I will sit down to discuss the matter." According to White's memorandum, the Secretary had the impression that Roosevelt had asked Eden because of Morgenthau's earlier report that Eden was "tough on the question of a policy toward Germany." The President also said: "Don't worry about Churchill. He is going to be tough too."[13]

A few hours later on the thirteenth, there was a formal conference dinner at the Citadel, Quebec. Besides the President and the Prime Minister, those present included Admiral William Leahy, Roosevelt's personal chief of staff as Commander in Chief, Admiral Land, the United States War Shipping Administrator, Lord Cherwell, Paymaster General and adviser to the Prime Minister, and Lord Leathers, Minister of War Transport. The two personal doctors of the two leaders, Admiral McIntire and Lord Moran, were also present.

The course of the table talk is described in another memorandum drafted by White, evidently to Morgenthau's dictation. White recorded that, though shipping was supposed to have been the subject that evening, "the discussion quickly turned to Germany." Roosevelt stated that he had asked Morgenthau to talk with Cherwell about Germany the following day, and the President now suggested that Morgenthau "explain the program he had in mind for Germany."[14]

However, following Morgenthau's description of the Treasury program dealing with the Ruhr, Churchill "indicated that he was strongly opposed to such a program. He said that all that was necessary was to eliminate the production of armament. To do what the Treasury suggested was 'unnatural, unchristian, and unnecessary.'"

According to a later newspaper article by Morgenthau, Churchill "turned loose on me the full flood of his rhetoric, sarcasm and violence. He looked on the Treasury Plan, he said, as he would on chaining himself to a dead German. He was slumped in his chair, his language merciless. . . . I have never had such a verbal lashing in my life. . . ."[15]

In White's record of the dinner, Admiral Land supported Morgenthau, but Admiral Leahy, on the other hand, "seemed on the whole unsympathetic to the Treasury program and to side with Churchill." Lord Leathers also apparently disagreed with Morgenthau. However, White's memorandum notes, "the President came back to the German problem several times very nicely and did not recede from his position. He reminded Churchill that Stalin at Teheran had said: 'Are you going to let Germany produce modern metal furniture? The manufacture of metal furniture can be quickly turned into the manufacture of armament.'"

Lord Cherwell, White noted, "seemed in sympathy with the Secretary's point of view." This accords with Moran's account of the dinner. Moran also remarks on the Prime Minister's "instinctive revulsion" from the Treasury program and his words: "I agree with Burke. You cannot indict a nation."[16]

With the end of the dinner at the Citadel, White recorded, Cherwell remarked "that he expected to talk with the Secretary about Lend-Lease assistance between the defeat of Germany and the defeat of Japan. The Secretary told him that he had been asked by the President to come to talk about Germany but after he would be glad to discuss Lend-Lease aid the following morning. . . ."

Despite Churchill's opposition, almost violently expressed, to the Treasury proposals, Cherwell was thus to meet with Morgenthau to discuss Germany the next day. Stage II Lend-Lease had also been drawn into the proposed conversations by the end of the dinner. Moreover, White was to attend the Cherwell-Morgenthau meeting. A minute of Morgenthau's postconference report to the Cabinet Committee in Washington records that the dinner at the Citadel "broke up with the suggestion that Mr. Morgenthau (and apparently Mr. White) should discuss the question [of Germany] with Lord Cherwell, which they did on the basis of the Treasury's memorandum."[17]

Clearly, at the dinner, Churchill had indeed been "tough," but not perhaps in the way envisaged by Morgenthau and White. The outlook for an understanding along the lines of the Treasury proposals on Germany was not auspicious. Morgenthau tells us, in his newspaper article that he spent "a sleepless night."

However, in the background to the subject of British Lend-Lease was Morgenthau's apparent belief, held since his trip to England in August, that the Treasury proposals on Germany would be of advantage to Britain. Moreover, by the time of the Octagon Conference, the British had clarified their Stage II Lend-Lease objectives. As a yardstick, the British Treasury now suggested in a memorandum for Roosevelt that during Stage II Lend-Lease munitions received by the United Kingdom should be in the same proportion to British munitions production as in 1944. Besides munitions, the British also asked for foodstuffs and raw materials to meet the needs of the tightly organized British economy. The aggregate requirements, Whitehall calculated, for the first year of Stage II would be about $3 billion, compared with about $3.9 billion in 1944.[18]

Churchill's agreement on Germany, and Roosevelt's on Lend-Lease, was brought considerably closer by the meeting held at ten o'clock on the morning of the fourteenth between Morgenthau, Cherwell, White and G. D. A. (later Sir Donald) MacDougall of Cherwell's staff. White then wrote a memorandum for Morgenthau's files.

Cherwell began by outlining the British case for Stage II aid, after he had initially stated that he would like to take up Lend-Lease first "since he thought it would be easier to dispose of than the question of policy towards Germany."

After listening to Cherwell, Morgenthau replied that "he had heard it all before." But the Secretary went on to say that he "didn't like the approach of determining the amount of Lend-Lease aid that Britain was to get that Cherwell presented. In his [the Secretary's] opinion the question should be approached from the point of view of just how much munitions the British need in the role that they are to play in the Pacific. The Secretary thought that food shipments could be handled all right but he felt that commercial goods could not appropriately go into exports."

Morgenthau was, at this juncture, apparently suggesting that British needs in the munitions category for the first year of Stage II should be based on a figure rather than on a percentage basis related to British production. According to White's record of the meeting, Morgenthau went on to stress that the subject should be handled "by a joint committee of British and Americans." Cherwell liked this idea, White noted, and asked Morgenthau if he himself would head the proposed committee. That was up to Roosevelt. Cherwell then suggested that White and MacDougall "attempt to draft a directive setting up such a committee so that if the Prime Minister and the President did agree on the idea they might get it out then and there. The Secretary agreed."

With Lend-Lease disposed of in this way, apparently to Cherwell's satisfaction, the meeting then turned to Germany. Cherwell hurriedly read through the first part of the Treasury program, expressing skepticism "as to whether organised Labour in the United States would approve a programme so drastic in character." Secretary Morgenthau thought that it would. Cherwell commented that he didn't understand why Churchill had taken so contrary a position the evening before. He (Cherwell) was surprised by Churchill's attitude and thought possibly that it was due to the fact that Churchill did not wholly understand what the Secretary was driving at.

Morgenthau then said that "the question came down to a choice of: 'Do you want a strong Germany and a weak England or a weak Germany and a strong England?' The Secretary said that he preferred to rely on a strong England and a weak Germany. Cherwell thought the proposal could be dressed up in a way to be more attractive to the Prime Minister and the Secretary said that he would be very glad to have Cherwell try it."

Morgenthau and Cherwell then left to see Roosevelt and Churchill. Later, White, MacDougall and another British official met to draft the directive on the Lend-Lease committee suggested by Cherwell. Morgenthau and Cherwell then returned, reporting that the two leaders liked the idea of a committee. They wanted it to set up on an informal basis, to be formalized after the presidential election. Morgenthau later told White that Churchill had suggested Harry Hopkins as chairman, but the President wanted Morgenthau.[19]

During the negotiations on Lend-Lease, Morgenthau had found Cherwell "wonderful to work with," and Professsor Blum remarks, "together they brought negotiations to the point where Roosevelt and Churchill were quickly able to reach agreement."[20] That agreement, reached verbally on the same day as the Morgenthau-Cherwell conference, September 14, was then put into writing and initialed by Roosevelt the following day, but after the Quebec understanding on Germany had been reached by the two leaders.

The talks on Germany between Morgenthau and Cherwell had also been successful from the Treasury viewpoint, for Morgenthau recorded in a later newspaper article that, when he met the Prime Minister later on the fourteenth, "Churchill, without a word about the night before showed himself much more reasonable on the subject of weakening the German economy."

According to Morgenthau's account to the Cabinet Committee in Washington a few days after Quebec, the Treasury proposals on Germany having "convinced" Cherwell, the latter discussed the matter with Churchill. The proposals apparently "appealed to the Prime Minister on the basis that Great Britain would acquire a lot of Germany's iron and steel markets and eliminate a dangerous competitor." Morgenthau told the Cabinet Committee that Churchill "came round completely and proved to be an advocate of the Treasury policy."

As Cherwell told Moran at Quebec, "I explained to Winston that the [Morgenthau] Plan would save Britain from bankruptcy by eliminating a dangerous competitor. Somebody must suffer for the war, and it was surely right that Germany and not Britain should foot the bill. Winston had not thought of it that way, and he said no more about the cruel threat to the German people."[21]

Nevertheless, the actual written agreements of September 15 were not reached without some preliminaries. On the morning of that day, Morgenthau told White that during the Roosevelt-Churchill talks on Lend-Lease the previous afternoon, "the President delayed initialling the memorandum on the creation of the Lend-Lease committee by interrupting with stories. Churchill was nervous and eager to have the memorandum initialed and finally he burst out: 'What do you want me to do? Get on my hind legs and beg like Fala?' "[22]

In another memorandum on a conference in Morgenthau's office at Quebec at 11 A.M. attended by White and Cherwell, White recorded Morgenthau's dissatisfaction with Cherwell's draft of the Roosevelt-Churchill understanding on Germany the previous day. Morgenthau said that "they ought to begin where Churchill left off and go forward. In the first conversation [i.e., at dinner on the thirteenth] Churchill had been shocked by the proposal, but on the following day he seemed to accept the program designed to weaken the German economy. The memorandum ought to take that for granted. Churchill had already spoken of diverting Germany to an agricultural state...."[23]

In the event, when Morgenthau and Cherwell went to meet Roosevelt, Churchill and Eden at noon on the fifteenth, Cherwell's draft on Germany was not presented. The Prime Minister restated the understanding on Germany, but was not satisfied with the subsequent Morgenthau-

Cherwell draft. Churchill then personally dictated another version to his secretary. The Quebec memorandum on Germany was then initialled by Roosevelt and Churchill as it stood:

Top Secret　　　　　　　　　　　　　　　　　　September 15, 1944
Quebec Directive on Germany

At a conference between the President and the Prime Minister upon the best measures to prevent rearmament by Germany it was felt that an essential feature was the future disposition of the Ruhr and the Saar.

The ease with which the metallurgical, chemicals and electric industries in Germany can be converted from peace to war has already been impressed upon us by bitter experience. It must also be remembered that the Germans have devastated a large portion of the industries of Russia and other neighboring allies, and it is only in accordance with justice that these injured countries should be entitled to receive the machinery they require in order to repair the losses they have suffered. The industries referred to in the Ruhr and the Saar would therefore be necessarily put out of action and closed down. It was felt that the two districts should be put under some body under the world organization which would supervise the dismantling of these industries and make sure that they were not started up again by some subterfuge.

The program for eliminating the war-making industries in the Ruhr and the Saar is looking forward to converting Germany into a country primarily agricultural and pastoral in its character.

The Prime Minister and the President were in agreement upon this program.

　　　　　　　　　　　　　　　　O.K.　　　　F.D.R.
　　　　　　　　　　　　　　　　　　　　　　W.C.
　　　　　　　　　　　　　　　　　　　　　　15.9.[24]

The Quebec memorandum clearly indicated a shift away from the taut policy of postponing decisions on Germany by Roosevelt and Churchill, but there were several features that distinguished it from the Treasury Plan.

There was no mention of German partition, and the specific industries mentioned for removal from the Ruhr and the Saar indicated perhaps an attempt to limit the effects of deindustrialization. On the other hand, an indication of the haste with which the Quebec discussions took place, the Saar was bracketed with the Ruhr, although it had been scheduled for cession to France in White's successive drafts of the Treasury Plan. These measures, it will be noted, were related to the first cause of German aggression.

However, the Quebec memorandum was not a treaty or a governmental agreement, but a statement of intention. As the Russians were not included, it could not be a tripartite statement of Allied views on Germany. Yet in its references to closing down some of the crucial Ruhr industries, and to reducing Germany to "a country primarily agricultural and pastoral in character," it seems clear why White and Morgenthau could regard "the Quebec directive" as a triumph.

Eden was angry at Churchill's assent to the document, and an argument broke out between the two men. In his memoirs Eden remarks that he did not like the Morgenthau Plan, "nor was I convinced that it was to our national advantage." The United States Treasury proposals were thoroughly disliked in Whitehall, and a message conveying this disapproval had been sent to Churchill by the War Cabinet, arriving, however, in Quebec after the agreement on Germany. The Foreign Office and the British Treasury considered that, while there were good arguments for weakening Germany as a security measure, if the country was unable to manufacture it would be unable to pay for imports. World trade would suffer and British exports with it. This made nonsense, Eden considered, of the United States Treasury claim that the plan would bring benefits to Britain.[25]

Following the signing of the memorandum on Germany, the President now initialled another paper, on Stage II Lend-Lease for Britain. This recorded the agreement verbally reached by Roosevelt and Churchill the previous day, September 14.

In this "Record of Conversation between the President and the Prime Minister at Quebec on September 14, 1944," Roosevelt initally agreed that during Stage II Britain should continue to receive assistance to cover "reasonable needs," calculated on the proportional basis noted above. The "Record" goes on:

Mr. Morgenthau however suggested that it would be better to have definite figures. He understood that munitions assistance required had been calculated by the British at about three and a half billion dollars in the first year on the basis of the strategy envisaged before the Octagon conference. The exact needs would have to be recalculated in the light of decisions on military matters reached at the conference. The non-munitions requirements had been put at three billion dollars gross against which a considerable amount would be set off for reverse Lend-Lease. The President agreed that it would be better to work on figures like these than on a proportional basis. The Prime Minister emphasized that all these supplies would be on Lend-Lease. The President said that this would naturally be so.

In addition, Lend-Lease articles were not to be sold for profit, or exported by the British, but it was essential, the "Record" noted, that the United States should "not attach any conditions to supplies delivered to Britain on Lend-Lease which would jeopardize the recovery of her export trade. The President thought this would be proper."

The "Record" also noted that a joint Anglo-American committee would be set up to implement these decisions, headed by Morgenthau.[26]

Later in the day, a third matter was settled between Roosevelt and Churchill, when the President, after what Churchill calls "a considerable correspondence"[27] agreed that the British should take the northwestern occupation zone of Germany, as defined by the EAC. The United States, of course, would occupy the southwestern zone. There is a post-Quebec suggestion by Morgenthau to the Cabinet Committee, recorded by White, that Roosevelt wanted the British to be in charge of the Ruhr "so that they would have to implement the policy which was outlined in the memorandum [on Germany] initialled by Churchill and himself."[28]

But, for White, these arrangements on Lend-Lease and the German occupation zones must surely have been secondary to the importance of the Roosevelt-Churchill understanding on Germany. As a private achievement, the events leading to the Quebec memorandum of September 15, 1944, may have been as satisfying to him as the public acclaim at Bretton Woods had been two months previously.

As White and Morgenthau now returned to Washington from Quebec there was surprise, consternation and anger among those who had opposed the Morgenthau Plan in the intense secret debate on the future of Germany which had preceded the Octagon Conference.

It had been announced from Quebec on September 13 that Morgenthau's presence at the conference would assist the President "in dealing with some of the serious economic issues arising out of world conditions."[29] Stimson was by now preparing to sign a third memorandum for Roosevelt opposing the Treasury proposals, a paper which had been drafted largely by McCloy. The memorandum, "pitched on a higher level than anything else," as it is described in Stimson's memoirs, stated that the Treasury Plan would be "just such a crime as the Germans themselves hoped to perpetrate upon their victims—it would be a crime against civilization itself . . . an open confession of the bankruptcy of hope for a reasonable economic and political settlement of the causes of war."[30]

Hearing of the Quebec agreement, Stimson still sent the memorandum, dated September 16, to Roosevelt at Hyde Park, where the two leaders had repaired after the conference. The Quebec memorandum, as we have seen, modified the Treasury proposals on Germany, but it was now hardly surprising that McCloy told James Forrestal, the Navy Secretary, on September 18 that Roosevelt "had decided to go along with Morgenthau." Morgenthau obviously thought so too, for the next morning at a group meeting in the Treasury attended by White and others, he told his staff that "the thing up at Quebec, all together, was unbelievably good . . . it was the high spot of my whole career in the government. I got more personal satisfaction out of those forty-eight hours than with anything I have ever been connected with."[31]

The next day, September 20, Morgenthau, with White in attendance, reported his victory at Quebec to the Cabinet Committee. Besides Hull and Stimson, Freeman Matthews and McCloy were present at this meeting in Hull's office.

After Morgenthau's account of how agreement between Roosevelt and Churchill was reached at Quebec, with Cherwell's assistance, Stimson asked whether there was any connection between Churchill's acceptance of the proposals on Germany and the arrangements on Stage II Lend-Lease. Morgenthau pointed out, according to White's minute of the meeting, that the agreement on Lend-Lease was not drafted until the final day and that Churchill had agreed to the policy on Germany prior to the drafting of the agreement by Roosevelt on aid to Britain.

Stimson seems to have accepted Morgenthau's assurance that there was no formal connection, but Hull, angry and upset, was not convinced. The Secretary of State was triply outraged by the proceedings at Quebec. His jurisdictional domain had been dramatically invaded by Morgenthau and White, the President had ignored the State Department's painstaking work on Germany, and the Quebec arrangements, he told the meeting, threw away the "bait" of Lend-Lease in obtaining British concessions on his liberal commercial policies, a goal pursued with such single-mindedness ever since the signing of Article VII.

The whole development at Quebec, Hull remarks in his memoirs, "angered me as much as anything else that had happened during my career as Secretary of State." Reversing his earlier stand, Hull now emerged as a determined opponent of the Treasury proposals on Germany and the Quebec memorandum.[32]

There seems no reason to doubt Morgenthau's view that there was no formal "deal" at Quebec, and that instead Cherwell's advocacy was decisive with Churchill. As Paul Y. Hammond has pointed out, the original Treasury proposals were partly toned down in the Roosevelt-Churchill memorandum, and it seems hardly likely that the Quebec agreement would have been almost casually dictated by the Prime Minister if a formal bargain had been struck.[33]

Nevertheless it is conceivable that some sort of informal understanding may have emerged during the talks between Morgenthau, Cherwell and

White on September 14. R. H. (later Lord) Brand, the British Treasury representative in Washington during 1944 has recorded that during the Octagon Conference he was sent by his department to Quebec "to try and stop this lunatic idea." Like Eden's mission, Brand's journey was part of Whitehall's opposition to the United States Treasury proposals on Germany.

Hurrying northward from Washington, Brand arrived too late in Quebec. Roosevelt and Churchill were already locked up in "the Fort" discussing "high strategic matters," and when Brand expressed his disagreement on the United States Treasury proposals for Germany to Cherwell, he gathered that Churchill's adviser took "a different idea." Cherwell told Brand that Britain would be "very much more likely to get the loan if he got Winston to sign the document," an attitude Brand found "irresponsible."[34]

Perhaps, too, as Brand hints, Cherwell's advocacy to Churchill may have been influenced by his own favorable view of the White-Morgenthau proposals. Apropos of Brand's comments, Cherwell's biographer writes that although Cherwell was "in favour of depriving Germany of her capital industrial machinery so that she could not be in a situation to start another war, he considered that the Morgenthau Plan went much too far and could only result in our having to support Germany. But he did feel very strongly that after the war we should discourage the rebuilding of German industry, especially heavy industry, and should make an all-out effort to capture the German export market which was far more important than seeking industrial reparations from Germany in the form of manufactured goods."[35]

However, if Cherwell were in favor of "depriving Germany of her capital industrial machinery," he may have been in sympathy with part of the White-Morgenthau proposals as he sought to persuade Churchill to reverse his initial stand on Germany at Quebec. Moreover, in a recent memoir, Jock Colville, Churchill's Assistant Private Secretary at the time, who attended the Octagon Conference, remarks that while elimination of Germany had no place in Churchill's considered views, which envisaged a reunited European family with an honorable place for Germany, Cherwell at this time possessed "an obsessive hatred of Germany."[36]

At Quebec, therefore, Cherwell, whose great contributions to the Allied cause as Churchill's scientific adviser are well known, presented not only the case for the White-Morgenthau proposals on Germany, but may have linked those proposals with Stage II Lend-Lease as he discussed the matter with Churchill. Evidently Brand thought there was a connection. And as a cryptic sentence in Churchill's account of Octagon indicates, the Prime Minister was hardly unaware of a possible relationship between Lend-Lease and the Morgenthau Plan. "At first," Churchill writes, "I violently opposed this idea. But the President, with Mr. Morgenthau—from whom we had so much to ask—was so insistent that in the end we agreed to consider it."[37]

White himself had little doubt that the agreements on Germany and Lend-Lease at Quebec were "tied up." A month after the conference, he suggested to Morgenthau that there was a *quid pro quo* relationship between the two matters. Morgenthau disagreed, arguing that, as he had told Stimson, the Quebec memorandum had been signed before Roosevelt agreed in writing to the understanding on Lend-Lease. White persisted:

> You put special stress [to Stimson] on when they signed the document, but if I may remind you, what Churchill said to the President when he was trying to get the President to agree on the [Lend-Lease] document, you remember he said, "What do you want me to do, stand up and beg like Fala?" And the document was signed on Lend-Lease after, but there was practically an oral commitment before. It was just to be put in writing.

White then recalled that Cherwell had come to Morgenthau's office at Quebec, when he was present, as noted above, to discuss both Lend-Lease to Britain and the future of Germany: "But in any case the more significant thing in my mind is that you tied them both up together."[38] While there seems to have been no explicit understanding, Professor Blum writes, "Morgenthau realized then and later that the two questions had some bearing on each other at Quebec, but he never thought he and Churchill struck a bargain in any direct sense."[39]

Probably, therefore, some tacit understanding emerged between Morgenthau, Cherwell and White and then later between Roosevelt and Churchill as the Octagon discussions proceeded. But the conflicting motives of those concerned, the way in which understanding was reached, and the opposition to the memorandum as an international agreement on Germany would now mean that the triumph of White and Morgenthau at Quebec was compromised.

Whatever the qualifications of the Morgenthau Plan in the Quebec memorandum, the Cabinet Committee on September 20 showed that Hull and Stimson assumed that the Treasury had won a major victory. At the same time the Draft Interim Directive for Eisenhower's use in the immediate postsurrender period was now being written, as we shall see, not only with Treasury participation, but in line with ideas on the postwar

German economy that White had outlined since Redrice. Such principles, the Treasury now implied, were authoritatively underlined on the
highest level by the President. And it was assumed that this Directive
would have "Combined" Anglo-American status, like CCS-551, the presurrender directive sent to Eisenhower.

Meanwhile, on the battlefront three Anglo-American airborne divisions were fighting to clear a corridor across the lower Rhine and perhaps into the heart of Germany. On the afternoon of the twentieth,
James Gavin's men from the United States 82nd Airborne Division had
captured the northern end of the Nijmegen Bridge, and while the para-
troopers from Urquhart's 1st British Airborne Division were invested at
Arnhem the battle could still conceivably go either way. If there were a
sudden collapse of the Reich, Allied intentions might well be influenced
by the Quebec memorandum.

Now, on Thursday, September 21, Drew Pearson's syndicated column,
"Washington-Merry-Go-Round," appeared in the Washington *Post* with
a dramatic, pro-Treasury account of the *Handbook* episode of the previous month.

"War and State Department officials are still quaking in their boots
after President Roosevelt blew up last month over their failure to achieve
any clear plan for civil administration on Germany," Pearson reported.
The column went on to describe how "joint British and American army
units" had spent most of the summer writing and rewriting the civil
administration *Handbook* for Germany. When the book arrived in Washington "late in August" it was "a completely negative set of instructions
with no clear and workable recommendations concerning labor problems, food problems, industrial problems." Civil administrators studying
the book were given no reason to believe that the American and British
governments "even desired to oust Nazis from important posts in Germany."

"In disgust," Pearson went on, "Treasury Secretary Henry Morgenthau
and Harry White, director of the Treasury's monetary research division,
took the proofs to the White House, tossed them on the President's bed,
and asked him to look them over." Roosevelt "threw the book down
indignantly: 'Feed the Germans,' he said, 'I'll give them three bowls of
soup a day with nothing in them. Control inflation! Let them have all the
inflation they want. I should worry. Control industry! There's not going
to be any industry in Germany to control.'"

Pearson went on to relate that Roosevelt had asked Morgenthau, Stimson and Hull to prepare for him "a detailed plan" for the administration
of Germany, then wrote Stimson a letter "blistering" the proposed *Handbook*. No "final plan" was reached, Pearson concluded, but by the time

Roosevelt left for Quebec the President "had some very clear ideas on this policy even though it was not yet fully formulated."

Those against the Morgenthau Plan immediately realized that Pearson's report, with its probable origins in the Treasury, was an illustration of the department's confidence that the President would follow the White-Morgenthau policy on Germany. Moreover, Pearson's column presaged further reports in the same vein, and the opponents of the Treasury Plan now decided to fight back by publicizing the split in the Cabinet Committee, so taking the issue to the press and the public.

One recent account reports that "having discussed the issue with Stimson who apparently did not quite approve of the proposed course of action, Cordell Hull went into a strategy meeting with one of the President's assistants, who, he knew, was also worried about Morgenthau's new role and who thoroughly disapproved of the Morgenthau Plan."[40] But whatever the precise source of the leak, publication at this moment of the details of the Treasury proposals could only strengthen the opposition, particularly in the State Department. A briefing was now prepared, and Arthur Krock of the New York *Times* writes of the episode in his memoirs, "One day at the hour known to the South as bull-bat time, I was summoned to partake of liquid refreshment with an official just below the Presidential echelon."[41]

Following the briefing, Krock broke the story of the significance of Morgenthau's attendance at Quebec. Morgenthau, Krock wrote in the New York *Times* of September 22, had become "the central civilian government official" concerned with postwar Germany. The Secretary's views, Krock went on, were more in line with Roosevelt's than with those of the President's other advisers. Krock's story was only the beginning.

The next day, September 23, a detailed account of the Morgenthau Plan and the Cabinet opposition written by Alfred F. Flynn appeared in the *Wall Street Journal*. Flynn outlined the Treasury proposals on German partition and deindustrialization and went on to write that "the Treasury Plan is designed to bring about fundamental changes not only in physical Germany, but in the German way of living and thinking . . . supporters of the Treasury plan say it would encourage more than thirty million persons to move to other portions of the world and that this, in itself, would be a major contribution to peace."

An Associated Press dispatch on similar lines, datelined from Washington the same day, appeared on the front page of the New York *Times* on the morning of the twenty-fourth. The story described the split in the Cabinet Committee over the Plan, stated that the Treasury proposals had the "general approval" of the President and that Churchill had found them "acceptable" at Quebec. The same day, the first of a series of three detailed stories on the Plan by John Hightower appeared in the Washington *Evening Star*. The wire services now carried the story of the Morgenthau Plan all over the world.

In the mounting uproar, the Morgenthau Plan was criticized in the American and British press and attacked in the House of Commons. Eden was able to parry questions by answering that "I have seen reports in the Press, but on the whole it is judicious on these matters not to found oneself exclusively on reports in the Press."

> MR. STOKES. May I ask my right honorable Friend whether it is totally inaccurate that this matter was discussed at Quebec?
> MR. EDEN. No, Sir, I am afraid that my right honorable Friend will not draw me out on that.[42]

But dissociation from the Morgenthau Plan was not always possible. In Germany the story was taken up by the Nazi propaganda apparatus. It was orchestrated by Goebbels, together with the themes of Unconditional Surrender and the R.A.F.'s area bombing, into his last great campaign, warning the German people to fight on against those who wished to annihilate them and turn the Reich into a potato patch. One headline in the German press read: ROOSEVELT AND CHURCHILL AGREE TO JEWISH MURDER PLAN! In *Das Reich* Goebbels asserted that "it hardly matters whether the Bolshevists wish to destroy the Reich in one fashion, and the Anglo-Saxons propose to do it in another. They both agree on their aim; they wish to get rid of thirty to forty million Germans. . . ." "The Morgenthau Plan," Albert Speer writes, "was made to order for Hitler and the Party, insofar as they could point to it for proof that defeat would finally seal the fate of all Germans. Many people were actually influenced by this threat."[43]

German resistance was stiffening in any case as the Wehrmacht was forced back to Reich soil in the autumn of 1944, and the Nazi leaders were pledged to fight to the end. But Roosevelt's domestic political opponents were also able to capitalize on the revelations of the Treasury Plan. At the end of the presidential election campaign, Thomas Dewey, the Republican candidate, was claiming that the news of the Plan was "as good as ten fresh German divisions." Once the story broke, therefore, Roosevelt's approval of the Quebec memorandum was obviously a major political liability.

White, like Morgenthau, was understandably disturbed by the mounting speculation, and in a Treasury group meeting on September 25 the tone of the discussion was, uncharacteristically, a defensive one. Walter Lippmann had been to see White before the weekend, "discussing why he thought it would be a mistake to move to an agrarian or pastoral coun-try."[44] Morgenthau canceled a press conference for that day while Hull, meanwhile, had issued a bland press statement mentioning neither the Morgenthau Plan nor the Cabinet split, so in effect confirming the press reports.

The tension continued in the Treasury on September 26 when Roose-velt dissolved the Cabinet Committee on Germany. One of the con-tinuing press stories had named White as "largely responsible for the preparation of the Plan," and this, White remarked, was "no pleasure" for him. Two days later, as the storm continued, Elmer Davis, Director of the Office of War Information, asked Morgenthau how 15,000,000 Germans were going to be prevented from starving. Davis needed selling "very badly," Morgenthau considered, and an appointment was arranged with White.[45]

By the twenty-ninth White was persuaded that it would be best to attempt to ride out the storm for the time being, without engaging in too much debate on Germany until after the election. That morning Krock had returned to the attack in a knowing *Times* piece which stated that at Quebec the British had lent an interested ear "to descriptions of the beneficial effect on their hard-pressed economy if Germany were turned into an agricultural nation. The British Lend-Lease debit with us is now six or seven million." Krock judged that "familiar signs" pointed to Roo-sevelt's abandonment of the Morgenthau Plan following the press pub-licity.

In the Treasury group meeting that morning, White "was positive when I got to reading that Krock article that that was State—Hull or Matthews." But, White told Morgenthau, "after all that has been said and done . . . I think you will have to take whatever rap is coming during the next month of the election. Publicly, I think that the President will do whatever he thinks is of interest to him politically . . . after the election it will be a different story.[46]

As White implied, Roosevelt had already begun to move away from Morgenthau and the Quebec understanding. Shortly after the Cabinet Committee meeting of September 20, Hull had gone to see the President, inveighing against the Morgenthau Plan and the Quebec arrangements. He bitterly attacked the Treasury proposals, which he describes in his memoirs as "a plan of blind vengeance," telling the President that they were "out of all reason." No expert of the American or any other govern-ment had had anything to do with their preparation, and, Hull went on, 40 percent of the German population would die if the country were converted to an agricultural basis.

Hull told Roosevelt that he was "satisfied" that the British had joined with Morgenthau at Quebec to obtain Lend-Lease credits, and that such negotiations should be handled by the State Department. He concluded that if the President were connected with the Treasury proposals "it would greatly injure him politically." Roosevelt apparently said very little "except to indicate that he had not actually committed himself to Morgenthau's proposals." Hull followed up this visit by sending a memorandum on September 25 stating that it was "highly advisable" that the United States should have the support of Britain and Russia on German policy. The paper rightly implied that there was no indication that the British government would support Churchill's position at Quebec, as there was no evidence that Whitehall wanted the "complete eradication" of the industrial Ruhr.[47]

Following the dissolution of the Cabinet Committee on the twenty-sixth, Roosevelt told Stimson on the telephone the next day that he did not "really intend" to make Germany "a purely agricultural country." The State Department was privately told by the President that it alone was "to study and report" upon the German problem, and "high administration sources" informed the media that Roosevelt did not favor the Morgenthau Plan and that he had never really adopted it. Interest was further diverted by Roosevelt's press conference on September 29 when a presidential letter to the Foreign Economic Administration was released directing that agency to make studies of what should be done about the postwar German economy. When asked about reports of the Cabinet split, Roosevelt replied that "every story that came out was essentially untrue in its basic facts."[48]

Moreover, Roosevelt sent a memorandum to Hull on September 29 emphasizing that "the real nub" was to keep Britain from bankruptcy after the war, and that "no one" wanted to eradicate the Ruhr and to make Germany an agricultural country. Before this paper reached Hull, the Secretary of State went to Roosevelt on October 1 with a paper of his own, also dated September 29, which outlined in some detail his department's moderate views on postwar Germany which, of course, were at complete variance with White's. It was Hull's "last important item of business" before his collapse and resignation in late November.[49]

Roosevelt lunched with Stimson on October 3, when the President, thanks to strenuous efforts, had largely been dissociated in the public eye from the Morgenthau Plan. The President grinned and said that Morgenthau had "pulled a boner." When Stimson read out parts of the Quebec memorandum, Roosevelt was "frankly staggered" and said that "he had no idea how he could have initialled this."[50]

As the presidential election campaign was now in full swing, Morgenthau and White avoided conspicuous participation in any administration discussion on policy toward postwar Germany during October, 1944.

Morgenthau was also sensitive to the charges that his Plan had contributed to the stiffening of German resistance on the West Wall. But White was now to supervise the writing of a book by Treasury staff explaining and defending the Morgenthau Plan, eventually published a year later under Morgenthau's name as *Germany Is Our Problem*. However, Morgenthau told McCloy at this time that after the elections he "intended to get back into the German picture in a big way."

In any case, with the failure of the Arnhem drop at the end of September, public interest in postwar policy for Germany waned as it became likely that the Reich would fight on until the spring. And Roosevelt, while appearing to move toward the State Department position, more likely edged back toward the policy of postponement on Germany. Answering Hull's paper of September 29 on October 20, the President wrote, "I dislike making detailed plans for a country we do not yet occupy."[51] The next day, in a carefully phrased speech before the Foreign Press Association in New York, Roosevelt stated that "The German people are not going to be enslaved. . . . But it will be necessary for them to earn their way back. . . ."

At Downing Street there was an equally unmistakable retreat from the Quebec memorandum which, as Churchill later put it, "dropped on one side," and never reached the Cabinet. The matter was raised by Attlee in the Armistice and Postwar Committee of the Cabinet, who said that Churchill had asked for an examination of the Quebec proposals on Germany. The Committee "were doubtful" of them and they were sent to the Economic and Industrial Planning Staff in Whitehall, which had been set up earlier in 1944 to examine the economic aspects of the German armistice terms. At the end of the year the E.I.P.S. delivered a "most unfavourable" report; Eden considered that the Cabinet need do nothing more about the Quebec proposals unless the President "raised them again."[52]

In early January, 1945, Churchill indicated to Eden that, as with Roosevelt, the policy of postponement was once again in the ascendant with him. "It is much too soon," wrote the Prime Minister on the postwar treatment of Germany, "for us to decide these enormous questions . . . it is a mistake to try and write out on little pieces of paper what the vast emotions of an outraged and quivering world will be either immediately after the struggle is over or when the inevitable cold fit follows the hot."[53]

Ten years later when the cold fit was well in the ascendant Churchill remarked guardedly in *Triumph and Tragedy* that at Quebec it did not seem unfair to agree that German "manufacturing capacity need not be revived beyond what was required to give her the same standards of life as her neighbours. All this was of course subject to the full consideration of the War Cabinet, and, in the event, with my full accord, the idea of pastoralising Germany did not survive."[54]

It was not White's intention, as we have seen, to give Germany the same standards of life as her neighbors. Perhaps Churchill's frankest words on the events surrounding the Quebec memorandum were to the House of Commons in July, 1949, during a Foreign Affairs debate:

> Another matter to which the Foreign Secretary referred, about which I do not by any means feel so confident in my conscience as to the judgment of my actions, is the Morgenthau Agreement at the second [Quebec] conference—the document published by Mr. Morgenthau of the conference. There is an agreement; it was initialled by President Roosevelt and by me, and it undoubtedly proposed treatment of Germany which was a harsh treatment, in respect of largely limiting her to being an agricultural country. But that was not a decision taken over the heads of the Cabinet. It was not one that ever reached the Cabinet. It never reached the Cabinet because it was only *ad referendum*; it was disapproved by the State Department on the one hand and by my right hon. Friend and the Foreign Office Committee on the other, and it just dropped on one side. I must say that it never required a Cabinet negative; it never had any validity of any sort or kind.
>
> Nevertheless, I must say that I do not agree with this paper, for which I none the less bear a responsibility. I do not agree with it, but I can only say that when fighting for life in a fierce struggle with an enemy I feel quite differently towards him than when that enemy is beaten to the ground and is suing for mercy. Anyhow, if the document is ever brought up to me I shall certainly say, "I do not agree with that, and I am sorry that I put my initials to it." I cannot do more than that. Of course many things happen with great rapidity, but to say it was done over the heads of the Cabinet, or anything like that, is quite untrue, and the Cabinet never agreed to it for a moment.[55]

Not only the Quebec memorandum on Germany, but also the Octagon agreement on Stage II Lend-Lease was to prove a will-o'-the-wisp.

In early October, as the Lend-Lease negotiations promised at Quebec approached, Morgenthau told White that he considered that "the spirit of the Quebec Conference" was to prevail during the discussions. The British dollar balances, Morgenthau said, had not entered into the agreement between Roosevelt and Churchill, but he considered that these balances were not a yardstick any longer. White objected to incurring any responsibility for putting England back on her feet. The United Kingdom, he argued, "could absorb endless billions of dollars, and any vague commitment to England's future prosperity would threaten both the financial and political position of the United States in the postwar world."[56]

However, following detailed talks with a British mission led by Cherwell and Keynes, Morgenthau, Under Secretary of State Edward R. Stettinius, White and other American negotiators reached agreement on Stage II Lend-Lease. A basis of $5.5 billion was agreed, to cover both munitions and non-munitions, and a greater degree of freedom for the British export trade, in the context of the "export White Paper," was achieved. At the end of November, following the conclusion of the Anglo-American negotiations, Churchill gave an enthusiastic and optimistic report to the House of Commons.

But no formal undertaking or protocol was signed for, understandably, what the Anglo-American committee proposed, Congress disposed. The United States Joint Chiefs of Staff believed also that Lend-Lease deliveries should be made only in the case of materials which could actually be used in the conflict; and Roosevelt, according to Admiral Leahy, his Chief of Staff, recognized that the projected program could not constitute any formal agreement as the schedules were subject to the changing demands of strategy, procurement and allocation. Moreover, even if Stage II deliveries to Britain went ahead as planned, Lend-Lease aid could not be used after the end of the Pacific war. In April, 1945, Congress specifically legislated that such aid could not be used for postwar reconstruction or rehabilitation.[57]

As we have seen, at the outset of the Octagon Conference, the British planners had envisaged that Stage II Lend-Lease would help to solve part of the British transitional problem. But now, within a few months, it appeared that no binding commitment could be made as a result of the Conference; and, in any case, what if the Pacific war ended less than eighteen months after the defeat of Germany—or suddenly? Lend-Lease was thus of no more potential use in solving the British transitional problem than the Bretton Woods program. Hence Keynes's remark in London to an emissary of Roosevelt's in the spring of 1945, "The only possible solution for Britain's problems today would be another brainwave by your President Roosevelt—like Lend-Lease."[58]

Inevitably, therefore, the spirit of Quebec soon waned, but the two major problems of postwar Germany and the British transition remained. We shall return below to White's views on the British transitional problem as he piloted the Bretton Woods legislation through Congress in the spring of 1945. But his immediate concern in the winter of 1944–45 remained Germany, for the absence of any firm Anglo-American agreement on the postwar Reich meant that the problem had to be considered in a tripartite context—the Yalta Conference.

However, the uproar over the Morgenthau Plan and the retreat from the Quebec memorandum by Roosevelt and Churchill obscured the fact that the American, short-term, postsurrender "Draft Interim Directive" for occupied Germany, which incorporated some of White's prominent provisions for the conquered Reich, had already been approved by the American government.

THE VITAL PARAGRAPHS

... you will take no steps looking toward the economic rehabilitation of Germany nor designed to strengthen the German economy.
—THE INTERIM DIRECTIVE, JCS 1067, September, 1944

THE PUBLIC uproar over the Morgenthau Plan and the apparent retreat from the Quebec memorandum by Roosevelt and Churchill obscured the fact that in the immediate aftermath of Octagon the postsurrender "Draft Interim Directive" for Germany had been approved by the President and the Cabinet Committee before its dissolution. In some of its most important provisions, the Directive, an official secret document known as JCS 1067, followed the spirit of the Treasury proposals for Germany. It reflected in particular White's belief, expressed to Eisenhower in England during the previous month, that the German economy should be given "an opportunity to settle down."

In Washington, however, the progress of the Directive toward official approval, while closely intertwined with the development of the Morgenthau Plan, was separate. As we have already noted during the meeting on September 2 of the Cabinet Committee deputies, when White had first put forward his sweeping Treasury proposals for the postwar Reich, it had been agreed that work should start at once on a short-term Interim Directive for Eisenhower. This Directive would then be issued pending high-level agreement on long-term policy for Germany. It was hoped that following American approval, the document would then be cleared by the Combined Chiefs, so becoming an Anglo-American document for the Supreme Commander Allied Expeditionary Force (SCAEF), analogous to CCS-551, the presurrender Directive.

Following the meeting of the deputies, the next day the War Department gave the Treasury its Draft Interim Directive.[1] The paper stated that Germany would be treated as "a defeated enemy nation," emphasized the complete authority of SCAEF, put forward proposals for denazification, and also emphasized the discretionary nature of SCAEF's powers over the German economy. Although, as we have seen, Eisenhower had been concerned during August that maintenance of this economy might incur too much responsibility for SCAEF in conditions of total collapse, such discretionary power left the question of the postwar German economy an open one.

As White was now involved in the drafting of the successive versions of the wider Treasury proposals for Germany—Morgenthau, it will be remembered, had returned from Fishkill to the Treasury on September 4—a member of the Division of Monetary Research, W. H. Taylor, produced, on September 5, a Treasury draft of the Interim Directive.[2] In its financial and economic provisions the Treasury draft differed considerably from that of the War Department in that it severely restricted SCAEF's discretion to maintain the German economy.

The Treasury draft stated that in the imposition and maintenance of economic controls, "German authorities will to the fullest extent practicable be ordered to proclaim and assume administration of such controls." SCAEF was to control the German economy only to the extent necessary to safeguard his forces, assure the cessation of German war production, and prevent serious disease and unrest: "Except for the purposes specified above you will take no steps (1) looking toward the economic rehabilitation of Germany nor (2) designed to maintain or strengthen the German economy." Responsibility for price controls, rationing, distribution, transportation etc. would be left in German hands, in line with the provision in all three of White's drafts of the Morgenthau Plan that "the sole purpose of the military in control of the German economy shall be to facilitate military operations and military occupation."[3]

Before, during and after the Quebec Conference, negotiations continued between State, War and Treasury, with the latter department stiffening the successive drafts of the Interim Directive and advocating the reduction of SCAEF's discretionary powers in an attempt, perhaps, as Hammond puts it, "to force the compliance of an agent expected to be hostile." However, on this very issue of limiting command discretion in enforcing the Directive, the Treasury now found a decisive ally against State in the War Department itself, although of course Assistant Secretary McCloy was as opposed as Stimson to the punitive provisions of the Morgenthau Plan.

The grounds of this Treasury-War alliance, which was to endure during the revising of the Directive in the months to come, lay in the War Department's concept of limited liability toward its responsibilities in military government, now reinforced by Eisenhower's fears of German collapse. This attitude, of course, had already been demonstrated, as we have seen, in earlier negotiations with State over the German occupation when the Army had wished to be kept out of policy-making. Hence for quite differing reasons, both the Treasury and War departments now "wanted the Army clearly absolved from any responsibility for maintaining the German economic system in operation; the Treasury because it did not want the Army to be authorized to build up the German economy, and the War Department because it did not want to have the responsibility which clearly overreached its capabilities."[4]

Moreover, with the promising military situation in mid-September, there was a compelling need, from the War Department's viewpoint, to get a German postsurrender directive to Eisenhower, perhaps *any* agreed directive. Finally, the Treasury's hand was immeasurably reinforced when on September 16 the news of the Quebec memorandum on Germany reached Washington, with its authoritative statement of intent by the two leaders. McCloy now had a Draft Interim Directive prepared which at least presented the negative Treasury provisions on the German economy as an exception to the purposes for which the economy would be controlled. Thus the Directive, in the form in which it was sent to Eisenhower, now read that SCAEF would assume control of the German economy for the purposes of stopping German war production, preventing disease and unrest which might endanger the occupation, and preventing dissipation of resources which might be needed for restitution and reparation pending a decision by the Allied governments. However, the Directive then went on:

> Except for the purposes specified above, you will take no steps looking toward the economic rehabilitation of Germany nor designed to maintain or strengthen the German economy. Except to the extent necessary to accomplish the purposes set out above, the responsibility for such economic problems as price controls, rationing, unemployment, production, reconstruction, distribution, consumption, housing or transportation will remain with the German people and the German authorities.[5]

The Treasury accepted this draft, and in the meeting of the Cabinet Committee on September 20, when Morgenthau reported his triumph at Quebec, White told McCloy that this latest draft was "an excellent job and we were quite pleased by it." According to White's minute, McCloy remarked that the State Department, too, was in agreement except for "the paragraph on economic control." White replied "that is a vital paragraph," but the concord between War and Treasury on this "vital paragraph," quoted above, hardly presaged success for the State Department's objections.[6]

The showdown came on September 22 when agreement was reached by the three departments on the Treasury-War draft, including the economic control passage. In a report for Hull the next day, J. W. Riddleberger of the State Department noted that,

> at a meeting yesterday in the War Department on the Interim Directive for Germany in which representatives of State, War and Treasury participated, there were several developments of which I think you should be apprised. The Treasury representatives were Messrs. Pehle, Luxford and Taylor. In the course of the discussion, they made it altogether clear that in their opinion the Treasury Department, as a result of the establishment of the Cabinet Committee on Germany, should be consulted on all phases of German problems, including both political and economic. They participated vigorously in the discussion on the political directive and insinuated that the Treasury plan for the treatment of Germany had received the approval of the Cabinet Committee and the blessing of the President. They stated flatly that the economic documents, as approved by the Executive Committee on Economic Foreign Policy, had been repudiated both by Secretary Morgenthau and Secretary Hull, and that no further attention was to be given to these papers. They requested that certain other confidential memoranda be transmitted to them at once and implied that henceforth all such material should be immediately made available to the Treasury Department. In general they took the line that henceforth the Treasury must be consulted on all important matters respecting Germany and that was the purpose of the Cabinet Committee.[7]

Ironically, this meeting took place on the same day that Arthur Krock's first piece on the Quebec Conference began to break the story of the Cabinet split on the Morgenthau Plan. But the very fact of the Quebec memorandum meant that the State Department was virtually overruled, and that the War Department had to swallow its reservations over the economic provisions of the Draft Interim Directive, which, of course, reflected White's views. In his thoughtful essay on JCS 1067, Walter Dorn has succinctly summed up the interrelationship between White's original memorandum on Germany of September 1, the Quebec memorandum of September 15 and the approval of the Draft Interim Directive:

> When on 22 September 1944 Harry Hopkins called the deputies of the members of the Cabinet Committee to meet in Mr. McCloy's office for an all-day session to draft the interim directive for General Eisenhower, the Treasury representatives declared that the original White memorandum had been approved by the President. This put an end to all further opposition on the part of their colleagues from the War and State Departments. Thus it happened that the original version of JCS 1067 became largely a Treasury document. Although written in accordance with the limited liability theory of the War Department, its principal features were of Treasury origin and none of the basic State Department policy recommendations were incorporated in its clauses. By forbidding the American Army to maintain price, wage and market controls, it literally decreed, as a State Department official put it, economic chaos. In this way the Treasury view that the extreme disruption of German economy was not in conflict with Allied interests became official American policy . . . the Cabinet Committee, including Mr. Hull, approved this directive. As it stood JCS 1067 was an impracticable directive. The War Department accepted this document knowing that it was impracticable but so long as Mr. Morgenthau had the ear of the President no other directive was obtainable and an immediate directive, indeed any directive, was a necessity required by the military situation, a circumstance which State Department, thinking largely in political terms, was inclined to forget. . . .[8]

Following this meeting on the twenty-second, the Directive was approved by Hull, cleared with Roosevelt, and recommended by the United States Joint Chiefs of Staff for discussion by the Combined Chiefs, acquiring the file number JCS 1067 in the process. Then, on September 27, following transmittal to Eisenhower, the Interim Directive was sent to Ambassador Winant in London by the State Department "for background information and guidance."[9]

However, on October 3, 1944, JCS 1067 was rejected by the British in a Combined Chiefs meeting. Thus the Interim Directive did not become a Combined Directive, but remained the guideline for Eisenhower in his capacity as the United States Commanding General in Europe, applicable for the American zone of Germany. The agreed Anglo-American Directive for Germany remained CCS-551, with its reconstructionist principles, but applicable only preceding German defeat.

Moreover, the Interim Directive was valid only pending agreed long-term policy by the three Allies, and in the meantime the British would occupy the Ruhr, and the Russians East Germany.

On the other hand, there can be little doubt that, as official American zonal policy for Germany, JCS 1067 as approved in September, 1944, was a considerable triumph for White in that in its economic provisions it was a clear break with the positive principles that had been taken for granted in considering the postwar German economy up until two months previously. As we shall see the final revised version of the Directive issued to Eisenhower immediately after VE-Day in May, 1945, still retained the language and the spirit of White's "vital paragraph."

In any case, during the winter of 1944–45 Morgenthau remained close to the President; and White in particular and the Treasury in general had to be represented in any further interdepartmental negotiations. The War Department was loath to reopen a sensitive matter, so maintaining its tacit alliance of convenience with the Treasury. Within the Treasury Department, under White's supervision, drafting continued, as we have seen above, of a book explaining and defending the Morgenthau Plan, to be issued under the Secretary's name.[10] The momentum acquired by the Interim Directive, propelled as it was by the Quebec memorandum, thus endured.

Illustrating the Treasury's confidence, at the end of October, Morgenthau severely criticized a collection of detailed British draft directives for Germany, designed for long-term policy to be negotiated in the EAC. In a memorandum drafted by his staff, reflecting White's views, Morgenthau complained that the British directives failed to deal adequately with German partition and the "elimination or destruction" of German industry. He held that the Interim United States Directive was the appropriate document for immediate Anglo-American discussion. The Treasury criticisms were given to Cherwell, who thought that the British should adopt a draft following Morgenthau's views. Churchill, who had not seen the British drafts, sent a memorandum to Eden and the Chiefs of Staff commenting that Morgenthau's criticisms seemed "very cogent," but this manifestation of the spirit of Quebec fell on deaf ears. The Foreign Office and the War Office in London considered the criticisms of the British drafts as "ill-founded and impertinent."[11]

It was left to the State Department to soldier on against the Treasury policy on Germany. The department sent two long papers on its postwar German objectives to Roosevelt during November, but the President's abbreviated reply to Stettinius, who succeeded Hull on December 1, was not too encouraging. Roosevelt thought Germany should be allowed "to come back industrially to meet her own needs, but not to do any exporting for some time," and that "we are against reparations."[12]

From London, Ambassador Robert D. Murphy, Eisenhower's political adviser, argued that large-scale removal of German governmental and industrial officials would create a vacuum "that would in turn encourage chaotic social and economic conditions." Murphy's plea for the revision of the Interim Directive so that the occupation authorities could take steps to prevent inflation was rejected by the Treasury.[13]

The State Department even lost ground in this direction when it attempted to revise JCS 1067 for negotiation in the EAC, where it would be subject to British and Russian discussion. The revision was at first cleared by the new State-War-Navy Coordinating Committee on January 6, 1945, and was essentially unchanged from the September version. It was then sent to Winant in London, but without agreed financial provisions.

Meanwhile in London, Colonel Bernard Bernstein, who had shown Morgenthau and White the SHAEF *Handbook*, had by this time been appointed Director of the Finance Division of the new United States Group, Control Council, Germany. This group, and its British counterpart, had replaced the joint SHAEF "German Country Unit" during the late summer of 1944 with separate national cadres for the task of governing conquered Germany. Colonel Bernstein still wore his hat as Chief of the Finance Division, Civil Affairs Division, SHAEF, and was thus well informed about developments over the plans for Germany as they continued to be discussed by the military and by Winant's advisers in London. He kept White and the Treasury informed of these plans, and the extent to which they conformed to JCS 1067, through L. C. Aarons, a Treasury representative in London, as we have seen earlier.[14]

In January, 1945, Colonel Bernstein returned to Washington, and during discussion with White and other departmental staff the financial provisions of the revised Interim Directive for Winant were if anything stiffened. The internal German banking and financial structure was to be further broken up, German foreign trade forbidden, and the responsibility for finance and taxation put on the German authorities, so further removing control of inflation from the occupation regime. The War Department agreed with the Treasury provisions, and the State Department had to go along. The revised Financial Directive was then issued to Winant in February, 1945.[15]

As we have seen, the provisions of the Interim Directives were explicitly short-term. Now, as the Yalta Conference approached in early 1945, White was active in the preparatory discussions in Washington over United States long-range policy toward Germany and Russia. Here the Assistant Secretary of the Treasury was involved in perhaps the most wide-ranging of all his proposals for the postwar world.

"Harry White, a man of about 50 years old, of medium height and wearing glasses, is very businesslike and sociable," reported I. Zlobin, a member of the Soviet delegation to Bretton Woods, in October, 1944. Writing in the Moscow journal *War and the Working Class* on "Meetings in America," Zlobin recounted that at Bretton Woods he had become acquainted and established business contacts with many "influential financiers of America and some other countries." These included Morgenthau, Keynes and White.

White and Morgenthau, Zlobin went on, had displayed a lively interest in the Soviet Union, and this interest of "practical Americans" was far from idle, as it was dictated by a realization of the fact "that in the postwar period the problem of economic collaboration with the Soviet Union would play an important role for America." Later Zlobin had visited the Whites at their home outside Washington, but the chief interest of this article is perhaps the informal sketch it gives of White at the height of his career. The games enthusiast of Everett High, thirty-five years before, had not lost his interest:

> White is a passionate sportsman. He has a special passion for volleyball and tennis. In Bretton Woods, between meetings, we have for the first time met our skill in a game with him in volleyball. He was head of the American team, and Comrade Chechulin was captain of the Soviet Command. At first we won, and with a substantial score. White was very much disappointed and has threatened that for the next game he will get together such a team that will literally crush us; and sure enough he has gathered such a command and the most important thing is that he has invited a well-known sportsman from South America and has finally succeeded in beating us. Later on, whenever there was an occasion that we had to put through some decisions of interest to us, White would always jokingly say, "All I can place at your disposal are our own votes and the votes of the 22 Latin American Republics. . . ."[16]

White had always played to win ever since his early Boston days, as Comrade Chechulin discovered. By the end of 1944 he was one of the most powerful men in the Treasury, and also perhaps one of the most influential, yet unknown, figures in the Anglo-American world of the later war years. Moreover, White's responsibility for his department's foreign relations, and for liaison with the armed services, meant that in effect, as Director of Monetary Research, he was in charge of a small but effective organization inside the Treasury that virtually paralleled the work of the State Department. Yet, formally, as an assistant to Morgenthau and as Director of Monetary Research, White held the same positions in late

1944, as the end of the war approached, as he had on the day America entered the conflict.

Morgenthau now moved to give White the formal title to go with the authority of Assistant Secretary which had been given him on the day following the Pearl Harbor attack. On November 17, 1944, the Secretary spoke on the telephone to Robert E. Hannegan, the Democratic Party National Chairman. Assistant Secretary of the Treasury John L. Sullivan was leaving, Morgenthau said, and he had recommended White in his place. The President thought White had earned the position, and (as a matter of protocol) Roosevelt had asked Morgenthau to mention the matter.

Hannegan was doubtful about White from a party manager's perspective—"you can't find anyone around that knows that fellow from a political standpoint"—but Morgenthau insisted, pointing out that White was a Democrat, and "that's more than you can say for the Army and Navy."[17] Later in December, 1944, as the opening of the new Congress approached, Morgenthau sent Roosevelt a memorandum supporting White's nomination. Remarking that Congress was hoping to consider the Bretton Woods legislation in the new session, Morgenthau went on, "In connection with Harry White, I sincerely hope you will send his name up as Assistant Secretary of the Treasury on the first day. He will have to carry the brunt of the fight of the Bretton Woods legislation and the additional prestige of being Assistant Secretary will be most useful. He has earned this award many times over. The Administration needs him in the field in which he has distinguished himself so brilliantly. White has been more than a match for people like Lord Keynes. I strongly recommend his promotion."[18]

Accordingly at the beginning of the new session of Congress, in early January, Roosevelt sent White's name up. The nomination was, almost automatically, approved by the Senate Finance Committee and the Senate. White resigned his two offices in the department on January 23, and the following day took the oath to "support and defend" the Constitution as an Assistant Secretary of the Treasury. White was to continue, under a Treasury order signed by Morgenthau, to supervise both the work of Foreign Funds Control, which had been placed under his responsibility the previous month, and his old Division of Monetary Research. Frank Coe then formally took over the Division in the middle of the following month.[19]

The social attention understandably given to White at this time is shown in a wartime Washington comedy of errors during 1944. A humble carpenter in the city, Harry D. White by name, began receiving a deluge of White's mail. The carpenter was invited to the White House, to a reception for General Charles de Gaulle, and asked to contribute to a

$100-a-plate Washington Day dinner given by the Democratic National Committee. The carpenter and his wife were reluctant to enter this Cinderella land, they told a newspaper, because they were scared. At Christmas, 1944, gifts from the Soviet Embassy appeared at the carpenter's home, Russian wines and cigarettes.

Eventually the carpenter received a telephone call from the Assistant Secretary of the Treasury. White proposed that the carpenter keep half the gifts and return the other half. "I was going to send them all back to him," the wary carpenter told a newspaperman, "but I thought 'He's the kind of fellow that if I did send them all back, will still think I kept half.' So I did."[20]

With the approach of the Yalta Conference in early 1945, Allied long-term policy over Germany became a major concern of White and Morgenthau. The Quebec memorandum, in the Treasury's view, had committed Churchill to the policy of reducing Germany to a country "primarily agricultural and pastoral in its character." It also seemed probable at the turn of the year that the essence of JCS 1067 could be sustained in the negotiations over the revision for Winant. Yet it remained doubtful whether the British War Cabinet would go along with the Quebec memorandum, and JCS 1067 as the Interim Directive was explicitly short-term, besides lacking "Combined" Anglo-American status.

Moreover, in the position papers that it had submitted to Roosevelt in November, which we have noted above, the State Department was shrewdly differentiating between a stern short-term policy on Germany, to take account of the President's wishes, and longer-term moderate objectives which could only be carried out gradually. But if, of course, the Russian position on Germany at Yalta continued to follow the lines of the peace envisaged by Stalin at Teheran, and if the Western Allies were brought formally to agree to this position, then the Treasury's long-term objectives for Germany could conceivably be implemented in some form or another.

Therefore, in early October, 1944, immediately following the press reports in the United States on the Morgenthau Plan, White had asked Ambassador Gromyko where the Russians stood on the Treasury proposals for Germany. According to White's report to a group meeting in the Treasury on October 5, Gromyko had replied, "I don't know anything official, but I would think they [the Soviet government] stand very close or closer to what is spoken of as 'The Morgenthau Plan.'" White went on to report that the Russian ambassador had said, of his government, that "they want reparations, but reparations all at once, machinery—that sounds all right to him."[21]

At this time Stalin had apparently not changed his mind from his general approach on Germany as outlined at Teheran. Churchill records that at Moscow in mid-October he and Stalin discussed "the merits and drawbacks" of the Morgenthau Plan. Then, in a message to Roosevelt on the way home, Churchill reported that he and Stalin had talked informally on the future of Germany. Stalin wanted to see Vienna as the capital of a South German confederation; and as for Prussia, Churchill went on, "U.J. wished the Ruhr and the Saar detached and put out of action and probably under international control and a separate state formed in the Rhineland. He would also like the internationalisation of the Kiel canal. I am not opposed to this line of thought. However, you may be sure that we came to no fixed conclusions pending the triple meeting."[22]

Clearly there was an obvious parallel between the territorial provisions of the Morgenthau Plan and Stalin's informal ideas on this occasion. And as the "triple meeting" in the Crimea approached in January, the tentative Russian view on German reparations still seemed to follow Gromyko's opinion that Moscow would like reparations "all at once."

On January 20 Ambassador Harriman in Moscow recorded in a conversation with Ivan Maisky, the Assistant Foreign Commissar, that while Moscow had not reached precise conclusions, the Soviet government felt that Germany should be broken up, and that the Rhineland and the Ruhr should become a separate state. There might also be "a Catholic republic" including Bavaria and Württemberg. Maisky thought that Germany should be demilitarized industrially, with a cut to about 25 percent of previous production. Heavy industry would be allowed to furnish Germany's "own needs," but as the Soviet government was primarily concerned with security, Moscow would not ask for reparations "which would call for strong heavy industries." Instead, Soviet demands would be "to strip Germany's heavy industries of their machinery and equipment and other products not involving heavy industry."[23]

A few days later, on January 25, Treasury Assistant Secretary Herbert Gaston reported to Morgenthau that in a conversation with a *Tass* correspondent, Vladimir Pravdin, he had been told that "it is the general Russian view . . . that German heavy industry should be sharply curtailed and . . . the idea of physically removing and distributing to neighboring countries German equipment is a good one. Their real solution of the problem, however, is a Socialist solution . . . I would say that in general Pravdin's concept of the Russian ideas with respect to the treatment of Germany in the economic sphere checks very closely with yours."[24]

No doubt, from White's perspective, such tentative, yet apparently authoritative indications of the Russian attitude toward Germany as that given by Ambassador Gromyko showed that at any forthcoming Allied conference the work begun with the Quebec memorandum might be extended into a three-power, long-range agreement. If the United States and the Soviet Union could agree on the lines of the Treasury proposals for Germany, the British might have to agree with their Allies, no matter what the reservations in London over the Quebec memorandum.

It also seems clear, however, that White understood at this time that a drawback in the Treasury proposals for Germany, as far as the Soviet was concerned, lay in the low level of recurrent reparations provided for Russia. But could American credits be a substitute for reparations? As early as March, 1939, as we have seen, White had advocated a $250,-000,000 credit to the Soviet Union, and the amount had grown to $500,-000,000 in his proposed American-Soviet-Japanese Pacific arrangements of May, 1941.

Then, in March, 1944, in reply to a request by Morgenthau on the feasibility of a postwar credit to Russia, White had proposed a $5 billion loan. This amount would be in exchange for such strategic raw materials as Soviet manganese, chrome, tungsten and mercury provided over a thirty-year period. The arrangement, White suggested in this paper, would expand trade between the two countries, let the United States have these raw materials "expected to be in short supply in the U.S. after the war," and "would provide a sound basis for continued collaboration between the two governments after the war."[25]

This Cobdenite belief that trading arrangements per se were conducive to settling international differences was not only a conviction of White's, but was shared in varying degrees by other postwar planners in Washington, and above all by Cordell Hull. Indeed, as we have seen with the evolution of the White Plan, the Bretton Woods agreements to some extent reflected the conviction that commercial rivalries were primarily a cause and not a symptom of international political tension. The prospect of postwar aid for Russia gave an added impetus to this line of thought.

Nevertheless, during the later war years discussions between the Americans and the Russians on transitional reconstruction aid for the Soviet had shown the difficulties of the approach. At the time of the Moscow Conference in 1943, Hull "had in long discourses tried to win Stalin and Molotov over to the program he had in mind for the world. Toward his efforts Molotov had shown polite but unhelpful admiration. He seemed impressed with Hull's idealistic zeal and genuinely perplexed as to how Hull's doctrines of freer trade could be harmonized with the Communist trade methods. . . ."[26]

Throughout most of 1944, the talks on postwar transitional aid between Moscow and Washington proceeded hesitantly, following Mikoyan's suggestion of a billion-dollar credit at one-half percent interest in the February of that year. The Russians also hoped to obtain some postwar supplies through Lend-Lease; but the difficulties, as we have seen, of using Mutual Aid for this purpose were appreciable. Moreover, Averell Harriman, the American ambassador in Moscow, hoped to use American credits as an instrument of diplomatic negotiation with the Russians, while Stalin and his colleagues assumed that, in order to avoid an inevitable postwar depression, the United States would be eager to advance credits to the Soviet Union. These subterranean differences of approach, compounded anyway by mutual miscalculation, hardly made for immediate agreement. Hence, by the end of 1944 the entire question of American credits as a source of transitional aid began to assume added importance from the Soviet viewpoint, especially with the approach of the Yalta Conference and the end of the war. From White's perspective, therefore, the larger the credits supplied by the United States, perhaps the greater chance of acceptance by Moscow of the Treasury proposals on Germany.[27]

The Treasury now entered, or rather jumped into, the scene with a letter from Morgenthau to Roosevelt on January 1, 1945. Morgenthau wrote that "during the past year I have discussed several times with Ambassador Harriman a plan which we in the Treasury have been formulating for comprehensive aid to Russia during her reconstruction period. We are not thinking of more Lend-Lease or any form of relief but rather of an arrangement that will have definite and long range benefits for the United States and for Russia." Morgenthau was convinced that such a plan for reconstruction aid "would contribute a great deal toward ironing out many of the problems we have been having with respect to their problems and policies." If such a plan interested the President, Morgenthau would be glad to discuss it with him.[28]

Two days later, on January 3, with the forthcoming Big Three conference evidently in mind, the Soviet government made a formal request for an American loan. Molotov gave Harriman a memorandum suggesting a $6 billion credit at 2¼ percent, to be repaid over thirty years. In a message to Stettinius on January 6, Harriman reported that Molotov had made it plain that the Soviet government placed high importance on a large American credit as basis for the development of postwar Soviet-American relations. It was Harriman's opinion that the credit "should be tied into our overall diplomatic relations with the Soviet Union." Harriman considered that the United States should stand firm in current negotiations over the fourth Lend-Lease protocol with the Russians, which had been dragging on for some months. The timing of the note's delivery, he considered, meant that the Russians would expect the subject to be discussed in the forthcoming three-power conference.[29]

Now, in a vintage example of attempted "all-out" diplomacy, White, assisted by other Treasury staff including Harold Glasser and J. E. Du-Bois, produced a "Memorandum for the President" from Morgenthau, dated January 10, 1945. This paper suggested a $10 billion loan to the Russians. Essentially the memorandum was based on White's paper to Morgenthau of March, 1944, which had suggested a $5 billion credit. The new enlarged version suggested that "consideration be given to a financial arrangement with the U.S.S.R. to provide her with $10 billion credits for the purchase of reconstruction goods in the U.S., with provision for repayment to us chiefly in strategic materials in short supply in the U.S."

The memorandum proposed an interest rate of 2 percent, the capital repayable over thirty-five years, and envisaged that the United States would conserve its depleted resources "by drawing on Russia's huge reserves for current needs of industrial raw materials in short supply here." White concluded that the credit would be "a major step in your program to provide sixty million jobs in the postwar period." An attached schedule outlined the estimated American reserve domestic supply of such strategic materials as tungsten, chrome and manganese: "The U.S.S.R. could provide substantial quantities of strategic materials for an annual basis within five years after the close of the war. . . ."[30]

The paper drafted by White and his colleagues suggesting a $10 billion loan to Russia was only part of the Treasury's efforts to bring its views to Roosevelt in the weeks preceding the Yalta Conference. On January 10, the date of completion of the paper on the proposed Russian credit, Morgenthau's staff produced another "Memorandum for the President" which was soon sent by the Secretary to Roosevelt.

The paper, which clearly reflected White's views and language, pointedly began by saying that if Germany was to be deprived of the ability to make war again within a few years, "it is absolutely essential that she be deprived of her chemical, metallurgical and electrical industries." (The Quebec memorandum had envisaged the closing down of these industries in the Ruhr-Saar area, rather than the whole of Germany.) This by itself would not guarantee peace. But it was one of the steps, and this conclusion was based on the premises that the German people "have the will to try it again," that programs for democratic reeducation could not destroy that will in a short time, and that heavy industry was the core of Germany's war-making potential.

"The more I think of this problem," the paper went on, "and the more I hear and read discussion of it, the clearer it seems to me that the real motive of most of those who oppose a weak Germany is not any actual disagreement on these points. On the contrary, it is simply an expression of fear of Russia and Communism. It is the twenty-year-old idea of a 'Bulwark against Bolshevism'—which was one of the factors that brought this present war down on us."

The memorandum asserted that those who held this view were unwilling "to come out in the open," and threw up "all sorts of smoke screens" to support the proposition that Germany must be rebuilt. Examples of these fallacious arguments were:

(a) The fallacy that Europe needs a strong industrial Germany.

(b) The contention that recurrent reparations (which would require immediate reconstruction of the German economy) are necessary so that Germany may be made to pay for the destruction she has caused.

(c) The naïve belief that the removal or destruction of all German war materials and the German armament industry would in itself prevent Germany from waging another war.

(d) The illogical assumption that a "soft" peace would facilitate the growth of democracy in Germany.

(e) The fallacy that making Germany a predominantly agricultural country, with light industries but no heavy industries, would mean starving Germans. . . .

The memorandum ended, "There is nothing I can think of that can do more at this moment to engender trust or distrust between the United States and Russia than the position this Government takes on the German problem."[31]

Prior to meeting with Stettinius and other State Department officials on January 17, White told Morgenthau that "we all feel that it would be easier and helpful if you would in your discussions leave yourself a little vague in the treatment of the [German] coal mines . . . we think one of the strongest objections of the other side will be centered on the closing of the coal mines and the elimination of industry and they pick on that one point and assume that it is indicative or illustrative of your entire program. . . ."[32]

Morgenthau continued to insist on the closing of the coal mines, and in the subsequent meeting attended by himself and White for the Treasury there was no meeting of minds between the two departments on either large credits to Russia or over the Treasury proposals for Germany. The Secretary disagreed with Harriman's cable of January 6 that the United States should remain firm with the Soviets on current Lend-Lease negotiations and considered that new proposals should be made. Referring to the Treasury memorandum to Roosevelt advocating a $10 billion loan to Russia, Morgenthau felt that "we should go beyond" the Soviet suggestion of a $6 billion loan, offering them instead $10 billion credit linked with optional repayment in strategic materials. Morgenthau went on to suggest to Stettinius, who was about to leave for the Crimea, "that they should both suggest to the President that he make a concrete proposal to Stalin at the forthcoming meeting."

Following a résumé by Morgenthau of the familiar Treasury proposals for removing German heavy industry, White commented that Germany would still be left "with some types of industry, a transportation system, utilities etc." Stettinius emphasized that the State Department was thoroughly in agreement in making Germany permanently incapable of aggression, but another State official, Emile Depres, conceded in a little jewel of understatement that "there was a difference of emphasis between the State Department and the Treasury regarding the economic measures appropriate to that objective." White and Assistant Secretary of State James C. Dunn were then designated "to discuss these matters further."[33]

The next day, the State Department, where morale was relatively high with the promised attendance of Stettinius at Yalta, the only wartime conference where the Secretary of State would be present from beginning to end, submitted its formal briefing papers on Germany to Roosevelt. These position papers, running to more than 10,000 words, supported the concept of a stern short-term occupation of Germany. But in their longer-term provisions they restated in general the approach of the State Department which had been approved by the E.C.E.F.P. on August 4, 1944, two days before White had flown to England, so beginning the upheaval over the Treasury proposals for Germany. "In the long run," summed up one of the State Department briefing papers, ". . . the best guarantee of security, and the least expensive, would be the assimilation of the German people into the world society of peace loving nations."[34]

The impasse between the State and Treasury departments immediately preceding the Yalta Conference was once again illustrated in the meeting arranged between White and Dunn, with other departmental staff, on January 19.

A revision of the comprehensive Treasury memorandum on Germany of January 10, which had been sent to Roosevelt, was circulated by White and read aloud. This position paper on the "long-range program for Germany" was based on the proposal that "the elimination of [German] heavy industry is one of the essential steps we must take now" in order to prevent a third world war. There was no "panacea" to guarantee peace. The paper listed the same five allegedly fallacious arguments employed by those who thought otherwise, as in the earlier memorandum sent to Roosevelt.[35]

In the course of this meeting on the nineteenth, according to a report by W. H. Taylor of the Division of Monetary Research, White once again put forward strong reasons for deindustrializing the Ruhr on the pattern of the Treasury arguments of the previous five months. When Assistant Secretary of State William Clayton advocated an international regime for the Ruhr, White insisted that only if heavy industry were removed first would an international solution present no great problem. Controls might not be adequate, and, said White, deindustrializing the Ruhr would have two fundamental advantages. It would tend "to set a pattern toward agrarianism in Germany . . '. furthermore it would tend to gain for the Allies a breathing space of, say, ten, fifteen, twenty years. . . ."[36]

The State Department was not convinced, and the matter was to be discussed further. Moreover, the department was hardly enthusiastic over the Treasury's proposals for a $10 billion credit to Russia. Clayton told Stettinius that Congressional restrictions made it impossible to offer post-war credits to Russia, and that "it would seem to be harmful for us to offer such a large credit at this time and thus lose what appears to be the only concrete bargaining lever for use in connection with the many other political and economic problems which will arise between our two countries." Harriman concurred in this, Clayton wrote, and invoking a note of common sense he pointed out the Soviets themselves had only asked for $6 billion. There was also the question whether the Soviet Union would be willing to bind itself to supplying strategic materials over a long period.

These considerations were repeated in cable a week later from Acting Secretary of State Joseph C. Grew to Harriman. The matter of Russian credit had been discussed with Roosevelt, Grew reported, and he had displayed "keen interest." Roosevelt believed that the matter should not be pressed further pending discussion with Stalin.[37] Relatively, perhaps, on the long-range program, despite all White's efforts, the Treasury was not in a particularly advantageous position vis-à-vis the State Department as the Yalta Conference drew near. By the end of January, Roosevelt was on the USS *Quincy*, en route for Malta, the Crimea and the last of his conferences with Churchill and Stalin, "Argonaut."

In these weeks preceding the Yalta Conference White had renewed his strong advocacy of his proposals for postwar Germany, specifically as a long-term program. At the same time, and closely connected with his views that recurrent reparations should not be made available from a Germany stripped of its heavy industry, White and the Treasury had proposed very large American credits to the Soviet Union. These measures were clearly aimed at providing important American economic, and perhaps political, ties with Russia in the postwar period, ties which would be linked with the supply of Russian strategic raw materials. In the words of White's March, 1944, paper to Morgenthau, it was hoped such arrangements would "provide a sound basis for the continued collaboration between the two governments after the war."

Yet here one may ask: How could White reconcile this sweeping program, which was apparently designed to bring the Soviet Union into the world economy in a dramatic extension of the Bretton Woods agreements, with his proposals for Germany? In the view of many distinguished critics, as we have seen, the Treasury proposals for Germany would have meant virtually the ruin of Europe. Much odium, moreover, would have been incurred by the countries which would have imposed this solution on Germany, even if it were possible to do so in the first place. Could the hoped-for multilateral trading regime, sponsored under American auspices, have ever been created in such conditions?

In a letter to the writer, Ansel F. Luxford, a veteran of the Bretton Woods negotiations who also worked with White on the Treasury proposals for Germany, comments:

You ask how one can reconcile White's espousal of the Morgenthau Plan with his enthusiasm for postwar multilateral trade and a multilateral political framework. Having participated in Treasury councils in both areas I believe I know how White and other exponents of the Morgenthau Plan reconciled their position; indeed their analysis may have been prophetic in part. White and others, including myself, were deeply disturbed that the end of the fighting after World War II would see a breakdown of relations between Russia and the Western world including particularly the United States. . . . In short White saw the issue of world peace after World War II as essentially one of whether the United States and Russia could learn to live together. This was not a matter necessarily, of their becoming friendly allies; rather it was a question of whether their positions made World War III inevitable. In that context the White group concluded that the greatest risk to World War III was a defeated Germany strong enough to become the balance of power between the West and the U.S.S.R.—and once acquiring this strength, willing to throw its weight one way or another and trigger the war (e.g. World War III). I may add that this part of the premise was shared by a great many people in Government who could not buy the Morgenthau "solution" (including me). . . . It is enough to say, I believe, that White's position on the Morgenthau Plan (at least in his own mind and in that of many others) did not contradict his general position on multilateralism. Indeed White believed in a multilateralism which included (not excluded) the U.S.S.R. . . . My judgment is that White was seeking a

broader multilateralism than that connoted by the term today . . .
[Luxford's italics]

Moreover, Luxford goes on:

> I believe that in his concept of the term multilateralism he probably
> viewed the United Kingdom and the U.S.S.R. in much the same way—
> both major factors to be weighed and dealt with but with no more
> love nor trust for one than the other. I think White's reading of his-
> tory convinced him that the U.K. was an enemy of full multilateralism
> in the sense that the term is inconsistent with balance of power poli-
> tics. More than that, as a serious liberal he could not condone the
> then British colonial policy; its policy under Chamberlain; its Pales-
> tine policy; indeed its social and class attitudes at home. . . .[38]

It was within this framework, perhaps, that White attempted to link
the Treasury proposals for Germany, the large-scale credits for Russia,
and the world of Bretton Woods. White's views on the necessity of
avoiding an Anglo-Saxon "gang-up," expressed to Keynes in London in
October, 1942, his attitude toward the British dollar balances and the
precarious British economy into which billions of dollars could be poured
indicate clearly that, whatever his involvement with the British in the
Fund negotiations, he by no means believed in an exclusive Anglo-
American association. Bretton Woods was perhaps but one of the means
toward that "broader multilateralism." Moreover, many in the Roosevelt
administration looked forward, as we have seen, to that postwar world
free of what Hull called those "special arrangements" which had bedeviled the "unhappy past."
  Yet what perhaps distinguished White, as he sought these ambitious
objectives at the height of his career, was his special enthusiasm in their
pursuit, and, certainly in the case of his proposals for postwar Germany,
a certain liberation from conventional prescriptions of the past. In other
ways, too, White may have regarded himself as freed from conventional
constraints as he pursued these objectives.

John L. Snell, an historian of the conference held at the Livadia Palace,
Yalta, February 4–11, 1945, has written, "the prospects of Germany's
early collapse had brought the Western statesmen face to face at last
with the greatest European dilemma of the twentieth century: How can
the threat of German power be eliminated from Europe without leaving
Soviet power dominant throughout the Continent?"[39]
  During the conference, as is well known, Churchill, Roosevelt and
Stalin discussed many issues, and we shall note below, for example, their

agreement on the Far East in the context of White's policy on the American gold shipments to China. But no issue was of greater importance than the future of Germany, and on this subject the views of Roosevelt and Churchill had evidently changed since Quebec, five months previously. As far as the President was concerned, in spite of his belief in continued great-power collaboration after the war, both the lion and the fox were in evidence during Roosevelt's last great conference:

> Roosevelt was no conscious advocate of the balance-of-power concept but, like other American statesmen since Wilson, he supported a principle which was its corrollary: that it was not in the interest of the United States for any one state in Europe to dominate the whole. Churchill, on the other hand, consciously followed a balance-of-power policy on his negotiations with the Russians concerning the future of Germany. Thus it came about that the discussions of German questions at Yalta revealed beneath the verbiage of conciliation towards Russia the hard rock of Anglo-American solidarity and moderation towards Germany. . . .[40]

Early in the conference, Roosevelt told Churchill and Stalin that he "did not believe that American troops would stay in Europe much more than two years."[41] With such traditional military means of controlling defeated Germany apparently ruled out as far as the United States was concerned, three-power political harmony and a significant reduction of German industrial potential were clearly imperative as a security measure. But could Roosevelt and Churchill maintain the front of Allied harmony, without agreeing to the total reduction of German power by formal partition and deindustrialization?

Understandably, Stalin was quick to bring up the question of German partition, which the Big Three had discussed at Teheran and which featured so prominently in the White-Morgenthau proposals for Germany. On February 5, he asked his two colleagues if they were still in favor of partition as informally approved at Teheran. The partition of Germany was then agreed in principle by Roosevelt and Churchill. But significantly, substantive discussion was postponed once again, this time for twenty-four hours, pending study by the foreign ministers:

> PRESIDENT. I ask that . . . the three foreign secretaries bring in tomorrow a plan for dismemberment.
>
> PRIME MINISTER. You mean a plan for the *study* of the question of dismemberment, not a plan for dismemberment itself? [Italics in original]
>
> PRESIDENT. Yes, for the study of dismemberment.[42]

Eventually, after further discussion, the foreign ministers agreed that a committee to study the procedure for German partition should be set up in London, consisting of Eden, Winant and F. T. Gusev, the Soviet ambassador to Britain. This decision to postpone further formal consideration of the dismemberment of Germany was then recorded in the Yalta Protocol.[43] Moreover, on a subject connected with partition—territorial cession—Roosevelt and Churchill did not agree in plenary session with Stalin's suggestion that the western borders of Poland should be formally extended to the Oder-Western Neisse line in compensation for the eastern Curzon Line border of the new Poland. Instead the Yalta Protocol records that Poland was to receive "substantial accessions of territory in the North and West." The Red Army was, of course, overrunning these areas, but formal Western recognition remained to be used as a bargaining point at Potsdam.

On the question of reparations and the deindustrialization of Germany, the Western leaders bargained with rather more tenacity than on the question of partition. After all, whatever happened at Yalta, the Russians were in any case promised a large zonal area of Germany in the forthcoming occupation; as Roosevelt presciently remarked to Churchill and Stalin, "the permanent treatment of Germany might grow out of the zones of occupation, although the two were not directly connected."[44]

The Yalta reparation discussions were begun on February 5 by Molotov, who remarked that, as well as reparations in kind, he hoped the United States "would furnish the Soviet Union with long-term credits." As Russian losses during the war were incalculable, clearly, the application of the strategy of postponement at this stage would require some skilled stonewalling by the Western leaders as they fought to avoid too many substantive concessions on the theme of German deindustrialization.

Maisky soon made clear that, as Gromyko had said to White during the previous October, the Russians expected to receive reparations "all at once." The Soviet Assistant Foreign Commissar then called for two types of reparations in kind, by physical transfer of German heavy industry, and by recurrent reparations from remaining production.

But the primary Soviet emphasis was on the capital removal of Germany's heavy industry.

"Sounding like Morgenthau every minute,"[45] Maisky said that it would be necessary to reduce, by physical withdrawal, 80 percent of all German heavy industry. By heavy industry he meant iron and steel, electrical power and chemical industries. Specialized military industry, such as aviation and synthetic oil refineries etc., would be completely removed. These removals would be made within two years, and further reparations from remaining current German production would be taken in yearly deliveries over a period of ten years. An Allied reparations commission would meet in Moscow, and the total value of German reparations asked by the Soviet in both capital withdrawals and yearly payments would total $10 billion.

Churchill was concerned that the Soviet Union "would get nowhere near the sum which Mr. Maisky had mentioned from Germany," while Roosevelt recalled that after the previous war the United States had really financed German reparations, a mistake not to be repeated. Rather ambiguously, Roosevelt concluded that "he was in favor of extracting the maximum in reparations for Germany but not to the extent that the people would starve." Both Roosevelt and Churchill now assented to the creation of a three-power Moscow Reparations Commission, which, of course, further postponed agreement. In addition, Churchill remarked that "differences arising in the Commission must be referred to and settled by the three governments," so insisting on the veto power of any member of the Commission.[46]

Haggling over the reparations issue continued throughout the conference as the Russians sought agreement on the terms of reference for the Moscow Reparations Commission. A Soviet draft proposal on reparations on February 7 omitted the suggestion to reduce German heavy industry by 80 percent, but kept the figure of $10 billion reparations to be paid to the Soviet Union by both capital transfer of industry "in a single payment" and by recurrent reparations over ten years. The capital transfer of industry would be for "the purpose of military and economic disarmament of Germany." Total reparations from Germany were put at the figure of $20 billion.

Eventually, after further discussions between the three foreign ministers and "a lengthy and at times heated discussion between Marshal Stalin and Churchill on the question of reparations,"[47] agreement was reached on the guidelines for the Reparations Commission at the end of the conference. But even the revised Soviet position of February 7 had been moderated by the Western stand. Reparations in kind were to be extracted from Germany by capital removals of industrial plant over two years, by annual deliveries of goods over a period "to be fixed," and by forced labor. The Moscow Reparations Commission was to "take in its initial studies as a basis for discussion" the sum of $20 billion, half of which, it was suggested by the Russians, should go to the Soviet Union.

But the British refused to commit themselves to this figure, in the Yalta Protocol, even as "a basis for discussion," believing no figure should be mentioned. Moreover, the language of the Soviet draft which had proposed capital removals for "the purpose of military and economic disarmament of Germany" was not adopted. Instead the protocol on reparations included the language of the British draft which stated that such removals were to be for the rather narrower purpose of "destroying the war potential of Germany."[48]

Clearly the three allies were agreed on large reparations from Germany, but the *amount*, and the precise proportion between capital removals and payments from current German production remained to be negotiated in yet another round of the strategy of postponement. Moreover, it will be noticed that the thrust of the Russian compromise proposals on reparations at Yalta, following the Western resistance to Maisky's advocacy of an 80 percent removal of German heavy industry, was to demand recurrent reparations as well as capital payments. The Morgenthau Plan, of course, explicitly precluded such recurrent reparations. As Professor Snell has written, "all in all the reparations decision at Yalta constituted a thinly disguised defeat for the Russians and clear-cut rejection of the Morgenthau Plan and the Quebec agreement. Nor was there any compensating assurance for the Russians that they would obtain postwar credits in the United States; by agreeing to Stalin's figure 'as a basis of discussion' the Americans had successfully sidetracked the Soviet movement for American aid."[49]

But it also seems clear that Soviet policy toward Germany was more flexible than White might have supposed. In the wartime conferences, as we have seen, Stalin had proposed the partition of Germany, along with the demand for huge Soviet reparation of capital equipment. However, by the creation of the "National Committee for Free Germany" and other prisoner groups on Russian soil, tacitly appealing to German nationalism, Moscow retained another option, whether Germany was formally partitioned or not. By the end of the war in Europe, three months after Yalta, this latter approach was explicit in Stalin's victory address of May 9, 1945: "The Soviet Union celebrates victory, although it does not intend either to dismember or destroy Germany."

Nevertheless, in general, the differences between the Allies over Germany had been plastered over at Yalta. And Roosevelt and Churchill evidently still looked forward to postwar Allied harmony. The public communiqué recorded formal Big Three agreement over the occupation arrangements and the Allied Control Commission for Germany, which had earlier been negotiated in the EAC. German Nazism and militarism was to be destroyed, and German industry that could be used for military production was to be eliminated or controlled.

On March 1, Roosevelt, exhausted after his exertions at Yalta, reported to Congress that the Crimea Conference "spells—and it ought to spell—the end of the system of unilateral action, exclusive alliances, and spheres of influence, and balances of power and all the other expedients which have tried for centuries and have always failed. . . ."

In the aftermath of Yalta, White took a prominent part in two Treasury campaigns in defense of its policies on Germany. The first, which was short, sharp and victorious, resulted in a new official affirmation of the Interim Directive, JCS 1067. The second concerned the work of the Reparations Commission set up at Yalta.

Following his return from Yalta, Roosevelt asked Secretary of State Stettinius, on February 28, to see that the conclusions of the conference, except in the military sphere, were carried out. Stettinius was away, but department officials, under Assistant Secretary James Dunn, began drafting a new directive for the German occupation. The revised version of JCS 1067, it will be recalled, had been sent to Winant for negotiation in the EAC, but now the State Department told Winant not to present the Directive as it had been superseded by the Yalta agreement.

The State Department quickly prepared a "Draft Directive for the Treatment of Germany," dated March 10, applicable for the tough, initial period of occupation which would yield to the regime of reconciliation which the department had always envisaged. The new Directive thus emphasized that policy for Germany must be worked out in collaboration with the other Allies, and that a substantial amount of centralized economic control would be necessary, even in the initial period of the occupation. These provisions quite clearly clashed both with the Army's emphasis on the administrative necessity of zonal autonomy and the Treasury's policy of letting the German economy "stew in its own juice." Without consulting the Treasury and War departments, Roosevelt initialed the State Department's Draft Directive of March 10, 1945, which now replaced JCS 1067.

The State Department's victory was to last only for a matter of days. On the fifteenth, Stettinius announced the formation, with Roosevelt's approval, of a new high-level committee, the Informal Policy Committee on Germany (IPCOG). The chairman was Assistant Secretary of State William Clayton, Stimson named McCloy as his representative, and Morgenthau named White, with Frank Coe as White's alternate.[50]

Stettinius presented the "Draft Directive" of March 10 to the new committee. But understandably from its viewpoint, the Treasury reaction was a violent one as the "Draft Directive" would have meant a decisive defeat for its German policies. Moreover, the War Department was also opposed to the new Directive as it compromised the military's zonal authority in the forthcoming occupation. Thus the tacit alliance of the previous autumn between the two departments was reforged. On March 20, after tense meetings in the Treasury, White produced two memoranda for Stettinius and Roosevelt attacking the Draft Directive, both of which were signed by Morgenthau. These papers urged the retention of

JCS 1067, and criticized the Draft Directive of March 10 as inconsistent with the Yalta decisions.[51]

The rout of the State Department was soon complete. During luncheon with Morgenthau on March 20, Roosevelt indicated that he wished to withdraw the Draft Directive. Then, after further negotiations, in which the Treasury played a major part, the President on March 23 approved a War Department paper which McCloy felt represented Roosevelt's views. The paper emphasized the role of the zonal commander, and German responsibility for the economy. This Presidential Policy Statement of March 23 was signed "O.K. F.D.R. superseding memo of March 10, 1945," and was Roosevelt's last policy statement on the subject; it was also signed by Morgenthau, McCloy and Clayton.[52]

The Informal Policy Committee on Germany now proceeded, on the basis of the Presidential Policy Statement of March 23, with the final revision of JCS 1067 for Eisenhower, "but it is perhaps of more than symbolic significance that IPCOG held its plenary session in the Treasury office of Mr. Morgenthau."[53] As the Anglo-American armies crossed the Rhine toward the end of March, 1945, therefore, the Interim Directive remained little changed from the previous autumn, still the only detailed official American document on German occupation policy.

As Morgenthau's representative on IPCOG, White was closely involved in the final drafting of JCS 1067, but his battle was of course really won with the collapse of the State Department's ill-timed initiative of March 10. Rather more important now was White's participation in the negotiations which would lead to the drafting of the instructions for the American delegation to the Moscow Reparations Commission, for this centrally involved the "Long-Range Program" for Germany.

Following his return from Yalta, Roosevelt had appointed Isador Lubin, a labor economist, to lead the American delegation to Moscow. As we have seen, Roosevelt and Churchill had resisted the virtually unlimited Russian demands on the postwar German economy at Yalta, and the figure of $20 billion reparations was a Soviet-American one to be used as "a basis of discussion."

But clearly the composition of reparations from Germany—not defined precisely in the Protocol—as between capital transfer of industry and recurrent payments was of great importance in affecting the extent of German deindustrialization. As Walter Dorn has written,

Yalta did have its Achilles heel in the secret protocol on the reparations problem. What is surprising about the final Yalta reparations protocol . . . was less the mention of twenty billion dollars reparations total as a basis of discussion which the Russians later misinterpreted, than the complete absence of any reference to what the Americans considered a basic principle, namely the setting of an upper limit on reparations from current production which was necessary for the maintenance of a self-sustaining German economy. Hence, this protocol made far greater concession to the Russians than the United States could actually support, if it did not wish to feed the population of Germany out of its own resources.[54]

White was a friend of Lubin's, and now, with unerring understanding of this Achilles heel, in another "vital paragraph" in the Reparations protocol White tried to convince the American reparations group being formed that, in the words of E. F. Penrose, "reparations should take the form of large scale removal of German industrial equipment. Reparation in the form of periodical deliveries of raw material or manufactured goods would only preserve or increase the productive capacity which Germany could turn to war purposes later."[55]

In this way, as Penrose remarks, reparations could be reconciled with "deindustrialization" by taking away industrial plant instead of destroying it with explosives, as envisaged in the Morgenthau Plan. With the assistance of the Treasury, Lubin, at the end of March, 1945, prepared a memorandum on the subject for Roosevelt. When Clayton saw the document, he considered it the "toughest" paper on the subject he had seen, "tougher than any document that had come out of the Treasury."[56]

Clearly, yet another round of the unresolved policy debate on Germany was at hand between the Treasury, State and War departments. Yet White was undoubtedly playing from a position of strength after the Treasury's victory over the State Department in March. At this juncture, in late March, 1945, Roosevelt left Washington to recuperate at his retreat at Warm Springs, Georgia. As so often before, the President's physical resilience was taken for granted.

18

THE NEW PRESIDENT

I felt as if I had lived five lifetimes in my first five days as President. . . .
But very few Vice-Presidents have been in complete agreement with the
policies of the Presidents with whom they have served. . . .
— HARRY S. TRUMAN, *Year of Decisions*

As THE new cycle of negotiations on the German reparations issue began
in Washington in early April, 1945, White had never been so closely
involved in major issues of international affairs.

These were weeks of preparation for his piloting of the Bretton Woods
agreements through the appropriate Congressional committees. From
Chungking, as we shall see, T. V. Soong, the Chinese Foreign Minister,
was about to arrive in Washington to settle the issue of the American
gold shipments to China. This was another matter in which White was
centrally concerned, and which involved as well wider Sino-American
relations in the period following Yalta. In addition, on March 24 Morgenthau had nominated White as the Treasury "technical adviser" to the
American delegation at the founding conference of the United Nations.
The United Nations Conference on Organization, which was to draft the
Charter, was to open in San Francisco on April 25, 1945.[1]

But "the basic issue" remained Germany, and on April 7 an important
departmental meeting was held in Assistant Secretary Clayton's office in
the State Department. Under discussion were the instructions to be given
to the American delegation to the Moscow Reparations Commission set
up at Yalta. The leader-designate of the delegation, Isador Lubin, was at
the conference, and White, Harold Glasser and J. E. Du Bois represented
the Treasury. During this meeting there was considerable discussion of
Lubin's draft proposal that the American government should favor a
reparations period as long as possible "with annual recurrent payments as

315

small as possible." This of course was in line with White's view that reparations should come from German capital equipment and not from recurrent payments which would build up German heavy industry.

The State Department opposed this position, arguing instead for "a short period of time with larger amounts." The department suggested that the United States did not want a long occupation, inasmuch as it would be necessary to keep occupation troops in Germany to collect such reparations, and "it would be politically undesirable to withdraw United States troops from Germany while Russian troops still remained in Germany." White and his colleagues argued that small payments would avoid the dependence of the recipients on Germany, and "would avoid rebuilding the German economy." They also argued that if recurrent reparations "were collected in small amounts annually this would not require maintenance of troops in Germany to collect such reparations" as the terms of the occupation would be decided by other factors.

Evidently White won his point, for finally Clayton suggested that the United States "merely announce a statement of principle to the effect that recurring reparations should be fixed so as to avoid the dependence of the recipients on the German economy and so as to avoid the building up of the German economy." Perhaps this meeting marks the high-water mark of White's influence on American government policy, as such, over Germany.[2]

On April 11, four days after the meeting in Clayton's office, Morgenthau spent the evening at Warm Springs, at Roosevelt's invitation. Slightly less than two months before, on February 15, during their last post-Yalta farewells on board the *Quincy* moored at Alexandria, Churchill had considered that the President "seemed placid and frail. I felt that he had slender contact with life." About the same time, at the beginning of the year, Vice President Truman had seen what "the long years in office" had done to Roosevelt: "The very thought that something was happening to him left me troubled and worried."[3]

Morgenthau had also been disturbed for some time about the President's health, and now, on April 11, he was "terribly shocked" when he saw the President. But the two men spent a pleasant evening over supper. Other friends of Roosevelt's were present, and Morgenthau obtained the President's enthusiastic approval to go ahead and publish his book on Germany, which of course was being drafted in the Treasury. One of the book's chapters, Morgenthau hoped, would explain how 60,000,000 Germans could feed themselves.[4]

Roosevelt died the following afternoon, April 12, 1945, and for his Dutchess County friend of thirty years it "was a catastrophe. He had lost his sponsor, his chief and his closest friend. For years he felt the shock of personal deprivation. From the first, as he suspected immediately, he faced also the lesser loss of support without which he could no longer even effectively pursue his public purposes, his plan for Germany not the least. That evening of April 11 was, in a special sense, the last evening of Morgenthau's public career. . . ."[5]

In different ways the shock of Roosevelt's death carried much the same message for other members of his administration. Harry Hopkins told Robert Sherwood in the author's Georgetown home on the fourteenth that he was going to resign from government service, and he thought the whole government should do likewise, with the exception of Stimson and Forrestal, the War and Navy Secretaries. Morgenthau, Hopkins considered, should "stay long enough to see the next war bond drive through." But Hopkins went on, "Truman has got to have his own people around him and not Roosevelt's: If we were around we'd always be looking at him and he'd know what we were thinking, 'The *President* would do it that way.' "[6]

The effect of Truman's succession was rather more complex as far as White was concerned. Some of White's influence depended on his intellectual ascendancy over Morgenthau, which had made him perhaps the Secretary's closest adviser, and then on the unique friendship between Morgenthau and Roosevelt. This conjunction, together with the resources of the Division of Monetary Research, and the urgent and extraordinary events of the wartime years, had laid the basis of most of White's influence outside the traditional preserves of the Treasury.

But as the Treasury's leading authority on the Bretton Woods institutions, which were central to the American government's professed internationalist goals for the postwar world, and indisputably within Treasury jurisdiction, there was no apparent reason why White should not survive a change of command in both the White House and his own department. In any case, Truman was apparently committed to following Roosevelt's policies. When, therefore, White notified Morgenthau on April 21 of his impending departure for San Francisco,[7] where he would remain until May 9, there was no reason for him to assume that there were any significant changes under way in Washington which would affect him.

However, in the wider field of foreign policy involving American relations with Russia, with which White was so concerned, the arrival of the new President had quickly meant new attitudes in the White House.

The effects of the change of perspective which Truman brought with him were, of course, gradual and not fully apparent, perhaps, until the Potsdam Conference three months later. But as early as April 15, an important change in the administration decided by Truman looked forward to a contraction in the Treasury's role in foreign affairs. On that day, during the return journey to Washington from Roosevelt's funeral at

Hyde Park, Truman had offered the post of Secretary of State to James F. Byrnes, until a short time before a powerful Director of War Mobilization.[8]

Byrnes, a vice presidential aspirant in 1944, a former Supreme Court Justice and a Democratic Senator, was by no means well disposed toward Morgenthau. This feeling was cordially reciprocated by the Secretary who, on the same journey back to Washington from Hyde Park, had unsuccessfully lobbied against Byrnes's appointment with the party chief, Robert Hannegan.[9] But Byrnes's appointment was not to be announced publicly until after the San Francisco Conference, in deference to the presence there of Stettinius, the current Secretary of State, and Truman's choice thus remained unknown to Morgenthau and White for some weeks.

The new President, moreover, possessed what Dean Acheson has called "a passion for orderly procedure,"[10] and so liked to work through formal channels. Such methods were the antithesis of the administrative chaos upon which Roosevelt had sometimes thrived, and which had of course maximized the influence of Morgenthau and White on foreign policy, as, for instance, in the development of the Treasury proposals for Germany. In Truman's view foreign policy was the domain of the State Department.

Perhaps the most significant of all the changes ushered in with the new President, who had been opposed to the Morgenthau Plan even as a Senator, was the emergence of a new approach toward negotiations with the Russians.

Truman was not personally committed in the way that Roosevelt had been to the concept of Big Three collaboration. In any case, by April, 1945, in a strictly military context, Soviet help was not needed in defeating Germany. The problem of Japan was more complex in view of the Yalta accords on China and the promised Soviet entry into the Pacific war within three months of VE-Day. Here, as we shall see in the next chapter, events pointed toward the postponement of any showdown with the Russians. But as early as April 24, in view of the rapid development of American air and sea power in the western Pacific, the Joint Staff planners had advised the Joint Chiefs of Staff that early Russian entry into the Pacific war was "no longer necessary" to make the invasion of Japan feasible.[11]

In addition, on the evening of April 12, within a few hours of Roosevelt's death and immediately after Truman's first Cabinet, Stimson had told the new President that he wanted him "to know about an immense project that was under way—a project looking toward the development of a new explosive of almost unbelievable destructive power." Truman had not known of the Manhattan atomic project when Roosevelt died, and the next day Byrnes added to the impact of the news by telling the President further details of "an explosive great enough to destroy the whole world."[12]

Truman's attitude toward the Soviet was made quite clear on the subject of broadening the provisional Polish government, where accord had been apparently reached at Yalta. However, since the conference differences had arisen between the two Western governments and Moscow. There had been a threat that Molotov would not attend the San Francisco Conference. Now, on April 20, eight days after Roosevelt's death, the American ambassador in Moscow, Harriman, told Truman that the Soviet government was pursuing two simultaneous policies. One was a course of cooperation with the United States and Britain, while the other aimed at extending Russian control over neighboring states "by independent action."

In Harriman's opinion Moscow did not want to break with the United States, because American reconstruction aid was needed. The ambassador considered that, in his judgment, the United States was faced with a "barbarian invasion of Europe," but he was not pessimistic because it was possible to arrive at a workable basis with the Russians. This would require "a reconsideration of our policy and abandonment of any illusion that the Soviet Government was likely soon to act in accordance with the principles to which the rest of the world subscribed." In any international negotiations there was give and take, Harriman said, going on to outline the Polish issue. Truman ended the meeting by remarking that he intended "to be firm" in his dealings with the Soviet government.[13]

Three days later, on April 23, the new President was as good as his word as he met with his senior advisers before talking to Molotov. Present were Stimson, Stettinius, Forrestal, Leahy, Marshall, Harriman and, among others, Assistant Secretary of State James Dunn. Truman supported the "firm" position on the Polish problem, and according to Charles E. Bohlen, the State Department's Soviet expert, "The President said . . . that he felt that our agreements with the Soviet Union had so far been a one-way street and that he could not continue; it was now or never. He intended to go on for the plans for San Francisco and if the Russians did not wish to join us, they could go to hell."[14]

When Molotov later arrived to discuss Poland, Truman records he went "straight to the point." Molotov should understand that American cooperation was only available on the basis of the mutual observation of agreements and not on the basis of a one-way street. Truman continued: " 'I have never been talked to like that in my life,' Molotov declared. I told him, 'Carry out your agreement, and you won't get talked to like that.' " Two days later, on the twenty-fifth, Truman was fully briefed for the first time on the atomic project by the Secretary of War. Stimson told the President that if expectations were realized the weapons would have "a decisive influence on our relations with other countries . . . in all probability success would be attained within the next few months."[15]

Whatever the implications of the new Presidency for any future foreign policy initiatives by White, his continuing influence on the United States Interim Directive, JCS 1067, was clearly established when he left Washington for San Francisco.

Throughout April, as the Allies occupied Germany, drafting had continued on the second major revision of JCS 1067, with Morgenthau, by virtue of his seniority, *de facto* chairman of IPCOG. (The first revision, which it will be remembered, was sent to Winant in London for negotiation by the EAC, had been superseded by the Yalta Conference.) By April 26 this second revision of the directive was approved by IPCOG and sent to the Joint Chiefs of Staff for clearance. The directive amplified certain Treasury concepts dating back to the first draft of the previous September.

The directive noted that the war had made "chaos and suffering" inevitable in Germany, that the objective of the occupation was to prevent Germany from "ever again" becoming a threat to the peace of the world, and that as the directive dealt with the initial post-defeat period it was not intended to be an "ultimate statement" of policies on Germany. Yet the provisions of this detailed and lengthy fifty-two-clause directive were comprehensive. In the absence of agreed policy by the four-power Control Council, JCS 1067 was to be followed by the military authorities in the American zone. Then the temporary could become permanent.

In its vital economic and financial provisions, the objectives of JCS 1067 were negative. As Walter Dorn has written, "what is so striking about JCS 1067 is not that it was a punitive document—it could not have been otherwise—but that it was an exclusively punitive document."[16] The "industrial disarmament" of Germany was prescribed first by prohibiting the production and acquisition of war products and associated facilities, and second by prohibiting and preventing the production of iron and steel, chemicals, nonferrous metals, machine tools, electrical equipment and heavy machinery. These provisions did not go so far as those of the Morgenthau Plan, but they were also "not the minimum alternative which would have all industries which operated for a direct military purpose converted to nonmilitary production."[17]

Equally significant, in view of the Treasury objective of letting the German economy "stew in its own juice," were the economic provisions in Paragraph 16 that, except to carry out the "basic objectives" of the occupation, the zonal commander was to "take no steps (a) looking toward the economic rehabilitation of Germany, or (b) designed to maintain or strengthen the German economy." The financial provision of JCS 1067, Paragraph 44, emphasized in the same vein that you "will take no steps designed to maintain, strengthen or operate the German financial structure except in so far as may be necessary for the purposes specified in this directive."

Specific orders against economic controls were seen as a way of enforcing this program. Paragraph 5 stipulated that controls would only be imposed to protect the occupation forces and to "assure the production and maintenance of goods and services required to prevent starvation or such disease and unrest as would endanger these forces." Paragraph 38 specified that the Control Council should direct the German authorities to establish controls to prevent inflation that would endanger the occupation, and that pending such action the zonal commander could take necessary action. But the directive went on:

Prevention of restraint of inflation shall not constitute an additional ground for the importation of supplies, nor shall it constitute an additional ground for limiting the removal, destruction or curtailment of productive facilities in fulfillment of the program for reparation, demilitarization and industrial disarmament.[18]

The thrust of the instructions for the American representative on the Moscow Reparations Commission, which were completed at the beginning of May and cleared by IPCOG, also reflected White's preoccupation with removing German heavy industry. The complex instruction specified, in one clause, that "to . . . the maximum extent possible, reparations should be taken from the national wealth of Germany existing at the time of the collapse, with the primary emphasis on the removal of industrial machinery. . . ." In line with White's arguments of April 7, the instructions also emphasized that recurrent reparations from manufacturing production should be as small as possible.

But illustrating the stiff fight put up by the State Department during the latter phases of the drafting, other clauses specified that the American government opposed paying for German reparations, and that the first charge against reparations exports should be for Allied imports into Germany. Moreover, unlike JCS 1067, the Reparations Instructions had to be negotiated on a tripartite basis in Moscow; the $20 billion sum agreed by the United States and Russia at Yalta was, of course, to be taken "as a basis for discussion." The substantive matter still remained open for the new President to negotiate.[19]

Truman signed the JCS 1067 Directive and the Reparations Instructions on May 10, the day following White's return to Washington from the United Nations Conference in San Francisco. But a last-minute revision in the directive was insisted on by the Joint Chiefs of Staff over Morgenthau's opposition.

The American zonal commander was now given discretionary authority to waive prohibition of production of synthetic rubber and oil, magnesium and aluminum without special clearance through the JCS in Washington. This gave the American military in Germany greater leeway in running the German economy, and probably saved these specialized plants from destruction. Here, in a hint of his future attitude on the German economy, the new President disagreed with Morgenthau.[20]

The fully revised directive, JCS 1067/8, was issued to Eisenhower on May 14. But when the policy directive "became available to the planning staff of the American Army at Versailles on May 21, 1945, it caused something like consternation and dismay. General Lucius Clay was shocked by it, shocked not so much by its exclusively punitive realities as by its failure to consider the basic economic realities which confronted the Army of Occupation in a ruined country. . . ."[21] Not until July, 1947, was the directive "purged of the most important elements of the Morgenthau Plan."[22]

The German surrender had been signed at Rheims and Berlin on May 7 and 8, 1945—the defeat of the thousand-year Reich that had conditioned so much of White's career in government. When White arrived back in Washington from San Francisco on May 9, therefore, the Treasury's successful involvement with the drafting of the Interim Directive, JCS 1067, was completed. At the same time, White's role in the gold shipments to China had been brought to a head by T. V. Soong's visit to Washington, although not perhaps with the outcome for which White had hoped.

CHINA: GOLD SHIPMENTS RESUMED

I understand that you were troubled about the letter of the two hundred million. Mr. Secretary, we have always taken the position that we had absolutely no legal grounds for withholding the gold; that what we were doing was skating on thin ice. . . .
         —WHITE TO MORGENTHAU, May 10, 1945

PRESIDENT Truman's accession had come at a critical time not only in the development of American policy in Europe. The Yalta Agreement on the Far East of February, 1945, with its concessions made to the Russians at China's expense by Roosevelt, had been seen at the time as a necessary price to be paid for Soviet entry into the Pacific war within two or three months of Germany's collapse.

But military considerations were not everything, and the well-known Yalta concessions to Russia over the Manchurian railroads, Port Arthur, Dairen and the status of Outer Mongolia had wider political purpose in that they looked forward to continuing great-power collaboration in this part of the world. The Yalta concessions, it was hoped, would prevent direct Soviet interference in the incipient Chinese civil war, and in any case the Russians could have taken more than they were given at Yalta with the impending collapse of Japan in the background.

Hence, the Big Three had agreed in the Crimea that the claims of the Soviet Union in the Far East would be "unquestionably fulfilled" after the collapse of Japan, and that the agreement regarding Manchuria and Outer Mongolia would require the "concurrence" of Chiang: "The President will take measures in order to obtain this concurrence on advice from Marshal Stalin." For his part, Stalin had therefore agreed that the Soviet Union would sign "a pact of fellowship and alliance" between the Soviet Union and China. Tang Tsou has drawn these threads together by summing up that the Yalta Agreement on the Far East "can be interpreted as an attempt to prevent the balance of power from being totally upset by a resurgent Soviet Union working in coordination with the Chinese Communists."[1]

Clearly Chiang would have to pay a price for the implementation of this agreement, which had been reached behind his back, but if the Chinese Communists could be neutralized this price might be worth paying. Moreover, following the doldrums of the post-Cairo-conference period, American policy had again begun to emphasize, certainly with the Henry Wallace mission to Chungking in June, 1944, the necessity of peaceful unification in China. Whatever his faults, Chiang was the man for this, it was believed. Stilwell had been dismissed, and "just as in the case of the policy of making China a great power, traditional principles, military considerations, and political planning for the postwar world appeared to converge perfectly in a program of peaceful unification of China."[2]

At the end of the Pacific war, therefore, as at its beginning, and despite intervening Sino-American differences, circumstances appeared to "converge perfectly" in sustaining the Generalissimo. For without his support, it was argued, not only was Chinese unification hardly possible, but neither was agreement with the Russians over the wider horizons of the postwar world in the Far East.

With these wider hopes in the background during the winter of 1944–45, the issue of the gold shipments from the $500,000,000 1942 credit now gradually came to the foreground of Sino-American relations as the economic conditions inside China continued to deteriorate no matter what plans were laid for the postwar world in the Far East. Between December, 1944, and August, 1945, for example, the average price index in Nationalist China rose from 755 to 2,647.

As we have seen, in October, 1944, White had told Morgenthau that he had "stalled" in sending gold to China because of the difference between the official and the free market price. The reader will remember that $20,000,000 of gold had been transferred to Chinese earmark in New York in February, 1943, and this amount had gradually been sent to China in the next eighteen months.

Morgenthau had then promised the Chinese government, in writing, on July 27, 1943, that they could draw a further $200,000,000 of gold from the 1942 credit whenever they wished. In January, 1944, Roosevelt had told Morgenthau and White that Chiang should be told that "we would send them about $25 million of gold a month."

Following White's foot-dragging on the issue, the Chinese had gradually increased their representations in the autumn of 1944, and the firs

$20,000,000 from the $200,000,000 had been transferred to Chinese earmark in New York in October, 1944. Two consignments of gold amounting to about $6,000,000 had then been sent by sea in November and
December, 1944. But no more gold was then sent to China until April 14,
1945, when a shipment of $1,200,000 was sent by sea, which meant that
no metal actually arrived in Chungking between January 26 and June 14,
1945.[3]

Morgenthau, as noted, was displaying no great interest in the gold
shipments in October, 1944. Responsibility was with White and, according to Professor Blum, "in assessing the state of affairs in China, Morgenthau turned neither to his subordinates who were aggressively bearish
about Chiang Kai-shek's future, nor to his own judgment." Rather, Morgenthau looked to Major General Patrick Hurley, Roosevelt's special representative in China.[4]

Hurley had been sent to Chungking as the President's personal representative in August, 1944. Following Stilwell's recall on October 19, his
replacement in the China command by General Albert C. Wedemeyer
and the resignation of Ambassador Gauss soon after, Hurley had been
nominated as the new American ambassador to China at the end of
November. Hurley understood his mission as one which would maintain
and sustain the Generalissimo, harmonize relations between the United
States and Chiang, and unify all military forces in China for the purpose
of defeating Japan.

On his way out to Chungking, Hurley had been told by Molotov in
Moscow that the Chinese Communists were "in no way at all" related to
Communism but were expressing their dissatisfaction with economic con-
ditions. The Soviet government, Molotov said, should not be associated
with these "Communist elements," and Moscow would be glad to see the
United States "taking the lead economically, politically and militarily in
Chinese affairs."[5]

Hurley, who according to the China White Paper made "frequent references" to this conversation with Molotov in his subsequent reports to
Washington, considered what he called the "so-called Communists" in
China neither dedicated nor formidable revolutionaries. According to
Tang Tsou, Hurley's "key assumption was that since the Soviet Union
would support America's policy of sustaining Chiang, the Chinese Communists would eventually have to accept Chiang's term." In general,
therefore, as Feis puts it, Hurley took "a friendly and favorable view of
the plight and intentions of the Chinese government. In his opinion it
merited support and help. If aided, he thought that in time it would
correct its faults and failures."[6]

In a message to Morgenthau in mid-November, Hurley mentioned
Molotov's conversation in Moscow, criticized the selfishness of some

Chungking officials, while dissociating himself from the tough approach of Stilwell and Gauss. Hurley now hoped to adopt a more constructive approach, and in his felicitations on Hurley's appointment as ambassador on December 13, Morgenthau promised every assistance from Adler, who was then about to return to China from the United States after a visit of some months.[7]

Yet behind these amiable high-level exchanges the problem of the gold shipments remained unresolved as the Chinese stepped up their requests. On December 9, in a memorandum to Morgenthau, White stated that the Chinese had been pressing to send gold by commercial vessels, but the Treasury insisted on military transportation. "We have stalled as much as we have dared," White wrote, "and have succeeded in limiting gold shipments to $26 million during the past year. We think it would be a serious mistake to permit further large shipments at this time."[8]

A few days later, following Morgenthau's note of congratulation on Hurley's appointment, White again reported that the Chinese were demanding accelerated shipments of gold. White considered it unwise in the "very uncertain state" of political development in China to get out as much gold as the Chinese wanted: "What we would like to do is to raise a lot of objections. . . . We can continue to stall indefinitely. Is that all right with you?" Morgenthau approved, "as long as we let Ambassador Hurley know what we are doing."[9]

White then followed up with a memorandum to Morgenthau on December 23 for presentation to Roosevelt. The gold was being sold in China in such a way that it chiefly benefited speculators, White maintained, and it was having practically no effect on the inflationary situation. While gold sales gave Chungking an additional source of revenue, this was by sacrificing valuable national assets at low prices. Despite pressure, the Treasury had held back gold shipments to China, while the existing shipments clearly showed support for Chungking.

White's memorandum suggested use of gold shipments as a "bargaining weapon" to get Chungking to accept "your China program." Morgenthau did not present White's memorandum to Roosevelt.[10] The Chinese, doubtless, would have answered White with the arguments for gold shipments they had already advanced, as we have seen, in the meeting with White in the Treasury on October 2. Without gold at hand, they insisted, it was impossible during a time of inflationary crisis to attempt to control the market and to keep official and free market rates in line.

White's explicit references to delaying the Chinese gold shipments from the 1942 credit came at the time of a government reshuffle in Chungking. Toward the end of 1944, H. H. Kung resigned as Finance Minister, and was succeeded by O. K. Yui. Kung was ill and remained in the United

States for treatment, where he continued to press the Treasury over the gold shipments. At the same time, however, T. V. Soong, after a period of eclipse, was restored to favor by the Generalissimo, and while retaining his post of Foreign Minister became Acting President of the Executive Yuan (Cabinet) in Chungking.

As we shall see, there may have been a growing awareness on the Chinese side that White was chiefly responsible for the delay in the gold shipments, but probably Soong's elevation meant that a new urgency was felt in the Chinese requests for the gold. Soong had negotiated the original credit with Morgenthau, and in a few months' time he was to tell Morgenthau, when he came to Washington to ask for the gold, that he felt that he was sitting on top of a volcano in Chungking.

In addition, more than many on the American side, Soong may have felt that the Pacific war was going to end very suddenly, and that Chungking needed immediately all its promised resources before being confronted with a new set of circumstances; nine months before the first atomic test at Alamogordo in New Mexico in July, 1945, Soong had told Ambassador Gauss "that the war would be won by a secret weapon which the United States was developing."[11]

On December 30, 1944, as the opening shot of the new Chinese campaign to expedite the gold shipments, Kung forwarded to Morgenthau a fresh request from the Chinese Finance Minister, Yui, for large-scale deliveries of bullion totaling $180,000,000. A few days later on January 5, Morgenthau replied to Kung that he was giving the matter his "close attention," and that he hoped to be able to give Kung his decision in the near future. Morgenthau then sent a cable to Adler in Chungking telling him that the Chinese were asking for larger gold shipments but in view of the "current situation" in China, and the need for the Chinese to conserve their foreign resources, he had not given permission for the request. Cautiously, Morgenthau wanted Adler to discuss the matter thoroughly with Hurley and inform him of the ambassador's views.[12]

Kung wrote again to Morgenthau on January 18 emphasizing the urgency of sending bullion and gold tokens. During February the Chinese government also requested 23,000 tons of textiles to be sold, like the gold, for anti-inflationary purposes. Soong considered the importation of textiles of "paramount importance"; tonnages flown over the Hump had now greatly expanded, and the Stilwell Road, linking India with the Burma Road into China, had just been opened.

On February 26, Kung returned to the attack in a long letter to Morgenthau reviewing the entire Chinese financial situation. He stressed the dangers of inflation to China's economic structure, emphasizing that the sale of gold to drain off notes was but a financial expedient and "it is only the financial emergency that justifies this policy." The Chinese hoped to replace the sale of gold by consumer goods. Again asking for gold, Kung wrote that only just over $7,000,000 of gold out of the $200,000,000 "made available" by the United States from the 1942 credit had been sent to China.[13]

Clearly, the Treasury was standing by White's policy of delay. At this time, on January 24, White was formally appointed Assistant Secretary of the Treasury, and two days later Morgenthau ruled in a Treasury order that the Division of Monetary Research was to continue under White's supervision. Frank Coe was appointed White's successor on February 16.[14]

However, although Donald Nelson, the former head of the War Production Board, told White and Morgenthau in mid-January, following a visit to China, that Chiang "was giving definite evidence of his desire to cooperate fully with the United States," Adler's reports to White were less optimistic. One of his letters, written in mid-January and passed by White to Morgenthau on February 7, commented that "the economic and financial situation continues to deteriorate apace." In another February letter to White, shown to Morgenthau on March 19, Adler considered that the Hurley mission was a fiasco, and that the ambassador was "a stuffed shirt playing at being a great man . . . very much in T.V.'s pocket."

Adler commented that unconditional support for the Chungking regime would be the best way to make civil war inevitable, and that "without a change in the present situation there seems to be no alternative for the Treasury to adopt or rather maintain a *negative* policy toward China." (Italics in original.) Adler considered that "we should continue to send as little gold as possible to China," and that "we should turn down Chinese requests for goods on civilian Lend-Lease for the ostensible purpose of combating inflation. There is no escaping the fact that inflation cannot be combated in the present setup."[15]

Support for at least some of Adler's views now came from Hurley himself, who cabled Morgenthau at the end of February from Chungking, where the involved negotiations between the Nationalists and the Communists had made little progress. Hurley hoped for improvements in China, but recommended "holding down gold shipments to about the same magnitude as in past years."[16]

Hurley's message could hardly have come at a worse time as far as Kung's latest request for gold on February 26 was concerned. On March 2 Coe sent a memorandum to Morgenthau about Kung's message, along with a suggested reply. The new Director of Monetary Research remarked that since the situation in China was unchanged, "you will probably wish to continue the policy of permitting only small gold shipments to China. It will be recalled that Ambassador Hurley agreed with you on holding down gold shipments to approximately the same magnitude as in the past." Coe suggested that Kung be told verbally that $7,000,000 of gold would be sent to China within the next three months, one-half of it to pay for tin exports from China to the United States.

The same day, in a note to Morgenthau, White recommended against granting a $16,000,000 Export-Import Bank reconstruction loan to China on the grounds that it was "premature," that China had ample American dollars, and that the political and military situation in China made such a loan "a very serious risk at this time." Morgenthau then wrote to Kung on March 3 mentioning the "many difficulties" involved in exporting gold to China, and that as "military necessity" took precedence he had instructed his men "to raise again with the military the possibilities of shipping gold to China during the next few months. They will inform your representatives of their findings on this matter."[17]

On March 11, as the Treasury still stalled on gold shipments, Adler reported direct to Morgenthau by telegram from Chungking. The Chinese government, he said, was now relying on the sales of the gold it held as "a main source of revenue." The free market price of gold was now over C$39,000 per ounce while the official price had been maintained (at C$24,000, including tax). Three-quarters of the gold revenue was from forward sales, and Adler considered that the official claim that raising the official price of gold would push up prices could not be taken seriously as "prices were skyrocketing in any case." Adler also considered that "the official pretext that price [of gold] cannot be raised without an adequate supply on hand does not hold water." He concluded that "since inflation has now entered snowball phase, future sales of gold at current rate will have ever smaller effect as brake on inflation." Adler's message was hardly a recommendation for the resumption of gold shipments. There was a complete impasse between Chungking and the Treasury.[18]

The Chinese of course were still convinced, or so they insisted, that spot gold was necessary to control the market, and once again on March 30 Kung was writing to Morgenthau for gold shipments as "the inflationary danger is reaching alarming proportions." The situation was so grave that he considered exceptional measures justified. Effective the same day, the official price of gold per ounce was raised abruptly from C$24,000 to C$35,000 in Chungking in an attempt to level with the free market. But within hours the free market had already jumped to C$60,000 per ounce, and the cost of American dollar notes increased from C$525 to C$660. According to the Chungking press, "Numerous commodities followed suit."[19]

In mid-April, 1945, T. V. Soong, in the United States for the United Nations Founding Conference at San Francisco, came to Washington to plead the case for gold shipments to China. The issue now had to be settled on the highest level.

In a Treasury conference on April 20, White told Morgenthau that Soong "is here . . . primarily to get as much gold as possible. The story that they have appears to be a very defensible one that they are going to re-establish order, reforms in China, but that is not the real reason in either Soong's mind or the Generalissimo's mind. . . . And the political ramifications are the most important things, Mr. Secretary, that are on the docket." White went on to say that after Soong had discussed the matter with Truman, the President would probably not be satisfied "with just a no answer." White considered that Morgenthau, who had been immersed in the ramifications of occupation policy for Germany, would "have to go into it in more detail."[20]

Coe now prepared a paper to brief Morgenthau, dated the same day of his talks with Soong. He wrote that the Chinese government was trying to get as much as possible from the United States and continued to misuse the assistance it had been given. The Chinese were now attempting to withdraw $180,000,000 of gold from the $240,000,000 which remained on the books of the Treasury from the $500,000,000 credit. Altogether about $27,000,000 of gold had been sent to China, where it was being sold at low prices to speculators.

Continuing, Coe remarked that the Chinese government avoided taking effective measures to retard inflation. Adverting to the sale of the dollar securities in 1942–43, he wrote that there was "little doubt" that persons "intimately connected" with T. V. Soong and H. H. Kung had purchased millions of dollars of these securities. As for the textiles which the Chinese wanted to import, "as in the case of the gold sales, the anti-inflationary effects of the sales of such textiles would be very small." The next day Coe sent a detailed memorandum to Morgenthau on the sale of the dollar securities inside China which itemized purchases by persons and organizations allegedly connected with Soong and Kung. Coe wrote that "a highly reliable source" had reported, through Gauss and Adler, that Madame Chiang and Madame Kung had between them purchased $50,000,000 of the securities.[21]

After talking with Truman, Morgenthau consulted with the State and War departments, while Soong continued to lobby in Washington before temporarily leaving for San Francisco. From Chungking came renewed requests for gold, culminating in a desperate cable from the Central Bank on April 28 stating that "we cannot over emphasize the serious effect in consequence Doctor White's default in meeting its [sic] more obligations." As both sides rallied their forces for Soong's coming confrontation with Morgenthau, White left Washington for the United Nations San Francisco Conference, to which he was a technical adviser. White was based in San Francisco's Sir Francis Drake Hotel from April 22 to May 9.[22]

However, Coe continued with the presentation of what was essentially White's policy on the gold shipments, with the State and the War departments now apparently beginning to align themselves with the Treasury. On May 1 Coe reported to Morgenthau that another request for gold had been received from the Chungking Finance Ministry; the Treasury was being "repeatedly bombarded with cables of this type."

In another, longer paper the same day, Coe outlined a comprehensive Division of Monetary Research policy on the Chinese gold requests. He told Morgenthau that these views had been discussed with the State and War departments, and that he thought "we can get their agreements on all the points below."

Coe went on to suggest that the Treasury should continue to oppose all except minimum shipments of gold, and that the Chinese should be told the Americans expected them to drop all forward sales of gold immediately. Any gold sent to China should be from Chinese external assets which totaled, with the $240,000,000 balance of the 1942 credit, about $900,000,000. Coe then wrote that Morgenthau should tell the Chinese that this balance of the 1942 credit, together with a sum from the Chinese assets, should be formed into a $500,000,000 stabilization and reconstruction fund, "in accordance with an agreed program, to go into effect at an agreed date."

"If the Chinese are not willing to accept this proposal," Coe wrote, "we think it wise policy to allow no further depletion of the loan."[23]

On the afternoon of May 8, 1945, VE-Day, representatives from State, War and the Foreign Economic Administration met in the Treasury with Morgenthau in the chair to discuss the gold shipments with Soong. The State Department was represented by Assistant Secretary of State William Clayton. Coe, Adler and Friedman were present from the Division of Monetary Research. White was still in San Francisco and flew back to Washington from the West Coast the next day.

Coe had expanded his longer memorandum of May 1 to Morgenthau into a Treasury "Memorandum for Dr. T. V. Soong," of which he read parts at the opening of the meeting.

The paper recommended the setting up of a $500,000,000 Chinese currency stabilization fund to be constituted from the remaining $240,-000,000 of the 1942 credit and China's existing external assets. Envisaged was a broad anti-inflationary program involving Chinese banking, exchange and administrative organizations, directly involving the United States: "The Fund would be set aside with firm mutual commitment on the part of China and the United States as to its purpose."

Criticized in the paper were the forward sales of gold in China. The

Treasury would make "limited quantities" of gold available to China with due regard for "scarce transport facilities," but gold shipments should come from China's foreign assets and not from resources put aside for the proposed stabilization fund, that is, not from the balance of the 1942 credit. The memorandum proposed that China should investigate and cancel sales to gold speculators. It concluded by stating that it was "most unfortunate" that the impression had arisen in America that the $200,-000,000 of United States dollar securities "and the gold sold in China" has gone into relatively few hands "with resultant large individual profits. . . ."

Coe had also resubmitted a memorandum dated the same day, to Morgenthau listing the alleged purchasers of the dollar securities in China, and repeating the report that Madame Chiang and Madame Kung had purchased between them $50,000,000 worth of these securities.

The Chinese request for textiles (and trucks) was not mentioned in the "Memorandum for Soong," but General Somervell, speaking for the Army, said the trucks would be available. No decision could be made at present on textiles which were in short supply. In response to Morgenthau's query, there was common agreement on the approach outlined in the memorandum from all agencies represented at the meeting.

Soong now entered the conference with two colleagues, and Coe read aloud the memorandum addressed to him. The Chinese Foreign Minister commented urbanely on this virtual *demarche* by saying that the proposals therein were very constructive, but he wanted to know how the suggested $500,000,000 fund would be used to fight inflation. Morgenthau replied that until China had an open seaport, the fund would be a more orthodox way than gold sales to deal with inflation.

The situation in China would not allow him to wait, Soong said, and that was why he had come from the San Francisco Conference to Washington. It was true the Treasury had not been consulted in the forward sales of gold, but there was a "definite commitment" to supply gold by Morgenthau. Obviously prepared for this moment, which demolished the Treasury position, Soong read aloud Morgenthau's letter of July 27, 1943, to Kung which promised $200,000,000 of gold from the 1942 credit "on receipt of requests from the Government of China." (See Chapter 11.)

Morgenthau hesitated, thinking the sum involved was $20,000,000, having overlooked the original commitment. But Soong insisted, going on to remark that there was no commitment to consultation by the Chinese in the 1942 credit agreement, which he had had the honor of signing with Morgenthau. It will be remembered that with the signing of the credit agreement in March, 1942, Soong had merely written a letter to Morgenthau saying that China would keep the United States "fully informed" as to the use of the loan.

Soong went on to say that confidence in his government was closely connected with the gold sales, and that in Chungking he had felt that he "was sitting on top of a volcano which may erupt at any moment." He was prepared to tax gold speculators and investigate the sale of dollar securities in China. There was no disposition on the part of his government to allow speculation. When told of the shortage of textiles for which the Chinese had asked, Soong commented: "Prague was taken yesterday or the day before. This country that first got beaten up by the aggressor will be the last to be rescued. . . ."[24]

On the next morning, May 9, Morgenthau reprimanded Coe, Adler and Irving Friedman, who had known of the 1943 commitment, for not reminding him of his promise: "Look, you people, I think you should be severely criticized for letting me go into court and try my case before T. V. Soong. . . . After all, you were so worried about saving face, what about my face? I have given, in writing, the Chinese Government a firm commitment that they have two hundred million dollars worth of gold and you—I don't remember it, I can't remember it. I do ten things a day . . . it's impossible for me to remember, and you put me in an absolutely dishonorable position and I think it's inexcusable."

The previous evening, Morgenthau went on, "I was worried wholly independent of this." Then Clayton had telephoned and had given him material on China's war effort. Admiral King, the Chief of Naval Operations, had also told him that morning that "the Chinese are doing much better . . . they are really getting somewhere . . . and here I am acting like a huckster over something which has been settled . . . I don't like it."

Morgenthau went on to tell Coe that "we should promptly begin to move this gold." Of the $200,000,000, $8,000,000 had been sent, Coe said. The Chinese were now asking for the remainder to enable them to cover forward commitments and then go on to spot sales. Morgenthau also directed that Coe's memorandum was to be redrafted to tell the Chinese the gold would be sent, while containing a request to set up a stabilization fund.[25]

Following lunch with Soong on what he described as "a very courteous plane," Morgenthau told Adler and Friedman that Soong had thrown in the fact "that he had gotten along so well with the Russians, and Molotov is insisting that he go to Russia . . . and if I would strengthen his hand it would make possible the success of his mission to Russia . . . the success or failure of his trip depended on what I did, and this was an opportunity to bring two great nations together."

Then, in yet another Treasury meeting with Soong later in the day Morgenthau said that he was ready to fulfill any commitment that was made, but that he hoped that the Chinese would set up a fund so that matters could be made easier for him: "We will immediately study the gold question as to how we can accelerate the shipment of gold."[26]

Following these discussions with Soong, it began to appear that the question of gold shipments was at last resolved. White, returning from San Francisco, met with Morgenthau the next afternoon, May 10. The Secretary then dictated a letter to Soong confirming their new understanding, and there was a general discussion. According to the transcript in the Morgenthau Diaries, White brought up the July, 1943, pledge to send the $200,000,000 of gold to China:

MR. WHITE. I understand that you were troubled about the letter of the two hundred million. Mr. Secretary, we have always taken the position that we had absolutely no legal grounds for withholding the gold; that what we were doing was skating on thin ice and offering excuses and we were getting away with it so long as we could and remember because I said we are getting away with it that you had better get the President's backing when they begin putting on the heat. It's because I said we have no basis for it. We have been successful over two years in keeping them down to twenty-seven million and we never understood why the Chinese didn't take it in there and do what they are now doing. The history is that we had no basis for it.

H. M., JR. I can't remember things that happened and when he flashed that letter on me it caught me sort of off guard. I didn't remember it.

MR. WHITE. That letter grew out of what you thought the President promised Madame Chiang Kai-shek.

H. M., JR. They refreshed my memory but the trouble is that, Harry, I think that the Army and the State Department have advised me very badly on this thing last week and suddenly Will Clayton woke up to that fact himself entirely on his own, and all the indications are that the Chinese are really going to fight. This man comes here now and gets a cold shoulder, gets bounced around, he gets nothing. He may get four thousand trucks and this is the money which we have committed ourselves to, and I have sort of come to the decision that I don't know how far I'll go, but I certainly want to loosen up, and I think this is a psychological time for the Treasury to demonstrate we can be a friend to China when they really need it, with their own money.

MR. WHITE. This isn't the same way I'd do it. I'll drop that. . . .

Probably misjudging the Secretary's mood, White went on to tell Morgenthau that what "you need now is an exchange of letters from you to the President indicating the money is badly used." White thought the only basis for sending gold to China was "military necessity."[27]

White now decided to make a last stand on his policy over the gold shipments to China. On May 12 an "urgent" telegram was sent by Coe to the American embassy in Chungking asking that "as soon as possible digest of newspaper information or comment on gold scandal" should be forwarded to the Treasury.[28]

Then, in a meeting on the gold shipments in the Treasury on May 15, 1945, White opened by telling Morgenthau that "we have a memorandum prepared." The paper, White said, had been sent to the State Department for their concurrence as it had not been possible to clear it first with Morgenthau. Coe then read to the meeting the draft "Memorandum for the President, Subject: China," which could, if forwarded to Truman by Morgenthau, have reopened the entire issue of the gold shipments on the White House level.

The memorandum, a redraft of Coe's paper of May 8, criticized the gold sales program as ineffective, prophesied scandal in China and the United States over the program, and re-recommended the establishment of a $500,000,000 fund from the balance of the 1942 credit and other Chinese assets. It ended with the suggestion that Soong be told by Morgenthau that both the State Department and President agreed "that it is in the best interests of Chinese-American relations that China withdraw for the time being her request for immediate heavy shipments of gold."

Morgenthau reacted immediately, and ordered the draft memorandum to be retrieved from the State Department. He told White that he was going to keep his word: "I mean you keep on going over the same ground, the same ground, the whole time. This doesn't make it plain to the President of the United States that these people own this gold, that I, over my signature, told them they could have two hundred million dollars worth of gold."

White continued to argue that behind all the discussion lay the assumption that the Chinese were supposed to be using the loan wisely.

Morgenthau pointed out that there was no written commitment to that effect, and that the memorandum went back on what he had already promised to Soong the previous week. He thought the Treasury, up until this time, had been correct, but he had now changed his mind:

We have two targets . . . one is we have to first defeat Japan, and the other target is to liberate China. . . . The Chinese are beginning to fight now. That seems to be fairly well substantiated . . . that means saving lives, many lives, and it's an inexpensive investment. . . . Now I was going along with these fellows up to a point and I suddenly made up my mind that this was all wrong, and I'm just going to turn a somersault on this thing, and I want to do it; and particularly when I see my written word and the promise of Franklin Roosevelt is at stake. . . . Even if the Chinese weren't fighting with a letter over my signature that they could have this, I think I'd be inclined to say it's yours. Now I'm through. . . .

When White argued that there was a way of "wriggling out" of the commitment, Morgenthau again insisted that he did not want "any part" of the memorandum produced at the opening of the meeting. He was going to recommend to the President that the gold be sent to China.[29]

But before seeing the President the next morning, May 16, Morgenthau met with White, Coe, Adler and others of his staff, together with Clayton from the State Department. The Secretary again reprimanded his advisers, remarking that, contrary to what he had been told in Coe's memorandum, there was no reason to assume that Soong and Kung had personally benefited from the purchase of dollar securities by firms in China: "You boys have been telling me right along that Soong owns most of this stuff, and that's misleading." Morgenthau complained that he had "been told three times that these people individually had purchased gold."

White considered, apropos of Coe's "Memorandum for Soong" of May 8 on the purchase of dollar securities, that "all you have to do is reword it a little differently. Say the purchasers have been these companies and from our information T. V. Soong is an important director or large shareholder of each one of these or something like that." But after further discussion, in which the State Department view was that it wished "to maintain" Chiang, Morgenthau stated, to be supported by Clayton, that he was going to tell Truman that "we fulfill our contract. . . . I'm sorry, Harry, that's final."[30]

When Soong called on Morgenthau following his meeting with Truman, the Secretary remarked that he and the President recognized "that the United States Government has made this commitment and we are prepared to carry it out." He pointed out to Soong that the use of the gold would influence the American government over further assistance to China.[31]

Then, that afternoon, in the presence of White, Under Secretary Daniel Bell, Coe and Adler, Morgenthau signed the letter to Soong authorizing the shipment of the balance of the first $20,000,000 of Chinese gold on earmark in New York. The remaining $180,000,000 of the promised $200,000,000 would follow in three monthly installments of $60,000,000 from May to July, 1945. The letter also urged the Chinese to constitute a $500,000,000 stabilization fund. (A fund for eventual monetary stabilization of that amount was set aside by the Chinese government in February, 1946.)

Morgenthau also obtained a formal letter, to cover his flank, from Acting Secretary of State Joseph C. Grew which, while expressing reservations over the gold-sales program, recommended "that the Treasury, if transportation is available, deliver the gold to China in accordance with the time schedules put forward by Dr. Soong."[32]

The turnabout on the gold shipments was not communicated at the time to Hurley in Chungking. The ambassador was not consulted. Eventually commenting on the news to the Treasury in early June he observed that he could not see that the creation of a stabilization fund would arrest inflation in China. But if Washington really thought so, said Hurley, it should have made gold shipments conditional on the promise to establish such a fund. He had great respect for the power of suggestion, but in this case would have relied on the power of $200,000,000.[33]

By now Morgenthau had developed greater confidence in the Chinese Nationalists. He was urging the Army and the Foreign Economic Administration to send the requested textiles to China, and on May 23 visited the White House to press these shipments. Truman pounded the desk: "What the hell is the matter with these people. . . . Don't they know we have a war on our hands? . . . I want to give China some cotton."[34]

On June 1, Morgenthau delivered to the White House a joint report on Chinese requests by a committee of the Treasury, State and War departments, together with the Foreign Economic Administration. It confirmed the shipment of gold, as requested by Soong, and textiles and trucks were also being sent. The final point of the committee's report noted that "Further operations under the Anti-Inflation program will be carried out through regular channels and procedures."[35]

For skaters on administrative thin ice as a new era began in Washington, possibly, it was a warning.

As Hurley's message to Morgenthau at the end of May indicated, many besides Stilwell on the American side, and including some who disagreed with the General's specific policies and personal approach to Chiang, came to believe in some sort of application of the *quid pro quo* policy in negotiating with Chungking. As we have seen, several factors contributed to this pervasive feeling of disillusion with Nationalist China. There was disappointment with Chungking's war effort, the fiasco of the dollar securities, and the hard negotiations over American military costs in China, all of which helped to bring War Department and State Department into apparent tentative agreement with the Treasury on its gold shipments policy by early May, 1945.

White, as we have seen, had originally conceived of delaying the gold transfers to China from the $200,000,000 promised by Morgenthau in July, 1943, as early as the September of that year. At first the policy of "being tough" was based on supplying gold only as quickly as it could be sold in China, a sensible enough approach. But by January, 1944, as we have seen, Roosevelt evidently thought that $25,000,000 of gold monthly was being sent over the Hump. Later, there was White's suggestion that the gold be used as a "bargaining weapon," recalling a preoccupation, in different circumstances, which we have noted in connection with the British reserves. Then during 1944–45, as the economic and military situation in China deteriorated, and as Chinese requests became more insistent, the policy on gold shipments became one of virtual embargo. Concurrently, the wider policy of the American government sought to strengthen the Chungking regime, regardless of the wartime differences between the two sides.

However, by his omission to remind Morgenthau of his written commitment to the Chinese over the gold, White made sure, willy nilly, by "skating on thin ice," that when Morgenthau discovered from Soong that his word was in doubt the gold would have to be sent without insistence on Chinese concessions. Hence the gold was denied as a palliative to the Chinese at a time of inflationary crisis, and when it was eventually sent the Treasury was unable effectively to suggest the creation of a currency stabilization fund in China. Although White had been sympathetic toward the Chinese Nationalist cause in the earlier period of the Sino-Japanese struggle, when both the United States and Soviet Russia, for their differing reasons, had supported Chiang, clearly his attitude had changed by the later war years. The upshot was that China was denied gold when the necessity of checking inflation was greater than ever.

On the other hand Morgenthau had been a staunch friend of Nationalist China in the past, quickly ordered the gold shipments when his undertaking was pointed out to him, and, fully briefed earlier, might have been able to persuade the Chinese to set up some form of stabilization fund as he wished. The apparent belief of White and the Division of Monetary Research that little could be done by the gold sales program may be balanced by the view of another observer, Arthur Young, that it was the American "much more than the Chinese action that prevented the [gold] sales operation from accomplishing what it could and should have accomplished."[36] In the event, the withholding of the gold may well have exacerbated, to a degree that of course cannot be measured, the Chinese inflation.

Paradoxically, however, in a final illustration of the cross-purposes and conflicting motives that surrounded the shipment of gold to Chungking, White's last stand in favor of delaying the gold in May, 1945, came at the very time when the American government was being drawn closer to Chiang as part of its post-Yalta diplomacy. But in the gold negotiations involving the Treasury these latest developments were only barely hinted at by such comments as Soong's remark on May 9 that he had "gotten along so well with Molotov," or Truman's unspectacular assurance to Morgenthau on May 16 that the administration intended to "carry out" its promises over the Chinese gold.

For in the background of the Soong mission to Washington with its objective of expediting the gold lay the concern of Truman and his closest advisers, not including Morgenthau and White, about the implementation of the Yalta accord on the Far East. This came at the same time that the new President was urgently reconsidering American policy toward Moscow over the Polish question. But in the Far East, as the war with Germany ended, some weeks still remained to tell Chiang of the Yalta agreement and to have the terms codified in a comprehensive Sino-Soviet agreement.

With an ebbing of faith in Soviet intentions in Washington, it has been plausibly suggested, the question that came to be debated by Stimson, Grew, Navy Secretary James Forrestal, Averell Harriman, American ambassador to Moscow, and a few other close advisers to the President was whether or not to postpone some sort of clarification with the Russians over the implementation of the Yalta agreement. And would it be best to postpone such a clarification—or confrontation—until the American government had successfully tested the almost completed "S-1," the secret atomic weapon?[37]

Now on April 23, as White began his two weeks' stay in San Francisco, George Kennan, the American chargé in Moscow, cabled home to Harriman that he believed Soviet policy in China would be "a fluid resilient policy directed at the achievement of maximum power with minimum responsibility on portions of the Asiatic continent . . . it would be tragic if our natural anxiety for the support of the Soviet Union at this juncture were to lead us into an undue reliance on Soviet aid or even Soviet acquiescence in the achievements of our long term objectives in China."[38] This cable was read by the President.

Moreover, at the same time the President's diplomatic advisers were speculating on the possible political disadvantages of Soviet entry into Manchuria and North China, his military advisers, as we have seen, were beginning to doubt that such entry was absolutely imperative to defeat Japan. Would it therefore be better to attempt to strengthen the American bargaining position in the Far East by procrastinating over the arrangements implementing the Yalta accord? Such was the question implied in a closely written paper put by Grew to the Secretary of War (Stimson) and the Secretary of the Navy (Forrestal) on May 12.

After discussion on this level, at the same time as White was making his last attempt to prevent the gold from being sent to China, Truman and Grew met with Soong on May 14. The President was sympathetic to what Dr. Alperovitz calls "the strategy of delay" in the Far East and thus Chinese cooperation in general and Soong's in particular was absolutely necessary. Soong, after all, was the Chinese Foreign Minister and would personally have to negotiate any Sino-Soviet accord with Molotov. In Truman's talk with Soong, the Yalta accord was still not mentioned, and it was agreed that consideration of Soong's journey to Moscow be postponed, although Soong was at first anxious to proceed there to enlist Stalin's help against the Chinese Communists. Instead, the matter of Soong's Moscow mission, according to Grew's memoirs, "was left open."[39]

The next day, May 15, Morgenthau rejected White's advice to withhold the Chinese gold. The same evening Stimson, illustrating the intensity of the moment, wrote in his diary that in the problem of Russian relations with Manchuria and North China, "over such a tangled weave of problems [the atomic bomb] secret would be dominant and yet we will not know until after that time [of the coming Big Three conference] whether this is a weapon or not. We think it will be, shortly afterwards, but it seems a terrible thing to gamble with such big stakes in diplomacy without having your master card in your hand."[40]

On the morning of the sixteenth Truman saw Morgenthau, and confirmed the promise to send the gold to China. That afternoon, as we have seen, Morgenthau finally signed, in the presence of White, the letter to Soong expediting the gold shipments. Lastly, and perhaps most important of all, after a meeting later in the day with Truman, Secretary Stimson felt that the President agreed with him on the necessity to postpone negotiations with the Russians.[41] But Truman still retained a negotiating option, for he had already arranged for Harry Hopkins to visit Moscow at the end of May.

In the Far East, Soong's docility was clearly necessary for such diplomacy to be implemented, and with "such big stakes" at hand until "the master card" was ready, the Chinese bullion was surely of secondary consideration. On the presidential level, the overriding problem now was how to implement a muted *quid pro quo* policy, not with the Chinese, as White had been advocating, but with the Russians. To ease the path of President Truman's new diplomacy, with its apparently exciting vistas, slightly less than $200,000,000 of gold was surely not too expensive a price to pay. But White was by now rather far from the center of decision on such matters.

Yet, no matter what the terms of the Morgenthau-Soong rapprochement and the new, involved calculations of Truman's diplomacy, prices continued to rise in China.

Following Morgenthau's letter to Soong on May 16, five gold shipments left the United States before the end of the month, and ten consignments in June. But these shipments still went by sea, and only on June 16 did air shipments begin, the first arriving in Chungking on June 26. Between July and October, 1945, over $100,000,000 of gold arrived in China.

Probably the gold arrived too late, as the market had already gyrated out of control during the summer, adding another twist to the inflationary spiral. By early June, the official price of gold had been raised again from C$35,000 to C$50,000 per ounce. But as there was no spot gold for immediate sale, by the end of that month the free market price had reached C$185,000. A $1,200,000 consignment of gold, dispatched from New York in April, and sent by sea, arrived at Chungking on June 14, the first to arrive since January. But by now the market had collapsed and on June 25 official gold sales were suspended for the remainder of the Pacific war. During July the free market price ranged uncontrollably from C$167,000 to C$225,000.

Following Japan's defeat in August, the free market price dropped, and as the gold arrived from the United States the government in Chungking settled its forward commitments, setting the official price at the end of September at C$89,000.[42]

The average price index in Nationalist China, as we have noted, had risen from 755 in December, 1944, to 2,647 in August, 1945. But following VJ-Day prices began to fall. Then, in October, 1945, prices resumed their upward course, and by December the index stood at 2,491. There was no further reversal of this course.

White had hoped to exert political pressure on the Nationalist government by virtually declaring a one-man embargo on the gold promised under the 1942 credit. Yet essentially, his actions implied that some sort of American solution might be valid for China, if the right leverage could be found. On quite a different level, Roosevelt, for his part, had attempted to make China one of the Big Four. In Chungking, Stilwell had perhaps seen himself as a latter-day "Chinese" Gordon who could mobilize the masses denied leadership by the Generalissimo.

But, as the Nationalist government began the long slide toward the final catastrophe in the summer of 1945, it soon became clear that there could be no external solution for China's problems; only a Chinese one.

CONGRESS PASSES THE FUND

A new era seemed to be dawning. Issues of monetary and financial policy
were easily confused with other issues—regionalism and universalism,
war and peace, isolationism and internationalism.
—RICHARD N. GARDNER, *Sterling-Dollar Diplomacy*

IN EARLY 1945, President Roosevelt had sent the Bretton Woods Agreements to Congress recommending their approval as one of the cornerstones of postwar international cooperation. A few months later, in the
spring of that year, White took a major part in piloting Bretton Woods
through Congress, appearing before the appropriate committees of the
House and Senate.

The impending defeat of the Axis, the wide hopes for great-power
cooperation in the postwar period, and the general enthusiasm surrounding the United Nations founding conference at San Francisco in April,
1945, all combined to emphasize the apparent demise of political isolationism in the United States. Congress would have to decide, in considering the Bretton Woods Articles of Agreement, whether economic
isolationism had also suffered the same fate.

But the opposition to the Bretton Woods program did not come only
from traditional isolationist quarters, but from influential sections of the
American financial community. Most of the New York press was cool
toward Bretton Woods. In general, Wall Street considered that the Bretton Woods institutions favored the debtor rather than the creditor, that
the Fund's provisions on exchange rates were too loose, and that the
financial interests and bargaining power of the United States would not
be adequately protected. Loans on a private, bilateral basis were seen as
a viable alternative to Bretton Woods.

There were anxieties, too, about the problem of transitional finance, as well as over the Bretton Woods liquidity provisions and methods of adjustment. One of the most influential critics of Bretton Woods was Professor John H. Williams of Harvard University and vice-president of the New York Federal Reserve Bank. Williams suggested a large loan or grant to cover the transitional demands of the United Kingdom, combined with an attack on the sterling balances and a bilateral stabilization agreement linking the two key currencies. Other countries would join the Anglo-American agreement as gradual progress was made in postwar reconstruction.

The "key-currency" proposal was based on the undoubted fact that, as in the preliminaries to Bretton Woods, close agreement was necessary between the United States and Great Britain before any postwar multilateral trading regime could work. At the same time, however, the key-currency proposal conflicted with the widespread demand for universal institutions to deal with postwar economic problems. And the very concept of the Fund and the Bank, as we have seen, was designed from the beginning to prevent such exclusive arrangements.

In addition to these criticisms of the Bretton Woods program, the technical structure of the Fund and the Bank, together with their anticipated complementary relationship was hard to project at a time which saw the climax of the war. The United States Treasury thus promoted a powerful public relations campaign on the Bretton Woods institutions during 1944-45. Articles appeared in journals ranging from *Foreign Affairs* to the *Reader's Digest*, and the case was taken directly to the public, sometimes through the many organizations with which the Treasury had worked on the war bond campaigns.

A veteran of the Treasury negotiations on the financial institutions, Ansel Luxford, who was also Morgenthau's agent for public relations during the passage of the Bretton Woods agreements, has remarked that "the battle in Congress was won only because the issue was taken to the people who in turn applied the pressure to Congress. The Treasury then was no neophyte at reaching the public—it had a whole staff of 'pros' managing the war bond program and in turn they knew the opinion makers in the media field. . . . Parenthetically, the Treasury also had the money to finance this program—it controlled the Stabilization Fund from the devaluation of the dollar and its use was not subject to scrutiny or audit by any other authority. I am not suggesting that the Treasury bought public opinion, but it had no budgeting problems in turning Bretton Woods into a War Bond drive."[1]

As Morgenthau's chief agent for Congressional relations during the Bretton Woods debate, White had already nailed his colors to the mast in a *Foreign Affairs* article in January, 1945. Here he deployed a number of preemptive arguments which were to be heard throughout the debate on Capitol Hill in the following spring.[2]

First White pointed out that a return to the Gold Standard was "not a policy we can hope to see widely accepted." The British especially appeared to be convinced that many of their economic troubles between the wars were due to the overvaluation of the pound in the 1920's to its pre-1914 parity.

The Fund, on the other hand, obtained many of the stabilizing advantages of the Gold Standard without the rigidities which had led to the competitive depreciation of the prewar years. White maintained that the world "needs assurance that whatever changes are made in exchange rates will be solely for the purpose of correcting a balance of payments which cannot be adjusted in any other way. The world needs assurance that exchange depreciation will not be used as a device for obtaining competitive advantage in international trade. . . ."

A generation later, in our own time, when inflation has become a major source of financial instability in the Western community, criticism of the fixed exchange rates favored by the International Monetary Fund is commonplace. A frequent comment, for example, is that the Fund's rules that each country must attempt to maintain the official price of its currency within 1 percent of its value in dollars precludes efforts to let national exchange rates reflect differing stages of economic growth and inflation. But as we can see from White's defense, one of the primary preoccupations of the men of Bretton Woods was not inflation, but deflation and the consequent competitive devaluation common in the 1930's.

White's emphasis here was clearly on domestic correctives, implying some measure of deflation, as the usual means of adjusting a country's balance of payments. But, White went on, the Fund "would not force upon a country a rigid exchange rate that can be maintained only by a severe deflation of income, wage rates, and domestic prices. Nor if a change in exchange rates is necessary to correct a fundamental disequilibrium, could the Fund object on the grounds of the domestic social or political policies of a country: it cannot be placed in the position of judging such policies. . . ." The Fund therefore provided for "a stable and orderly pattern of exchange rates without restrictive rigidity."

One of the major criticisms of Bretton Woods in the United States was that it would put American resources into the control of an international organization. Hence, in his *Foreign Affairs* article, on this sensitive question of international liquidity, White repudiated charges that the Fund was a device for lending dollars cheaply. Given the revolving structure of the Fund, "the fact is that if over a period of time all countries were to maintain their international payments in equilibrium, the distribution of the Fund's resources would not only be restored to its original position, but because of the growth in monetary reserves, even strengthened."

White also repudiated that argument that the "scarce-currency" clause would mean unlimited liability for the United States: "Very definitely this country assumes no moral responsibility for a scarcity of dollars. The technical representatives of the United States have made it clear to other countries . . . that a scarcity of dollars cannot be accepted as evidence of our responsibility for the distortion of the balance of payments. . . ." White stressed that the responsibility for the correction of a maladjustment was not a unilateral one placed on "the country whose currency is scarce." Debtor countries also had responsibilities. Here White was implying the "active" conditional nature of the Fund's operation, as opposed to the "passive," unconditional interpretation favored by Keynes.

Therefore it was a basic error to assume that the purpose of the Fund was, in White's words, "to provide additional exchange resources. Primarily the Fund is the means for establishing and maintaining stability, order and freedom in exchange transactions." Administration spokesmen thus emphasized throughout the Bretton Woods debate the conditional access to the Fund's resources, as a country's right to assistance was predicated upon the harmony of its policies with the wider purposes of the Fund. It was pointed out that in any case, exchange controls and other such restrictions would be abolished in the coming multilateral trading regime.

White's emphasis on the "soundness" of the Fund, therefore, meant that he stressed in this *Foreign Affairs* essay that exchange rates would be altered only when a trading imbalance could not be cured "in any other way." This implied the primacy, as we have noted, of internal correctives before depreciation as a means of payments adjustment, hardly the emphasis given by Keynes and other British spokesmen. So, too, was White's interpretation of the "scarce-currency" clause and the conditional, "active" nature of the Fund's operations different from the British interpretation. But it was clearly understandable why White should use the ambiguities in the Agreements to defend the internationalist and idealistic aspects of the Fund.

The pervasive "key-currency" argument, however, was ultimately based less on the orthodox concept of sound finance than on the mutual dependence of the United States and Great Britain. In his *Foreign Affairs* article on the Monetary Fund, White used "Universal" arguments to rebut Professor Williams's thesis. He stated that the British share of world trade in 1937 was 15 percent, and that of the United States 12 percent. He went on to ask: "Is it of no importance to achieve currency stability in the countries carrying on nearly 75 percent of world trade among themselves?" White considered that "the emphasis on the key currencies in which international payments are made seems to me completely mistaken. The dollar and sterling are of course the most important currencies; but the currencies of other countries are also important to the extent that they affect volume of international trade and investment."

White went on to cite the example of New Orleans cotton in 1931, the price of which had dropped drastically as a result of devaluations abroad. Moreover, a loan to Britain would burden that country with a postwar dollar debt. "On the other hand," the Fund and the Bank would be "a real help" in providing a sound postwar trading pattern. The general thrust of White's comprehensive defense of Bretton Woods was to insist that the new institutions would be adequate to deal with the problems of both the postwar transitional period and after.

In an article accompanying White's, Morgenthau emphasized, in much the same key, the internationalist aspects of Bretton Woods as opposed to isolationism and "power politics."[3] He invoked the fate of the Versailles Treaty, and suggested that "we must always keep in mind that other nations are anxiously asking whether the U.S. has the desire and ability to cooperate effectively in establishing world peace." Morgenthau warned that the problem of postwar finance was a general one, and that "the establishment of an exclusive Anglo-American condominium would not be the appropriate means of dealing with international monetary problems."

Clearly, the Treasury's general strategy was to meet its critics head on in the debate on Bretton Woods.

However, in addition to these arguments deployed by the defenders of Bretton Woods as the enabling legislation passed through Congress between April and July, 1945, the administration also decided on a significant legislative concession to conservative opinion. Written into the Bretton Woods Agreements Act was the creation of a National Advisory Council on International Monetary and Financial Problems. This was a Cabinet-level committee chaired by the Secretary of the Treasury which would, in effect, oversee the operations of the Fund and the Bank.

Thus the American executive director of the Fund would need to have the Council's approval before casting his vote on any necessary matter. The Council, for example, would have to approve before the American director could vote the dollar a scarce currency. The American director was also to oppose any use by the Fund of its resources for relief and reconstruction. This concession to Congressional sentiment meant, of course, that those provisions of the Fund stating that its resources were only conditionally available were reinforced. In a wider political sense, it was an astute concession by the administration which was bound to influence critics of Bretton Woods, concerned that the Fund and the Bank might not be operated in the national interests of the United States.

With the Treasury's flank covered by the creation of the National Advisory Council, the way was open to insist on the overall advantages of the Fund and the Bank. Administration spokesmen affirmed that the resources of the Fund would not be unconditionally available, that exchange restrictions and controls would soon disappear, and that removal of financial controls would be matched by progress in liberating commercial policy. A provision was written into the Bretton Woods legislation stating that the financial obligations enshrined in the Fund would have to be complemented by parallel concessions in the field of commercial policy.[4] The multilateral regime of the postwar planners would soon be at hand, it was optimistically implied.

Moreover, in defending the Bretton Woods Agreements before the House committee, White strongly emphasized the value of the Fund and the Bank as a contribution to peace:

> MR. PATMAN. . . . Dr. White, if we had adopted something like the Bretton Woods Agreements back in the early twenties, and it had worked as you expect this to work, would that have had any effect in preventing the war we are in now?
>
> MR. WHITE. I think it would very definitely have made a considerable contribution to checking the war and possibly might even have prevented it. . . .
>
> MR. SMITH. Do you think we must have this fund?
>
> MR. WHITE. I think we will make a very serious error if we do not have it. I think history will look back and indict those who fail to vote the approval of the Bretton Woods proposals in the same way that we now look back and indict certain groups in 1920 who prevented our adherence to an international organization designed for the purpose of preventing wars. . . .[5]

At the end of May, 1945, the House Committee on Banking and Currency reported favorably on the enabling legislation. On June 7 the House of Representatives voted overwhelmingly for Bretton Woods, 345 to 18.

However, in the succeeding hearings before the Senate Committee on Banking and Currency, there was a slightly different emphasis in the arguments against the Bretton Woods legislation. Here the leading conservative Republican opponent of Bretton Woods, Robert A. Taft, made an issue of the "key-currency" arguments. Would it not be preferable to abandon Bretton Woods in favor of a possible arrangement with the British inside the framework of an international economic conference?

The administration stuck to its guns. It considered that a key-currency agreement was unnecessary, and in any case, perhaps, such an arrangement would not have been politically possible at this time. The Fund and the Bank could cope with the reconstruction problem, helped by relief measures and orthodox financing through existing institutions.

Moreover, from the very beginning of the development of the White Plan, its author, as we have seen, had envisaged the Fund and the Bank as supplanting such bilateral arrangements as that proposed by the supporters of the key-currency approach. It will be recalled that White had told Keynes in London in October, 1942, that it was necessary to avoid an Anglo-Saxon financial "gang-up." At the same time, the working of the Fund still depended on the prior achievement of postwar economic equilibrium, and here sterling clearly had an important world role that had to be sustained. However, according to Ansel Luxford, White now "dug in . . . and took an irrevocable position on this issue."[6]

A few months later, Senator Taft stated that in executive session before the Senate Committee, White had said that the British did not need a loan, or if so, it could be worked through the Export-Import Bank: "He was afraid it would interfere with the Bretton Woods Agreements."[7] Quite consistently White was already on public record as to the unnecessary alternative of special transitional aid to Britain:

> Some critics carry the key currencies concept so far that they completely identify postwar monetary problems with the British balance of payments in the postwar period. . . . A loan to Britain to enable her to establish exchange stability and freedom from exchange control will not of itself help significantly with Britain's problem, or with the world's problem of establishing a sound postwar pattern of international payments. Such a loan might burden Britain with a dollar debt while making no real contribution toward balancing Britain's international payments. On the other hand, the Fund and the Bank, by providing the favorable conditions necessary for expanding world trade and investment, would be of real help in establishing a sound postwar pattern of international payments and would contribute substantially to prosperity in this country and abroad.[8]

Clearly, the difficulties of attempting to defend additional transitional aid to Britain, even in defense of American interests, posed obvious problems to the Treasury. Yet behind the universalism of the language in which Bretton Woods was presented to Congress there lay the reality that any multilateral regime would depend on the closest possible collaboration between the United States and Great Britain. Moreover, the world of 1937 was certainly not the world of 1945 as White had half implied in his defense of the Fund.

But White's position did not go completely unchallenged in the Senate hearings. Professor Williams, who had come to see the key-currency conception and the Bretton Woods program as complementary, had already deprecated the presentation of the Fund and the Bank as an alternative to transitional aid. He continued to emphasize in the hearings the "extremely difficult" transition problem of the United Kingdom.[9]

In the broader aspects of the debate there was widespread support for Bretton Woods in the Senate committee. As Senator Fulbright put it, "there is a feeling that we must do something a little different. . . . There is a tendency to say we must take a chance."[10] Concurrently with these hearings, the United Nations Charter had been unanimously signed at San Francisco on June 26, 1945, and in the words of Richard Gardner, "A new era seemed to be dawning. Issues of monetary and financial policy were easily confused with other issues—regionalism and universalism, war and peace, isolationism and internationalism. There was a natural temptation to exploit the temporary enthusiasm for international cooperation and to claim all good things for the Bank and the Fund."[11]

Accordingly, after a debate on the floor of the Senate in which Senator Taft was isolated from his internationalist Republican colleagues, the Bretton Woods Agreements Act was approved on July 19 by a vote of 61–16. After all vicissitudes the amended White Plan, the result of so much devoted labor by the American and British negotiators, had passed through Congress. But by now Morgenthau's successor had already been named by President Truman, and White's position in the department could hardly be the same.

21

"TERMINAL"

The problem which presents itself is how to render Germany harmless
as a potential aggressor, and at the same time to enable her to play her
part in the necessary rehabilitation of Europe. . . .

—STIMSON TO TRUMAN, July, 1945

. . . the United States possessed a new weapon, the atomic bomb, which
could defeat any aggressor.

—TRUMAN TO DE GAULLE, August, 1945

AT THE beginning of July, 1945, White could justifiably feel some sense
of achievement. The Bretton Woods Agreements were proceeding almost
triumphantly through Congress. The Interim Directive, JCS 1067, had
been dispatched to Eisenhower. And though gold shipments to China
had been accelerated, White would apparently continue to be closely
involved in the Treasury's operations in the Far East.

On May 4, as heavy fighting on Okinawa presaged a coming Allied
invasion of Japan, Coe reported to Morgenthau that General Douglas
MacArthur was willing to have "a Treasury staff move forward to the
Philippines." It was felt, Coe wrote, that the office should be established
as a "general Treasury office capable of assuming broader responsibilities
as the situation warrants. As in the case of other Treasury field offices, it
will report to and receive directions from Harry White as Assistant Secretary."[1]

However, of all the policy issues in which White had been involved,
"the basic issue" still remained to be resolved at the forthcoming Big
Three conference at Potsdam, "Terminal," scheduled for mid-July. This
was the question of the future of Germany.

On June 29 in a Treasury conference with Morgenthau, White thought that "if somebody ought to go to Berlin, I have a good nomination, Harry White. I think it's important, and I think Treasury ought to be represented there and if it is important enough for Assistant Secretary [of State] Clayton to go, certainly the Treasury ought to have someone there on this Peace Conference and German business, and it seems that only next to yourself can I support your point of view and help it along."

Morgenthau said that the only thing that worried him was that White would be so tired during the next month when he, Morgenthau, went to Moscow. White thought that he would "rest up in Moscow after Berlin. That was the general idea." The Secretary remarked that he was going to raise the question of who was going to Berlin with President Truman, and that he did have White in the back of his mind.[2]

In the event, White did not attend the Potsdam Conference, nor "rest up" in Moscow, obviously unaware as he was of the extent of Truman's opposition to the Treasury policy on postwar Germany. In a significant passage in his memoirs, Truman records that on May 16 he met with Stimson to discuss the rehabilitation of Europe. The President "expressed the fear of famine in Europe which might lead to chaos. I made it clear that also I was opposed to what was then loosely called the Morgenthau Plan. . . . I had never been in favor of that plan when I was in the Senate, and since reaching the White House I had come to feel more strongly about it."

Truman recalled to Stimson his discussions with his friend Senator Elbert Thomas of Utah: "The problem, as Senator Thomas and I talked about it, was to help unify Europe by linking up the breadbasket with the industrial centers through a free flow of trade." Clearly Truman had believed, like Stimson, from the very outset of his Presidency, that the German economy was necessary for a stable, peaceful and democratic Europe. During June, therefore, the President, in consultation with the British, ordered Eisenhower to take "all steps necessary" to increase coal production in Western Germany.[3]

Specifically, Truman's attitude on the economic future of Germany was illustrated by the development of his policy toward the proceedings of the Moscow Reparations Commission created at Yalta. It will be recalled that the Americans and the Russians had agreed at the Crimea that the Commission "should take in its initial studies as a basis of discussion" the Soviet figure of $20 billion, half of that figure going to the Soviet Union. The British had reserved their position over a precise figure. But clearly the emphasis at Yalta, where the problem of security from Germany was still a pervasive factor in the discussions, was on compensation from the Reich and industrial disarmament rather than on preserving a viable German economy with the "ability to pay" for imports.

Truman—like White—had quickly realized the significance of the vagueness of the Yalta reparations agreement, and on April 27 he replaced Lubin as American representative on the Moscow Reparations Commission with the former California oil executive, Edwin A. Pauley. Lubin was to remain as his deputy. Truman felt that the position "required a tough bargainer, someone who could be as tough as Molotov." Moreover, Truman writes, Pauley "understood my attitude on the reparations question."[4]

It will be recalled that the instructions to the American representative on the Moscow Reparations Commission, approved in May, were ambiguous in that they contained both clauses emphasizing that Germany should retain the ability to pay for imports and that there should be heavy capital reparations, as emphasized by White. Truman's attitude, which Pauley understood as his "tough" negotiator, was to stress the former rather than the latter provisions. In his memoirs, Truman makes incisively clear that there was "one pitfall" he intended to avoid in the peace settlement: "We did not intend to pay, under any circumstances, the reparations bill for Europe. We wanted a European recovery plan that would put Europe on its feet. We did not intend to send billions of dollars to Russia just because there was no possible way for Germany to pay vast reparations—although morally she should have been made to pay."[5]

When, therefore, the Moscow Reparations Commission met in June, it was still American policy, as enshrined in Pauley's instructions, to dismantle or remove industry associated with the German war machine. But Pauley was to insist that enough German industrial capacity should be left to pay for imports into Germany, as a first charge, before reparations payments were delivered. As Feis describes it, "Pauley had wished to stipulate that only excess of exportable German products as were not needed to pay for essential imports into Germany should be allocated as reparations." With slightly different emphasis Alperovitz writes that "in this fashion, the American interest in a reasonably strong German economy would be given first priority, while reparations would be residual."

Moreover, using much the same "first charge on imports" formula, the British Chancellor, Sir John Anderson, had submitted a "decisive paper" on reparations to the War Cabinet in March, 1945. This had stressed that to avoid paying for German reparations, the United Kingdom should insist that "any supplies necessary to put Germany in a position to pay for reparations should be a first charge on reparation and must be paid for by those receiving deliveries."[6]

In this shift away from not only the White-Morgenthau proposals on Germany, but from the substance of the Yalta reparations agreement, Pauley at Moscow thus refused to accept the $20 billion figure. He personally believed in avoiding a fixed target figure in favor of percentages. The State Department was not ready to move completely away from a fixed target figure but thought that $20 billion was too high, and instead told Pauley there was no objection to discussing a figure in the $12–14 billion range. The Russians, of course, continued to insist on the $20 billion figure. Once again the issue, and with it the future of Germany, was stalemated at Moscow, and postponed for consideration by the Big Three at Potsdam. While adhering to the form of the Yalta reparations agreement, therefore, Truman was moving away from its content as his "tough" negotiator insisted on the German "ability to pay" for imports.[7] In this framework of negotiation it is difficult to see what place there was for White at Potsdam, at least as an American negotiator.

By the end of June, 1945, President Truman had already replaced six members of Roosevelt's cabinet with his own men. At the beginning of that month, Morgenthau had asked Truman if the rumors of Byrnes's forthcoming appointment as Secretary of State were true. The President had replied noncommittally, and the rumors continued. Then, on June 30, the appointment of the new Secretary of State was announced, and on July 3 Byrnes was sworn in. He would, of course, accompany the President to Potsdam.

Two days later, on July 5, Morgenthau called on Truman, and asked if he could go with the President to Potsdam. According to Truman's account of the meeting, in which he writes that "he did not like" the Morgenthau Plan, he told Morgenthau that the Secretary of the Treasury was badly needed in the United States, more so than in Potsdam. Morgenthau replied that it was necessary for him to go, and that if he could not he would have to quit. Truman goes on: "'All right,' I replied, 'if that is the way you feel, I accept your resignation right now.' And I did. That was the end of the conversation and of the Morgenthau Plan."[8]

White, along with the other senior Treasury staff, was quickly told the news by Morgenthau, and the event was announced on the fifth. But no announcement was made of Morgenthau's successor, and at first Truman had intended that the news should be withheld until after his return from Europe. However, a few hours before he was due to leave the White House for Potsdam on the night of July 6, the President announced that on his return from Europe Fred Vinson, the Director of War Mobilization and Reconversion, would be nominated as the new Secretary of the Treasury. Vinson had been a Congressman for Kentucky for many years, as well as a judge. A few days later Judge Samuel Roseman told Morgenthau that Truman had been "under great pressure" because of "the succession" and that Vinson, who had been expected to go to Potsdam, had been "pulled off the boat" at the last minute on the afternoon of the sixth. President Truman had decided to leave Vinson in Washington as the senior Cabinet officer while he was in Europe.[9]

There were other reasons besides the obvious policy ones for Morgenthau's removal. Under the nineteenth-century succession law then in operation, after the succession of Vice President—which was provided for, of course, in the Constitution—the line ran from the Vice President to the Secretary of State to the Secretary of the Treasury and so on following the seniority of Cabinet departments. (A new succession law was passed in 1947.) One of the reasons for Stettinius' replacement by Byrnes as Secretary of State had been the desire of the party managers to have a formally elected senior official (and a good party man) next in line to Truman. The precipitate arrangements involving Morgenthau's replacement by Vinson at the last minute before the President's departure for Europe meant similar considerations had been invoked against the untoward event of both Truman and Byrnes not returning to Washington from their journey across the Atlantic.

With this fundamental matter settled, Truman left the White House late on July 6. He and Byrnes then embarked the following morning aboard the heavy cruiser *Augusta*, moored at Newport News, Virginia. "It was a wonderful crossing," Truman records in his memoirs, "the *Augusta* had a fine band which played during the dinner hour each evening. . . ."

On July 9, the United Press reported from Washington that a "host of advisers and assistant secretaries" would leave the United States Treasury with Morgenthau. Only two subordinates had a chance of remaining, the story went on. One was Under Secretary Daniel Bell, who was popular with "bankers and businessmen as well as with the President." The other was Harry Dexter White, who would remain for the rather different reason that "he was one of the few men in the country who fully understood the proposed International Monetary Fund set up by the Bretton Woods plan."[10]

A few days later on July 14, Morgenthau discussed the fate of the 900 volumes of the Morgenthau Diaries with White and other Treasury staff. The retiring Secretary wanted the Diaries to be placed, under restrictions for twenty-five years, at the Roosevelt Memorial Library, Hyde Park, a government institution. Daniel Bell told Morgenthau that there were some things in the Diaries "which would be embarrassing to a lot of people. We have talked quite frankly in your conferences about a lot of people." Mrs. Klotz agreed that it would be "very embarrassing," while John Pehle thought twenty-five years' restriction would cover all eventualities. Pehle, like Bell, thought that a Congressional Committee could subpoena the Diaries. In one of his last wisecracks in a Morgenthau conference, White remarked that "I just want time enough to get out of town. (Laughter)"[11]

On July 23, 1945, a few days after the Senate had passed the Bretton Woods legislation, Vinson took up his duties as Secretary of the Treasury. With the exception of Albert Gallatin of Pennsylvania, Morgenthau had served longer than any other incumbent of the United States Treasury when he left after more than eleven and a half years in office.

White remained behind as Assistant Secretary of the Treasury. On July 21, he wrote to Morgenthau at his home on Connecticut Avenue. "Dear Mr. Secretary," the letter began, "you have given a big slice of your life to the affairs of the nation and the world. To my mind your leaving the Treasury deprives this country not only of an upright public servant, but also of a leader with vision and drive. You owe it to the people to continue the good fight. May the way be found soon! It has been a privilege to have worked with you in these crucial years toward our common objectives."

Morgenthau replied on August 4, thanking White. A postscript to his letter added that "I am sure we will have many opportunities to work together in the Public Interest." But this letter ended the formal association between the two men.[12]

At the Potsdam Conference, the Big Three had still not reached agreement on Germany when Morgenthau left the Treasury. Attlee replaced Churchill. Then, at the close of the conference a virtual "package deal" was arrived at which decided the future of Germany for years to come.

For their part, the Anglo-Americans, "pending the final determination of Poland's western border," accepted the demarcation of this border along the Oder-Western Neisse line. The former German territories to the east were to be placed under "the administration of the Polish state," in the language of the Potsdam Protocol.

No agreement on reparations had been possible within the Yalta framework, and the British and American delegations had resisted the Soviet arguments on very large industrial reparations. There had been no Western response to Soviet suggestions that the Ruhr should be placed under four-power control. Byrnes had stuck to his position that American imports would have to be paid for before reparations would be delivered.

Eventually, agreement was reached on the basis that the United States and the United Kingdom would satisfy their reparation claims from their own zones of Germany, and the Russians would take theirs, and that of the Poles, from the Soviet zone. In addition, 15 percent of German industrial capital equipment not needed for the peacetime German economy was to be sent to the Soviet Union from the Western zones in exchange for Soviet deliveries of coal, food, timber and other commodities. Another 10 percent of German industrial capital equipment not necessary for the peacetime economy was to be sent to the Soviet Union without any exchange.

But illustrating the tortuous nature of the Potsdam compromise, excluding these deliveries, "payment of reparations should leave enough resources to enable the German people to subsist without external assistance." Thus proceeds of exports from current production would be available "in the first place" to pay for Allied Control Council-approved imports.

Within the framework of a nominal central administration of occupied Germany by the four-power Control Council, a *de facto* economic partition of Germany had been decided. There would be Western dismantling of German war industry, and JCS 1067 would remain in force, but essentially the Anglo-Americans had negotiated at Potsdam the suspension, rather than the destruction, of German industrial power in their zone. This power, it came to be realized, could be revived given a favorable climate of opinion in the West.

This was hardly "the long-range program" for which White had fought so hard the previous year. Central to White's advocacy of destroying Germany as an industrial power was the thesis, frequently expressed as we have seen, that only by such measures could a future German resurgence be prevented and "peace" ensured. And even as late as June, 1945, with the basic issue of security from Germany to be solved, Truman had still not completely jettisoned the framework of the Yalta reparations agreement, which at the least envisaged large-scale industrial reparation from the Reich. "The problem which presents itself," Stimson wrote to Truman at Potsdam on July 16, "is how to render Germany harmless as a potential aggressor and at the same time to enable her to play her part in the necessary rehabilitation of Europe."[13]

That same day, July 16, 1945, the problem outlined by Stimson and which had lain at the center of all the wartime debates on the future of Germany was solved, as Truman soon saw. Later, on the sixteenth, Stimson received a brief coded message from Washington which told him that the first atomic bomb had been exploded earlier that day in the New Mexico desert. Another short coded message followed the next day, and then a full report arrived at Potsdam from General Leslie Groves, the Manhattan Project director, on July 21.

Groves reported that "in a remote section of the Alamogordo Air Base, New Mexico, the first full-scale test was made of the implosion type atomic fission bomb. For the first time in history there was a nuclear explosion. . . . The test was successful beyond the most optimistic assessment of anyone. . . ." Groves, the engineer in charge of building the Pentagon, went on, "I no longer consider the Pentagon a safe shelter from such a bomb."[14] When Stimson read Groves's extraordinary message to Truman, the President was "tremendously pepped up by it . . . and said that it gave him an entirely new feeling of confidence."[15]

The atomic bomb had thus resolved, for Truman, the dilemma of European security from Germany which had been posed by Stimson in such succinct terms on July 16, 1945. With the bomb there was now no overwhelming need for the total "industrial disarmament" of Germany, still less for the measures White had advocated. And for Truman, perhaps, whatever the public expectations at the time, the atomic bomb made less necessary the preservation of the wartime grand alliance about which he had had such doubts since the beginning of his Presidency in April, 1945. In his memoirs, Truman writes that during his return home from Potsdam, he considered that the conference had enabled him "to see what we and the West had to face in the future." The Russians, Truman considered, were "relentless bargainers," their foreign policy was based on the premise of a major American depression, and Stalin wanted the Black Sea straits.[16]

Two weeks after returning from Potsdam, and a week after Japan had sued for peace, the President pulled the threads of his German policy together when he met with General de Gaulle in the White House on August 22. Truman told the General that there was no longer any need for specific guarantees against Germany such as international control of the Ruhr for "the United States possessed a new weapon, the atomic bomb, which could defeat any aggressor."[17]

By this time, White's effective career in government was largely over. The momentum of that great career was to persist for over eighteen months, carrying White during 1946 from the Treasury to the International Monetary Fund. But on August 21 or 22, 1945, Elizabeth Bentley had at last reported to the FBI in New Haven, Connecticut. By November, White himself was under FBI surveillance and was to remain so for most of the rest of his life.

PART V

LAST ACT

1945–48

FUND EXECUTIVE DIRECTOR

It has been our belief from the beginning that the Fund constitutes a very powerful instrument for the coordination of monetary policies, for the prevention of economic warfare, and for an attempt to foster sound monetary policies throughout the world. . . .
— HARRY DEXTER WHITE, SAVANNAH, March, 1946

WHATEVER White's incursions into higher foreign policy during the course of the war, there can be little doubt that the author of the White Plan was also a genuine idealist for international trade. But the abrupt ending of the Pacific war on August 15, 1945, now brought to the forefront of Anglo-American relations the state of the postwar world in which the Bretton Woods institutions were expected to begin their work. A leading Anglo-American issue was the transitional problem of the British economy. Could the Bretton Woods institutions cope with this problem?

In the Congressional hearings on the Bretton Woods Agreements, it will be recalled, White had emphasized that the Fund and the Bank would make transitional assistance for Britain largely unnecessary. Bretton Woods had been presented as an alternative to transitional measures. Moreover, it will be recalled, White had expected that the Fund and the Bank would operate in an increasingly united and peaceful world.

Despite portents in Washington that Lend-Lease would be cut off with the ending of hostilities, it was expected in London that British transitional financing would be greatly helped by the Stage II Lend-Lease promised at the Octagon Conference. At Quebec it was assumed that Stage II, the period between the defeat of Germany and that of Japan, would last eighteen months.

But at the climax of the war, with public attention in both the United

States and Great Britain understandably focused on apocalyptic military events, there was still little appreciation in either country of the precariousness of the British economy. This economy, together with the role of sterling, was expected to be one of the two main pillars of the forthcoming multilateral trading regime. However, the facts were not too reassuring. After six years of total war, a paper submitted to the British War Cabinet in August, 1945, noted that without new aid from the United States the country would be "virtually bankrupt."[1]

Following VJ-Day, the Truman administration was almost under statutory obligation to end Lend-Lease, and on August 21 the President announced that all programs would be discontinued. Terms would have to be negotiated for goods in the "pipeline." In view of the administration's promises and the language of the Lend-Lease legislation, it seems unlikely that anything much more than temporary tapering arrangements could have been made pending the transitional agreements which would now have to be negotiated. At one stroke had come "the end of the principal link which had bound the economies of the Grand Alliance together."[2]

Attlee, never given to overstatement, told the Commons on August 24 that Britain was "in a very serious financial situation."[3] The Fund, of course, was specifically precluded from financing relief and reconstruction, and the once-ambitious scope of the Bank as an instrument of transitional aid had been scaled down before Bretton Woods. In any case, the Bretton Woods insitutions were not yet in being. Keynes was now to lead a British delegation to Washington to wind up the Lend-Lease account and to negotiate new measures of aid for Britain.

White did not take part in the Washington negotiations which led to the famous American loan to Britain. His pre-eminent position in the Treasury had ended with Morgenthau's departure. He had staked his claim on Bretton Woods rather than on special transitional measures, and in any case, as one of the Washington negotiators told the writer, White probably didn't believe in the loan.

The loan negotiations formally began on September 13, 1945, after Keynes and Halifax had led the British delegation into the Federal Reserve Building on Constitution Avenue. Keynes frankly presented his case for American assistance on mutual self-interest. Without such assistance, Britain would have to maintain wartime controls, and perhaps develop bilateral trading relations. With transitional help, Britain would move as quickly as possible to a worldwide liberal trading regime, as envisaged at Bretton Woods.

But the contrasting domestic political background to the negotiations in the two countries was not propitious. British opinion tended to regard American aid as a matter of right for wartime sacrifices. In the United States, on the other hand, where confidence was at its height, a swift advance to a liberal trading regime was envisaged, with a lowering of wartime political barriers to the free exchange of goods and services. In this period, when the sterling area was considered a potential rival to American interests, some months before a major Soviet threat to the West was discerned, "there was a feeling that the various Western nations whose freedom and integrity had been saved from a deadly threat, must now fend for themselves and settle down with discipline to the task of repairing their own homes."[4]

Moreover, personal relations between Vinson and Keynes were not good. Some of Keynes's shafts were not appreciated by the new Secretary of the Treasury, who regarded his objective as one of discovering "the popular will and translat[ing] that into government policy." The American popular will in September, 1945, was understandably not too concerned with international events. To some sally by Keynes, Vinson would reply: "Mebbe so, Lord Keynes, mebbe so. But down where I come from, folks don't look at things that way."[5]

There were also differences between them over substantive points. Keynes had originally hoped for a grant-in-aid of perhaps $6 billion, and when it was realized that this was out of the question the negotiators moved on to consider the interest and size of the loan. It was agreed that the interest should be the very reasonable figure of 2 percent, repayable over fifty years, with a waiver clause for bad times when Britain did not earn an adequate amount of foreign exchange.

The size of the loan was really based on a figure thought to be acceptable to Congress. Vinson suggested $3.5 billion, Clayton and the State Department, $4 billion. At this stage of the negotiations White still retained some of his previous influence in the Treasury, and as we have seen, during the Bretton Woods hearings he had deprecated the need for transitional British finance in addition to the Fund and the Bank. At this time, differences had developed between White and two of his senior colleagues, Edward M. Bernstein and Ansel F. Luxford, who were more in sympathy with British needs.

During the loan negotiations, when a technical committee was set up by White to advise on the British financial position, Bernstein and Luxford were deliberately excluded. The committee produced "extremely moderate" estimates of British needs for American assistance and, alarmed, Bernstein and Luxford on their own initiative sent Vinson a memorandum. They thought that the technical committee's estimates were too low, that the Anglo-American arrangements would break down, and that the administration would be forced again to come to Congress for more aid to Britain.[6]

"In this context," Luxford remarks of the joint memorandum,

> I do not believe that White was opposed to a British loan, although definitely he was on the low side, and we were on the high side. My friendly criticism is that he did not fight as hard as he should have for a proper figure and deluded Vinson and others into believing the loan figure was adequate. But Vinson had informal advice before the execution of the loan agreement that the amount was too small [the Bernstein-Luxford memorandum Gardner refers to]. He acknowledged the validity of our position but stated it was impossible to get a high figure through Congress.[7]

In the event, President Truman split the difference between the Treasury and the State Department, setting the figure for the "line-of-credit" at $3.75 billion. Vinson, who was, of course, convinced of the necessity for the loan, strongly defended the Anglo-American agreement in the subsequent Congressional hearings. In the circumstances of the time, bearing in mind the state of Congressional opinion, there cannot be much doubt that, inadequate as the amount probably was, "American generosity was stretched to what at that point was its limit."[8]

The British loan was only one of several agreements reached in the Washington negotiations with the same general objective of expediting the multilateral trading regime. Of great importance was the remarkably generous Lend-Lease settlement, a "complete and final" ending of the account. It could be argued that in view of the principle of "equality of sacrifice" this was no more than was due from one ally to another, yet the administration was under pressure from Congress to exact some sort of payment. By removing this potential debt, the Lend-Lease settlement, it was hoped, would also facilitate the advent of the expected liberal trading regime.[9]

Over $20 billion in wartime Lend-Lease from the United States to Britain was written off. Another $6 billion in American Lend-Lease supplies in the United Kingdom, together with American war surplus property, was transferred to Britain for $532,000,000. For "pipeline" supplies delivered after hostilities $118,000,000 was charged. The $650,000,000 outstanding was to be paid for at the same terms of the loan. Reverse Lend-Lease of $6 billion was erased at the same time.

The Lend-Lease settlement took note of the common benefits received by the two governments "in their defeat of their enemies." But the settlement also took note of the "general obligations assumed by them in

Article VII of the Mutual Aid Agreement of February 23, 1942, and the understandings agreed upon this day with regard to commercial policy." Discussions were to continue to achieve the multilateral objectives mentioned in Article VII. Thus this pledge by the British in the Lend-Lease settlement could be presented to Congress as the "benefit" which the administration had received as the "consideration" for Lend-Lease, as demanded by the legislature in 1941.

Closely linked, therefore, with these pledges was the Anglo-American understanding on commercial policy also negotiated on Washington in late 1945. It will be recalled that the commercial policy talks on tariffs, preferences and other associated matters had been initiated during the 1943 Law Mission to Washington. Further informal Anglo-American talks had been held in London in early 1945. Now in Washington, toward the end of that year, Anglo-American agreement was reached on the principles of liberalizing trade and embodied in the "Proposals for Consideration by an International Conference on Trade and Employment."[10]

Publication was, regrettably perhaps, timed to coincide with the loan agreement so that the American government could claim the commercial agreement on the "Proposals" as one of the benefits for the loan and the Lend-Lease settlement. But the British government, for reasons of domestic sensitivity over the issue of Imperial Preference, was not willing to appear as one of the joint sponsors of the "Proposals." Instead, the Joint Statement by the two countries, published at the same time as the Financial Agreement on December 6, 1945, said that the British government was "in full agreement on all important points in these proposals and accepts them as a basis for international discussions; and it will, in common with the United States Government, use its best endeavours to bring such discussions to a successful conclusion, in the light of views expressed by other countries...."[11]

But the most important instrument of multilateralism agreed at Washington was the Anglo-American Financial Agreement signed on December 6, 1945, by Vinson and Halifax. One of the primary purposes of the $3.75 billion "line-of-credit" was "to assist the Government of the United Kingdom to assume the obligations of multilateral trade, as defined in this and other agreements." Chief among the multilateral obligations enshrined in the loan was the famous provision making current account sterling convertible within one year of the loan agreement coming into effect.

The feelings aroused by both the Bretton Woods Agreements and the loan in Britain were ventilated within a few days of the signing of the Financial Agreement. On December 12 Parliament was asked to vote for a composite resolution approving Bretton Woods, the Lend-Lease settlement, the financial Agreement, and also to "welcome the initiative" of the American government in presenting the commercial "Proposals."

In a stormy Commons debate on December 12 and 13, a leading opponent of the multilateral view, Robert Boothby, called the loan agreement "our economic Munich." The Conservatives, including Churchill and Eden, officially abstained, although many voted against, and the resolution was finally approved 345 to 98.

Keynes, in the last great public act of his life, delivered the most effective defense of Bretton Woods and the loan, turning the tide of public opinion. On December 18, speaking in the House of Lords debate, he ridiculed the opponents of Bretton Woods as those who wished "to build up a separate economic bloc which excludes Canada and consists of countries to which we owe more than we can pay, on the basis of their agreeing to lend us money they have not got, and buy from us and one another goods we are unable to supply." Keynes thought it "crazy" to prefer the world of rival trading blocs, and considered that truly international trade "is plainly an essential condition of the world's best hope, an Anglo-American understanding, which brings us and others together in international institutions which may be in the long run the first step towards something more comprehensive. . . ."[12]

A few weeks later, in January, 1946, in forwarding the Anglo-American Financial Agreement to Congress, President Truman said with unintended ambiguity that the loan "would set the course of American and British economic relations for many years to come."

With the loan, pending Congressional approval, thought to be the instrument for dealing with Britain's transitional problem, plans were now made to implement the Anglo-American understanding on commercial policy agreed at Washington. In February, 1946, a Preparatory Committee of nineteen countries was set up by the United Nations Economic and Social Council to write a convention for consideration by an International Conference on Trade and Employment. The agenda would have as a main item the courses in the "Proposals" drafted in Washington in late 1945 by the British and American negotiators. It was agreed that the Preparatory Committee would meet in London in October, 1946, to begin work on a Charter for the proposed International Trade Organization (ITO).

Now, with the Anglo-American loan signed, and with these developing plans on commercial policy, the Fund and the Bank could come into their own. The inaugural meeting of the two Bretton Woods institutions was scheduled to take place in Savannah, Georgia, in March, 1946.

On January 23, President Truman nominated Harry Dexter White as the first American executive director of the International Monetary

Fund. The nomination was approved by the Senate on February 6, when White was confirmed for a term of two years.

White's final promotion by the American government gave him a position of much potential power and authority in the new organization. The prestige of the post of American executive director was enhanced by the fact that at this time, before the serious deterioration of East-West relations and the birth of the Marshall Plan, the Fund stood at the center of the administration's foreign economic policy.

Moreover, according to Mr. Truman in 1953, "it was originally planned that the United States would support Mr. White for the election to the top managerial position in the International Monetary Fund—that of managing director—a more important post than that of a member of the board of executive directors."[13]

On January 18, 1946, W. H. Taylor and W. M. Tomlinson of the United States Treasury called on Keynes in his London office. The United States, they reported, now planned to hold the inaugural meeting of the Governors of the Fund and the Bank at Savannah, Georgia, in March. White was looking forward to seeing Keynes there.

The Conference would determine the site of the two Bretton Woods institutions, as well as the salaries and functions of the executive directors. Such decisions would influence the operation of the Fund and the Bank from their very inception.

In this conversation with Tomlinson and Taylor, Keynes remarked that in his view the Fund should start out "with a very small and compact organization. . . . He would be very disturbed if the decision as to the size of the staff of the Fund should precede a determination of its functions."

A few days later on January 24, in a further talk with W. H. Taylor, Keynes remarked that he had seen the news of White's nomination as Fund executive director. He hoped this would not rule out White standing for the post of Fund managing director. Again expressing an implied view on the future structure of the Fund, Keynes told Taylor that "it was a British thought that their executive director would spend only a portion of his time in the U.S. and that probably the U.K. Treasury representative in Washington would be designated as the British alternate to carry out the routine functions."

Keynes also thought, according to Taylor's note, that during the passage of the British loan through Congress, "the one criticism that he felt would really contain some truth would be the charge that by making this loan to England, America would be underwriting British policy in other parts of the world."[14]

Nevertheless, whatever Keynes's thoughts at this time about the coming meeting, during February he considered that Savannah would be "just a pleasant party." Instead, at this conference where White and Keynes faced each other for the last time, "all turned out quite differently. There was a clash of wills and bitter frustration."[15]

For behind the apparently secondary matters of a site for the Bretton Woods institutions and the functions of the executive directors, lay rather more important issues of the Fund's structure at which Keynes had hinted in London. There was an issue here which had existed from the very beginning of the White-Keynes negotiations over the financial institutions and which would now have to be settled at Savannah:

Were the Fund and the Bank purely financial institutions whose direction could be entrusted to a group of international civil servants? Or did their operations have such economic and political implications as to require close control by member governments? The Articles of Agreements signed at Bretton Woods made no clear choice for either alternative. It remained for Savannah to decide between them.[16]

Vinson was in the chair at Savannah, assisted by White as the senior Treasury representative. The thrust of the conference was soon apparent. It will be remembered that the British had reserved their position at Bretton Woods on the placing of the new institutions in the United States. Keynes now thought that New York was the best site, away from "the politics of Congress and the nationalistic whispering galleries of Embassies and Legations."

However, immediately preceding the conference, Vinson had told Keynes that the American delegation had decided that the headquarters of both institutions should be placed in Washington and that "this was a final decision the merits of which they were not prepared to discuss." Vinson had taken his proposal to President Truman "to obtain his authority to make this an absolute instruction."[17]

New York, of course, was suspect in some quarters of Congress as the center of American banking and finance, and the overwhelming ascendancy of the United States in the immediate postwar world pointed to Washington. Whatever the merits of the debate, the decision to place the Fund and the Bank in Washington, was, Richard Gardner has written, "an important victory for the idea of close national control of the Bretton Woods institutions. It was to have a profound effect on their future development."[18]

A second Anglo-American dispute took place over the duties of the Fund executive directors. Article XII of the Articles of Agreement had stated that the Fund directors should "function in continuous session at the principal office of the Fund and shall meet as often as the business of the Fund shall require." (Similar language was used in the Bank Articles.) The extent of the directors' commitment had a clear bearing on the extent to which the Fund would be subjected to national control. Keynes, as we have seen, had hoped that the directors would have other work so minimizing the influence of national governments on the daily operations of the Fund.

The United States, on the other hand, supported by a majority of the delegates, wanted to have a clear role in the operations of the Fund on a daily basis, and so desired the directors and their alternates to give full-time attention to the task of running the Fund. It was decided at Savannah that it was the duty of a director and his alternates "to devote all the time and attention to the business of the Fund that its interests require, and between them, to be continuously available at the principle office of the Fund."

There was still some ambiguity here, but the American suggestion, adopted at Savannah, of highly salaried executive directors, who would clearly be employed full-time, settled the issue. The directors were voted $17,500, but Keynes refused to give British approval to the figure, "a decisive victory for the American conception" of the Fund.[19]

The Anglo-American differences at Savannah resulted from contrasting views of the Fund which had been debated, as we have seen, from the very beginnings of the White Plan and the Keynes Plan in 1942. The debate had continued through the Washington negotiations of 1943 to Bretton Woods, when a compromise had been reached. Was the Fund "active" or "passive" in its operations? Could it exercise discretion in answering members' requests for its resources? Could members withdraw a substantial part of their quota without what Keynes had once described as "policing"?

Originally, as we have seen, the larger resources of Keynes's Clearing Union would have dispensed credit more or less automatically. When the British realized that White's "limited liability" Fund would have to be adopted, they sought a compromise to make its resources unconditionally available. The Bretton Woods compromise, in Article V, as we have noted, stated that a country would be "entitled" to buy currency from the Fund provided that it was "presently needed" for payments consistent with the purpose of the Fund. But the Fund could limit resources if it thought a member was using its dispensation contrary to Fund purposes. Perhaps such language was inherent in the structure of a smaller Fund as opposed to Keynes's Clearing Union with its virtually unrestricted resources.

While Keynes had seemed to suggest to Parliament in May, 1944, that the Fund's resources would be automatically available, Congress had also been assured—and White was on record—that Fund resources were not freely obtainable in this manner. The ambiguity in the Article of Agreement had to be decided at Savannah, and the American conception of the role of the Fund's executive directors given an authoritative glossing.

It should be recalled, moreover, that during the Bretton Woods hearings, to head off Congressional criticism, the American executive directors of the Fund and the Bank had been subordinated to a Cabinet-level National Advisory Council. This, of course, further propelled the Bretton Woods organizations away from the concept of "purely financial institutions."

On March 16, 1946, the author of the White Plan emphatically laid down the conditional aspect of the Fund's operations during the discussion at Savannah on the salaries of the executive directors:

> The controversy stems from the issue as to what is the major role which the Fund and the Bank, and particularly the Fund, shall play. It has been our belief from the beginning that the Fund constitutes a very powerful instrument for the coordination of monetary policies, for the prevention of economic warfare, and for an attempt to foster sound monetary policies throughout the world. As part of the necessary machinery to implement those objectives, it was regarded by the United States and others as essential that there should be large resources available to the Fund. But I should like to call your attention to the fact that those large resources were regarded as one of the instruments to make possible the broader purposes of the Fund.

Remarking that the issue now separating the delegates at Savannah went back to the "very first conversation that we had with our British friends," White considered that the majority of members at Bretton Woods did not agree with the British approach. The Fund Articles of Agreement, White considered, contained the American view of the Fund as an active supervisor of exchange practices:

> We feel that any attempt to weaken that aspect of the Fund's operations is a threat to the Fund. . . . We submit that the thesis that salaries should be lower than necessary to attract competent men is not only a blow at the prestige of the group, not only a threat to the competence of the group, but may become, I hope undesignedly, an instrument to divert the purposes and divert the general policy

of the Fund so that it will come closer to the hearts of those who foresee in the Fund little else than a source of credit. . . .[20]

In this last debate with Keynes, White finally won his point. The executive directors were voted the salaries Keynes opposed, and future operations of the Fund tacitly reflected White's interpretation of the conditional nature of the institution's loans. Although, perhaps, it may be remarked here that with the large increases in the Fund's resources in the 1960's, with such devices as Special Drawing Rights (SDR's), providing liquidity in accordance with the needs of world trade, Keynes also won his point, but some twenty years later.

For Keynes, the outlook at Savannah was bleak. He thought the conference meant that the Americans had abandoned their agreement over the Fund, "slipping back to the old ideas of the schoolmistress." He had always repudiated those who had questioned American goodwill in the great debates on Bretton Woods: "Now at Savannah, it seemed that all his fine protestations on behalf of American goodwill and cooperativeness were belied. . . . They no longer discussed. They settled matters in advance. His castles were falling around him. . . ."[21] During the return to Washington from Savannah, Keynes was taken ill.

In London, Keynes's resilience asserted itself. During these months he had written an article on the American balance of payments, taking a relatively optimistic view of the transitional problem. In a salute to the classical economists, he considered that "there are in these matters deep undercurrents at work, natural forces one can call them, or even the invisible hand, which are operating towards equilibrium."[22]

In a closing contact between the two leading practitioners of sterling-dollar diplomacy, on March 27 White returned the proofs of the article to Keynes in the British Treasury. Agreeing on the whole with Keynes's assessment, White's letter ended: "Altogether the possibility of scarcity of dollars during the next five years seems to me, as it does to you, to be remote—barring of course untoward international political developments."[23]

On Easter Sunday, April 21, 1946, Keynes died at his home in Sussex.

With the issue of the Fund's powers finally decided in White's favor at Savannah, the Bretton Woods institutions were to begin work in May, 1946. As we have noted, the full-time role of the executive directors, to which Keynes had objected, meant that in practice there would not be automatic dispensation of the Fund's resources.

In any case, in the circumstances of the time, with an acute world "dollar shortage," when there was no absolute certainty that Fund resources would be repaid on schedule, it was understandable why the

United States should not wish to leave allocation of the Fund's considerable dollar resources to "international civil servants." When world financial equilibrium had been restored, Keynes's conception of automatic liquidity would again flourish.

However, there were also wider political aspects of the Fund's day-to-day running. These were now, at the very moment of the Fund's activation, to clash with White's original view of the organization as almost a supranational body "fostering monetary policies throughout the world," as he had put it at Savannah.

As we have seen, there was a strong idealistic, almost utopian, element in the events surrounding the inception of White's Stabilization Fund in the early war years. Morgenthau was envisaging "a New Deal for a new world." Now, within a few days of the Savannah meeting, Morgenthau had written a letter to Truman and Vinson—over a proposed Wall Street appointment to the World Bank—stating that during his years as Treasury Secretary it had been his objective "to move the financial center of the world from London and Wall Street to the United States Treasury and to create a new concept between nations on international finance." The Bretton Woods Agreements, Morgenthau wrote, were to have been "the crystallization of that program."[24]

But as Richard Gardner has written, what White and Morgenthau had failed to see was that this program of transferring the control of international finance from Wall Street to Washington "might actually increase the nationalistic and political exponents of international financial policy."[25] The creation of an American National Advisory Council to oversee the American executive directors of the Fund and the Bank during the Bretton Woods debates in Congress had been an important portent.

Moreover, Vinson, with his awareness of the Congressional mood, and his border-state conservatism, represented in some ways a rather different approach from the White-Morgenthau view with its New Deal associations. Besides, in the politically uncertain world of 1945, Fund and Bank decisions would inevitably affect the national interest—and perhaps the national security, it soon came to be thought—of the United States.

In a *Foreign Affairs* article in the summer of 1946, Vinson wrote that "the business of the Fund and the Bank involves matters of high economic policy. They should not become just two more financial institutions. . . . And discussion of the operation of the World Fund and the Bank must take note of the special position and responsibility of the United States. . . . Ours is a position of tremendous power, and is, therefore, also a position of tremendous responsibility."[26]

In short, the traditional world of Hobbesian international relations was emerging from beneath the temporary superstructure of the wartime

alliance. Inevitably, the twin institutions designed by White to implement global multilateral financial cooperation would be subject to the
same pressures from which differences between the wartime Allies over
Germany had emerged. Gradually, the United States began to assume
that economic considerations would have to be subordinated to the calculations of national power and policy.

White, perhaps more than some administration figures during the winter
of 1945–46, remained committed to the assumption of great-power harmony in the postwar world. The corollary of this assumption to White
was that the chief emphasis in international relations should be on Soviet-
American understanding. In an unaddressed memorandum among his
papers at Princeton, dated November 30, 1945, he wrote that since Roosevelt's death "the international situation has deteriorated sharply." But
White was confident that it was possible "to change the trend of affairs."
He went on:

> The major task that confronts American diplomacy—and the only
> task that has any real value in the major problems that confront
> us—is to devise means whereby continued peace and friendly rela-
> tions can be assured between the United States and Russia. Every-
> thing else in the field of international diplomacy pales into insignifi-
> cance besides this major task. It matters little what our political
> relationships with England become or what happens in the Balkans
> or the Far East if the problems between the United States and Russia
> can be solved. Contrariwise, if we cannot discover ways to assure
> sincere friendship and military alliance between those two countries,
> the international maneuvering in the Balkans, the Far East and in
> Europe can only accentuate the fear of war, and if anything enhance
> the chances of major conflict. Let us therefore examine the situation
> anew. . . .[27]

However, in the period between Keynes's arrival in the United States
to negotiate the British loan in September, 1945, and White's assumption
of his new responsibilities in the Fund in May, 1946, "the trend of
affairs" became irreversible. There was a steady deterioration of East-
West relations, and a new importance came to be placed on British-
American political relations as the loan slowly passed through Congress
in the first half of the new year. But as the cautious reaction in the
United States to Churchill's "Iron Curtain" speech in Fulton, Missouri, in
March, 1946, showed, the shift in American public opinion was by no
means a dramatic or hasty one during this period.

In general, during these months, the impasse at Potsdam had been followed by renewed controversy between Moscow and Washington over the recognition of the new Eastern European regimes. There was friction over the Black Sea Straits and Soviet claims on northern Iran. The British presence in Greece was a source of complaint by the Russians. Early in the new year, "persecuted democratic citizens" were in action against the British-backed Athens regime. At the same time, the American administration was acutely concerned over Iran. In January, 1946, following what he regarded as the "unreal" success of the Foreign Ministers' Conference in Moscow, Truman read Byrnes a stern letter which stated that "unless Russia is faced with an iron fist and strong language another war is in the making."[28]

In China, moreover, the easy wartime assumptions quickly evaporated. With the ending of the Pacific war, on September 4, Yenan announced: "We hold the entire region stretching from Kalgan to the Yangtse, and from Shensi to the China sea, except for the largest cities and some fortified points along the railroads." As the inflationary spiral plumbed new index figures, throughout north China "the situation was out of hand," Feis records. Although the subsequent Marshall mission to reconcile the Nationalists and the Communists had some initial success, heavy fighting had again broken out in Manchuria in April, 1946. By July the civil war had begun, as the China White Paper put it, "with the spread of hostilities to various points in China proper."[29]

Perhaps above all, there was growing evidence of East-West tension in Germany. Here, where a deluge of Soviet-printed AM marks flooded all four zones, the conquerors ruled over the ruined and defeated Reich. In the American zone, JCS 1067 was the basis of administration. But in December, 1945, with a slight relaxation of Washington's attitude toward the reconstruction of the peacetime German economy as laid down at Potsdam, Colonel Bernard Bernstein returned home to fight against this drift in policy and resign from American Military Government.[30] In the wider arena, the Anglo-Americans came to believe that the Russians were not fulfilling their exchange deliveries to the West under the Potsdam agreement, and on May 3, 1946, General Lucius Clay, American Deputy Military Governor, suspended reparations deliveries to the East from the American zone. This remained a landmark in the postwar history of Germany.

Equally significant, perhaps, was the fact that by the spring of 1946 it had become clear that the Russians were not going to ratify the Bretton Woods Agreements. One of the effects of this development was that the American voice in the councils of the Fund and the Bank would be increased accordingly at the very time when tension between the two countries could no longer be ignored. Testifying on the British loan before the House Banking and Currency Committee on May 15, Vinson remarked that "there is no way at this time to avoid two economic groups but we have got to take the world as it is."[31]

Two months later the British loan cleared Congress after a stormy debate in the House, and was signed by the President. The decisive argument in Congress had been the necessity of obtaining British political and strategic support against Soviet Communism, rather than the benefits of the multilateral regime which the loan was supposed to expedite. Politics had taken precedence over economics. While six months before Keynes had thought that "the one" criticism against the loan might have been the argument of underwriting British policy, this was now seen, in July, 1946, as the critical advantage for the loan in an increasingly divided world.[32] Truman signed the Bill on July 15, 1946, bringing the loan agreement into effect.

With these events, a new element had been injected into American foreign policy which White, like many others, had not foreseen. Moreover, these developments came at a time when, as we have seen, American ascendancy in the Bretton Woods institutions had been reaffirmed, and when the administration had come to recognize that the affairs of the Fund and the Bank involved "not just two more financial institutions."

It was against this background of swiftly changing world events that White wrote to President Truman on April 30, 1946, resigning as Assistant Secretary of the Treasury, effective the next day, May 1. The Fund would begin work on May 6, White continued, and he would do his best "to carry out the policies of international economic cooperation which you have fostered."

Replying in a letter the same day, the President accepted the resignation, stating that his regret was lessened by the knowledge that White was taking up new duties with the Fund. "I am confident," Truman ended, "that in your new position you will add distinction to your already distinguished career with the Treasury."[33]

White launched the work of the International Monetary Fund on the morning of May 6, 1946, when twelve executive directors assembled under his temporary chairmanship. The meeting was held in the Washington Hotel on Pennsylvania Avenue, where the Fund had found temporary accommodation. Welcoming the executive directors, White spoke briefly:

We have the honor to meet as the Board of Executive Directors of an organization new in the annals of international monetary practice. I am sure that we are assuming the responsibilities of our office in that spirit of humility which our difficult task and profound obligations to the world evoke. The opportunity which we have for helping to promote monetary stability, a high level of international trade and world prosperity is very great. We want to meet that challenge.

The problems before us, as we all appreciate, are extremely complex. They will demand all that we possess of wisdom, experience, goodwill and economic statesmanship. Our hope of helping lies in being able to pool these resources for the benefit of all countries.

I need not remind you that we are pioneering. There is much that we must explore, there is much that we have to learn. We must proceed very carefully and not be discouraged because accomplishment does not keep pace with our desire. Our chief function is to counsel, guide and help. In proportion as we earn the confidence of the world our influence toward sound monetary policy will increase.

I want to welcome all of you here on behalf of the American people. They have taken an active interest in the development of the International Monetary Fund and of the International Bank. The American people and their government are eager to help us fulfill the promise this organization holds for the world.[34]

The White Plan had become a major international institution.

23

A PROBLEM OF NATIONAL SECURITY

Investigation of this matter is being pushed vigorously. . . .
— HOOVER TO THE WHITE HOUSE, November, 1945

WHITE's assertion of the active role of the Fund at Savannah, together with his subsequent assumption of the post of first American executive director in May, 1946, completed his decisive part in the creation of the Bretton Woods institutions.

Yet such is the paradox of White's career that his formal appointment as Fund executive director in February, 1946, only barely survived scrutiny by Truman, Byrnes and Vinson, the three senior officials of the American government, on February 6 of that year. By this time, as a result of Elizabeth Bentley's disclosures, White had already been under FBI surveillance for some three months.

Moreover, according to Mr. Truman, speaking in November, 1953, the White nomination to the Fund, following its approval by the Senate, was only allowed to take its normal course pending an FBI investigation. Then, according to Mr. Truman, White was "separated from the Government service promptly when the necessity for secrecy concerning the intensive investigation by the FBI came to an end."[1]

The train of events which led to the conclusion of White's official career in 1947 had begun when Miss Bentley, disillusioned as we have seen with the underground, yet hitherto reluctant to make a full break with all it entailed, had gone to the FBI field office in New Haven, Connecticut, on August 21 or 22, 1945. These dates were supplied in her initial public appearances before HUAC in 1948. As events developed, according to Miss Bentley's testimony and her story of *Out of Bondage*, she gave the "highlights" of what she had to say to the FBI in New

Haven. Subsequently, the FBI were interested in her keeping her contacts, so that they could investigate matters further.

On or about October 17, 1945, Miss Bentley goes on, under FBI instructions and surveillance—for she had seen one of their agents the previous day—she met one of her former contacts, "Al," in New York City. Miss Bentley was given $2,000, a sum which "Al" described as "part of her salary," and which Miss Bentley turned over to the FBI. This man was later identified as Anatol Gromov, first secretary of the Soviet Embassy. Another contact was made on November 21, also supervised by the Bureau. But by now Gromov was probably growing suspicious, and in any case left the United States within the next few weeks. Miss Bentley found she was not able to renew her underground contacts, but conversely she records in *Out of Bondage*, by the new year "I knew the FBI believed my story."[2]

It should be noted, however, that there is a possible discrepancy in Miss Bentley's account of these weeks between August and November, 1945, which became apparent only later, in the events following Attorney General Herbert Brownell's Chicago speech on November 6, 1953—to which we will return—in which he stated that Mr. Truman had appointed White to an important position knowing that he was a Communist spy. In the subsequent melee, Truman, Brownell and Hoover all made statements on "the White case," Truman on radio and television, Brownell and Hoover in sworn testimony before a Senate subcommittee. As we have seen in our earlier account of Miss Bentley's story and White's place in it, Mr. Hoover testified on this occasion that "all information furnished by Miss Bentley which was susceptible to check has proven to be correct."[3]

However, in his examination of the Bentley story, Professor Packer, from whose analysis of the case we have already quoted, has commented that, while Mr. Hoover on this occasion in 1953 stated that the FBI did know about the allegations against White at the time of the Bentley contact with Gromov on November 21, 1945, Hoover did not specifically state that the FBI also had this information at the time of the earlier October meeting with Gromov. Some evidence from one of Miss Bentley's court appearances, cited by Packer, indicates that Miss Bentley may not have been able to see the FBI in mid-October. Moreover, in his November, 1953, statement on the White case, Hoover suggested that Miss Bentley did not fully inform the FBI with details of her espionage career until November 7, 1945.

Professor Packer therefore concludes that there are four matters which have never been fully corroborated on this period in Miss Bentley's story. Did Miss Bentley begin telling her espionage story to the FBI in August,

1945, as she says she did? Did she meet Gromov on October 17, 1945, under FBI instructions? Was she under FBI surveillance at this time? If not, how soon after did she give the FBI the $2,000?[4]

Of course, it would still be possible that Miss Bentley was acting in some form of contact with the FBI on this occasion. Perhaps her initial account to the Bureau in August, 1945, was so general that she did not give the names of her espionage contacts. And, as we have seen earlier in our narrative, her occasional disdain for detail may have led her to think that her account to the FBI and any subsequent arrangements made were more specific than would have been thought by the counterespionage organization.

There may have been a failure of coordination in the Bureau, and perhaps the FBI had to show some caution in accepting her story before taking it to the highest levels of the Bureau. As one writer has described it, "It took some time before she talked freely. To FBI officials, the outline of her story was not news. But the names she earnestly mentioned staggered them. . . . Even to men whose work was counterespionage, her story was unbelievable. Wary that she might be a plant, or worse, a double agent, they refused to take her seriously."[5]

What does seem reasonably certain is that doubts were resolved by November 7, 1945, during the period of the Washington negotiations on the American loan to Britain. On that day, in Hoover's words, Miss Bentley "advised special agents of the FBI in considerable detail of her career as an espionage agent."[6] On November 8, Hoover went on, a letter was sent by him to Brigadier General Harry Vaughan, the presidential military aide and liaison for FBI matters in the White House. This letter of November 8 was a "preliminary flash" warning of Miss Bentley's story and the first of three communications which implicated White in the alleged activities of Soviet Intelligence in the United States. His name was second on the list it contained.

Hoover's letter to General Vaughan began:

As a result of the Bureau's investigative operations, information has been recently developed from a highly confidential source indicating that a number of persons employed by the Government of the United States have been furnishing data and information to persons outside the Federal Government, who are in turn transmitting this information to espionage agents of the Soviet Government. At the present time it is impossible to determine exactly how many of these people had actual knowledge of the disposition being made of the information they were transmitting. The investigation, however, at this point has indicated that the persons named hereinafter were actually the source from which information passing through the Soviet espionage system was being obtained, and I am continuing vigorous investigation for the purpose of establishing the degree and nature of the complicity of these people in this espionage ring.

The Bureau's information at this time indicates that the following persons were participating in this operation or were utilized by principals in this ring for the purpose of obtaining data in which the Soviet is interested. . . .

The letter then listed the names, in the following order, of Silvermaster, White, Silverman, Currie and Perlo, before going on to name a number of individuals recognizable to us as some of Miss Bentley's alleged "independent" contacts. Hoover's letter of November 8 noted that American government documents were furnished to Silvermaster, who photographed them, and that the undeveloped film was then turned over to a contact of the Soviets in Washington or New York. The letter ended: "Investigation of this matter is being pushed vigorously, but I thought that the President and you would be interested in having the foregoing preliminary data immediately."[7]

Later in November, "a detailed summary memorandum was then prepared consisting of 71 pages, exclusive of the index, setting forth the highlights of Soviet espionage in the United States . . . this memorandum included information on Harry Dexter White" (Hoover). This memorandum was dated November 27, 1945, and it was delivered to General Vaughan for the President on December 4. Copies were sent to Secretary of State Byrnes, Attorney General Tom Clark and later to heads of other government agencies.

According to Attorney General Brownell's sworn Congressional testimony on November 17, 1953, this report of November 27, 1945, "named many names and described numerous Soviet espionage organizations. Harry Dexter White and the espionage ring of which he was part were among those referred to in this report. The index list refers to his activities in three different places." This report, Brownell went on, summarized "White's espionage activities in abbreviated form, but no reasonable person can deny that the summary, brief though it may be, constituted adequate warning to anyone who read it of the extreme danger to the security of the country in appointing White to the International Monetary Fund or continuing him in Government in any capacity."

This report of November 27, 1945, was not made public in the Brownell-Hoover statements of November, 1953, although fragments of it are published elsewhere in the subcommittee's hearings.[8]

The FBI had by now initiated an investigation of White, and according to Hoover, he was put under surveillance in November, 1945. Surveillance was continued throughout 1946, and at times in 1947 and 1948. Hoover pointed out that as the IMF had extraterritorial privileges, surveillance of White was "hampered," presumably during the year from May, 1946, to May, 1947, when White was with the Fund.[9]

Following the delivery of the second FBI memorandum to the White House on December 4, over six weeks elapsed. The period was an eventful one on the international scene. Then, on January 23, White was nominated by the President as the American executive director of the Fund. As we have seen, according to Mr. Truman's statement of November, 1953, White was also being considered for the post of Fund managing director at the time.

Of the persons named in the two FBI reports given to General Vaughan, White was the most senior in government service. His very importance now helped to build a trap around him, for according to Hoover's testimony, as soon as the knowledge of the Fund nomination was announced, the FBI prepared a special report on White for the President. This information "secured from sources whose reliability has been established either by inquiry or long-established observation and evaluation" was put into a twenty-eight-page summary dated February 1, 1946.

The report was delivered to General Vaughan on February 4, with copies sent to Byrnes and Attorney General Clark. Hoover went on to say that "the information contained therein came from a total of thirty sources, the reliability of which had been previously established." It was at this stage in his testimony on White that Hoover gave his endorsement of Miss Bentley's reliability, that "all information furnished by Miss Bentley, which was susceptible to check, has proven to be correct."[10]

With the twenty-eight-page report on White went a letter of transmittal to General Vaughan from Hoover who noted that White had been nominated as American delegate to the Fund. Hoover went on:

In view of this fact, the interest expressed by the President and you [Vaughan] in matters of this nature, and the seriousness of the charges against White in the attachment, I have made every effort in preparing this memorandum to cover all ramifications. As will be observed, information has come to the attention of this Bureau charging White with being a valuable adjunct to an underground Soviet espionage organization operating in Washington, D.C. Material which came into his possession as a result of his official capacity allegedly was made available through intermediaries to Nathan

Gregory Silvermaster, his wife Helen Witte Silvermaster, and William Ludwig Ullmann. . . .

The letter of transmittal went on to outline that Ullmann photographed the documents, which were then taken, with other information, by courier to Jacob Golos, and following his death, through other individuals to Gromov of the Soviet Embassy. Hoover went on:

This whole network has been under intensive investigation since November, 1945 and it is the results of these efforts that I am now able to make available to you. I also feel it is incumbent upon me at this time to bring to your attention an additional factor which has originated with sources available to this Bureau in Canada. It is reported that the British and Canadian delegates to the International Monetary Fund may possibly nominate and support White for the post of president of the International Bank or as executive director of the International Monetary Fund. The conclusion is expressed that assuming this backing is forthcoming and the United States acquiescence, if not concurrence, resulting, White's nomination to this highly important post would be assured. It is further commented by my Canadian source that if White is placed in either of these positions, he would have the power to influence to a great degree deliberations on all international financial arrangements.

This source which is apparently aware of at least some of the charges incorporated in the attached memorandum against White, commented that the loyalty of White must be assured, particularly in view of the fact that the USSR had not ratified the Bretton Woods agreement. Fear was expressed that facts might come to light in the future throwing some sinister accusations at White and thereby jeopardize the successful operation of these important international financial institutions. . . .

Like the "Summary of Soviet Espionage in the United States" dated November 27 and given to General Vaughan on December 4, the special twenty-eight page report on Harry Dexter White of February 1, 1946, was not made public. This was because, as Brownell explained in November, 1953, it might jeopardize confidential sources and intelligence techniques. But the purpose of the report as stated in its opening paragraphs was quoted verbatim by Brownell:

The purpose of this memorandum is to relate all of the information available at this time concerning Harry Dexter White, his activities and contacts in order that an overall picture may be available for review, action or future reference. This information has been received from numerous confidential sources whose reliability has been established either by inquiry or long-established observation and evaluation. In no instance is any transaction or events related where the reliability of the source of information is questionable. It is with these factors in mind that the following material is set forth.

Brownell then went on to summarize the February, 1946, report on White. He stated that information had come from a confidential source to the FBI that White was engaged in espionage activities "at least as early as the latter part of 1942 or early in 1943." It was reported "that White was supplying information consisting of documents obtained by him in the course of his duties" to N. G. Silvermaster and W. L. Ullmann. The material, the FBI report went on, consisted of varied reports on the financial activities of the American government, "particularly if they related to foreign commitments." Reports from other departments and agencies were also made available through these channels.

The material supplied, Brownell went on, consisted of notes, verbatim copies, and sometimes "the original documents themselves were seen." This material was photographed in the Silvermaster house on 30th Street, N.W., in Washington and delivered through channels to Jacob Golos, "a known Soviet agent." Brownell stated that the FBI investigation had shown that "a complete photographic laboratory did in fact exist in the basement of the Silvermaster home." The report presumed that material of primary interest was forwarded by diplomatic code to Moscow, while the rest was sent in the diplomatic bag.

Brownell stated that according to the information received by the FBI, and incorporated in the report, White "was considered one of the most valuable assets in this particular parallel of Soviet Intelligence." He went on to say that this view was taken because "those individuals whom this group were anxious to have assigned there could be placed in the Treasury Department." Among the persons in this category. were Mrs. Sonia Gold, who "through arrangement with White" obtained a position in the Treasury as a secretary. Mrs. Gold obtained documents from White's office which she copied, and then made her notes available to Mrs. Silvermaster. The information which Mrs. Gold obtained in a general way concerned the Treasury Department's opinions and recommendations concerning applications for loans by the Chinese and French governments.

It was also reported, Brownell went on, that another parallel of Soviet Intelligence within the American government was headed by Victor Perlo. The report pointed out that Harold Glasser was alleged to be in this branch of Soviet espionage. Glasser, who was "rather closely associated with White," was able to supply general information concerning the activities of the United States Treasury. Another source had reported to the FBI that George Silverman, formerly employed by the Railroad Retirement Board and the United States Army Air Forces, was a member of the underground. Silverman had "worked through close friends who were indebted to him, including Harry Dexter White."

In July, 1945, Brownell said, continuing with his summary of the FBI report on White, a clerical employee of the Passport Division of the State Department, formerly employed as a clerk by the Soviet Purchasing Commission, was allegedly stealing information from the State Department's official records to give to unknown persons. This individual apparently admitted that he had collected the information in the course of his duty, and that he knew a man who would pay him $1,000 for it. This individual had listed White as a reference, and was highly recommended by White.

The FBI report went on to state that White had been interviewed by the Bureau in connection with the *Amerasia* case, "particularly concerning Irving S. Friedman, who according to the report, was known to be one of the sources in the Treasury Department . . . that had been furnishing documents to Philip Jacob Jaffe, editor of *Amerasia*. White told the FBI that Friedman was an employee of the Treasury Department handling matters dealing with monetary affairs in the Far East, and admitted that he had brought Friedman into the Treasury Department five or six years earlier."

Brownell stated that the FBI report on White contained "much corroborative evidence which cannot be made public either because it would disclose investigative techniques of the FBI or might be harmful to the national interest. It can be pointed out, however, that over a period of three months beginning in November of 1945 the activities of Harry Dexter White were entirely consistent with all previous information in the report. White was in frequent close personal contact with nearly every one of the persons named as his associates in the spy ring."[12]

Clearly, from the list of names in the FBI report quoted by Attorney General Brownell, we can see the outline of Miss Bentley's story. Presumably if thirty sources were involved, as Hoover stated, additional information had been obtained by the Bureau. Moreover, if as Chambers stated, he had given White's name to the FBI in 1942, that report may have been filed in the arcana of the Bureau. It will be recalled also that Chambers had mentioned White's name to the State Department security officer, Ray Murphy, in March, 1945, in a discussion on the underground. But in a revealing remark about the FBI report on White, Mr. Truman stated that "this report showed that serious accusations had been made against White, but it pointed out that it would be practically impossible to prove these charges."[13]

Hence the note of caution in the Hoover letter to the White House on November 8, 1945, when the FBI director wrote that at that time it was impossible to determine how many of the people in the alleged spy ring had knowledge of the disposition of the material transmitted. Again, in his covering letter to General Vaughan, on February 1, 1946, Hoover, with caution, wrote that information received charged White with being "a valuable adjunct" of the spy ring, and that material had been forwarded through intermediaries to Silvermaster. As we shall see below, both Brownell and Hoover, in their Congressional statement on the events of February, 1946, said that the matter to be decided at this time did not relate to criminal proceedings in court against White.

What was now to be decided, with the transmittal of the FBI report on White to the President, was whether he could be allowed to remain in government service.

The special FBI report on White, dated February 1, was delivered to General Vaughan on February 4, 1946. There was no dispute that the two previous FBI memoranda in which White was mentioned, those of November 8 and 27, 1945, had been delivered to General Vaughan.[14] Evidently the reports had been overlooked, for in his address of November, 1953, Mr. Truman said that "as best as I can now determine, I first learned of the accusations against White early in February, 1946, when an FBI report specially discussing the activities of Harry Dexter White was brought to my attention. The February report was delivered to me by General Vaughan and was also brought to my personal attention by Secretary of State Byrnes."[15]

It will be recalled that White's nomination as Fund executive director had been sent to the Senate on January 23. The Senate Committee on Banking and Currency had approved the nomination on February 5, the same day that Byrnes received the FBI report. On February 6, according to Mr. Truman's 1953 account, he sent a copy of the FBI report to White's immediate superior, Fred Vinson, Secretary of the Treasury, suggesting that he and Byrnes should confer with him "and find out what we should do."[16]

Byrnes later recalled the events of that day:

The following day, after I had read the report, I requested an engagement with the President. That afternoon I was invited to come to the White House. I told President Truman I had received a copy of the report sent to him by Mr. Hoover, that I was shocked by its contents, and I asked what he intended to do about it. The President stated that he had read the report and that he also was surprised. When I asked about the status of the nomination of Mr. White, he said it was still pending in the Senate. I told him, in view of the nature of the charges contained in Hoover's report, I thought he should immediately ask the Senate to withhold action and then withdraw the nomination.

The President had a member of his staff telephone to Mr. Leslie Biffle, the Secretary of the Senate. The President asked Mr. Biffle the status of the nomination, but did not give any reason for his inquiry. Mr. Biffle stated that the nomination had been favorably acted upon that afternoon. The President apparently was as disappointed as I was by the statement of Mr. Biffle. In further discussing the matter, I suggested to the President he might ask someone in the Senate about moving to reconsider the vote by which nomination was approved. He did not think well of that suggestion. I then suggested to him that the only thing he could do would be to refuse to issue a commission to White. He said he had been advised on a previous occasion that once the Senate had acted he could be required to sign a commission. I told him that if he should send for White and tell him about Hoover's report, White would never resort to the courts.

I got the impression that the President was disposed to follow that course. However, he said he wanted to think it over.

During our conversation the President told me that he appointed White on the recommendation of the Secretary of the Treasury, Mr. Vinson. Later that afternoon Mr. Vinson came to my office. He said that the President had told him of what had occurred and of my recommendation. Mr. Vinson was quite worried about it. However, I got the impression that he agreed with my suggestion that the President refuse to commission White. He said he was going to talk with the President again about it.

I heard no more from either of them about the matter, but I later noticed in the press that White was commissioned by the President, and became Executive Director of the International Monetary Fund.[17]

Following these consultations in the White House on February 6, Vinson was to see the Attorney General, Tom Clark, and "other officials," as Truman put it in his November, 1953, statement on White. The subject of this high-level activity was now preparing for the coming Savannah conference on the Bretton Woods institutions. In White's office at Room 3434 in the Treasury, February 6 had been a normal day. There had been a "Bretton Woods meeting," and the Navy Department had wanted to know whether the Treasury had any objection to a proposal to revert to dollars "for sundry supplies and services in China." White had lunched with Governor Graham Towers of the Bank of Canada, and "Mr. Kaplan called yesterday and said he would like to see you."[18]

Two weeks later, in a meeting with Hoover on February 21, Attorney General Clark told the FBI Director that he had spoken with Truman and Vinson. Clark felt, according to Hoover's account of the meeting, that the President should personally tell White that it would be best for him not to serve on the Fund. Hoover told Clark that he felt it would be "unwise" for White to take up the Fund appointment. In reply to a question, Hoover stated that he had also told Clark that he considered White "unfit" to serve.[19]

The next day, February 22, there was "a lengthy conference" (Hoover) between Vinson, Clark and the FBI Director on White. Hoover was told that the problem was one of what could be done to prevent White from taking his oath of office. Vinson did not want White to serve on the Fund, and neither did he wish him to continue as Assistant Secretary of the Treasury. Hoover, concerned with his sources, told Vinson and Clark that "the character of the evidence was such that it should not be publicly disclosed at that time in view of the confidential nature of the sources involved."

Vinson and Clark now decided, according to Hoover, that they would see Truman and suggest to the President that there were three alternatives: The President could dismiss White and make no statement; the President could tell White he had changed his mind about his Fund appointment and ask for his resignation; the President could sign the commission and instruct the Attorney General "to continue the investigation vigorously." Hoover emphasized that he did not enter into any agreement to shift White from the Treasury to the Fund. That was not within his purview, and there was no agreement while he was present, except that Vinson and Clark should suggest the three alternatives to Truman. Hoover was not present in any subsequent discussion of the matter.

Four days later, on February 26, Clark told Hoover that he had seen Truman and that an effort would be made "to remove" White, although the Attorney General was doubtful if this "would work out." Clark went on to tell Hoover that "he felt that White would go into the job and would then be surrounded with persons who were specially selected and who were not security risks. He further stated that the President was interested in continuing the surveillance." Hoover then said that if that was the wish, the FBI "would continue the investigation."[20]

It seems reasonably clear, therefore, that by the end of February, 1946, two months before he went to the Fund, the course of White's official career had been decided.

But it should be noted that, as Attorney General Brownell put it in his November, 1953, statement to the Senate Internal Security Subcommittee, "in considering the facts in this case it is well to keep in mind that the matter to be decided in January and February of 1946 did not relate to criminal proceedings in court. It was not a question of whether White could at this time have been formally charged before a grand jury with espionage. The matter to be determined by Mr. Truman and his associates was whether Harry Dexter White should be advanced to a post of high honor, great trust and responsibility and of vital importance to the security of our country."[21]

Similarly, in his concluding remarks to the same Senate subcommittee, Mr. Hoover said that he had called the attention of the authorities to the facts, as alleged by reliable sources, "which were substantial in pointing to a security risk." This was the context in which White's future had been decided in February, 1946, by President Truman.

Some of the background to this investigation of White was given by Hoover before the Senate subcommittee. Speaking almost didactically, Hoover outlined the difference between an "intelligence operation" and an "allout open investigation looking toward eventual prosecution." These were two different things, Hoover said. He went on to state that in the period between November 8, 1945, and February 22, 1946, the first course of the FBI—as a counterintelligence organization—was "to safeguard the Government from infiltration by subversive elements and in this approach the objective of pointing attention to security risks must not be confused with prosecutive action." Clearly, during this initial period following the full recital of Miss Bentley's confession, the Bureau had been primarily concerned, as we have seen, with checking her story, and with attempting to restore her contacts. The primary object was to find out more about the methods, objects and personnel of the alleged Washington spy networks.

Thus Hoover had taken "a strong stand" against the premature disclosure which would result if prosecution were initiated: "The evidence necessary to sustain convictions in indictments for law violation is entirely different from that necessary to establish the existence of security risks in sensitive posts in the Government. Some of the evidence, while of an irrefutable nature, was not admissible in a court of law." Hence the apparent note of certainty in the lengthy FBI report on White of February, 1946, as described by Brownell, could not be sustained in court with anonymous undercover agents, incomplete links, hearsay evidence and testimony based, as Brownell told the Senate subcommittee, on wiretap information not admissible before a grand jury or a Federal Court.

Hoover's testimony made clear that from the FBI viewpoint the intensified investigation into the persons named by Miss Bentley—and which led, Hoover claimed, to some dismissals from government as early as the spring of 1946—meant the beginning of the end of the intelligence operation. In any case, Miss Bentley had not renewed her contacts. As Hoover put it, "had it been the intent of the FBI to handle the Harry Dexter White case and other related cases solely as an intelligence operation, the widespread dissemination of the information that was furnished to the branches of the government would not have been undertaken." Clearly, the impending Fund appointment of White had marked a change of emphasis in the investigation. The FBI had not been a party, Hoover stated, to the decision to keep White in public service. But the Bureau had asked that its sources be protected.

On February 26, 1946, Hoover concluded in his 1953 Congressional statement, he had told Attorney General Clark that White "might have received some notice of the cancellation or impending cancellation of his appointment as U.S. delegate to the International Monetary Fund." According to Hoover, this information was "absolutely reliable." The possibility remains, therefore, that White might have had some knowledge of the secret debate around his future.[22]

The outcome of the episode was outlined by Mr. Truman in his national broadcast on the White case in November, 1953. The former President stated that after the results of the consultations on White had been reported to him, the conclusion was reached that the appointment of White to the Fund "should be allowed to take its normal course. The final responsibility for this decision was of course mine."

Truman went on to say that hundreds of FBI agents were involved in an investigation, and that any unusual action with regard to White might have alerted all the persons involved. A second reason for retaining White was that his contemplated appointment as Fund managing director was abandoned. As an executive director "his position would be less important and much less sensitive—if it were sensitive at all—than the position held by him as Assistant Secretary of the Treasury." This course, Mr. Truman said, "protected the public interest and security and at the same time permitted the intensive FBI investigation, then in progress, to go forward."

Later, Mr. Truman said, White "was separated from the Government service promptly when the necessity for secrecy concerning the intensive investigation by the FBI came to an end."[23]

With White's assumption of the post of Fund executive director in May, 1946, the FBI investigation therefore continued. Hoover told the Senate subcommittee during his 1953 appearance that between November, 1945, and July, 1946, "seven communications went to the White House wherein Harry Dexter White's name was specifically mentioned."[24]

A further series of FBI reports was circulated within the various branches of the Federal government beginning in the spring of 1946. These included reports on Silvermaster, Ullmann, Glasser, Perlo, Coe, Adler and others later named publicly by Miss Bentley. Silvermaster resigned from government service at the end of 1946, Ullmann and Perlo in March, 1947, and Glasser at the end of 1947.[25]

As we shall see below, White wrote a letter of resignation to President Truman on March 31, 1947. In the context of Truman's remarks, noted above, presumably by this time the FBI had given up any hope of restoring Miss Bentley's contacts.

In a further ratchetlike motion toward the eventual publication of Miss Bentley's story, a Federal Grand Jury of the Southern District of New York was impaneled in New York City in March, 1947, to hear evidence on Communist activities in the United States. The Grand Jury would sit behind closed doors to hear evidence and consider possible indictments. It would question Miss Bentley, and some of those named by her, including Harry Dexter White.

ONE WORLD, TWO WORLDS

. . . I doubt if any responsible official of the member governments in spring of 1944 believed that by 1948—only three years after the cessation of hostilities—the tensions between certain of the major powers would have been so pronounced and that the world, instead of drawing together during these years, would have moved so precipitously toward a split. . . .

—HARRY DEXTER WHITE, May, 1948

FOLLOWING his address to his fellow executive directors with the activation of the Fund in early May, 1946, White was soon busy with his new duties. The executive directors met frequently, and White was also involved with interviewing prospective staff, besides holding regular consultations with representatives of Fund member countries. The Fund headquarters was moved during June, 1946, from its temporary location at the Washington Hotel to 1818 H Street, N.W., where premises were shared with the Bank. Frank Coe became Secretary of the Fund.

There was also the task of building up the Fund archives, as with any new organization. On July 18, White telephoned Harold Glasser of the Treasury, "with regard to having certain files pertaining to the International Monetary Fund transferred here for our historical records." Glasser mentioned "the large number of files which had been removed from the Treasury by various men." White was to speak to them individually concerning files which should not have been taken. Glasser said he would look over the files to which White referred, and see if there was objection to transferring them to the Fund.[1]

In a wider sense, the outlook for the Fund and the Bank in these later months of 1946 still reflected the wartime assumptions that the multilateral trading regime would be implemented once the postwar transitional difficulties were overcome. To the Bretton Woods institutions had now been added the Anglo-American Financial Agreement; and as we have seen, the Preparatory Committee was to meet in London in October, 1946, to begin the drafting of the ITO Charter on commercial policy.

Some of the hopes that underlay these developments were brought out during the meeting of the Board of Governors of the Fund and the Bank in Washington during September, 1946. In the course of this meeting the new Secretary of the Treasury, John W. Snyder, who had replaced Vinson on the latter's elevation to the Supreme Court, had spoken of "speedily activating" the Fund.

Evidently Snyder meant that the Fund's monitoring powers would be activated, not that the Fund could provide financial aid for solving transitional difficulties. Such aid was of course precluded by the Fund's Articles. In any case, following Congressional wish, the American executive director, White, had obtained an interpretation that Fund resources were to be used for short-term stabilization purposes rather than for transitional reconstruction. At this stage, the techniques for policing the expected multilateral regime were clearly considered of great importance.

Equally, the British government was concerned with the maintenance of full employment, and obtained a Fund interpretation of the Articles to protect the right of sterling devaluation if such full employment were threatened. The wartime concern with the techniques of implementing the multilateral trading regime, and of safeguarding full employment within that regime, continued to be in the forefront of official thought as the economic position of Western Europe continued to deteriorate.[2]

Throughout the year, American administration spokesmen continued to make optimistic assertions that the Bretton Woods institutions, combined with measures of emergency aid, could deal with the transitional-reconstruction problem. In London, during October, 1946, Hugh Dalton, the Chancellor, spoke of "a song in my heart," and hoped that the postwar frustrations and shortages which had afflicted Britain would soon "disappear like the snows of winter and give place to the full promise of springtime."

As late as December, 1946, Richard Gardner has noted, the experts of the American Federal Reserve Board estimated that the world's need for dollars in 1947 would amount to but $3.5 billion. These needs could be satisfied by existing foreign holdings, the American loan to Britain, and Export-Import Bank loans. The remainder of the world's needs could be satisfied "without excessive strain by the new international institutions. . . ."[3]

✻   ✻   ✻

In what was probably his last letter to Keynes in March, 1946, White, as we have seen, considered that a world dollar scarcity was remote, "barring untoward international political developments." The makers of the Bretton Woods institutions had proceeded on the assumption that, following a period of postwar adjustment, the world would move toward political and economic equilibrium. Now, in the early months of 1947, not only the impending collapse of the economy of Western Europe but "untoward international political developments" shattered the commonly held wartime assumptions.

In international trade, the disequilibrium between the United States and Western countries was becoming critical, and quite clearly could not be dealt with by existing measures and institutions. The export surplus of the United States in 1946 was $8.2 billion, but during 1947 the figure rose to $11.3 billion. The consolidated deficit of the European countries with the rest of the world was $5.8 billion in 1946, and $7.5 billion in 1947.[4]

Moreover, there was a structural imbalance between North America and Western Europe caused by the disappearance of the pre-1939 pattern of world trade. During the war the United States had switched, of necessity, to Latin America for the source of some of its imports. With the end of the war, trade between Western and Eastern Europe was curtailed for political reasons, making Western Europe that much more dependent on North America.

The legacy of wartime controls and shortages also meant that trade between the Western European countries themselves was restricted, in addition to the problems created by wartime destruction. The "dollar shortage" was not only the absence of hard currency, or even the "reconstruction" problem, but also represented the breakdown of the old world trading system with all its intricate links. Without the restoration of a new equilibrium, clearly neither the Fund nor the Bank could function as designed.[5]

Closely entwined with this economic crisis of the West was the increasing polarization of East-West relations in early 1947, which from now on was to affect all aspects of American economic foreign policy.

In France and Italy, for example, weak governments were faced by strong indigenous Communist movements. The Greek civil war, and the tension between Turkey and its great northern neighbor were further manifestations of growing differences between East and West. Germany, hitherto a political and economic vacuum, where dismantling of industry was still continuing, was now on the verge of becoming another arena between the Western Allies and Russia as the last semblances of wartime understanding dissolved in recrimination.

Although above all the Truman administration was concerned with

Western Europe, events in China were also symptomatic of an increasingly divided world. Here, in the early months of 1947, the inflationary spiral entered the ultimate stage of hyper-inflation, which has been described as beginning "in the month the rise in prices exceeds 50 percent."[6] In January, 1947, the Communist armies of General Lin Piao went over to the offensive in Manchuria. From this time on, the military balance in China tipped against the Nationalists.

The link between the international economic and political crisis, which finally spelled the end of optimistic wartime hopes, was the prolonged blizzard which ravaged Britain in the late winter of 1947. The country's chances of a decisive economic recovery vanished, forcing London to relinquish many of its commitments in Greece and Turkey.

From now on the world's attention was on a virtual strategic and ideological confrontation between Washington and Moscow. In a Congressional briefing in late February, 1947, at the beginning of the "fifteen weeks" which changed the course of American foreign policy, Under Secretary of State Dean Acheson considered that "only two great powers remained in the world . . . divided by an unbradgable ideological chasm . . . for the United States to take steps to strengthen countries threatened with Soviet aggression or Communist subversion was not to pull British chestnuts out of the fire; it was to protect the security of the United States—it was to protect freedom itself."[7]

A few weeks later, on March 12, 1947, President Truman, in an address to Congress, announced a new economic and military aid program to Greece and Turkey. The program was presented by the President as part of a wider policy to assist "free peoples to work out their destinies in their own way."

The Truman Doctrine was followed on March 21 by the issue from the White House of Executive Order 9835, which consolidated earlier federal security procedures. From this time on, the standard for the refusal of government employment, or the removal from federal service on loyalty grounds, was that "on all the evidence, reasonable grounds exist for the belief that the person involved is disloyal to the Government of the United States." The order was to come into force later that year.[8]

Three months later, in June, 1947, Truman was asked after a Cabinet meeting what the United States would do if confronted by a Russian *démarche* and simultaneous *coups* in France and Italy. According to James Forrestal the President's reply was that,

We would have to face that situation when it arose . . . he said he was afraid the answer would have to be found in history—of the struggle between the Romans and Carthage, between Athens and

Sparta, between Alexander the Great and Persia, between France and England, between England and Germany. . . .[9]

The effect on White of these developments can be imagined. The breakup of the wartime alliance was a matter of regret in both the United States and Great Britain. But, George Kennan has written, "it should be remembered that nowhere in Washington had the hopes entertained for postwar collaboration with Russia been more elaborate, more naïve, or more tenaciously (one might say almost ferociously) pursued than in the Treasury Department."[10] However, White's belief that there were common interests between the United States and the Soviet was not entirely invalidated by the events of 1947. Eventually, indeed, the two powers would be drawn together, but by the necessities of the nuclear age, rather than by the hopes of the strange wartime alliance.

These events now seriously affected the Bretton Woods institutions at the very moment when they began to function. With the acute dollar shortage most countries invoked the transitional period provisions of the Fund articles which sanctioned the retention of wartime exchange restrictions. When, therefore, the Fund began operations in March, 1947, such restrictions were the rule rather than the exception.

At the same time the operations of the World Bank were affected, for in the uncertain economic and political climate of 1946–47, few member governments were willing or able to guarantee loans floated by the Bank. The Bank had only restricted resources of its own, and thus private investors had to be approached. As the United States was the largest source of private capital, the confidence of Wall Street was essential. Moreover, at a time when Congressional control of the purse strings would be all-important to the administration's unprecedented proposals for peacetime foreign aid, the new Republican Congress had to be reassured that the Fund and the Bank would be run on strictly orthodox lines.

Accordingly, in early 1947, changes occurred in the personnel of the Bretton Woods institutions, replacing those associated with the beginnings of the Fund and the Bank. In February, 1947, John J. McCloy, a Wall Street lawyer and the former Assistant Secretary of State for War replaced Eugene Mayer, who had resigned the previous December, as the Bank president. In March, the Wall Street financier Eugene R. Black was appointed the new American executive director of the Bank, following the resignation of Emilio G. Collado.

Special factors, of course, may have been involved in White's departure from the Fund, which coincided with the changes above. On March

31, 1947, White wrote a letter of resignation to President Truman, which was accepted a week later:

31 March 1947

Dear Mr. President,

I am writing to submit my resignation as U.S. Executive Director of the International Monetary Fund. I have for some time cherished the idea of returning to private enterprise but did not want to leave the Government until the Bretton Woods organizations, in which I am so deeply interested, were well launched. The work of the Fund is now off to a good start. The period of active operations is just beginning, and this is an opportunity for my successor to take over.

In the absence of Mr. Gutt, who is in Europe on business for the Fund, I am Acting Chairman, and have promised to remain until he returns in the early part of May.

I want to thank you, Mr. President, for your confidence in me and for the opportunity you gave me as U.S. Executive Director of the Fund, to help bring the Bretton Woods proposals to realization. I shall continue to follow their work closely and will of course be glad to help any time I am called upon.

It has been a source of satisfaction and encouragement to me to know of your keen interest in the Fund and your policy of bending every effort toward achieving a stable and prosperous world economy. I shall always remember with pleasure my connection with your Administration.

Please accept my warm personal regards and good wishes.

Respectfully yours,

HARRY D. WHITE

7 April 1947

Dear Mr. White:

With sincere regret and considerable reluctance I accept your resignation as U.S. Executive Director of the International Monetary Fund, effective on Mr. Gutt's return from Europe.

I know you can view with a great deal of personal satisfaction your career in public service, crowned as it has been by your ceaseless efforts to make a real contribution to the stability of international trade through the International Bank and the International Monetary Fund, which hold so much promise to a world desperately anxious for a lasting peace.

You have filled with distinction your present assignment as United States Representative on the Board of Executive Directors of the

International Monetary Fund, and your unfaltering efforts have been a source of great pride to me.

I wish you the very best of luck and will feel free to call upon you from time to time for assistance in dealing with problems we will be continually facing in which your background and abilities make you peculiarly able to help us.

Very sincerely yours,

HARRY S. TRUMAN[11]

Pending the President's formal acceptance of his resignation, White, in a last official appearance on Capitol Hill on April 3, outlined to the Senate Finance Committee the interdependence of the Fund, the Bank and the proposed International Trade Organization.[12]

The exchange of letters between Truman and White was released on April 8, 1947. The New York *Times* reported the next day, April 9, that the resignation was announced "without prior indication that it would occur." The story continued that White's resignation "marked the close of the first phase of participation by the United States in the Bank and Fund, and forecast for the early day when all the original personnel that took part in creating the $8 billion international finance twins would depart." Financial spokesmen, the *Times* said, had explained that White had "recently suffered a serious illness."

The New York *Herald-Tribune* reported that White's resignation stirred speculation whether the Fund was following the Bank "in shifting from government to bank-trained men in American personnel. In any event, it emphasized the general departure of high level New Dealers from government and semi-government offices. . . ."

The same day that these reports appeared in the press, the Executive Board of the Fund passed a formal resolution "upon the occasion of learning of the resignation of Mr. Harry D. White, executive director from the United States":

Whereas Harry D. White has been preeminent in the establishment of the International Monetary Fund and the International Bank for Reconstruction and Development, inasmuch as he conceived and developed the first plans for these organizations, conducted for the Government of the United States the negotiations with many countries which resulted in the Joint Statement by Experts on the Establishment of an International Monetary Fund of the United and Associated Nations, as a delegate to the Bretton Woods conference played an important role in framing the Agreements concerning the Fund and the Bank which were adopted by the conference, and as

Executive Director appointed by the United States has worked tirelessly, unselfishly, and wisely to establish the International Monetary Fund and to make it useful to all peoples of the world; and

Whereas Harry D. White is now resigning his position as Executive Director of the Fund:

Therefore, it is hereby resolved by the Executive Board of the International Monetary Fund:

That the Fund expresses its thanks to Harry D. White for the outstanding services he has rendered the Fund and its members; and

That in appreciation of the extraordinary labors of Harry D. White in the establishment of the Fund, and as a tribute to his statesmanship in the field of international finance, the Fund will present a suitable testimonial to him; and

That there is created the special position of Honorary Adviser to the International Monetary Fund, which position shall be occupied by Harry D. White so that, from time to time, with his consent, his advice and counsel may be obtained.[13]

Evidently, with the ending of his involvement with the Fund White decided to leave Washington. On April 10 he wrote to the Mayor of New York, William O'Dwyer, at City Hall:

Dear Bill,

As you see by the enclosed, I shall soon be on my own. After all the years in Washington it will seem like a holiday to have no Government responsibility. I intend to make my headquarters in the world's financial center—your fair city—and be a doctor to the world's monetary ills. And there sure are plently of such ills.

I look to you to get me a place to live (I'll take any one or two-bedroom apartment). I expect to be in New York soon and expect to talk with you further about that plan for creating the biggest and the best international trade center in the world in New York City.

Just keep your good health and good spirits. The Democratic Party needs you.

H. D. WHITE[14]

White, as he had stated in his letter to the President, remained as acting chairman of the Board of the Fund until Camille Gutt, the managing director, returned from Europe on May 10, 1947.[15] On May 15, White wrote again to Mayor O'Dwyer telling him that he had been able to obtain an apartment in Manhattan.[16] With the move to West 86th Street, White now left Washington after thirteen years.

He was succeeded as the American executive director of the Fund by Andrew N. Overby, former assistant vice-president of the Federal Reserve Bank of New York, a special assistant to the Secretary of the Treasury during 1946–47, and earlier, of the Irving Trust Company of No. 1 Wall Street.

White's departure from the Fund and from the Washington scene took place at the very moment of the launching of the Truman administration's historic measures to save Western Europe.

On May 8, 1947, at Cleveland, Mississippi, Dean Acheson spoke of the interdependence of lasting peace and prosperity. Acheson stated that the United States would have to undertake "further emergency financing of foreign purchases" in 1948 and 1949 if countries were to be sustained. Requests for aid, Acheson said, might be of a type that existing institutions were not equipped to handle: "But we know that further financing, beyond existing authorizations, is going to be needed." Following a visit to Western Europe, Under Secretary of State William Clayton was also a powerful advocate of further measures.

A month later on June 5, in his Harvard address, Secretary of State George C. Marshall outlined the origins of the Plan that bears his name. Planning for the transitional period, Marshall said, had not grasped the full extent of the dislocation of the European economy. More time and effort than had been anticipated would be needed: "The United States should do whatever it is able to do to assist in the return of normal economic health in the world, without which there can be no political stability and no assured peace." The European nations, Marshall went on, would have to agree among themselves on measures "to give proper effect to whatever action might be undertaken by this Government."

With the speeches of Acheson and Marshall, the American government had reacted just in time. Within the next few months the legislative progress of the European Recovery Program in Washington was matched by the joint consultations between the Western European countries themselves. The Marshall Plan now came inevitably to overshadow the work of the Fund and the Bank, although perhaps it could not have been conceived of in the first place without the principle of international economic cooperation that had been established at Bretton Woods. But as a detailed, unified and comprehensive scheme, "transcending any measures of international aid conceived in the past," as Penrose has put it,[17] the Marshall Plan finally dealt with the hitherto intractable transitional problem in the wider context of restoring the Western economy.

Moreover, the Marshall Plan pointed rationally toward a "long-range program" for Germany which was the very opposite of that so strenuously advocated by White during his intense involvement with postwar German policy during 1944–45. Byrnes' Stuttgart speech of September, 1946, had already called for increased German production levels, and the

Anglo-American zones had been merged in January, 1947. Now, following the deadlock over Germany in the Moscow foreign ministers' conference in March and April, 1947, the United States moved to abandon finally the JCS 1067 policy in its zone. In July, 1947, a revised directive, JCS 1779, was issued, in which the earlier directive "was purged of the most important elements of the Morgenthau Plan." Following the London conference of the Western Allies, the communiqué of March, 1948, recorded that the Western zones of Germany were to be "fully associated" in the European Recovery Program.[18]

Wartime destruction, dismantling, reparations and a perhaps inevitable punitive occupation policy by the victors had brought about virtual economic standstill in occupied Germany during the immediate postwar years. A major contributory factor was the inflationary deluge of Soviet-printed AM marks from the duplicate plates delivered to the Russians; as we have seen, the three Western Allies put into circulation about 10.5 billion occupation marks, while according to one recent "very conservative estimate" the Russians issued at least 78 billion AM marks.[19] As Germany began to return to a preindustrial economy, "the whole of economic life threatened to break down since a modern industrial economy cannot function by barter. It gradually became clear to everyone that money must somehow be made to serve its proper purpose again...."[20]

As Vladimir Petrov has written, "the victor's insistence on utilising his power for the maximum destruction of the vanquished's economic potential and social structure leads to an increase in the political and economic costs of the occupation. The moment finally comes when these costs become so prohibitive as to make the continuation of a strictly punitive regime a self-defeating operation."[21]

That moment had come for the Western powers at some time in 1947, and from now on what Churchill had called "the inevitable cold fit" was in the ascendant. Along with other measures, by the end of 1947 the Anglo-Americans had provisionally agreed to a currency reform. Thus White's concept of "deindustrializing" Germany began to pass into history. Rather, from this time on, West Germany was seen as a potential ally in the new alignment of the great powers.

These developments on the world stage during 1947–48 meant that in the months after White's departure from the Fund the Bretton Woods institutions were inevitably subordinated to the Marshall Plan and the wider interests of American policy. The Russians, as we have seen, had not ratified the Bretton Woods agreements. Events now decreed that the development of the twin institutions, which had been conceived of as almost supranational, universal bodies, was played out in a way which seemed rather different from that originally envisioned by White and other postwar planners.

In June, 1947, the Fund executive directors stated that they could "look behind" applications for assistance to see whether in fact loans asked of the Fund were in line with the Articles. The Fund was again insisting on conservation of resources, and that loans were not going to be granted for reconstruction purposes. Hence, at this time, the Fund was almost inactive. Then, in the year beginning July, 1947, the Fund extended over $600,000,000 to member countries, money which was hardly needed for short-term stabilization purposes, but which was necessary as a stopgap until the Marshall Plan came into its own during 1948.

With the launching of the ERP, the Fund once again lapsed into inactivity, making virtually no exchange operations during the early years of the Marshall Plan. By mid-1949, the fourth report of the executive directors wrote the epitaph of the wartime hopes for multilateralism. The report stated that, four years after the end of the war, "dependence on bilateral trade and inconvertible currencies is far greater than before the war."[22]

Operations of the Bank were similarly subordinated to the Marshall Plan, which offered grants on terms more advantageous than the Bank. Wider political factors in harmony with American policy were also taken into consideration by the Bank directors in conserving their resources. In November, 1947, for example, it was reported that the Bank had refused a loan to Poland on the grounds that the country's refusal to attend the Paris conference on European recovery opened doubts about its independence from Russia and "its standing as a good credit risk."[23]

During the same general period of 1947–48, wartime hopes of significant advances in liberalizing commercial policy, complementary to the Bretton Woods agreements and the later loan to Britain, died away. Although the protocol of the General Agreement on Tariffs and Trade (GATT) was signed at Geneva in October, 1947, so creating a valuable permanent framework for tariff reform, progress at the time was less than expected. A few months later, in March, 1948, the International Trade Organization Charter was signed at Havana. Earlier negotiations had taken place in Geneva the previous year. But the ITO Charter was never ratified by the United States, and was thus stillborn.[24]

Finally, the suspension of the sterling convertibility provisions of the Anglo-American Financial Agreement in August, 1947, with Britain in the throes of a serious balance-of-payments crisis, had removed the third prop of the expected multilateral trading regime. The British loan, it was recognized, had largely failed as an instrument of multilateralism. American policy now moved decisively from encouraging global multilateralism to the regional emphasis of rebuilding Western Europe as a first practical step.

In this context, Britain was no longer seen as a third major world power, or as a possible trading rival to the United States. This assumed rivalry had been an undercurrent in many of the wartime negotiations and had been symbolized above all by the tariff-preference issue. Rather, with the events of 1947, came a much more realistic assessment in Washington of Britain's reduced power and its role as an American ally in facing the entirely new circumstances of a changed world. The diplomacy of a new alliance now replaced the sterling-dollar diplomacy in which White had played such a leading role.

With his departure from the International Monetary Fund in May, 1947, and his subsequent move to New York, White was now far from "the natural point of control" where he had been for so long. For the first time since he had left Lawrence College in June, 1934, to work for the Treasury, his work was no longer involved with the United States government.

In line with his letter to Mayor O'Dwyer in April, 1947, White told the House Committee in August, 1948, that following his departure from government service he was a "sort of financial and economic consultant."

From August, 1947, until he was taken ill a few weeks later White worked part-time under a technical committee of the Council of Jewish Federation and Welfare Fund. According to a later statement by the Council's president, White worked under this committee "to outline the specific types of additional studies that would be most appropriate and helpful to the projected Institute on Overseas Studies."[25]

In addition, in a brief undated memorandum of this time in White's papers, he recorded that "I am working as a consultant to the Bank of Mexico under an oral arrangement. For the time being I am to receive payment at the rate of $18,000 a year." On November 12, 1947, White filed registration forms with the United States Department of Justice covering "my employment as an economic consultant by the Bank of Mexico." But it was White's understanding that he did not have to register under the Foreign Agents Registration Act since his work for the Bank of Mexico constituted "normal business activity" under the meaning of the Act. A few weeks later, on January 21, 1948, White was thanked by an official of the Bank of Mexico for submitting a memorandum on "Suggestions for a Program of Close Economic Cooperation Between Mexico and the United States."[26]

Meanwhile, with his move to New York, White had also bought a small farm, Blueberry Hill, some three miles outside Fitzwilliam, New Hampshire, about eighty miles northwest of Boston. Here, in the austere and remote beauty of the Monadnock region of southern New Hampshire, he spent some time in the summer of 1947.

How did White regard the development of the Bretton Woods institutions in the perspective of the crisis of 1947–48 which seriously affected the earlier hopes held of the Fund and the Bank? We can see the development of his thought in two papers, one written in the spring of 1947 and a second a year later.

In a generally optimistic survey of the Fund's "first year," published in July, 1947, but probably written in April, before he left the Fund, White considered that "the major accomplishment so far is that the paper plan of a year ago has been transformed into a living reality. The Fund is now a going concern."[27]

White went on to write that an international staff had been recruited and that a library was being formed. The Fund Articles, White pointed out, were "a synthesis of different views. At times varying views and presumed national interests could be harmonized only by the adoption of more general or more ambiguous language than many of us would have liked." Thus in the Fund's first year, by-rules and working rules had evolved to "make it possible for the Fund to perform its day to day business."

Parity agreements had been reached with thirty-two countries, White wrote, mostly on the basis of existing exchange rates. What White described as "political situations" had to be taken into account in this process, perhaps implying the necessity for accepting overvalued rates in the immediate postwar period. But, White wrote, "we hope that the world will rapidly approach a relatively high degree of economic and political stability at a high level of production."

White stated that, although the Fund had been ready to begin exchange operations on March 1, 1947, "no member country eligible to purchase foreign exchange from the Fund has applied." It had been said that the absence of such requests was "an indication of failure, of breakdown, or of something wrong." This was "absurd."

White supposed that such comments arose from a confusion between the role of the Fund, with its exchange operations, and the Bank, which already had a number of requests for loans before it. Many member countries did not want to buy exchange from the Fund at present, were able to supply their needs from accumulated wartime resources or were unable to get their foreign orders filled. But sooner or later, White thought, many countries would avail themselves of the Fund's reserves.

In conclusion, White warned that the truly difficult tasks were to come when the world "seller's market" then in existence would be replaced by a "buyer's market"; when competition for world markets would characterize world trade; "and when world prices decline markedly and the international accounts of many countries appear to reflect the development of serious basic disequilibria. . . ."

The hopes expressed in this paper of course reflected the Bretton Woods view of the postwar years. This view was, as we have seen, received opinion until the crisis of early 1947. Similarly, White's remark on the dangers of an approaching decline in world prices, with its inference of possible deflation and depression, was another preoccupation of the wartime years. The true danger, perhaps, in the transitional period and after was inflation rather than deflation on the pattern of the interwar years. When White expressed these views in 1947, unhappily the Bretton Woods institutions had already been overtaken by events.

A year later, when the attempt to restore global multilateralism had been decisively overtaken by the new measures to rebuild Western Europe, White again turned to the problem of the Bretton Woods institutions. On May 19, 1948, a year after his departure from the Fund, he drafted a statement to introduce an amendment to the Fund Articles. The draft survives in White's papers at Princeton.[28]

White now wrote that " a candid appraisal of the contributions which both institutions have so far made toward the stated objectives would force us to the conclusion that achievement has been much less than anticipated . . . the small progress that has been made would be much less disturbing if there were any substantial hopes that in the next few years the situation would change. But there is no such hope. There can be none until existing world tensions disappear."

White went on to outline what he considered the two basic reasons for this state of events. The first was the rise in world prices which had almost doubled since 1944 and thus cut the value of the subscriptions to the Fund and the Bank almost in half.

But there were "other, more serious reasons," White then wrote, in a passage we have noted earlier. In 1944 it was expected "that the early postwar years would witness a degree of unity and goodwill in international political relations among the victorious allies never before reached in peacetime. It was expected that the world would move rapidly toward . . . 'One World.' . . . No influential person as far as I can remember expressed the expectation that international relations would worsen. . . .

"I doubt if any responsible official of the member governments in the spring of 1944 believed that by 1948—only three years after the cessation of hostilities—the tensions between certain of the major powers would have been so pronounced and that the world, instead of drawing together during these years, would have moved so precipitously toward a split."

White considered that the economic consequences of worsened international relations had "become almost catastrophic." Military expenditures, lack of confidence, and fear of war "on a scale unprecedented and unimaginable in its destructive potentialities" had delayed economic recovery and impeded world trade. Political developments since 1945 had in short thrown a moneky wrench into "the delicate machinery of world economic development and reconstruction." The British loan and the Marshall Plan, White went on, had helped enormously, "but these efforts are not enough to compensate for the losses sustained by the world because of the split of One World into at least two."

White's last plan, which he now tentatively outlined in this draft, proposed "to narrow the gap between the expectation and accomplishment, between need and the power to meet the need." It was characteristically ambitious as he proposed in effect to increase drastically Fund liquidity. The proposal both recalled the wider suggestions of the Keynes Plan and looked forward to the Special Drawing Rights which the Fund eventually developed twenty years later.

White's modifications were designed, first, to provide "an international medium of exchange to supplement IMF resources for the purpose of making possible increases in international trade among the member countries." Second, White hoped to accomplish this without further increasing the financial burden on countries already providing economic aid; presumably a suggestion that no great increases in Fund quotas was envisaged. Third, White hoped "to bring about a balance of world trade at a higher level than can possibly be reached with present instrumentalities."

The means proposed by White to achieve this new increase of world liquidity was "trade gold," the issue of which would be sponsored by the Fund.

It could not have been easy for White to acknowledge that the Bretton Woods institutions had proved a disappointment. This statement was never delivered, and it was not until the middle of the next decade that the Fund and the Bank came into their own. In the late 1940's the political tensions of a divided world took precedence over any financial planning. One world had become two worlds, as White had recognized. Now in a last act, he was personally involved in issues raised by this division.

THE COMMITTEE

. . . Laskell thought how much of life was being conducted as a transaction between guilt and innocence. Even among people who were devoted only to ideas of progress and social equality and not at all to action, there had grown an unusual desire to discover who was innocent and who was guilty, who could be trusted and who needed to be watched. . . .

—LIONEL TRILLING, *The Middle of the Journey,* 1947

AT THE beginning of September, 1947, four months after leaving the International Monetary Fund, White suffered "a very severe heart attack" and remained confined to his bed from Labor Day to December of that year.[1]

Meanwhile, in early 1947, as we have seen, a Federal Grand Jury had been impaneled in the Southern District of New York to inquire into Communist activities, including possible espionage, in the United States. The Grand Jury would hear Elizabeth Bentley's story. In early October, 1947, a Federal Marshal called at White's house at 334 West 86th Street in New York, and left a summons for White to appear before the Grand Jury.

Mrs. White wrote a letter on October 12 to the Federal Attorney, John F. X. McGohey, at the United States District Court, Foley Square, New York. She noted that the Federal Marshal had called the previous Friday (October 10) and went on to write that "unfortunately my husband is ill of a heart attack and it will not be possible for him to attend." A letter was enclosed from White's doctor.[2]

Three months later, in January, 1948, White was convalescing in St. Petersburg, Florida. Now, in a last political commitment, he apparently came to support the Third Party presidential candidacy of Henry Wallace, which had been declared the previous month.

A draft letter in White's papers, written from an address in St. Petersburg, and dated January 17, 1948, begins "Dear Henry, Along with millions of others I am grateful that you have come out to lead a third party." White went on to write that "it seems to me unquestionably the right thing to do now that the Democratic Party can no longer fight for peace and a better America. I want you to know that you can count on me to do anything my health permits." White ended this draft letter by saying that he had suffered a heart attack and had been *hors de combat* for some months. His improvement had been steady and he "expected to be back in the spring."[3]

Three years earlier, when writing to Wallace on the latter's confirmation as Secretary of Commerce in March, 1945, White had considered that "this is only an early round of what is going to be a battle royal extending over a number of years, and I know that in the years to come you are going to continue to put up a tremendous fight for things you stand for. The common man is indeed fortunate in having you to champion his cause in the many coming battles."

Wallace wrote to White a few months later, in July, 1945, thanking him for his "helpfulness and interest" in the early stages of the preparation of Wallace's book *Sixty Million Jobs*.[4]

In September, 1946, President Truman had asked Wallace to resign from the Cabinet following his Madison Square Garden speech attacking Byrnes' hardening approach toward the Russians. During the next year, Wallace came to think in terms of a Third Party in the 1948 presidential election led by himself and "dedicated to the proposition that the Russians earnestly wanted peace."[5]

Clearly, Wallace's approach, at a time of increasing East-West tension, represented the views of some Democrats who were unhappy with the administration's new foreign policy. Besides, Wallace was not only associated with the New Deal, but with the Midwestern progressivism which White had so enthusiastically supported in the person of La Follette nearly a quarter of a century before. And, despite what Irving Howe has called the "slick enveloping operation" by Communists and fellow travelers as the march of Gideon's Army got under way in the summer of 1948, Wallace himself of course was not a fellow traveler, let alone a Communist. Rather, Dwight MacDonald has suggested, Wallace land was "a region of perpetual fogs, caused by the warm wind of the liberal Gulf Stream coming in contact with the Soviet glacier."[6]

With the support of such disparate elements, what the Wallace movement lacked in mass support it made up in enthusiasm, an enthusiasm described in a story sent out by a New York feature agency in April, 1948. Wallace, "with his special exhilaration," it was reported, was now predicting twenty million votes in the forthcoming Presidential election.

Such votes could conceivably win him the election in a three-way race, "if they came from states with large electoral votes." "Fantastic as it seemed," the reporter went on, the Wallace brain trust had been Cabinet-making. The proposed Cabinet, "which has been thought about by Wallace and/or close advisers," included Harry Dexter White as Wallace's Secretary of the Treasury.[7]

Other Wallace choices were Supreme Court Justice William O. Douglas as Secretary of Defense, Supreme Court Justice Hugo Black as Secretary of State, and Albert Fitzgerald, president of the United Electrical Workers, as Secretary of Labor.

But it seems doubtful, after all, if Wallace's Secretary of the Treasury-designate was able to take to any active part in this final "battle royal" for the common man. (Wallace eventually polled little over a million votes.) In May, 1948, as Gideon's Army began to mobilize, White wrote to Senator Charles W. Tobey of New Hampshire. He was now "functioning again, though at a slower tempo. I manage to keep myself sufficiently occupied in my field of special interest as economic and financial consultant. . . ."[8]

During White's illness and convalescence, the Federal Grand Jury, meeting in New York, had continued with its work. It had called before it many of those named by Miss Bentley. White testified, under the subpoena sent him, on March 24–25, 1948.[9]

In this general period, FBI inquiries into Miss Bentley's story continued, although she had, of course, been unable to take up her Soviet contacts again. Chambers, who did not appear before the Federal Grand Jury prior to his public appearances before the House Committee in August, 1948, records that from 1946 to 1948 special agents of the FBI were "frequent visitors." They were interested, Chambers writes, in Harry Dexter White, Victor Perlo, Harold Glasser and others who, of course, had been named by Miss Bentley to the Bureau.[10]

Another line of inquiry which involved White's name had been instigated in the State Department, apparently as a result of Adolph Berle placing the notes of his September, 1939, conversation with Chambers at the disposal of the authorities [11]

As we have seen, Chambers had not mentioned White in the Berle interview of 1939. But in March, 1945, during a conversation on the underground between Chambers and Ray Murphy, the State Department security officer, it was noted that "Harry White of the Treasury was described as a member at large but rather timid. He put on assistants in the Treasury, Glasser, a member of the underground group, and an Adler or Odler, another party member. The two Coe brothers, also Party members, were also put on by White."

This conversation with Ray Murphy took place some five months before Miss Bentley went to the FBI. In August, 1946, in another meeting with Chambers, Murphy noted that "Harry White was reported to be a member of one of the cells, not a leader, and his brother-in-law, a dentist in New York, is said to be a fanatical Communist."[12] But at this stage, of course, as we have seen, Chambers had "suppressed" (as he puts it in *Witness*) any mention of espionage in his account of the underground to the security authorities.[13]

By the spring of 1948, the Federal Grand Jury had not returned any indictments against the people named by Miss Bentley. Instead, the thrust of the inquiry was now changed, and in July, 1948, indictments were returned against twelve leaders of the American Communist Party for alleged violation of the 1940 Smith Act, which had forbidden the advocacy of overthrowing the government by force.

Clearly, the Grand Jury in hearing Miss Bentley's story had faced considerable difficulties. As we have seen, Attorney General Brownell stated in November, 1953, that wiretap evidence was not admissible in the proceedings. Perhaps other FBI information was not available as no evidence could have been submitted to the Grand Jury which was not available in open court. The penalties for espionage, moreover, were not lenient; a maximum of thirty years or death in wartime, and a maximum of twenty years in peacetime.[14]

A lesser charge of conspiracy, presumably, could have been considered, and there was no statute of limitations on wartime espionage. But as we have seen, Miss Bentley had not produced material evidence of White's alleged underground activities, and she had not personally met White. The Federal Grand Jury had evidently failed to find her story credible enough to return a formal indictment.

Paradoxically, the tacit abandonment of the possibility of any espionage indictments by the Federal Grand Jury now at last made public the story of the Washington spy networks. For with the indictment of the Communist leaders on July 20, 1948, Miss Bentley was technically free of her Federal subpoena.

Within the next few days, a series of sensational feature articles appeared in the New York *World Telegram*, telling the story of the "red spy queen" of Soviet espionage in the nation's capital. Miss Bentley appeared as "Mary," and other principals were enigmatically described as "a Presidential adviser" and "a high Treasury official."

On July 30 Miss Bentley appeared for the first time on Capitol Hill, before Senator Homer Ferguson's Investigations Subcommittee of the United States Senate Committee on Expenditures in the Executive Departments. Before the subcommittee, Miss Bentley named one of her "independent" contacts, William Remington.

Miss Bentley's story had also come to the attention of the House Un-American Activities Committee, or House Committee. On July 31, following her unspectacular appearance before the Ferguson subcommittee, she testified before the House Committee in a hearing room in the old House Office Building. For the first time she told in public the story of her career as a courier for Soviet Intelligence, naming the alleged personnel of the Silvermaster and Perlo groups.

She was asked about White's participation, after stating that he had worked with the Silvermaster group. Miss Bentley said that she did not know whether White was "a card-carrying Communist or not":

> Mr. Stripling. What was the extent of his cooperation with your group?
>
> Miss Bentley. He gave information to Mr. Silvermaster which was relayed to me.[15]

Miss Bentley said that White knew where the information was going, but preferred "not to mention the fact." White would also help to get people of Communist sympathies into government employment, said Miss Bentley. Her statements on White were based on what Silvermaster had told her.

Of some thirty former government officials named by Miss Bentley, Harry Dexter White was of course the most senior and the most distinguished. Interviewed on the telephone at his New York home by the United Press, White said that Miss Bentley's charges were "fantastic" and that he was "shocked." He would seek permission to testify before the House Committee and "refute these charges." The UP dispatch noted that all thirty former officials named by Miss Bentley would be subpoenaed by the committee.[16]

On August 3 Chambers appeared before the committee, outlining his conspiratorial activities in a lengthy statement. He went on to describe the structure of the Ware group, his role as a courier for the Communist underground, and the way in which J. Peters had suggested that "an elite group" was to be taken out of the Ware apparatus. The "paramount objectives" of this elite group were "power and influence," infiltration rather than espionage. "It was also decided," Chambers said, "to add to this group certain other people who had not originally been in that [Ware] apparatus. One of these people was Harry White." The elite group was connected with J. Peters, head of the Communist underground, through Chambers.

Chambers told the House Committee that he could not say positively whether White was a "registered member" of the Communist Party, "but he was certainly a fellow traveller so far within the fold that his not being a Communist would be a mistake on both sides." When Chambers had left the Party he had asked White to break from the Communist movement: "He left me in a very agitated frame of mind and I thought I had succeeded. Apparently I did not."[17]

Although Chambers had excluded charges of espionage from his testimony, he had of course stated that White was known personally to him, which Miss Bentley had not done.

Two days later, in the middle of his election campaign, President Truman termed the committee's investigation a "red herring." Over a week was now to elapse before White appeared in the hearing room. The emphasis of the committee's inquiries was already shifting to the confrontation between Chambers and Hiss, named, as is well known, as both a member of the Ware group and the "elite group."

On Friday, August 13, 1948, White appeared before the House Committee. It was a remarkable occasion, and the drama—and the ambiguity —of the hearing are evident from the transcript.[18]

White took the oath, outlined his formal career, and stated that he was now a "sort of financial and economic consultant." He was given permission to read a statement:

I voluntarily asked to come here before the Committee, and the Committee has been kind enough to grant my request. I have read in the newspapers charges that have been made against me by a Miss Elizabeth Bentley and a Mr. Whittaker Chambers. I am coming before you because I think it is important that the truth be made known to the Committee, and to the public, and I am prepared to answer to the best of my ability any questions that any member of the Committee may wish to ask.

I should like to state at the start that I am not now and never have been a Communist, nor even close to becoming one; that I cannot recollect ever knowing either a Miss Bentley or a Mr. Whittaker Chambers, nor judging from the pictures I have seen in the press, have I ever met them.

The Press reported that the witnesses claim I helped to obtain key posts for persons I knew were engaged in espionage work to help them in that work. That allegation is unqualifiedly false. There is and can be no basis of fact whatsoever for such a charge.

The principles in which I believe, and by which I live, make it impossible for me ever to do a disloyal act or anything against the interests of our country, and I have jotted down what my belief is for the Committee's information.

My creed is the American creed. I believe in freedom of religion, freedom of speech, freedom of thought, freedom of the press, freedom of criticism and freedom of movement. I believe in the goal of equality of opportunity, and the right of each individual to an opportunity to develop his or her capacity to the fullest.

I believe in the right and duty of every citizen to work for, to expect and to obtain an increasing measure of political, economic and emotional security for all. I am opposed to discrimination in any form, whether on grounds of race, color, religions, political belief or economic status. I believe in the freedom of choice of one's representatives in Government, untrammeled by machine guns, secret police or a police state. I am opposed to arbitrary and unwarranted use of power or authority from whatever source or against any individual or group.

I believe in a government of law, not of men, where law is above any man and not any man above law.

I consider these principles sacred. I regard them as the basic fabric of our American way of life, and I believe in them as living realities and not as mere words on paper. That is my creed. Those are the principles I have worked for. Together those are the principles that I have been prepared in the past to fight for, and am prepared to defend at any time with my life if need be.

That is all I am going to say at this time. I am ready for any questions you may wish to ask.

Following White's opening statement, he was asked about his colleagues in the Division of Monetary Research who had been named by Miss Bentley. As we have seen, White readily agreed that Coe, Glasser, Ullmann, Adler, Mrs. Sonia Gold and others had worked for him. Currie, Silverman and Silvermaster were old and good friends. Later in the hearing, White was asked if he did not think it strange that eight or nine of all those named by Miss Bentley or Chambers had worked for him and that two others were close friends. White commented that it was "disconcerting but I would not say strange." The Treasury was probably the largest economic department, they needed all the good people they could get, and White considered that he "was a pretty good judge of the competence in that field."

White had played ping-pong in the Silvermasters', but he could not recollect whether there was any photographic equipment there. He did know that Ullmann was "interested in photography," and he had taken "excellent pictures" of White's children. The questioning circled back to Silvermaster on several occasions, described by White as "a very charming chap and a very fine chap." White had known Silvermaster for about ten years, and he had taken him to Bretton Woods as "more than an interpreter," but Silvermaster had fallen ill. White was convinced that Silvermaster was not a Communist, and when asked about his attempts in 1942 to intervene on Silvermaster's behalf when the security authorities were trying to remove him from the Board of Economic Warfare White concluded, to applause from the public, "I believe he is innocent."

White quickly dominated the committee. When he said that he had played ping-pong at the Silvermasters', the Chairman, J. Parnell Thomas, ineptly remarked to White that "for a person who had a severe heart condition you certainly can play a lot of sports." This was a reference to White's request for rest periods during the hearing because of his heart condition. White replied, to applause, that the heart attack had taken place the previous year, while he had played games for many years before that: "I hope that clears that up, Mr. Chairman. . . ."

In another round of questioning over his connections with Victor Perlo, who had worked for the Treasury, White reminded the committee, in an exchange terminated by further applause, that "our country was founded, amongst other things, on the principle that there shall be no Star Chamber proceedings." Such proceedings, White went on, were contrary to the Bill of Rights and to "all the paraphernalia of Anglo-American justice. . . ." Representative Richard Nixon countered by saying that Star Chamber proceedings were "conducted in such a way in which people were not allowed to present their side of the case. They were conducted secretly." The committee, on the contrary, favored open hearings.

When White was asked at one stage if he were the author of the Morgenthau Plan, he shot back: "Did you hear that I was the author of the famous White Plan by chance?" After saying that he had "participated in a major way in the formulation of a memorandum which was sent to—which was given to the President, to the proper authorities," White's offer to comment further on the Morgenthau Plan was turned down flat by Representative McDowell.

However, during one round of questions on the successful attempt by the security authorities, including the Office of Naval Intelligence, to extrude Silvermaster from the Board of Economic Warfare in 1942, White and the committee were obviously in complete agreement on one matter. In terms which would probably have been commended by Mr. Hoover, White emphasized that "I can well understand and thoroughly sympathize with the view that if there is the slightest question of a man's being a Communist, he ought not to be in a position—ought not to hold a position where there was any confidential information being passed; that even though there was no evidence or proof, a mere suspicion was enough."

Nevertheless, the loose investigative procedure of the committee, used on other occasions to the disadvantage of a witness, was actually a boomerang in the case of White's testimony. Each Congressman tried to develop differing points; with one exception there was no real attempt at sustained questioning, and White, with his experience of Congressional committees, was in effect able to ridicule his interrogators as he quickly came to command the situation.

But one committee member, eschewing open-ended questions relating to Communist sympathies or the alleged structure of the Silvermaster group, concentrated on the elementary (but critical) issue of whether White knew Chambers. This issue did not exist between White and Miss Bentley, who had never met. But Chambers, on the other hand, had stated he had known White, and known him well enough to ask him to break from "the Communist movement." White, for his part, in his opening statement to the committee had insisted, "judging from the pictures I have seen in the press," that he had not met Chambers. It would appear that there was a simple issue of fact between White and Chambers, irrespective of the ideological or conspiratorial issue, the truth or falsity of which might be established by close questioning of both men in turn.

Therefore, Representative Richard Nixon asked could there have been any conceivable circumstances in which White could have met Chambers, known by his underground name of Carl, during the years in question? If this could be established, then perhaps other issues could be explored. But as a beginning, could White have met Chambers in 1935 or 1936? Pictures of Chambers taken in August, 1948, were produced:

WHITE. I say I have no recollection of ever having met him. It was twelve or fifteen years ago. I must have met anywhere from 5 to 10,000 people in the last fifteen years, but I have no recollection. It may be that he did meet me, and it may be that I did chat with him.

NIXON. In the event that you had met that individual, Mr. White, on say, as many as three or four occasions, would you recollect whether you had or had not met him?

WHITE. The oftener I was supposed to have met him, the more nearly would it be that I would have remembered. It partly depends on where, what the conversation was. I should think so, three or four times, I do not know.

NIXON. Well, assuming that a meeting did occur on as many as four occasions, would your testimony be that you do not recollect having met this person?

WHITE. My testimony would have been the same. I do not recollect ever having met him. It is possible that I may have met a chap like that in any one of a dozen conferences or cocktail parties or meetings.

NIXON. Suppose you had met this individual on four occasions by himself, and were engaged in conversations with him, would you recollect whether you did or did not?

WHITE. I should think I would—I should think I would, but I am not sure.

NIXON. And you do not want to say then that if you had met him on three or four occasions, whether you do or not remember having met him?

WHITE. I do not recollect ever having met him.

NIXON. You do not recall having met any person who was known to you by the name of Carl during that period?

WHITE. No; I do not. Something I remember very definitely though, judging from the papers, and I am quoting only from the papers, that the gentleman said that he had met me and was convincing me or tried to convince me, either to go into or leave—I do not remember precisely—the Communist party or the Communist ring. That I would have remembered. And that I can confirm without any qualification or hesitation or shortness of memory or breath could not possibly have been so. . . .

NIXON. Your testimony is that you did not during the year 1935 or 1937—

WHITE. I do not recollect having met that individual.

NIXON. I am sorry, but I did not hear you. You what?

WHITE. I said I do not recollect ever meeting that individual. I am merely repeating what I said before. . . .

NIXON. In other words, the point I want to clear up is that you are stating for the record that at no time did this man by the name of Carl discuss with you the fact that he was leaving the Communist Party, and discuss also the matter of your, shall we say, ceasing to be a friend of the Communist Party—shall we put it that way?

WHITE. The first, certainly, not to my recollection. The second, I certainly would have remembered, and the answer is "No."

Perhaps Nixon's persistence indicated some private skepticism over White's denial of Chambers' charges. Yet White's denial could hardly have been more emphatic. To be sure, however, this firm denial now existed as a hostage should Chambers in turn, under further questioning, elaborate on his alleged relations with White.

But at the time, surely, what was important for White was his virtual triumph in the hearing. His credo would be printed in the papers the next day as the words of a patriot. And he was now apparently cleared of both the Federal Grand Jury and the House Committee. "He was reminiscent of a wise old college professor," wrote one columnist, Thomas Stokes, on White's appearance, "—he had been one once—a salty philosopher who roved far and wide over the whole field of human knowledge and experience and who does not get overly excited about anything that human beings can do—it has all happened before...."[19]

Following the committee hearing in Washington, White returned home to New York, where he saw his doctor the next day, August 14. Later that day he left by train for his summer place at Blueberry Hill, Fitzwilliam, New Hampshire. He was taken ill with chest pains on the train. The next day White was seen twice by Dr. George S. Emerson, the elderly, widely respected local general practitioner who lived in Fitzwilliam. Heart trouble was diagnosed. On August 16, White was again seen twice by Emerson, but apparently little could be done, so serious was the heart attack.

Late on the afternoon of Monday, August 16, 1948, White died at his summer home at Blueberry Hill.

White's family was with him, but Emerson was not present. Ever since it has been rumored, incorrectly, that White's death was not a natural one, or that there was some mystery surrounding it. The facts were set out by Dr. Emerson in an interview with the Boston newspaperman, Charles L. Whipple, in November, 1953.

Emerson told Whipple "very definitely that Harry Dexter White died of a heart attack and didn't think it at all pertinent that he was not present when White died." Whipple's account goes on:

Dr. Emerson says he got a phone call from the White home right after he arrived on the 14th. He said that while on the train he had had severe attacks of terrible pain in his chest. The next day I saw him twice. The second time he called me, I wasn't here, and while they tried to reach me, they finally got Dr. Herbert E. Flewelling of Peterboro, then a young doctor in Jaffrey. We got there about the same time. He brought his electrocardiograph machine and we took an electrocardiogram. It showed definite heart trouble.

He said nothing of the trouble he'd been through in Washington and I didn't know about it at the time. The next day, the 16th, I saw him twice again but I left before he died. There's nothing to this suicide talk. I don't believe he could have died from an overdose of digitalis. That night when they came to get the body, I was on a maternity case in Keene, and they went there and got me to sign the death certificate.

Emerson went on to tell Whipple that this was about 10:30 on the morning of August 16, and that he had listed the cause of death as "coronary heart attack due to disease of coronary arteries and heart." The State of New Hampshire death certificate was reproduced with Whipple's interview in the Boston *Globe*. Following Whipple's talk with Emerson, the newspaperman spoke on the telephone with Dr. Herbert E. Flewelling of Peterboro, who had, of course, also attended White. Dr. Flewelling said that he

remembered the case well because of all hullabaloo afterwards. I'll try to look up the cardiogram. We both felt strongly at the time that it was a typical death caused by heart trouble. I remember distinctly it was an abnormal cardiogram definitely indicating he had heart trouble. He was having a very severe episode of pain. It was a very definite thing, of the kind we see often. I saw nothing about the case at the time that seemed suspicious to me, such as taking poison. I saw nothing on the cardiogram that would suggest his taking too much digitalis.

Flewelling later found the cardiogram and told Whipple that "it confirmed what he said before."[20]

When Dr. Emerson signed the death certificate at Keene, only a few miles away from Fitzwilliam, arrangements were already in hand to remove White's body to Boston for the funeral. At 7:30 on the evening of August 16, the Boston undertaking firm of J. S. Waterman & Sons received a telephone call from Abraham White, one of Harry White's brothers, who informed them that Harry Dexter White had died at 5:45 P.M. that day and asked them to look after the funeral arrangements.

A hearse was sent from Boston to Fitzwilliam, and the driver obtained Dr. Emerson's signature on the death certificate, in the circumstances noted above. Besides the death certificate, a burial permit was also signed at about midnight on the day that White died by Willard M. Blodgett, town clerk of Fitzwilliam. White's body was then driven through the night to his native city of Boston.[21]

On August 18, the news of White's death was a front-page story in the New York *Times*. At Waterman's, the funeral proceedings were "routine," and the next day the burial papers were filed in Boston City Hall. A funeral service was then held at Waterman's chapel in Boston at 11 A.M. on August 19, officiated by Rabbi Irving Mandel of the city's Temple Israel, where White had been married. It was attended by about thirty-five people.

Later that day White's body was cremated at Forest Hills cemetery, in the Jamaica Plains area of south Boston, a few miles away from his birthplace at Lowell Street. Nearby are the old districts of Roxbury and Dorchester where White had lived briefly as a young man in the years before the First World War, when he had worked at J. White's Sons.

With his death in August, 1948, White's name dropped out of the head-lines, overshadowed by the tragic confrontation between Hiss and Chambers and tumultuous events in world politics. But the half-forgot-ten case lived on. Five years later it would become a hotly debated national issue involving both Mr. Truman and General Eisenhower.

This chain of events began with the Bentley-Chambers testimony of the summer of 1948 and was taken a step further three months after White's death, when Chambers produced documents containing govern-ment information which he claimed Hiss and White had given him ten years earlier. This charge, of course, broadened the original accusation of Communist infiltration by the "elite group" to include espionage for the Soviet. But here we must only recapitulate events concerning White.

On November 14, 1948, so Chambers tells us, he retrieved from the Brooklyn dumbwaiter the documents which he had secreted ten years before as a "life preserver" against the revenge of the underground. Besides the documents which appeared in the Hiss trials, Chambers tells us, he also retrieved "a long memo on yellow foolscap in the handwriting of Harry Dexter White," the so-called White Memorandum. These pa-pers were shown to Chambers' lawyers the next day, and, Richard Nixon told the House of Representatives in January, 1950, the alleged White documents were turned over to the United States Department of Justice on November 17, 1948.[22]

Three months later, in February, 1949, a staff member of the House Committee gave photostatic copies of the White Memorandum, along with photostatic copies of White's handwriting from the Treasury files, to a government handwriting expert. The handwriting expert, Harold Ge-sell of the Veterans' Administration, reported that after "careful exami-nation and comparison" of the documents submitted, "It is concluded" that "Harry D. White is the author of the questioned writings purporting to be notes involving State Department activities." (The notes, rather, involved some foreign operations of the United States Treasury, as we have noted.) Gesell also reported that "the above conclusion is subject to rectification upon examination of the original documents."[23]

Later that year, during the second Hiss trial, Chambers stated in court that, apart from Hiss, the main sources of his apparatus were Julian

Wadleigh and Harry Dexter White. Chambers told the court "that White had given him many documents, some of them even in his own handwriting."[24]

In January, 1950, the trial jury found Hiss guilty on two charges of perjury before the Federal Grand Jury, and on January 25, Hiss was sentenced to five years' imprisonment.

The next day, January 26, Richard Nixon delivered a speech on the background of the Hiss case on the floor of the House. During this speech he noted that Chambers had testified in open court that White was a source of information for the Soviet espionage ring, and that Chambers had received various documents from White which he had turned over to the Soviet. Nixon went on to say that since December, 1948, he had possessed photostatic copies of eight pages of documents "in the handwriting of Mr. White" which Chambers had turned over to the Justice Department on November 17, 1948. Since Chambers testified that he had received documents from White, "I think the public is entitled to see and consider the evidence."

Nixon then went on to say that "these facts have definitely been established." First, a government handwriting expert, Harold Gesell, had "established the documents were in Mr. White's handwriting." Second, Chambers, a self-confessed espionage agent, "had the documents in his possession." Third, "a substantial portion of the information contained in these documents was of a confidential nature."

Richard Nixon then read the text of the White Memorandum into the *Congressional Record*.[25]

Eighteen months later, in August, 1951, as we have seen, both Chambers and Elizabeth Bentley testified again on White before the Senate subcommittee.

Miss Bentley elaborated on how White had passed information to Silvermaster for transmission to her. She stated that White had used his considerable influence to place Communists in American government departments. She alleged that White had not only devised a plan to "integrate" intelligence for the underground gained from the numerous interdepartmental committees on which he sat, but that the plan had been put into effect. Miss Bentley concluded by saying that during 1944 the Russians, for security reasons, "had intended to put White directly in contact with a Soviet superior" and that she was "convinced" that the plan had gone through.

Chambers' testimony on this occasion was heightened by his personal knowledge of White, whom he said he had known "rather well." The witness reiterated that White was one of his sources for Colonel Bykov and Soviet Intelligence, and that he passed both original government documents and a weekly or fortnightly summary of confidential information in his own handwriting. Referring to the alleged White Memorandum, Chambers said that one of these handwritten reports was in the custody of the Department of Justice.

Chambers summed up by saying that White's character was such that he enjoyed being of the Communist Party, but not in the Party and subject to its discipline: "In that relationship he was willing to go to great lengths to assist them."[26] The following year, Chambers published *Witness*, which repeated this story of White's involvement with the underground.

By the time Elizabeth Bentley and Chambers testified on White in the summer of 1951, the charge of alleged "Communists in Government" had become a major issue in American politics, exacerbated by the attacks of Senator Joe McCarthy. In the Presidential campaign of 1952, the charge featured prominently in the Republican criticisms of the Democratic administration. The issue lived on after General Eisenhower succeeded Mr. Truman in the White House in January, 1953.

However, by this time the White case itself seemed half-forgotten. Then, in November, 1953, White's name was catapulted into the political arena in a speech by the Attorney General, Herbert Brownell. On November 6, 1953, in a speech defending the new administration's vigilance in security matters, given to the Executives' Club of Chicago, Attorney General Brownell stated,

> Harry Dexter White was a Russian spy. He smuggled secret documents to Russian agents for transmission to Moscow. Harry Dexter White was known to be a Communist agent by the very people who appointed him to the most sensitive position he ever held in Government service.
>
> . . . I can now announce officially, for the first time in public, that the records in my department show that White's spying activities for the Soviet Government were reported in detail by the FBI to the White House . . . in December of 1945. In the face of this information, and incredible though it may seem President Truman subsequently on Jan. 23, 1946, nominated White who was then Assistant Secretary of the Treasury, for the even more important position of Executive Director for the United States in the International Monetary Fund.[27]

Mr. Truman then stated, in words later withdrawn, that he knew nothing of any FBI report: "As soon as we found White was disloyal, we fired him." Soon after, Truman said that, "White was fired by resignation."

Brownell had discussed his speech with Sherman Adams and James

Hagarty, the White House press secretary, and, in a vague way, without going into details, with Eisenhower. In the mounting uproar, Chairman Harold Velde of the House Committee attempted, unsuccessfully, to subpoena Truman. James Byrnes issued the statement, already noted, of events in the White House on February 6, 1946, the day that White's nomination to the Fund passed the Senate.

President Eisenhower, for his part, now moved to dissociate himself from charges which evidently impugned Mr. Truman's patriotism. He told his press conference that he considered it inconceivable that Truman would knowingly do anything to damage the United States. In this atmosphere of universal accusation, clearly affecting the office of the Presidency, the White case had become a national issue. White's name now became known for the first time to millions in the United States and abroad.

On November 16, Mr. Truman, in a national radio and television address, strongly defended his actions in the White case. He stated that Brownell's charges against him were false. He went on to tell his national audience that when Brownell made his charges "I was unable to remember the precise documents to which he referred, just as President Eisenhower was unable to remember that he had met with Harry Dexter White and Secretary of the Treasury Morgenthau in 1944." In his news conference, a few days earlier, Eisenhower had stated that he did not know anything about White. It had then been pointed out that Fred Smith's article on the origins of the Morgenthau Plan, which we have noted, had described a supposedly seminal meeting between Eisenhower, Morgenthau and White in England in 1944.

Mr. Truman then outlined the events, noted earlier, which had led to his decision in February, 1946, to retain White in government service pending an FBI investigation. White, said the former President, was then "separated from the Government service promptly" when the necessity for secrecy concerning the FBI investigation ended. Truman concluded his address by vigorously attacking the administration which had "fully embraced, for political advantage, McCarthyism."[28]

The next day, November 17, 1953, the administration replied to Truman's address with the appearance of both Brownell and J. Edgar Hoover before the Senate Internal Security Subcommittee.[29] It was on this occasion that the series of FBI documents sent to the White House between November, 1945, and February, 1946, on Harry Dexter White were partly declassified. Photostats of the White Memorandum were also released, as we shall see below.

Brownell, who was accompanied by the Deputy Attorney General, William P. Rogers, later Secretary of State, appeared to modify some of the statements in his Chicago speech. He stated that the case against

White, as we have seen, did not relate to criminal proceedings, but whether White should be promoted to the Fund. Brownell told the subcommittee that the FBI warning sent to the White House in December, 1945, "constituted adequate warning to anyone who read it of the extreme danger to the security of the country" in appointing White to the Fund. Brownell also stated that he did not mean to impugn Mr. Truman's loyalty in his Chicago speech, but that he considered him "blind on this score."

In his testimony, the Attorney General outlined the nature of the FBI documents sent to the White House which we have noted earlier in discussing the events of 1945–46. Some of the documents were quoted verbatim.

Hoover also dealt in some detail, as we have seen, with the events of 1945–46, summarizing the relevant FBI reports and letters. The FBI Director emphasized that White had not been retained in government service on the FBI's agreement. He had told Tom Clark, then Attorney General, that he considered it "unwise" for White to go to the Fund, as he was "unfit." But Hoover pointed out that evidence necessary to sustain court conviction was quite different from that necessary to establish "the existence of security risks in sensitive posts in the Government."

Both Brownell and Hoover evidently considered that the production of the alleged White documents by Chambers removed any doubt about White's involvement with Soviet Intelligence.

Brownell considered that "no one could with any validity, suggest today that there is any doubt that White was in this espionage ring. Some of the White espionage reports, written by him in his own handwriting for delivery to agents of the Red Army Intelligence, were recovered in the fall of 1948 and are now in the Department of Justice." The Attorney General then released copies of the White documents allegedly given to Chambers.

Later in his testimony, Brownell went on to say that "much of this evidence" against White was received by wiretap not admissible before a Federal Grand Jury or a Federal court in a criminal case. Referring to the wiretap evidence Brownell said that "therefore, that information was not available to the Grand Jury and, secondly, when the pressure came, when the conclusive evidence came of these papers in 1948, shortly after his death, of course that had not been discovered at that time."

In much the same way, Hoover, referring to the White Memorandum, told the committee:

Miss Bentley's account of White's activities was later corroborated by Whittaker Chambers, and documents in White's own handwriting concerning which there can be no dispute, lend credibility to the information previously reported on White. Subsequent to White's death on August 16, 1948 events transpired which produced facts of an uncontradictable nature which clearly established the reliability of the information furnished in 1945 and 1946.

Evidently for Brownell and Hoover, the matter was closed, and at the time of writing these remain the last official comments on "the White case." Shorn of its partisan element, much of Brownell's original statement of the facts concerning the delivery of the FBI reports to the White House had been essentially correct. But the case against White, however plausible on "security" grounds, had not been established by courtroom standards in February, 1946, as we have seen. At the same time, it seems clear that President Truman had found out about the FBI reports on White too late to have White's nomination to the Fund withdrawn by the Senate.

Following the Brownell-Hoover statements on White to the Senate Subcommittee, President Eisenhower hoped that no more would be heard of the matter. On November 19, an editorial in the New York *Times* considered that in 1945 and 1946 there was "ample reason" to question White's loyalty. The newspaper criticized both the timing and method of Brownell's original speech and some of the security procedures of the previous administration, so setting the episode in some sort of perspective. In his memoirs, *Mandate for Change*, published a decade later, General Eisenhower, in a brief passage on the events of November, 1953, referred to the "incontrovertible evidence" against White.[30]

There were two further episodes involving the White case before the matter finally disappeared from public attention.

On June 1, 1955, Henry Morgenthau, Jr., voluntarily testified on Harry Dexter White before the Senate Subcommittee, where he was received with deference. Morgenthau's appearance was consequent upon the Brownell speech of November, 1953, and the Senate Subcommittee's continuing interest in the White case. It was the first time that Morgenthau had testified on White since the latter's name had first been mentioned in the House hearings of 1948. Morgenthau reviewed White's career in the Treasury during his own term of office, from 1934 to 1945. He went on: "The entire time I was in office I had no reason to suspect White's integrity or his loyalty to the United States. No security agent and no individual ever reported or suggested to me that there was any doubt about White's loyalty. It was some time after I resigned that I learned that any charge of disloyalty had been made against him. I was shocked and surprised when those charges were first brought to my attention."

Morgenthau went on to say that he had not had access to any classified documents since his resignation from the Treasury in 1945, and in the circumstances he did not think that he could attempt to assess the charges against White. If the charges had been brought when he was in office, "I . . . should immediately have suspended White and ordered a full investigation."

The subcommittee's chairman, Senator Eastland, thanked Morgenthau for his cooperation; earlier Morgenthau had agreed that subcommittee staff could examine his Diaries. The chairman went on to say that Morgenthau was to be commended for his "objective attitude with respect to the question of possible disloyalty in high places." Such an attitude, the chairman considered, "one might look for in a real elder statesman." Responding to the chairman, Morgenthau, who was shortly leaving for a holiday in Europe, thanked the subcommittee for its consideration, stating that if in the future they wanted anything "you will get my whole-hearted cooperation." On this note of mutual esteem, Morgenthau departed.[31]

A few weeks later, in July, 1955, the White summer home at Blueberry Hill, Fitzwilliam, was searched "upon proper process" by the Attorney General of New Hampshire (later Congressman), Louis C. Wyman. He was accompanied by a special assistant, Joseph Gall, and Sheriff Frank Walker of Keene. An earlier search had been made on the authority of the State Attorney General in November, 1953.

Now, in a final ceremony, some of White's papers from Blueberry Hill, which had been found during the two searches, were placed into the Senate Subcommittee's records during a special hearing in the State House, Concord, New Hampshire, on August 30, 1955.[32]

But by this time, the passions of the early 1950's were beginning to ebb. Stalin had died in 1953. Two years later, in the summer of 1955, President Eisenhower had attended the Geneva Conference with the Soviet leaders, and the consequent "spirit of Geneva" was in the air. Issues which had fired much of White's career, such as the new international financial order, relations with Russia, or the place of Germany in the postwar world, now appeared solved, after a fashion.

In spite of the uneasy peace, and recurrent alarms and excursions, the next few years were a relatively tranquil time in the West. It was even a time which some men would look back to later, as a time between two turbulent eras.

Was the evidence against White "conclusive" (Brownell), "uncontradictable" (Hoover), or "incontrovertible" as General Eisenhower wrote in his memoirs? If so, how may we attempt to assess White's career as a whole?

In the first place, surely, it should be emphasized that White was not tried by any court of law in his lifetime. Presumably, in the light of White's statements to the House Committee in August, 1948, had a later perjury prosecution ever been initiated against him on the basis of the documents produced by Chambers, the "two-witnesses" rule, designed to protect the defendant on such a prosecution, would have obtained. The prosecution would have had to prove to the court's satisfaction that the documents were in White's hand, and that White had given the documents to Chambers.

We have also seen that, as well as the silent evidence of the documents produced by Chambers, the so-called White Memorandum, his story and that of Elizabeth Bentley were partly corroborated by each other. For Chambers had mentioned White to the FBI in 1942, and to the State Department security officer, Ray Murphy, in 1945, before Miss Bentley went to the authorities. We have also noted the comments of Professor Packer that "it seems most reasonable to assume that what probably happened was what appears to have happened, namely that Miss Bentley and Chambers, independently and without knowledge of each other's stories," named White to the authorities at two different times. And that, Professor Packer concluded, "is corroboration of a kind that cannot lightly be dismissed."

Clearly, as we have seen, there were a number of inconsistencies and inaccuracies in the Bentley-Chambers testimony. Miss Bentley, moreover, never met White, and Chambers did not charge White with espionage until the documents were produced after White's death. But, taken as a whole, are these considerations central or peripheral? The writer considers that the arguments against the credibility of Miss Bentley and Chambers on the central issue regarding White are not sustained. Absolute certainty, of course, can only be established on very few issues in history. But until any evidence in the future refutes the Chambers-Bentley story on White, it is tentatively assumed here that, on the whole, the story of the witnesses regarding White was correct.

Finally, perhaps, the answer lies in White's character. With his justly deserved success in the Treasury, following the doldrums of his later Harvard career, White became increasingly brash and overconfident. "He could be disagreeable," Henry Morgenthau told Professor Blum years later, "quick tempered, overly ambitious, and power went to his head."[33]

Moreover, these characteristics which went with White's high responsibilities and great achievements may have been harnessed to a view of government that did White no good. As we have seen from the memoranda he wrote in presenting his Pacific peace proposals in 1941, White believed in "all-out" diplomacy as he castigated the "traditional method" with its "atmosphere of high secrecy." "Where we should speak openly and clearly, we engage in protocol, in secret schemes and subtleties."

Modern diplomacy, White considered, "called for swift and bold action," a prescription that may have led White into circumventing ordinary channels of government in what he regarded as a good cause. It is of interest to note that Professor Blum, in the passage noted above, considers that White "appointed some assistants who were almost certainly members of the Communist Party, though Morgenthau did not know they were, and those assistants, in White's view, were as free to pass along information about Treasury policy to the Russians as was Averell Harriman, for example, free to talk to the British. . . ."

Such an attitude could mean that White was led from one step to another. Yet, clearly, the author of the White Plan was a man who wished to remake the world, and it was second nature for him to propose large schemes on a grand scale. Many of the impulses in his official career, with the marked exception of the Treasury Plan for Germany, were decent and honorable ones. Like many men of his time White looked forward, as we have seen in these pages, to a new, unified world which would replace the old. If some of White's large schemes involved the Soviet Union, such as his successive proposals for credits, what seems most likely is not that White was a Communist, but rather, as Lord Robbins has suggested, "a sentimental and highly indiscreet fellow traveller."[34]

Yet those who place themselves above the accepted laws and loyalties of the world, whatever the cause, have frequently to pay some penalty. There is also the possibility that White was the victim as well as the agent of what Rebecca West has described as "some grimly compulsive force": "It is impossible not to feel that Harry White, this gifted and playful man, began by putting his finger in every pie but ended in giving his whole body to the rack."[35]

In our prologue we suggested that there was some difficulty in assessing White's historical role. The answer, it is suggested, is that the Bretton Woods institutions will remain White's enduring monument. Of White's own fate, perhaps it suffices to suggest that hubris may have led to nemesis with his abrupt fall from grace in the winter of 1945–46. *Requiescat.*

EPILOGUE

A POSTSCRIPT ON BRETTON WOODS

On August 15, 1971, President Richard Nixon suspended the dollar's convertibility into gold, so allowing the dollar to float on the world's exchanges. A 10 percent surcharge was imposed on American imports. A few days later the President was quoted as saying that "the old monetary system" which had originated over a quarter of a century earlier at Bretton Woods was "crisis-prone" and could not be "patched up."

The President's actions and words in August, 1971, recognized that its role as the world's banker had become too great for the United States. The virtual impossibility of changing by American action the value of the dollar in relation to other countries, the rigidity of the world's exchange rates, and in commercial policy, the problems posed by the rise of Japan's economic power and the new trading area of the European Economic Community had all led to the great dollar crisis.

Remedial measures since August, 1971, have included the new parities of the Smithsonian Agreement of December, 1971, which also devalued the dollar, the second U.S. devaluation of February 1973, and the decision the following month to float the world's major currencies against the dollar. Yet the open world economy of the postwar era, pivoted on the Fund, the Bank, and GATT, the latter born from the same spirit of wartime Anglo-American collaboration as Bretton Woods, remains threatened. A new protectionism may arise unless a reform of the Bretton Woods system, along with new arrangements in commercial policy, are negotiated.

In a rapidly changing world, what remains the legacy of the devoted work of White, Keynes and their associates some thirty years ago?

Perhaps it should be remembered in the first place that the architects of sterling-dollar diplomacy in the negotiations which culminated at Bretton Woods worked at a time when there were but two major world trading currencies. Today there are powerful economic forces in Western Europe, Japan, and the United Kingdom itself has entered the European Economic Community. The very need for a reform of the Bretton Woods system is a comment on the passing of the special role of sterling and the dollar in the world economy. Moreover, the Anglo-American negotiators worked at a time when there was a unique stimulus toward agreement in the form of the wartime alliance.

On the other hand, as we have seen in the pages above, the political difficulties surmounted by White and Keynes, as committed advocates of new world monetary arrangements, were very considerable. The forces of economic nationalism were strong in both countries, and it seems to one observer at least a historic achievement that White and Keynes were able to play such an effective role in establishing the Bretton Woods institutions. Probably the difficulties faced and overcome by White and Keynes at that time were even greater than those faced by today's multilateral negotiators over new exchange parities, wider margins, and the future role of the Fund Special Drawing Rights. But they persisted and won their case. The achievement remains.

The first legacy, therefore, of the men of Bretton Woods is the necessity for the political will to reach agreement on the best solution. Such a will White and Keynes showed many times as they hammered out the intricacies of the Fund Articles in 1942–44: "Well, Harry, what shall it be today—passivity, exchange stability, or the role of gold?"

The second legacy of Bretton Woods remains the twin institutions themselves created by White and Keynes, institutions which certainly did not come about by accident. For despite the turbulent events of the last thirty years, leading to the breakdown of "the old monetary system," the Fund and the Bank (with GATT) still remain an indispensable institutional framework for implementing those wartime hopes of the Anglo-American negotiators.

Within this framework the United States and the United Kingdom, albeit in a very changed world, can still continue that movement toward a liberal international trading order that lies very much in their interest. It was such an order that the author of the White Plan envisaged in early 1942. Surely White's own words in inaugurating the work of the Fund in May, 1946, are just as apposite today: "The problems before us . . . are extremely complex. They will demand all we possess of wisdom, experience, goodwill and economic statesmanship. Our hope of helping lies in being able to pool these resources for the benefit of all countries. . . ."

APPENDICES

If Japan repeats another incident like the "Panay" incident, Treasury machinery is all ready to embargo Japanese imports into U.S. & freeze her dollar balances. This was done at the Pres. orders. It remains unknown outside of Treasury.

We have just agreed to purchase 50 million more oz. of silver from China. China will have left (almost all in London) about 100 million oz. of silver. Her dollar balances are almost all gone.

Bullit just called to Sec. (copy not available) comment by Herriot, Blum, Reynaud, to him. Herriot says if he were premier he would quickly strengthen ties with U.S.S.R. & recover Czech. that France will at once come to her military aid and if Germany enters Czech. He also stated that if U.S.S.R. goes to aid of Czech. she would cut through Roumanian resistance "like butter". and would also get through quaking Esthonia against their wishes. Herriot doesn't think there is any chance, however, of his

PAGE Q2 reverse of "The White Memorandum," allegedly given by Harry Dexter White to Whittaker Chambers in 1938. The full text is reproduced in Appendix A. Used with permission of the U.S. Department of Justice.

APPENDIX A

Text of "The White Memorandum" produced by Whittaker Chambers at Baltimore, November 17, 1948

Photostat Q1 obverse

1/10/38. Taylor tried to press the Secretary (indirectly through Feis to Hull to Sec.) to hurriedly accept an offer from Hungary of settlement of her 2 million dollar debt to U.S. Govt. The payment offered was trivial. Sec. refused to be hurried & said did not want to establish a pattern on these int. debt settlements without considering the whole problem. The fact that the Hungarian amount involved was trifling was no reason to accept the offer as it raised matters of principles, precedent, policy etc.

(What is behind Taylor's (and possibly Feis) desire to press M. into a debt settlement arrangement of that character at this time. Why didn't Taylor try to convince Sec. directly instead of surreptitiously via Feis.)

1/19/38. U.S. Naval Captain Ingersoll will remain in London until English want to communicate anything to us with respect to Japan boycott or exchange controls. He is to act solely as agent of communication and not discuss matters. English are now interested in

Q1 reverse

in economic boycotts if against Japan. Some incident may develop which will lead them to be desirous of our cooperation. We are likely to act alone only if unusually "bad" incident occurs such as another Panay incident.

Japan according to Col. Strong, has increased greatly its storage facilities for oil. Tanks built underground with two layers of thick cement and air space between as protection against bombing. Reported yesterday through private Jap banking connection (unknown but supposed to be important) that J. will not declare war on China for some time at least.

Sec. reading Red Star Over China and is quite interested.

Q2 obverse

We have just discovered evidence of Japanese "dumping" of textiles into U.S. and are requiring importers to put up 100% bond against imports. I expect evidence of dumping will increase.

About 1 month ago the Pres. asked Sec. M. to secretly place as many obstacles in the path of imports from Japan as possible under existing regulations. Our purchases from Japan are declining [*illegible word crossed out*] steadily mostly

433

on items other than silk. Our imports average about two-thirds of last years average. Part of the decline is due, of course, to our reduction in purchases from all countries.

Japans dollar balances in the U.S. are not declining much. They are about 50 million dollars.

Purchases of Japanese goods by
       are decreasing sharply while our exports to these countries are increasing.

State Dept. believes British moves towards Italy and Germany will reduce substantially European fear of war in the near future.

Q2 reverse

If Japan repeats another incident like the Panay incident Treasury machinery is all ready to embargo Japanese imports into U.S. & freeze her dollar resources. This was done at the Pres. wishes.

It remains unknown outside of Treasury.

We have just agreed to purchase 50 million more oz. of silver from China. China will have left (almost all in London) about 100 million oz. of silver. Her dollar balances are almost all gone.

Bullitt just called to Sec. (copy not available) comment by Herriot, Blum, Reynaud to him. Herriot says that if he were premier he would quickly strengthen ties with U.S.S.R. & reassure Czech that France will at once come to her military aid if Germany enters Czech. He also stated that if U.S.S.R. goes to aid of Czech she would cut through Roumanian resistance 'like butter' and would also go through quickly Latvia and Estonia against their wishes. Herriot doesn't think there is any chance, however, of his

Q3 obverse

becoming Premier.

Reynaud believed the solution of French economic situation is to permit a sharp drop in the franc. Also to form a national cabinet that would include all elements. Blum claims he doesn't want to be premier at this time.

Marchandeau tried feebly to get Eng. & U.S. to agree to support the franc. (Not the slightest chance) The prospects of continued depreciation of franc are very strong.

I have heard nothing as to Capt. Ingersolls mission in England beyond my earlier explanation. So far as Treasury is concerned he is supposed to be there in case of another incident with Japan. In that event he would serve as secret liaison man between Eng. and U.S. unknown to anybody as to the nature of his mission. Chamberlain turned us down at the time of the Panay incident when we asked him whether he would cooperate with us in placing exchange restrictions against Japanese operations in case we decided to do so, but another Knatchbull incident may bring them around.

State Dep't was eager to accept Hungary's debt offer & sold idea to Sec M. & president. But Congress doesn't want to begin debt negotiations with Hungary.

Q3 reverse

The Van Zeeland report was not taken seriously here.

Q4 obverse

(via Cochrane)
Bachman of the Swiss. Nat Bank said 2/15/38 that the Japanese have recently put out a feeler to some of his banks for a loan for industrial development in Manchouko. "However, his bankers have not sufficient interest in such a proposition even to submit it to their National Bank for consideration and possible approval.

"Schact impressed me—and some of my friends also—as finding some hope in Van Zeeland report as a basis for a possible approach between German and the British and French."

"Schact said he positively did not know what had taken place at the meeting between Hitler and Schuschnigg."

Q4 reverse

65 big sheets
4 little slips

SOURCE: U.S. Department of Justice. The photostat copies of the original documents were released by the United States Attorney General on November 17, 1953.

Report by Harold Gesell, Handwriting Expert of the Veterans' Administration, on the "White Memorandum," March 2, 1949

March 2, 1949.
EI/HJEG: ml.
#1829.

Director, Inspection-Investigation Service.
Chief, Identification & Detection Division.
Examination of handwriting of Harry D. White
(Committee on Un-American Activities).

1. On February 21, 1949, Investigator Owens, of the Committee on Un-American Activities of the U.S. House of Representatives, personally and informally submitted three photostatic copies of documents purporting to bear the known writings of one Harry D. White, which are identified as follows:

K-1 Photostatic copy of letter dated June 11, 1934, addressed to "Dr. Jacob Viner, Treasury Department, Washington, D.C." and signed "Harry D. White".

K-2 Photostatic copy of Personal History Statement (Standard Form No. 6) which purports to be the Personal History Statement of Harry Dexter White, understood to bear certain writings made by Harry Dexter White.

K-3 Photostatic copy of final portion of Personal History Statement (Standard Form No. 6) purporting to bear the known writings of Harry D. White.

Investigator Owens also submitted eight pages (photostatic copies) of questioned writing herein identified as Q-1 through Q-8.

2. It was requested that an examination and comparison be conducted of the purported known writings of Harry D. White (identified as K-1, K-2, and K-3) with the questioned writings (identified as Q-1 through Q-8), to determine whether Harry D. White is the author of the questioned writing. It was also requested that the documents as submitted be photographed, and that several copies of each document be attached to the report.

3. A careful examination and comparison was conducted regarding the afore mentioned writings and as a result of such a study, it is concluded that the person responsible for the writings appearing on K-1, K-2, and K-3, purporting to be the known writings of Harry D. White, also is responsible for all of the writing appearing on Q-1 through Q-8. In other words, Harry D. White is the author of the questioned writings purporting to be notes involving State Department activities.

4. The above conclusion is subject to verification upon examination of the original documents.

5. Photostatic copies of the documents as submitted, together with three photographic copies of each document, are attached.

HAROLD J. E. GESELL

Atts

SOURCE: Committee on the Judiciary, Internal Security Subcommittee, *Institute of Pacific Relations*, Hearings, 82nd Congress, 2nd Session (1951–2), p. 5488.

Average retail market prices in the cities of Nationalist China, 1937–48

1937		1943	
July	1.0	June	132
December	1.2	December	228
1938		1944	
June	1.4	June	466
December	1.8	December	755
1939		1945	
June	2.3	June	2,167
December	3.2	August	2,647
1940		December	2,491
June	4.9	1946	
December	7.2	August	5,485
1941		December	8,613
June	11	1947	
December	20	June	36,872
1942		December	129,384
June	33	1948	
December	66	June	1,335,303
		20 September	8,740,600

SOURCE: Arthur Young, *China's Wartime Finance and Inflation, 1937–1945* (1965), pp. 348, 358. Used by permission of Harvard University Press.

Average Gold prices, Retail prices, Exchange rates and American dollar equivalents of Gold prices in Nationalist China during the Second World War

(Retail Prices, January–June, 1937 = 100. The Chinese ounce or *tael* is roughly comparable with the Troy ounce.)

End of year	Retail market prices, average	Gold price, average per Chinese ounce	Free market exchange rate per US$	Equivalent value of gold per ounce, average
1937	118	C$ 115	C$ 3.35	US$ 34.40
1938	176	210	6.10	34.50
1939	323	400	13.30	30.10
1940	724	750	18.00	41.70
1941	1,977	2,400	28.00	86.00
1942	6,620	6,150	49.00	125.00

End of quarter	Retail market prices, average (continued)	Official price	Free price	Average	Based on Official prices	Free prices
1943 (4th)	22,800	12,500	12,977	83	150	157
1944 (1st)	33,300	17,000	17,895	170	100	105
(2nd)	46,600	18,500	18,803	203	91	93
(3rd)	56,200	18,500	20,070	209	89	96
(4th)	75,500	22,500	28,932	441	51	66
1945 (1st)	142,000	24,500	38,235	558	44	69
(2nd)	216,700	39,500	92,477	1,060	37	87

SOURCE: Arthur Young, *China and the Helping Hand* (1963), p. 444. Used by permission of Harvard University Press.

APPENDIX C

Extract from national radio-television address by
former President Harry S. Truman on the White Case,
November 16, 1953

. . . I have had my files examined and have consulted with some of my colleagues who worked with me on this matter during my term of office. The facts, as I have determined them in this manner, are these:

In late 1945, the FBI was engaged in a secret investigation of subversive activities in this country. In this investigation, the FBI was making an intensive effort to verify and corroborate certain accusations of espionage made by confidential informants.

A lengthy FBI report on this matter was sent to the White House in December, 1945. The report contained many names of persons in and out of government service concerning whom there were then unverified accusations. Among the many names mentioned, I now find, was that of Harry Dexter White, who had been in the Treasury Department for many years and who was at that time an Assistant Secretary of the Treasury.

As best I can now determine, I first learned of the accusations against White early in February, 1946, when an FBI report specifically discussing activities of Harry Dexter White was brought to my attention. The February report was delivered to me by General Vaughan and was also brought to my personal attention by Secretary of State Byrnes.

This report showed that serious accusations had been made against White, but it pointed out that it would be practically impossible to prove these charges with the evidence then at hand.

Immediately after the matter was brought to my attention, I sent a copy of the report, with a covering note signed by me, to White's immediate superior, the Secretary of the Treasury, Fred Vinson. In this note dated February 6, 1946, I said:

"I am enclosing you a memorandum from the Secretary of State which came to me this morning.

"I suggest that you read it, keeping it entirely confidential and then, I think, you, the Secretary of State, and myself should discuss the situation and find out what we should do." That's the end of the quotation from my note to Mr. Vinson.

Later—I believe it was the same day—I discussed the matter with Secretary Vinson as well as with Secretary Byrnes.

As I have mentioned, Mr. White was at that time an Assistant Secretary of the Treasury. It had been planned for some time that he should be transferred from that position to be the United States member on the board of executive directors of the International Monetary Fund, a new international organization then in process of being set up.

His appointment had been sent to the Senate for the new position, and it was confirmed on February 6, shortly before I saw Secretaries Byrnes and Vinson, and in this situation, I requested Secretary Vinson to consult with the appropriate officials of the government and come back to me with recommendations.

Secretary of the Treasury Vinson consulted with Attorney General Tom Clark and other government officials. When the results of these consultations were reported to me, the conclusion was reached that the appointment should be allowed to take its normal course.

The final responsibility for this decision was, of course, mine. The reason for this decision was that the charges which had been made by the FBI against Mr. White also involved many other persons. Hundreds of FBI agents were engaged in investigating the charges against all those who had been accused.

It was of great importance to the nation that this investigation be continued in order to prove or disprove these charges and to determine if still other persons were implicated.

Any usual action with respect to Mr. White's appointment might well have alerted all the persons involved to the fact that the investigation was under way and thus endanger the success of the investigation.

It was originally planned that the United States would support Mr. White for election to the top managerial position in the International Monetary Fund —that of managing director—a more important post than that of a member of the board of executive directors.

But following the receipt of the FBI report and the consultations with members of my Cabinet, it was decided that he would be limited to membership on the board of directors.

With his duties thus restricted, he would be subject to the supervision of the Secretary of State, and his position would be less important and much less sensitive if it were sensitive at all—than the position then held by him as Assistant Secretary of the Treasury.

Tonight, I want the American people to understand that the course we took protected the public interest and security and, at the same time, permitted the intensive FBI investigation then in progress to go forward. No other course could have served both these purposes.

The appointment was accordingly allowed to go through, and the investigations continued. And in 1947 the results of the investigation up to that time were laid before the Federal grand jury in New York by the Department of Justice. Mr. White was one of the witnesses called before the grand jury. The grand jury did not indict Mr. White, although it was the same grand jury which indicted the twelve top Communists in the country.

All this was done in the American way, by due process of law. In the meantime, Mr. White, in April, 1947, resigned his office referring to reasons of health. Although my recent off-hand comment concerning his resignation was in error, the fact is that he was separated from the Government service promptly when the necessity for secrecy concerning the intensive investigation by the FBI came to an end. He died in 1948 after appearing before the Un-American Activities Committee of the House. . . .

SOURCE: New York *Times*, November 17, 1953.

APPENDIX D

A preliminary draft of the White Plan, early 1942.

H. D. White

Suggested Plan for a United Nations Stabilization
Fund and a Bank for Reconstruction of
the United and Associated Nations

It is yet too soon to know the precise form or the approximate magnitude of post-war monetary problems. But one thing is certain. No matter how long the war lasts nor how it is won, we shall be faced with three inescapable problems: to prevent the disruption of foreign exchanges and the collapse of monetary and credit systems; to assure the restoration of foreign trade; and to supply the huge volume of capital that will be needed virtually throughout the world for reconstruction, for relief, and for economic recovery.

How prepare to satisfy these needs? If we are to avoid drifting from the peace table into a period of chaotic competition, monetary disorders, depressions, political disruption, and finally into new wars within as well as among nations, we must be equipped to grapple with these three problems and to make substantial progress toward their solution.

Clearly the task can be successfully handled only through international action. In most discussions of post-war problems this fact has been recognized, yet to date—though a number of persons have pointed to the solution in general terms—no detailed plans sufficiently realistic or practical to give promise of accomplishing the task have been formulated or discussed. It is high time that such plans were drafted. It is

D-1

SOURCE: The Harry Dexter White papers, Princeton University Library. Reproduced with permission of Princeton University.

An early draft of the Keynes Plan sent to
Harry Dexter White in August 1942.

PROPOSALS FOR AN INTERNATIONAL CLEARING UNION.

I.—PREFACE.

ABOUT the primary objects of an improved system of International Currency there is, to-day, a wide measure of agreement :—

(*a*) We need an instrument of international currency having general acceptability between nations, so that blocked balances and bilateral clearings are unnecessary; that is to say, an instrument of currency used by each nation in its transactions with other nations, operating through whatever national organ, such as a Treasury or a Central Bank, is most appropriate, private individuals, businesses and banks other than Central Banks, each continuing to use their own national currency as heretofore.

(*b*) We need an orderly and agreed method of determining the relative exchange values of national currency units, so that unilateral action and competitive exchange depreciations are prevented.

(*c*) We need a *quantum* of international currency, which is neither determined in an unpredictable and irrelevant manner as, for example, by the technical progress of the gold industry, nor subject to large variations depending on the gold reserve policies of individual countries; but is governed by the actual current requirements of world commerce, and is also capable of deliberate expansion and contraction to offset deflationary and inflationary tendencies in effective world demand.

(*d*) We need a system possessed of an internal stabilising mechanism, by which pressure is exercised on any country whose balance of payments with the rest of the world is departing from equilibrium in either direction, so as to prevent movements which must create for its neighbours an equal but opposite want of balance.

(*e*) We need an agreed plan for starting off every country after the war with a stock of reserves appropriate to its importance in world commerce, so that without due anxiety it can set its house in order during the transitional period to full peace-time conditions.

(*f*) We need a method by which the surplus credit balances arising from international trade, which the recipient does not wish to employ for the time being, can be set to work in the interests of international planning and relief and economic health, without detriment to the liquidity of these balances and to their holder's faculty to employ them himself when he desires to do so.

(*g*) We need a central institution, of a purely technical and non-political character, to aid and support other international institutions concerned with the planning and regulation of the world's economic life.

(*h*) More generally, we need a means of reassurance to a troubled world, by which any country whose own affairs are conducted with due prudence is relieved of anxiety, for causes which are not of its own making, concerning its ability to meet its international liabilities; and which will, therefore, make unnecessary those methods of restriction and discrimination which countries have adopted hitherto, not on their merits, but as measures of self-protection from disruptive outside forces.

2. There is also a growing measure of agreement about the general character of any solution of the problem likely to be successful. The particular

2424~   B

*The partition of Germany proposed in White's second draft
of the Morgenthau Plan, September 5, 1944.*

SOURCE: *Diary of Henry Morgenthau, Jr.*, Volume 769, p. 3, September 5–6,
1944. Reproduced with permission of the Franklin D. Roosevelt
Library, Hyde Park, New York.

Abbreviations

Alperovitz	Gar Alperovitz, *Atomic Diplomacy* (1966).
Bentley, *Out of Bondage*	Elizabeth Bentley, *Out of Bondage* (1952).
Blum I, II, III	John Morton Blum, *From the Morgenthau Diaries*, vol. I, *Years of Crisis 1928–1938* (1959); vol. II, *Years of Urgency 1938–1941* (1965); vol. III, *Years of War 1941–1945* (1967).
Chambers, *Witness*	Whittaker Chambers, *Witness* (1952).
China White Paper	*U.S. Relations with China, with Special Reference to the Period 1944–1949* (1949).
Currency Hearings 1947	Committee on Appropriations, Armed Services, and Banking and Currency, *Occupation Currency Transactions*, Hearings, 80th Congress, 1st Session (1947).
Currency Hearings 1953	Committee on Government Operations, Permanent Subcommittee on Investigations, Subcommittee on Government Operations Abroad, *Transfer of Occupation Currency Plates—Espionage Phase*, Hearings, 83rd Congress (1953).
Diary (China)	*Morgenthau Diary (China)*, 2 vols., with foreword by Anthony Kubek (1965).
Diary (Germany)	*Morgenthau Diary (Germany)*, 2 vols., with introduction by Anthony Kubek (1967).
FDR	Franklin Delano Roosevelt
FRUS Japan II	*Foreign Relations of the United States, Japan 1931–41*, vol. II (1943).
FRUS 1941 IV	*Foreign Relations of the United States, 1941*, vol. IV, *The Far East* (1956).
Gardner	Richard N. Gardner, *Sterling-Dollar Diplomacy*, rev. ed. (1969).
Hammond	Paul Y. Hammond, "Directives for the Occupation of Germany: the Washington Story," in *American*

Civil-Military Decisions, ed. Harold Stein (1963).

Harrod, *Keynes*	R. F. Harrod, *The Life of John Maynard Keynes* (1951).
HDW	Harry Dexter White
Hearings	Committee on the Judiciary, Internal Security Subcommittee, *Interlocking Subversion in Government Departments*, Hearings, 83rd and 84th Congress, 30 pts (1953–5).
HM	Henry Morgenthau, Jr.
Howe and Coser	Irving Howe and Lewis Coser, *The American Communist Party: a Critical History (1919–1957)* (1958).
HUAC Hearings	House Committee on Un-American Activities, *Communist Espionage in the United States Government*, Hearings, 80th Congress, 2nd Session (1948).
IPR Hearings	Committee on the Judiciary, Internal Security Subcommittee, *Institute of Pacific Relations*, Hearings, 82nd Congress, 2nd Session (1951–2).
Jowitt	Lord Jowitt, *The Strange Case of Alger Hiss* (1953).
Latham	Earl Latham, *The Communist Controversy in Washington* (1966).
Penrose	E. F. Penrose, *Economic Planning for the Peace* (1953).
Petrov	Vladimir Petrov, *Money and Conquest: Allied Occupation Currencies in World War II* (1967).
Potsdam Papers	*Foreign Relations of the United States: the Conference at Berlin (Potsdam)* (1960).
Scope of Soviet Activity	Committee of the Judiciary, Internal Security Subcommittee, *Scope of Soviet Activity in the United States*, Hearings, 84th Congress, 2nd Session, pts 34, 35 and 42 (1956–7).
Stimson and Bundy	Henry L. Stimson and McGeorge Bundy, *On Active Service in Peace and War* (1948).
Teheran Papers	*Foreign Relations of the United States: the Conferences at Cairo and Teheran, 1943* (1961).
Whipple	Charles L. Whipple, "The Life and Death of Harry Dexter White," in Boston *Globe*, 12 pts (Nov., 1953).
White, *Loyal American*	Nathan I. White, *Harry D. White Loyal American* (1956).
White Papers, Concord Files, *Hearings*	Committee on the Judiciary, Internal Security Subcommittee, *Interlocking Subversion in Government Departments*, Hearings, 83rd and 84th Congress, 30 pts (1953–5) pt 30.
White Papers, PUL	Papers of Harry Dexter White, Princeton University Library.

Yalta Papers	*Foreign Relations of the United States: the Conferences at Malta and Yalta, 1945* (1955).
Young, *China's Wartime Finance*	Arthur Young, *China's Wartime Finance and Inflation, 1937–45* (1965).
Young, *Helping Hand*	Arthur Young, *China and the Helping Hand* (1963).

Prologue: Cards of Identity

1. IMF press release, April 9, 1947; White Papers, Concord Files, *Hearings*, p. 2584.
2. Harrod, *Keynes*, pp. 538–9.
3. Latham, pp. 177–8.
4. New York *Times*, November 17, 18, 1953. See ch. 23 below.
5. Ernest Havemann, "Close-up of a Ghost," *Life*, November 23, 1953, p. 32.
6. Walter Goodman, *The Committee*, p. 163.
7. *Ibid.*, p. 226.
8. *HUAC Hearings*, pp. 503, ff.
9. White, *Loyal American*, p. 403.
10. *HUAC Hearings*, pp. 563, ff.
11. HDW's testimony on August 13, 1948 is in *ibid.*, pp. 877–906.

Chapter 1.   Boston Boyhood

1. HDW's birth is recorded by the Registrar of Births, Marriages and Deaths in Boston City Hall. Cf. Whipple, pt II.
2. *Ibid.*; White, *Loyal American*, p. 269.
3. White, *Loyal American*, p. 269; Whipple, pt II.
4. *Ibid.*; Federal Immigration records, U.S. Circuit Court Records, Federal Building, Boston. Jacob Weit's 1892 petition is filed as vol. 225, p. 120; that of 1897 as vol. 300, p. 192.
5. See telegram HDW to Westbrook Pegler, June 28, 1946: White Papers, Concord Files, *Hearings*, p. 2647.
6. Date of HDW's entry into Eliot School and absence of discharge date, Principal, Michelangelo School, Michelangelo-Eliot-Hancock District, Boston Public Schools, to writer, March 3, 1970. Other family details above based on Whipple, pt II, and White, *Loyal American*, pp. 269–70.
7. *Ibid.*, pp. 270–1.
8. Based on Boston city directories quoted in Whipple, pt III.
9. Henry Adams, *The Education of Henry Adams* (1918), pp. 19–20.
10. H. G. Wells, *The Future in America*, pp. 316–30.
11. Richard J. Whalen, *The Founding Father: the Story of Joseph P. Kennedy*, p. 42.
12. Date of HDW's enlistment, April 12, 1917, is in Whipple, pt III.

Chapter 2.   Soldier and Student

1. See White, *Loyal American*, p. 271, for these details.
2. Whipple, pt III, gives details of HDW's Boston marriage.

3. Office of the Chief of Military History, Historical Services Division, to writer, August 22, 1969. C. E. Dornbusch to writer, October 3, 1969. White, *Loyal American*, p. 271, is apparently in error when it gives HDW's two regiments as part of the 27th and 42nd divisions.

4. Office of the Chief of Military History to the writer, August 22, 1969; Whipple, pt III.

5. See HDW's entry in *Current Biography 1944* and White, *Loyal American*, p. 271, for this 1919–22 period.

6. *Current Biography 1944* says that HDW "did not decide on an academic career until he had reached his late twenties."

7. *Time*, November 23, 1953.

8. Dates of HDW's Stanford degrees, Office of the Registrar, Stanford University, to the writer, February 27, 1970.

9. Whipple, pt IV.

10. White Papers, Concord Files, *Hearings*, pp. 2541–2.

11. For a recent account of the issues of this period, see Arthur S. Link, *Woodrow Wilson and the Progressive Era 1910–1917*, rev. ed. (1963).

12. Howe and Coser, p. 132.

13. *Ibid.*, p. 141.

14. See Theodore Draper's discussion of this point in *The Roots of American Communism*, pp. 34–7. *Cf.*, Howe and Coser, pp. 27–8, who point out that this period followed one of the great waves of immigration to the U.S., that many of the immigrants had come from eastern Europe and that many of them had been forced to seek work in the lowest-paying industries. Hence some of the reasons for the influence of the Slavic federations on the left.

Chapter 3.   A Major Turning-Point

1. Details of HDW's connection with Harvard, Harvard University Archives to the writer, February 9, 1970.

2. Whipple, pt IV.

3. HDW, *The French International Accounts 1880–1913*, p. i.

4. See Whipple, pt IV, for these two comments on HDW at Harvard.

5. Whipple, pt V.

6. *Ibid.*

7. This Harvard University Press book was published by Oxford University Press in Britain.

8. See HDW, *French International Accounts*, pp. 301–12.

9. C. R. Whittlesey, in *American Economic Review*, vol. 23 (December, 1933), pp. 721, ff.

10. *Journal of Political Economy* (August, 1934), pp. 542–5.

11. *Economic History Review* (Economic History Society, Cambridge, England), vol. 6 (October, 1935), pp. 109–11.

12. Boston *Transcript*, July 22, 1933.

13. *Books* (weekly literary supplement of New York *Herald-Tribune*), August 6, 1933.

14. J. K. Galbraith, *Great Crash*, p. 12.
15. The above figures are from Galbraith, *Great Crash*, pp. 16 and 152, and Arthur M. Schlesinger, *The Age of Roosevelt: the Coming of the New Deal*, pp. 27, 87.
16. White Papers, PUL, file 29.
17. *Ibid., Cf.*, Schlesinger, *New Deal*, pp. 185–6.
18. Galbraith, *Great Crash*, pp. 164–6. *Cf.*, Herbert Stein, *The Fiscal Revolution in America*, ch. 2.
19. HDW's review in the *Quarterly Journal of Economics* (Harvard University Press), vol. 48 (August, 1934), pp. 727–41, discussed "two outstanding books on the theory of international trade." These were Gottfried Haberle's *Der Internationale Handel* (Berlin: J. Springer, 1933) and Bertil Ohlin's *Interregional and International Trade* (Cambridge, Mass.: Harvard University Press, 1933).
20. *Cf.*, the *Economic Journal* (Royal Economic Society, London), vol. 43 (March, 1933), pp. 143–5, for this review by J. B. Condliffe of *The Theory of Protection and International Trade* by Michael Manoilesco (London: P. S. King, 1931. The reviewer was skeptical of the author's claim that he had discovered "a fundamental justification for tariff protection, true for all countries and for all times . . ."
21. White Papers, Concord Files, *Hearings*, p. 2570.
22. *Ibid.*, p. 2587. Prof. Viner, an adviser to the U.S. Treasury over many years, has been described by Lord Robbins "as being in this age the outstanding all-rounder in our profession" (*Autobiography of an Economist* [London: Macmillan, 1971], p. 220). He died in 1970.
23. *Hearings*, p. 1096.
24. *Hearings*, p. 2587.

Chapter 4. The Natural Point of Control

1. HDW's report to Viner is in White Papers, PUL, file 1.
2. HDW's Civil Service "Statement of Federal Service" from June 20, 1934, to April 30, 1946 (when he left the Treasury for the IMF), together with most of his letters of appointment, are in *Hearings*, pp. 947–58.
3. New York *Times*, May 8, 1933.
4. Schlesinger, *Coming of the New Deal*, p. 185.
5. *Ibid.*, p. 223.
6. HM, "The Morgenthau Diaries: the Paradox of Poverty and Plenty," *Collier's Magazine*, October 25, 1947. For the background of Acheson's "spectacular row" below, see his *Present at the Creation*, pp. 3 and 9–11, and *Morning and Noon*, pp. 213–14.
7. For an excellent account of the silver issue, which draws on the Morgenthau Diaries, against the general background of these years, see A. S. Everest, *Morgenthau, the New Deal, and Silver*. Everest writes (p. 63) that "most of the nation was unaware of the silver issue, concealed by so

much other New Deal legislation," while to HM the silver program was the "only New Deal monetary fiscal policy I cannot explain or justify." Schlesinger, *Coming of the New Deal*, p. 252.

8. Robert Neustadt, *Presidential Power*, pp. 161–6.

9. Schlesinger quotations and Tugwell's remark are from *Coming of the New Deal*, ch. 32, "The Dynamics of Decision." James M. Burns' *Roosevelt: the Lion and Fox* (New York: Harcourt Brace, 1956) also explores these problems with great insight.

10. Based on Blum I, ch. 1.

11. Henry Adams, *The Life of Albert Gallatin*, p. 267.

12. Blum I, p. 119.

13. *Ibid.*, p. xv.

14. *Ibid.*, p. ix. Besides *Years of Crisis 1928–1938*, John Morton Blum's three-volume official biography of Morgenthau, based on the Diaries, includes *Years of Urgency 1938–1941* and *Years of War 1941–1945*. Sections of the Diaries concerning the background of the White case have been published by the Senate Internal Security Subcommittee in parts 28 and 29 of *Hearings* and in parts 34, 35 and 42 of *Scope of Soviet Activity*. Most of the latter passages have been collected in *Diary (China)*. See also *Diary (Germany)*. The original source cited in the Morgenthau Diaries is included in the reference to these committee publications.

15. Blum I, p. xv.

16. Blum II, p. 3.

17. Whalen, *Founding Father*, p. 196.

18. Schlesinger, *Coming of the New Deal*, p. 577.

19. Blum I, p. 485.

20. William L. Langer and S. Everett Gleason, *The Challenge to Isolation*, pp. 3–10.

21. Roberta Wohlstetter, *Pearl Harbor: Warning and Decision*, p. 230.

22. William L. Langer and S. Everett Gleason, *The Undeclared War 1940–1941*, p. 181.

Chapter 5.   Apprenticeship

1. "Selection of a Monetary Standard for the United States," pp. 320–2; White Papers, PUL, file 1.

2. *Ibid.*, pp. 331, 341.

3. "Outline Analysis of the Current Situation," February 26 and March 5, 1935; White Papers, PUL, file 2.

4. "Recovery Program: the International Monetary Aspect," March 15, 1935; White Papers, PUL, file 6.

5. See Blum I, pp. 131–8, for the general development of the Treasury's view on stabilization at this time.

6. Blum I, p. 139.

7. White Papers, Concord Files, *Hearings*, p. 2611.

8. *Hearings*, pp. 2281–2 (vol. 5, pp. 12D and 12E).

9. "Summary of Conversations with Men Interviewed in London"; White Papers, PUL, file 4. See also in the same file HDW to Haas, "Personal Report on London Trip, April–May, 1935."

10. Blum I, pp. 159–82, has a full account from HM's viewpoint of the developments leading to the Tripartite Pact; cf., William Shirer, The Collapse of the˙ Third Republic (London: Heinemann, 1970), ch. 17, for a recent account of the political background from the French side. Cf., Survey of International Affairs 1937 (London: Royal Institute of International Affairs, 1936), pp. 175, ff.

11. "Stabilization Funds and International Trade," n.d.; White Papers, PUL, file 6.

12. Blum I, pp. 160–1.

13. See HDW's letters of appointment for this period in Hearings, pp. 947, ff.

14. White Papers, Concord Files, Hearings, pp. 2561, 2608, 2610.

15. HDW's successive addresses at this time are listed under Treasury Department, Congressional Directory, from April, 1936, his first mention, to December, 1938. According to the Congressional Directory, his address listed in December, 1936, February, 1937, and May, 1938, was 4707 Connecticut Avenue. By December, 1938, he had moved to 6810 Fairfax Road, Bethesda.

16. Blum I, p. 381.

17. Harrod, Keynes, p. 449. See Arthur M. Schlesinger, The Politics of Upheaval, pp. 400–8, for an account of Keynes and the New Deal. Cf., Frances Perkins, The Roosevelt I Knew, pp. 225–7.

18. Blum I, pp. 387–90; Marriner S. Eccles to writer, April 30, 1970.

19. "Monetary Possibilities," memorandum, March 22, 1938; White Papers, PUL, file 2.

20. Blum I, p. 423. Cf., Stein, Fiscal Revolution in America, for an interesting account of FDR's options on the economy during 1937–9.

21. "The Sterling Decline and the Tripartite Accord," HDW to HM, September 6, 1938; White Papers, PUL, file 4.

22. Treasury Order no. 18 is in Hearings, pp. 2609–10.

23. Ibid., p. 2283 (vol. 120, p. 265).

24. Langer and Gleason, Challenge to Isolation, p. 11, ff.

25. Everest, Morgenthau, the New Deal, and Silver, ch. 8, has a full account of the effect of the silver buying program on the Chinese economy: cf., Blum I, pp. 211–28.

26. Blum I, p. 225. Ibid., p. 227 gives details of the subsequent silver arrangement with the Chinese.

27. "Economic Situation in China"; White Papers, PUL, file 3.

28. Young, China's Wartime Finance, p. 132. Cf., Chou Shun-hsin, The Chinese Inflation 1937–1950, pp. 116–17.

29. Young, China's Wartime Finance, pp. 132, 191.

30. Ibid., p. 192.

31. Everest, Morgenthau, the New Deal, and Silver, p. 130; Blum I, 481–2.

32. Young, China's Wartime Finance, pp. 98–102; F. F. Liu, A Military History

of Modern China (Princeton University Press, 1956), pp. 162–73; John Erickson, *The Soviet High Command* (London: Macmillan, 1962), pp. 400, 466–9, 490–1. While having a common interest with Chiang in checking the Japanese, Erickson emphasizes Stalin's caution in avoiding provocation.

33. Stuart Schram, *Mao Tse-tung* (Harmondsworth: Penguin, 1966), pp. 194–200; Charles B. Maclane, *Soviet Policy and the Chinese Communists 1931–1946* (New York: Columbia University Press, 1958), pp. 79–92.
34. Erickson, *Soviet High Command*, p. 400.
35. Young, *China's Wartime Finance*, p. 119.
36. Blum I, pp. 452–3.
37. Cordell Hull, *The Memoirs of Cordell Hull*, pp. 207–8.
38. This draft of October 10, 1938, is in White Papers, PUL, file 3.
39. HM's letter of October 17, 1938, to FDR; White Papers, Concord Files, *Hearings*, pp. 2631–3. Another copy is in White Papers, PUL, file 14. *Cf.*, Blum I, pp. 524–7.
40. See Young, *China's Wartime Finance*, pp. 102–5, 344, for the details of the successive U.S. purchase credits to China, 1937–41. *Cf.*, Blum II, pp. 58–64, 123–8, 345–8.
41. Blum I, p. 527.

Chapter 6. The Secret Agent

1. Quoted in Schlesinger, *Politics of Upheaval*, pp. 181–3.
2. Martin Esslin, *Brecht: a Choice of Evils* (London: Mercury Books, 1965), pp. 150–1.
3. Chambers, *Witness*, p. 441.
4. Latham, pt I, is an excellent account of the rise of the Popular Front and its various manifestations in the U.S.
5. Howe and Coser, p. 335.
6. Chambers, *Witness*, p. 269.
7. Bruce Paige, *et al.*, *Philby: the Spy Who Betrayed a Generation* (London: André Deutsch, 1968), p. 143.
8. Quoted in Latham, p. 96.
9. Leslie Fiedler, *An End to Innocence* (Boston, Mass.: Beacon Press, 1955), p. 18.
10. The songbooks, found in HDW's Fitzwilliam papers in 1953, included two volumes of a "Workers' Song Book" for 1934 and 1935. These included such rousing titles as "Mount the Barricades," "Lenin—Our Leader," "Comintern" and "Chinese Red Soldier's Song." Two similar volumes from 1937 included "Songs of the People" and "Spain Marches," while two wartime volumes from 1942–3 in English and Russian were titled *The Most Popular Songs from the Soviet Union* and *Sascha, Pascha, Yascha*. White Papers, Concord Files, *Hearings*, pp. 2418–92, 2553–7.
11. The development of the Chambers–Hiss story has been told, from differing approaches, in, for example, Alistair Cooke's *A Generation on Trial*, and Ralph de Toledano and Victor Lasky's *Seeds of Treason*. But see also

Rebecca West's critique of Cooke's book in the *University of Chicago Law Review* (1951), pp. 662–77, and Diana Trilling's critique of *Seeds of Treason,* "A Memorandum on the Hiss Case," in *Claremont Essays* (London: Secker & Warburg, 1965). John Strachey has an excellent essay on Chambers in *The Strangled Cry* (London: Bodley Head, 1962), while two other studies—Walter Goodman's *The Committee* and Latham—seem indispensable.

12. Chambers, *Witness*, pp. 275–88. The Red Army's Fourth Section was one of the six sections of Soviet Military Intelligence. It set up agents, networks and communications outside Russia, running its own training schools for codes, ciphers, sabotage, etc., independently of the Comintern and the NKVD networks. In 1939 the overall Chief Military Intelligence Directorate (G.R.U.) of the General Staff was established. According to Chambers (*Witness*, pp. 27, 407), it was Maj. Gen. Walter Krivitsky, former head of the Fourth Section in Western Europe, who told him that he had been working for Soviet Military Intelligence.

13. *Ibid.*, p. 32. Latham, p. 43.

14. *Ibid.*, pp. 32, 309. Latham, p. 63.

15. *Ibid.*, pp. 331–47; *cf.*, Schlesinger, *Politics of Upheaval*, pp. 181–207, who writes: "They were passive rather than active revolutionaries, laying side bets on a Communist revolution while working hard at immediate tasks in a reform government." Of Chambers' account of the seven members of the Ware group in the Department of Agriculture, Latham writes (p. 107): "Independent confirmation of four of the members has been supplied by Lee Pressman . . . and of all of them by Nathaniel Weyl."

16. Chambers, *Witness*, pp. 30, 335–6, 353, 405.

17. *Ibid.*, p. 370.

18. *Ibid.*, pp. 29–30, 441, 334, 405–7. One of the discrepancies in *Witness* is that Chambers states that he did not know Bykov's true identity until two years later, from Gen. Krivitsky. But, according to Isaac Don Levine, this meeting was in spring 1939. White, *Loyal American*, pp. 161–2; Chambers, *Witness*, pp. 27, 407.

19. *Ibid.*, pp. 420–4, 383, 429.

20. *Ibid.*, pp. 383–4.

21. *Ibid.*, pp. 384, 28; *IPR Hearings*, pp. 491–3. During the second Hiss trial in November, 1949, Chambers said that one of the sixty-five typewritten Baltimore documents—Baltimore no. 10—submitted by him in the original Hiss-Chambers Baltimore defamation suit on November 17, 1948, might have come from HDW. Chambers had first stated that he got it from Hiss, then that perhaps it came from HDW, before finally coming back to his first story. Baltimore no. 10 was a copy of War Department Military Intelligence Report typed not on the Hiss Woodstock but on a 1936 Royal. See Cooke, *Generation on Trial*, pp. 110, 314, 320, and Jowitt, p. 229.

22. Chambers, *Witness*, pp. 407, 414–17, 429–30. There is no record of HDW's having owned such a rug.

23. *Ibid.*, pp. 75–80, 445, 26, 37–40, 735–6; *IPR Hearings*, pp. 491–3.

24. *Ibid.*, pp. 65–70. During the Hiss trials, Wadleigh stated that Chambers

had asked him to leave the underground in February or March, 1939. Jowitt, p. 185.

25. Chambers, *Witness*, pp. 463–70, 492. Chambers amended the date of this interview with the FBI, when HDW's name was first mentioned, to May 14, 1942, during the second Hiss trial. White, *Loyal American*, p. 125.

26. Chambers, *Witness*, pp. 420, 426–7.

27. *Ibid.*, p. 442.

28. Glasser's "biographical sketch," produced in 1953 with his other official federal records show that he entered the Treasury's Division of Research and Statistics, where HDW was then Assistant Director, in November, 1936, and went to the Division of Monetary Research on March 25, 1938, the same day that HDW became director in March, 1938. *Hearings*, pp. 90–1, 946. In April, 1953, when asked before the Senate Internal Security Subcommittee if he had known HDW, Glasser declined to answer on the ground of self-incrimination. He invoked the Fifth Amendment when asked about his work with HDW in the Treasury, whether he had known Chambers, and the references to him in *Witness*. On the same grounds he declined to say whether he had known Victor Perlo, with whose wartime espionage group he was alleged to have worked by Miss Bentley in August, 1948. *Hearings*, pp. 59, 73–80.

In August, 1948, following Miss Bentley's allegations that he had worked with the Silvermaster espionage group, Silverman stated that he was "deeply shocked" by the "slanders" against him. He invoked the Fifth Amendment to further questions. *HUAC Hearings*, pp. 835–50. For two recent views of the controversy over the Fifth Amendment at this time, see Latham, pp. 12–13, 391–3, and Goodman, *The Committee*, pp. 283, ff.

29. Jowitt, p. 182.

30. White, *Loyal American*, p. 124. Chs II, III and IV of this book by HDW's brother have an extended rebuttal of the charges against HDW by Chambers and Miss Bentley.

31. *Ibid.*, p. 125.

32. *Ibid.*, p. 159. See also Chambers, *Witness*, pp. 430–1, and Cooke, *Generation on Trial*, pp. 129, 151, 177, 297–8, for the Peterboro episode. *Cf.*, Jowitt, pp. 83–7. Chambers' testimony that he was with HDW for "about 15 or 20 minutes" in the property he believed to be Currie's is in the transcript of the second Hiss trial, vol. I, p. 278. This transcript is available in the Library of Congress.

33. White, *Loyal American*, pp. 143–5.

34. *Ibid.*, pp. 151–2.

35. Cooke, *Generation on Trial*, p. 147; Jowitt, p. 180; *IPR Hearings*, pp. 491–3; Chambers, *Witness*, pp. 29, 40, 429, 735–8.

36. Cooke, *Generation on Trial*, p. 141. See *Hearings*, pp. 1180–3, for the Ray Murphy memoranda of conversations with Chambers, March 20, 1945, August 28, 1946.

37. Jowitt, p. 101.

38. Toledano and Lasky, *Seeds of Treason*, pp. 122–5; Chambers, *Witness*, pp. 725–6, 739–40, 776–7. Chambers writes of his denial of espionage to

the Federal Grand Jury in October, 1948: "My no to the Grand Jury stands for all men to condemn."

39. Chambers, *Witness*, pp. 735–8.
40. See Nixon's speech in the House of Representatives on January 26, 1950, which includes most of the text of "the White Memorandum": *Congressional Record*, vol. 96, pt I, pp. 999–1007, 81st Congress, 1st Session. Nixon stated that he had possessed photostatic copies of the alleged HDW documents produced by Chambers since December, 1948, and repeats in *Six Crises*, pp. 51–2, that these documents were turned over to the Justice Department on November 17, 1948. In his January, 1950, speech, Nixon also stated that on November 17, 1948, Alexander Campbell, the Assistant Attorney General in charge of the Criminal Division, was called by counsel on both sides (in the Hiss-Chambers libel suit) "to come to Baltimore to pick up the documents." *Cf.*, Chambers, *Witness*, pp. 748–50.
41. The text and photostats of the White Memorandum are reproduced in White, *Loyal American*, pp. 81–97, while photostats are also printed in *Hearings*, pp. 1120–7. See text in App. A. The first two paragraphs of Q2 obverse are omitted in the *Congressional Record* text, vol. 96, pt I, p. 1003, and this text also has "Secretary Marshall" for "Sec M" on Q3 obverse where HM is obviously indicated. *Cf.*, Chambers, *Witness*, pp. 735–50.
42. White, *Loyal American*, p. 99.
43. *Ibid.*, pp. 99–107. Young in *China's Wartime Finance*, p. 190, writes that the U.S. silver purchases during the winter of 1937–8 "were not made public until the spring of 1938." The Ingersoll mission, which was concerned with a possible secret understanding with the Admiralty on joint action in case of a Pacific war with Japan, is discussed in *Hearings before the Joint Committee on the Investigation of the Pearl Harbor Attack* (Washington, D.C.: U.S. Government Printing Office, 1946), pt 9, pp. 4273–8. See White Papers, PUL, file 13, for a report drafted by HDW on January 10, 1938, concerning a meeting within HM's home on the Hungarian debt settlement, "which would have a bearing on our intergovernmental debt situation with other countries." *Cf.*, White, *Loyal American*, pp. 104–5, for this report.
44. *Ibid.*, p. 114; Cooke, *Generation on Trial*, p. 150. *Cf.*, n. 33 above.
45. *Ibid.*, pp. 106, ff.
46. *Ibid.*, pp. 109–10. *Cf.*, Fred J. Cook's discussion of this point in *The F.B.I. Nobody Knows*, pp. 350–5.
47. White, *Loyal American*, p. 111.
48. *Ibid.*, p. 117.
49. Jowitt, pp. 110–11.
50. Latham, p. 113, 179, f.
51. Herbert Packer, *Ex-Communist Witnesses* (Stanford University Press, 1962), p. 104. Nixon comments, *Congressional Record*, January 26, 1950, p. 1003. See n. 40 above.
52. Chambers, *Witness*, p. 426.
53. Hede Massing, *This Deception*, p. 184.
54. George Kennan, *Memoirs: 1925–1950*, pp. 518–19.

Chapter 7. War and the Treasury

1. Blum II, p. 48.
2. "Preliminary Report on Depriving Aggressor Nations of Strategic Materials," HDW to HM, April 8, 1939; White Papers, PUL, file 15.
3. Blum II, p. 90.
4. Langer and Gleason, *Challenge to Isolation*, p. 81.
5. *Ibid.*, p. 46. *Cf.*, Blum II, p. 46.
6. Blum II, p. 187. See H. Duncan Hall, *North American Supply*, for an official history of the entire complex British procurement story in the U.S., and the American response.
7. Copy in White Papers, PUL, file 14; and in *Hearings*, pp. 1455–6. This HDW-to-HM memorandum is also initialed "HDW: HG," presumably Harold Glasser, who was then a Principal Economic Analyst in the Division of Monetary Research; *Hearings*, p. 91.
8. Langer and Gleason, *Challenge to Isolation*, p. 111.
9. Blum II, p. 55.
10. Three papers, HDW to HM, June 6, 1939, September 19, 1939, March 27, 1940: White Papers, PUL, file 14.
11. White Papers, Concord Files, *Hearings*, p. 2611.
12. Blum II, p. 57. *Cf.*, Langer and Gleason, *Challenge to Isolation*, pp. 272–80.
13. *Hearings*, p. 2341 (vol. 304, p. 246).
14. See IIDW to HM, "Status of the Mexican Stabilization and Silver Negotiations," October 3, 1941, together with the draft Treasury-Mexican Government agreement: *Hearings*, pp. 2343–6 (vol. 447, pp. 355–63).
15. White Papers, Concord Files, *Hearings*, p. 2634.
16. *Hearings*, pp. 2311–15 (vol. 541, pp. 128–42).
17. *Hearings*, p. 1275, for Braden comment; *Report on Cuba*, International Bank for Reconstruction and Development (Washington, D.C., 1951), p. 539. *Cf.*, White, *Loyal American*, pp. 202–3.
18. *Hearings*, pp. 2335–8 (vol. 213, pp. 249–53).
19. Young, *Helping Hand*, pp. 130–3; *cf.*, Blum II, pp. 123–4.
20. *Hearings*, pp. 2339–2341 (vol. 223, pp. 99–103).
21. Young, *Helping Hand*, pp. 135–5; Blum II, pp. 347, 356–61; Langer and Gleason, *Challenge to Isolation*, pp. 724–8; *Diary (China)*, pp. 176–8 (vol. 282, pp. 290–300).
22. Blum II, p. 376.
23. For a clear and closely documented account of these stabilization negotiations, which tends to be critical of the Treasury's role, see Young, *China's Wartime Finance*, chs. 16 and 17, and *Helping Hand*, ch. 10.
24. Herbert Feis, *The Road to Pearl Harbor*, pp. 215–18, 248.
25. Winston S. Churchill, *Their Finest Hour* (London: Cassell, 1949), pp. 119–20.
26. Langer and Gleason, *Challenge to Isolation*, pp. 644–50; *Nazi-Soviet Relations* (Washington: Department of State, 1948), pp. 166–8.

27. Two untitled HDW memoranda, June 15 and August 13, 1940; White Papers, PUL, file 15.
28. *Nazi-Soviet Relations*, pp. 217–55.
29. Halder diary quoted in Saul Friedlander, *Prelude to Downfall: Hitler and the United States 1939–41* (London: Chatto & Windus, 1967), p. 114.
30. See James V. Compton, *The Swastika and the Eagle*, ch. 13, for an interesting discussion of this point.
31. *Ibid.*, pp. 127–8.
32. Erickson, *Soviet High Command*, pp. 567, 587.
33. Alan Clark, *Barbarossa* (Harmondsworth: Penguin, 1966), p. 172.
34. Langer and Gleason, *Undeclared War*, p. 569.
35. Robert E. Sherwood, *Roosevelt and Hopkins*, p. 162.
36. *Hearings*, p. 947.
37. *Ibid.*, p. 950.
38. Blum II, pp. 339–42; Foley's remarks to HM on HDW's part in Foreign Funds is in the transcript of Conference, December 8, 1941; *Hearings*, pp. 2298–9 (vol. 470, pp. 82, ff.).
39. *Diary (China)*, pp. 366–73 (vol. 389, pp. 112–24).
40. *Hearings*, pp. 2295, 2584, 2608–9.
41. *Ibid.*, pp. 2608, 2347–50.
42. *Ibid.*, p. 2353. Transcript of conference on October 20, 1941 (vol. 452, pp. 249–79).
43. Young, *Helping Hand*, pp. 193–4.

Chapter 8. All-out Diplomacy

1. Compton, *Swastika and the Eagle*, pp. 180–1, 203.
2. Chalmers Johnson, *An Instance of Treason*, p. 155. See Masao Maruyama, *Thought and Behaviour in Modern Japanese Politics* (London: Oxford University Press, 1963) for a discussion of some of the wider historical factors behind Japan's decision for war in 1941.
3. E. L. Woodward, *British Foreign Policy in the Second World War*, p. 569.
4. Feis, *Road to Pearl Harbor*, p. 178.
5. Langer and Gleason, *Undeclared War*, p. 836.
6. *Ibid.*, p. 477.
7. White Papers, PUL, file 16; Young, *Helping Hand*, pp. 193–4, 463.
8. Carlos Baker, *Ernest Hemingway: a Life*, pp. 426–35.
9. *Diary (China)*, pp. 457–63 (vol. 433, pp. 278–83).
10. *Pearl Harbor: Warning and Decision*, ch. 7; *cf.* Ladislas Farago, *The Broken Seal*, for an account both of Magic and the parallel secret race between the Japanese and the U.S. cryptanalysts which culminated in Pearl Harbor.
11. Feis, *Road to Pearl Harbor*, p. 264.
12. *Ibid.*, p. 273.
13. Langer and Gleason, *Undeclared War*, pp. 707–8, 902–3.
14. F. W. Deakin and G. R. Storry, *The Case of Richard Sorge*, p. 247. Sorge

was arrested on October 18, a few days after sending his last and most important report to Red Army Intelligence.

15. Wohlstetter, *Pearl Harbor*, p. 392.
16. Feis, *Road to Pearl Harbor*, pp. 296, 303; Farago, *Broken Seal*, pp. 265–7.
17. White Papers, PUL, file 16. *Cf.*, Langer and Gleason, *Undeclared War*, pp. 876–88.
18. Text in *FRUS 1941* IV, pp. 606–13.
19. Blum II, p. 385.
20. *FRUS 1941* IV, pp. 622–5. "How such a program," remark Langer and Gleason, "based on the proposition that Japan, in return for American financial and economic assistance, should renounce all its aspirations for expansion and content itself with the role of a well-behaved but unpretentious contractor for American rearmament, could have received serious consideration in the State Department remains a mystery." (*Undeclared War*, p. 877.)
21. *Pearl Harbor Attack*, pt 14, pp. 1103–7; *cf.*, Wohlstetter, *Pearl Harbor*, p. 237.
22. Feis, *Road to Pearl Harbor*, pp. 309–11.
23. Langer and Gleason, *Undeclared War*, p. 894.
24. Text of Telegram 812, Togo to Nomura, November 22, 1941, is in *Pearl Harbor Attack*, pt 12, p. 165: ". . . Let me write it out for you—twenty-ninth . . . this time we mean it, that the deadline absolutely cannot be changed. After that things are automatically going to happen. . . ." *Cf.*, Wohlstetter, *Pearl Harbor*, pp. 189–90, 237–8
25. Feis, *Road to Pearl Harbor*, p. 313.
26. Winston S. Churchill, *The Grand Alliance* (London: Cassell, 1950), p. 530.
27. White Papers, PUL, file 16.
28. Blum II, pp. 386–91.
29. Carter testimony of July, 1951, in *IPR Hearings*, pp. 153–4. *Cf.*, *Hearings*, pp. 1079–80.
30. Text in *FRUS Japan* II, pp. 766–70.
31. Feis, *Road to Pearl Harbor*, pp. 321, 313; Langer and Gleason, *Undeclared War*, p. 906.
32. Feis, *Road to Pearl Harbor*, pp. 332, 341. Coding delays meant that Hull received Nomura and Kurusu one hour after the first bombs fell at Pearl Harbor.
33. Farago, *Broken Seal*, p. 384.

Chapter 9. Assistant Secretary

1. Transcript of conference and Hull telephone call, December 8, 1941; *Hearings*, pp. 2298–2300 (vol. 470, pp. 82, ff.).
2. *Hearings*, Report, p. 29.
3. Blum III, p. 23.
4. *Ibid.*, p. 30.
5. *Ibid.*, pp. 43–4.

6. "A Fiscal Policy for the War Years," HDW to HM, September 22, 1942; White Papers, PUL, file 20.
7. Transcript of conference, January 31, 1944; *Hearings*, pp. 2394–8 (vol. 698, pp. 140, ff.).
8. Blum III, p. 76.

Chapter 10.   *The White Plan*

1. Blum III, pp. 228–9. Besides section 5 in J. M. Blum's biography, the account in this and ch. 14 below of the events leading to Bretton Woods is also indebted to Gardner; Harrod, *Keynes*; and Penrose. There is also an excellent account of "Developing Plans for an International Monetary Fund and a World Bank" by John Parke Young in the *Department of State Bulletin*, November 13, 1950.
2. New York *Herald-Tribune*, March 31, 1946. See also the paper's leader for the following day.
3. White Papers, PUL, file 24.
4. *Hearings*, pp. 2301–7 (vol. 528, pp. 296–303, 321–32).
5. John Parke Young describes the development of the administrative side, while Harley A. Notter, *Postwar Foreign Policy Preparation 1939–45*, is a full official account of the attempts to coordinate economic foreign policy during the war by the U.S. Government.
6. Harrod, *Keynes*, p. 528.
7. Acheson, *Present at the Creation*, p. 726. *Cf.*, *Memoirs of Cordell Hull*, pt VIII, and George Kennan's *American Diplomacy 1900–1950* (Chicago University Press, 1951).
8. Memorandum, HDW to HM, March 7, 1944, "Proposed U.S. Loan to the U.S.S.R."; White Papers, PUL, file 23. *Hearings*, pp. 1451–2.
9. Blum III, p. 123.
10. "Draft of Statement on Proposed Amendments to I.M.F. Articles of Agreement," May 19, 1948; White Papers, PUL, file 27.
11. Penrose, p. 20.
12. Lord Birkenhead, *The Prof in Two Worlds*, pp. 262–7. *Cf.*, R. F. Harrod, *The Prof: a Personal Memoir of Lord Cherwell* (London: Macmillan, 1959), pp. 222–4.
13. Harrod, *Keynes*, pp. 525–6.
14. Details in Gardner, pp. 54–68, and Penrose, pp. 11–31. The final version of Article VII is in Penrose, pp. 25–6, and the text of the full Mutual Aid Agreement was published as Cmd 6341 (London: H.M.S.O., 1942).
15. A log of this HDW-HM visit to Britian, October 15–27, 1942, "Diary of a Trip to Britain," may be found in White Papers, Concord Files, *Hearings*, pp. 2591–4. There is no mention of HDW's meeting with Keynes, and Penrose comments (p. 49) that "no official record was made by us of the meeting" as the State Department had not given permission to engage "in any form" of discussion on postwar matters. The meeting was held on the personal initiative of Ambassador Winant.
16. Penrose, pp. 47–9.

17. *Preliminary Draft Outline of an International Stabilization Fund of the United and Associated Nations*; *Proposals for an International Clearing Union*, Cmd 6347; *Preliminary Draft Outline of a Proposal for a Bank for Reconstruction and Development of the United and Associated Nations*.
18. HDW, "Postwar Currency Stabilization," *American Economic Review*, vol. 33, no. 1, supplement (March, 1943).
19. Harrod, *Keynes*, pp. 543–4.
20. *Ibid*., p. 560. Interview with Lord Boothby, September 5, 1972.

Chapter 11. Gold for China?

1. Winston S. Churchill, *The Hinge of Fate*, p. 119. No Allied personnel were seconded to this proposed Allied joint staff, and Stilwell continued to serve as one of Chiang's two chiefs of staff, along with the Chinese army chief of staff. HDW's comments on gold above are from a draft manuscript paper, "The Future of Gold," written early in the war. White Papers, Concord Files, *Hearings*, p. 2692.
2. Stimson and Bundy, p. 528.
3. John K. Fairbank *et al.*, *East Asia: the Modern Transformation*, p. 717.
4. Young, *Helping Hand*, p. 418.
5. *Diary (China)*, pp. 632–3, January 29, 1942 (vol. 490, pp. 1–4).
6. Quoted in Young, *Helping Hand*, p. 341. *Cf.*, pp. 245–52, 339–41, and *The Stilwell Papers*, ed. Theodore H. White (London: Macdonald, 1949) pp. 138–9.
7. *Diary (China)*, pp. 566–7 (vol. 484, p. 186); China White Paper, p. 477.
8. *Ibid*., p. 476.
9. *Diary (China)*, pp. 587–92 (vol. 485, pp. 207–17).
10. China White Paper, p. 478.
11. *Diary (China)*, pp. 634–5, January 29, 1942 (vol. 490, pp. 5–7).
12. *Ibid*., p. 689 (vol. 491, pp. 74–7).
13. China White Paper, p. 479.
14. For Soong letter, joint HM-Soong statement and terms of loan agreement, signed on March 21, 1942, see China White Paper, pp. 484, 510–12.
15. *Diary (China)*, p. 719 (vol. 494, pp. 1–22).
16. China White Paper, p. 470.
17. Young, *China's Wartime Finance*, pp. 299, 305; *cf.*, Chou Shun-hsin, *Chinese Inflation*, chs. 1 and 4, and Kia-ngau Chang, *The Inflationary Spiral: the Experience of China 1939–1950* (New York: M.I.T. Press/Wiley, 1958), ch. 10.
18. J. M. Keynes, *The Economic Consequences of the Peace* (London: Macmillan, 1920), pp. 220–1.
19. Fairbank, *East Asia*, p. 717.
20. Young, *Helping Hand*, pp. 234–40, has an account of the dollar-securities fiasco.
21. Herbert Feis, *The China Tangle*, p. 300.
22. China White Paper, pp. 488–9.
23. *Diary (China)*, pp. 452, 860, 1081–2.

24. Blum III, p. 105.
25. China White Paper, pp. 486–7.
26. *Ibid.*, pp. 487–8.
27. Young, *Helping Hand*, pp. 319–21; Blum III, p. 108; *Scope of Soviet Activity*, pt 35, pp. 1986–7 (vol. 666, p. 179; vol. 668, p. 68). See ch. 4, n. 14, above.
28. Young, *Helping Hand*, p. 321.
29. China White Paper, p. 488.
30. Young, *China's Wartime Finance*, p. 115. The U.S. eventually paid $392,-000,000 to China for *fapi* war costs to the end of 1944, as well as $48,-000,000 for strategic purchases. *Ibid.*, pp. 274–7.
31. *Stilwell Papers*, p. 131.
32. Latham, p. 252.
33. Young, *Helping Hand*, p. 296.
34. Feis, *China Tangle*, pp. 74–5.
35. *Stilwell Papers*, pp. 123, 305–6. "Only outside influence can do anything for China," Stilwell wrote in his diary on June 19, 1942, "either enemy action will smash her or some regenerative idea must be formed and put into effect at once."
36. Charles F. Romanus and Riley Sunderland, *Stilwell's Command Problems*, pp. 49–54, 362–4; Tang Tsou, *America's Failure in China, 1941–50*, pp. 59–74.
37. *Ibid.*, p. 94.
38. *Diary (China)*, pp. 1027–30, January 19, 1944 (vol. 695, pp. 176–9); the War Department's case on the exchange and ependiture issue is in China White Paper, pp. 496–502.
39. Hornbeck quoted in Young, *Helping Hand*, pp. 423–4; Feis, *China Tangle*, p. 61.
40. China White Paper, pp. 488–9.
41. HDW's minutes of the January 19, 1944, meeting are in *Diary (China)*, pp. 1027–30 (vol. 695, pp. 176–9); *cf.*, Young, *Helping Hand*, pp. 322–4; *Scope of Soviet Activity*, pp. 2026–7 (vol. 846, pp. 32–6).
42. Young, p. 323.
43. See, for example, *Diary (China)*, pp. 970, ff., 1061–8, 1215–16, 1305–24, 1411–15. According to Miss Bentley, one underground report considered that Adler was "not tending to business and influencing the quarters he should be. He was playing too much bridge with Madame Chiang Kaishek." *IPR Hearings*, p. 435.
44. China White Paper, pp. 05–0; Tsou, *America's Failure in China*, p. 82.
45. Minutes of meeting on October 2, 1944, are in China White Paper, pp. 502–4.
46. Young, *Helping Hand*, pp. 327–32, discusses some of the pros and cons of the October 2 meeting, giving *inter alia* the July, 1944, note issue of C$6.3 billion.
47. Blum III, p. 296.
48. China White Paper, p. 470.

Chapter 12. An Offensive Weapon of War

1. Petrov, p. 16. In addition to Dr. Petrov's study, Walter Rundell, Jr., *Black Market Money: the Collapse of U.S. Military Currency Control in World War II*, is a good narrative analysis of the general story.
2. *Annual Report of the Secretary of the Treasury, 1944–1945* (Washington, D.C.: U.S. Government Printing Office, 1946), p. 389 (Treasury statement, March 14, 1945).
3. Blum III, pp. 141–2.
4. "Diary of a Trip to Britain," White Papers, Concord Files, *Hearings*, pp. 2591–4.
5. Petrov, ch. 3, has an engaging account of these negotiations in North Africa which "became the pattern for financial relations with all the 'liberated' countries of Europe." For the political background, see Robert Murphy's *Diplomat among Warriors*.
6. *Hearings*, pp. 2315–18, gives the transcript of this discussion in HM's office with Bell and HDW and the subsequent text of the letter to HDW (vol. 611, pp. 50–5; vol. 612, p. 68).
7. Paul Y. Hammond, "Directives for the Occupation of Germany: the Washington Controversy," in *American Civil-Military Decisions*, ed. Harold Stein (University of Alabama Press, 1963), p. 348.
8. Testimony by Assistant Secretary of State John H. Hilldring in *Currency Hearings 1947*, pp. 115, ff.
9. Petrov, pp. 78–9, 84–6.
10. C. H. S. Harris, *Allied Military Administration of Italy, 1943–5*, p. 382. Harris gives (p. 91) an equivalent figure, calculated by the Bank of International Settlements, of 39 and 145 lire to the dollar and the pound respectively in mid-1943; Hammond, p. 349.
11. Blum III, pp. 165–77.
12. *Currency Hearings 1947*, p. 147. Most of this account of the case of the duplicate plates is drawn from these hearings and *Currency Hearings 1953*. Cf., Petrov, ch. 5, and Blum III, pp. 177–94.
13. HDW to Gromyko, February 9, 1944: *Currency Hearings 1947*, pp. 173–4.
14. *Ibid.*, p. 148.
15. Hall to Bell, March 3, 1944, *Currency Hearings 1953*, p. 45.
16. *Currency Hearings 1947*, pp. 179–80. HDW had lunched with Gromyko on March 3, White Papers, Concord Files, *Hearings*, p. 2782.
17. *Memoirs of Cordell Hull*, pp. 1314–15.
18. Sherwood, *Roosevelt and Hopkins*, pp. 798–9.
19. Winston S. Churchill, *Closing the Ring*, p. 342.
20. Howe and Coser, p. 433; cf., Paul Willen, "Who Collaborated with Russia?" *Antioch Review*, September, 1954.
21. Churchill, *Closing the Ring*, p. 318.
22. Petrov, p. 121.
23. *Currency Hearings 1947*, pp. 179–80.
24. *Ibid.*, pp. 180–2.

25. *Ibid.*, pp. 182–3.
26. *Ibid.*, p. 150.
27. Memorandum for the files by HDW, March 22, 1944; *ibid.*, pp. 183–4.
28. Harriman to Hull, April 8, 1944; *ibid.*, p. 151.
29. Petrov, pp. 122–3.
30. HDW to HM, March 7, 1944, "Proposed U.S. Loan to the U.S.S.R."; *Hearings*, pp. 1451–2.
31. *Currency Hearings 1947*, p. 45.
32. Memorandum for the files by Taylor and Aarons, April 13, 1944; *ibid.*, pp. 184–5.
33. Minutes of C.C.A.C. meeting, April 13, 1944; Hilldring 1947 testimony; *ibid.*, pp. 46–7, 119; Hilldring 1960 comments, Petrov, p. 125.
34. Marshall to HM, April 13, 1944; *ibid.*, pp. 45–6.
35. Two memoranda by A. W. Hall for the files, April 14 and 15, 1944; *Currency Hearings 1953*, pp. 52, 46. Hall noted that "From the first time the Russian request came to my notice I have strenuously objected in oral argument and in writing to furnishing duplicate glass positives of the mark currency to the Russian government. There may be serious repercussions when the transaction becomes public information."
36. Dunn memorandum; *Currency Hearings 1947*, pp. 152–3.
37. Morgenthau to Gromyko, April 14, 1944; *ibid.*, p. 186.
38. Crow to Taylor, April 15, 1944; *ibid.*, p. 187.
39. Petrov, pp. 196–200.
40. Bell to Hall, April 27, 1944; *Currency Hearings 1947*, pp. 192–3.
41. *Ibid.*, p. 132.
42. Blum III, p. 188.
43. Bentley, *Out of Bondage*, p. 198; *Currency Hearings 1953*, pp. 27, ff. *Cf.*, the Mundt Subcommittee's Interim Report, S.837, *ibid.*, December, 1953, and White, *Loyal American*, pp. 174–82, 325–32.
44. *Diary (Germany)*, pp. 384–5 (vol. 735, pp. 126, ff.); Blum III, pp. 188–9.
45. *Ibid.*, pp. 385–93 (vol. 738, pp. 80–96).
46. Blum III, pp. 190–1. *Cf.*, Petrov, pp. 193–4.
47. *Currency Hearings 1947*, pp. 240–2, 253; *Diary (Germany)*, p. 590 (vol. 770, p. 123). A Treasury press release of October 3 stated that "military forces under General Eisenhower are using allied military marks in German territory."

Chapter 13.   Miss Bentley's New World

1. Miss Bentley's initial 1948 testimony on the Washington espionage networks is in *HUAC Hearings*, pp. 507–21, while her further testimony on HDW's alleged involvement may be found in *IPR Hearings*, pp. 419–24. The Hart-Davis edition of Elizabeth Bentley's *Out of Bondage* (London, 1952) is cited here, not the Devin-Adair edition (New York, 1951).
2. Bentley, *Out of Bondage*, pp. 19, 27.

3. Rebecca West, "Hiss Case Hid Graver Issues," *Sunday Times*, March 22, 1953. Murray Kempton's fine study of the thirties, *Part of Our Time* (New York: Simon & Schuster, 1955), p. 221, has some robust comment on the contrast between Miss Bentley's homely style and the events she described.

4. Bentley, *Out of Bondage*, pp. 118–19, 123–4. In *HUAC Hearings* of August, 1948, p. 507, Miss Bentley said that Earl Browder, American Party Secretary, had given Golos the name of Silvermaster, but Browder was in Atlanta Penitentiary from March, 1941 to May, 1942. *Cf.*, Latham, p. 167.

5. Bentley, *Out of Bondage*, p. 135. Nathan Gregory Silvermaster died in 1964.

6. *HUAC Hearings*, pp. 525–7; Bentley, *Out of Bondage*, pp. 141–6.

7. *HUAC Hearings*, p. 511.

8. Bentley, *Out of Bondage*, p. 135.

9. *Ibid.*, p. 136.

10. *Ibid.*, pp. 144–6.

11. For Miss Bentley's testimony on HDW in August, 1951, see *IPR Hearings*, pp. 419–24. Currie, who was alleged by Miss Bentley to have given confidential information to the Silvermaster group during the HUAC Hearings of 1948, while not being a Party member, appeared before the committee the same day as HDW, August 13, 1948. Like HDW, he denied ever passing any confidential information to unauthorized persons. He stated that he did know Silvermaster, Silverman, Ullmann and others named by Miss Bentley and Chambers, and had visited the Silvermaster home. In the IPR Hearings, Miss Bentley repeated that Currie had passed secret information—"most of it was Far Eastern"—and stated that once when the U.S. authorities were about to break "the Soviet code" the news had been passed to the Russians via Currie, HDW and Silverman. See Currie's testimony in *HUAC Hearings*, pp. 851–77.

12. Quoting from a February, 1946, FBI report to President Truman on HDW, partly based on Miss Bentley's statements to the Bureau, Attorney-General Brownell stated to the Senate Internal Security Subcommittee in November, 1953, that the Silvermasters—"sometime in the summer or fall" of 1943—believed it desirable for someone to be placed in HDW's office to facilitate the flow of information for delivery to Soviet espionage agents. "One of the Communist functionaries" recommended Mrs. Sonia Gold and, said Brownell, "through arrangements with White" obtained a position as one of the secretaries in the Treasury: "As a result of this employment, Mrs. Gold obtained documents from White's office, which she copied and made her notes available to Mrs. Helen Witte Silvermaster. The information which Mrs. Gold obtained in a general way concerned principally the Treasury Department's opinions and recommendations concerning applications for loans made by the Chinese and French Governments." (*Hearings*, p. 1117. See Part IV below.) Following her identification by Miss Bentley as an alleged member of the Silvermaster group in 1948,

Mrs. Sonia Gold denied to the House Committee that she was a Communist or a member of the Silvermaster group. She had visited the Silvermasters, but had never been in their basement. (*HUAC Hearings*, pp. 912–15.)

13. By the summer of 1944 there were eighteen committees or boards on which HDW had represented the Treasury. These were:

The Interdepartmental Lend-Lease Committee
The Canadian-American Joint Economic Committee
The Executive Committee on Commercial Policy
The Executive Committee and Board of Trustees of the Export-Import Bank
The Interdepartmental Committee on Inter-American Affairs
The National Resources Committee
The Price Administration Committee
The Committee on Foreign Commerce Regulations
The Interdepartmental Committee on Postwar Economic Problems
The Committee on Trade Agreements
The National Munitions Control Board
The Acheson Committee on International Relief
The Board of Economic Warfare
The Executive Committee on Economic Foreign Policy
The Liberated Areas Committee
The U.S. Commercial Corporation
The O.S.S. Advisory Committee
The Interdepartmental Committee on Planning for Coordinating the Economic Activities of U.S. Civilian Agencies in Liberated Areas

Charles S. Bell, Administrative Assistant to HM, to Mrs. Frances P. Bolton, July 17, 1944; White Papers, Concord Files, *Hearings*, pp. 2579–80. *Cf.*, the letter by Sonia Gold, Division of Monetary Research, listing these committees, to HM's acting administrative assistant, July 6, 1944; *ibid.*, pp. 2607–8.

14. *IPR Hearings*, p. 424.
15. *HUAC Hearings*, p. 540.
16. Latham, p. 159.
17. *Ibid.*, pp. 159–60. See the account in *I. F. Stone's Weekly*, January 16, 1956, reprinted in White, *Loyal American*, pp. 343–4. Stone goes on to cite an affidavit made in the suit against the newspaper in which Miss Bentley referred to *Out of Bondage* as "fiction." According to Packer, *Ex-Communist Witnesses*, p. 60, this statement was later denied by Miss Bentley.
18. *I. F. Stone's Weekly*, April 25, 1955, reprinted in White, *Loyal American*, p. 336.
19. *Ibid.*, also p. 341.
20. *Ibid.*, p. 337; Latham, pp. 159, 162.
21. *I. F. Stone's Weekly*, January 16, 1956, quoted in White, *Loyal American*, p. 343. The details of the Byron Scott statement on Miss Bentley's credibility was inserted into the *Congressional Record*, May 24, 1955, app. A, p. 3591.

22. Packer, *Ex-Communist Witnesses*, p. 116.

23. *Ibid.*, pp. 102–20. *Cf.*, Latham, pp. 159, ff. and 23. Fred J. Cook, *The F.B.I. Nobody Knows*, pp. 345, ff.

24. Packer, *Ex-Communist Witnesses*, p. 104. As we have seen, in ch. 6 above, until November, 1948, Chambers' story was that HDW, though a fellow traveller, was not specifically involved in espionage.

25. Latham, pp. 159–61. *Cf.*, *ibid.*, pp. 107, 115–16, for Weyl's testimony.

26. Berle mémorandum of September 2, 1939, Chambers, *Witness*, pp. 466–9; also in *Hearings*, pp. 329–30. Ray Murphy memorandum of conversation with Chambers, March 20, 1945; *Hearings*, pp. 1182–3. Charles ("Bob") Coe did not work in the Treasury. He was associated with Farm Research, organized by Harold Ware, according to James Burnham, *The Web of Subversion*, p. 115. Chambers told the IPR Hearings (p. 493) in May, 1951, that J. Peters had informed him in 1936 or 1937 that Adler was sending a weekly memorandum to the American Communist Party with information on the U.S. Treasury. Adler joined the Treasury in December, 1936, and the Division of Monetary Research in March, 1938. White Papers, Concord Files, *Hearings*, Report, p. x. But Coe was in Toronto not Montreal University at this time.

27. Packer, *Ex-Communist Witnesses*, p. 105.

28. *Ibid.*, p. 105.

29. *Ibid.*, p. 83.

30. *Ibid.*, p. 107.

31. *Ibid.*, pp. 107–8.

32. *HUAC Hearings*, pp. 587, ff. In these 1948 Hearings Silvermaster denounced Miss Bentley as "a neurotic liar," but invoked the Fifth Amendment to further questions, declining to say whether he knew her. For the Civil Service Report, see *ibid.*, p. 613.

33. Packer, *Ex-Communist Witnesses*, pp. 111–12. Lord Jowitt has written (p. 16) that, if a witness refused to answer on grounds of self-incrimination, he feels "tolerably certain" that a (British) judge would "not support his candidature" in a club committee.

34. Details of the 1956 Coe-Ullmann testimony in White, *Loyal American*, pp. 410–15. In the 1948 House Hearings, Coe denied participating in espionage activities; in 1952 he invoked the Fifth Amendment to questions, before the Senate Internal Security Subcommittee, on espionage and Communist affiliations, before denying the espionage charge in 1956 before the same committee. On this latter occasion he invoked the Fifth Amendment to questions on Party membership. *Cf.*, Burnham, *Web of Subversion*, pp. 114–15. Ullman invoked the Fifth Amendment in 1953 to questions regarding Party membership and involvement in espionage: *Hearings*, p. 1200.

35. *Hearings*, p. 1145. See Part IV below.

36. Packer, *Ex-Communist Witnesses*, pp. 73–5, 96–102, 113. See Part IV below.

37. *Ibid.*, p. 109.

38. *Ibid.*, p. 114.

39. *Ibid.*, pp. 114–17.
40. *Ibid.*, p. 120.
41. *Ibid.*, pp. 222–3.
42. Cook, *The F.B.I. Nobody Knows*, p. 298.
43. Latham, p. 160.
44. White, *Loyal American*, p. 173.
45. Bentley, *Out of Bondage*, pp. 135–6.
46. Chambers, *Witness*, p. 427.
47. Latham, p. 118.
48. *IPR Hearings*, Report, pp. 179–81. *Cf.*, Latham, p. 306.
49. White testimony, *HUAC Hearings*, pp. 877, ff.
50. Silvermaster, in the House Hearings, declined to say whether there was a darkroom in his wartime home at 5515, 30th Street, NW, Washington, and the others in the alleged group had either not noticed or forgotten. When the house was sold after the war, the real estate advertisement in the Washington *Star* of May 3, 1947, referred to "the excellent photographic room" in the basement. Burnham, *Web of Subversion*, p. 37.
51. Coe testimony, *HUAC Hearings*, pp. 915–28.
52. Packer, *Ex-Communist Witnesses*, p. 57.
53. *Hearings*, pp. 985, 987, 999–1000, 99, 458, 401.
54. *Ibid.*, pp. 1184–1200.
55. Latham, pp. 93, 176; *Hearings*, p. 969. See also *HUAC Hearings*, pp. 851–77, for Currie's testimony emphatically denying Miss Bentley's allegations. Latham comments that Currie "got an exculpatory letter from Patterson for Silvermaster and the latter was allowed to stay with the Board of Economic Warfare, although his tour eventually proved to be short-lived." See Latham, p. 170.
56. *Hearings*, pp. 975–7; White Papers, Concord Files, *Hearings*, Report, p. xliii; Rebecca West, "The Surprising Mr. Kaplan," *Sunday Times*, March 29, 1953; Burnham, *Web of Subversion*, pp. 78–9.
57. Silvermaster testimony on Bretton Woods, *Hearings*, pp. 130–1, that of Ullmann on Bretton Woods and San Francisco Conference, *ibid.*, pp. 1207–8; *cf.*, official Treasury biographical press release on Coe, February, 1945, *ibid.*, p. 1000. HM letter nominating HDW as Technical Adviser to the delegates at San Francisco Conference, White Papers, Concord Files, *Hearings*, p. 2611.
58. *Report of the Royal Commission Appointed by the Canadian Government in February 1946 . . .* (Ottawa, 1946), pp. 175, 182–7, 226.
59. *Hearings*, Report, p. 21.
60. Latham, pp. 90–7.
61. Bentley, *Out of Bondage*, p. 198.
62. David Dallin, *Soviet Espionage*, p. 443.
63. *IPR Hearings*, p. 423. During the extended "round-table" discussion in the IPR Hearings 1951–2 between Chambers, Bentley and Hede Massing on the underground, Chambers commented that it was "special history" that he had managed to save documents from his time as an agent. (*Ibid.*, p. 4791.)

64. Dallin, *Soviet Espionage*, pp. 444–5.
65. Latham, p. 97.

Chapter 14. Toward Bretton Woods

1. HDW, "The Monetary Fund: Some Criticisms Examined," *Foreign Affairs* (New York), January, 1945, p. 208.
2. The progress of the Law Mission commercial negotiations is related in Gardner, ch. VI, and Penrose, ch. V.
3. Details of the preliminary Anglo-American negotiating positions on the Fund are in John Parke Young, "Developing Plans for an International Monetary Fund and a World Bank," *Department of State Bulletin*, November 13, 1950.
4. Harrod, *Keynes*, p. 565.
5. Cmd 6519. (London: His Majesty's Stationery Office, 1944).
6. Edward M. Bernstein to writer, April 27, 1971.
6a. John Parke Young, *op. cit.*, *DOSB*, November 13, 1950.
7. Gardner, pp. 113–14.
8. Harrod, *Keynes*, pp. 570–2. In the event, the scarce-currency clause was never invoked in the postwar period.
9. White Papers, PUL, file 24.
10. Interview with Dean Acheson, Washington, D.C., November 4, 1969.
11. Gardner, pp. 111–12.
12. Blum III, pp. 249–52.
13. Keynes to HDW, March 12, 1944, *Hearings*, pp. 2325–6 (vol. 710, pp. 190–2).
14. *Parliamentary Debates, House of Commons*, vol. 399, cols 1935–2046 (May 10, 1944).
15. 3914, Bucknell, American Embassy, London, to Secretary of State, May 13, 1944, White Papers, PUL, file 24.
16. *Parliamentary Debates, House of Lords*, vol. 131, cols 840–5 (May 23, 1944).
17. Blum III, pp. 252–7; Harrod, *Keynes*, pp. 576–7.
18. HDW, "The Monetary Fund: Some Criticisms Examined," p. 195.
19. *United Nations Monetary and Financial Conference: Final Act*, Cmd 6546. The Articles were not ratified by the U.S.S.R.
20. Blum III, pp. 276–7; *cf.*, HM, "Bretton Woods and International Cooperation," *Foreign Affairs* (New York), January, 1945. Acheson, *Present at the Creation*, ch. 10, discusses Bretton Woods with some interesting details of the Bank negotiations.
21. White Papers, Concord Files, *Hearings*, pp. 2561–2.

Chapter 15. The Carthaginian Peace

1. HM, "Our Policy Towards Germany," New York *Post*, November 24, 1947; *Diary (Germany)*, pp. 413–14 (vol. 763, p. 92); *cf.*, Blum III, ch. vi, "The Morgenthau Plan," for the development of the Secretary's views.

2. Churchill, *Closing the Ring*, p. 356; Cardinal Spellman's memorandum of the talk with FDR is printed in Robert I. Gannon, *The Cardinal Spellman Story* (London: Robert Hale, 1963), pp. 222–4.
3. Penrose, pp. 217–24, for the studies of the Malkin Committee, and Woodward, *British Foreign Policy in the Second World War*, pp. 445, 465–76, for the work of the Cabinet Committee. Michael Balfour and John Mair, *Four Power Control in Germany and Austria 1945–1946* (London: Royal Institute of International Affairs, 1956), discusses in some detail the policy background to the occupation of defeated Germany by by the wartime Allies.
4. For the Allied plans on German partition and the work of the European Advisory Commission, see in particular the two essays by Philip Mosely, "Dismemberment of Germany" and "The Occupation of Germany," in *Foreign Affairs*, April and July, 1950, reprinted, with commentary, in the author's *The Kremlin in World Politics*. Mosely was Winant's political adviser in EAC matters. Paul Y. Hammond's "Directives for the Occupation of Germany: the Washington Controversy," quoted above in ch. 12, is an excellent survey of the development of American occupation policy for Germany. *Cf.*, William M. Franklin, "Zonal Boundaries and Access to Berlin," *World Politics*, October, 1963.
5. Hammond, p. 319.
6. *Ibid.*, p. 328.
7. Text is in *Diary (Germany)*, pp. 679–89 (vol. 777, pp. 69–87); *cf.*, John L. Chase, "The Development of the Morgenthau Plan through the Quebec Conference," *Journal of Politics*, May, 1954, pp. 327–8. Hammond, pp. 342–7, discusses the work of the ECEFP in some detail.
8. HDW, "Memorandum for the Secretary's Files," August 31, 1944; HDW to HM, September 29, 1944, *Diary (Germany)*, pp. 462, 679 (vol. 767, p. 176; vol. 777, p. 69).
9. *Diary (Germany)*, pp. 398–9 (vol. 754, p. 184).
10. Fred Smith, "The Rise and Fall of the Morgenthau Plan," *United Nations World*, March, 1947; HM, "Our Policy Towards Germany," New York *Post*, November 24, 1947; Dwight D. Eisenhower, *Crusade in Europe*, pp. 314–15; Smith's 1953 comments in Whipple, pt VIII. *Cf.*, *Diary (Germany)*, pp. 413–14 (vol. 763, pp. 92, ff.).
11. Smith, "Rise and Fall of the Morgenthau Plan."
12. Penrose, pp. 244–6; HM, "Our Policy Towards Germany," November 25, 1947.
13. Smith, "Rise and Fall of the Morgenthau Plan."
14. Penrose, pp. 246–8.
15. Telephone interview with Professor Philip Mosely, Washington, D.C., November 5, 1969. Also see Mosely comments in Snell, *The Wartime Origins of the East-West Dilemma over Germany*, pp. 66–67.
16. Smith, "Rise and Fall of the Morgenthau Plan"; HDW to HM, "Memorandum for the Secretary's Files," London, August 13, 1944; *Teheran Papers*, pp. 881–2; HM, "Our Policy Towards Germany," November 25, 1947.

17. HDW to HM, "Memorandum for the Secretary's Files," London, August 15, 1944; *Teheran Papers*, pp. 883–4, and White Papers, PUL, file 22; Smith, "Rise and Fall of the Morgenthau Plan"; HM, "Our Policy Towards Germany," November 25, 1947; see Hammond, pp. 316, 336, 353, for the reference of the study of partition to the EAC subcommittee; *cf.*, Mosely, "Dismemberment of Germany."

18. *Memoirs of Cordell Hull*, p. 1615; Blum III, pp. 338–9; *Diary (Germany)*, pp. 414–15 (vol. 763, pp. 92–115).

19. *Diary (Germany)*, pp. 415–18 (vol. 763, pp. 202–5); "Our Policy Towards Germany," November 25, 1947; Blum III, pp. 342–3.

20. Hammond, pp. 348–9; Luxford, Pehle comments, *Diary (Germany)*, pp. 429, 617–19.

21. Chester Wilmot, *The Struggle for Europe*, p. 458; Stimson and Bundy, p. 566.

22. *Diary (Germany)*, pp. 434–42 (vol. 766, pp. 1–12); Hammond, pp. 352–3.

23. *Diary (Germany)*, p. 442; Lord Avon (Anthony Eden), *The Reckoning*, pp. 475–6. *Cf.*, the telegram of September 2 from Halifax to the Foreign Office mentioned in Woodward, *British Foreign Policy in the Second World War*, p. 471.

24. *Diary (Germany)*, pp. 425–7 (vol. 765, pp. 14–16); Blum III, pp. 347–9; Stimson and Bundy, p. 569.

25. *Diary (Germany)*, pp. 443–5 (vol. 766, pp. 166–70); Hammond, pp. 356–7; *Diary (Germany)*, p. 541 (vol. 769, pp. 118, ff.).

26. *Diary (Germany)*, pp. 453–62 (vol. 767, pp. 18, ff, 161, ff.); Blum III, pp. 351 2. For the conversation of the 28th.

27. Text, dated September 1, 1944, in *Diary (Germany)*, pp. 463–6 (vol. 768, pp. 1–22).

28. Chase, "Development of the Morgenthau Plan through the Quebec Conference," pp. 338–9.

29. Herbert Feis, *Churchill, Roosevelt and Stalin*, pp. 366–7.

30. Riddleberger to Stettinius, October 28, 1944, *Yalta Papers*, pp. 160–3.

31. Text of the State Department paper, "American Policy for Treatment of Germany after Surrender," September 1, 1944, is reproduced in *Diary (Germany)*, pp. 479–83 (vol. 768, pp. 68, ff.).

32. *Memoirs of Cordell Hull*, pp. 1607–8.

33. HM, "Our Policy Toward Germany," November 28, 1947; Blum III, pp. 352–4.

34. *Ibid.*, "Our Policy Toward Germany."

35. The transcript of these two group meetings of September 4 on "Disarmament of Germany" is in *Diary (Germany)*, pp. 483–502 (vol. 768, pp. 104, ff., 134–45). HDW's comments on the population "problem" are in *Diary (Germany)*, pp. 488–92.

36. HDW, "Dinner at the Secretary's Home," September 4, 1944, *Diary (Germany)*, p. 503 (vol. 768, p. 156); Morgenthau comments on the dinner conversation, *ibid.*, pp. 525–6 (vol. 769, pp. 9, ff.); Stimson and Bundy, pp. 568–9.

37. The State Department's "Suggested Recommendations on Treatment of Germany by the Cabinet Committee for the President," September 4, 1944, is printed in *Diary (Germany)*, pp. 519–21 (vol. 768, pp. 190, ff.). The version in Stimson and Bundy, p. 571, differs slightly in phrasing.

38. Stimson and Bundy, pp. 571–3. *Memoirs of Cordell Hull*, pp. 1605–6, tends to blur the story by confusing HDW's presentation of September 2 with HM's of the fifth, when the idea of wrecking the mines was probably first proposed outside the Treasury. Hull's narrative also fails to bring out that he first sided with HM against Stimson, before switching later in the month, after Quebec, to oppose the Treasury proposals. See the interesting discussion of this point in Hammond, pp. 452–3. *Cf.*, Penrose, pp. 252–3, and Walter Dorn, "The Debate over American Occupation Policy in Germany in 1944–45," *Political Science Quarterly*, December, 1957, p. 491.

39. "Suggested Post-Surrender Program for Germany," September 5, 1944, *Diary (Germany)*, pp. 548–53 (vol. 769, pp. 152–63).

40. Stimson and Bundy, pp. 573–4; Blum III, pp. 362–3; *Diary (Germany)*, 536, ff. (vol. 769, pp. 118, ff.).

41. *Diary (Germany)*, pp. 590–1 (vol. 770, pp. 148–50).

42. A facsimile of the memorandum given to HM on September 9 is printed as a frontispiece in HM's *Germany Is Our Problem*.

43. *Diary (Germany)*, pp. 591–604 (vol. 771, pp. 6–16); White Papers, PUL, file 22; *Hearings*, pp. 1453–4.

44. Stimson and Bundy, pp. 574–5, 579; HM, "Our Policy Towards Germany," November 28, 1947; Blum III, pp. 367–8. *Diary (Germany)*, pp. 612–15 (vol. 771, pp. 50, ff.), contains a full text of Stimson's memorandum of September 9.

Chapter 16. "Octagon" and After

1. Churchill, *Triumph and Tragedy*, p. 137.
2. Sherwood, *Roosevelt and Hopkins*, p. 818.
3. Churchill, *Triumph and Tragedy*, p. 141.
4. Penrose, p. 256.
5. See the discussion of this point in Gardner, ch. 9.
6. *Ibid.*, pp. 172–4.
7. Blum III, p. 123.
8. HDW, "Lunch at the Secretary's Invitation," November 17, 1943; White Papers, PUL, file 24.
9. Churchill to Roosevelt, March 9, 1944, in Churchill, *Closing the Ring*, pp. 611–12.
10. HDW, "Memorandum for the Secretary's Files," September 25, 1944, Meeting in Hull's Office, September 20, 1944, *Yalta Papers*, p. 138.
11. Feis, *Churchill, Roosevelt and Stalin*, p. 369.
12. The writer is grateful to Mr. William J. Stewart, Acting Director of the

Franklin D. Roosevelt Library, Hyde Park, New York, for making available
to him copies of these five memoranda when the Morgenthau Presidential
Diary was opened for research in 1971.

13. HDW, "Memorandum for the Secretary's Files, Secretary Morgenthau's
Conversation with the President, Quebec, Wednesday, September 13,
1944, 4:00 P.M.," Morgenthau Presidential Diary, p. 1511.

14. HDW, "Memorandum for the Secretary's Files, Dinner at Citadel, Quebec,
Wednesday, September 13, 1944, 8:00 P.M.," Morgenthau Presidential
Diary, pp. 1516–1517A.

15. HM, "Our Policy Towards Germany," November 29, 1947.

16. Lord Moran, *Churchill: the Struggle for Survival 1940–1965*, pp. 177–82.

17. H. Freeman Matthews, "Memorandum," September 20, 1944, *Yalta Papers*,
pp. 134–5. *Cf.*, HDW's record of the same meeting on the twentieth, *ibid.*,
pp. 136–41.

18. Blum III, pp. 311–12.

19. HDW, "Memorandum for the Secretary's Files, Conference in Secretary
Morgenthau's Suite, Quebec, Thursday, September 14, 1944, 10:00 A.M.,"
Morgenthau Presidential Diary, pp. 1514–15.

20. Blum III, p. 312.

21. HM, "Our Policy Towards Germany," November 29, 1947; H. Freeman
Matthews, "Memorandum," September 20, 1944, *Yalta Papers*, pp. 134–5;
Moran, *Churchill*, p. 178: "As Lord Cherwell spoke, I could see him producing from his pocket one of his graphs, with that quiet confident air
that he was right."

22. HDW, "Memorandum for the Secretary's Files, Memorandum of a Conversation, Friday, September 15, 1944, Quebec," Morgenthau Presidential
Diary, p. 1512.

23. HDW, "Memorandum for the Secretary's Files, Conference in the Secretary's Room, Quebec, Friday, September 15, 11 A.M.," Morgenthau Presidential Diary, p. 1513.

24. *Diary (Germany)*, pp. 620–1 (vol. 772, p. 1); *cf.*, Stimson and Bundy,
pp. 576, ff.

25. Avon, *Reckoning*, pp. 476–7. Perhaps some of the strong reaction in Whitehall may be explained by the realization there that, although the HDW-HM
proposals on Germany could be superficially compared with those Lord
Vansittart put forward in Britain during the war, there were significant
differences. The extent to which HDW's proposals, even those of his first
draft of the Treasury proposals of September 1, 1944, went beyond those of
Vansittart can be seen by reference to the latter's widely publicized Twelve-
Point article, "My Peace Terms for Germany," *Sunday Dispatch* (London),
December 5, 1943. While emphasizing strict demilitarization, denazification, "effective control" and, where required, the "closing down" of Germany's war potential "including aviation in all its forms," Vansittart envisaged that Germany would "be allowed to purchase an adequate number
of commercial machines abroad." All German war potential, Vansittart
held, "must be put under supervision . . . there must be control of the

German machine tool industry and rationing of the key raw materials of war." Vansittart advocated "breaking-up Prussia," but a unified Germany, under Allied control, was implicit in his program, for he emphasized that the Reich must be "adequately decentralised," and there is no mention of partition. Moreover, in speaking of the "restoration of, or compensation for loot, machinery and equipment removed, or destroyed" by the Nazis, Vansittart evidently envisaged recurrent reparations on a fairly large scale.

All these points are expanded in *Bones of Contention* where the emphasis is on strict industrial control and political decentralization. In addition, Vansittart was emphatic that Germany must be policed by all the Allies, and as befitted a former Foreign Office Permanent Under-Secretary, was emphatic that a balance of power must be preserved, otherwise "the powers of occupation might become two, Britain and Russia and then Russia only": *Bones of Contention*, pp. 62–7, 74–7, and ch. 14. *Cf.*, Vansittart's *Events and Shadows*.

26. "Record of Conversation Between the President and the Prime Minister at Quebec on September 14, 1944," September 15, *Diary (Germany)*, pp. 619–20 (vol. 771, p. 223). There is a shorter memorandum on the terms of reference of the joint committee, initialed by FDR, which accompanies the above.

27. Churchill, *Triumph and Tragedy*, p. 444.

28. HDW, "Memorandum for the Secretary's Files," September 25, 1944, *Yalta Papers*, p. 137 (meeting of September 20, 1944).

29. *The Times* (London), September 14, 1944.

30. Stimson and Bundy, p. 579.

31. *The Forrestal Diaries*, ed. Walter Millis and E. S. Duffield (New York: Viking, 1951), p. 11; *Diary (Germany)*, pp. 624–5 (vol. 772, pp. 132, ff.).

32. Besides the two memoranda on this meeting of September 20, by Freeman Matthews and HDW noted above and printed in *Yalta Papers*, pp. 134–41, see *Memoirs of Cordell Hull*, pp. 1614–15.

33. Hammond, pp. 370, 453–4.

34. "Lord Brand Talks to Kenneth Harris," *Observer* (London), January 8, 1961.

35. Birkenhead, *Prof in Two Worlds*, pp. 267–8.

36. See Colville's essay in *Action This Day: Working with Churchill*, ed. Sir J. W. Wheeler-Bennett, pp. 84–7, 101–2.

37. Churchill, *Triumph and Tragedy*, pp. 138–9.

38. HDW HM conversation, October 18, 1944; *Diary (Germany)*, pp. 714 ff (vol. 783, pp. 23–9).

39. Blum III, p. 374.

40. Petrov, pp. 158–9.

41. Arthur Krock, *Memoirs*, pp. 208–9.

42. *Parliamentary Debates, House of Commons*, vol. 403, cols 414–15 (September 28, 1944).

43. Anne Armstrong, *Unconditional Surrender*, pp. 71–7; Wilmot, *Struggle for Europe*, pp. 548–51; Forrest C. Pogue, *The Supreme Command*

(Washington, D.C.: U.S. Government Printing Office, 1954), pp. 342–3; Albert Speer, *Inside the Third Reich*, p. 433.

44. *Diary (Germany),* pp. 633–7 (vol. 774, pp. 123–7).
45. *Ibid.*, pp. 639–40 (vol. 775, p. 9), 662–3 (vol. 776, pp. 185–6).
46. *Ibid.*, pp. 668, ff. (vol. 777, pp. 1, ff.).
47. *Memoirs of Cordell Hull*, pp. 1616–18; Hull to FDR, September 25, 1944, *Yalta Papers*, p. 142.
48. Stimson and Bundy, p. 580; Blum III, pp. 379–81; Hammond, pp. 378–9.
49. Roosevelt to Hull, September 29, 1944, *Yalta Papers*, p. 155; Hull to FDR, September 29, 1944, *ibid.*, pp. 156–8; *Memoirs of Cordell Hull*, pp. 1619–22.
50. Stimson and Bundy, p. 581.
51. Blum III, pp. 381–2; Matthews to Stettinius, November 4, 1944, *Yalta Papers*, p. 165; FDR to Hull, October 20, 1944, *ibid.*, p. 158.
52. Woodward, *British Foreign Policy in the Second World War*, pp. 472–4. The E.I.P.S. concluded that "the destruction of German productive power would impoverish the countries with whom Germany traded."
53. Churchill to Eden, January 4, 1945; Churchill, *Triumph and Tragedy*, pp. 305–6.
54. *Ibid.*, pp. 138–9.
55. *Parliamentary Debates, House of Commons*, vol. 467, cols 1596–8 (July 21, 1949).
56. Blum III, p. 316.
57. See the account of the Stage II negotiations in *ibid.*, pp. 316–26, and Harrod, *Keynes*, pp. 586–91. *Cf.*, W. K. Hancock and M. M. Gowing, *British War Economy*, pp. 527–9, and Admiral Leahy's remarks in *I Was There* (New York: McGraw-Hill, 1950), pp. 279–80.
58. Gardner, pp. 180–4, is illuminating on this aftermath of the Octagon Conference.

Chapter 17.   The Vital Paragraphs

1. Hammond, p. 372; *cf.*, the undated text in *Diary (Germany)*, pp. 509–17 (vol. 768, pp. 167–8).
2. See the partial text in Hammond, pp. 372–3, who states that Taylor produced a draft "which reflected the views of his Department."
3. See ch. 15 above.
4. Hammond, p. 402. See also pp. 373–4 on this point.
5. "Directive to SCAEF Regarding the Military Government of Germany in the Period Immediately Following the Cessation of Organized Resistance (Post Defeat)," September 22, 1944, *Yalta Papers*, pp. 143–54. This is the first official version of the Interim Directive, JCS 1067, sent to Winant on September 27.
6. HDW, "Memorandum for the Secretary's Files," September 25, 1944, *ibid.*, pp. 140–1 (meeting of September 20).
7. Riddleberger to Hull, September 23, 1944, *ibid.*, p. 141. *Cf.*, Riddleberger's remarks to Stettinius, *ibid.*, pp. 162–3. The remarks of the Treasury repre-

sentatives on Hull's position referred presumably to his position, later abandoned, in the Cabinet Committee of September 5.

8. Dorn, "The Debate over American Occupation Policy in Germany," pp. 494–5.

9. Riddleberger to Winant, September 27, 1944, *Yalta Papers*, pp. 142–3. This letter is followed by the text of the Directive: See n. 5 above.

10. *Cf.*, the draft chapters by J. E. Du Bois and Ansel Luxford in White Papers, Concord Files, *Hearings*, pp. 2693–2730. An important theme was the Treasury's contention that opponents of the Morgenthau Plan wanted to build up Germany against Russia.

11. *Yalta Papers*, pp. 163–5; Woodward, *British Foreign Policy in the Second World War*, pp. 473–4.

12. Stettinius to FDR, November 10 and 22; FDR to Stettinius, December 4, 1944: *Yalta Papers*, pp. 165–74.

13. Blum III, pp. 388–9. On the wider aspects of the Morgenthau Plan, Ambassador Murphy comments, "I have little doubt that it could have led to Russian domination of the area. I remember Mr. Molotov's statement— 'as goes Germany, so goes Europe.' " Robert D. Murphy to writer, November 28, 1969.

14. Hammond, p. 387.

15. Details in *ibid.*, pp. 405–7, and Blum III, pp. 389–90.

16. I. Zlobin, "Meetings in America," *War and the Working Class*, no. 20 (October 15, 1944), trans. John Dorosh, Library of Congress: *Hearings*, pp. 1447–8.

17. *Diary (Germany)*, pp. 760–2 (vol. 796, pp. 29–32).

18. HM to FDR, December 28, 1944, White Papers, Concord Files, *Hearings*, p. 2510.

19. *Hearings*, pp. 2621, 2635, 956–7, 998–1000; *Diary (Germany)*, p. 907 (vol. 811, p. 376). HDW's full title was Assistant Secretary in Charge of Monetary Research and Foreign Funds.

20. Washington *Times-Herald*, December 28, 1944, "It seems Mr. White gets Mr. White's mail"; Chambers, *Witness*, p. 432, who describes seeing the reports when on *Time* magazine.

21. *Diary (Germany)*, pp. 700–1 (vol. 779, pp. 274, ff.).

22. Churchill to FDR, October 22, 1944: *Triumph and Tragedy*, pp. 209–11. *Cf.*, *Yalta Papers*, pp. 159–60.

23. *Ibid.*, pp. 176–8.

24. Gaston to HM, January 25, 1945: *Diary (Germany)*, p. 910 (vol. 812, p. 214).

25. HDW to HM, "Proposed United States Loan to the U.S.S.R.," March 7, 1944: *Hearings*, pp. 1451–2. Copy in White Papers, PUL, file 23.

26. Feis, *Churchill, Roosevelt and Stalin*, p. 642.

27. See the discussion in *ibid.*, pp. 641–7, and Gabriel Kolko, *The Politics of War*, pp. 333–40.

28. White Papers, PUL, file 23; *Yalta Papers*, pp. 309–10.

29. *Ibid.*, pp. 310–15.

30. Memorandum for the President, "A $10 Billion Reconstruction Credit for the U.S.S.R.," January 10, 1945; White Papers, PUL, file 23. The copy in *Yalta Papers*, p. 315, omits the two schedules on repayments and U.S. raw material resources.

31. Memorandum for the President, January 10, 1945: *Diary (Germany)*, pp. 858–60 (vol. 808, pp. 297–9).

32. *Ibid.*, pp. 876–8 (vol. 810, pp. 141–5).

33. *Ibid.*, pp. 879–83 (vol. 810, pp. 149–58). The version of this State Department minute in the *Yalta Papers*, pp. 319–21, omits HM's remarks on Germany.

34. *Yalta Papers*, pp. 178–97; Hammond, pp. 408–9.

35. Memorandum for the Department of the Treasury, "Long Range Program for Germany," January 19, 1945, *Yalta Papers*, pp. 175–6.

36. W. H. Taylor, "Meeting in Mr. Dunn's Office . . . ," January 19, 1945: *Diary (Germany)*, pp. 898–901 (vol. 811, pp. 95–8).

37. Clayton to Stettinius, January 20, 1945; Grew to Harriman, January 26, 1945: *Yalta Papers*, pp. 318–9, 321–3. For FDR's caution, see Blum III, pp. 305–6.

38. Ansel F. Luxford to writer, October 15, 1970.

39. John L. Snell, "What to Do with Germany?" in *The Meaning of Yalta*, ed. John L. Snell, p. 72.

40. *Ibid.*

41. *Yalta Papers*, p. 617.

42. *Ibid.*, pp. 626–7.

43. *Ibid.*, p. 978. Philip E. Mosely, who was Winant's assistant for the committee, comments in "Dismemberment of Germany" that the committee "never discussed the substantive questions," holding only two formal meetings.

44. *Ibid.*, p. 612.

45. *Meaning of Yalta*, p. 58.

46. *Yalta Papers*, pp. 620–3, 630–3.

47. Freeman Matthews minutes, *ibid.*, p. 909 (plenary session, February 10).

48. See the reparations protocol in *ibid.*, pp. 978–9, and the British draft, which also mentioned no figures, on p. 885.

49. *Meaning of Yalta*, p. 63; *cf.*, Kolko, *Politics of War*, pp. 354–6.

50. Hammond, p. 417.

51. Blum III, p. 405.

52. See the detailed account in Hammond, and Dorn, "The Debate over American Occupation Policy in Germany."

53. *Ibid.*, p. 497.

54. *Ibid.*, pp. 489–90.

55. Penrose, p. 281.

56. J. E. Du Bois, "Memorandum re Conversations with Lubin," March 27, 1945: *Diary (Germany)*, pp. 1095–6 (vol. 833, p. 17). Penrose comments (pp. 291–2) that, while the Russians asked for some reparations from current production, HDW and HM "uncompromisingly and even bitterly opposed" such reparations.

Chapter 18. The New President

1. White Papers, Concord Files, *Hearings*, pp. 2527, 2582, 2611.
2. J. E. Du Bois, "Memorandum of Meeting on Reparations," April 7, 1945: *Diary (Germany)*, pp. 1112–14 (vol. 835, pp. 56, ff.).
3. Churchill, *Triumph and Tragedy*, p. 348; Harry S. Truman, *Years of Decisions*, p. 1.
4. Blum III, pp. 416–19.
5. *Ibid.*, p. 420.
6. Sherwood, *Roosevelt and Hopkins*, pp. 880–2.
7. HDW to HM, April 21, 1945: *Hearings*, pp. 2413.
8. Truman, *Years of Decisions*, p. 326.
9. Blum III, pp. 68–70, 424–5, 460–1.
10. Acheson, *Present at the Creation*, p. 733.
11. Alperovitz, pp. 31–2. The report was officially adopted by the Joint Chiefs of Staff on May 10.
12. Truman, *Years of Decisions*, pp. 10–11.
13. *Ibid.*, pp. 70–2.
14. Bohlen notes, in *Forrestal Diaries*, p. 40; *cf.*, Truman, *Years of Decisions*, p. 77.
15. *Ibid.*, pp. 82, 87.
16. Dorn, "The Debate over American Occupation Policy in Germany," p. 498.
17. Hammond, p. 427.
18. The text of the second formal revision of April 26, JCS 1067/6, is in *Diary (Germany)*, pp. 1287–1303 (vol. 841, pp. 67-0-67YY), and the final revised version approved by Truman on May 10, JCS 1067/8, is printed in the *Department of State Bulletin*, October 21, 1945, pp. 596–607. E. F. Penrose, Winant's economic adviser, in *Economic Planning for the Peace*, p. 268, considers that JCS 1067 "may well rank amongst the most discreditable state documents ever written."
19. For the text of the reparations instructions to the U.S. delegate, see *Diary (Germany)*, pp. 1280–5 (vol. 841, pp. 67A–67M); *cf.*, the summary and discussion of the instructions in Herbert Feis, *Between War and Peace: the Potsdam Conference*, pp. 253–5.
20. Hammond, p. 425; Feis, *Between War and Peace*, p. 56.
21. Dorn, "The Debate over American Occupation Policy in Germany," p. 481.
22. Hammond, p. 443.

Chapter 19. China: Gold Shipments Resumed

1. Tsou, *America's Failure in China*, p. 239; text of Yalta "Agreement Regarding the Entry of the Soviet Union into the War against Japan," is in *Yalta Papers*, p. 984.
2. *Ibid.*, p. 156; *cf.*, Feis, *China Tangle*, chs. 22 and 23, *Meaning of Yalta*, ch. IV, "Yalta and the Far East."
3. Young, *Helping Hand*, p. 330.
4. Blum III, p. 296.
5. *China White Paper*, pp. 71–2.

6. Tsou, *America's Failure in China*, pp. 180–2; Feis, *China Tangle*, p. 260.
7. Blum III, pp. 296–7.
8. *Diary (China)*, pp. 1386–7 (vol. 802, pp. 1–3).
9. Blum III, pp. 297–8.
10. Young, *Helping Hand*, p. 327.
11. Feis, *China Tangle*, p. 317.
12. *Diary (China)*, pp. 1389–91 (vol. 807, pp. 257–9, 327–30).
13. *Ibid.*, pp. 1432–5 (vol. 824, pp. 230–7); Young, *Helping Hand*, pp. 352–3.
14. *Hearings*, pp. 956–7, 999–1000.
15. *Diary (China)*, pp. 1457–65 (vol. 829-II, pp. 329–44). Adler's remarks of mid-January are in *ibid.*, p. 1415.
16. Blum III, p. 300.
17. *Diary (China)*, pp. 1431–6 (vol. 824, pp. 230–7; vol. 825, p. 171).
18. *Ibid.*, pp. 1437–8 (vol. 827-I, pp. 53–5).
19. *Ibid.*, p. 1468 (vol. 836, pp. 252–3); Young, *Helping Hand*, p. 331. Percentage of note issue in Nationalist China absorbed by gold sales in the first quarter of 1945 was 52 percent but dropped to 28 percent in the second quarter. *Ibid.*, p. 445.
20. *Ibid.*, pp. 1469–72 (vol. 839, pp. 4–5).
21. *Ibid.*, pp. 1474–6 (vol. 839, pp. 40–3), pp. 1486–8 (vol. 839, pp. 139–43).
22. Young, *Helping Hand*, p. 326; White Papers, Concord Files, *Hearings*, p. 2517. *Cf.*, the general account of the Soong mission in Anthony Kubek, *How the Far East Was Lost*, ch. 8.
23. *Diary (China)*, pp. 1510–12 (vol. 843, pp. 217–18, 230–5).
24. *Ibid.*, pp. 1520–43 (vol. 845, pp. 211–50).
25. *Ibid.*, pp. 1543–8 (vol. 845, pp. 314–22).
26. *Ibid.*, pp. 1548–57 (vol. 845, pp. 329–45). Minutes of this meeting with Soong are printed in China White Paper, pp. 505–6.
27. *Scope of Soviet Activity in the United States*, pp. 2025–7 (vol. 845, pp. 32–6). HDW's figure of $27,000,000 of gold forwarded from the 1942 credit included the earlier shipment of $20,000,000 sent during 1943–4. This was, of course, over and above the $200,000,000 promised in July, 1943, by HM, of which about $7–8,000,000 had been sent by spring 1945.
28. *Diary (China)*, pp. 1561–2 (vol. 846, pp. 153–4).
29. *Ibid.*, pp. 1562–9 (vol. 847, pp. 33–44).
30. *Ibid.*, pp. 1570–83 (vol. 847, pp. 75–97).
31. *Ibid.*, pp. 1583–8 (vol. 847, pp. 101–11).
32. For text of HM's letter to Soong, and Grew to HM, May 16, 1945, see China White Paper, pp. 507–8.
33. Feis, *China Tangle*, p. 302; *cf.*, Blum III, p. 445.
34. Blum III, pp. 445–6.
35. *Diary (China)*, pp. 1626–7 (vol. 851, pp. 44–6).
36. Young, *China's Wartime Finance*, p. 297.
37. Alperovitz, ch. 4, "The Strategy of Delay in the Far East"; Feis, *China Tangle*, ch. 28. HM had not been told of the Manhattan atomic project. Blum III, pp. 13–14.

38. China White Paper, p. 97.
39. Joseph C. Grew, *The Turbulent Era*, pp. 1460–1.
40. Stimson Diary, May 15, quoted in Alperovitz, pp. 97–8; *cf.*, Feis, *Between War and Peace*, p. 80.
41. Alperovitz, pp. 99–100.
42. Young, *Helping Hand*, pp. 335–6.

Chapter 20. Congress Passes the Fund

1. Ansel F. Luxford to writer, October 15, 1970.
2. HDW, "The Monetary Fund: Some Criticisms Examined," *Foreign Affairs*, January, 1945, pp. 195–210.
3. HM, "Bretton Woods and International Cooperation," *Foreign Affairs*, January, 1945, pp. 182–94.
4. Gardner, p. 136.
5. U.S. Congress, House Committee on Banking and Currency, *Bretton Woods Agreements Acts*, Hearings, vol. I, pp. 139, 155.
6. Ansel F. Luxford to writer, October 15, 1970.
7. Quoted in Gardner, p. 241.
8. HDW, "The Monetary Fund: Some Criticisms Examined," p. 207.
9. *Bretton Woods Agreements Act*, vol. I, pp. 319–25, 332–5.
10. Senate Hearings, p. 314.
11. Gardner, p. 140.

Chapter 21. "Terminal"

1. Coe and Schmidt to HM, May 4, 1945: *Diary (Germany)*, p. 1442 (vol. 844, p. 242).
2. *Ibid.*, pp. 1606–7 (vol. 859, pp. 149, ff.).
3. Truman, *Year of Decisions*, pp. 235–7, 496.
4. *Ibid.*, pp. 106, 308, 323.
5. *Ibid.*, p. 323.
6. Feis, *Between War and Peace*, p. 254; Alperovitz, p. 163; Woodward, *British Foreign Policy in the Second World War*, pp. 524–6.
7. *Potsdam Papers*, pp. 547, 524–5, 510–12, 519–20. *Cf.*, the discussion in Alperovitz, pp. 162–4.
8. Truman, *Year of Decisions*, pp. 326–7. *Cf.*, the rather differing emphasis in Blum III, pp. 465–6. Cabell Phillips, *The Truman Presidency* (New York: Macmillan, 1966), pp. 144–8, has an interesting account of Truman's early cabinet-making.
9. Blum III, pp. 468–70.
10. Quoted in White, *Loyal American*, p. 397.
11. *Diary (Germany)*, pp. 1640–3 (vol. 863, pp. 260–5).
12. White Papers, Concord Files, *Hearings*, pp. 2530–1.
13. Stimson to Truman, Babelsberg, July 16, 1945: *Potsdam Papers*, pp. 754–7. *Cf.*, the discussion of the Potsdam decisions in D. C. Watt, "Germany,"

in *The Cold War*, ed. Evan Luard (London: Thames & Hudson, 1964), pp. 89–97: ". . . the compromise agreed on the reparations issue nevertheless recognised the economic division of Germany *de facto*. . . ."

14. "Memorandum for the Secretary of War: the Test," July 18, 1945: *Potsdam Papers*, pp. 1361–8.

15. Stimson Diary, July 21, 1945, quoted in Feis, *Between War and Peace*, p. 171.

16. Truman, *Years of Decisions*, pp. 411–12.

17. Charles de Gaulle, *Salvation* (London: Weidenfeld & Nicolson, 1960), Documents, pp. 285–6.

Chapter 22. Fund Executive Director

1. Woodward, *British Foreign Policy in the Second World War*, p. liii. About one-quarter of Britain's national wealth had been lost in the war, and exports in 1944 were one-third of prewar. See the figures in *Statistical Material Presented During the Washington Negotiations*, Cmd. 6706 (London: His Majesty's Stationery Office, 1945).

2. W. H. McNeill, *America, Britain and Russia: Their Co-operation and Conflict 1941–1946*, p. 674.

3. *Parliamentary Debates, House of Commons*, vol. 413, cols 955–7 (August 24, 1945).

4. Harrod, *Keynes*, p. 598. *Cf.*, Macneil, *America, Britain and Russia*, pp. 661–3.

5. Gardner, pp. 193, 199–200.

6. *Ibid.*, p. 195.

7. Ansel F. Luxford to writer, October 15, 1970.

8. Harrod, *Keynes*, p. 614. The text of the loan is published in *Financial Agreement Between the Governments of the United States and the United Kingdom*, Cmd. 6708.

9. "Settlement for Lend-Lease, and Reciprocal Aid, Surplus War Property, and Claims," pp. 6–8, Cmd. 6708 cited above; *cf.*, the discussion in Gardner, pp. 208–10, and Sir David Waley, "Lend-Lease" in Macneil, *America, Britain and Russia*, pp. 772–89.

10. Published as part of the wider *Proposals for the Expansion of World Trade and Employment* (Washington, D.C.: State Department, 1945). See the account in Penrose, ch. 6, of the London talks in early 1945. For the commercial negotiations later in 1945, see Gardner, ch. 8.

11. McNeill, *America, Britain and Russia*, p. 684; *cf.*, Gardner, p. 146.

12. See the Commons debate in *Parliamentary Debates, House of Commons*, vol. 417, cols 422–739 (December 12 and 13, 1945) and Keynes's speech in *Parliamentary Debates, House of Lords*, vol. 138, cols 789, ff. (December 18, 1945).

13. See the relevant extract of the Truman speech of November 16, 1953, in App. C.

14. W. M. Tomlinson, Memorandum for the Files, "Conversation with Lord

Keynes in Regard to Scheduling First Meeting of Governors under Bretton Woods Agreements," January 19, 1946; William H. Taylor, Memorandum for the Files, "Conversation with Lord Maynard Keynes at British Treasury," January 24, 1946," White Papers, PUL, file 27.

15. Harrod, *Keynes*, p. 625.
16. Gardner, p. 257.
17. Keynes, "Memorandum on Savannah," March 27, 1946, in Harrod, *Keynes*, p. 630.
18. Gardner, p. 259.
19. *Ibid.*, p. 260.
20. Meeting of the Board of Governors of the IMF, *World Fund and Bank Inaugural Meeting*, Fund Document 27, pp. 10–13 (March 16, 1946). Quoted in Gardner, pp. 261–6.
21. Harrod, *Keynes*, pp. 635–6.
22. "The Balance of Payments of the United States," *Economic Journal*, June, 1946, pp. 172–87.
23. HDW to Keynes, March 27, 1946: copy in White Papers, Concord Files, *Hearings*, pp. 2531–3.
24. New York *Herald-Tribune*, March 31, 1946. *Cf.*, the paper's editorial on April 1, 1946.
25. Gardner, p. 265.
26. "After the Savannah Conference," *Foreign Affairs*, July, 1946, pp. 622–32. One financial writer commented in May, 1946, that operations of the Fund and the Bank would be "as political as a troop movement." Gardner, p. 266.
27. White Papers, PUL, file 35, November 30, 1945.
28. Truman, *Year of Decisions*, pp. 550–2.
29. Max Chassin, *The Communist Conquest of China* (London: Weidenfeld & Nicolson, 1965), p. 53; Feis, *China Tangle*, p. 377; China White Paper, p. 171.
30. Following his posts in SHAEF and the U.S. Group, Control Council, Colonel Bernstein ended his army career as Director, Division of Investigation of Cartels and External Assets, OMGUS—Office of Military Government, United States: Hammond, p. 437.
31. *The Times*, May 16 and 17, 1946; New York *Times*, May 16, 1946. The Russians also decided not to attend the London meeting in October, 1946, to draft the International Trade Organization Charter on commercial policy; the U.S.S.R. had been one of the nineteen countries of the preparatory committee.
32. *Cf.*, the discussion of this point in Gardner, pp. 250–2, and Macneil, *America, Britain and Russia*, pp. 685–8.
33. *Hearings*, p. 958.
34. "Statement by Harry D. White, U.S. Executive Director of the IMF, May 6, 1946," White Papers, Concord Files, *Hearings*, p. 2582. The first permanent premises of the Fund and the Bank were at 1818 H Street, N.W., set up in June, 1946.

Chapter 23. A Problem of National Security

1. Truman address on White Case, November 16, 1953, is in the New York *Times* the next day. See extract in App. C.
2. Bentley, *Out of Bondage*, ch. 12; *HUAC Hearings*, pp. 540, ff.
3. The Brownell testimony of November 17, 1953, is in *Hearings*, pp. 1110, ff., that of Hoover of the same date in *ibid.*, pp. 1142, ff. Text of Brownell's Chicago speech, New York *Times*, November 7, 1953.
4. See the discussion in Packer, *Ex-Communist Witnesses*, pp. 68–75, 101–2. A communication from the FBI to the White House dated November 27, 1945, had one passage on the Silvermaster group which read: "This case first came to the attention of the Bureau on 8 November 1945 when Elizabeth Bentley . . . came into the New York office of the Bureau. . . ." *Hearings*, p. 1070.
5. Toledano and Lasky, *Seeds of Treason*, p. 137.
6. *Hearings*, p. 1143.
7. *Ibid.*, pp. 1113–14. This letter to General Vaughan was not given any further dissemination, according to the FBI dissemination list of the three reports concerning HDW sent to the President between November, 1945, and February, 1946. *Ibid.*, pp. 1169–70. Currie had left government service in the summer of 1945, while Silverman had been a civilian Army Air Force employee.
8. See Brownell-Hoover comment on this report, entitled "Summary of Soviet Espionage in the United States," in *ibid.*, pp. 1112–13 and 1144. Parts are printed in *ibid.*, pp. 71–3, 1022–5 and 1070.
9. *Ibid.*, p. 1148.
10. *Ibid.*, pp. 1144–5.
11. *Ibid.*, pp. 1115–16.
12. *Ibid.*, pp. 1116–20.
13. Truman statement, November 16, 1953, App. C. Brownell's original Chicago speech of November 6, 1953, had stated that it had been "established" that HDW was a spy in February, 1946, when the IMF appointment was approved. See the skeptical comments in *I. F. Stone's Weekly*, November 14 and 23, 1953, quoted in White, *Loyal American*, pp. 315–23. Cf., Cook, *The F.B.I. Nobody Knows*, pp. 354–9, and especially Ernest K. Lindley, "Key to the White Case," *Newsweek*, November 30, 1953. Lindley considered that in this context, in February, 1946, the evidence against HDW was "not conclusive."
14. Vaughan testimony, November 12, 1953: *Hearings*, pp. 1081–5.
15. Truman statement, November 16, 1953: see App. C.
16. *Ibid.*
17. "Statement of Gov. James F. Byrnes, November 9, 1953," *Hearings*, pp. 1085–6. Byrnes' brief note to Truman on February 5 is printed on p. 1087. This high-level activity on HDW's future coincided with the climax of the Canadian investigation into Soviet espionage. Following the defection of Igor Gouzenko, a Soviet Embassy cipher clerk in Ottawa, in September,

1945, the Canadian authorities had been investigating his story of Soviet activities in that country. The Canadian prime minister, Mackenzie King, had informed President Truman on the matter in September; the order for a Royal Commission had been signed on February 5, 1946, and the first public statement was made ten days later.

18. White Papers, Concord Files, *Hearings*, pp. 2790–1.
19. Hoover testimony, *Hearings*, pp. 1145, 1149.
20. *Ibid.*, pp. 1145–7.
21. *Ibid.*, p. 1112. In their Congressional testimony on November 17, 1953, both Brownell and Hoover said that later developments, with the production of the documents which Chambers had alleged had been given to him by HDW, meant that there was no doubt about HDW's involvement. Brownell referred to this evidence as "conclusive," Hoover spoke of its "uncontradictable nature which clearly established the reliability of the information furnished by the F.B.I. in 1945 and 1946." *Ibid.*, pp. 1139, 1145. See ch. 25 below.
22. *Ibid.*, pp. 1143, 1145–7.
23. Truman statement, November 16, 1953; see App. C. *Cf.*, the discussion of these events in G. F. Hudson, "The Dexter White Case," *Twentieth Century* (London), January, 1953. Truman noted that a Federal Grand Jury, called in 1947, did not indict HDW when the results of the FBI investigation were laid before it.
24. *Hearings*, p. 1144.
25. *Ibid.*, pp. 1219, ff., 1247, ff. Adler remained in the Treasury until 1950, and Coe, appointed in June, 1946, resigned as Secretary of the Fund in December, 1952, after invoking the Fifth Amendment to Congressional questions on his alleged Communist affiliations and espionage activities.

Chapter 24.   One World, Two Worlds

1. White Papers, Concord Files, *Hearings*, p. 2810.
2. Gardner, pp. 288–90.
3. *Ibid.*, pp. 291–2.
4. *Ibid.*, p. 294.
5. See the discussion in Penrose, ch. 10, "The Gathering Crisis."
6. Young, *China's Wartime Finance*, p. 398.
7. Joseph M. Jones, *The Fifteen Weeks*, pp. 138–41.
8. Eleanor Bontecou, *The Federal Loyalty–Security Program*, pp. 28–34, 280.
9. *Forrestal Diaries*, p. 280.
10. Kennan, *Memoirs 1925–50*, p. 292.
11. These two letters appear in White Papers, Concord Files, *Hearings*, p. 2612.
12. U.S. Senate, Committee on Finance, *International Trade Organization*, Hearings, 80th Congress, 1st Session (March–April, 1947) (Washington, D.C.: U.S. Government Printing Office, 1947), pp. 619, ff.

13. IMF press release, April 9, 1947: White Papers, Concord Files, *Hearings*, p. 2584.
14. *Ibid.*, pp. 2533–4.
15. White, *Loyal American*, p. 273.
16. White Papers, Concord Files, *Hearings*, p. 2534.
17. Penrose, pp. 345–6.
18. Hammond, p. 443; *Selected Documents on Germany and the Question of Berlin* (London: Her Majesty's Stationery Office, 1961), p. 98.
19. Petrov, pp. 199–201. Petrov comments that, as his calculations exclude the Berlin enclave, "this is admittedly a very rough estimate."
20. Balfour and Mair, *Four Power Control in Germany and Austria*, p. 148.
21. Petrov, p. 221. A sequel to the story of the duplicate plates was the large amount of AM marks accumulated by the GI's and British servicemen in occupied Germany, as a result of black-market activities, over and above their authorized pay. This redeemable "troop pay overdraft" cost the U.S. Treasury some $270,000,000, most of the notes being Soviet AM issue. The sum was written off against the dollar earnings of German POW's in in the U.S., and by other bookkeeping devices.

    The GI's British comrades-in-arms on the black market showed only a little less enterprise, as the British troop pay overdraft for Germany (and Austria) was £58,000,000 ($232,000,000). There can probably be little doubt that, as with the GI's, much of this sum was in Soviet-issue AM marks. Some £38,000,000 was written off by debiting a War Office surplus, but Parliament still had to grant a £20,000,000 supplemental appropriation, after angry protests by MP's. Rundell, *Black Market Money*, pp. 36, 88–90; Petrov, pp. 210, 216–18; *Parliamentary Debates, House of Commons*, vol. 433, cols 1073, ff. (February 18, 1947).
22. Gardner, pp. 296–8, 303. External convertibility for sterling and other European currencies was restored in December, 1958.
23. *Ibid.*, pp. 296, 304.
24. See the discussion in *ibid.*, ch. 17.
25. *Hearings*, pp. 1239–40.
26. White Papers, Concord Files, *Hearings*, pp. 2543, 2583, 2616.
27. HDW, "The International Monetary Fund: the First Year," *Annals of the American Academy of Political and Social Sciences*, July, 1947, pp. 21–9. A note on p. vii indicates that the papers in this issue were presented to the Society's annual meeting held in Philadelphia on April 18 and 19, 1947.
28. HDW, "Rough Draft of a Statement that Might Be Used to Introduce the Proposed Amendments on the Agenda," May 19, 1948: White Papers, PUL, file 27.

Chapter 25. The Committee

1. White, *Loyal American*, p. 71.
2. A copy of this letter is in White Papers, Concord Files, *Hearings*, p. 2586.

A Federal Grand Jury consists of from sixteen to twenty-three citizens impaneled by a Federal District Court to hear evidence and, if 12 or more concur, to return an indictment as a result of its investigations. The function is purely accusatory.

3. Facsimile in White Papers, Concord Files, *Hearings*, p. 2560.
4. HDW to Wallace, March 1, 1945 (copy); Wallace to HDW, July 30, 1945: White Papers, Concord Files, *Hearings*, pp. 2526, 2521.
5. Goodman, *The Committee*, p. 200.
6. Howe and Coser, pp. 471–5.
7. Malcolm Hobbs, "Wallace Aides Come Up with Startling Cabinet Notions," Overseas News Agency: White Papers, Concord Files, *Hearings*, pp. 2529–30.
8. *Ibid.*, pp. 2574–5.
9. These dates are given in Whipple, pt XII.
10. Chambers, *Witness*, p. 510.
11. Jowitt, p. 99.
12. Murphy interviews with Chambers, March 20, 1945, and August 28, 1946, *Hearings*, pp. 1181–3, also reproduced in Jowitt, pp. 260–4. In his November, 1953, Congressional statement, Attorney General Brownell stated that in the FBI report on HDW which was sent to the White House in February, 1946, it was recorded that Dr. Abraham Wolfson (who was HDW's brother-in-law) of Newark, N.J., was a Communist Party member, active in the Party under another name. *Hearings*, pp. 1118–19. Dr. Wolfson, in his first marriage, and HDW had married sisters; he died in July, 1952.
13. Chambers, *Witness*, p. 511.
14. Under Title 50, United States Code, Section 32, which was in force between 1937 and 1945 (Department of Justice to writer, August 5, 1970).
15. *HUAC Hearings*, pp. 511–2.
16. White, *Loyal American*, p. 403.
17. *HUAC Hearings*, pp. 574–7.
18. *Ibid.*, pp. 877–906 inclusive. Currie had testified immediately before HDW, denying Miss Bentley's charges of involvement in the Silvermaster group.
19. Column of August 18, 1948, Boston *Traveller*, reproduced in White, *Loyal American*, p. 73.
20. Whipple, pt I. The "informant" on the death certificate was Dr. Abraham Wolfson, of New Jersey, HDW's brother-in-law.
21. *Ibid.*, cf., Karl Hess, "Dead or Alive," *American Mercury*, April, 1956, Dr. Emerson told a *Mercury* reporter: "I did not see the body. I know I made a mistake."
22. Chambers, *Witness*, pp. 735–50; *Congressional Record—House*, 81st Congress, 2nd Session, p. 1003 (January 26, 1950); Nixon, *Six Crises*, pp. 51–2.
23. *IPR Hearings*, p. 5488. See App. A for full text.
24. Jowitt, p. 180.
25. Nixon House speech, January 26, 1950. Two paragraphs were omitted from

this text of the White Memorandum, photostats of which were released in November, 1953. See n. 29 below.

26. *IPR Hearings*, pp. 419–24 (Bentley) and 491–3 (Chambers).

27. New York *Times*, November 7, 1953. Sherman Adams writes in *Firsthand Report* (New York: Harper, 1961), p. 140, that Brownell hoped that "his accusation would take away some of the glamour of the McCarthy stage play." *Cf.*, the account of events following Brownell's speech in Latham, pp. 369–72.

28. New York *Times*, November 17, 1953; for parts of the speech dealing directly with HDW, see App. C.

29. *Hearings*, pp. 1109–54 (November 17, 1953). The photostats of the entire White Memorandum, produced five years earlier at Baltimore by Chambers, are found on pp. 1120–7 of these hearings.

30. Dwight D. Eisenhower, *Mandate for Change* (London: Heinemann, 1963), p. 315.

31. *Hearings*, pp. 2277–81. In his biography of HM, Professor Blum records how "the measure of Morgenthau's confidence in White" was shown in a "curious episode" in July, 1941. A man with "a strong German accent" telephoned HM and said that he wanted a reward for discovering papers of HDW's. These, HDW said, were "important papers" he had left in the Treasury car taking him home. He had telephoned his office and asked for the papers to be put on his desk. A Treasury Secret Service investigation yielded no further results, and the man with the German accent was not heard from again. HM was sure that HDW had done all he could to remedy his momentary carelessness. Blum II, p. 340.

32. White Papers, Concord Files, *Hearings*, pp. 2415, ff. Some of HDW's papers had already been given to Princeton University Library in early 1951 by Mrs. White. *Cf.*, *ibid.*, pp. 2504–5.

33. Blum III, p. 90.

34. Robbins, *Autobiography of an Economist*, p. 198.

35. Rebecca West, "Hiss Case Hid Graver Issues," *Sunday Times*, March 22, 1953.

BIBLIOGRAPHY

1. Papers and Publications of Harry Dexter White

White's surviving papers are found in two collections. The first, the Papers of Harry Dexter White, was deposited after White's death by Mrs. White in Princeton University Library. It consists of memoranda, studies and papers from the period 1930–48, and includes unpublished drafts of the plans for the Fund and the Bank, together with other papers relating to White's time in the United States Treasury and with the Fund.

A second, smaller collection, the Harry Dexter White Papers, comprises letters, manuscripts, documents and other memoranda, mostly from the war and postwar years, although there are some items from before this time. This collection is printed as part 30, pp. 2415–2816, *Interlocking Subversion in Government Departments*, Hearings, Internal Security Subcommittee, Committee on the Judiciary, United States Senate (Washington, D.C.: United States Government Printing Office, 1956). These papers were taken from White's former home near Fitzwilliam, New Hampshire, in 1953 and 1955, "upon proper process," on the orders of the Attorney General of the State of New Hampshire. They were then entered in the Subcommittee's records during a session at Concord, New Hampshire, in August, 1955.

In addition there are two particular sources that contain material on White's early life and background. These are: Nathan I. White, *Harry D. White— Loyal American*, privately published by Bessie (White) Bloom at Waban, Mass., 1956; and a twelve-part series of articles, "The Life and Death of Harry Dexter White," by Charles L. Whipple, in the Boston *Globe*, beginning November 15, 1953.

BOOKS BY HARRY DEXTER WHITE

The French International Accounts, 1880–1913 (Cambridge, Mass.: Harvard University Press, 1933).

ARTICLES BY HARRY DEXTER WHITE

"Haberler's *Der Internationale Handel,* Ohlin's *Interregional and International Trade,*" in *Quarterly Journal of Economics,* vol. 48, no. 4 (August, 1934), pp. 727–41.

"The International Monetary Fund: the First Year," in *Annals of the American Academy of Political and Social Science,* vol. 252 (July, 1947), pp. 21–9.

"The Monetary Fund: Some Criticisms Examined," in *Foreign Affairs,* vol. 23 (January, 1945), pp. 195–210.

"Postwar Currency Stabilization," in *American Economic Review,* supplement, vol. 33, no. 1 (March, 1943), pp. 382–7.

2. Official Documents and Government Publications

DEPARTMENT OF STATE

Foreign Relations of the United States: Japan 1931–1941, vol. II (Washington, D.C.: United States Government Printing Office, 1943).

Foreign Relations of the United States: 1941, vol. IV, *The Far East* (Washington, D.C.: United States Government Printing Office, 1956).

U.S. Relations with China, with Special Reference to the Period 1944–1949 (Washington, D.C.: United States Government Printing Office, 1949).

Foreign Relations of the United States: the Conferences at Cairo and Teheran, 1943 (Washington, D.C.: United States Government Printing Office, 1961).

Foreign Relations of the United States: the Conferences at Malta and Yalta, 1945 (Washington, D.C.: United States Government Printing Office, 1955).

Foreign Relations of the United States: the Conference at Berlin (Potsdam) (Washington, D.C.: United States Government Printing Office, 1960).

Notter, Harley A., *Postwar Foreign Policy Preparation, 1939–45* (Washington, D.C.: United States Government Printing Office, 1949).

Proceedings and Documents of the United Nations Monetary and Financial Conference, Bretton Woods, New Hampshire, 1–22 July 1944, 2 vols. (Washington, D.C.: United States Government Printing Office, 1948).

Young, John Parke, "Developing Plans for an International Monetary Fund and a World Bank," *Department of State Bulletin,* November 13, 1950.

DEPARTMENT OF THE TREASURY

Preliminary Draft Outline of an International Stabilization Fund of the United and Associated Nations (Washington, D.C.: United States Treasury, 1943).

Preliminary Draft Outline of a Proposal for a Bank for Reconstruction and Development of the United and Associated Nations (Washington, D.C.: United States Treasury, 1943).

DEPARTMENT OF THE ARMY

Romanus, C. F., and Sunderland, Wiley, *Stilwell's Mission to China* (Washington, D.C.: Department of the Army, 1953).

———, *Stilwell's Command Problems* (Washington, D.C.: Department of the Army, 1956).

UNITED STATES CONGRESS

House Committee on Banking and Currency, *Bretton Woods Agreements Act*, Hearings, 79th Congress, 1st Session (Washington, D.C.: United States Government Printing Office, 1945).

House Committee on Un-American Activities, *Communist Espionage in the United States Government*, Hearings, 80th Congress, 2nd Session (Washington, D.C.: United States Government Printing Office, 1948).

Senate Committee on Banking and Currency, *Bretton Woods Agreements Act*, Hearings, 79th Congress, 1st Session (Washington, D.C.: United States Government Printing Office, 1945).

Committees on Appropriations, Armed Services, and Banking and Currency, *Occupation Currency Transactions*, Hearings, 80th Congress, 1st Session (Washington, D.C.: United States Government Printing Office, 1947).

Committee on Government Operations, Permanent Subcommittee on Investigations, Subcommittee on Government Operations Abroad, *Transfer of Occupation Currency Plates—Espionage Phase*, Hearings, 83rd Congress, 1st Session (Washington, D.C.: United States Government Printing Office, 1953).

Committee on the Judiciary, Internal Security Subcommittee, *Interlocking Subversion in Government Departments*, Hearings, 83rd and 84th Congress, 30 pts. (Washington, D.C.: United States Government Printing Office, 1953–5).

———, *Institute of Pacific Relations*, Hearings, 82nd Congress, 2nd Session (Washington, D.C.: United States Government Printing Office, 1951–2).

———, *Scope of Soviet Activity in the United States*, Hearings, 84th Congress, 2nd Session, pts. 34, 35 and 42 (Washington, D.C.: United States Government Printing Office, 1956–7).

———, *Morgenthau Diary (China)*, 2 vols., with foreword by Anthony Kubek (Washington, D.C.: United States Government Printing Office, 1965).

———, *Morgenthau Diary (Germany)*, 2 vols., with introduction by Anthony Kubek (Washington, D.C.: United States Government Printing Office, 1967).

UNITED KINGDOM GOVERNMENT

Financial Agreement Between the Governments of the United States and the United Kingdom, Cmd. 6708 (London: His Majesty's Stationery Office, 1945).

Hall, H. Duncan, *North American Supply* (London: Her Majesty's Stationery Office, 1955).

Hancock, W. K., and Gowing, M. M., *British War Economy* (London: His Majesty's Stationery Office, 1949).

Harris, C. R. S., *Allied Military Administration of Italy, 1943–45* (London:

Her Majesty's Stationery Office, 1957).

Joint Statement by Experts on the Establishment of an International Monetary Fund, Cmd. 6519 (London: His Majesty's Stationery Office, 1944).

Proposals for an International Clearing Union, Cmd. 6437 (London: His Majesty's Stationery Office, 1943).

Statistical Material Presented During the Washington Negotiations, Cmd. 6707 (London: His Majesty's Stationery Office, 1945).

United Nations Monetary and Financial Conference: Final Act, Cmd. 6546 (London: His Majesty's Stationery Office, 1944).

Woodward, E. Llewellyn, *British Foreign Policy in the Second World War* (London: Her Majesty's Stationery Office, 1962).

3. *Memoirs, Autobiographies, Personal Records*

Acheson, Dean, *Morning and Noon* (Boston, Mass.: Houghton Mifflin, 1965).
———, *Present at the Creation* (New York: Norton, 1969).
Adams, Henry, *The Life of Albert Gallatin* (New York: Lippincott, 1879).
Avon, Lord (Anthony Eden), *The Reckoning* (London: Cassell, 1965).
Baker, Carlos, *Ernest Hemingway: a Life* (London: Collins, 1969).
Bentley, Elizabeth, *Out of Bondage* (London: Hart-Davis, 1952).
Blum, John Morton, *From the Morgenthau Diaries: Years of Crisis 1928–1938* (Boston, Mass.: Houghton Mifflin, 1959); *Years of Urgency 1938–1941* (1965); *Years of War 1941–1945* (1967).
Chambers, Whittaker, *Witness* (New York: Random House, 1952).
Churchill, Winston S., *The Hinge of Fate* (London: Cassell, 1951).
———, *Closing the Ring* (London: Cassell, 1952).
———, *Triumph and Tragedy* (London: Cassell, 1954).
Deakin, F. W., and Storny, G. R., *The Case of Richard Sorge* (London: Chatto & Windus, 1966).
Eisenhower, Dwight D., *Crusade in Europe* (London: Heinemann, 1948).
Forrestal, James, *The Forrestal Diaries*, ed. Walter Millis and E. S. Duffield (New York: Viking, 1951).
Grew, Joseph C., *The Turbulent Era* (Boston, Mass.: Houghton Mifflin, 1952).
Harrod, R. F., *The Life of John Maynard Keynes* (London: Macmillan, 1951).
Hull, Cordell, *The Memoirs of Cordell Hull* (New York: Macmillan, 1948).
Kennan, George, *Memoirs, 1925–1950* (Boston, Mass.: Atlantic-Little, Brown, 1967).
Krock, Arthur, *Memoirs* (New York: Funk & Wagnall, 1968).
Massing, Hede, *This Deception* (New York: Duell, Sloan & Pearce, 1951).
Moran, Lord, *Churchill: the Struggle for Survival, 1940–65* (London: Constable, 1965).
Murphy, Robert, *Diplomat among Warriors* (New York: Doubleday, 1964).
Robbins, Lord, *Autobiography of an Economist* (London: Macmillan, 1971).
Schlesinger, Arthur M., *The Age of Roosevelt: the Coming of the New Deal* (Boston, Mass.: Houghton Mifflin, 1958).
———, *The Politics of Upheaval* (Boston, Mass.: Houghton Mifflin, 1960).
Sherwood, Robert E., *Roosevelt and Hopkins* (New York: Harper, 1948).

Speer, Albert, *Inside the Third Reich* (London: Weidenfeld & Nicholson, 1970).

Stilwell, Joseph, *The Stilwell Papers*, ed. Theodore H. White (London: Macdonald, 1948).

Stimson, Henry L., and Bundy, McGeorge, *On Active Service in Peace and War* (New York: Harper, 1948).

Truman, Harry S., *Year of Decisions* (New York: Doubleday, 1955).

———, *Years of Trial and Hope* (New York: Doubleday, 1956).

Wells, H. G., *The Future in America* (London, Chapman & Hall, 1906).

Whalen, Richard J., *The Founding Father: the Story of Joseph P. Kennedy* (New York: Signet Books, 1966).

4. Secondary Sources

Action This Day: Working with Churchill, ed. J. W. Wheeler-Bennett (London: Macmillan, 1968).

Alperovitz, Gar, *Atomic Diplomacy* (London: Secker & Warburg, 1966).

Armstrong, Anne, *Unconditional Surrender* (New Jersey: Rutgers University Press, 1961).

Birkenhead, Lord, *The Prof in Two Worlds* (London: Collins, 1961).

Bontecou, Eleanor, *The Federal Loyalty-Security Program* (Ithaca, New York: Cornell University Press, 1953).

Burnham, James, *The Web of Subversion* (Boston: Americanist Library, 1965).

Chang, Kia-ngau, *The Inflationary Spiral: the Experience of China 1939–1950* (New York: M.I.T. Press/Wiley, 1958).

Chou, Shun-hsin, *The Chinese Inflation, 1937–1950* (New York: Columbia University Press, 1963).

Compton, James V., *The Swastika and the Eagle* (London: Bodley Head, 1967).

Cook, Fred J., *The F.B.I. Nobody Knows* (London: Cape, 1965).

Cooke, Alistair, *A Generation on Trial* (London: Hamish Hamilton, 1950).

Dallin, David, *Soviet Espionage* (New Haven, Conn.: Yale University Press, 1955).

Draper, Theodore, *The Roots of American Communism* (New York: Viking, 1957).

Everest, A. S., *Morgenthau, the New Deal and Silver* (New York: Columbia University Press, 1950).

Fairbank, John, et al., *East Asia: the Modern Transformation* (London: Allen & Unwin, 1965).

Farago, Ladislas, *The Broken Seal* (London: Arthur Barker, 1967).

Feis, Herbert, *The Road to Pearl Harbor* (New York: Atheneum Books, 1965).

———, *The China Tangle* (Princeton University Press, 1953).

———, *Churchill, Roosevelt and Stalin* (Princeton University Press, 1957).

Galbraith, J. K., *The Great Crash* (London: Hamish Hamilton, 1955).

Gardner, Richard N., *Sterling-Dollar Diplomacy*, rev. ed. (New York and London: McGraw-Hill, 1969).

Goodman, Walter, *The Committee* (London: Secker & Warburg, 1969).

Hammond, Paul Y., "Directives for the Occupation of Germany: the Washington Story," in *American Civil-Military Decisions*, ed. Harold Stein (University of Alabama Press, 1963).

Howe, Irving, and Coser, Lewis, *The American Communist Party: a Critical History (1919–1957)* (Boston: Beacon Press, 1958).

Johnson, Chalmers, *An Instance of Treason* (London: Heinemann, 1965).

Jones, Joseph M., *The Fifteen Weeks* (New York: Viking, 1955).

Jowitt, Lord, *The Strange Case of Alger Hiss* (London: Hodder & Stoughton, 1953).

Kolko, Gabriel, *The Politics of War* (London: Weidenfeld & Nicholson, 1969).

Kubek, Anthony, *How the Far East Was Lost* (Chicago: Regnery, 1963).

Langer, William L., and Gleason, S. Everett, *The Challenge to Isolation* (New York: Harper Council on Foreign Relations, 1952).

——, *The Undeclared War 1940–1941* (New York: Harper/Council on Foreign Relations, 1953).

Latham, Earl, *The Communist Controversy in Washington* (Cambridge, Mass.: Harvard University Press, 1966).

McNeill, W. H., *America, Britain and Russia: Their Co-operation and Conflict 1941–1946* (London: Royal Institute of International Affairs/Oxford University Press, 1953).

Morgenthau, Henry, Jr., *Germany Is Our Problem* (New York: Harper, 1945).

Mosely, Philip, *The Kremlin in World Politics* (New York: Vintage Books, 1960).

Neustadt, Robert, *Presidential Power* (New York and London: Wiley, 1960).

Nixon, Richard, *Six Crises* (New York: Doubleday, 1962).

Packer, Herbert, *Ex-Communist Witnesses* (Stanford: Stanford University Press, 1962).

Penrose, E. F., *Economic Planning for the Peace* (Princeton University Press, 1953).

Petrov, Vladimir, *Money and Conquest: Allied Occupation Currencies in World War II* (Baltimore: Johns Hopkins Press, 1967).

Rees, Goronwy, *Capitalism in Crisis* (London: Weidenfeld & Nicolson, 1970).

Robbins, Lionel, *The Great Depression* (London: Macmillan, 1934).

Rundell, Walter, Jr., *Black Market Money: the Collapse of U.S. Military Currency Control in World War II* (Baton Rouge: Louisiana State University Press, 1964).

Snell, John L., *The Wartime Origins of the East-West Dilemma over Germany* (New Orleans: Hauser Press, 1959).

The Meaning of Yalta, ed. John L. Snell (Baton Rouge: Louisiana State University Press, 1956).

Stein, Herbert, *The Fiscal Revolution in America* (Chicago University Press, 1969).

Toledano, Ralph de, and Lasky, Victor, *Seeds of Treason*, rev. ed. (Chicago: Regnery, 1962).

Tsou, Tang, *America's Failure in China 1941–1950* (Chicago University Press, 1963).

Vansittart, Lord, *Bones of Contention* (London: Hutchinson, 1945).

——, *Events and Shadows* (London: Hutchinson, 1947).

Whitehead, Don, *The F.B.I. Story* (London: Muller, 1957).

Wilmot, Chester, *The Struggle for Europe* (London: Collins, 1952).

Wohlstetter, Roberta, *Pearl Harbor: Warning and Decision* (Stanford University Press, 1962).

Young, Arthur, *China and the Helping Hand* (Cambridge, Mass.: Harvard University Press, 1963).

——, *China's Wartime Finance and Inflation, 1937–45* (Cambridge, Mass.: Harvard University Press, 1965).

5. Articles

Chase, John L., "The Development of the Morgenthau Plan through the Quebec Conference," *Journal of Politics*, May, 1954.

Dorn, Walter, "The Debate over American Occupation Policy in Germany in 1944–45," *Political Science Quarterly*, December, 1957.

Havemann, Ernest, "Close-up of a Ghost," *Life*, November 23, 1953.

Hess, Karl, "Dead or Alive?" *American Mercury*, April, 1956.

Hudson, G. F., "The Dexter White Case," *Twentieth Century*, January, 1954.

Keynes, Lord, "The Balance of Payments of the United States," *Economic Journal*, June, 1946.

Lindley, Ernest K., "Key to the White Case," *Newsweek*, November 30, 1953.

Morgenthau, Henry, Jr., "Our Policy toward Germany," New York *Post*, November 24–29, 1947.

——, "Bretton Woods and International Cooperation," *Foreign Affairs*, January, 1945.

Mosely, Philip, "Dismemberment of Germany," *Foreign Affairs*, April, 1950.

——, "The Occupation of Germany: New Light on How the Zones Were Drawn," *Foreign Affairs*, July, 1950.

"One Man's Greed," *Time*, November 23, 1953.

Smith, Fred J., "The Rise and Fall of the Morgenthau Plan," *United Nations World*, March, 1947.

Vinson, Fred M., "After the Savannah Conference," *Foreign Affairs*, July, 1946.

West, Rebecca, "Hiss Case Hid Graver Issues," *Sunday Times*, March 22, 1953.

——, "The Surprising Mr. Kaplan," *Sunday Times*, March 29, 1953.

ACKNOWLEDGMENTS

I WOULD like to thank the following, without whose help, in one way or another, this book could not have been written in its present form: The late Hon. Dean Acheson; Mr. John P. Baker, New York Public Library; Professor Arnold Beichman; Dr. Edward M. Bernstein; The Lord Boothby; Mr. C. E. Dornbusch; Mr. Marriner Eccles; Mr. David Footman; Mr. Thomas E. Hohmann and Mr. Mark G. Eckhoff, National Archives and Record Services; Miss Judith B. Johnston, Reference Librarian, Treasury Department; Mr. Arthur Krock; Mr. Ansel F. Luxford; Mr. R. R. Mellor, Foreign Office Library; Mrs. Marlene C. McGuirl, Library of Congress; Professor Philip E. Mosely; Ambassador Robert Murphy; Dr. E. F. Penrose; Mr. Luke A. Petrocelli, Boston Public Schools; The Lord Robbins; Miss Marie G. Stark, Chief, Records Division, International Monetary Fund; Mrs. Margot T. Sullivan, Boston Public Library; Mr. Stanley Yonge, Swansea Public Library; Mr. Joseph W. Marshall and Mr. William J. Stewart, Franklin D. Roosevelt Library; Mr. Charles L. Whipple; and Miss Joan Worth.

I would also like to thank the Warden and Fellows of St. Antony's College, Oxford, for research facilities; Mr. Alexander Clark and Mrs. W. M. Randall of Princeton University Library for their help in connection with the Harry Dexter White papers in that library; and Mrs. M. J. Baylis for her care and patience in typing the manuscript.

D.R.

Index